HOUSE HOME

HEART

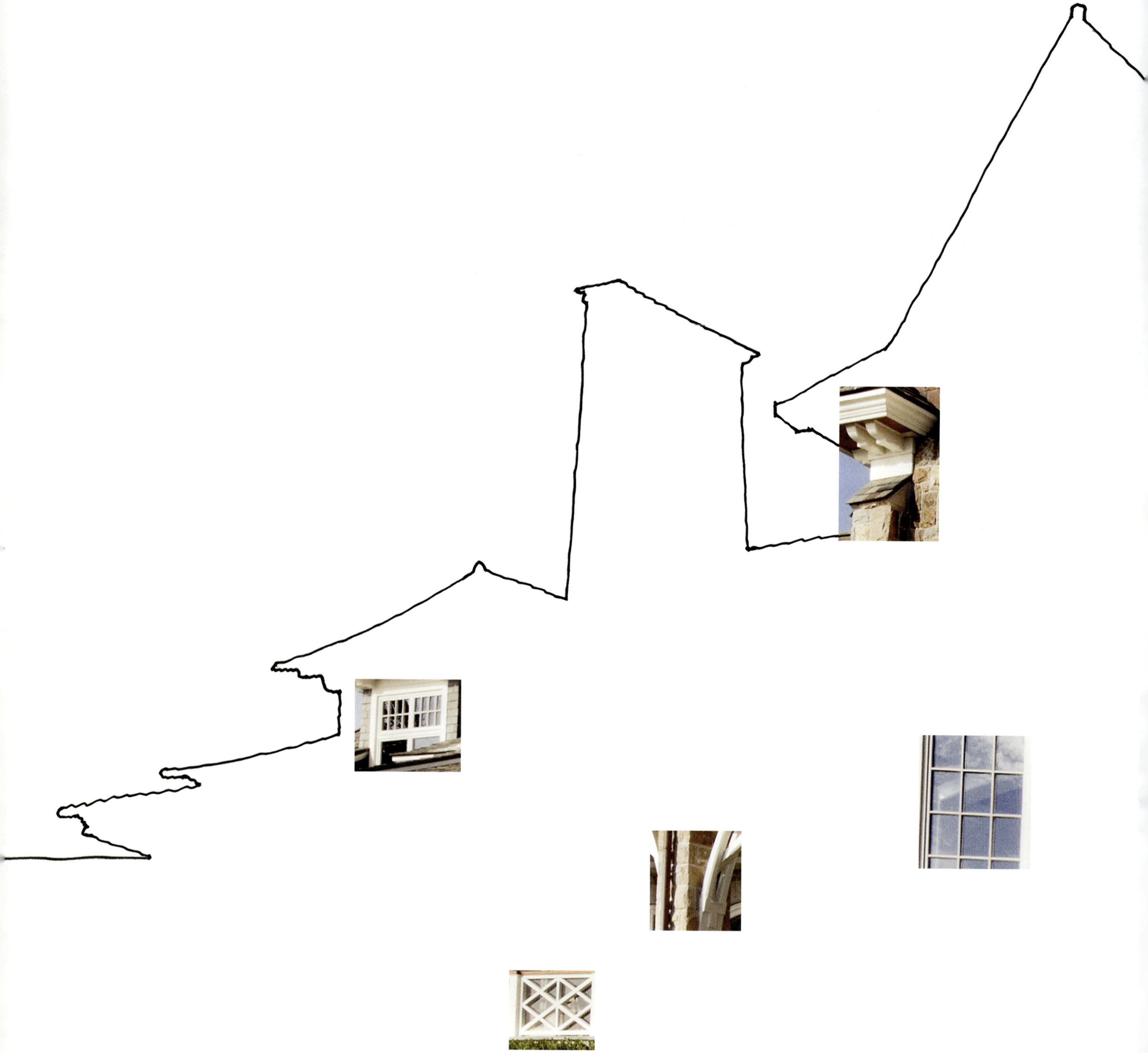

CONTENTS

14   FOREWORD   PAUL GOLDBERGER

20   INTRODUCTION   BERNARD M. WHARTON

60   THE DESIGN PROCESS   SHOPE RENO WHARTON

100 THE WORK   SEVENTEEN CONTEMPORARY
                           BUILDINGS

298 INDEX

300 BIBLIOGRAPHY

     ACKNOWLEDGMENTS

ARCHITECTURE THAT CELEBRATES TRADITION BUT CONTINUES TO REINVENT ITSELF
FOREWORD BY PAUL GOLDBERGER

It is not very hard to find an architect if you want to build a traditional house. Traditional houses are what most architects who specialize in residential work do. They design Cape Cod cottages and center-hall colonials and Georgian mansions and Shingle Style houses and Mediterranean villas, since people who build new houses tend to want something that will look more or less like the houses they have been looking at for most of their lives, and architects need to earn a living. Plenty of builders even put such houses up themselves, bypassing architects altogether. In a world in which the suburban landscape is littered with McMansions, traditional houses can sometimes seem more like a commodity than an act of architectural creativity.

All that only makes the work of Bernard Wharton all the more notable. Amid the noise, he produces architecture. Wharton and his firm, Shope Reno Wharton, have been designing traditional houses that rise above the din, you might say—traditional houses that are not churned out by the dozen, but are one-of-a-kind; houses that are not copies of anything else, but original works, designed with thoughtfulness and intelligence and fineness of detail. Wharton has as much respect for invention and imagination as any modernist, and as much determination to be creative. At a time when the ubiquitous McMansion has devalued the currency of traditional residential architecture, Wharton is one of the few architects in whose hands the idea of traditional house design continues to seem meaningful. He reminds us that there is potential for freshness in historical styles still—that these are not closed books, but languages ripe with opportunities for saying new things.

It is not for nothing that one of Wharton's favorite architects is Sir Edwin Lutyens, the great English eclectic whose creative imagination still staggers the mind. Lutyens could make a classic English country house seem more novel than a modernist villa, and at the same time feel as classic and English as Chatsworth. So, too, with the Shope Reno Wharton houses: The curving shingles and billowing surfaces in the Connecticut residence are not the details you expect to see in a Shingle Style house, but they somehow manage to make the house seem more connected to some essential quality of this style, accentuating its flowing space in a new way. Similarly, the projecting entrance pavilion of the stone-clad waterfront mansion, or the stair tower beside the entry portico in the suburban house, are not quite what you would be likely to see in a French country villa or an Adirondack camp, but they feel right.

Like Lutyens, Wharton is not a revivalist. He is a maker of architectural composition who uses elements from various historical styles, which he proceeds to expand, contract, stretch, compress, and combine in ways that emerge as much from his innate compositional sense as from any historical precedent. Maybe his instinct for composition is more important than his fondness for history; it is surely what gives his facades such movement, liveliness and texture, yet allows them to feel serene and balanced at the same time.

To be a successful compositionalist—and that is what Bernard Wharton is—requires much more than the ability to mix and match elements from the architecture of the past. It requires knowing architectural history and understanding it down to the smallest details, yes. But to design a traditional house well is not a matter of selecting bits and pieces of historical architecture as if they were laid out in a smörgasbord. In some ways it is the opposite: a process not of literally appropriating elements from the past, but of creating new ones that embody the spirit of one kind of architecture or another, interpreted in inventive ways. It is more a matter of being able to feel the essential qualities of one kind of architecture or another, of sensing what conveys the idea of Tudor or Georgian or what-have-you—and then of knowing what elements, new ones or variations on familiar ones, will enhance this idea, and give it fresh life.

In the end, what makes a house successful has very little to do with style, and certainly not with choice of style. What makes a house a good piece of architecture isn't whether it is French Renaissance or Georgian or Tudor or Mediterranean, but how strong its underlying bones are—how well proportioned its elevations and its interior spaces are, how well its rooms flow from one into the next, how its architect has handled light, what materials he has used and how well he has used them, how skillfully its small details have been thought through, and how conveniently and comfortably the house works for its occupants. By these measures, Wharton's houses succeed. They are luxurious but rarely grandiose or overbearing. They are, by and large, designed from a standpoint of reason.

But it is reason leavened with a bit of lyricism, even a certain quirkiness from time to time, a gentle undercurrent of wit. While these are serious houses for serious people, they are designed to amuse the eye, or at least to keep it occupied. Thus such elements as the big, low entry arch at Friar's Head, filling a low gable that is itself oddly but entrancingly placed nearly on the ground; or the exaggerated Serlian window over the front door of the house on the North Shore of Long Island, its white form playfully popping out of the shingled façade, or the six dormers in a line atop the garage wing of the house on the Connecticut shore, like a row of little hats, their rhythm playing off against the larger gables of the main house; or the entry tower of the house in New Jersey, which consists of a small pedimented porch at the base of a pyramidal shingled tower into which a high, three-part window has been cut. This may be the Wharton house that comes the closest to being openly whimsical—the entry tower is flanked by a one-story cylinder with a peaked roof that contains a library, and another cylinder, most of it windowed, that contains the stair; in that cylinder, the windows step up, echoing the profile of the stair. In some of the houses, Wharton will surprise with a great expanse of glass, not only a practical response to this age's demand for openness and natural light and views, but also, as in a hilltop house in Vermont, a way to play off new against old.

All of these houses are carefully sited to maximize views where there are views to be had, and privacy where that is the greatest benefit a property has to offer. Whatever the site, they generally seem to sit comfortably on the land, surely another happy result of Wharton's compositional skill. The large, embracing gables, the strong horizontal lines in counterpoint to a balancing array of chimneys, and the overall sense of texture and depth all contribute to a sense that these houses belong where they are.

A sense of appropriateness to place is more than a matter of a house feeling right for its own site, of course; there is also the challenge of how it fits into the larger community around it. Wharton does most of his work in the Northeast, where the eclectic architects who worked in the early decades of the twentieth century ranged freely from style to style, filling towns like Greenwich, Connecticut, with impressive houses in all kinds of architectural styles, ensuring that other prosperous American suburbs would not be constrained by the narrow stylistic identity of places like Montecito, with its Spanish colonial houses, or Santa Fe with its adobe—traditions of uniformity that have the virtue of preventing ugly outliers, but can also seem fetishistic and confining. Wharton has followed in their footsteps, both geographically and conceptually, doing most of his work amid the leafy precincts of luxurious suburbs and exurbs, and following the principle that there is no single prevailing architectural style. It's probably right for someone of Wharton's sensibility to be working in places like Greenwich, which put a value on pluralism, at least in the realm of architecture. Such towns are bastions of propriety and conservatism, but they have always offered a range of ways of achieving respectability: The town is happy to have you take the Georgian route or the Tudor route or the Renaissance route, so long as you do one of them, and stay within the prescribed bounds of taste. Wharton never violates those bounds, but at the same time, he rarely fails to challenge them. He starts out by speaking in familiar architectural languages, the easier to join the ongoing conversation over time that engages every town and village. But the more you study his work, the more you see how he uses those languages not only to celebrate the traditions he has inherited but to continue to innovate within them, and thus to keep the creative spirit of architecture flowing.

THE HOUSE AS A REFUGE, ARCHITECTURE AS A PIONEERING EFFORT FOR THE FUTURE
INTRODUCTION BY BERNARD M. WHARTON

"By Endurance We Conquer." This statement by Ernest Shackleton, the Antarctic explorer known for his qualities of leadership, is both powerful and poignant. It represents a self-determination that was to define the successes, and notably the failures, of a man committed to making a contribution that would prove instructive for generations to come. I feel as though the course of my life is predestined, as was his, in my pursuit of architecture. A stone carver inscribed Shackleton's quote in a stone that leads up to the front door of my house. As architects, we too are explorers.

Architecture is powerful. Our buildings are physical representations of how civilizations have lived in the past. We take the responsibility seriously when given the honor by a client to design a building. It is important that our buildings withstand the test of time. They must be beautiful, practical, well-built, and original. It is important to have an understanding of history while not being a slave to it. We do not design buildings that reflect any specific style. Our architecture is modern in thought and plan, while its imagery reveals a traditional skin.

When one is naïve and young, one has a sense of confidence that one will conquer the world. It is a great feeling to be young and brash, full of ideas and ideals. It fuels the fire to push forward. Years later, one can look back on the odyssey and feel a great sense of satisfaction. Could I have accomplished this body of work by myself? The answer is no. I have had the great privilege of working with wonderful and talented collaborators. You see, I am a believer in the team approach. This is not just one man's quest or odyssey. It involves many others, and their contributions have been invaluable.

What is the true meaning of odyssey? It was a journey described by Homer, and we have all read it. My quest through life has been an odyssey. We are always pioneers setting the path for the future. At the same time, a house will always be a home, a place of refuge and comfort, free from the strains of everyday life. This concept will never change. We are human beings, not machines, and our homes should never be machines for living.

I am blessed to have come from a family that has a history in the arts. This is deep rooted. My ancestors were writers, inventors, and scientists of note, all of whom made contributions to an emerging and growing nation which was establishing itself on the world stage. I was taught from an early age that making a contribution in life was mandatory and meaningful. There was no choice.

In creating my architecture, I always try to foresee the impact our buildings will have at a future point in time. Will they still be standing, enjoyed, treasured, and be relevant to our future society's fabric? Or will they become derelict and abandoned? If so, will they be beautiful and poignant as ruins? I have walked in and among some of the world's greatest ruins. Who were the people that created these great monuments? How did they live? Were they looking toward the future? Did they believe that their architecture was progressive and ground-breaking? Will someone be standing among the ruins of our buildings in a thousand years?

Many years ago I had the opportunity to visit one of Frank Lloyd Wright's Usonian houses. These houses were Wright's attempt to create small houses that would be more accessible to the masses. The house was modest on the exterior, but in its modesty, was highly thought-out and resolved. Once you entered the house, Wright began to work his magic. The progression of spaces, the volume of the rooms, and the careful placement of windows were enlightening, and had a lasting effect on this young architecture student. I have always been concerned with the progression of spaces. Our houses feature visual axes and the use of enfilades. Our façades are very carefully developed.

Over the years, our style of architecture has become our own. Without losing sight of what I have learned, I look toward the future. When I am asked to describe what historical style our houses represent, I am usually at a loss for words. Our style of architecture does not fit into any one historical category.

For our architecture to be deemed truly "American," one must understand how the country evolved from a demographic standpoint. The "melting pot" theory immediately comes to mind, where people of different origins come together to form a strong whole. Our work is an amalgamation of this theory: It is a powerful and honest expression of architecture that has its own sense of place and permanence.

There are two influences—one historical and one cultural—that I do happily acknowledge. The first is the influence of H.H. Richardson, one of the greatest American architects. In the third quarter of the 19th century, he took medieval influences and reconfigured them into what is called "Richardsonian Romanesque"—a unique architecture that took America out of the thin, provisional, wooden Eastlake style and into a mature expression of building. With Richardson's architecture, America became a grown-up country and a player on the world stage. Conversely, the other influence I have benefited from is the lightness and airy quality of Japanese architecture, with its sloping roofs that seem to lift buildings up toward the sky and its immutable walls, with their deceptive fragility.

We have been fortunate to work on all types of sites. They have been very geographically diverse and are usually extraordinary in their beauty. Each site offers its share of opportunities and constraints. Some of our most successful houses have been the product of sites that proved to be very challenging. Whether the site is on the waterfront, or in a rural or urban setting, we have a great responsibility to integrate the house with its surrounding environment. Our buildings must fuse with the land in an effortless way. They must become one with the land.

Architecture can become all-consuming and an obsession without balance with other aspects of life. It is fine to be romantic about your craft, but there are other wonderful outlets in life to be enjoyed. My escape is sailing. I relish the solitude and quiet. Being on the water gives me a different vantage point. I suspect this aspect of my life has been invaluable in our firm's ability to design waterfront houses.

I look at architecture in a holistic way. My journeys and life experiences have shaped the architecture of this firm. I had a wonderful professor at the University of Pennsylvania who had been a prominent architect in Cuba before Castro took over. Because of his experiences, he emphasized that, as architects, we could not be isolationists. We have to understand not only the physical aspects of architectural history, but what is happening socially that shapes the architecture.

I have been blessed with creative and talented partners who have contributed immensely to the success of the firm. They are Arthur Hanlon, Jerry Hupy, Michael McClung, John Gassett and Don Aitken. Without them and our diligent staff, the work in this book would not be possible.

My life and my career have intertwined in a wonderful and rewarding journey, made possible by the dedication and confidence that my collaborators and clients have had in my ability to chart a very important course. It has truly been "By Endurance We Conquer." It has been a journey filled with rich rewards. I hope you enjoy this book.

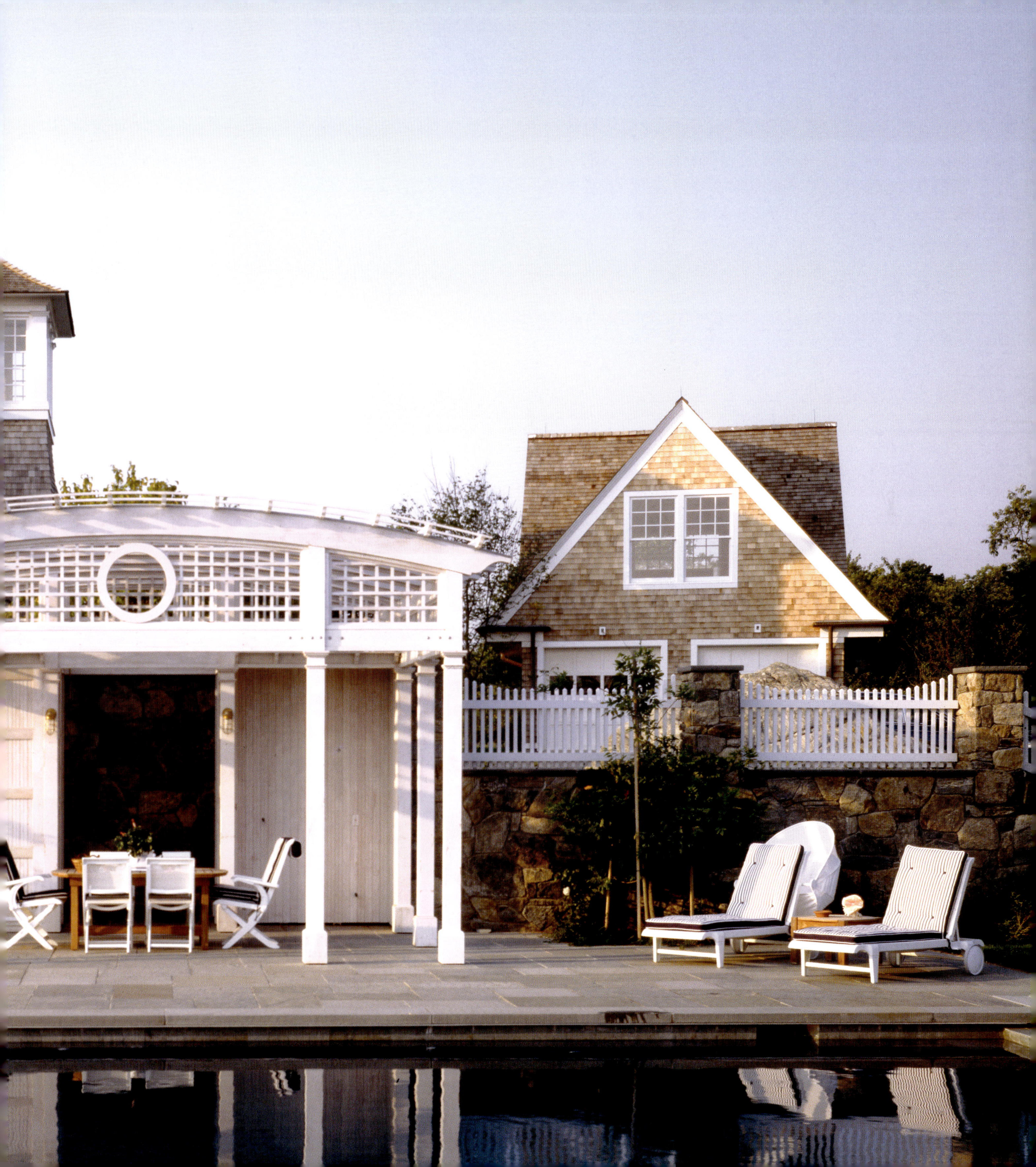

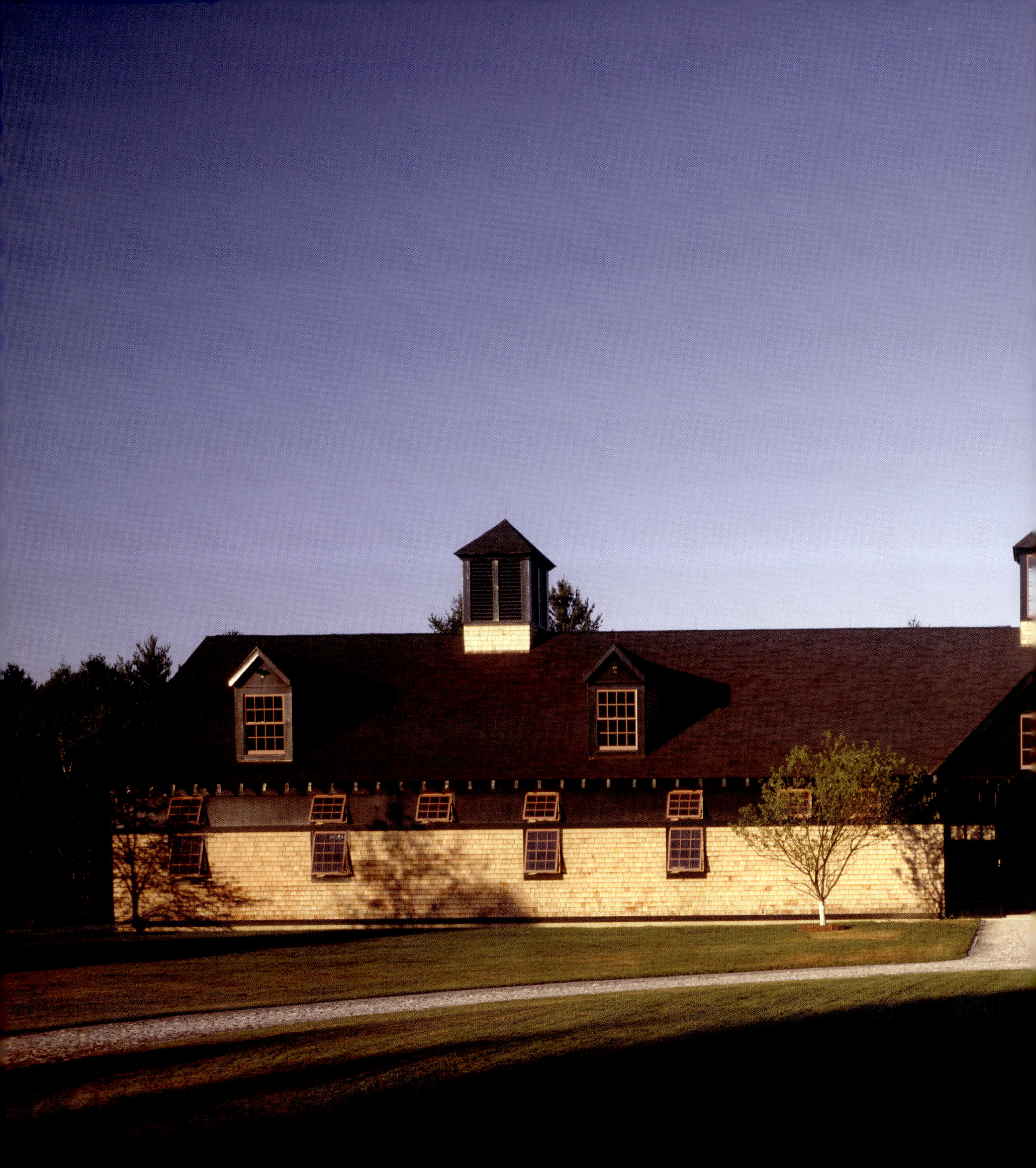

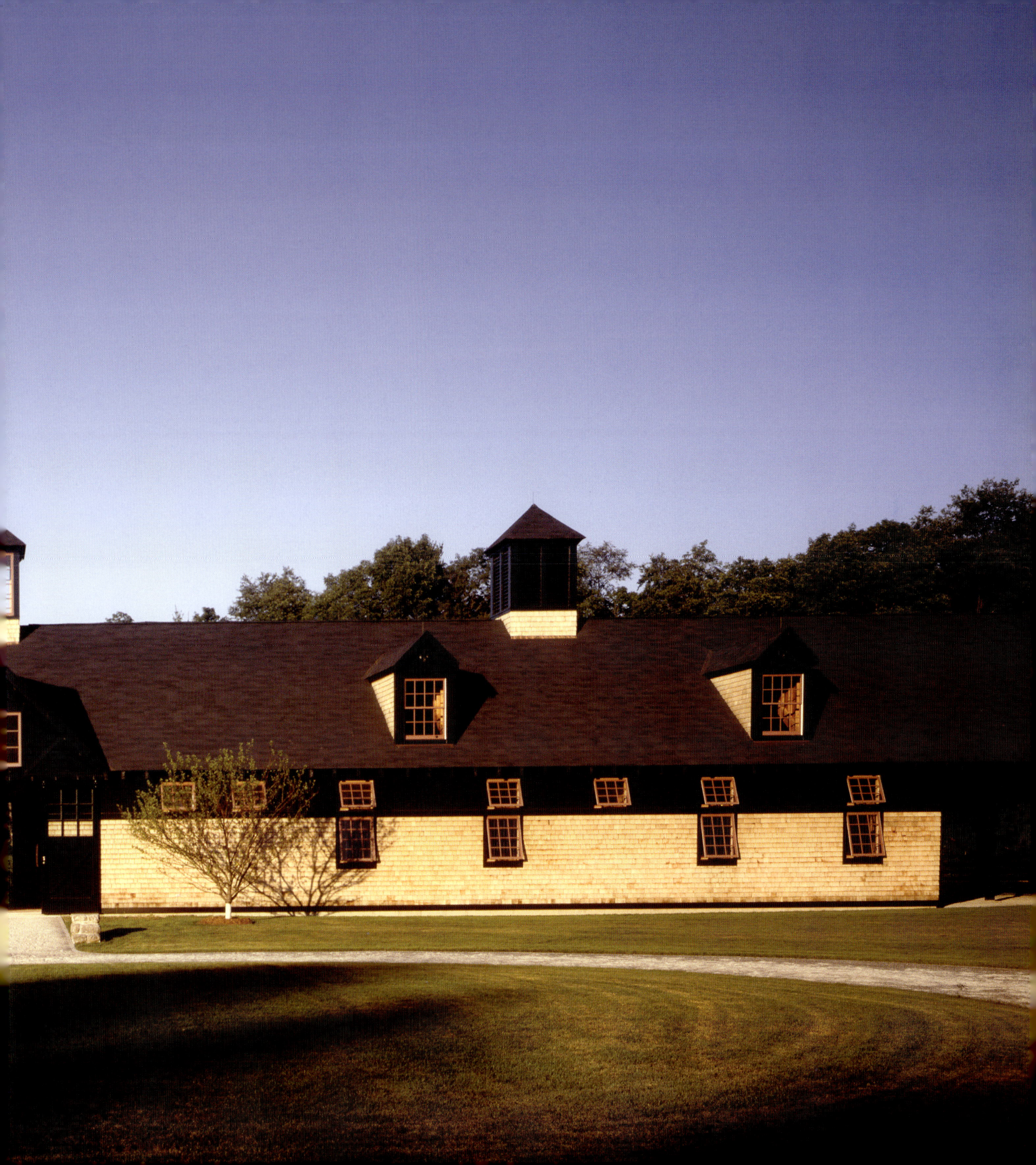

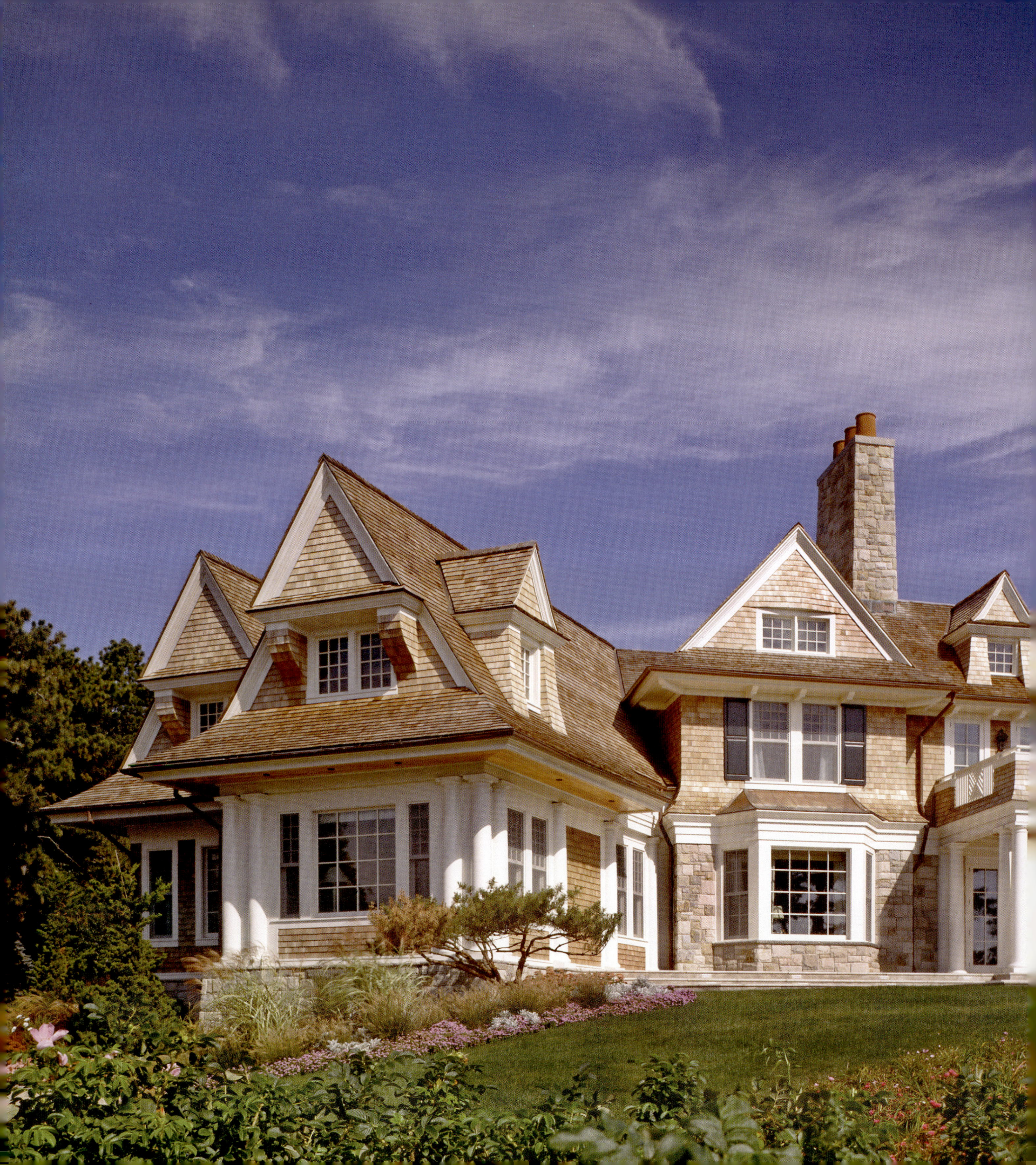

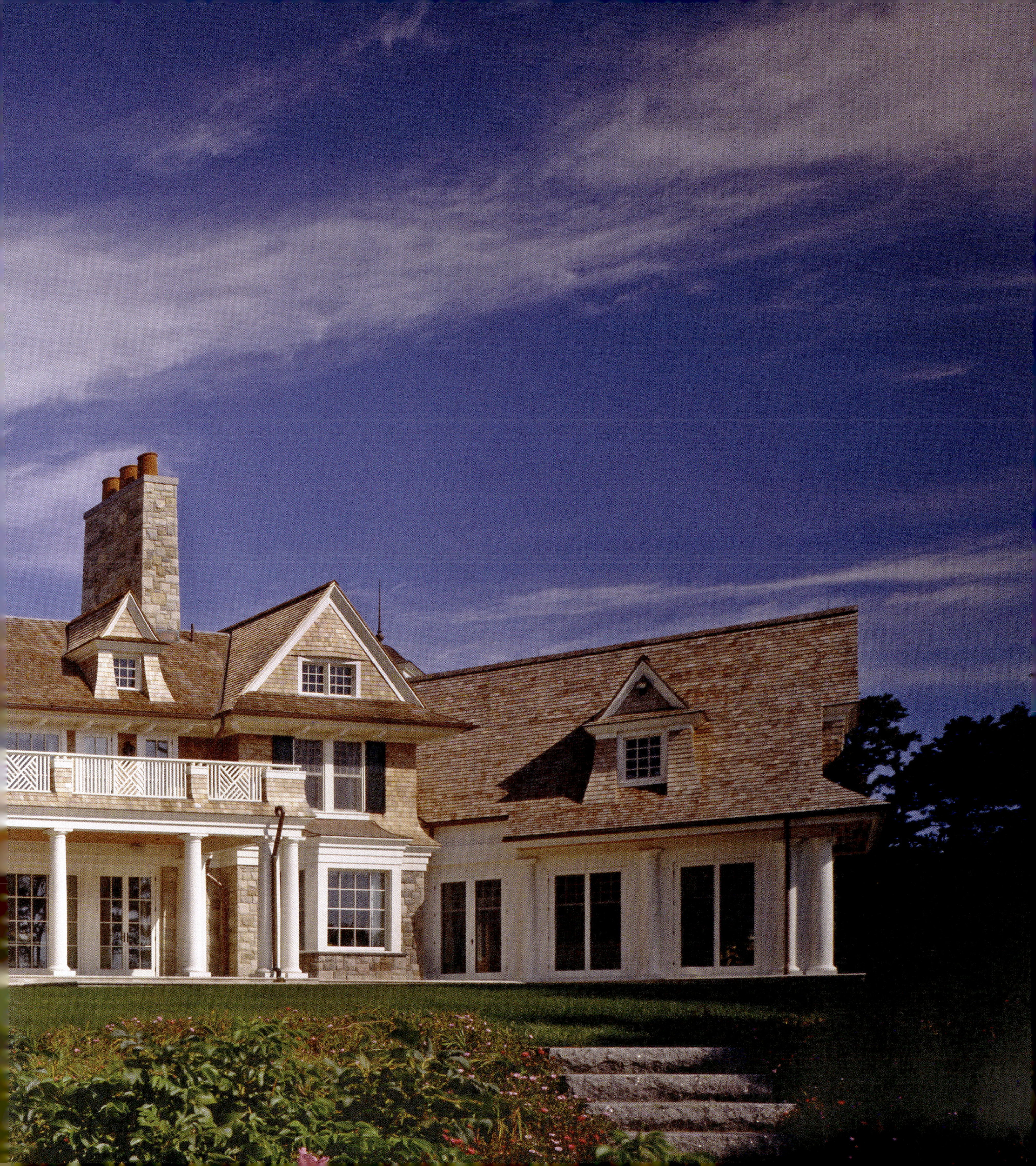

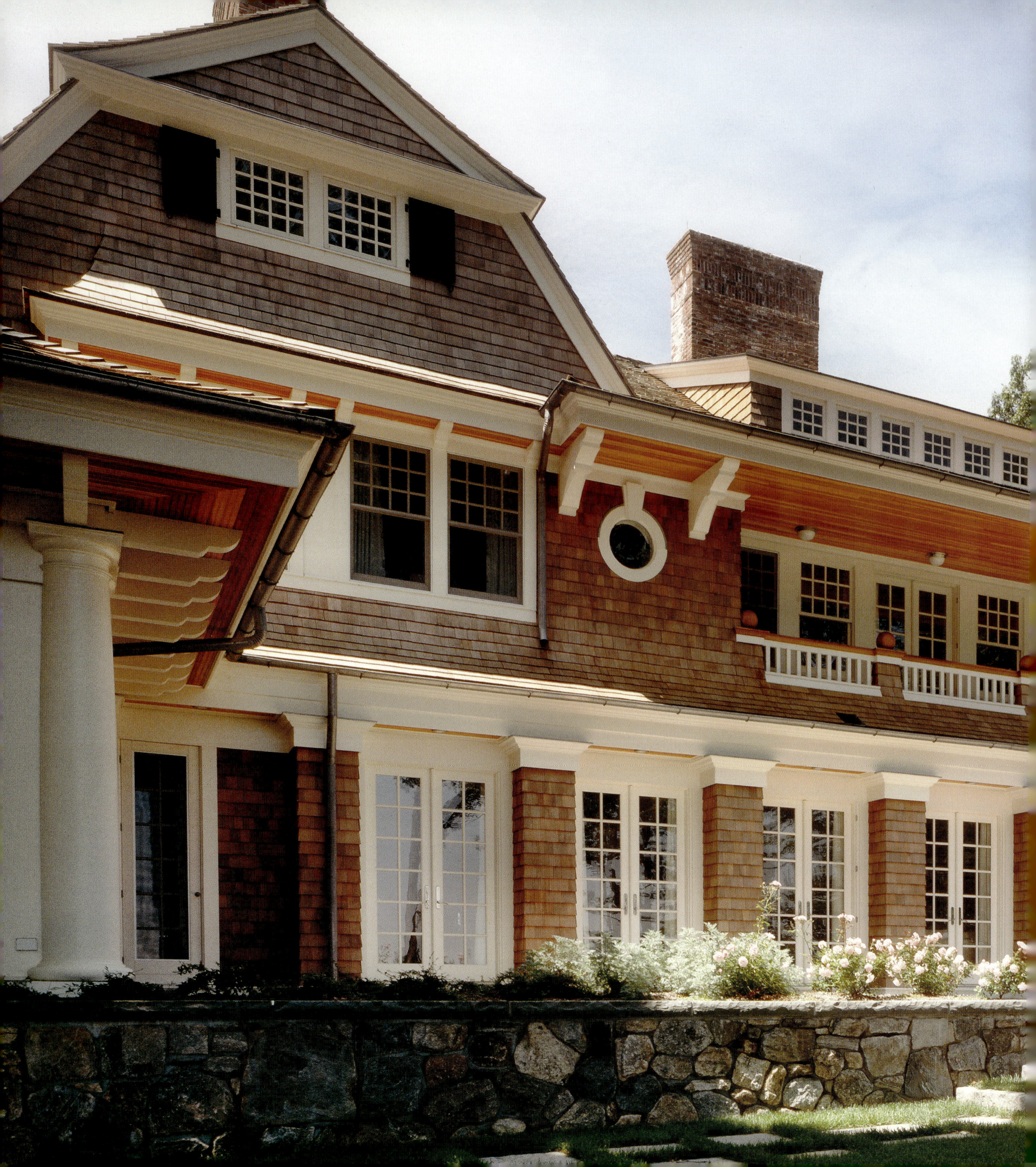

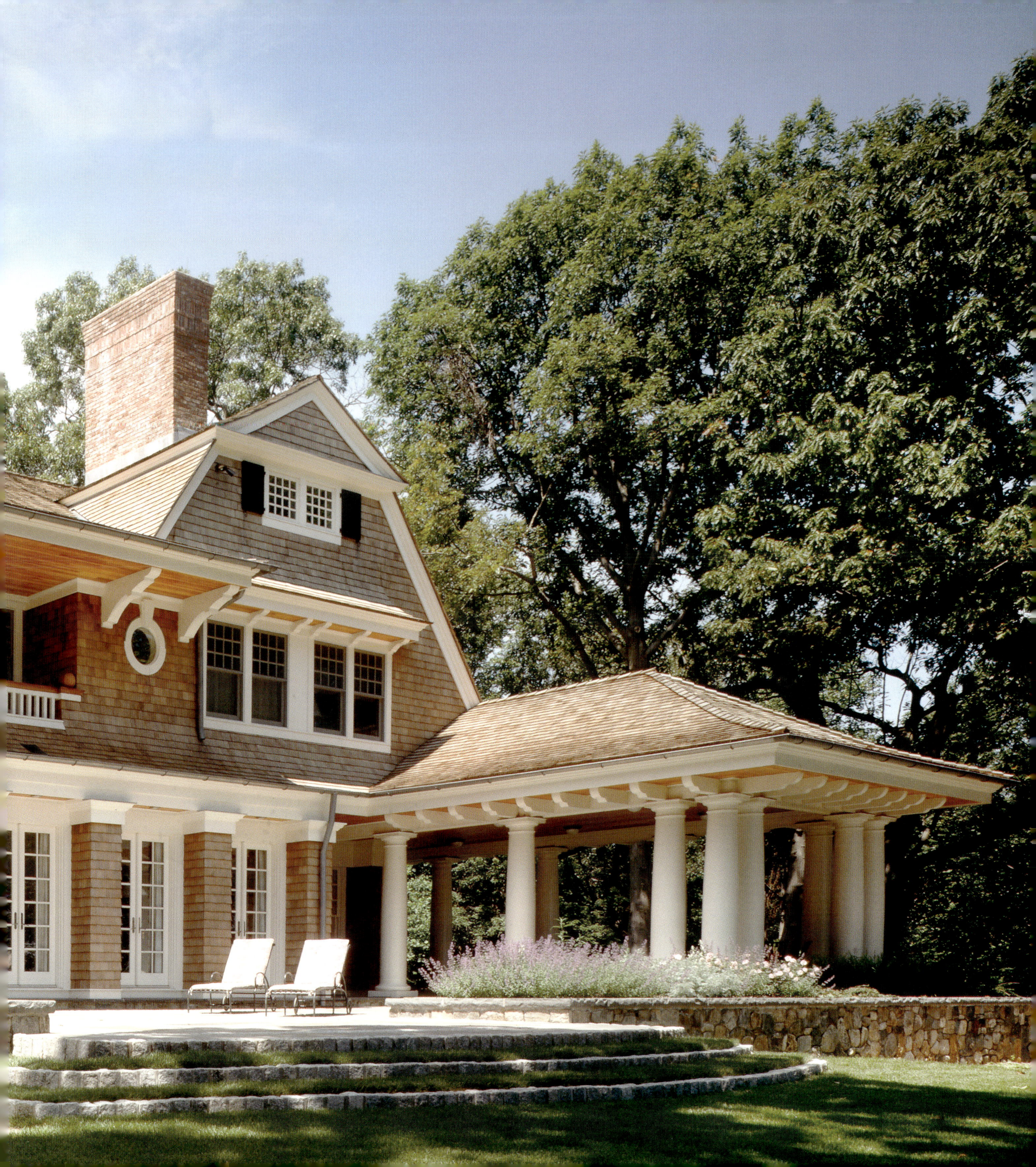

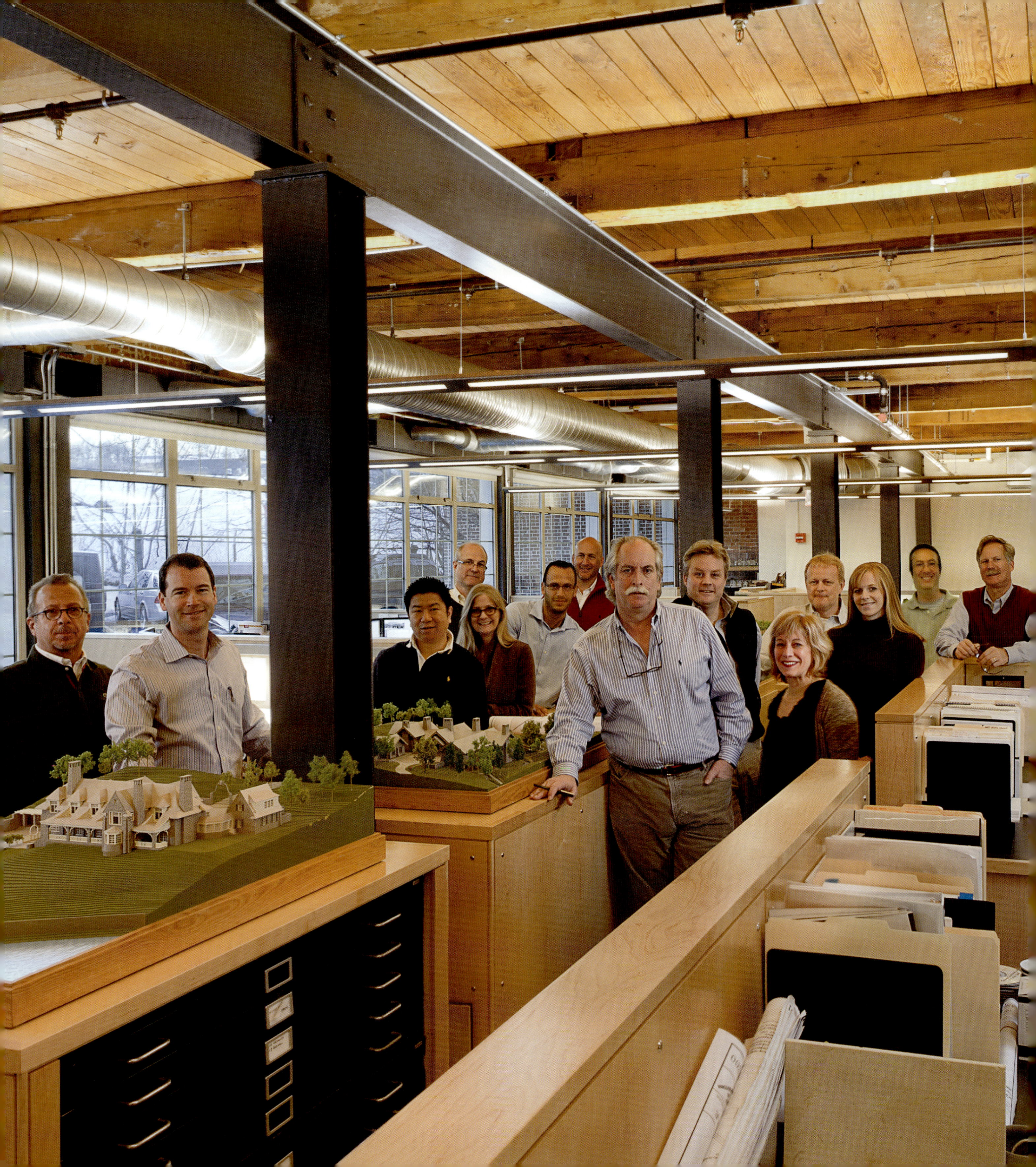

THE DESIGN PROCESS: CREATING A HOUSE IS NOT JUST DRIVEN LIKE A BUSINESS, BUT AS AN EVOLVING PIECE OF ART

A recently completed project in the Adirondacks, which we refer to as Big Rock, is a good model for explaining our design process from start to finish. A couple came from coastal California to find out about our office and share with us their dream house in the Adirondacks. Over the years, they had followed our work in periodicals, and were familiar with many of our projects. We are not sure that anything that we had done was exactly what they were after; however, we believe they sensed that we were good listeners, attentive to detail, and most importantly, passionate about the work. We thought the chemistry was there and the design possibilities abundant. The leap of faith a client takes is huge. With each commission, we applaud their gestures of good faith and belief in what we can do.

We went up to the Adirondacks, which has a very rich history (and a very different one from that of California), to spend time with the clients and to understand their site, which is a rocky and wooded peninsula overlooking an unbelievable lake view with dramatic mountains as a backdrop. The initial process was both ethereal and pragmatic. We talked about all of their wishes from how the house would relate to nature, to what they wanted inside the kitchen. On a site as beautiful as this, getting the approach correct was a huge responsibility. Simply stated: Successful houses are well sited.

The Adirondack lakes are great for families—for both kids and parents alike. Our clients wanted relief from the hectic pace of modern life and to be able to enjoy the outdoors. The Adirondacks have a great history of camps where people came to enjoy the sporting life and the fresh air. There were many trees on the site and there was a temptation to clear the site for panoramic views. We chose, however, to tread lightly on the land and work with select planned views through the trees. The design was going to be a success if we could minimally alter the site and capture the essence of the Adirondacks. The house, too, would need an organization that was flexible enough to capture those views, fulfill the clients' needs, and respect the camp tradition.

We wanted all of those things without becoming clichéd, or dare we say 'camp'. The design needed a little twist and an edge that was reflective of our artistic, visual, and nautical clients. At the same time, we needed to satisfy all of the programmatic requirements

The Shope Reno Wharton team was photographed in the firm's Norwalk, Connecticut offices. From left: Terry O'Halloran, Michael McClung, Patrick Lau, Bayard Cutting, Alice Weatherford, Jose Goncalves, Jerry Hupy, Bernard Wharton, Arthur Hanlon, Dorothy Susko, Don Aitken, Sara Murray, Paul Wise, and John Gassett.

with an eye on the project budget. Project budgets influence our response, as there is a dynamic between size, scope, and quality that cannot be overlooked. Zoning and land easements are also factors that need consideration at the beginning of any project. We have found over the years that the constraints of a site are often the genesis of strong design concepts that shape the layout and three-dimensional appearance of a design.

Armed with knowledge of our clients, a program, and an understanding of the site, we begin the schematic design process. Our first presentation usually happens approximately six weeks later. It typically includes an overall site plan, floor plans, and the primary elevations of the house. We add furniture to the plans to impart a sense of scale for the homeowner. The elevation drawings are typically done freehand to communicate the imagery and a looseness that is designed to convey the feeling of the house.

Over the years, Bernard Wharton has been the catalyst for the concept and initial ideas as well as sketches that start each project. The concepts and ideas developed show through in every SRW project—whether it be a shingled oceanfront home or a stone mountain estate. Typically, one of the five partners is involved from the start as the project architect and is supported by a team from the design studio. This was the process at Big Rock. Our office never separates design from production, and seeks to enhance the schematic concepts and imagery to fully developed statements. The studio is interactive and there is opportunity for enhancement that is ever present.

During the design-development phase, we work very quickly to transform the freehand plans and elevations to a more rigorous set of plans and elevations. It is during this time that we tinker with the plans and further develop the elevations, thinking about the structure from all sides. Too often, homes are designed from only one or two sides and the composition as a whole suffers. Our office works hard to make sure that we turn corners well as we perceive our buildings from all angles. Design development culminates in the production of a scale model. It is a physical affirmation of all of the decisions to date. While there are no big surprises for us, it does create a moment of glee for all when it is presented. We present our clients with a "brag book" that has all of the plans and elevations of the house, along with images of the model, often Photoshopped into the site. The model is a great tool to help clients envision, understand and appreciate what we are designing.

The construction documents and specifications come next and represent the legal contract between the owner and contractor. For us, however, it is also the opportunity to magnify the experience that we are trying to get across. Our drawings are highly detailed, showing every nook and cranny of the house. Structural systems, audio visual, millwork, plumbing, lighting, light fixtures, and trim (just to name a few) are all real components that need selection and integration during this phase. In this home, we made great efforts to reinforce the concept of simplified living while celebrating the unique nature of the

Adirondacks. We believe that we should detail our buildings to age well and look better as they weather. In a world of poor quality construction, we believe building something well for generations is the ultimate green. Passive technologies, such as overhangs and proper orientation, enforce design that is both beautiful and functional.

Our clients don't go away during the construction document phase—they are active participants and control the destiny of the house. We continue to be blessed with spirited clients, talented interior designers, and craftsmen who help create truly special homes. The relationships are intense and hopefully yield a final design greater than the sum of the individual parts. At the end of the construction documents, we have a fully developed piece of frozen music reflective of many perspectives that comes to life during construction. This was the case at Big Rock, where the furniture and decorative finishes reinforced the design of the interior hardscape. All of the little details create a richer whole.

During construction, the project architect is responsible for keeping the whole team—client, builder, interior decorator, and landscape architect—moving forward. Our design process and documentation is set up to minimize the improvisation that occurs when a design is not well thought-out. Inevitably, however, we will see certain things during the course of construction that we wish to make better. These tweaks can sometimes create angst and heated moments during construction. The role of the architect is to balance making a project the best it can be in the face of a schedule, time, and budget. We would venture to say a few of these tense moments have yielded some wonderful spaces that continue to delight, many years later. Our respect for the builders who navigate these waters and execute our dreams is immense—their contribution is great.

It can be about six months from sketches to the point of starting construction, and sometimes over two years before a home is completed. We like a process that has momentum and continuity and culminates in a special home that will last for years to come. After the clients move in, we often frame an initial sketch or two. We present them, and the client can compare the sketch to the built form. They can see how a sketch on yellow paper becomes the dream realized. We never get tired of people commenting that their house looks like the drawings and the model!

Shope Reno Wharton is not a business-centered practice. We are a practice-centered business in creating architecture as art. We deal with people whose dreams are challenging and wonderful and the relationships are as interesting and fun as the homes that we create. We have a great open studio and a great staff that is very competitive—we are our own toughest critics! The homes we create are the physical culmination of that collaboration. If we have done our job well, each client feels that his or her design is the best that we have ever created. We would not have it any other way.

Shope Reno Wharton Architecture, March 2011

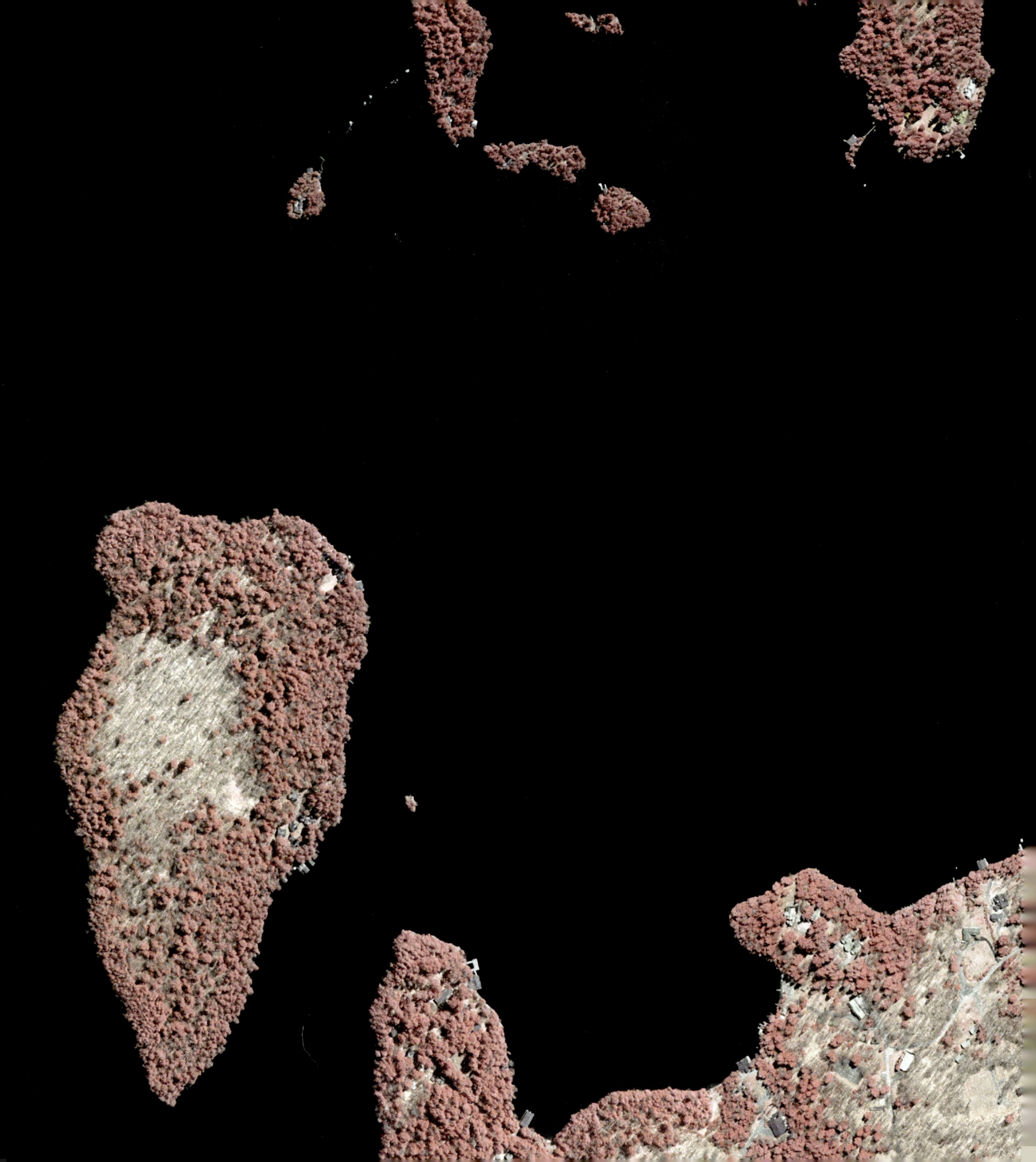

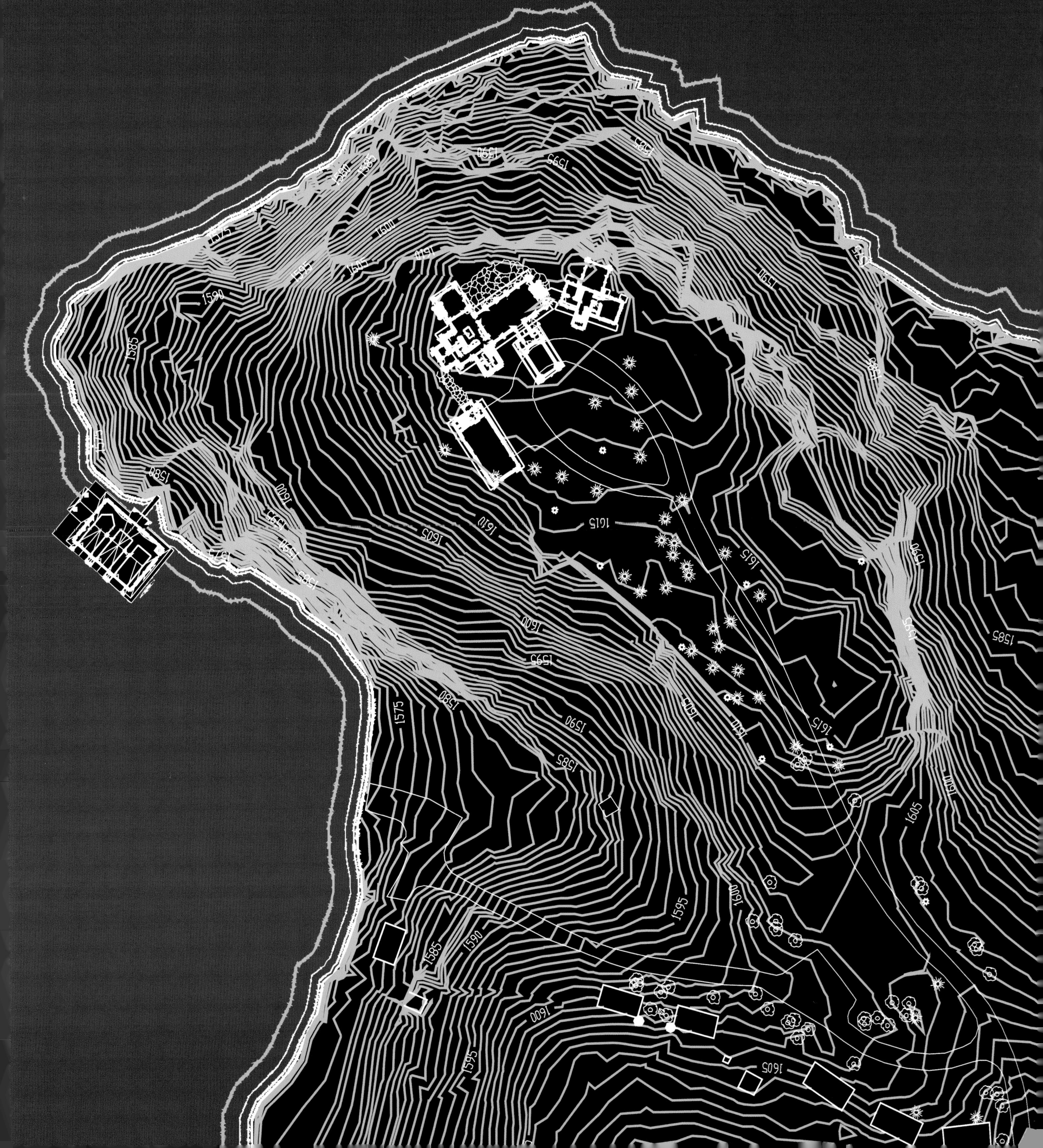

1575
1580
1585
1590
1595
1600
1605
1610
1615

views →

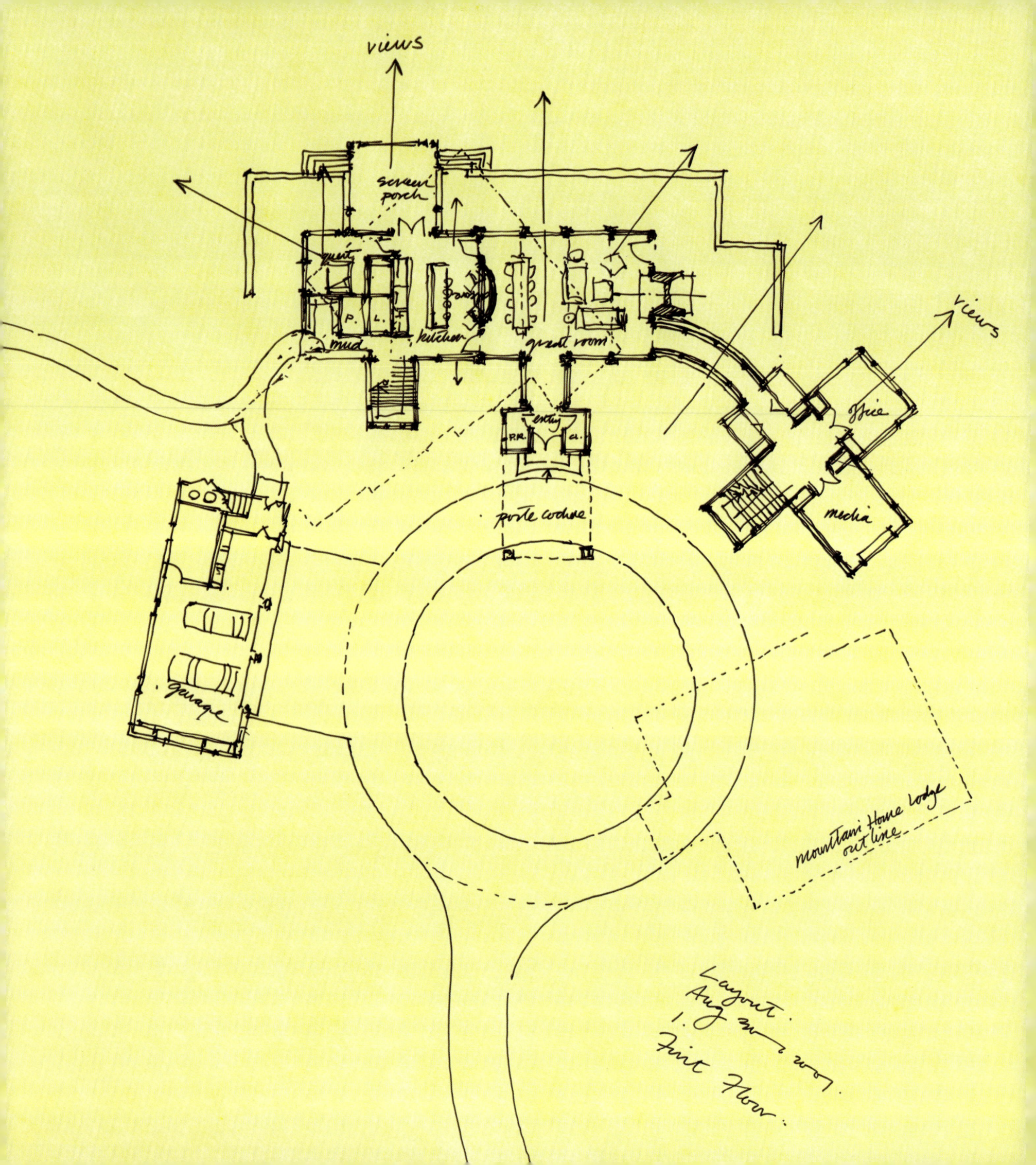

screen porch

guest — P.L. — mud — kitchen — great room — office

entry — P.R. — cl.

porte cochere

media

garage

mountain Home Lodge outline

Layout
August 30, 2007
First Floor

SITE PLAN

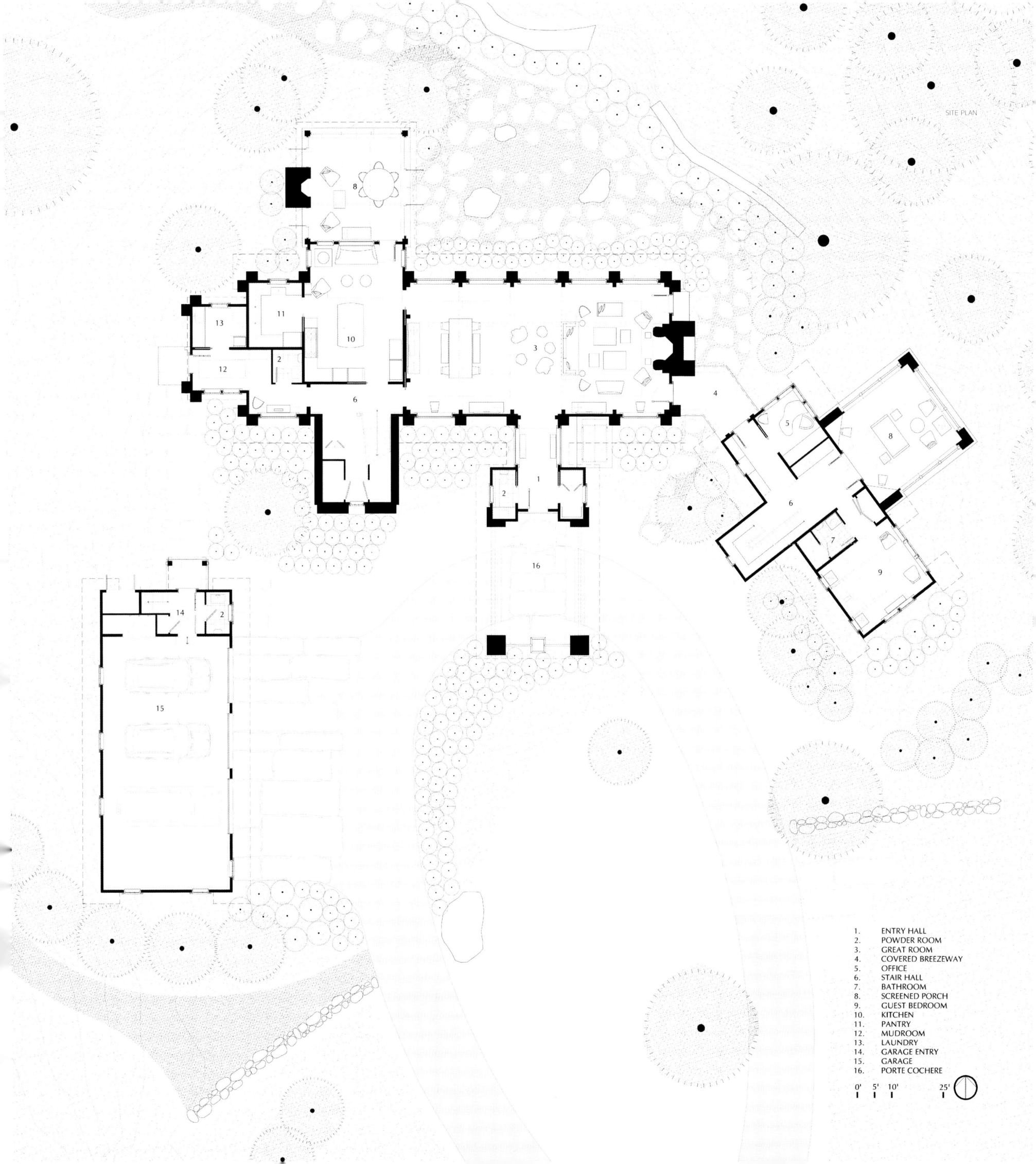

1. ENTRY HALL
2. POWDER ROOM
3. GREAT ROOM
4. COVERED BREEZEWAY
5. OFFICE
6. STAIR HALL
7. BATHROOM
8. SCREENED PORCH
9. GUEST BEDROOM
10. KITCHEN
11. PANTRY
12. MUDROOM
13. LAUNDRY
14. GARAGE ENTRY
15. GARAGE
16. PORTE COCHERE

0' 5' 10'   25'

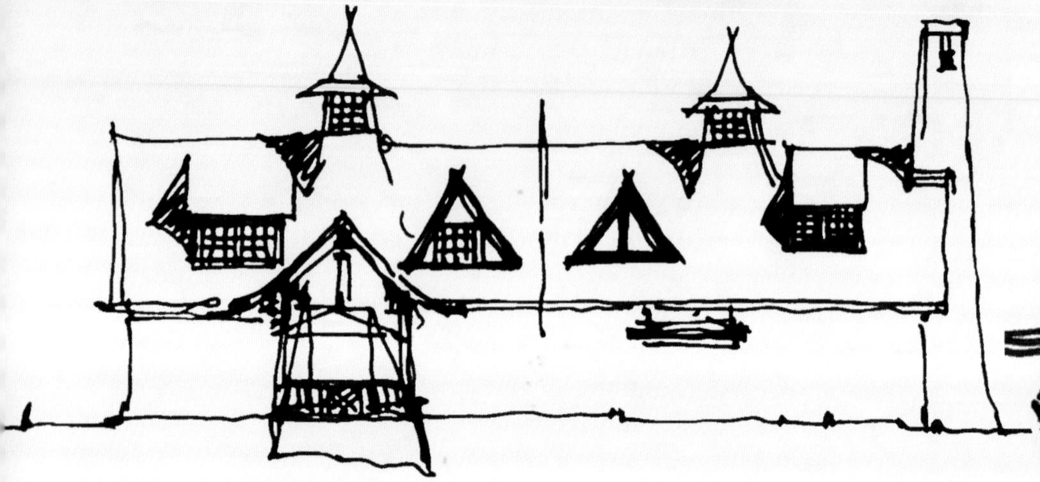

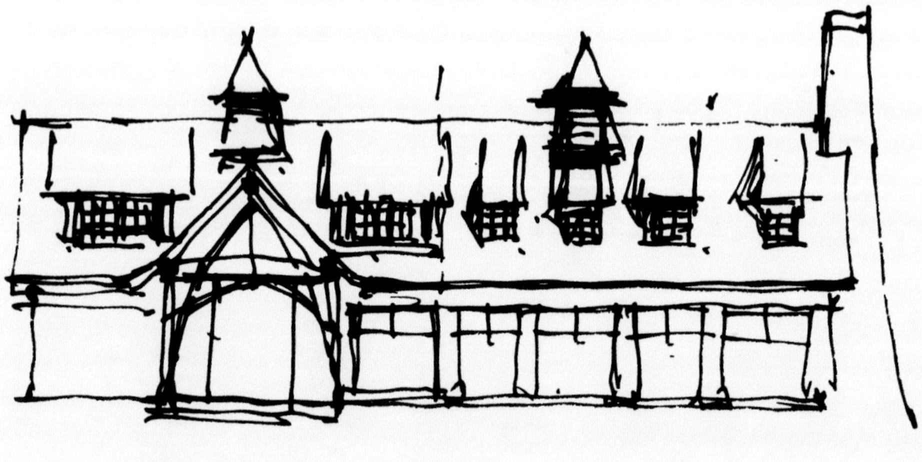

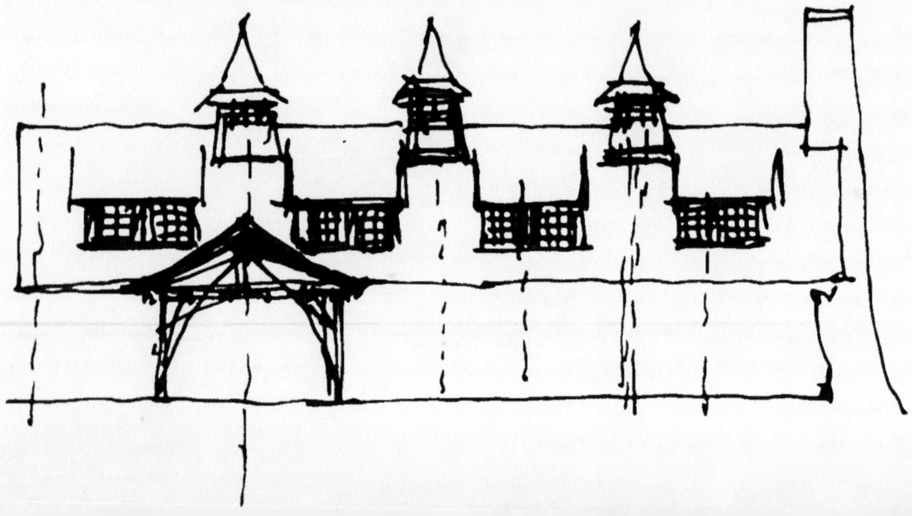

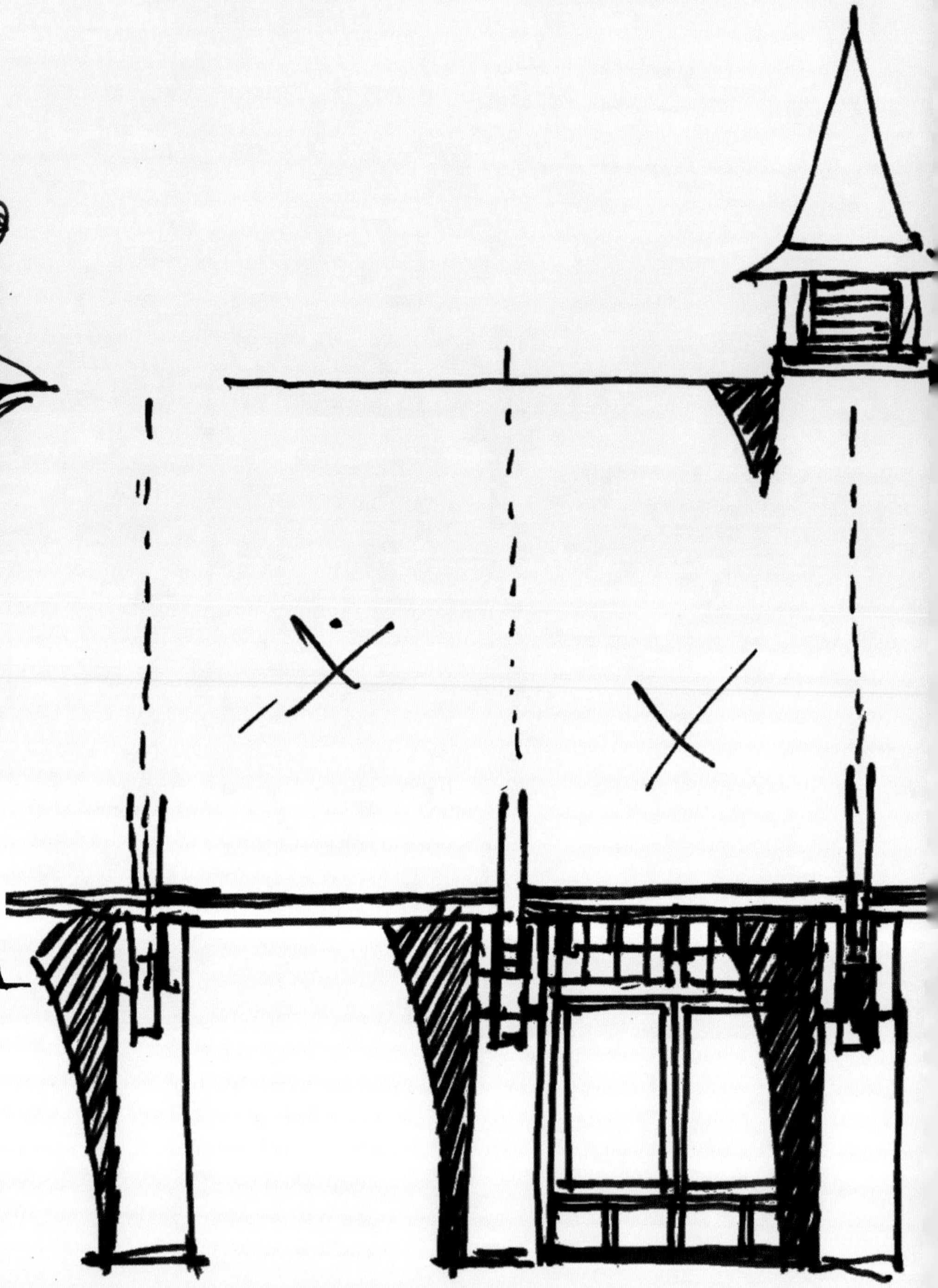

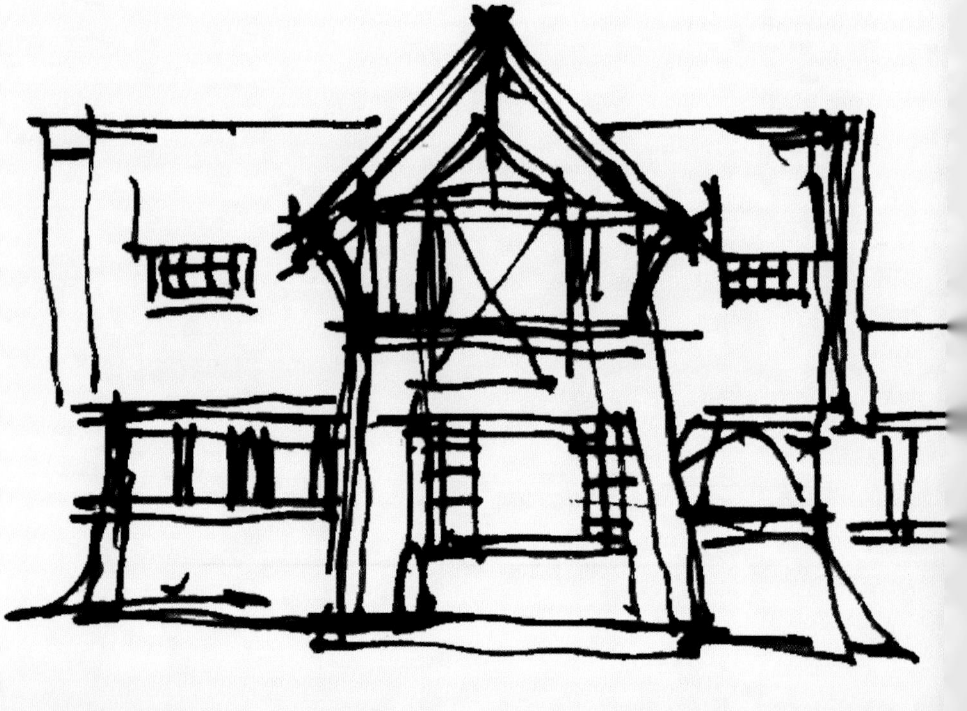

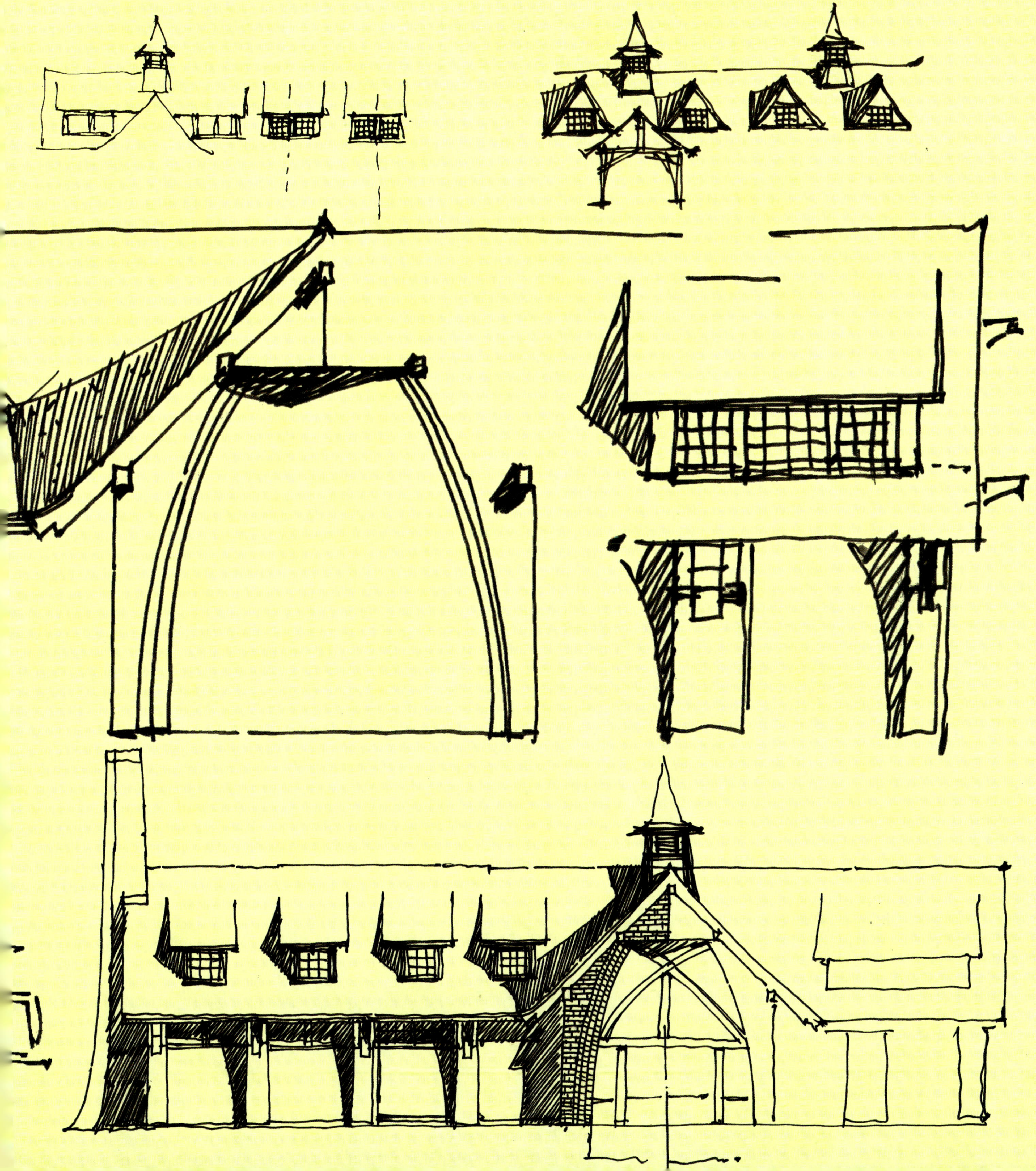

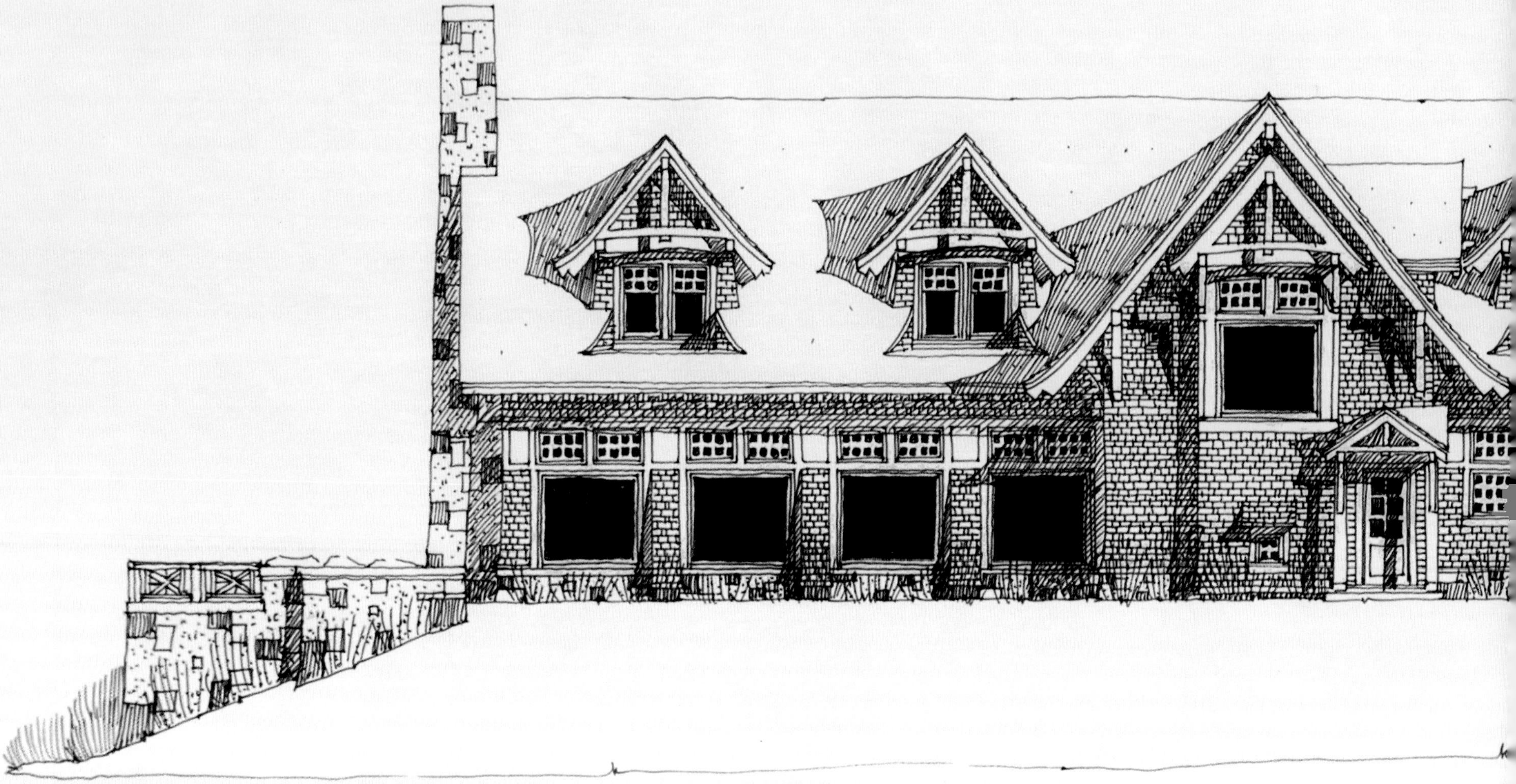

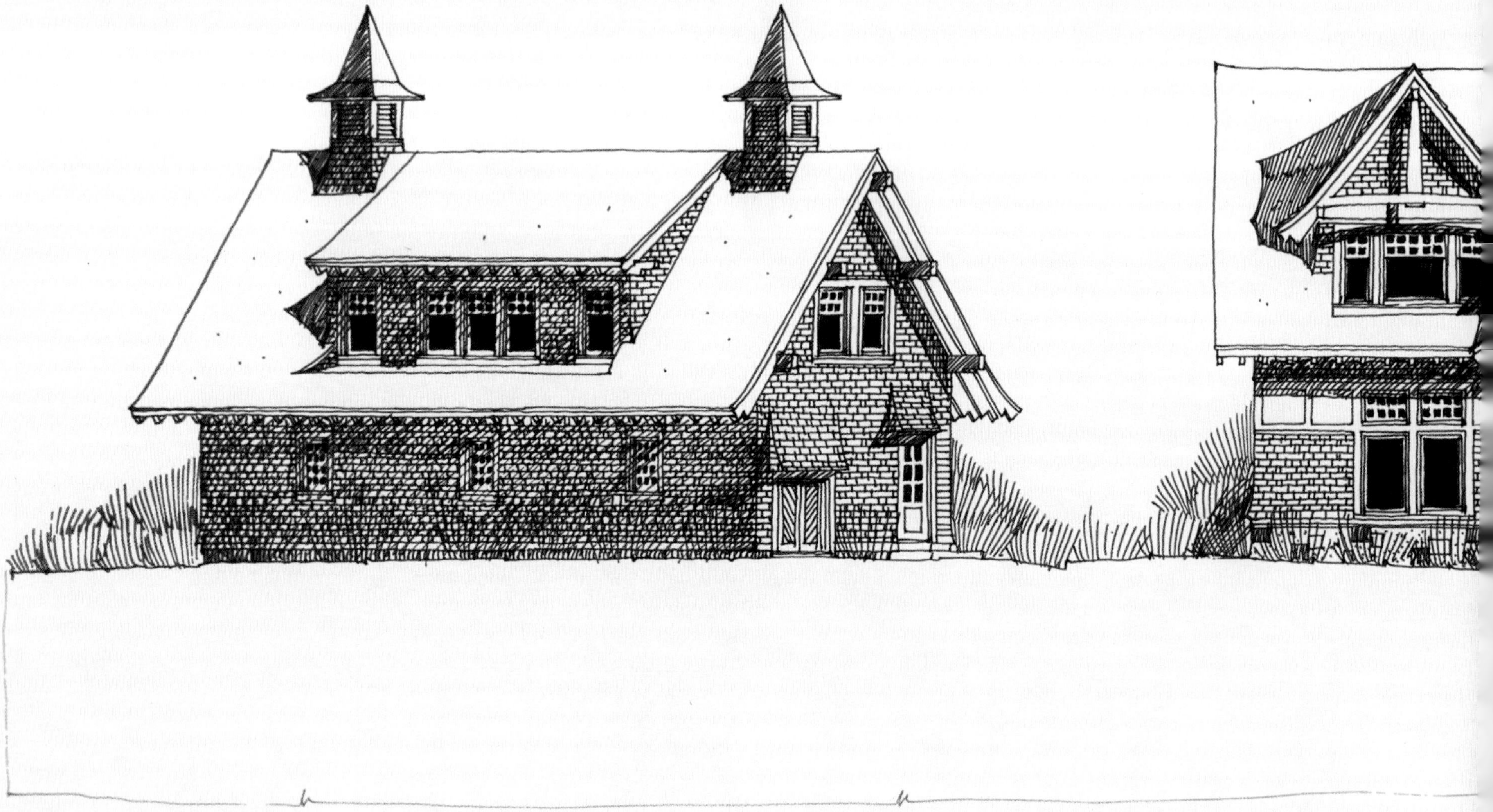

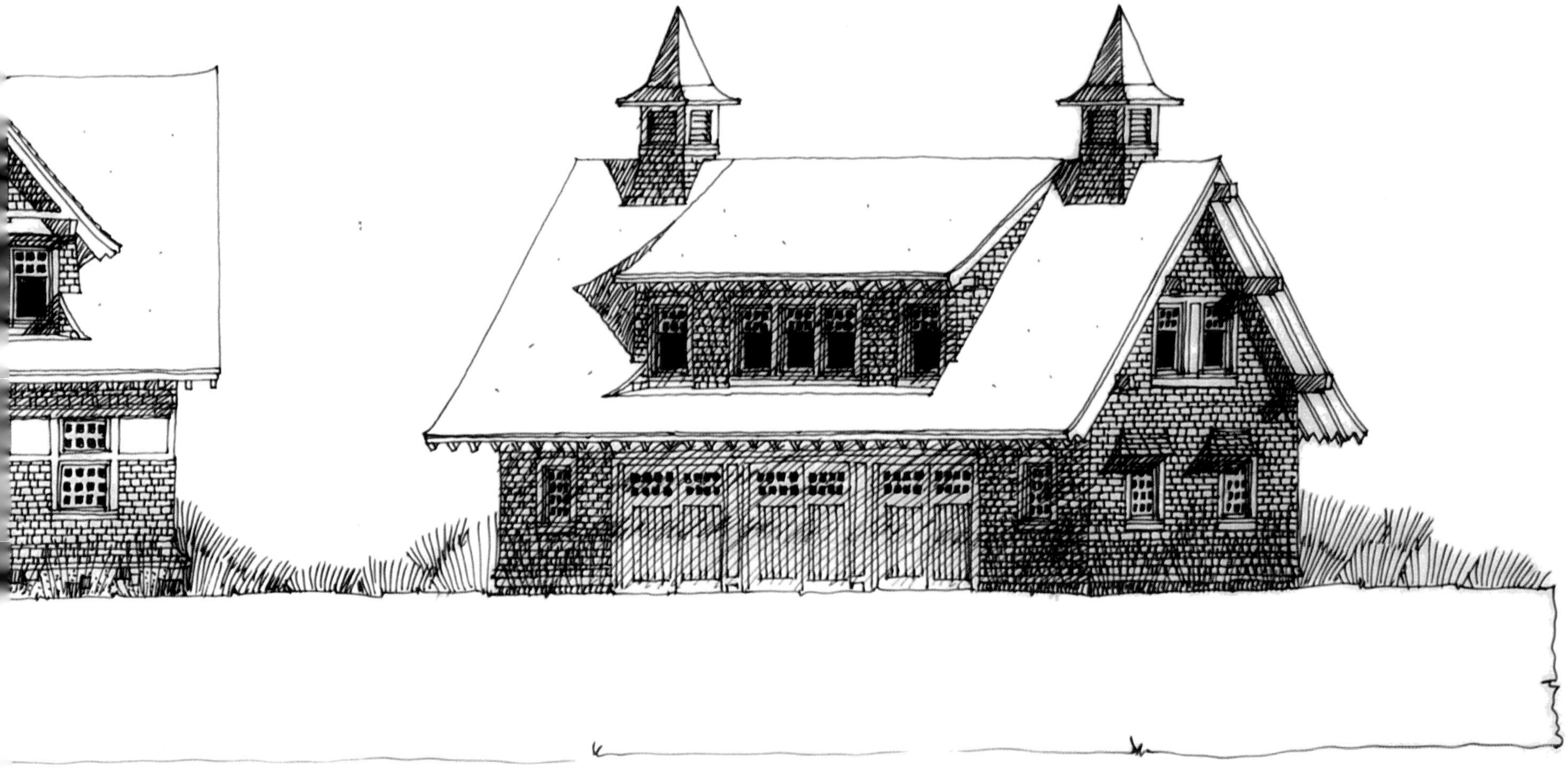

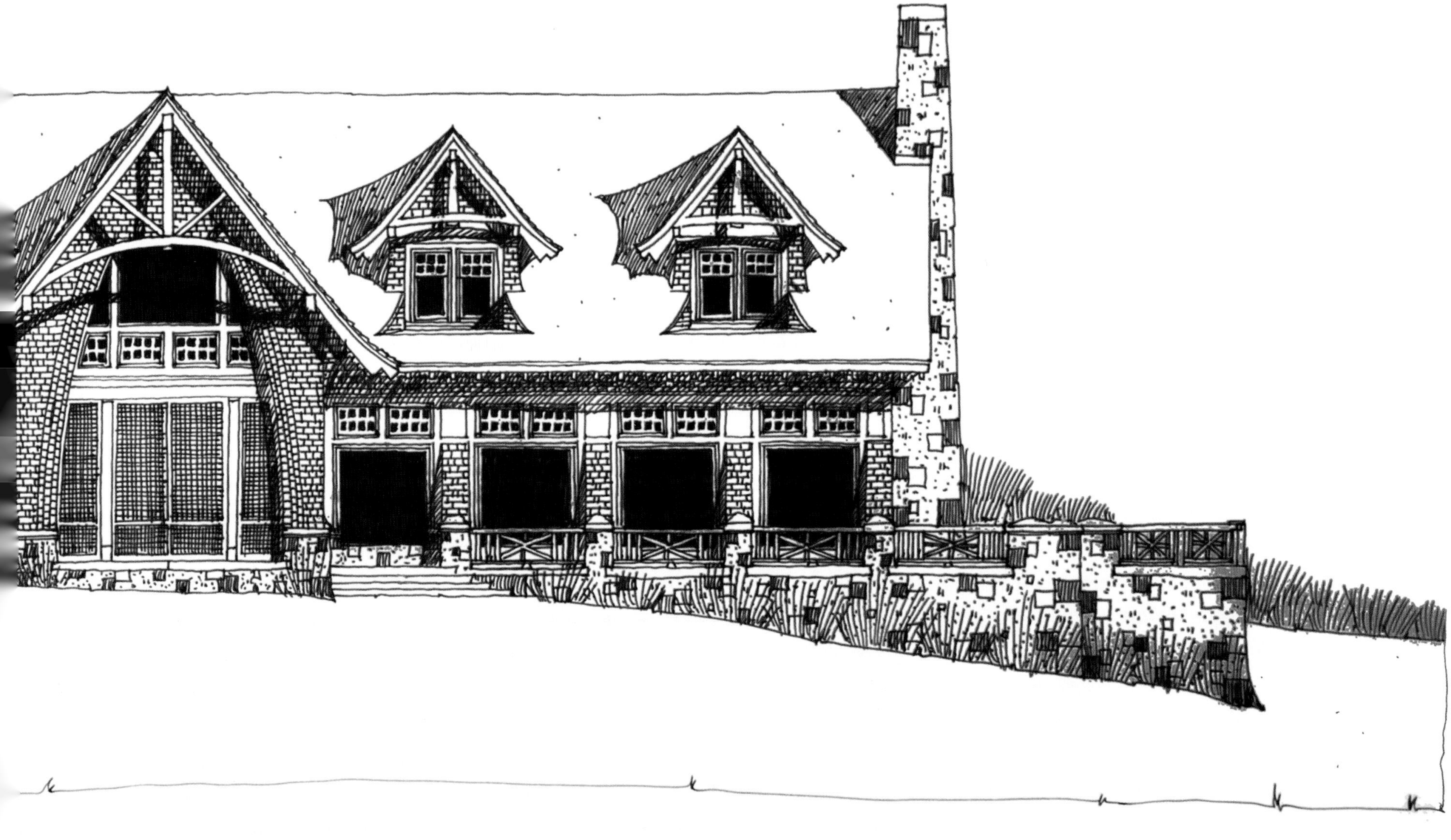

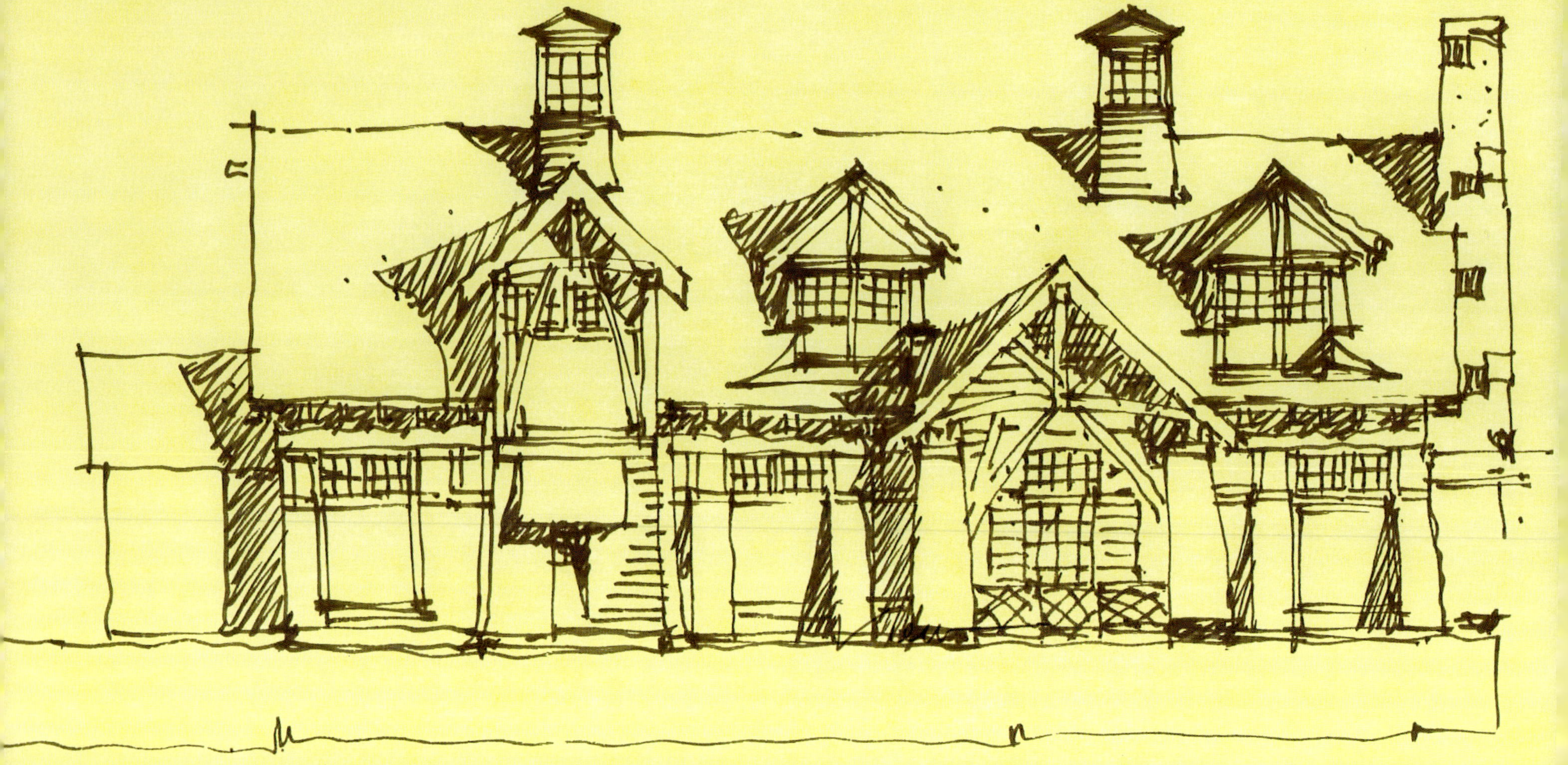

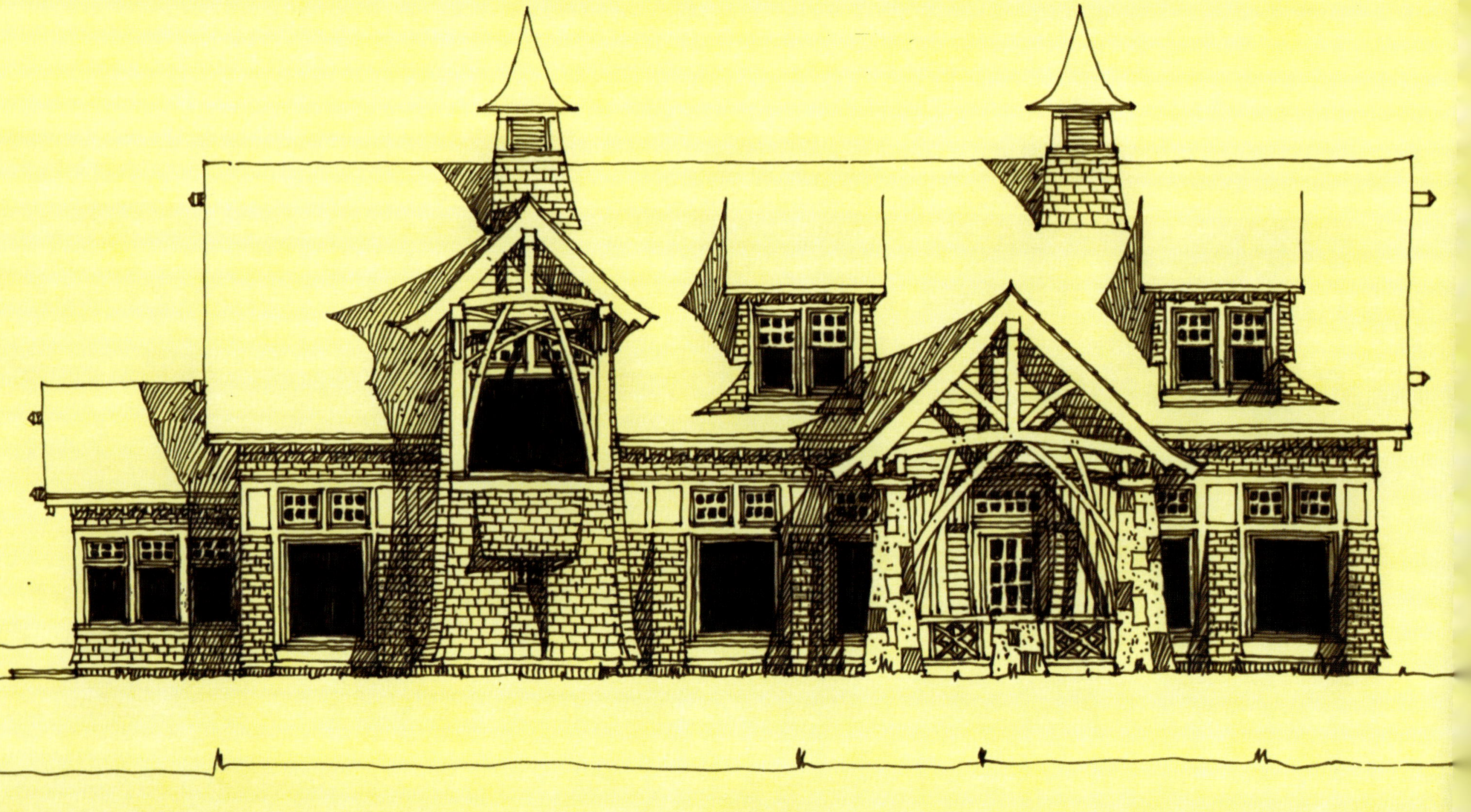

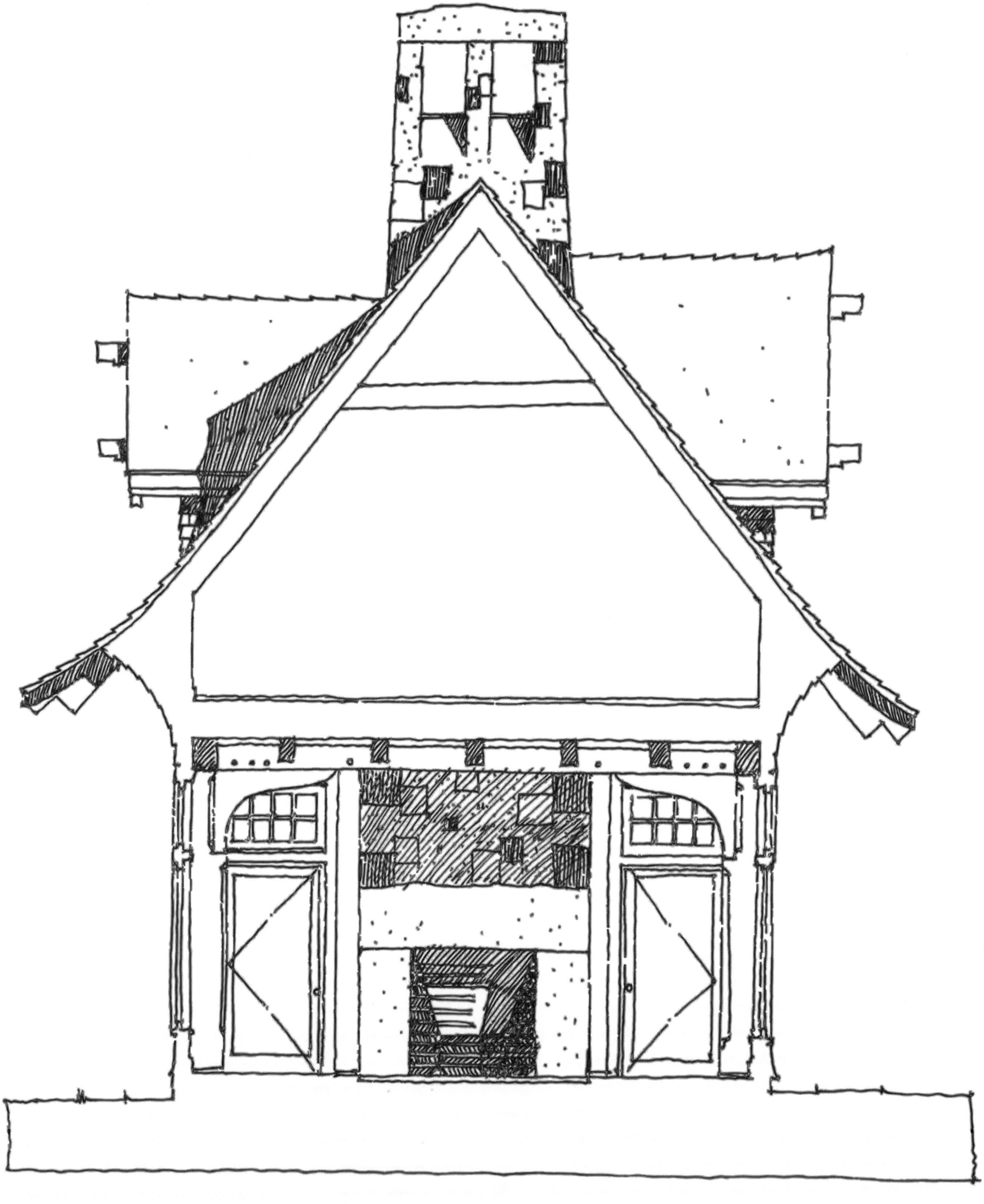

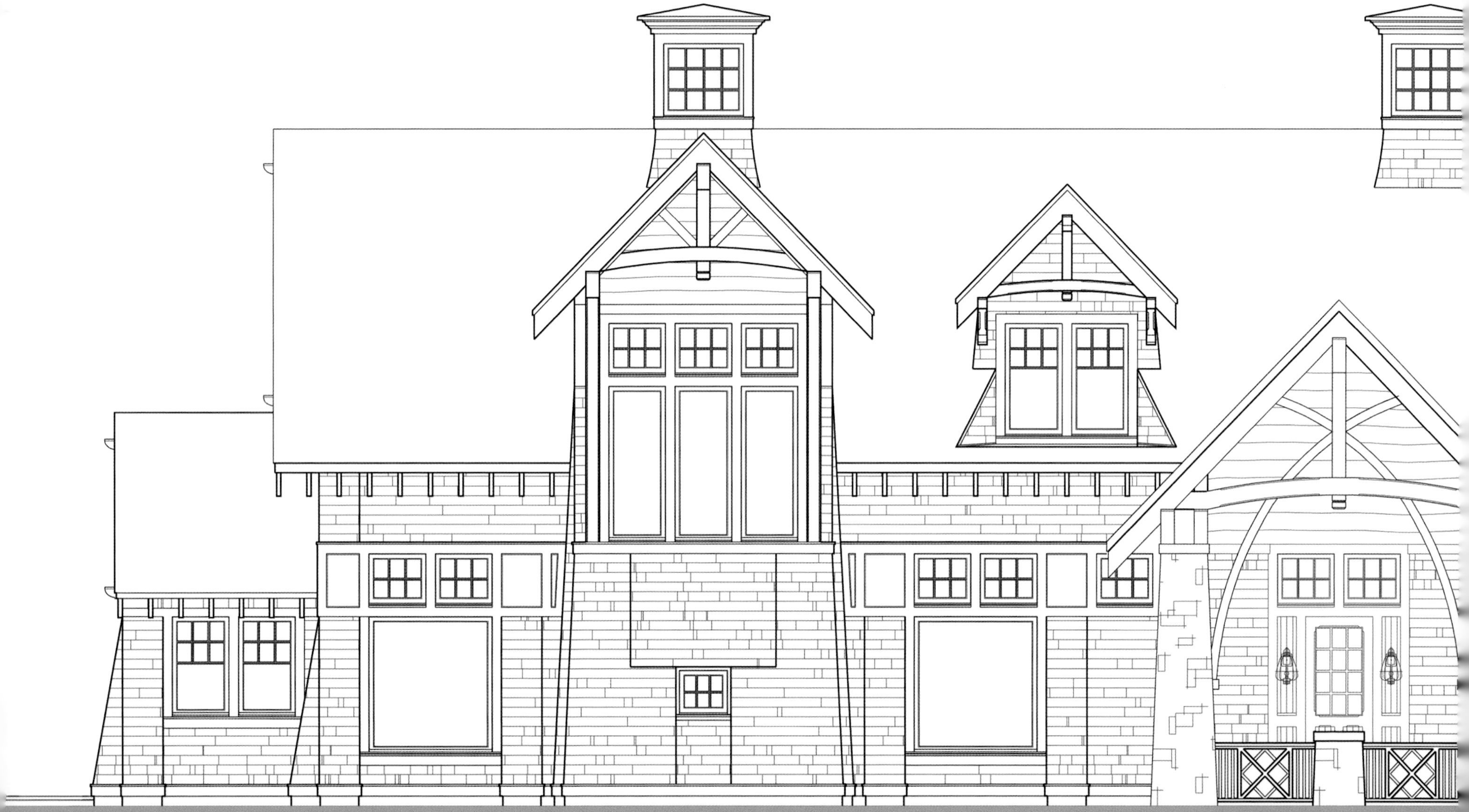

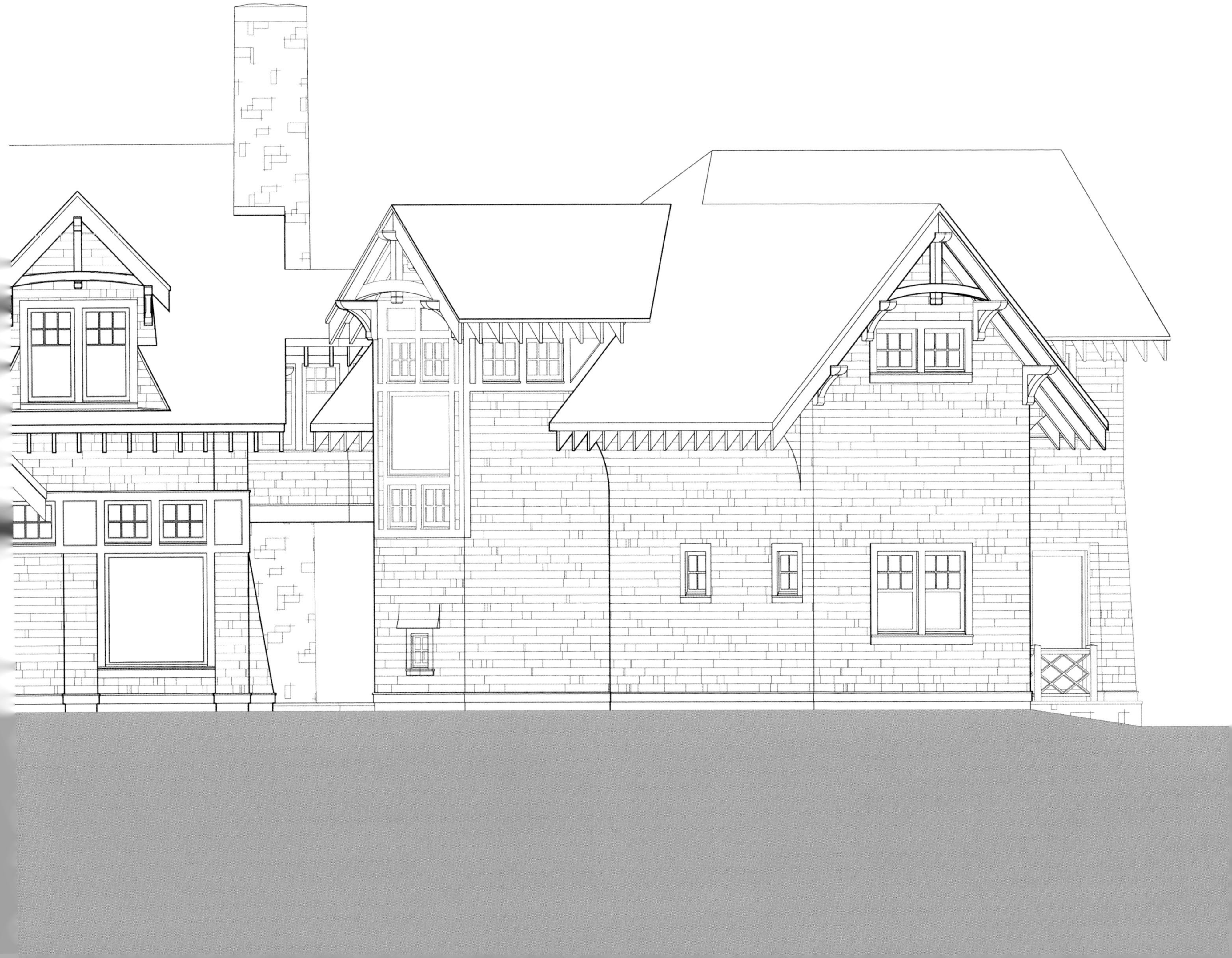

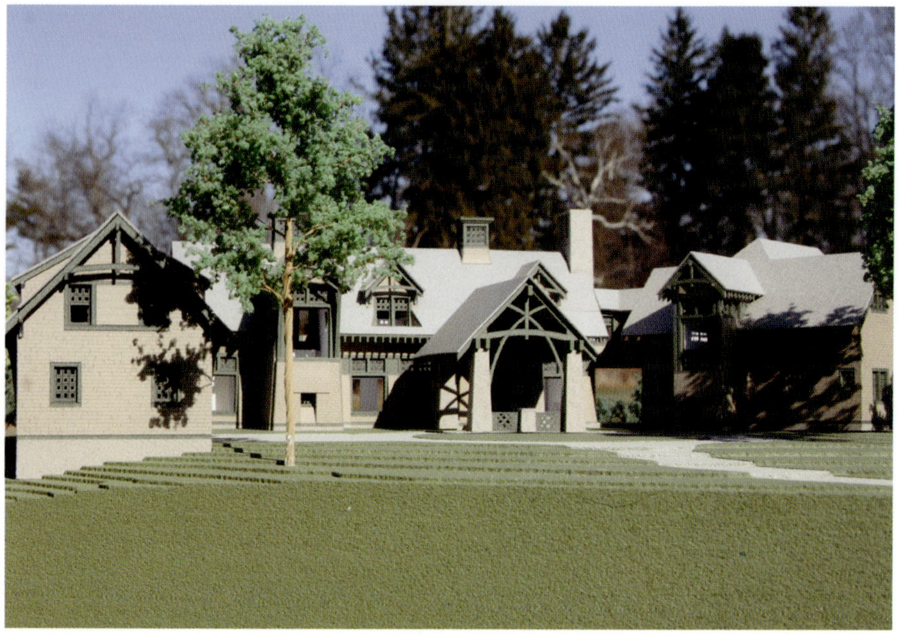
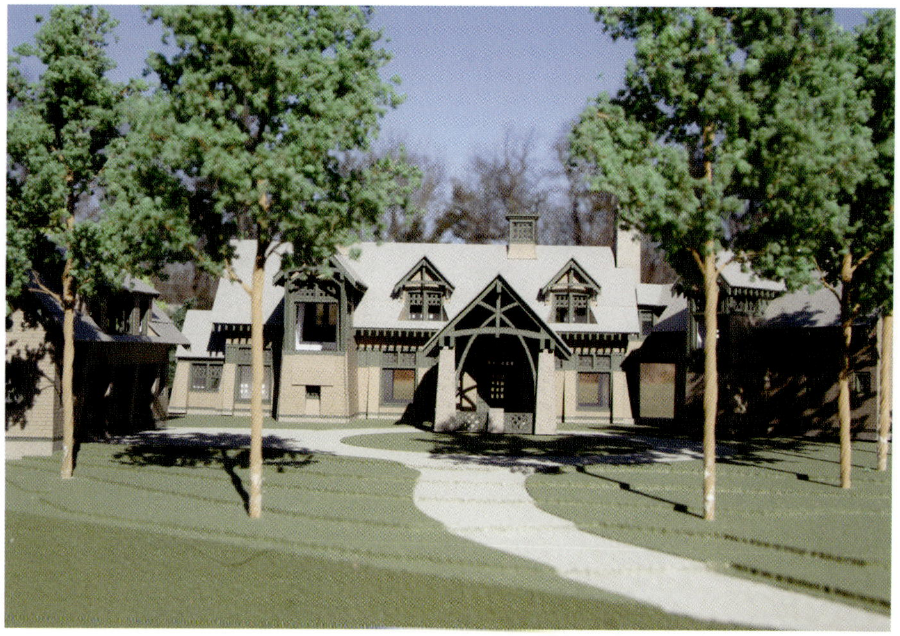
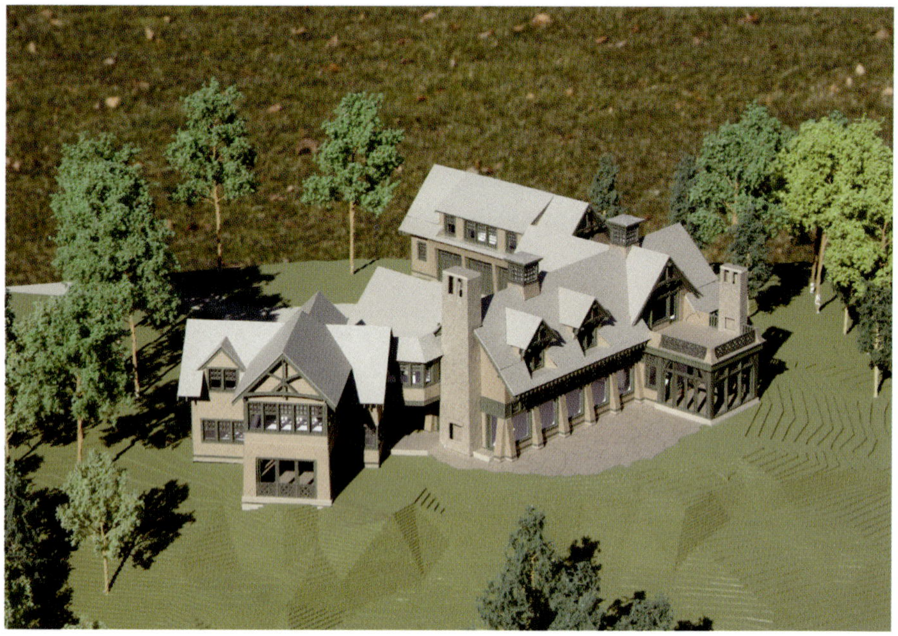
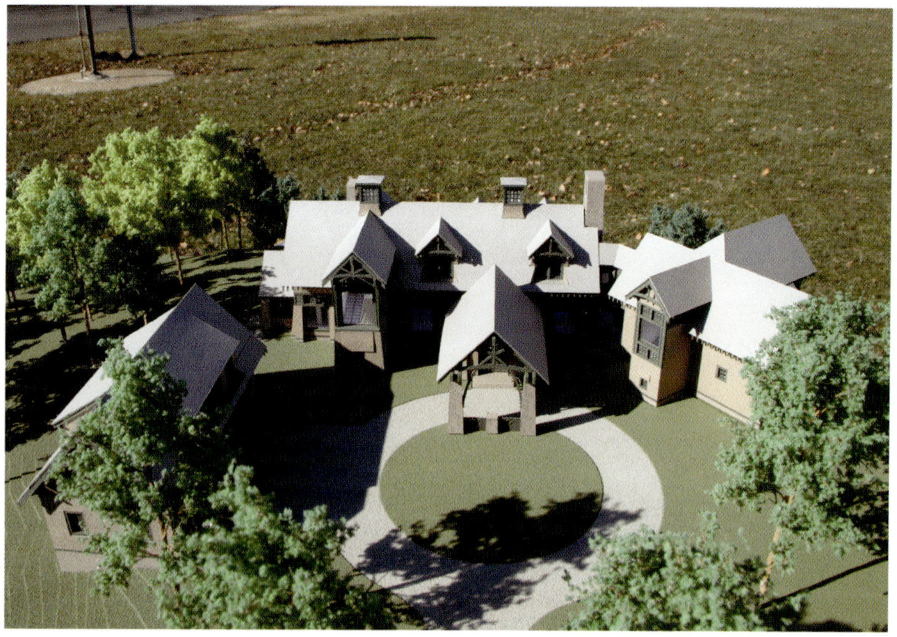
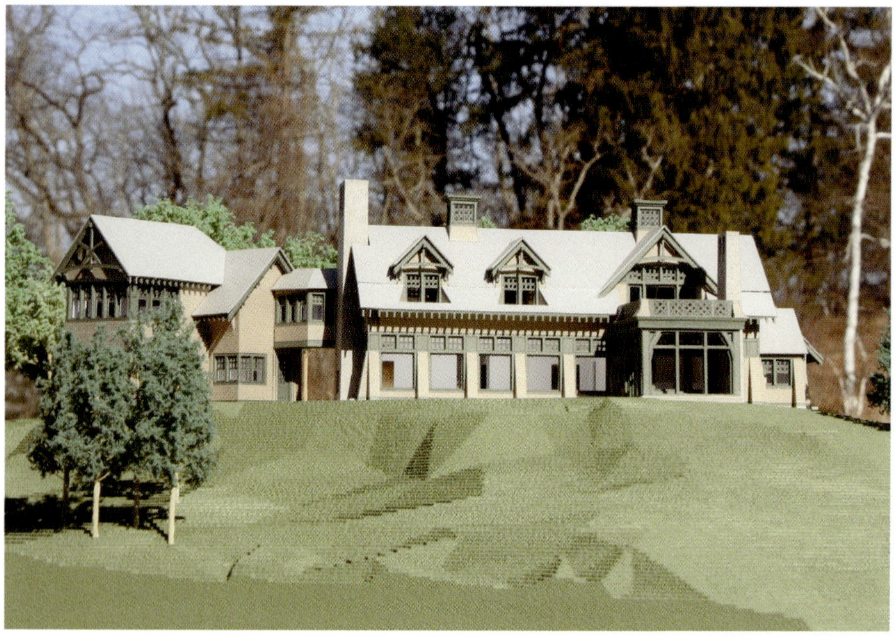
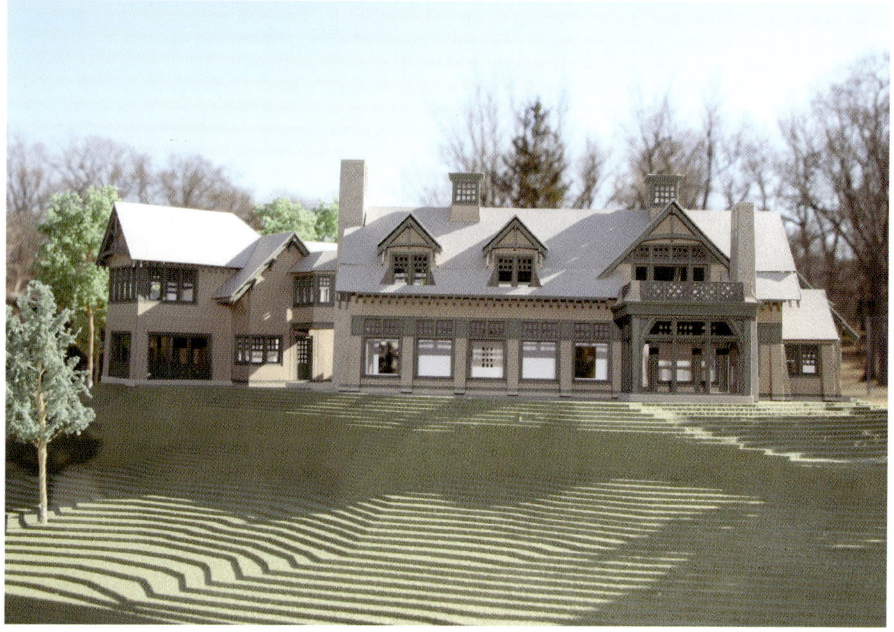

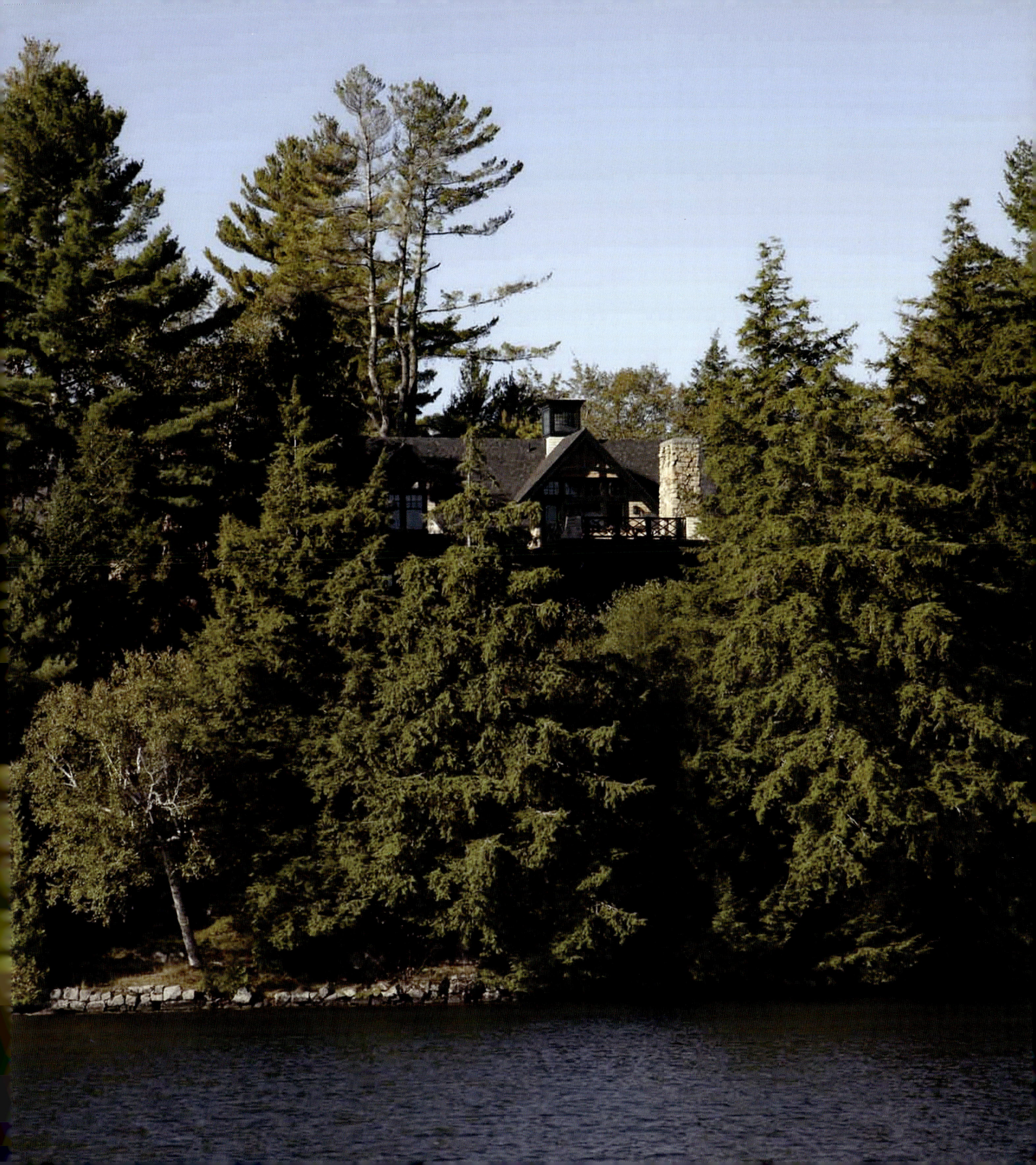

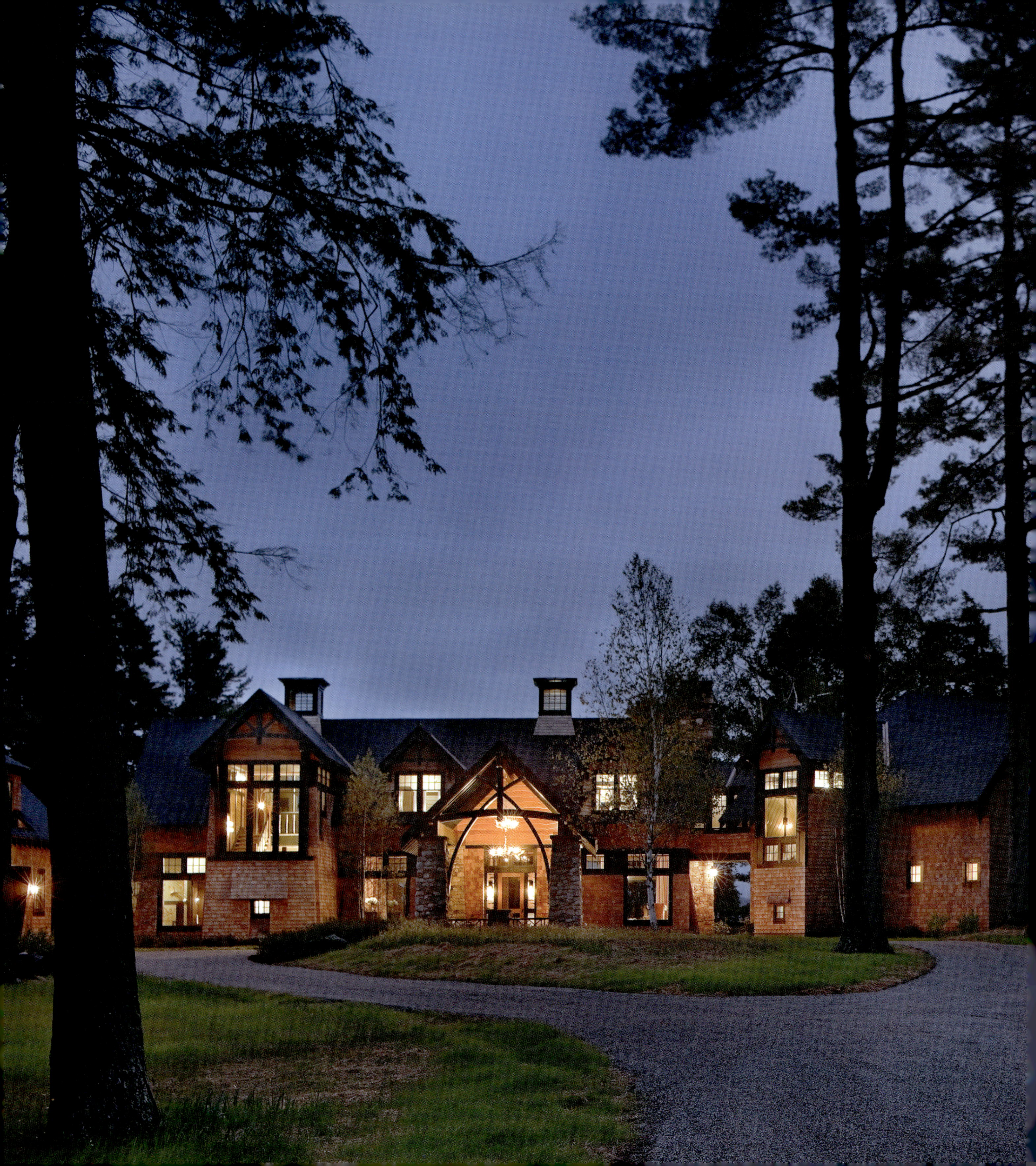

STYLE AND SECLUSION IN A RUSTIC SETTING ARE DEFINING CHARACTERISTICS OF THIS WOODED RETREAT

THE CLIENTS A couple from California with children were interested in building a house in the Adirondacks. They wanted their home to be a center for friends and family, and their property to be a place where they could hike, boat and swim. It was very important that their home be incorporated into its natural surroundings and that it fit in with the history of the area.

THE DESIGN BRIEF The clients were delighted with the idea of an Adirondack camp, but they wanted the house's amenities to be modern and up-to-date. When they found a 38-acre wooded and lakeside site, they were concerned about "treading lightly on the land"—they did not want any trees to be cut down for the sake of enhancing a view. The way the house related to the water and the trees would determine the architecture.

THE SOLUTION Rather than using logs—a typical material for an Adirondack camp—Bernard Wharton and Arthur Hanlon decided to sheath the house in red cedar shingles, which gave it a more contemporary look. One of the first elements to be designed was a large, windowed stair tower, which recalled the fire towers that once dotted the forest. The clients wanted the house to be a collection of buildings, which ultimately would contain 34 rooms spread over 9,300 square feet, recalling the old camps that usually had a kitchen building, a living room building, and several bedroom buildings. At Big Rock, the kitchen is the hub of the house. It sits between an outdoor screened-in porch and the Great Room, which encompasses the living room and dining room areas. Even though its appliances are twenty-first century, the kitchen is filled with the imagery of the rustic camps, with painted wood cabinets reminiscent of the turn of the twentieth century. The Great Room, which functions as the home's communal space, is anchored by a stone fireplace. There are broad expanses of glass in the large-paned windows that invite the surrounding woodlands into the room. The kitchen porch also has a fireplace, as does the upstairs terrace, from which one can watch the activities on the lake. A second porch off the master bedroom is equipped with cozy upholstered swings. Despite its wooded location, the house—or camp—sports some architectural virtuosity. At the entrance, a porte-cochère, with its peaked roof supported by stone pillars, balances the massive stair tower to the left, which also has a peaked roof. In the Great Room, the timber frame stretches from side to side which, rather than engaging with the ceiling, floats just below it. At the water's edge, a three-bay boathouse is nestled between a group of pine trees. Each bay has its own peaked gable. Living with nature, albeit in style and seclusion, characterizes this unique Adirondack retreat.

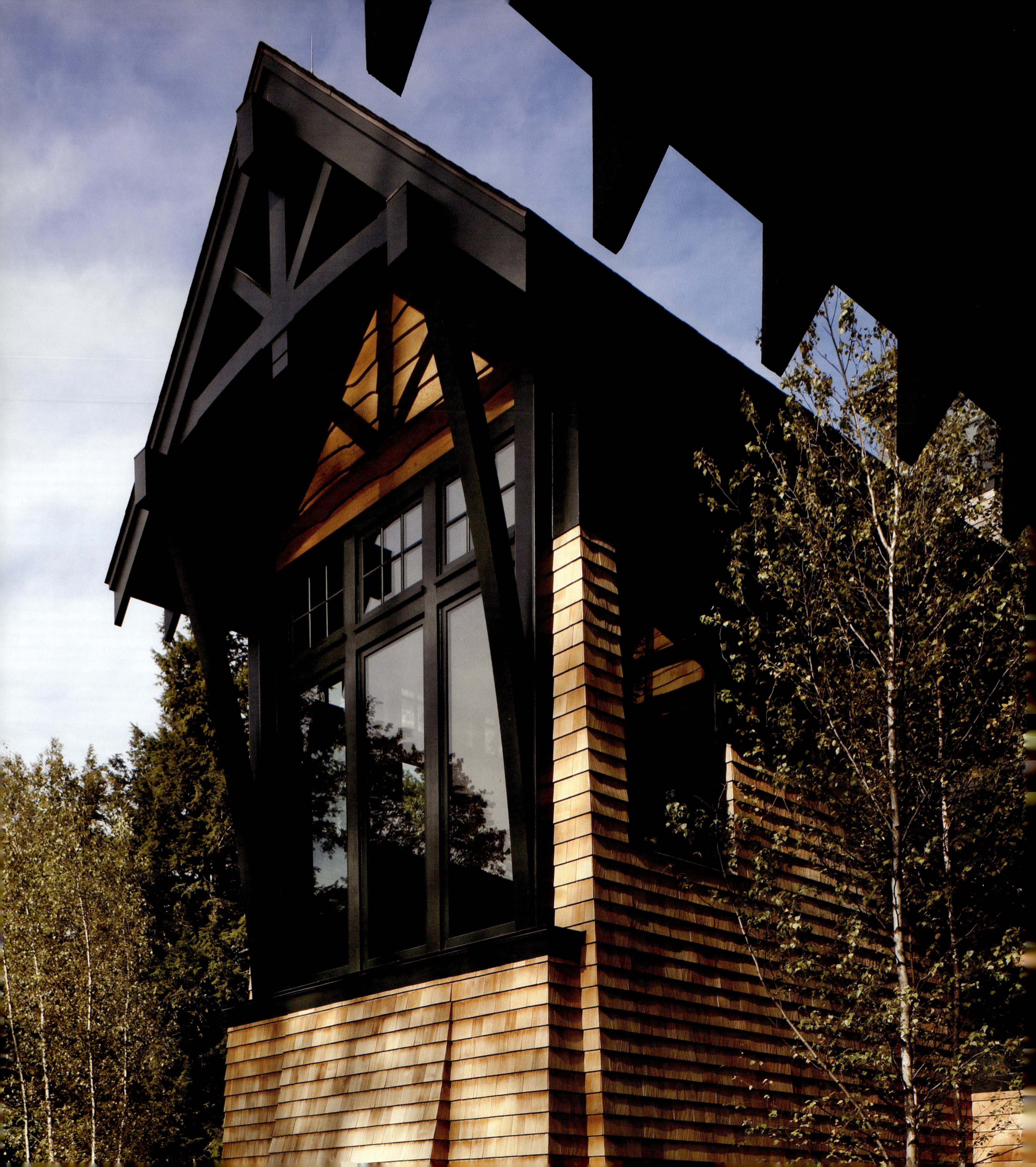

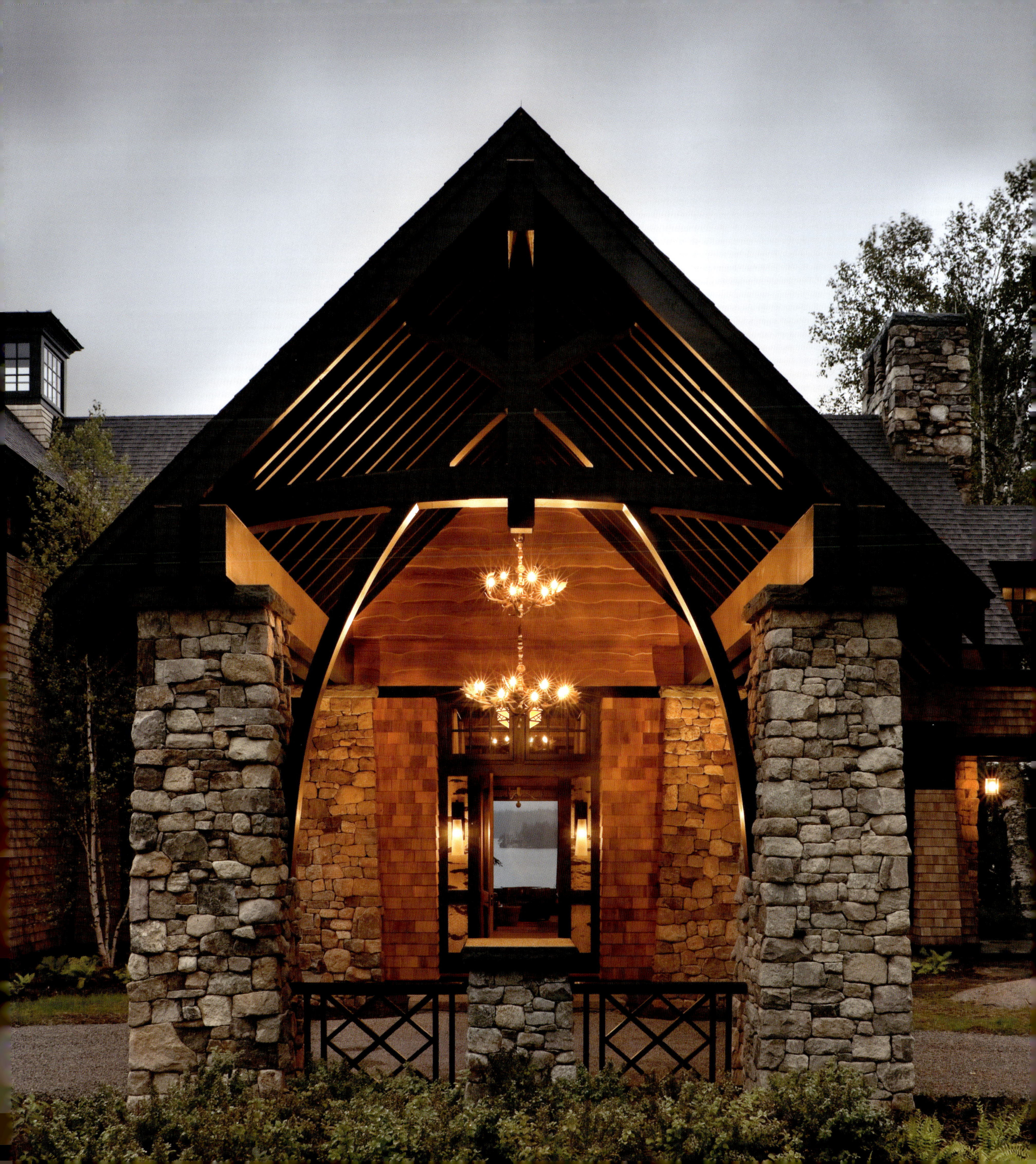

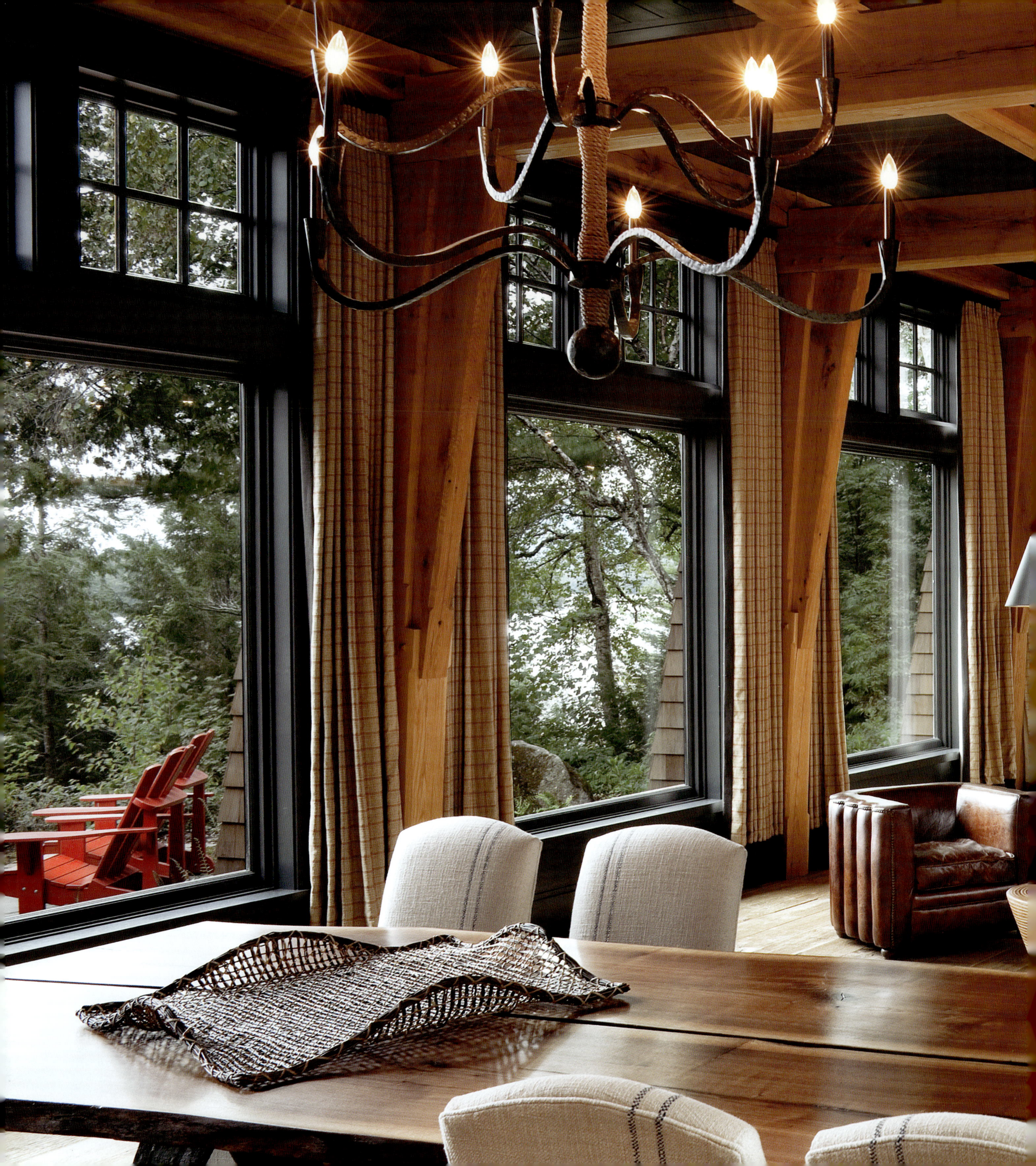

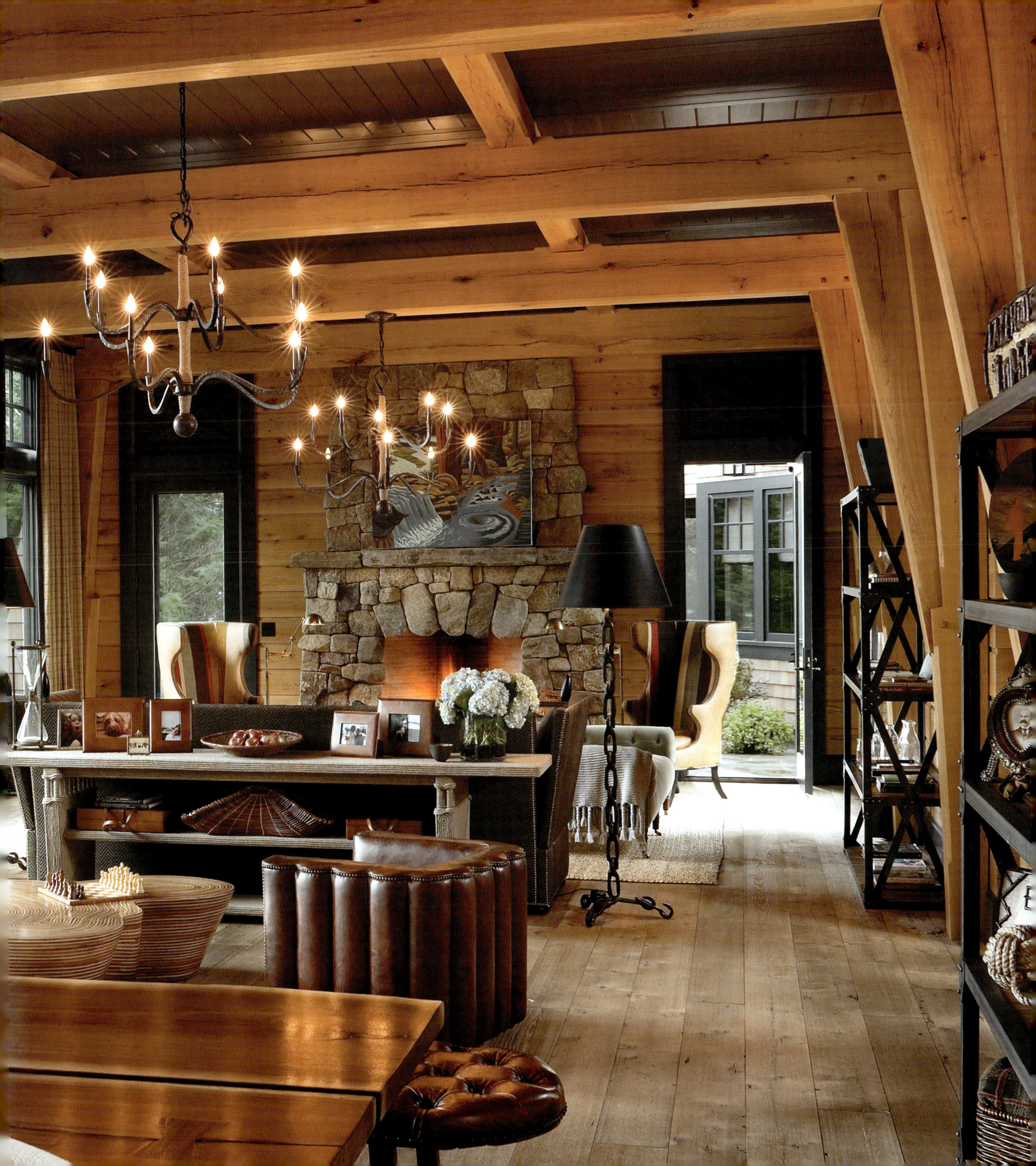

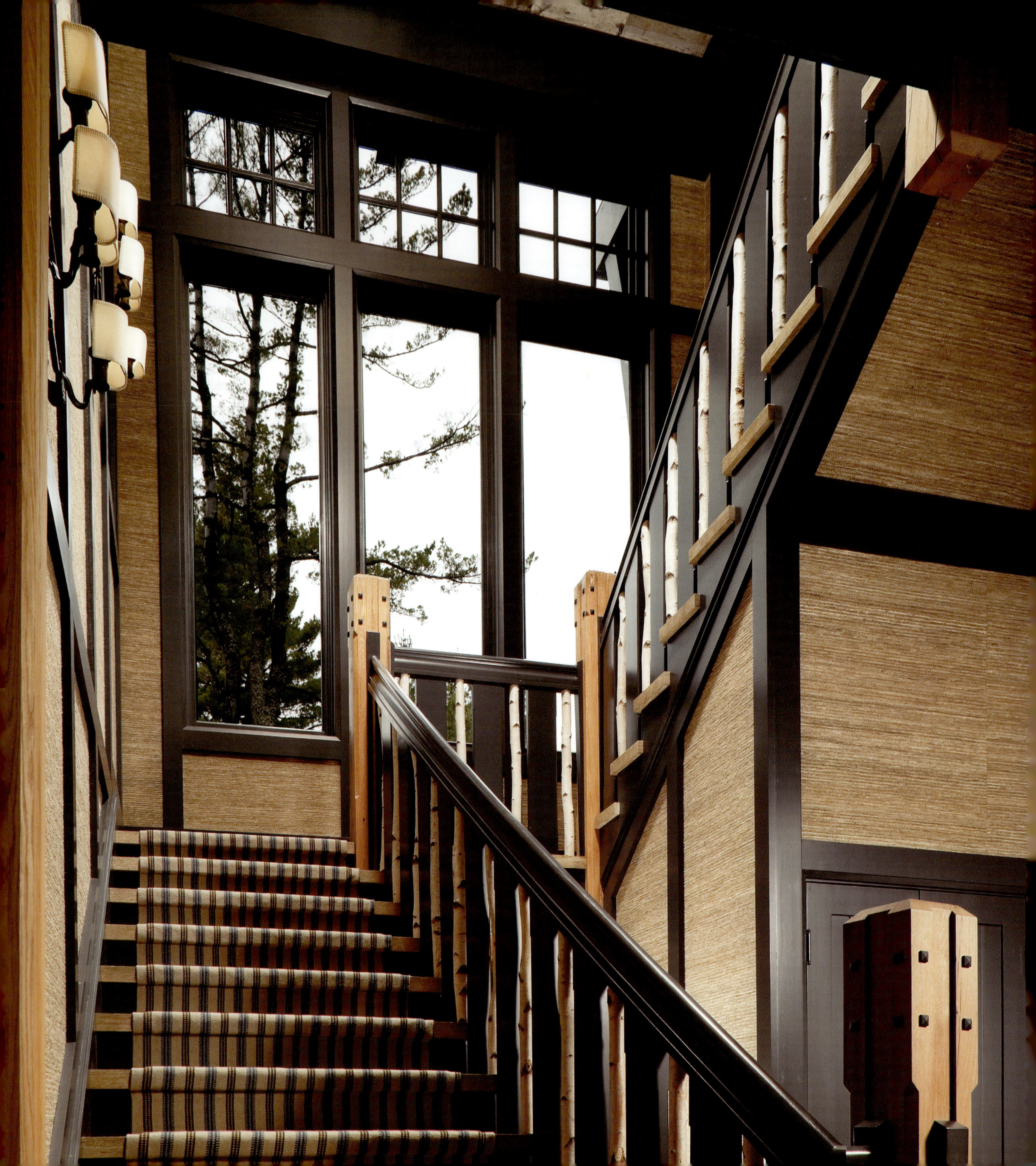

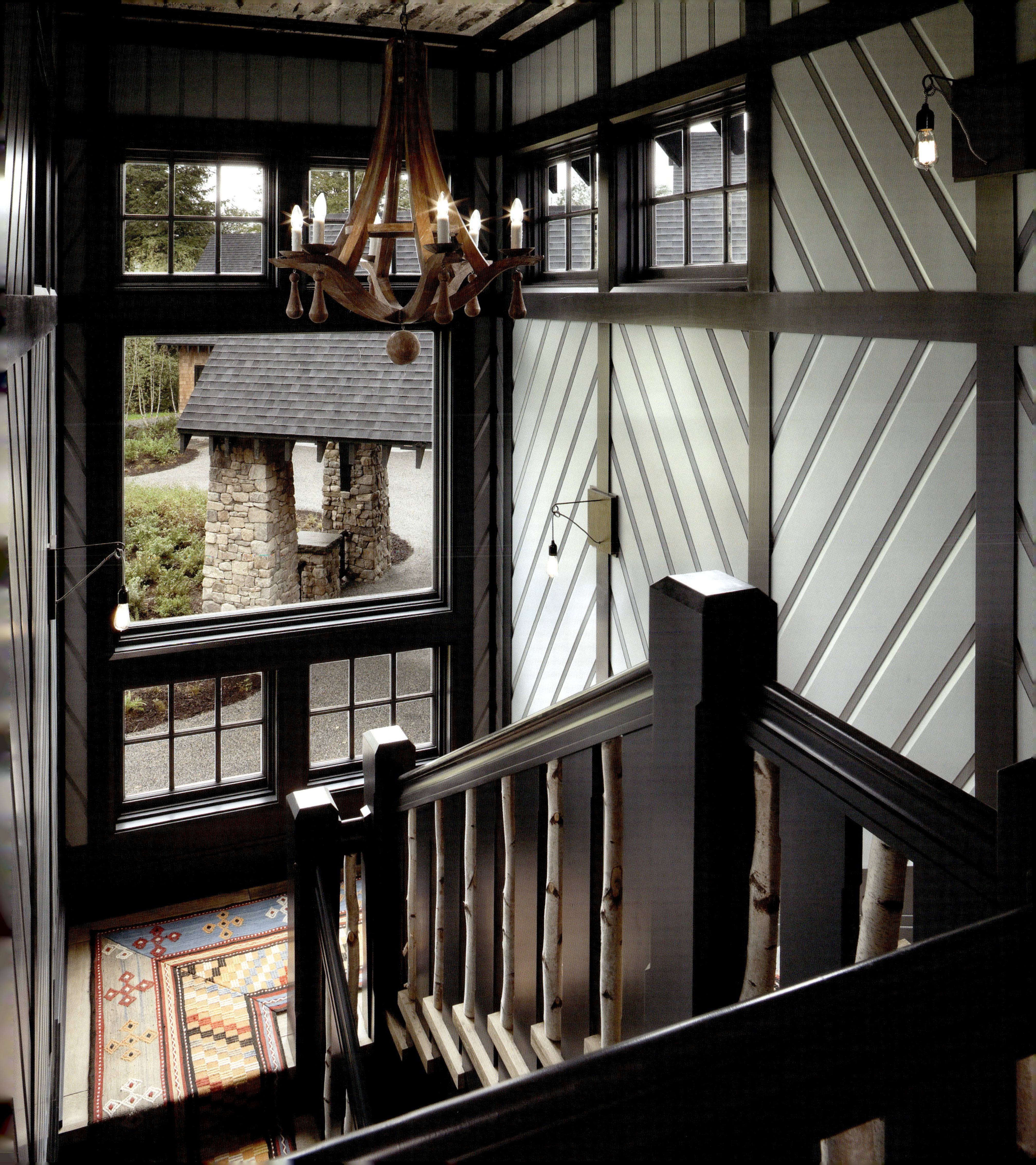

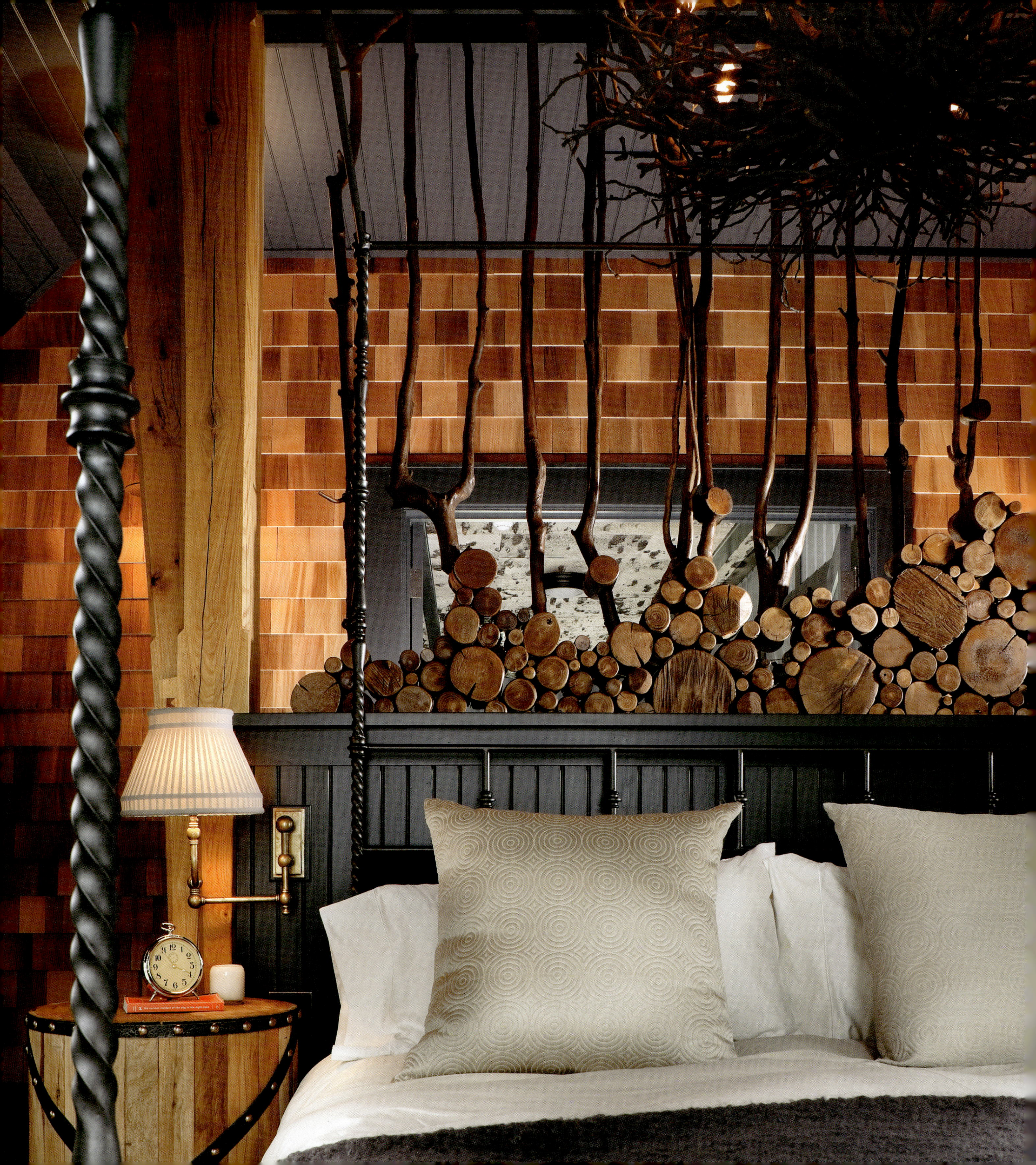

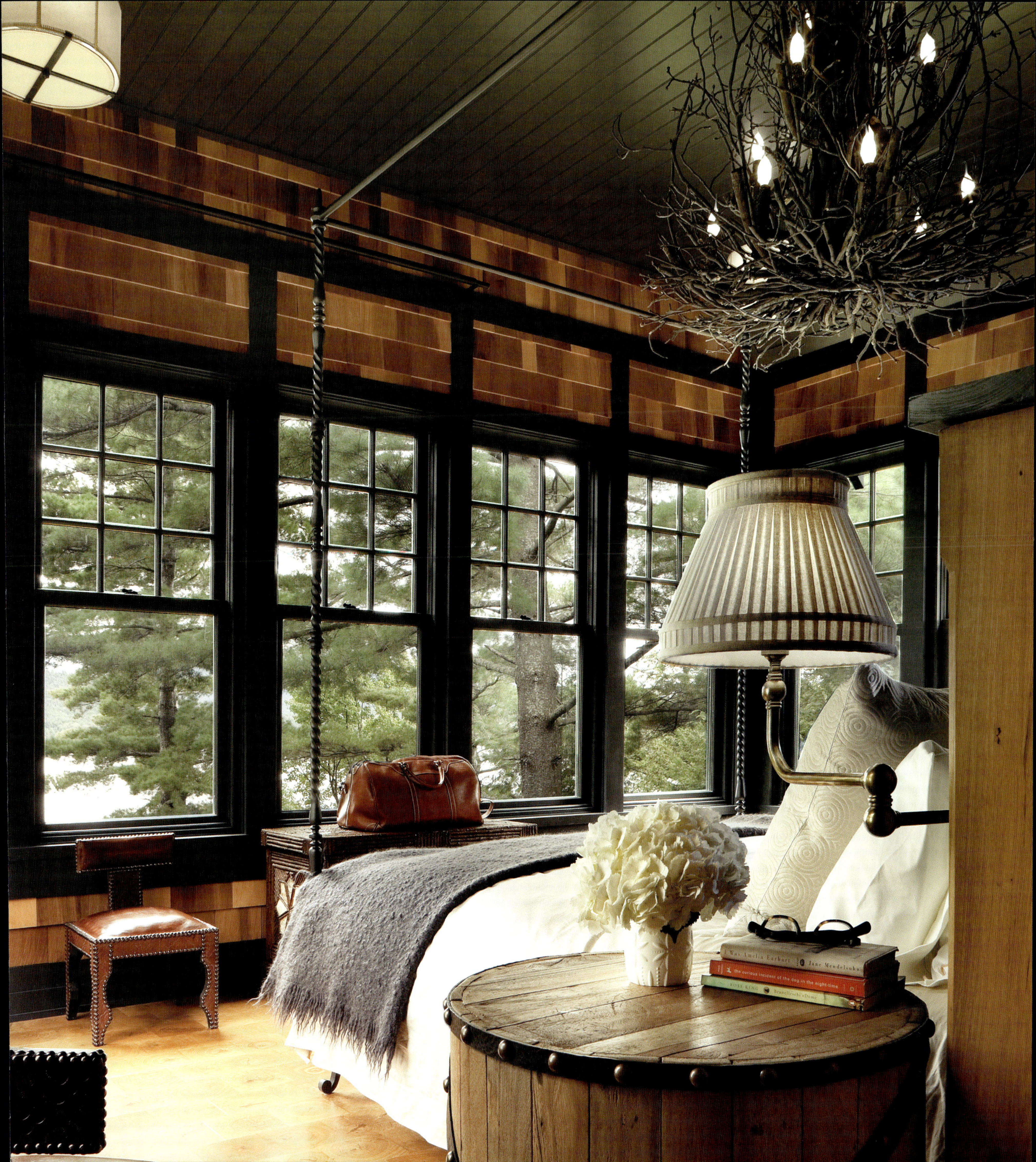

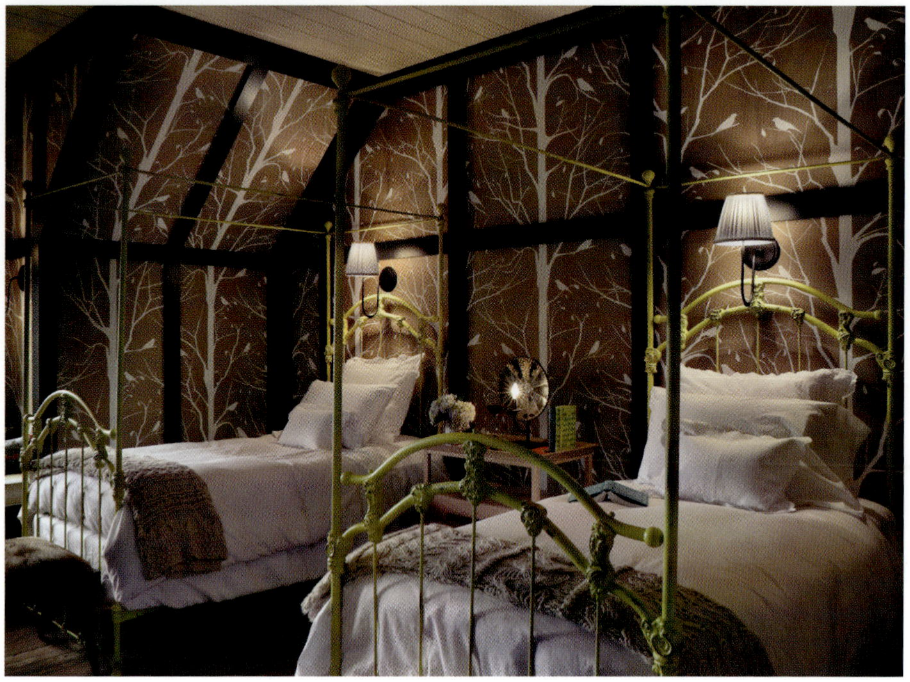

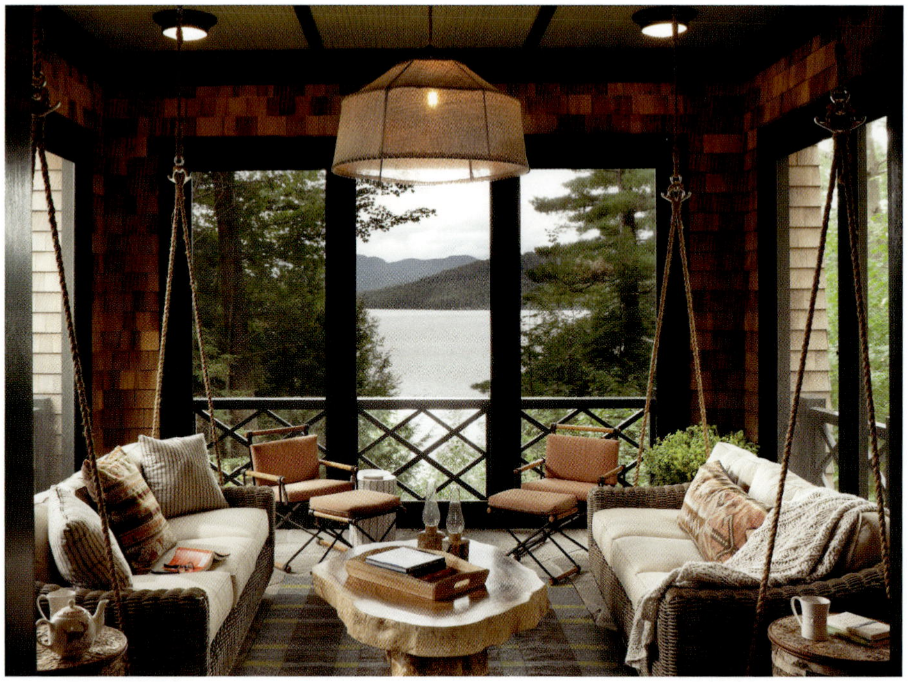

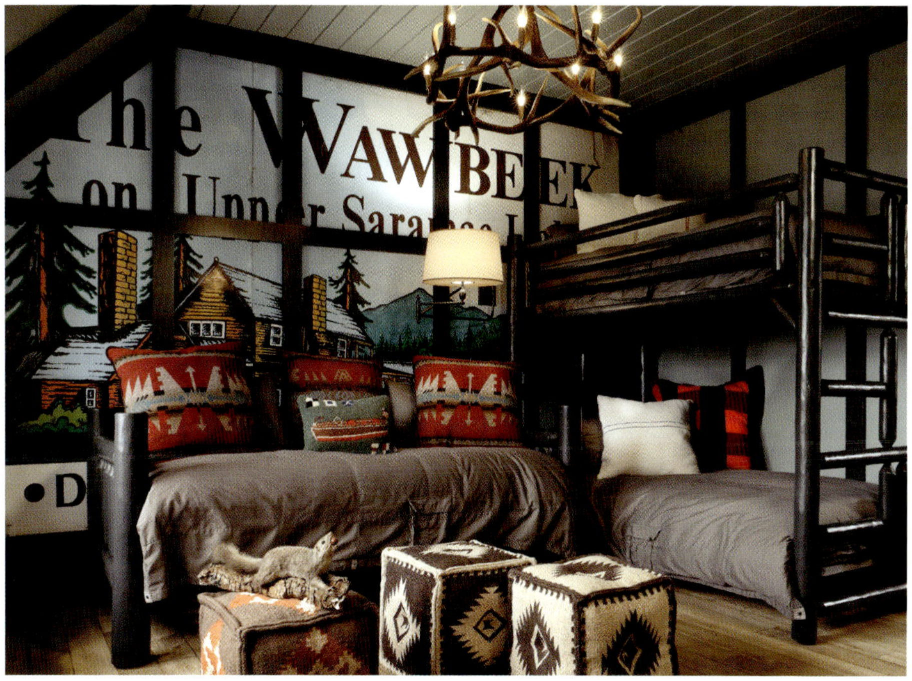

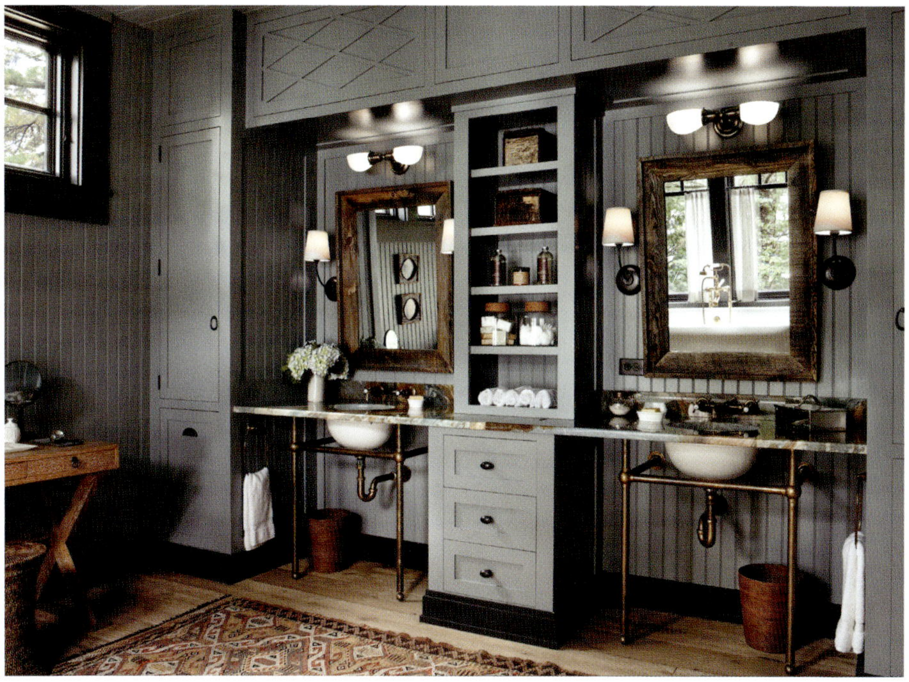

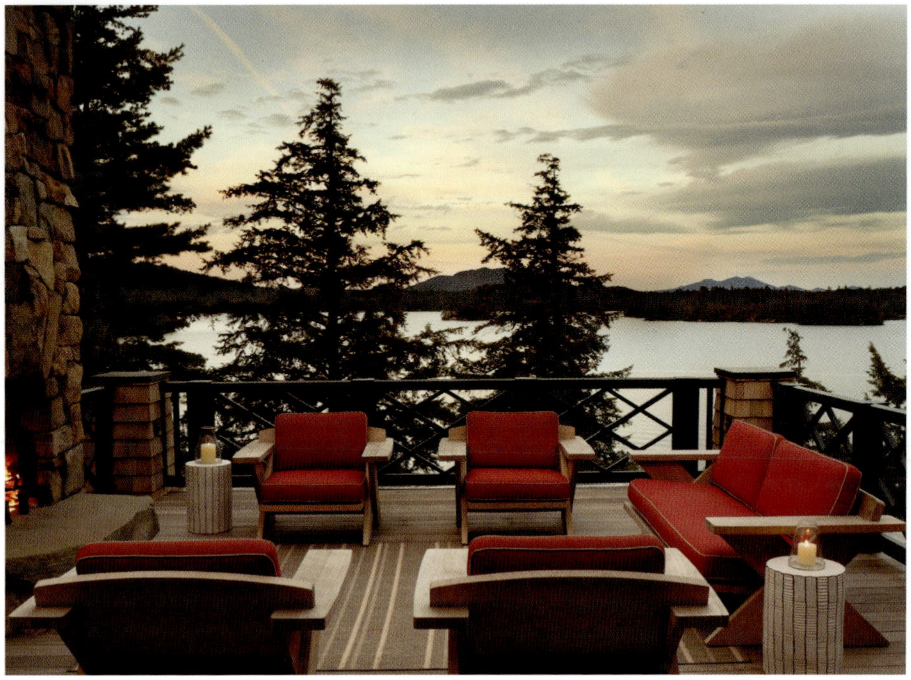

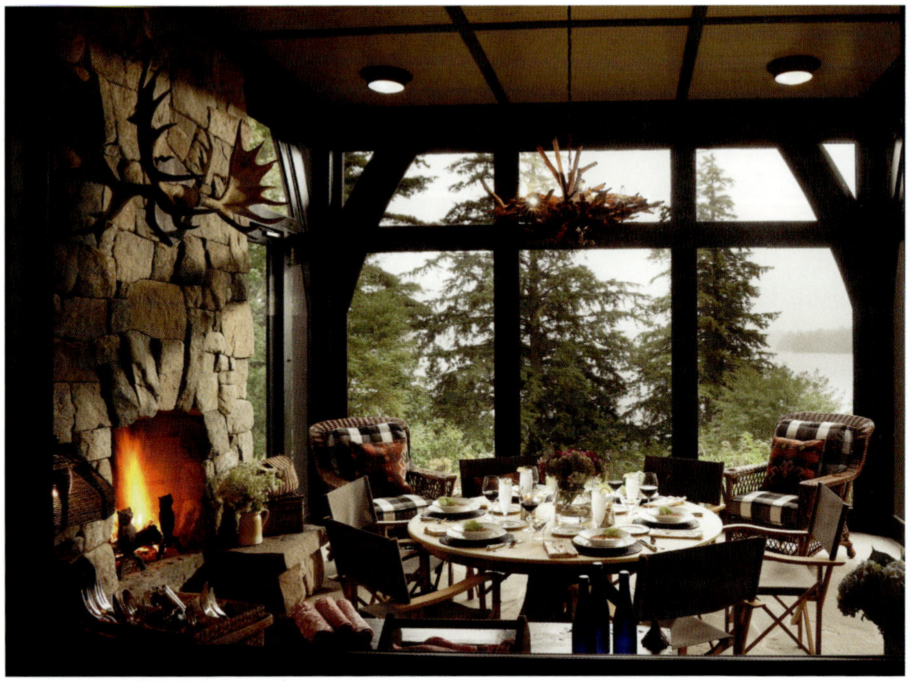

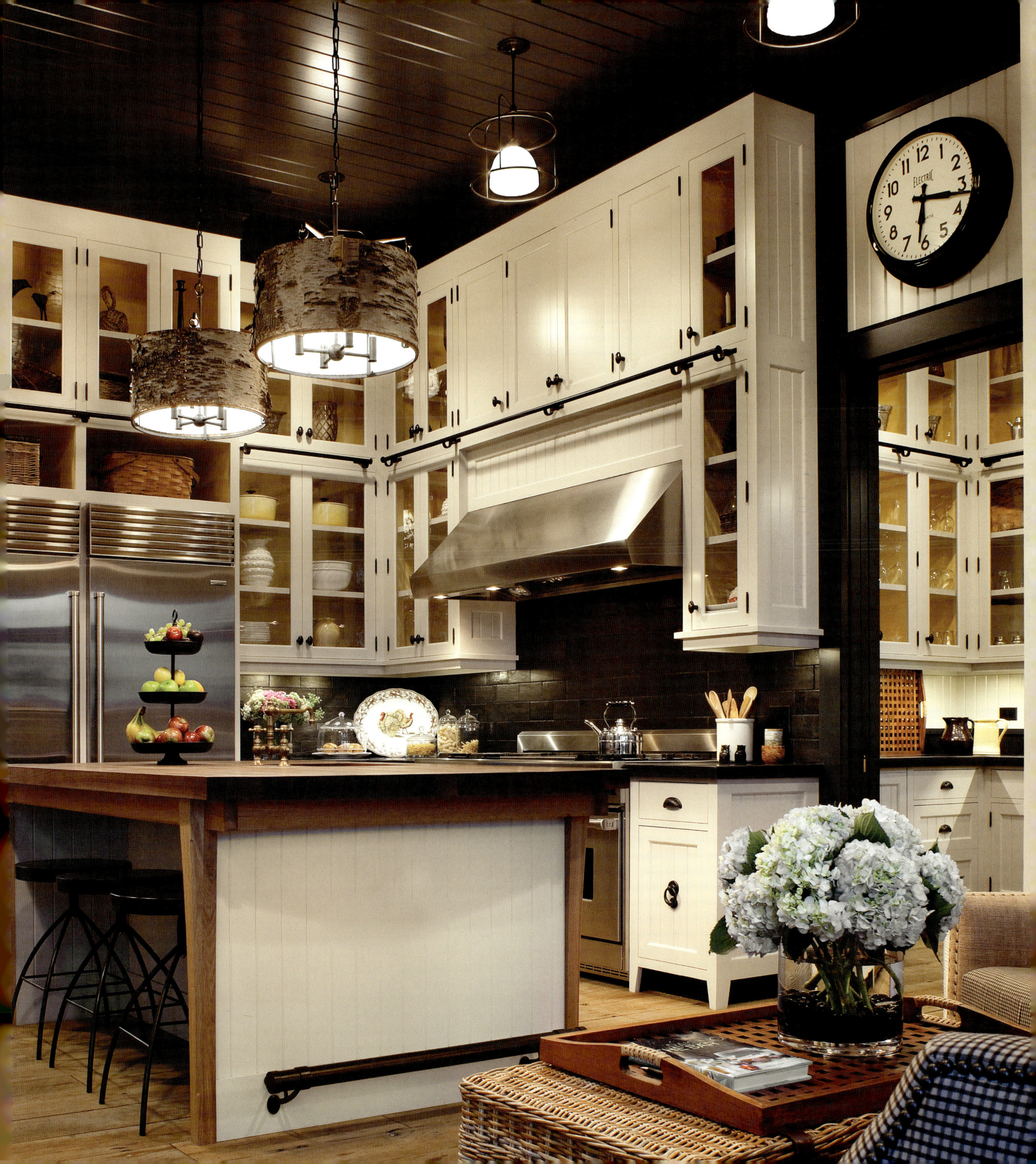
ELECTRIC

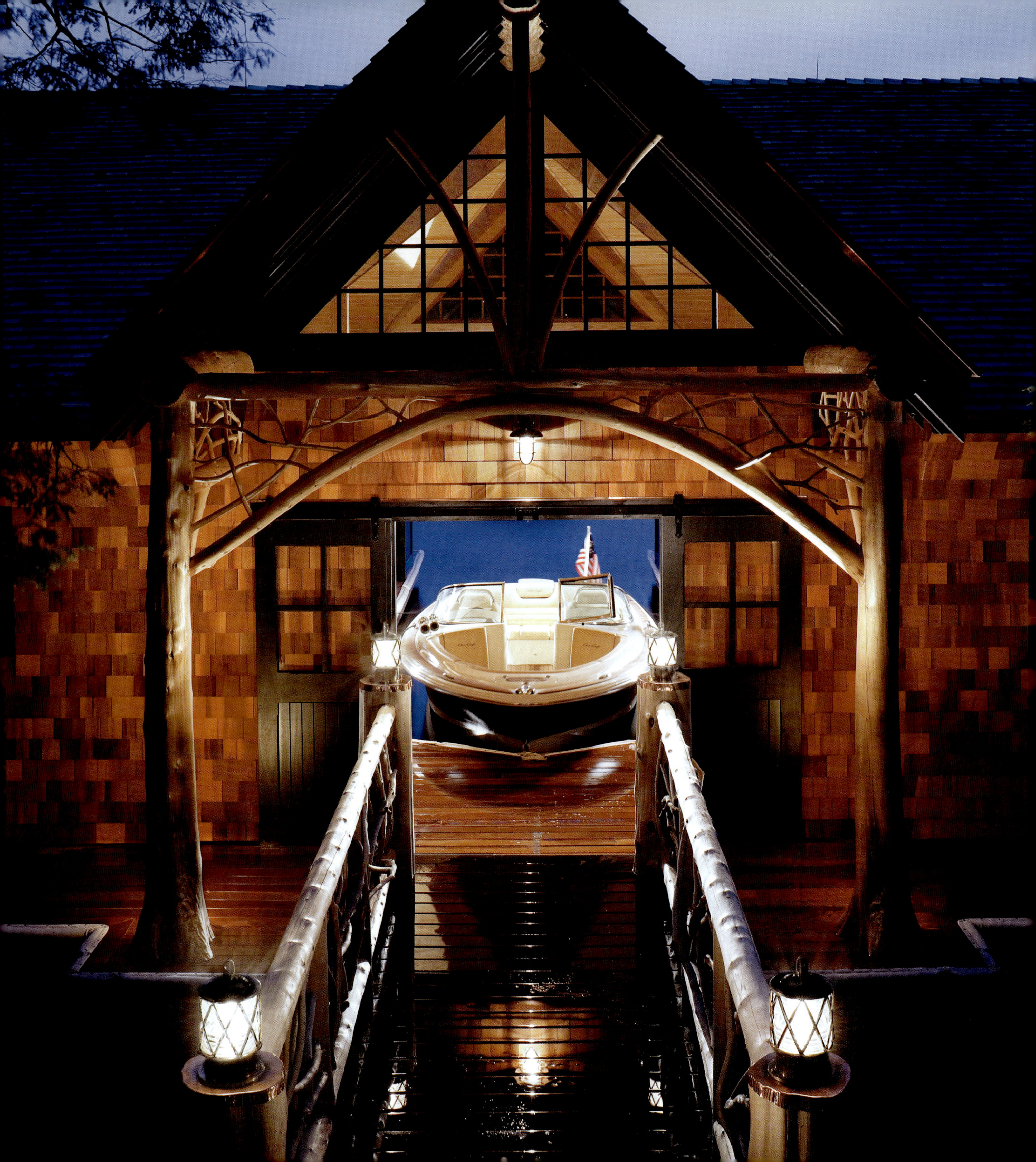

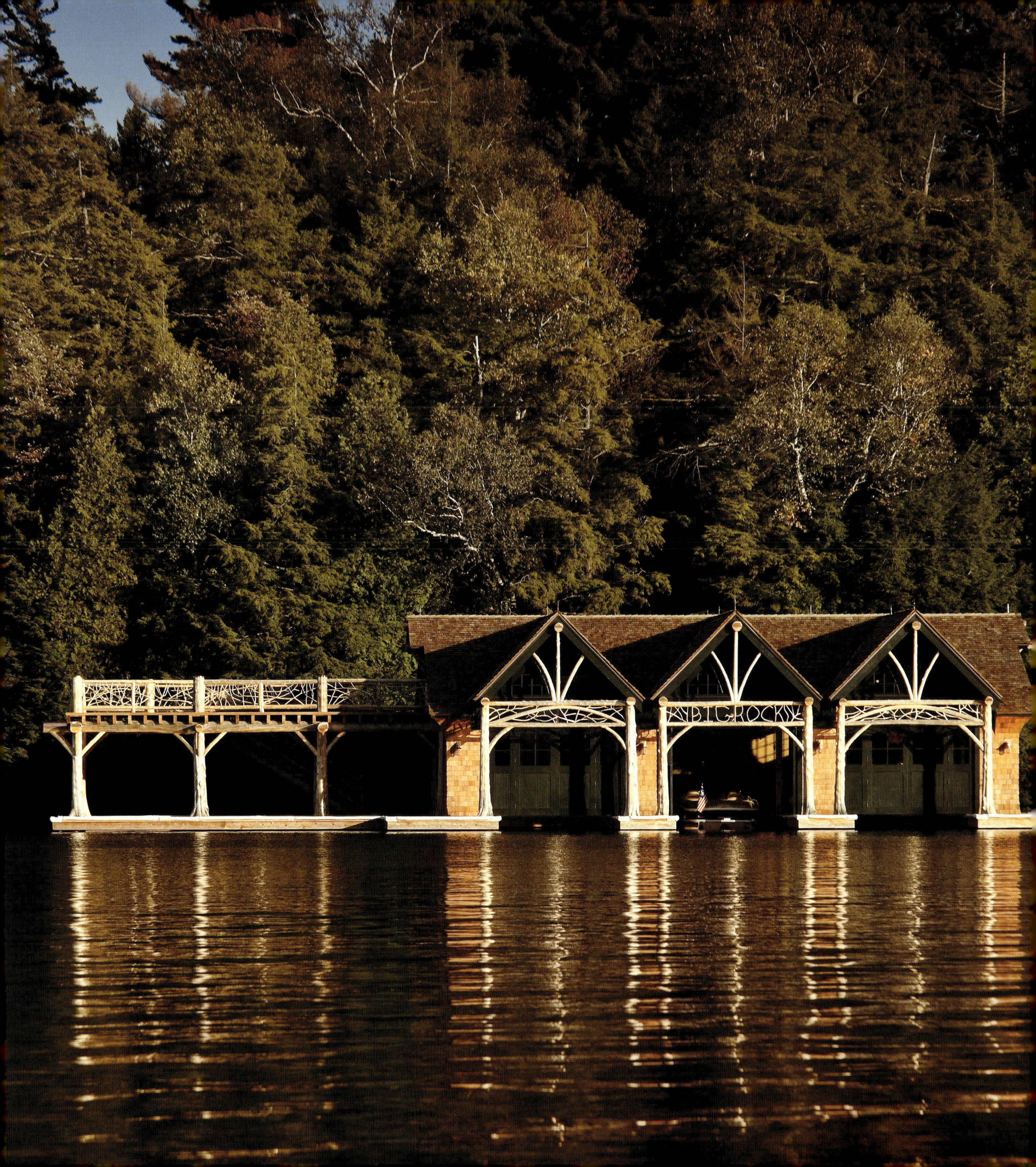
BIG ROCK

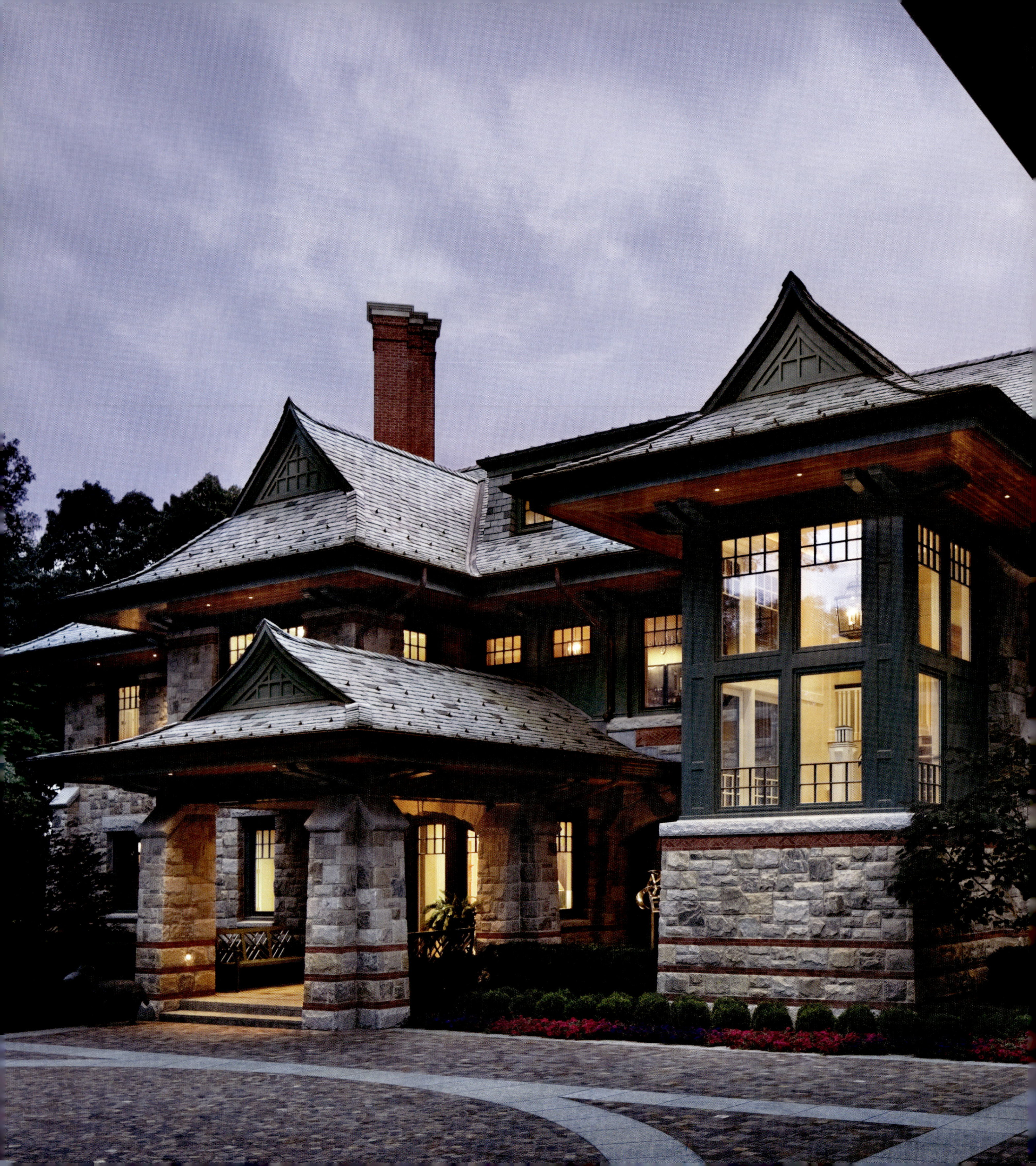

A HOUSE IN THE SUBURBS THAT REFLECTS ITS COMMUNITY'S RICH ARCHITECTURAL HISTORY

THE CLIENTS This house is the most recent one of several built by the same owners since the 1970s. They knew they wanted a house big and open enough for their children, their extended family, and to entertain their friends. But they also knew they wanted some more intimate spaces. "We'd been practicing on all the other houses," says the husband, "and this time it was perfect."

THE DESIGN BRIEF The house is located in the Boston, Massachusetts, suburb of Brookline, which has a history of significant architecture and where Henry Hobson Richardson, the historical predecessor who most influenced Wharton, had his studio. Adapting early medieval architecture to create a style known as Richardsonian Romanesque, the architects of the Shingle Style took up heavy massing, low rounded arches, and conical elements, which were contemporaneous with his later work. Richardson usually worked in stone, however, while the Shingle Style was a lighter and more fluid architectural presence, usually constructed in wood. Bold and strong in appearance, this house needed to convey a sense of timelessness through its massing, use of materials, and detailing. Granite, brick, and slate were mandated, as a varied texture of materials adds depth and quality to the façade. The sharply peaked and flared roofs, influenced by Japanese architecture and popular in Richardson's day, are mixed with solid granite buttresses and brick arches, giving the house a unique visual power.

THE SOLUTION One enters the five-acre site via a driveway that was designed to permit only glimpses of the house. Its scale cannot be fully appreciated until one enters the courtyard, which is defined by a dramatic stone-and-glass stair tower. The main block of the 9,600-square foot, 31-room house is an assemblage of architectural elements, some more transparent than others. The combination of long windows, heavy stone, and flared roofs work to break down the scale and create a façade with intriguing sequences. On the interior, the house is organized around a series of visual axes that create galleries for the clients' art collection. Massachusetts interior designer Nannette Lewis combined antiques with contemporary art, placing vintage sconces above the living room mantel on each side of a landscape painting by Wolf Kahn, who is known for his realism and colorfield work. The dining room wall hosts a grid of snowflake images created by identical twin artists, Doug and Mike Starn. The living room and dining room are embellished with fine millwork. The paint and upholstery are done in pale honey and butter colors, because Lewis wanted the palette to complement the copious sunlight. Nestled at the opposite end of the house there is a finely appointed library. The façade departs somewhat from the Richardsonian ideal with its bright red brick placed above a series of three arches, two tall chimneys, and two green painted bays. Because the architects applied such whimsy to the venerable and sturdy Richardson model, the house evokes curiosity from its visitors and, every day, a sense of marvel from its owners.

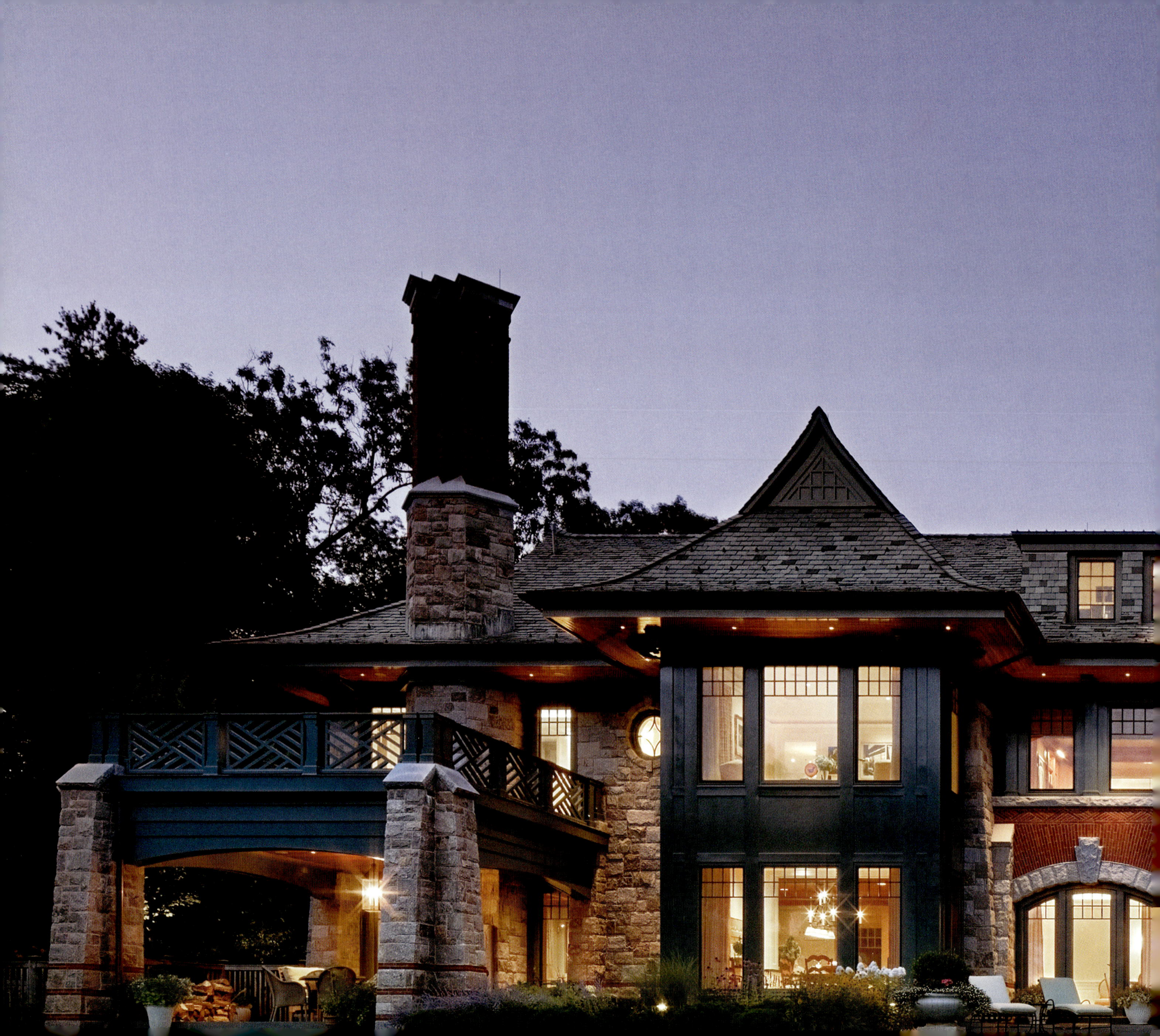

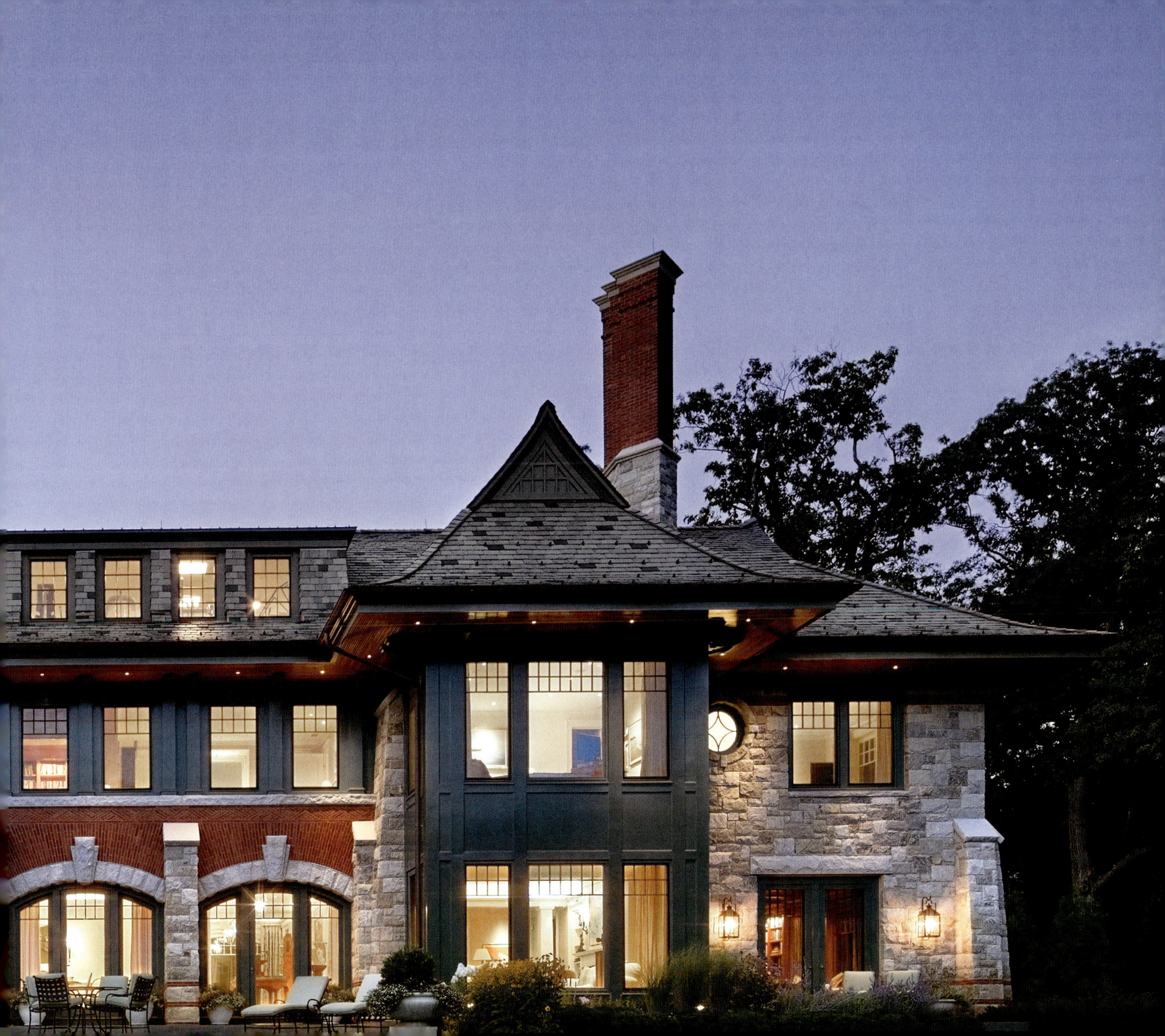

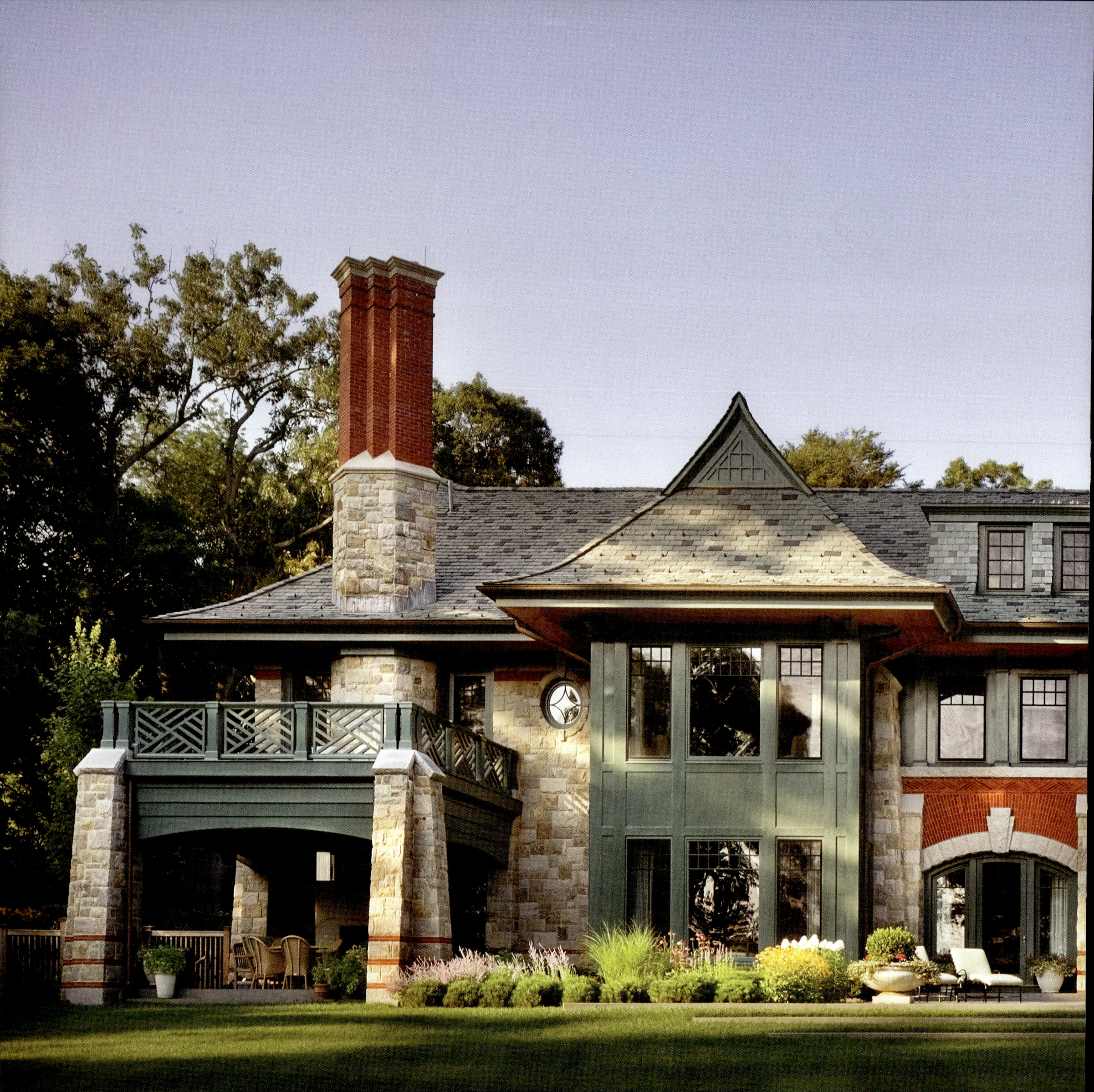

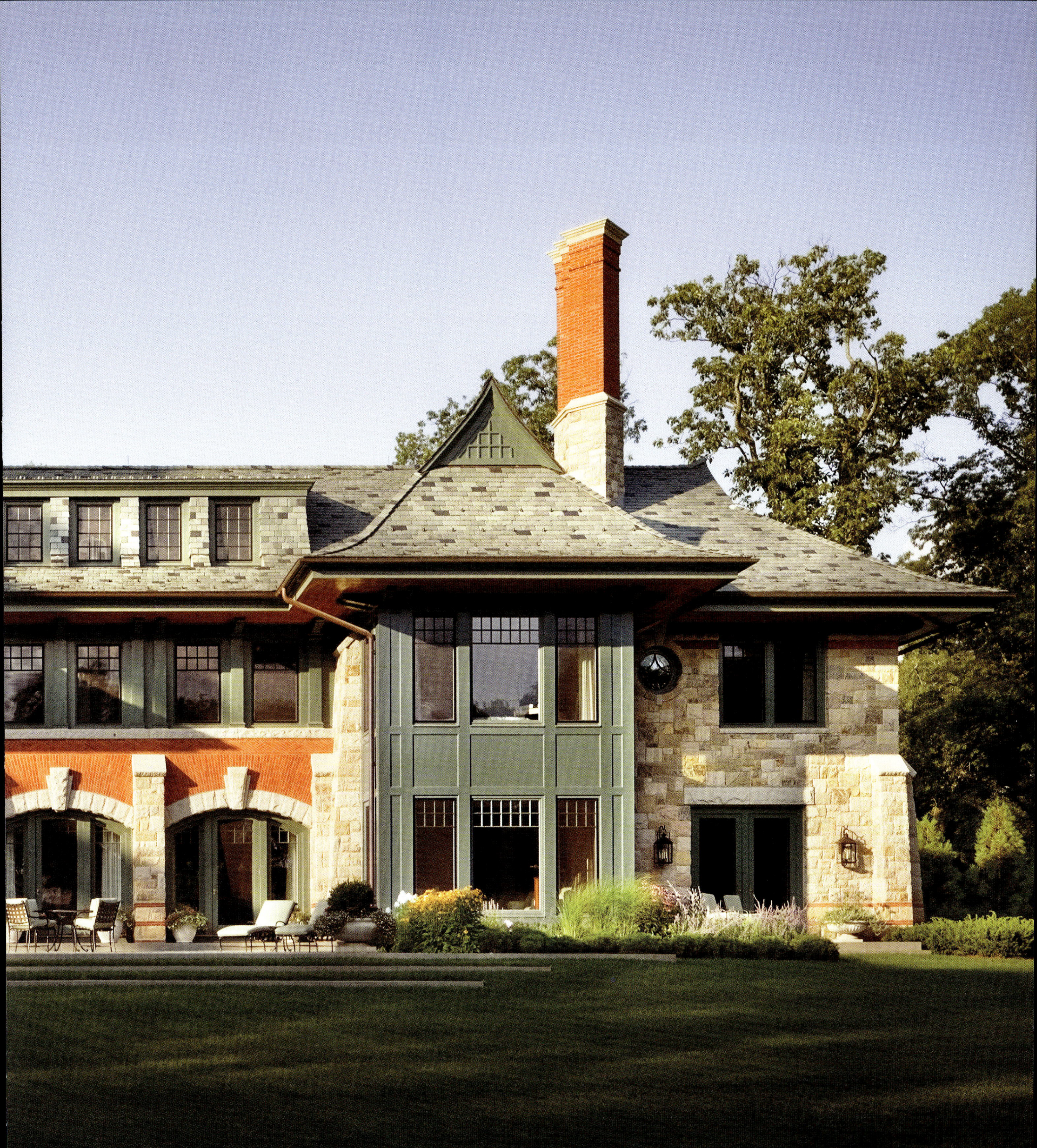

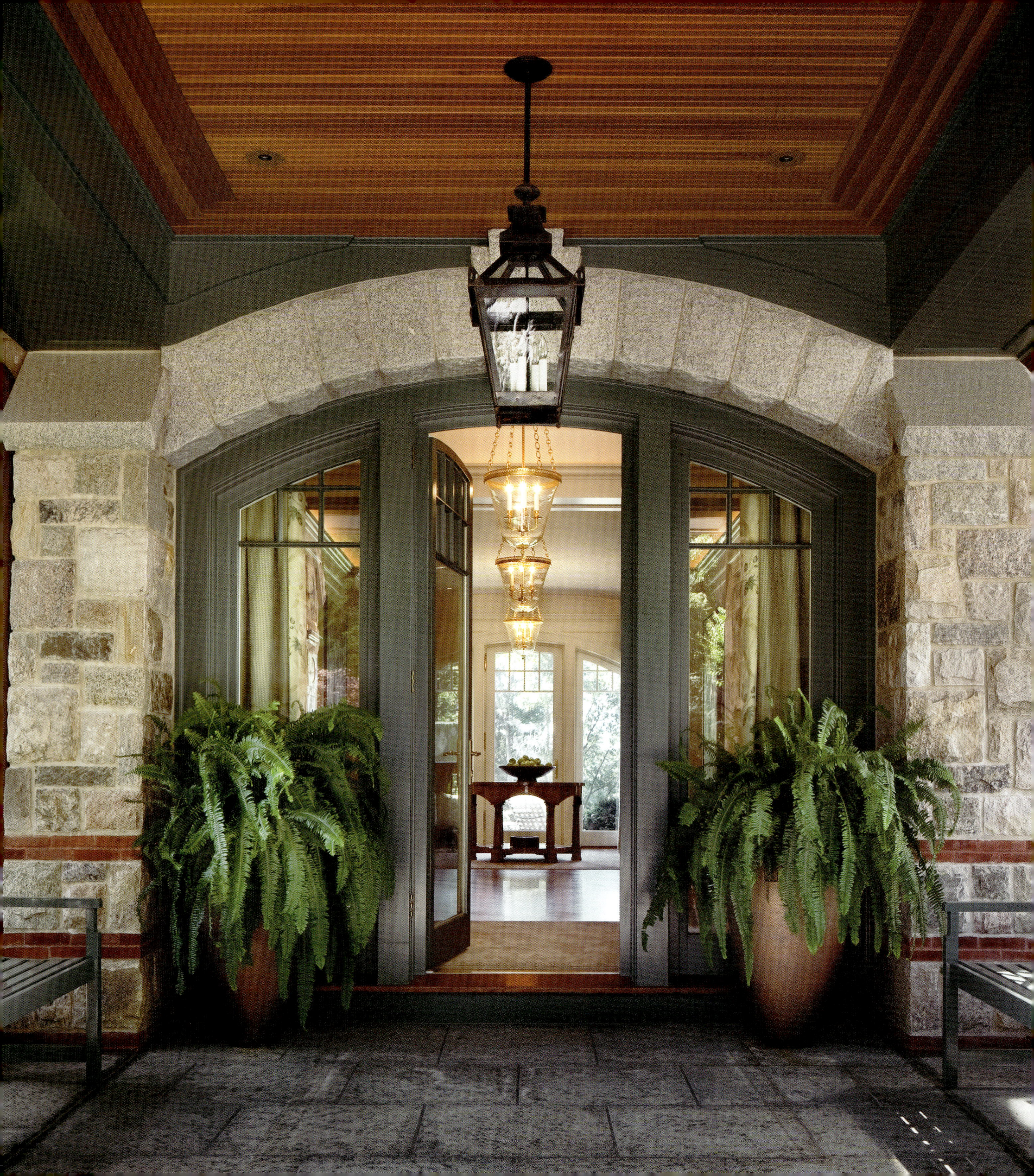

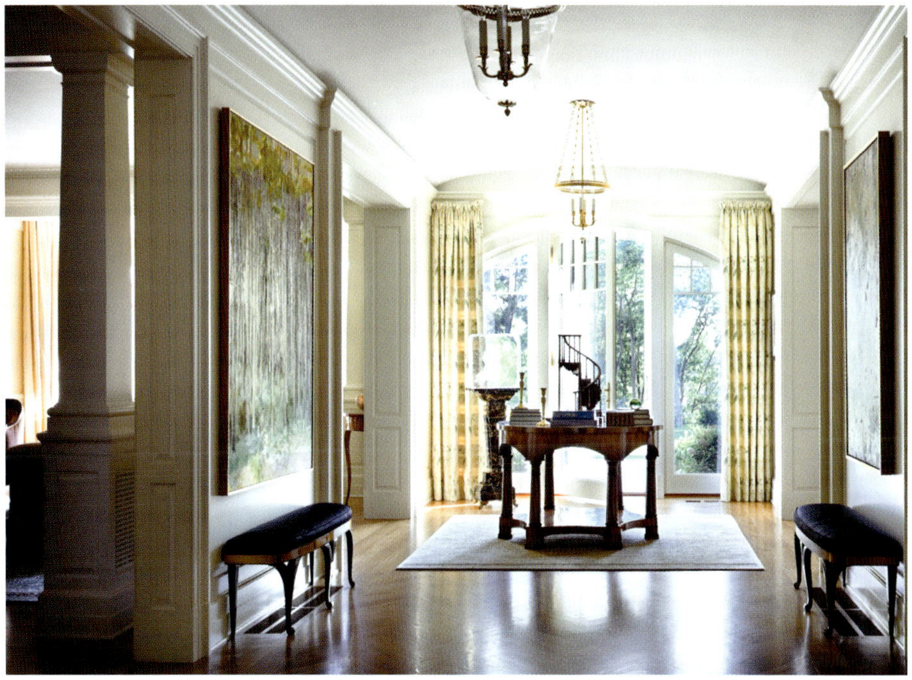

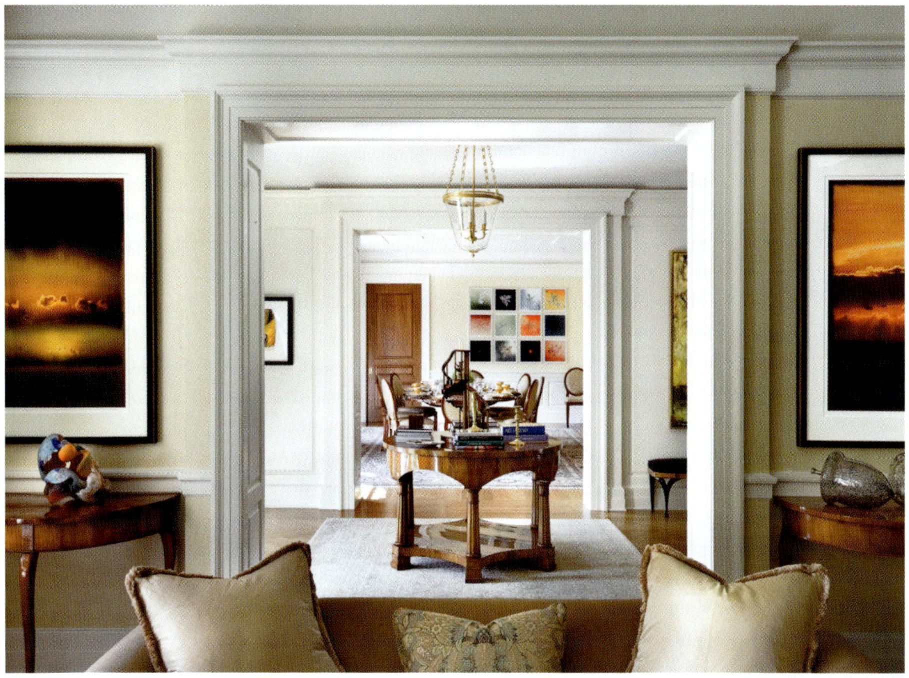

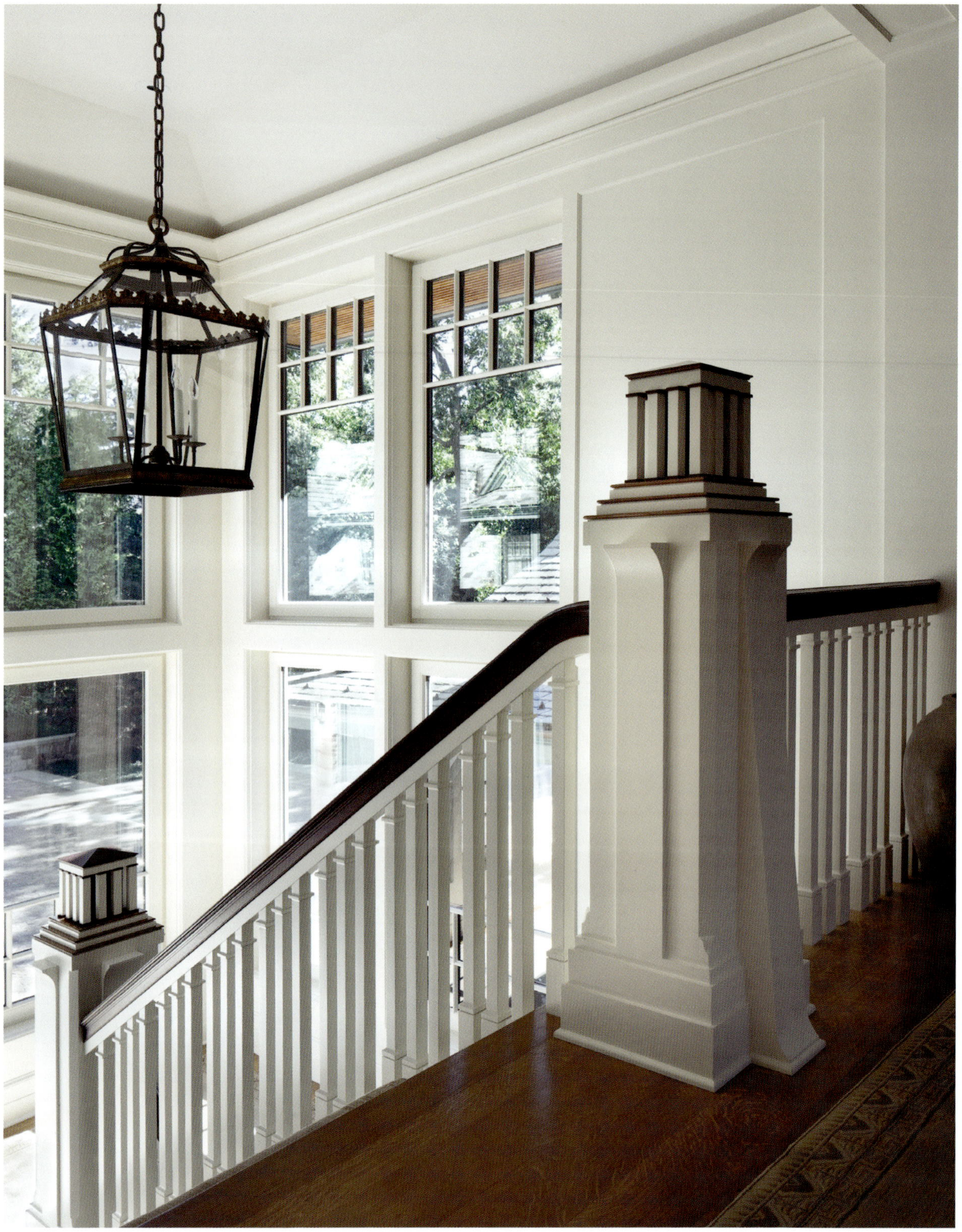

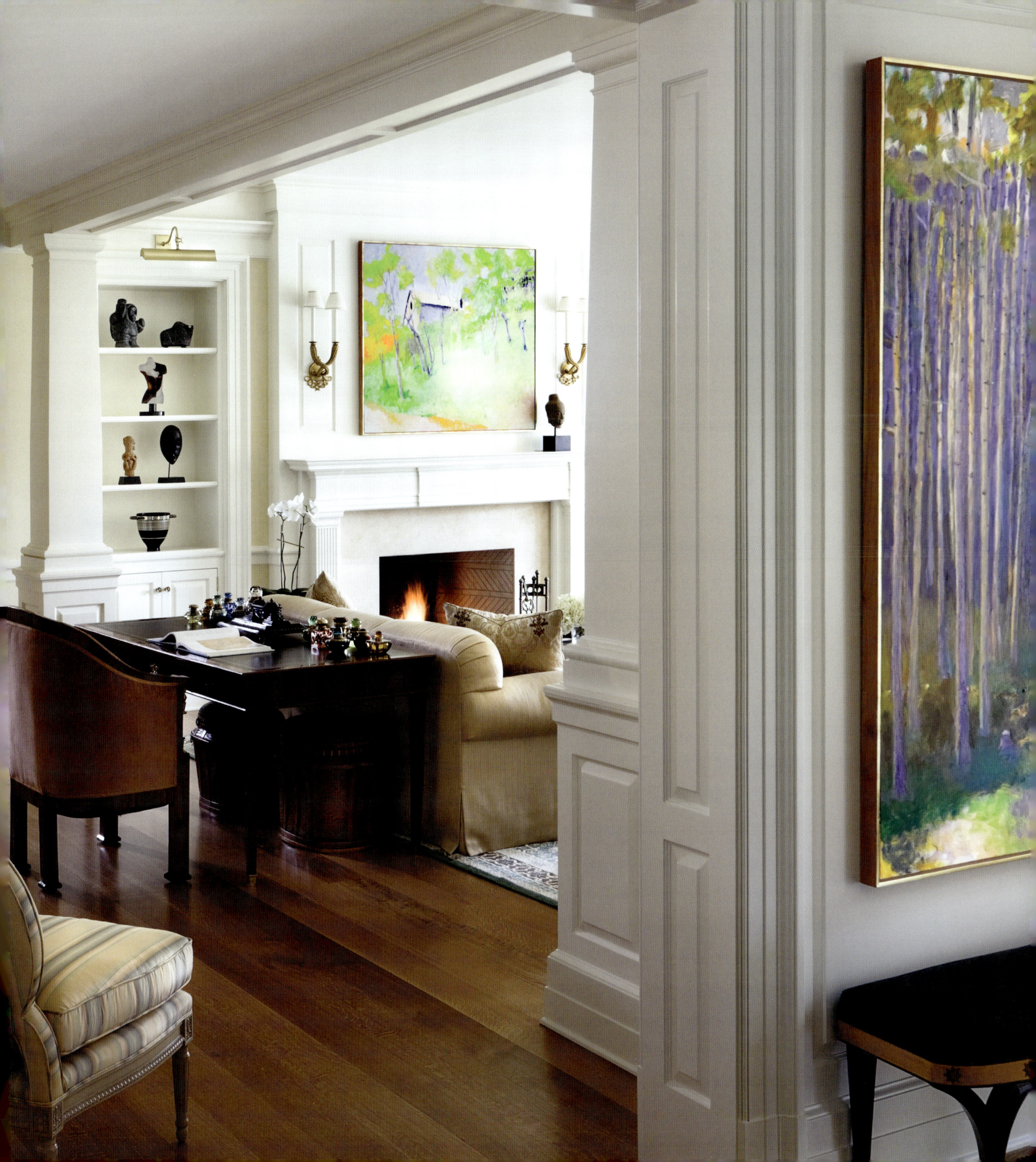

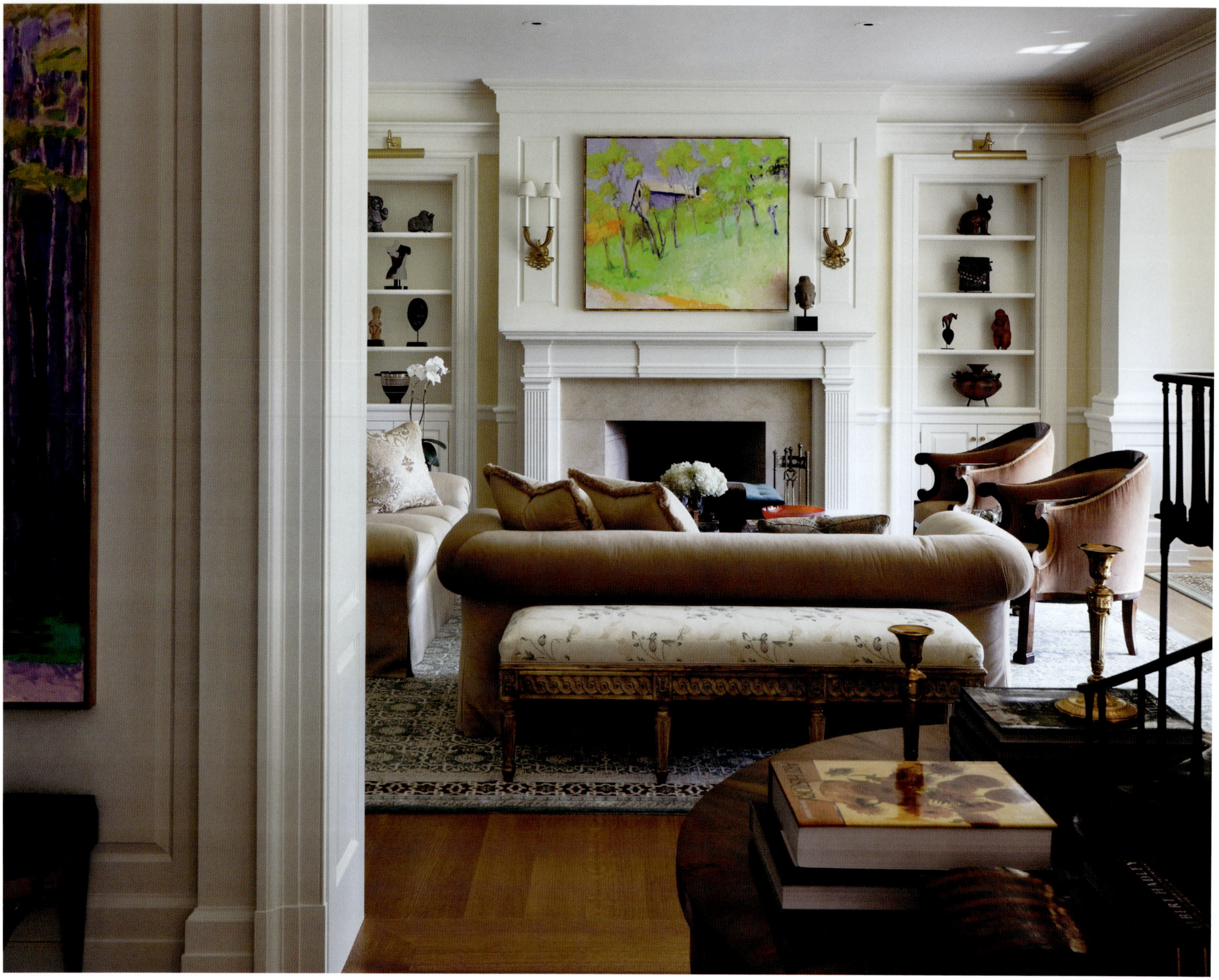

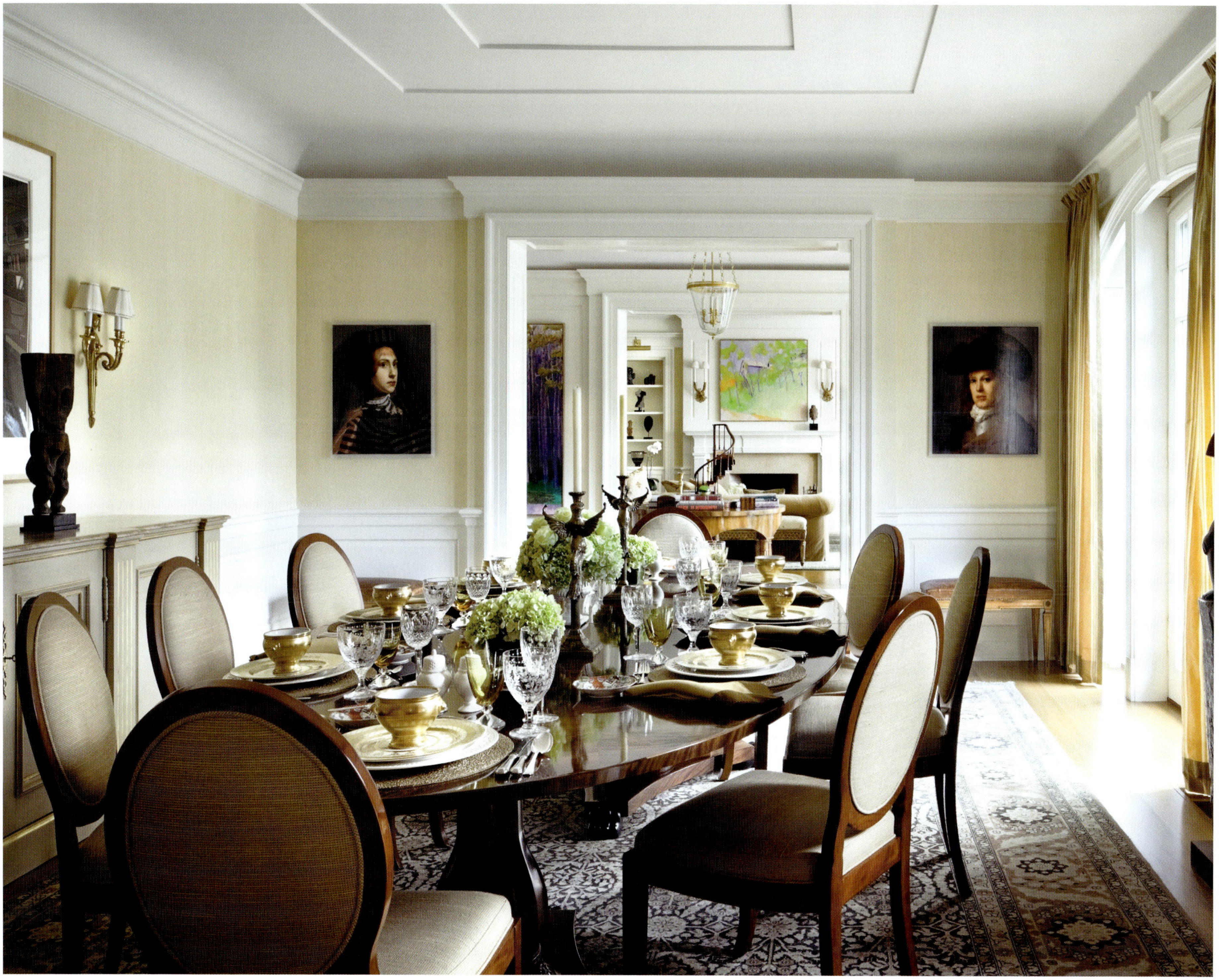

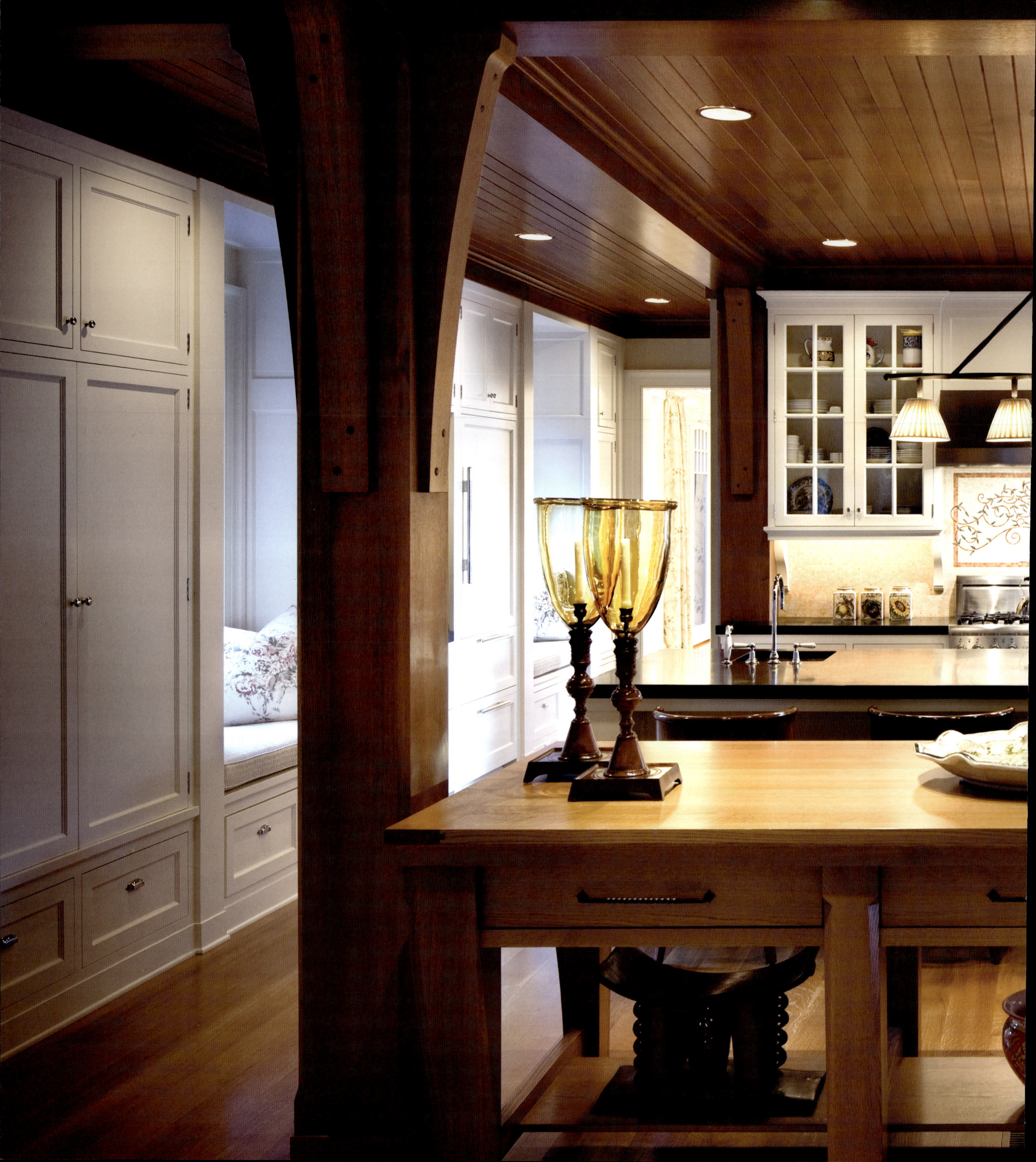

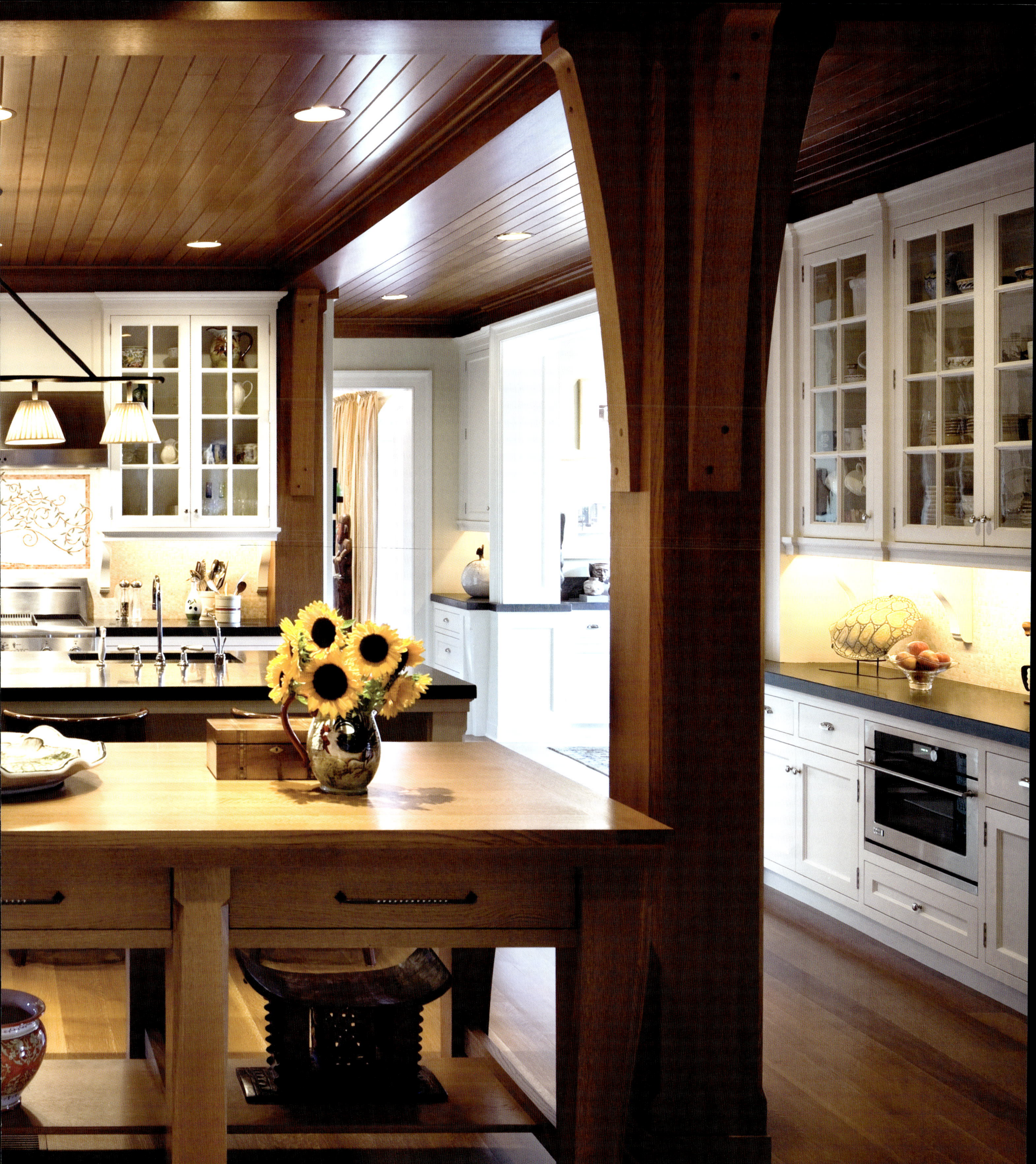

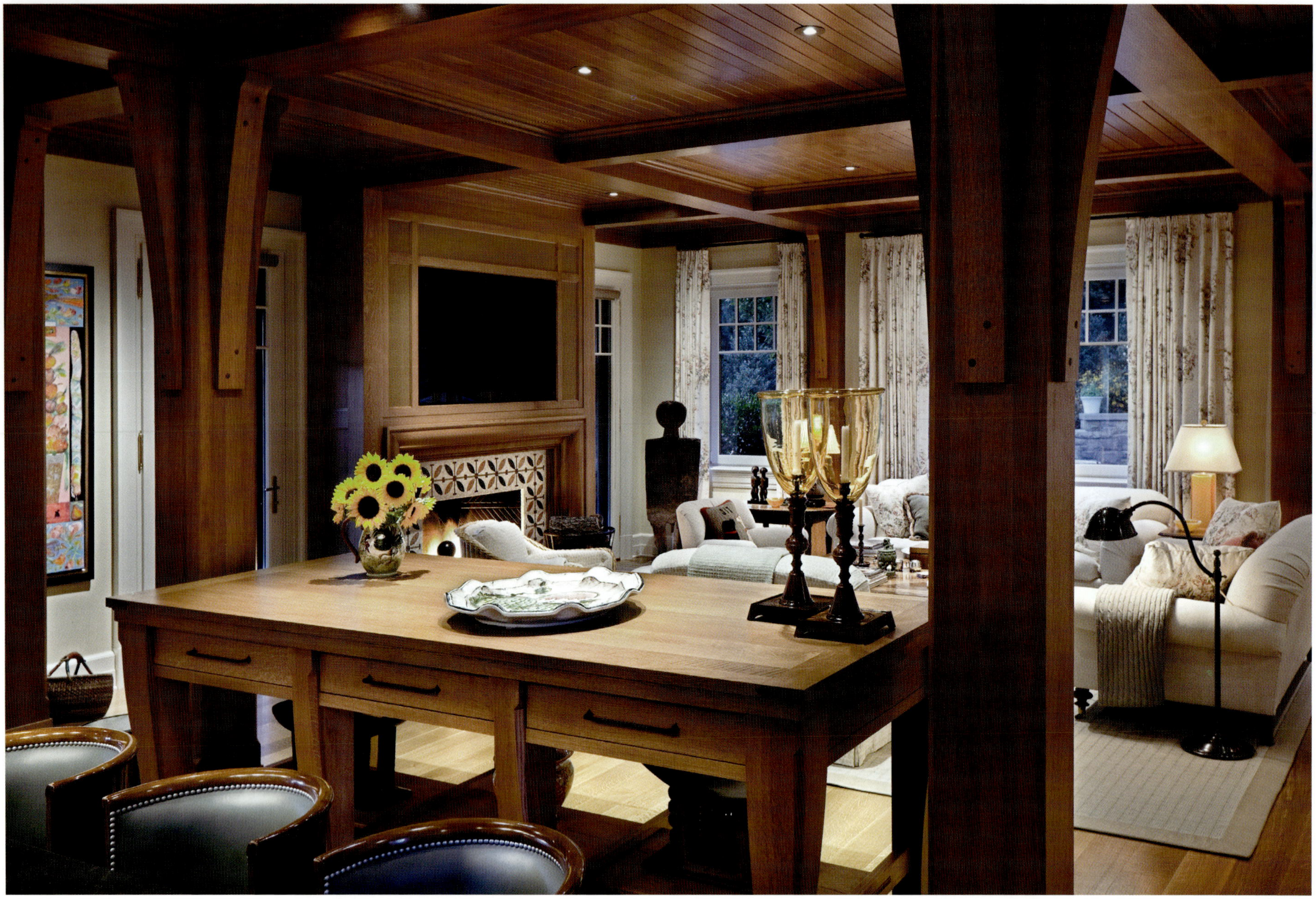

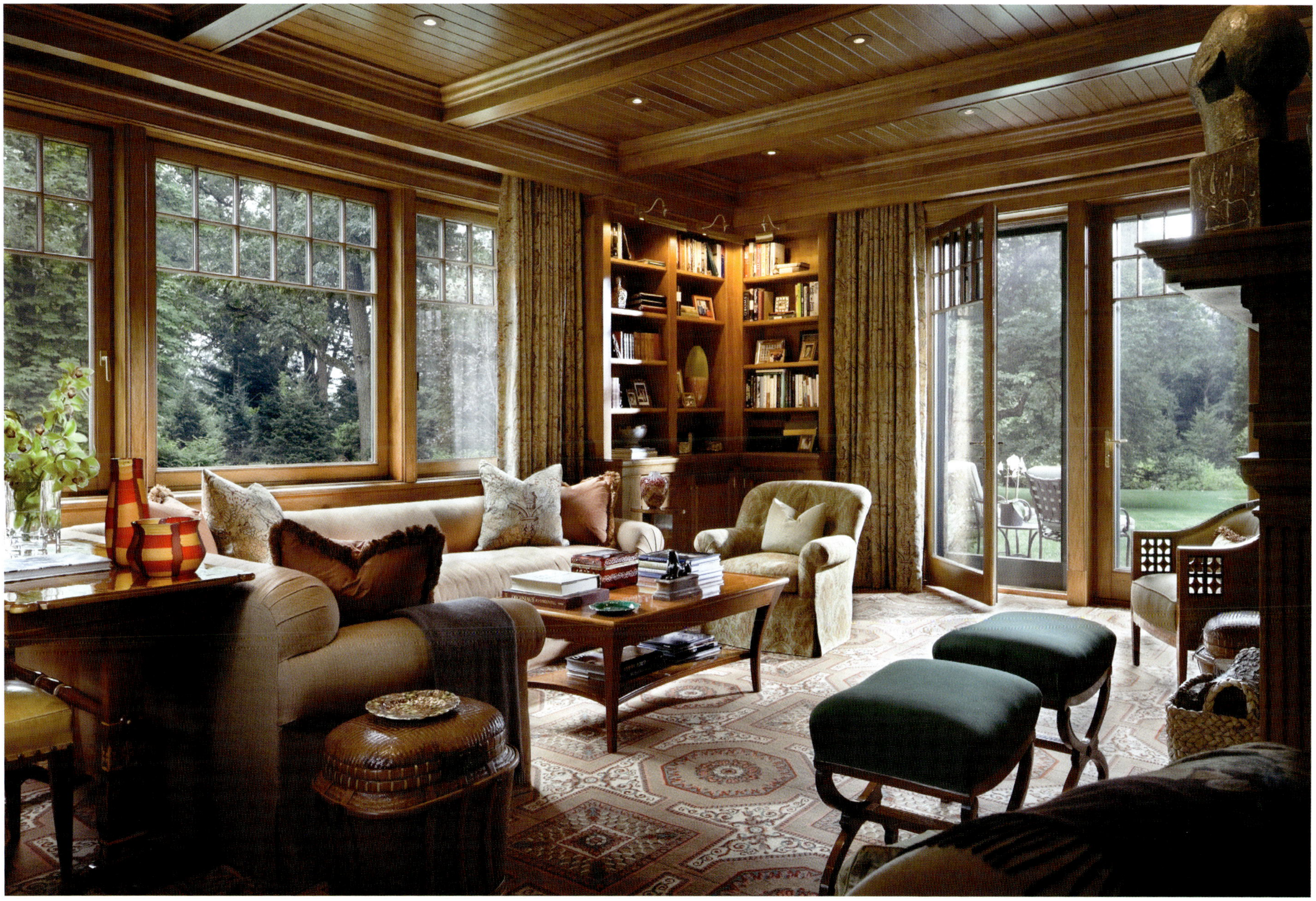

SITE PLAN

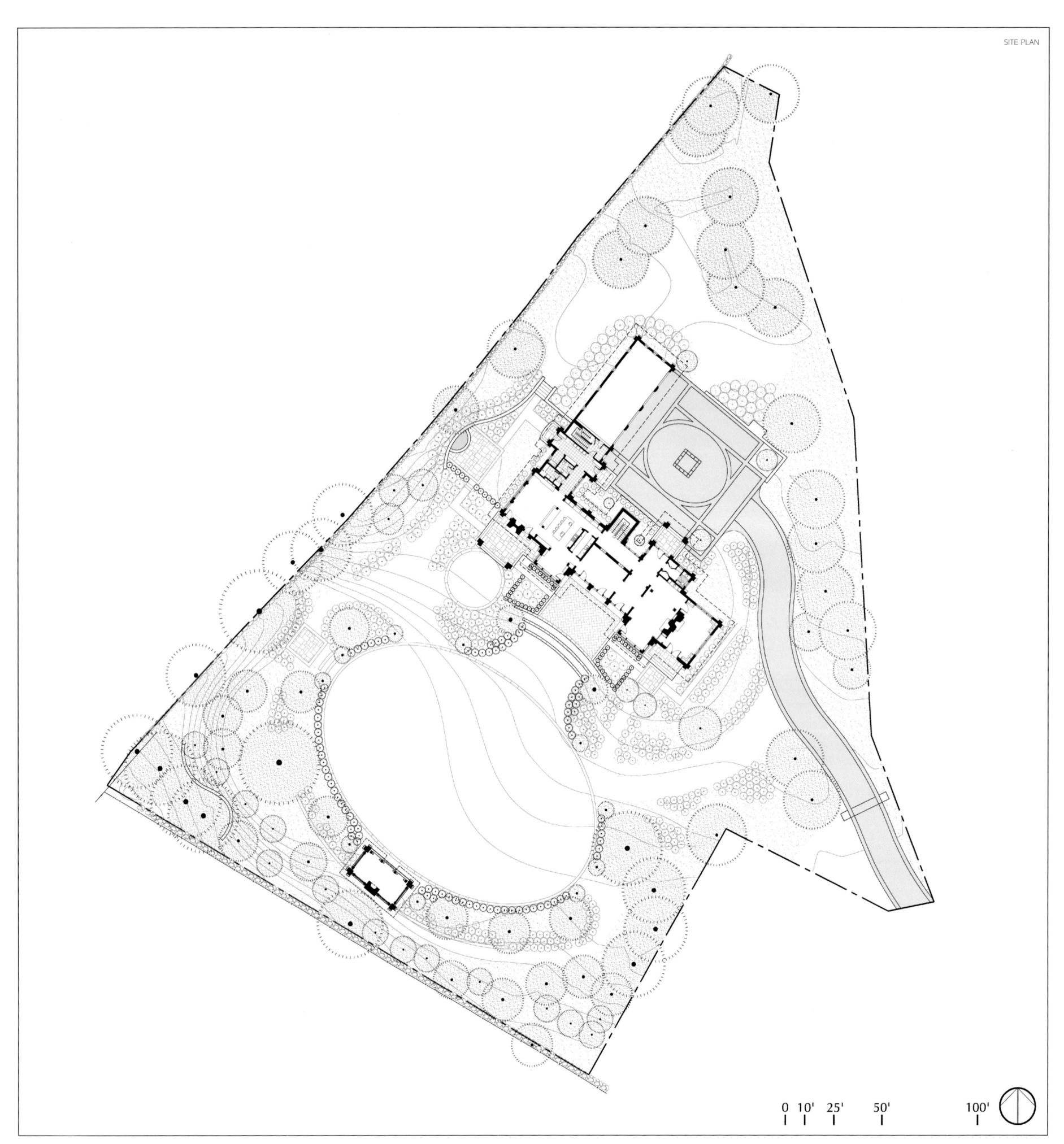

0 10' 25' 50'   100'

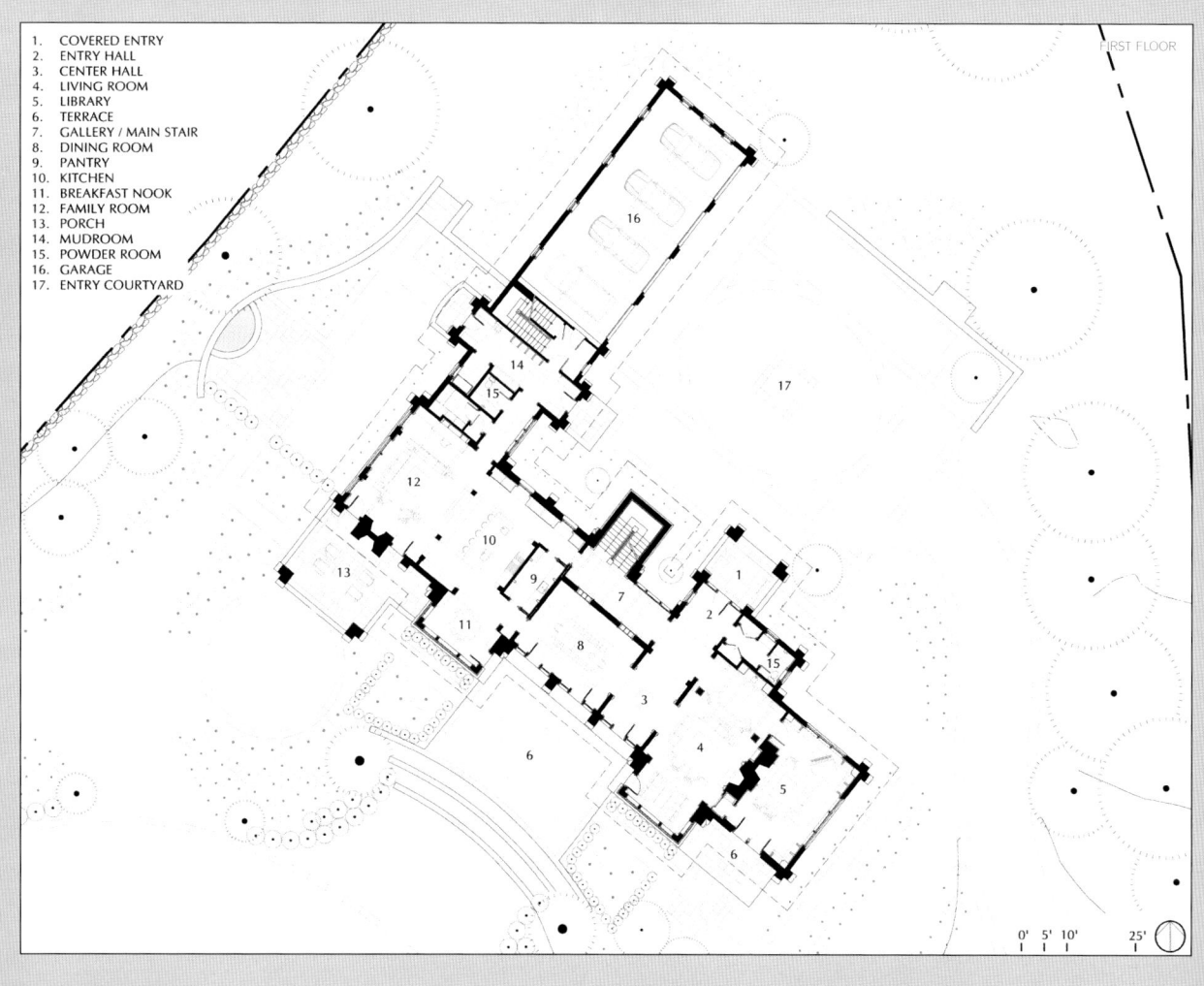

FIRST FLOOR

1. COVERED ENTRY
2. ENTRY HALL
3. CENTER HALL
4. LIVING ROOM
5. LIBRARY
6. TERRACE
7. GALLERY / MAIN STAIR
8. DINING ROOM
9. PANTRY
10. KITCHEN
11. BREAKFAST NOOK
12. FAMILY ROOM
13. PORCH
14. MUDROOM
15. POWDER ROOM
16. GARAGE
17. ENTRY COURTYARD

SECOND FLOOR

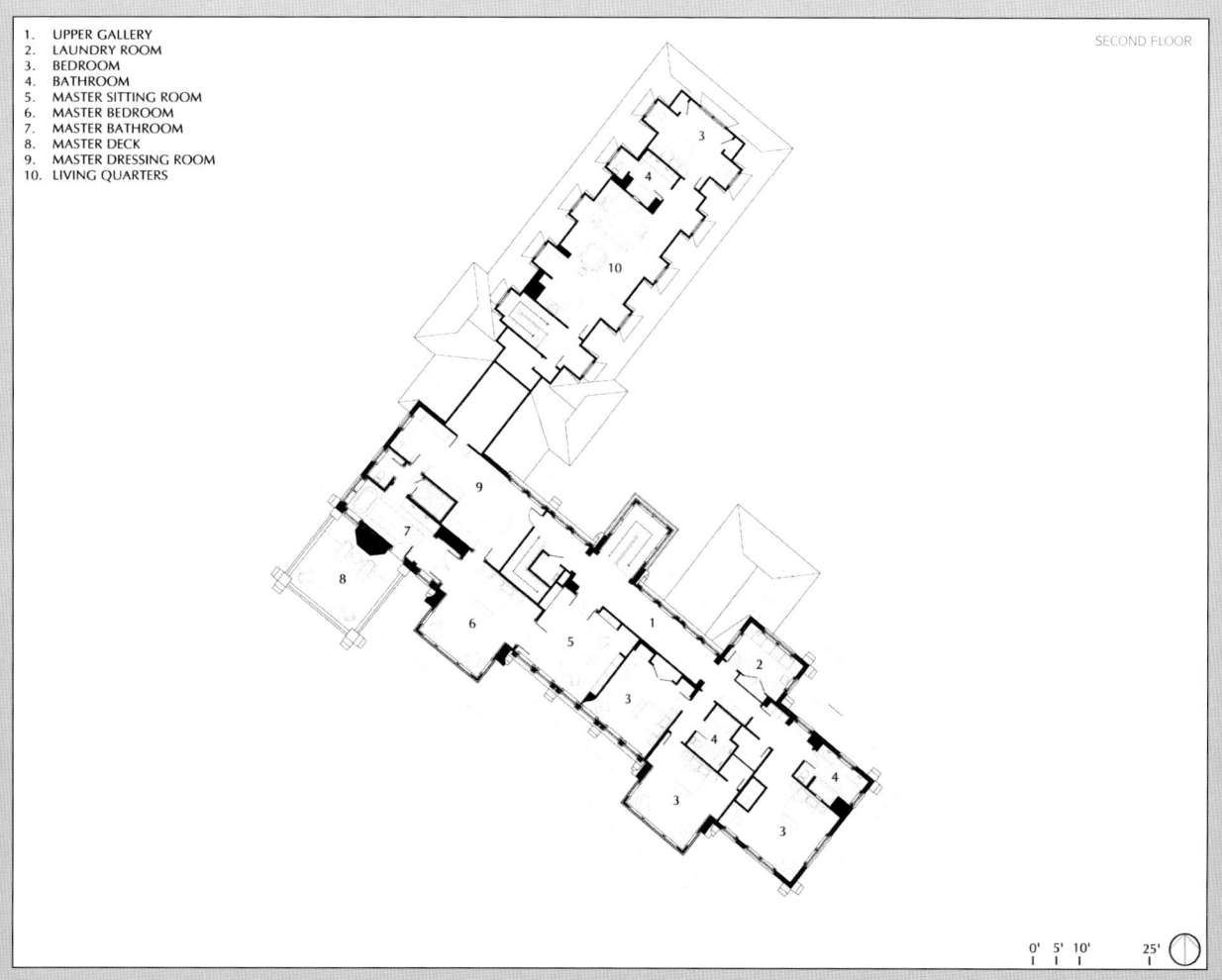

1. UPPER GALLERY
2. LAUNDRY ROOM
3. BEDROOM
4. BATHROOM
5. MASTER SITTING ROOM
6. MASTER BEDROOM
7. MASTER BATHROOM
8. MASTER DECK
9. MASTER DRESSING ROOM
10. LIVING QUARTERS

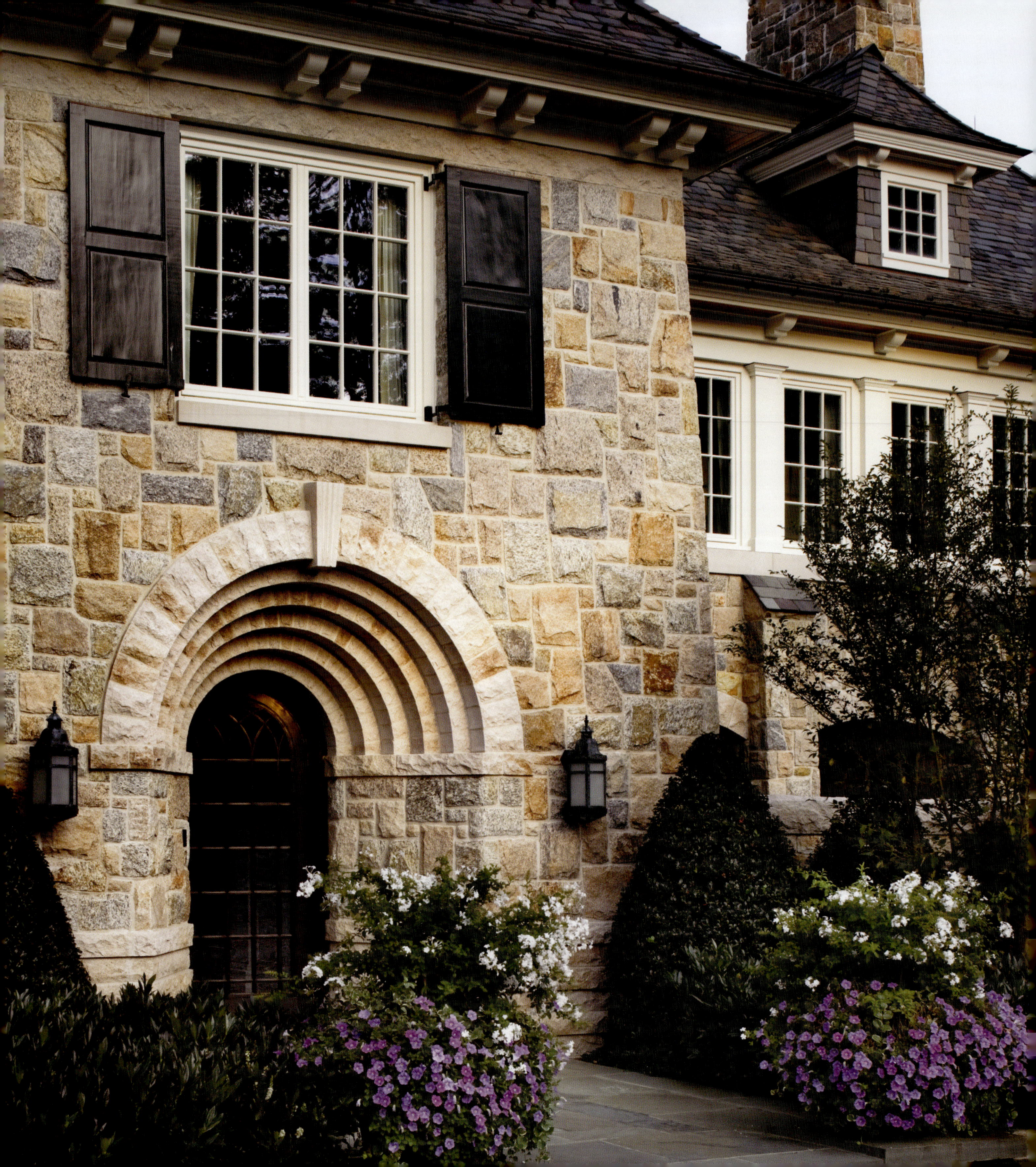

A BEAUTIFUL WATERFRONT SETTING, AND A DRAMATIC FOYER, ARE PART OF THE HOUSE'S STRONG PRESENCE

THE CLIENTS A young couple with small children have a versatile life. They entertained often for business and charity events, but they were also very family-oriented, and any home they had would have to be congenial to the rough and tumble of everyday life.

THE DESIGN BRIEF Because the 2.5-acre site is on a beautiful waterfront stretch on the Connecticut shore, the house needed to have a strong presence that would both anchor and enhance the surroundings. On its landward side, the house needed to welcome visitors, and on the other side, it had to be open to the Long Island Sound, providing views for the people inside and serving as a beacon for those on the water.

THE SOLUTION The 8,500-square foot house's strength is defined by its building material, a rough-cut granite, as well as by the homage to Wharton's continuing inspiration, the late-nineteenth century style of the American architect H.H. Richardson. At the end of the driveway, there is a cobblestoned courtyard giving onto the main front façade, in which an iron and glass entrance door has been set into a series of low, truncated arches. The two-story entrance hall is a point of departure for the rest of the house, with a stairway to the floor above, and French doors that open out to the porch and the view of the Sound beyond. The living room, which has a painted-wood coffered ceiling and French doors on both sides of the room opening onto porches, lies to one side of the entrance hall, with the library beyond. New York interior designer Thomas O'Brien had the living room ceiling painted a soft white. In contrast, the library glows with dark paneling and varnished oak ceiling beams that have an antique feeling. The deep porch on the water side of the house, anchored by granite piers with wooden brackets that suggest tree branches, provides a secluded shady refuge from which to look out at the movement of boats on the Sound. Despite the massive nature of the exterior, the more domestic parts of the interior are refreshingly open. White-painted cabinetry and a limestone floor brighten the kitchen, and the windows surrounding an adjacent breakfast room flood both spaces with light. Cummin Associates, a Stonington, Connecticut-based firm, was responsible for the landscape design. A swimming pool sparkles invitingly in the garden; it also provides access to a second, hidden pool tucked away beneath the planting beds. Skylights that filter soft natural light into the space illuminate the underground pool. This fortress of a house harbors a light spirit, which flourishes in a place of safety and happiness.

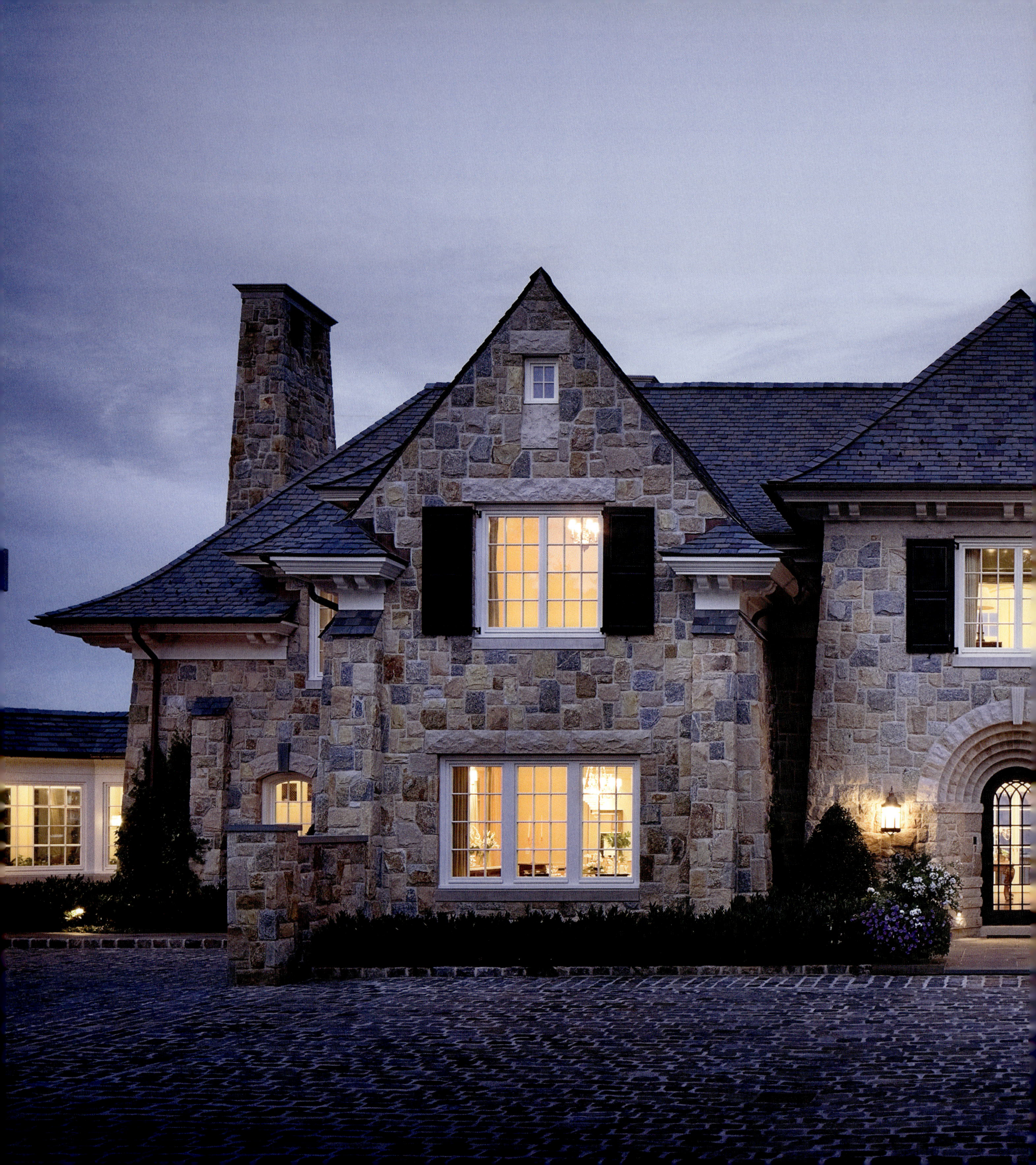

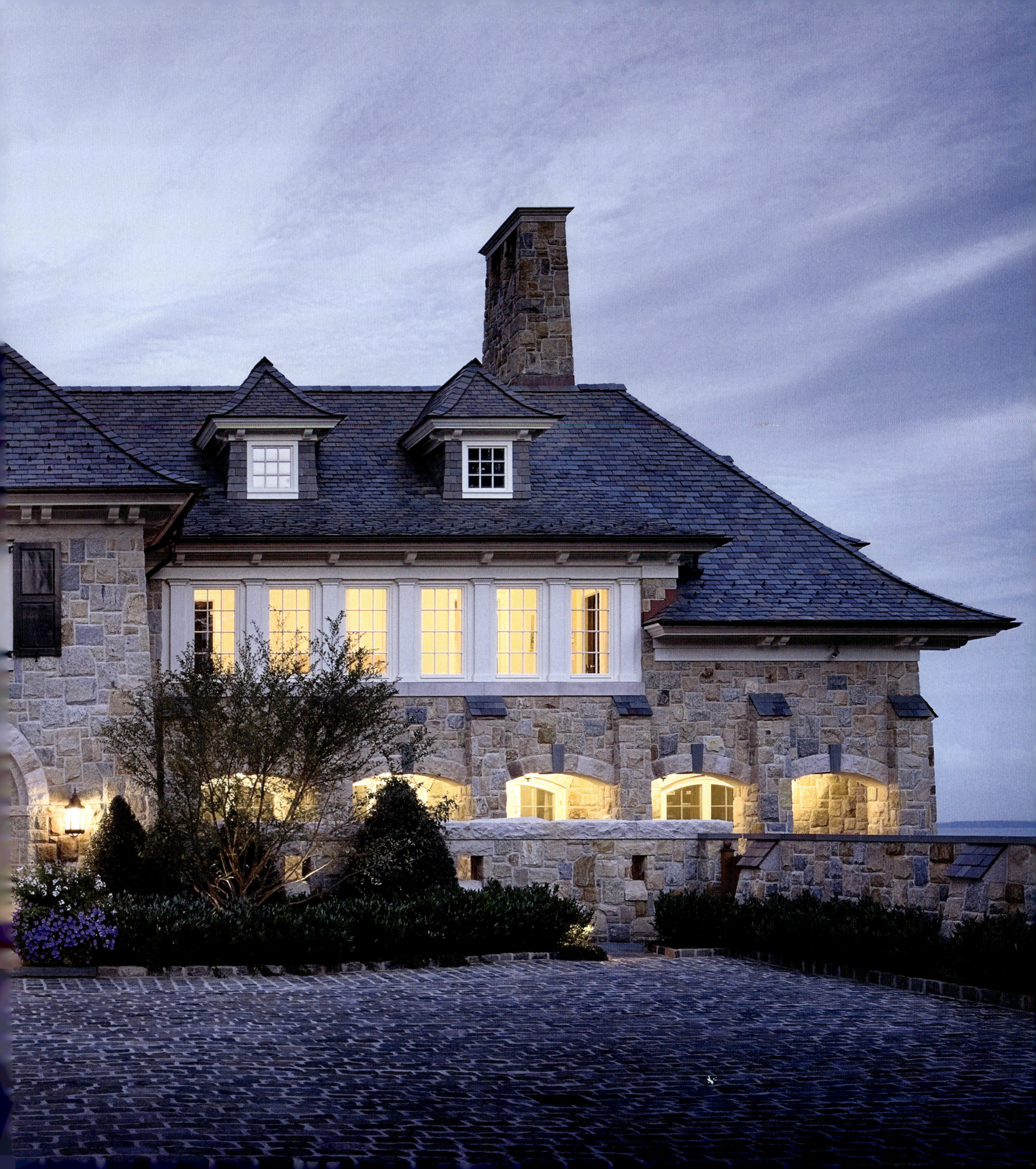

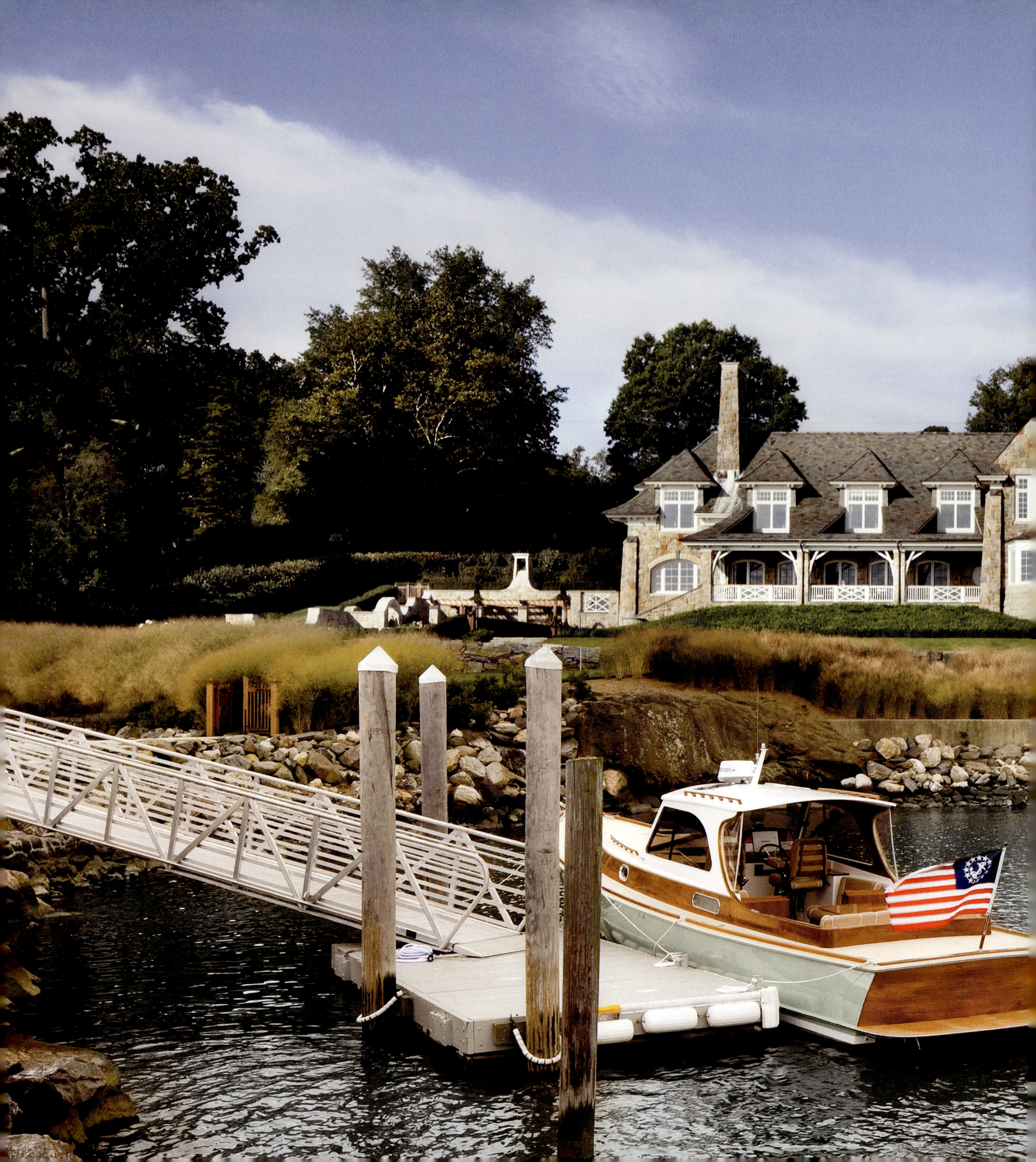

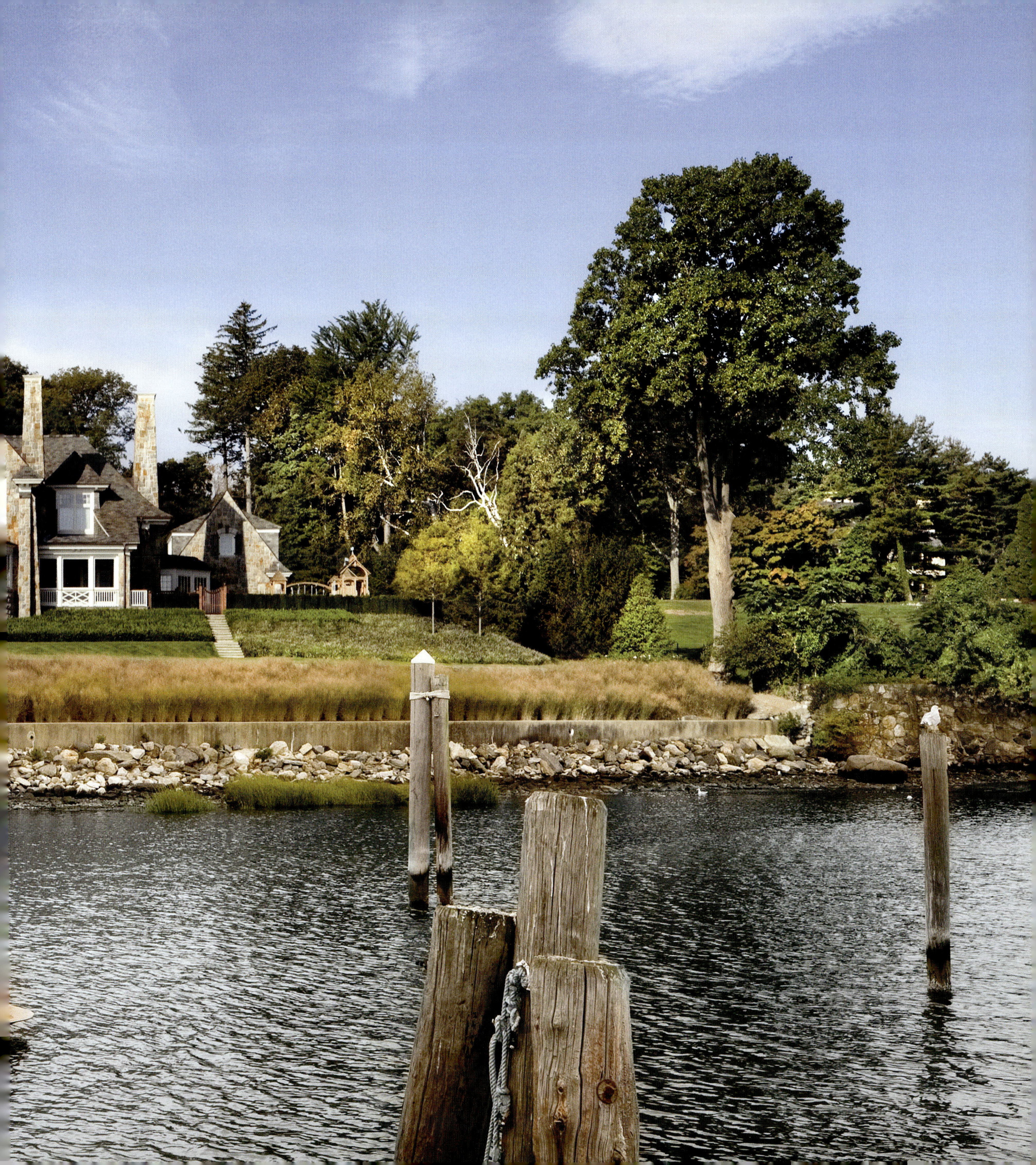

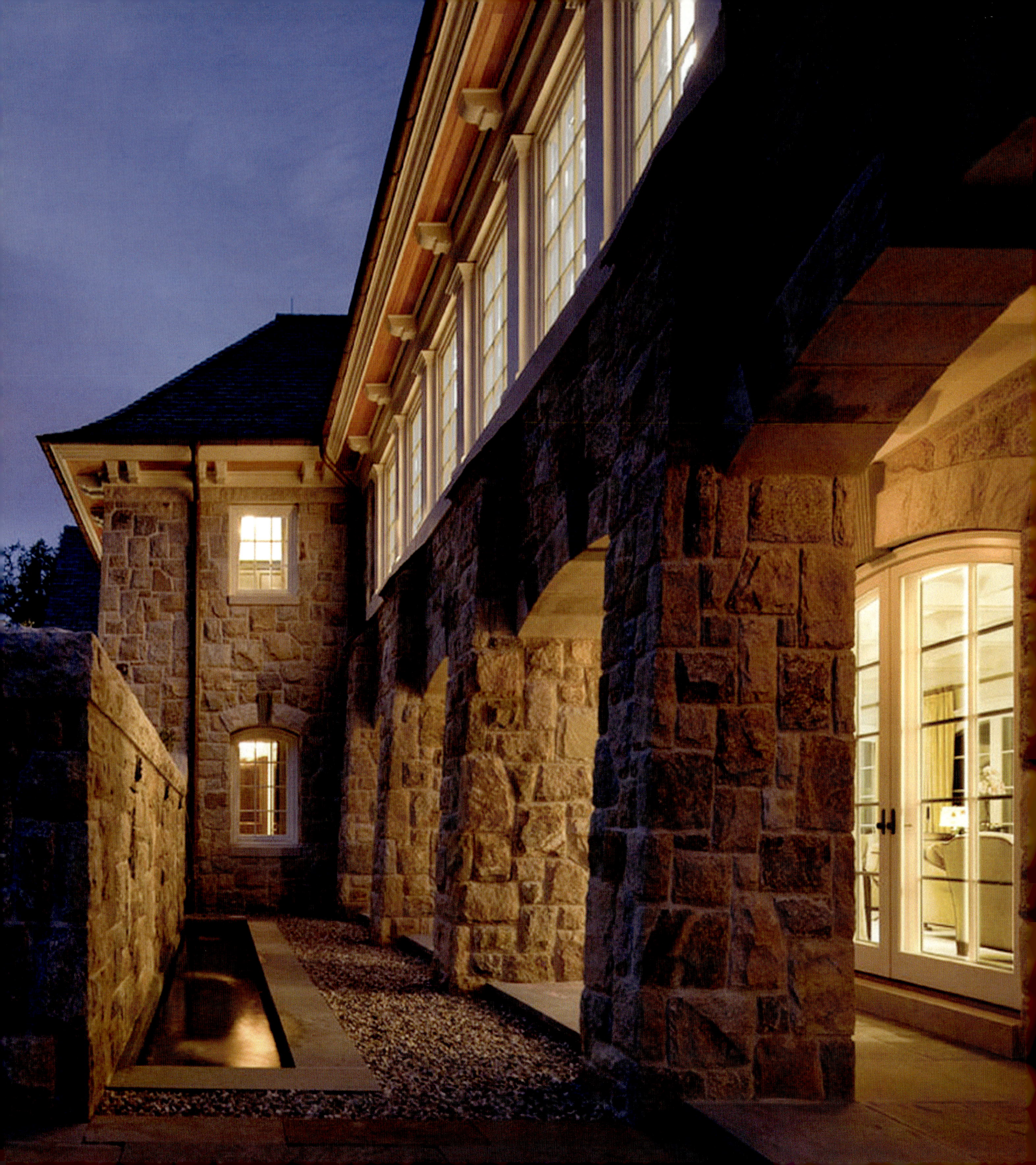

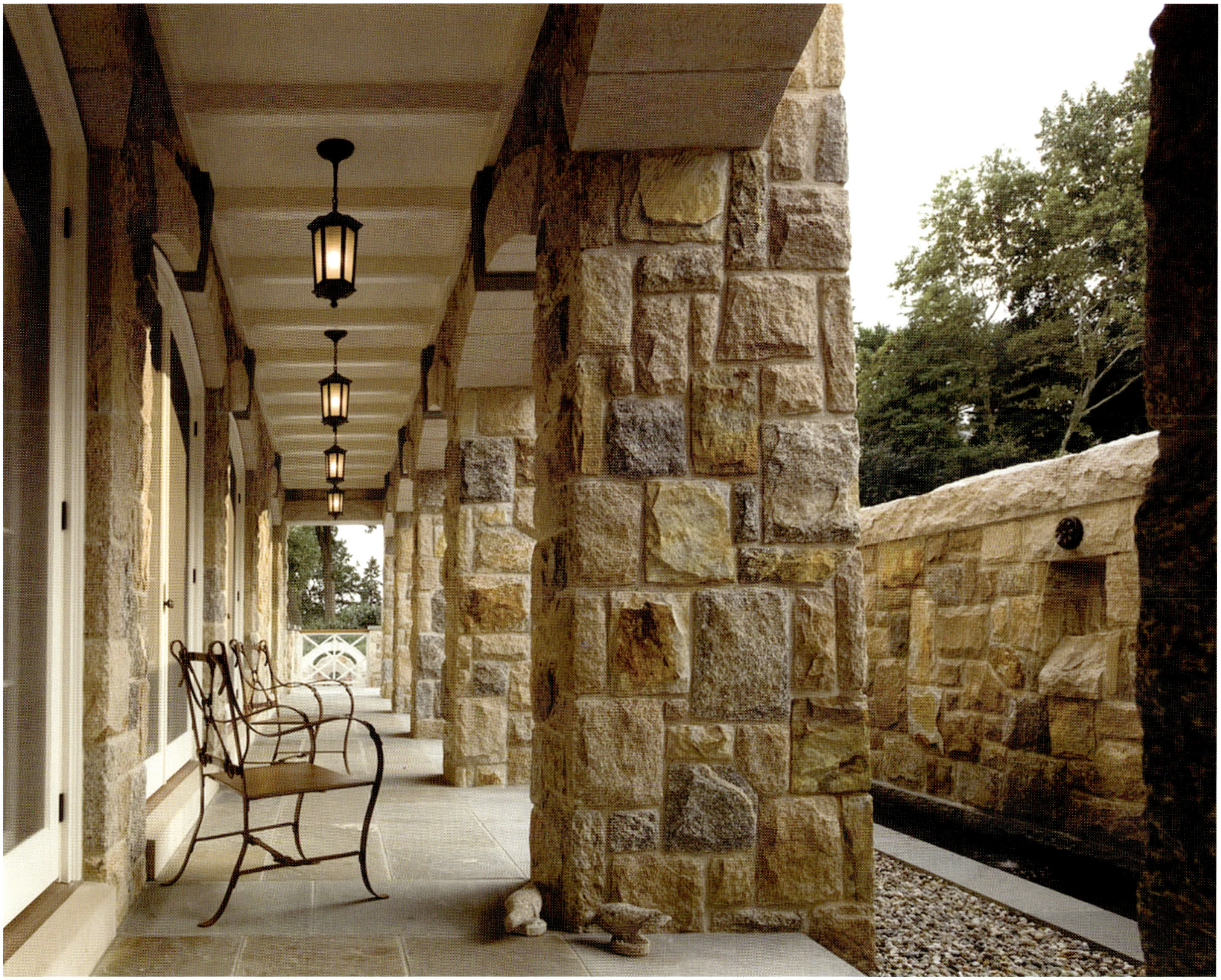

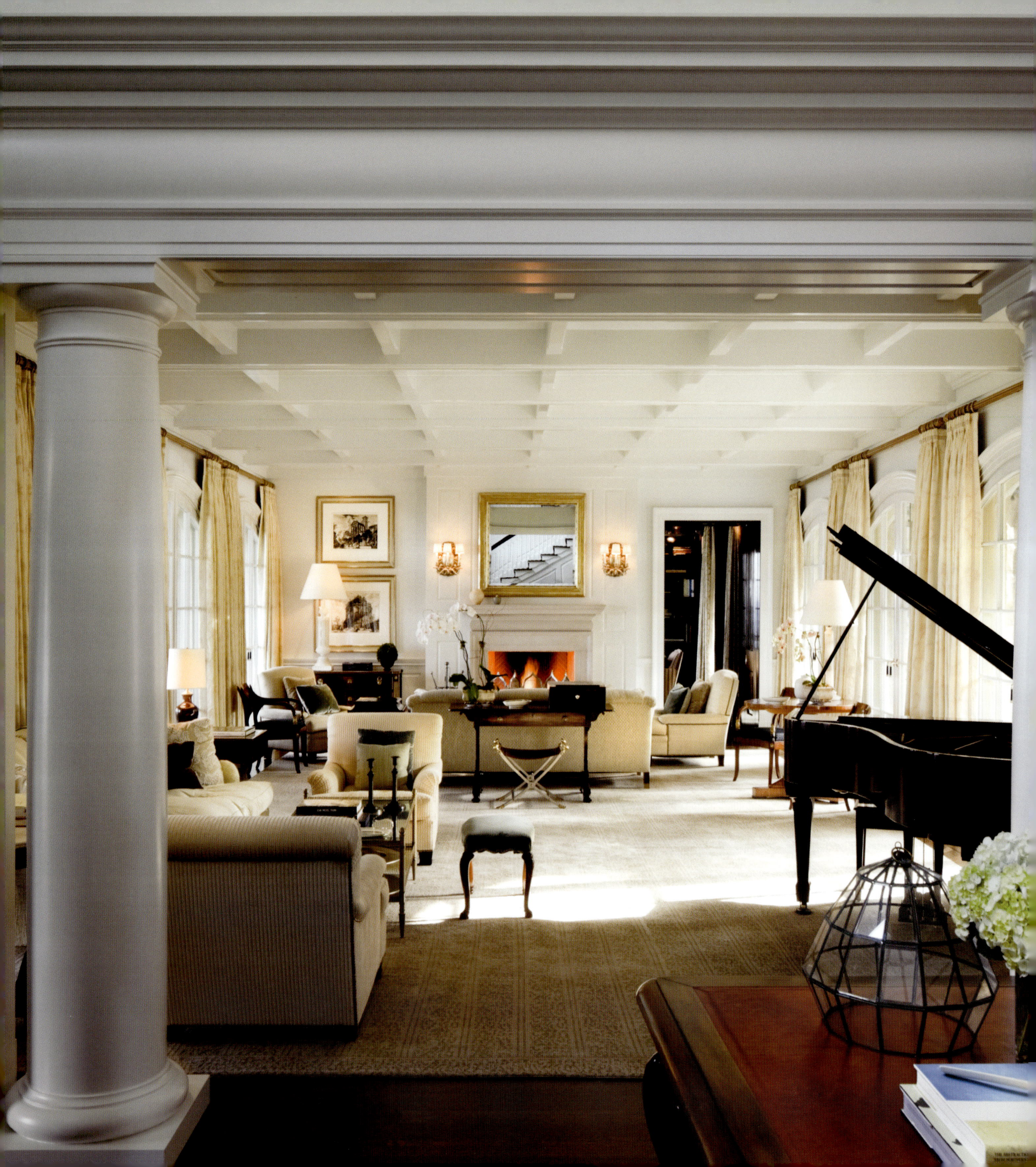

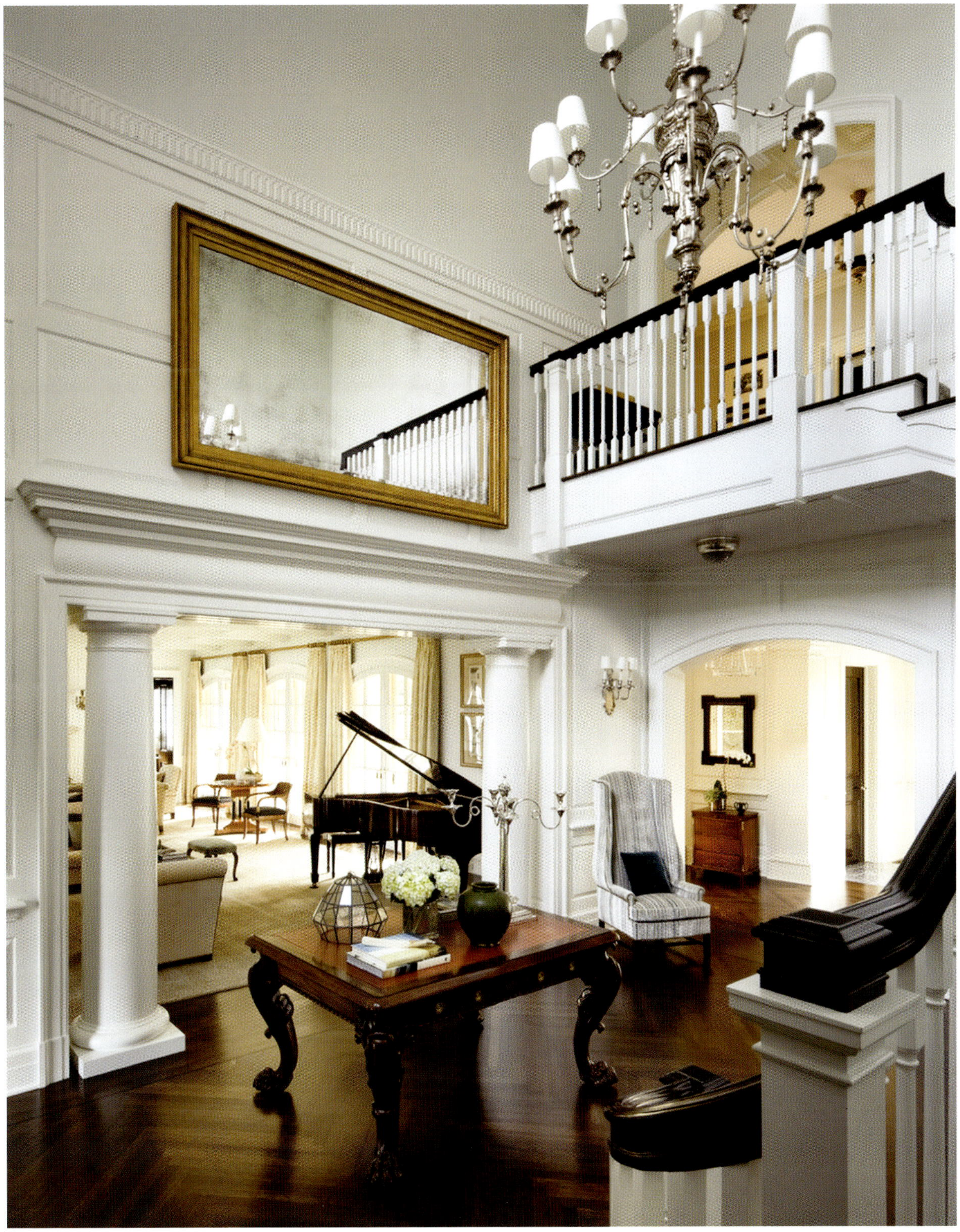

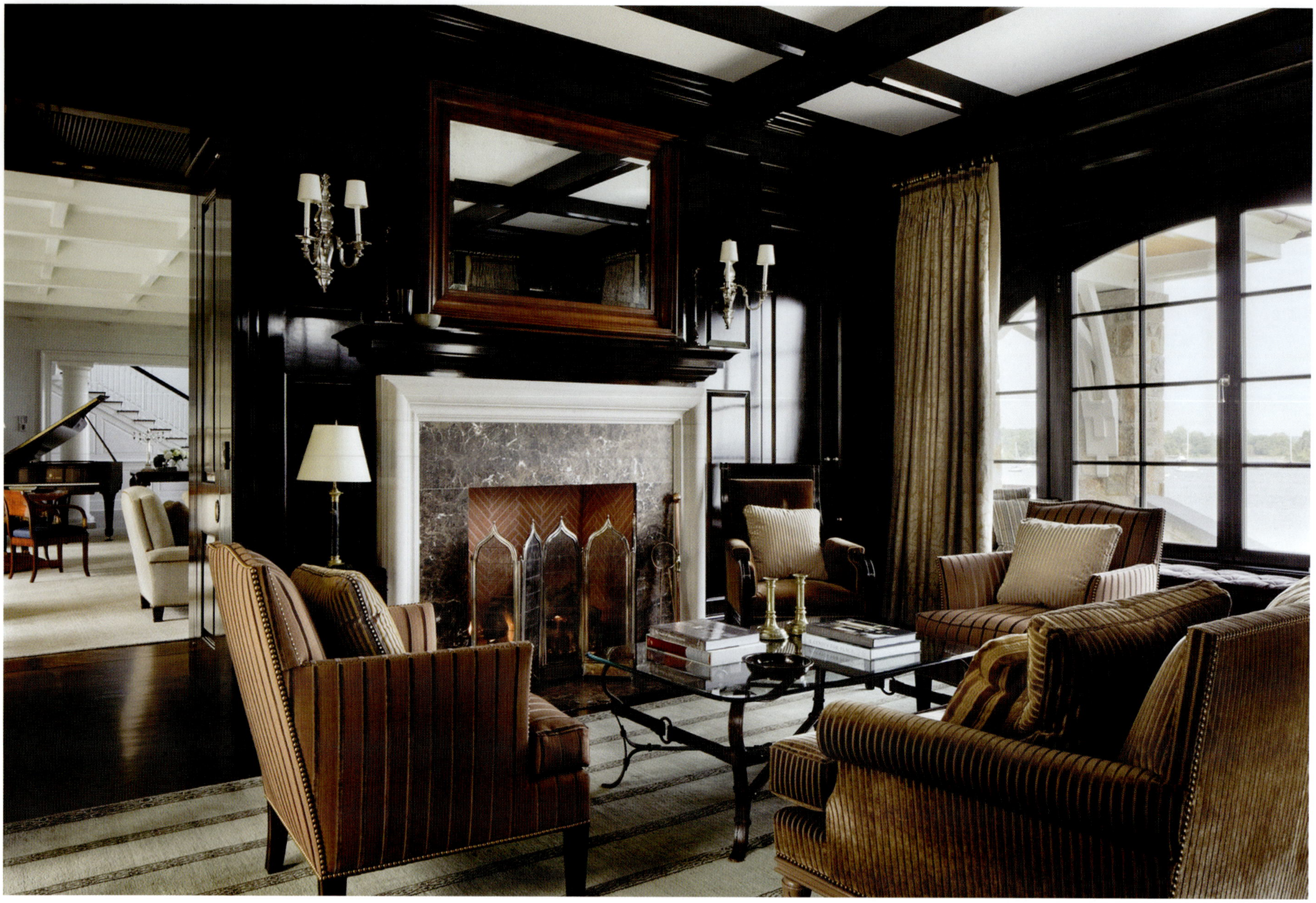

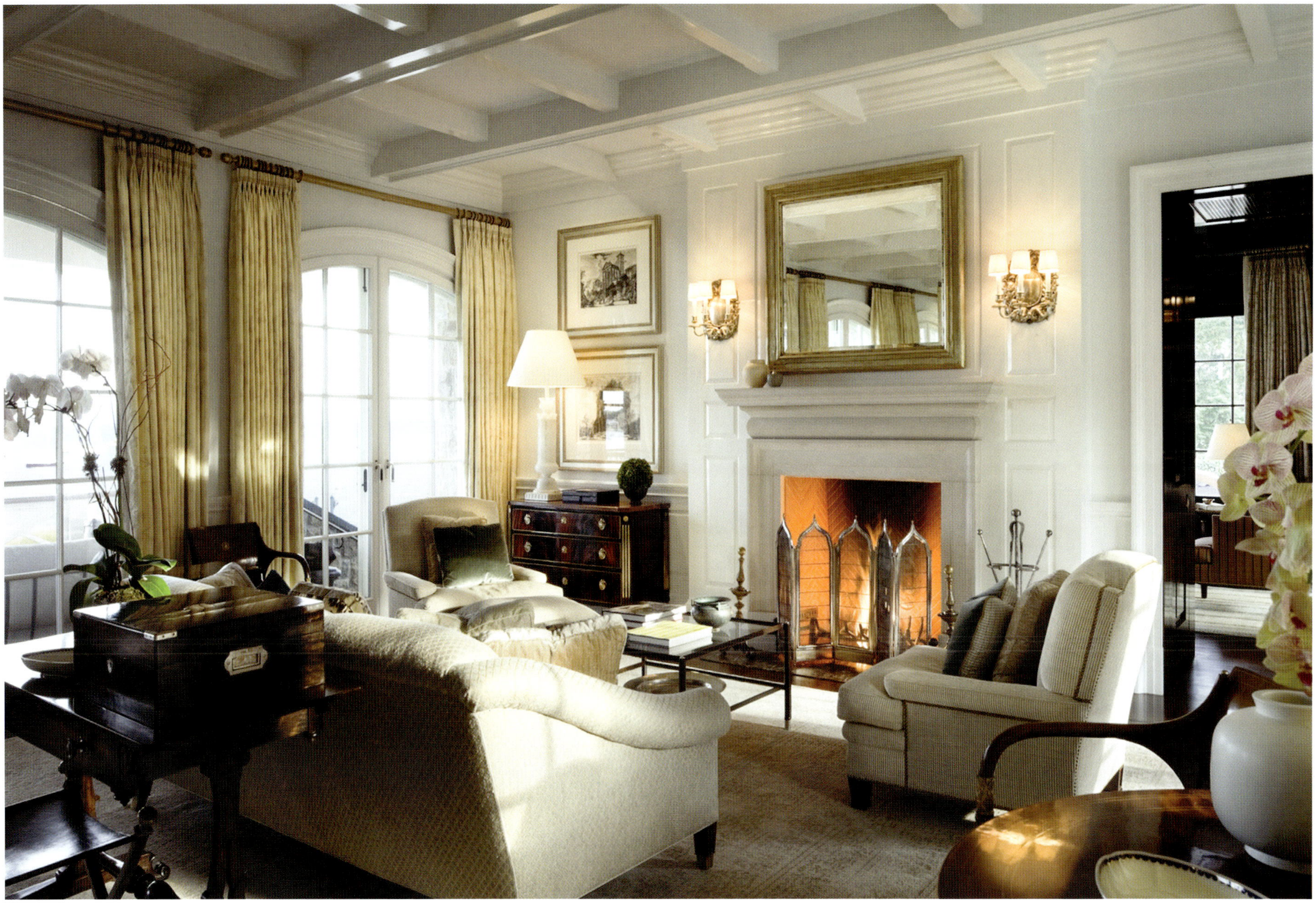

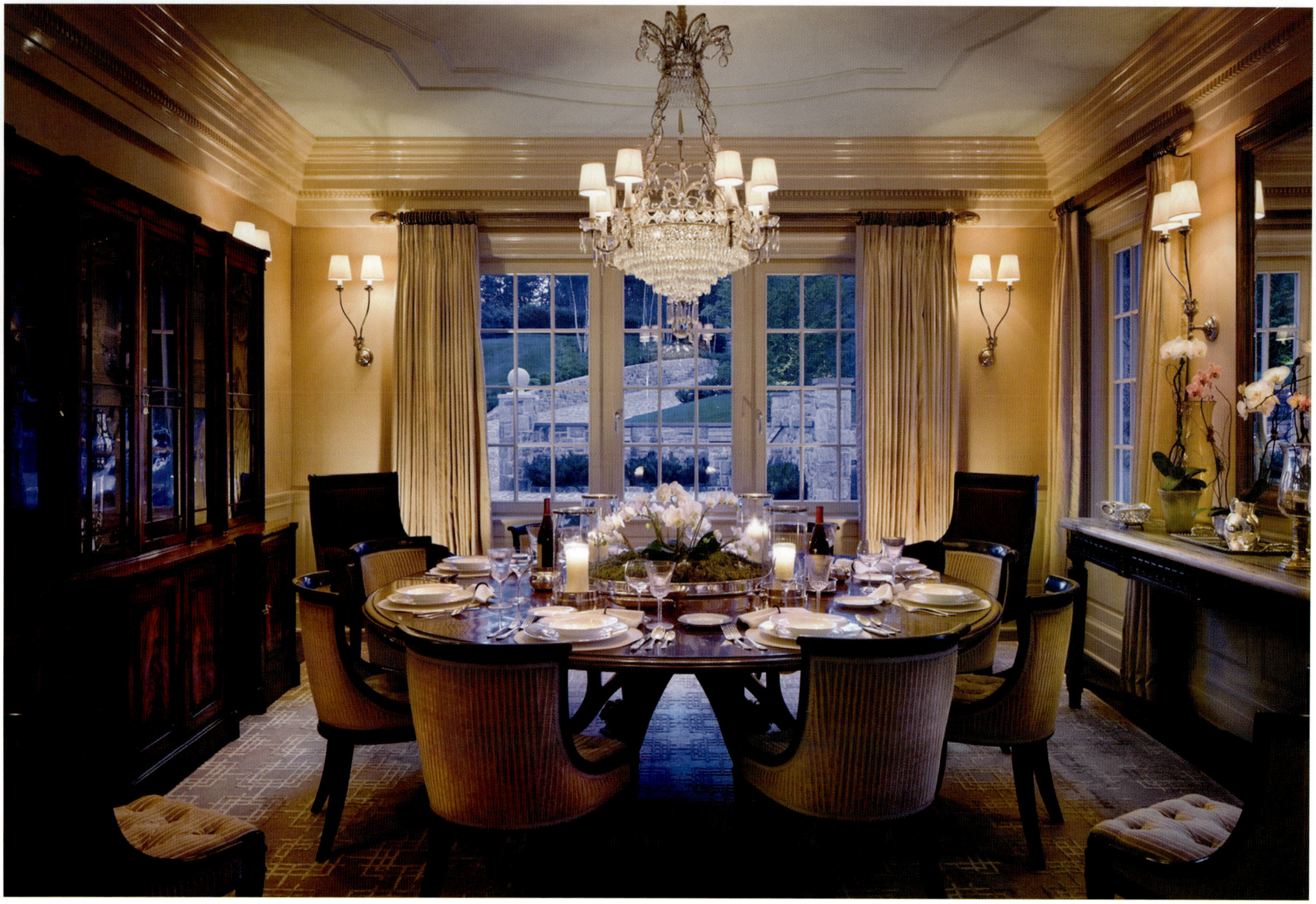

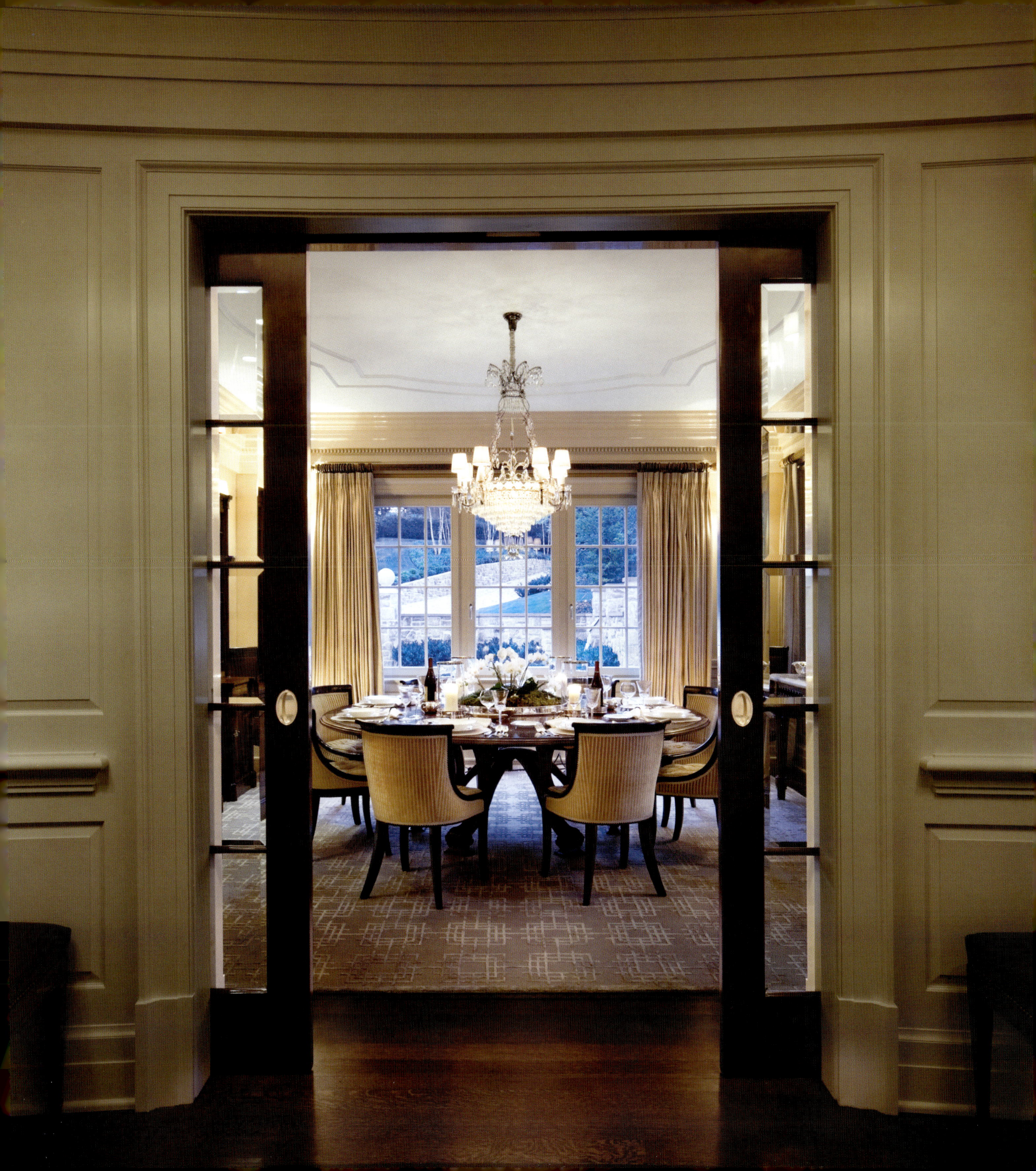

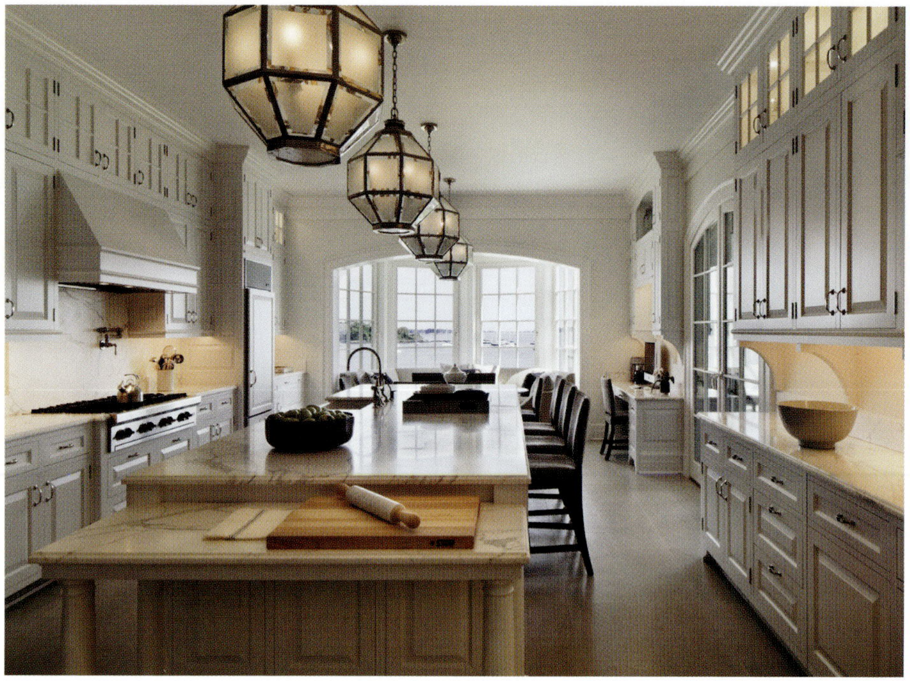

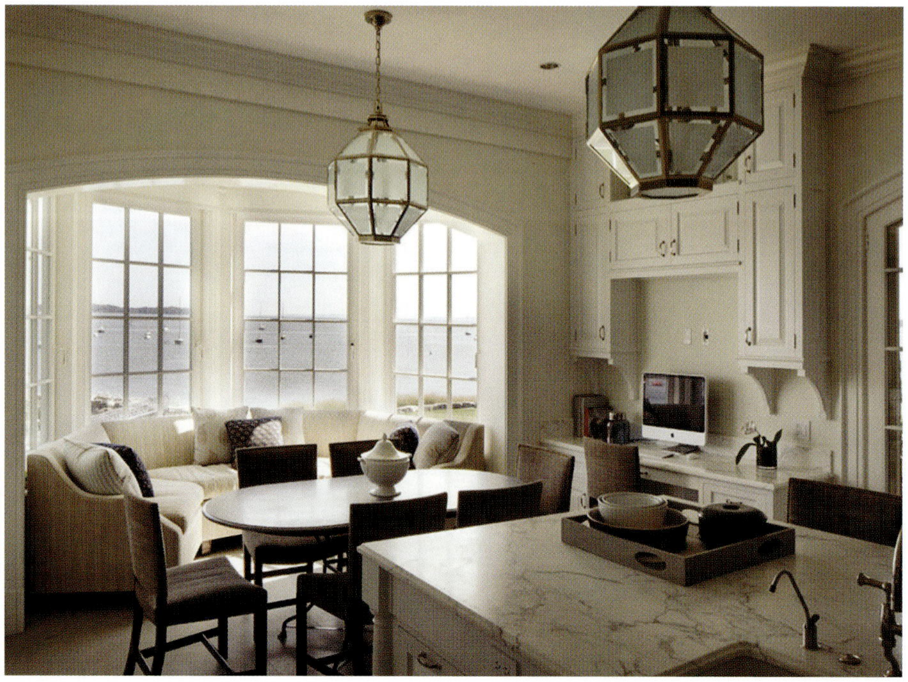

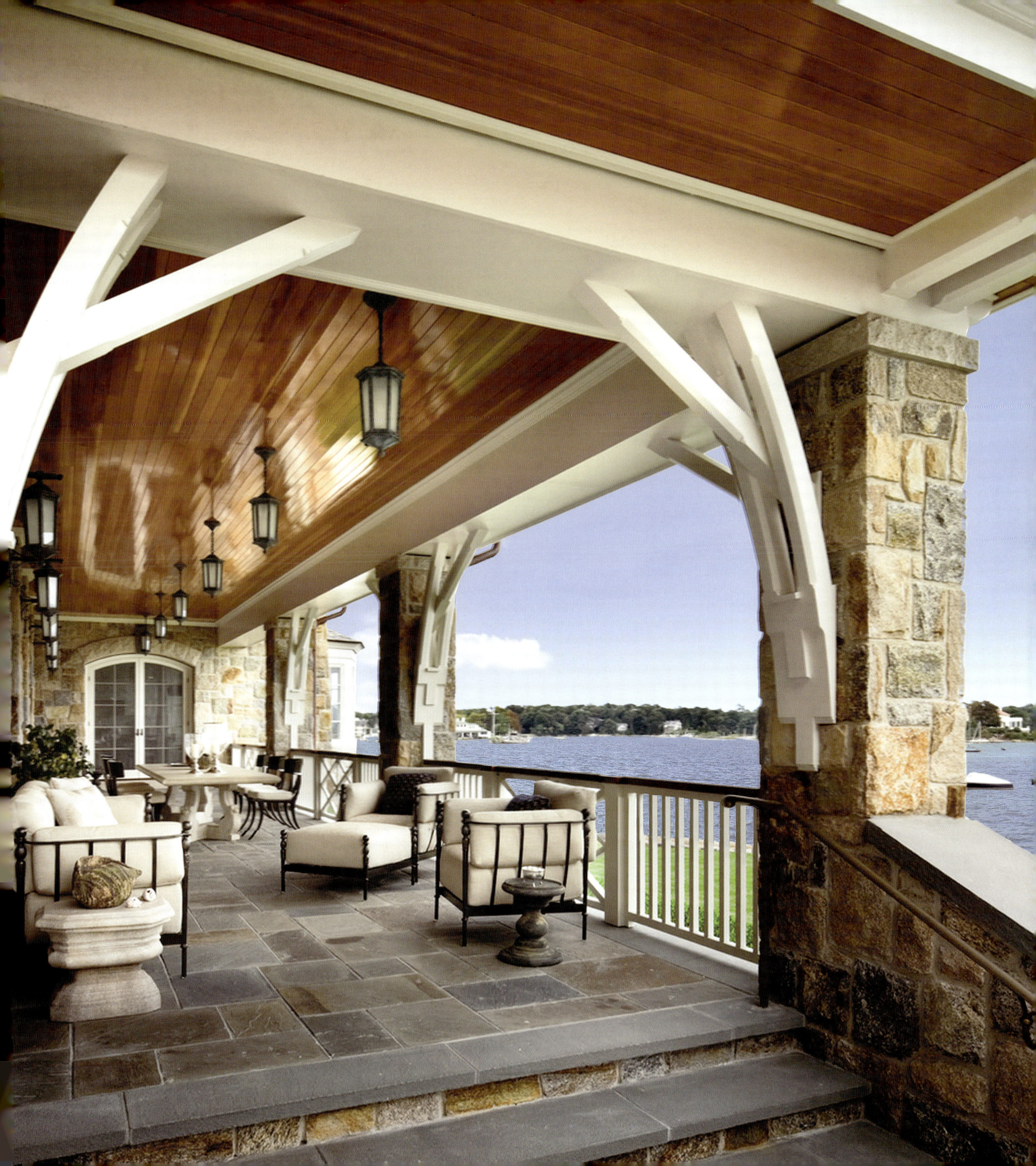

SITE PLAN

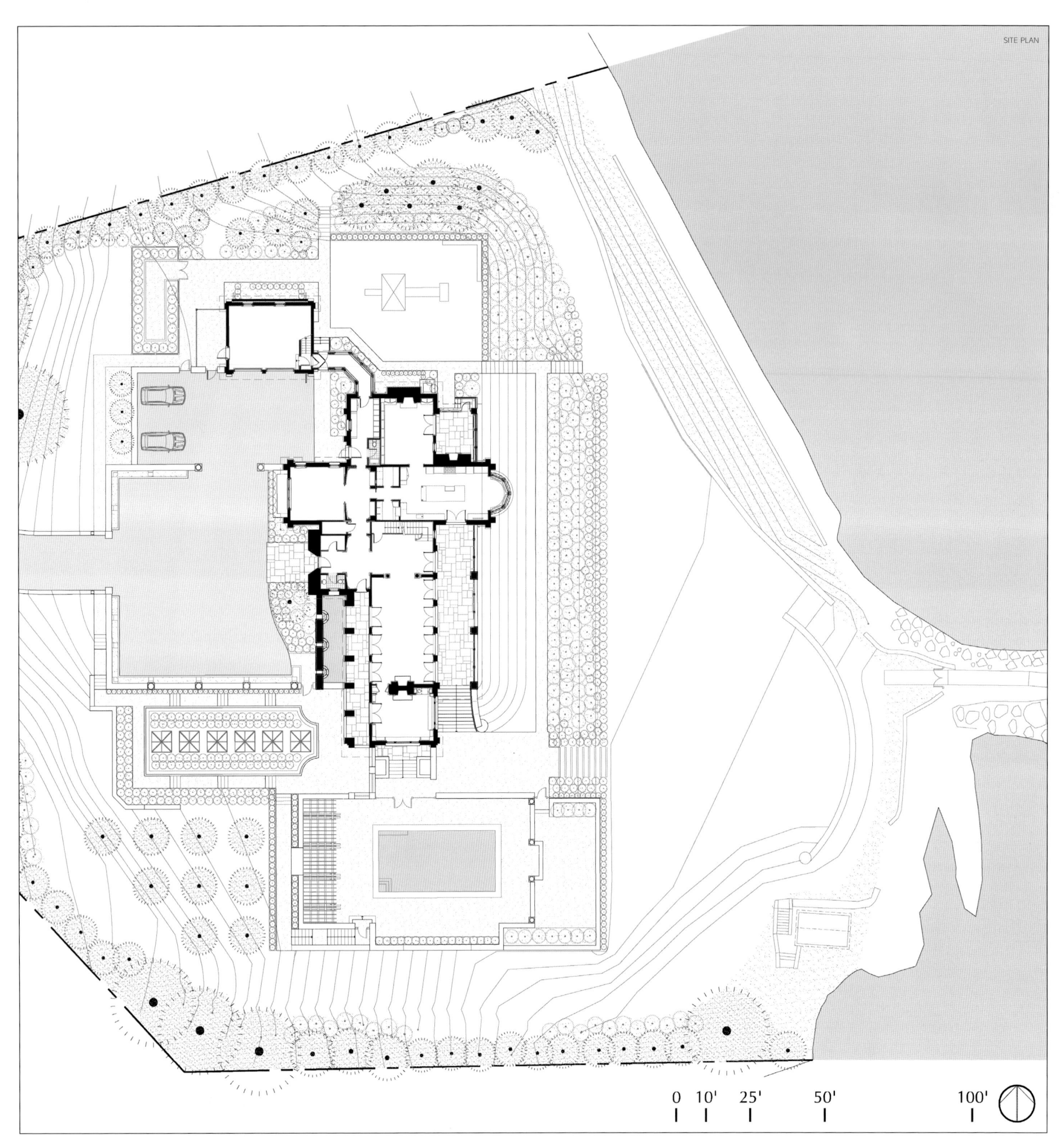

0 10' 25' 50' 100'

FIRST FLOOR

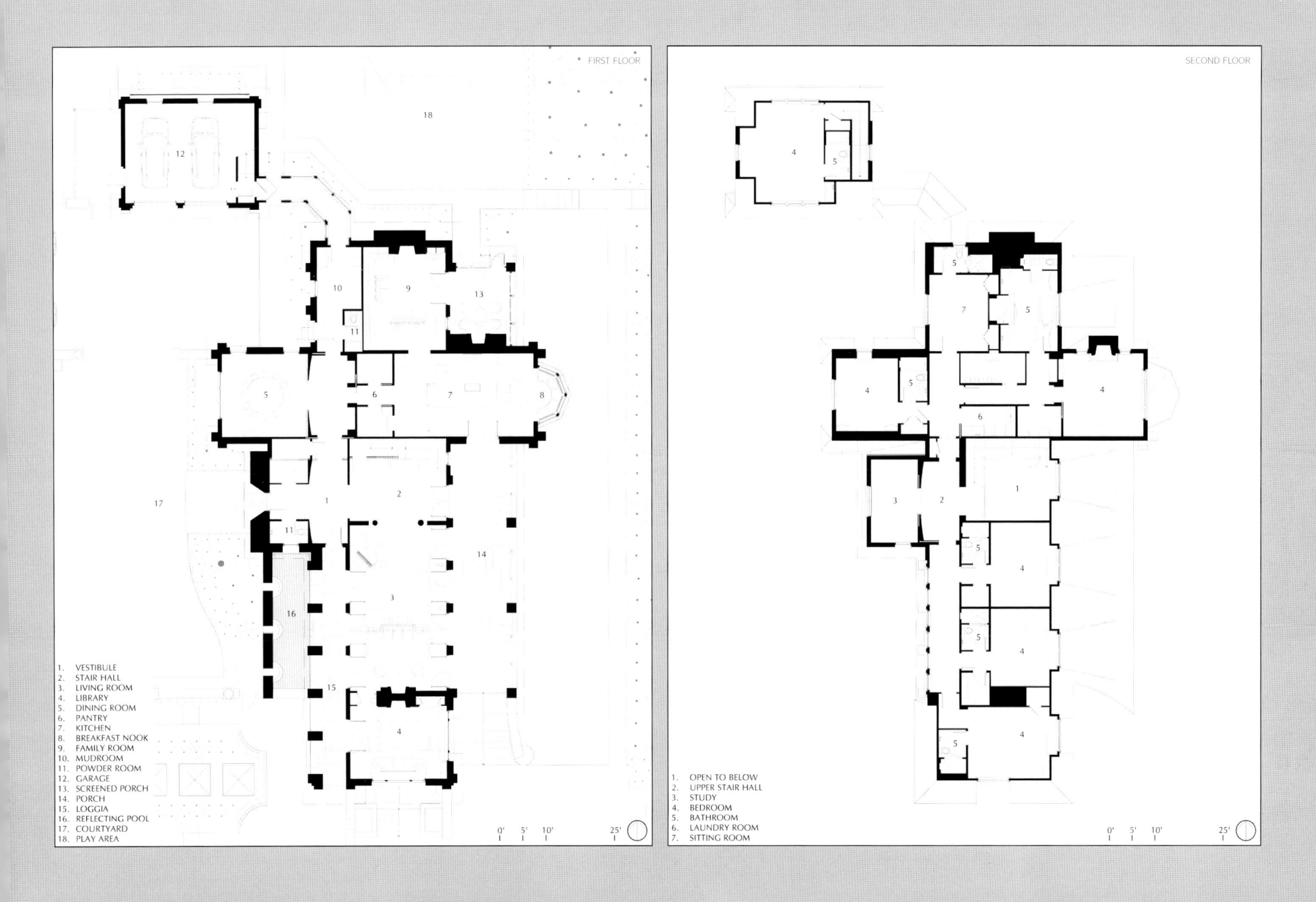

SECOND FLOOR

1. VESTIBULE
2. STAIR HALL
3. LIVING ROOM
4. LIBRARY
5. DINING ROOM
6. PANTRY
7. KITCHEN
8. BREAKFAST NOOK
9. FAMILY ROOM
10. MUDROOM
11. POWDER ROOM
12. GARAGE
13. SCREENED PORCH
14. PORCH
15. LOGGIA
16. REFLECTING POOL
17. COURTYARD
18. PLAY AREA

1. OPEN TO BELOW
2. UPPER STAIR HALL
3. STUDY
4. BEDROOM
5. BATHROOM
6. LAUNDRY ROOM
7. SITTING ROOM

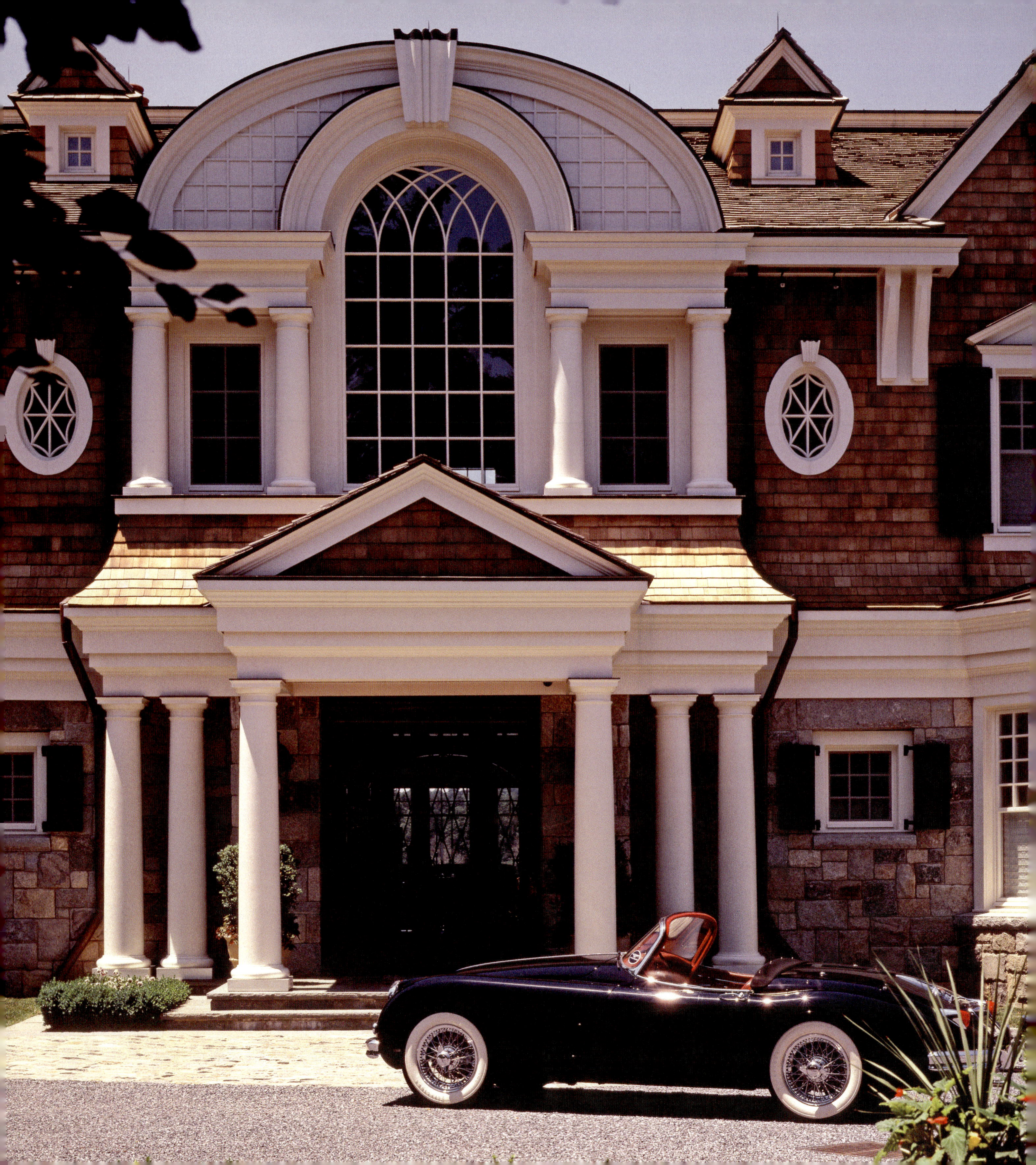

A PALLADIAN WINDOW, TWIN ROTUNDAS, AND A FEW SURPRISES ADD ROMANCE TO THIS RIVERFRONT HOME

THE CLIENTS An investment banker, who is also a former football star and a retired general, and his wife, acquired 10.4 acres on a point of land that juts out into the Navesink River in Rumson, New Jersey. The location was the reason the clients bought the property, and after they spent a year living in the house that already existed, they decided they wanted a new house that would be more open to the river. After coming across a residence designed by Shope Reno Wharton in a magazine, they were convinced they had found the architects who could realize their dream.

THE DESIGN BRIEF A house had to be designed with angles that conformed to the water frontage. Wharton felt that the late-nineteenth-century American Shingle Style, which he describes as "a very romantic, flowing kind of architecture with a certain casualness that permits some surprises and little embellishments," would suit the site and look as though it had been there for centuries.

THE SOLUTION Access to the house, which is clad in red cedar shingles and stone, is via a long driveway that ends in a view of the façade facing away from the river. The central block of the house has a pedimented and pillared entryway below a large Palladian window that makes a powerful visual statement. Angled wings are stretched out on either side to make a boomerang-shaped whole that follows the curves of the river. Inside, a two-story stairway hall dominates the layout. The living room lies directly ahead, through a large opening. Twin rotundas serve as anchors at opposite ends of the gallery. New York interior designer Sandra Nunnerley was asked to decorate the interior spaces of the 15,750-square-foot, 40-room house. "We wanted everything to be clean and pared down. The architecture stands by itself," says Nunnerley. To bring the rooms alive, she concentrated on strong, bold colors and very good English antiques. Working with New York color consultant Donald Kaufman, Nunnerley painted the living room a rich cinnabar shade. The living room opens out through large windows to the river beyond. The library and the dining room, which Nunnerley had painted a deep eggplant and where she used antique English chairs with glittering gilt detailing for accents, are connected to the living room through the rotundas off the hall. The kitchen has an open plan; the breakfast room is contained in a glass-walled pavilion; and the master bedroom suite occupies the center of the house on the second floor. The bedroom has access, through doors on either side of a Palladian window, to a deck with a Chinese Chippendale railing. The clients wanted a house that was timeless, with large open spaces for entertaining as well as intimate spaces for family functions. The scale and shape of the house was carefully crafted to fit the clients' needs. The Stonington, Connecticut-based firm Cummin Associates created the landscape design to enhance the watery environment of the site.

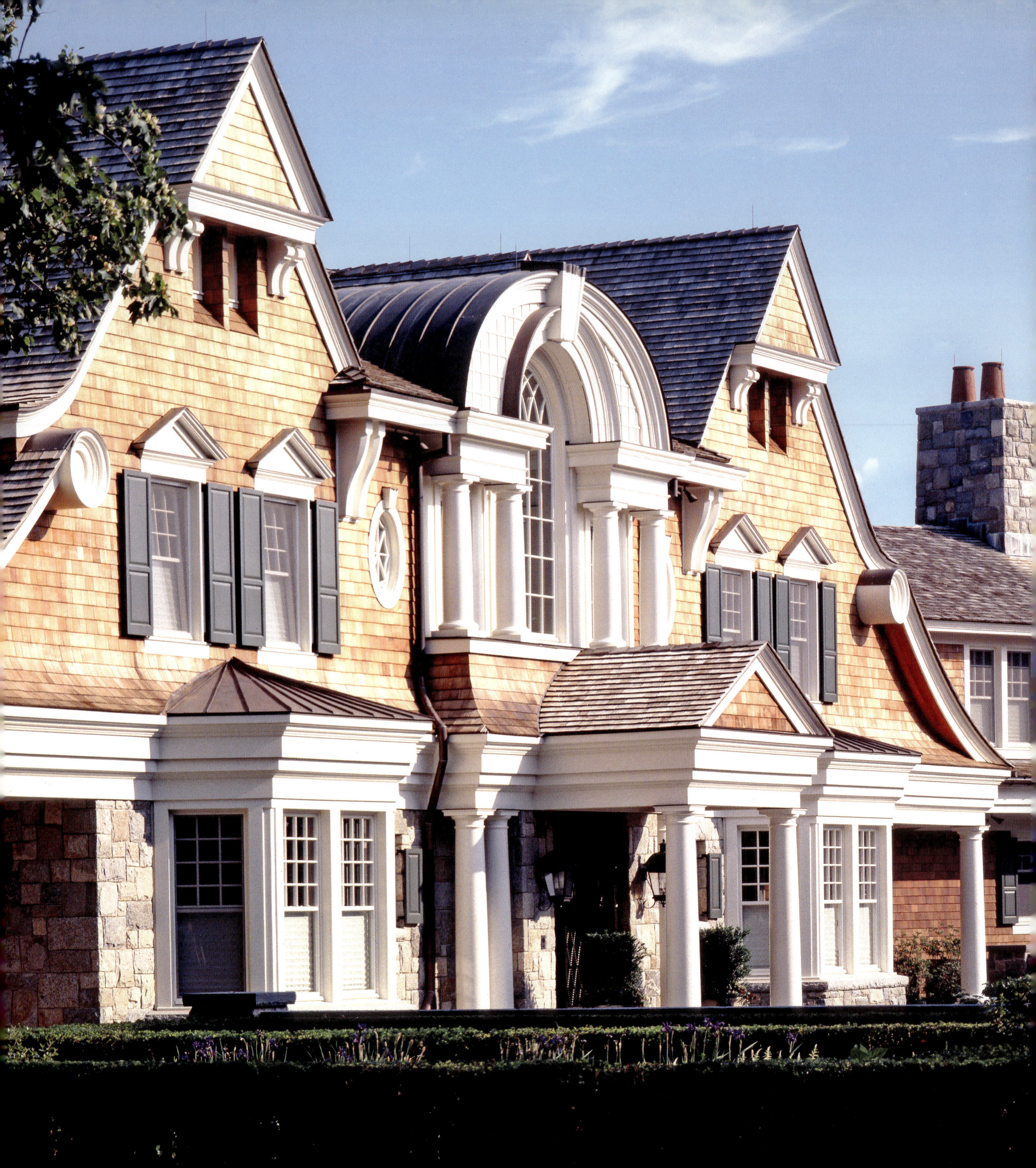

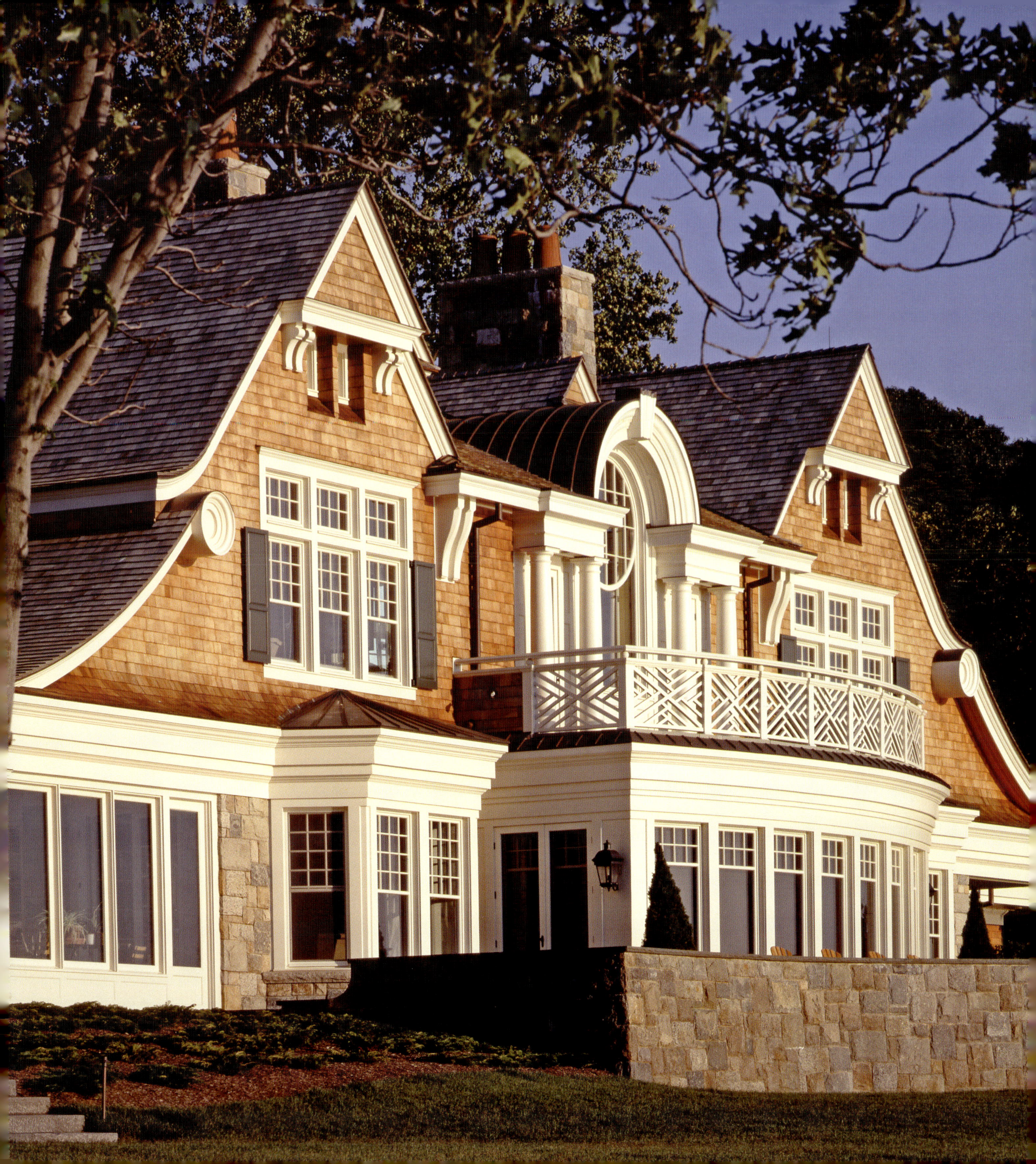

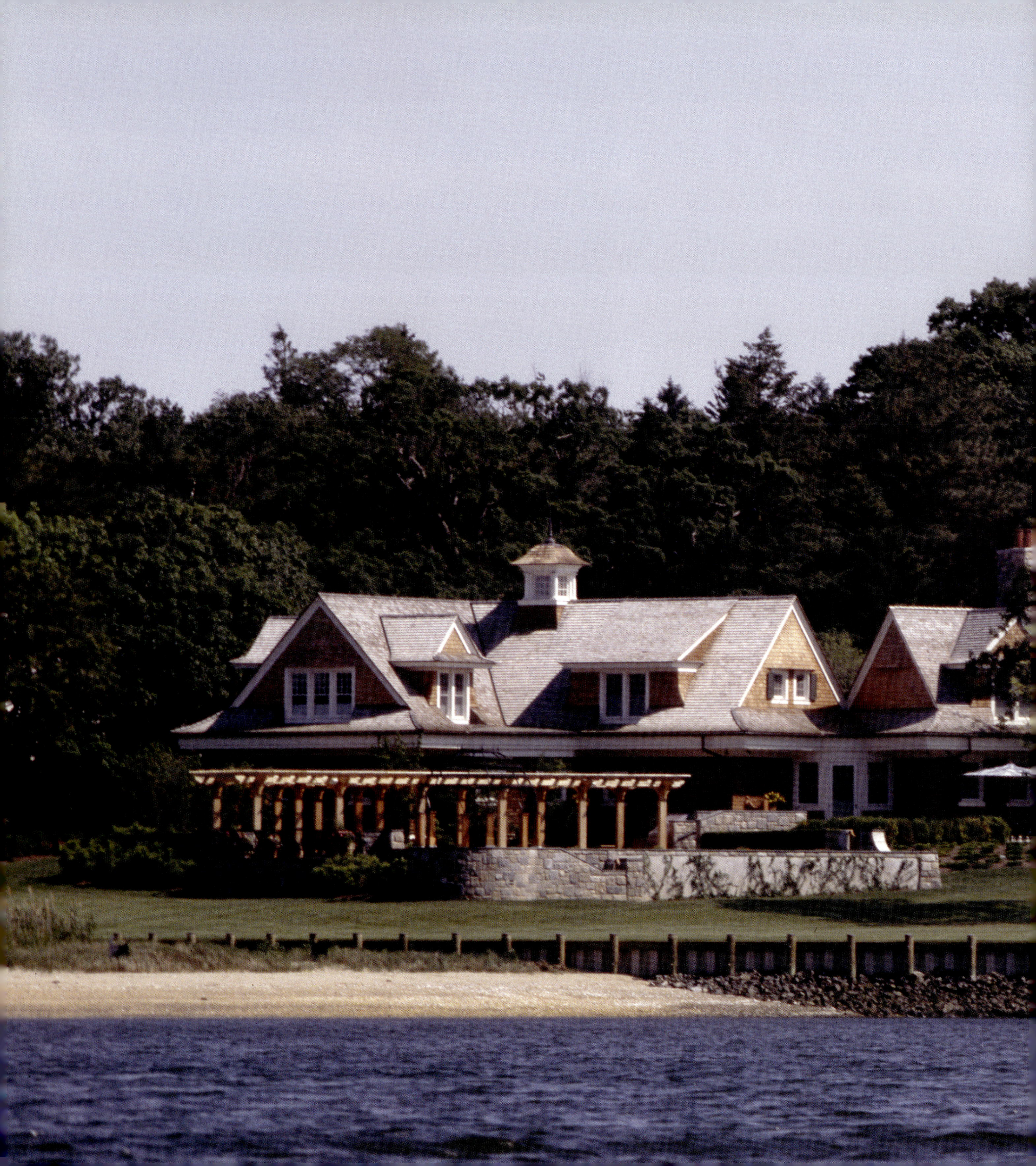

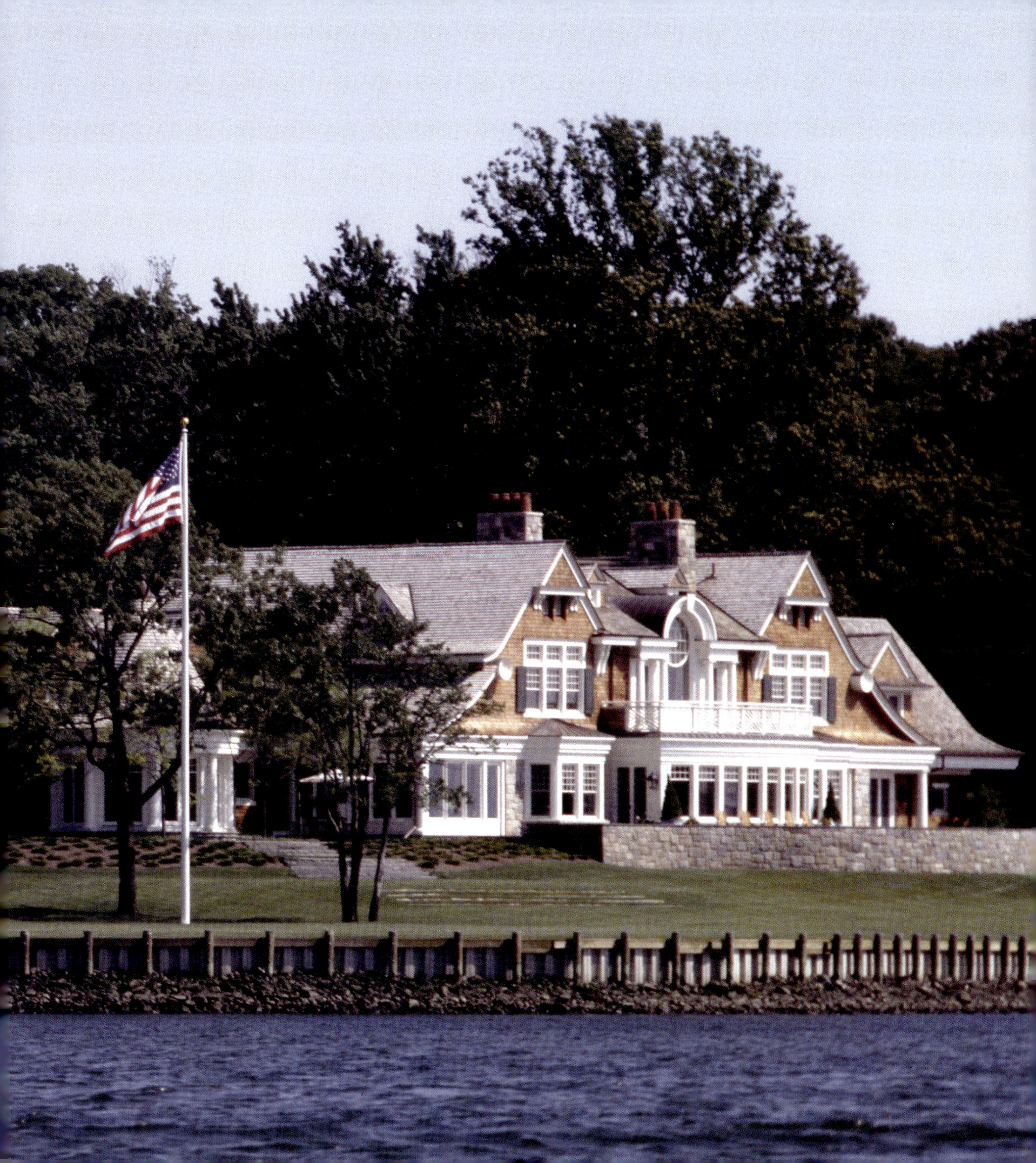

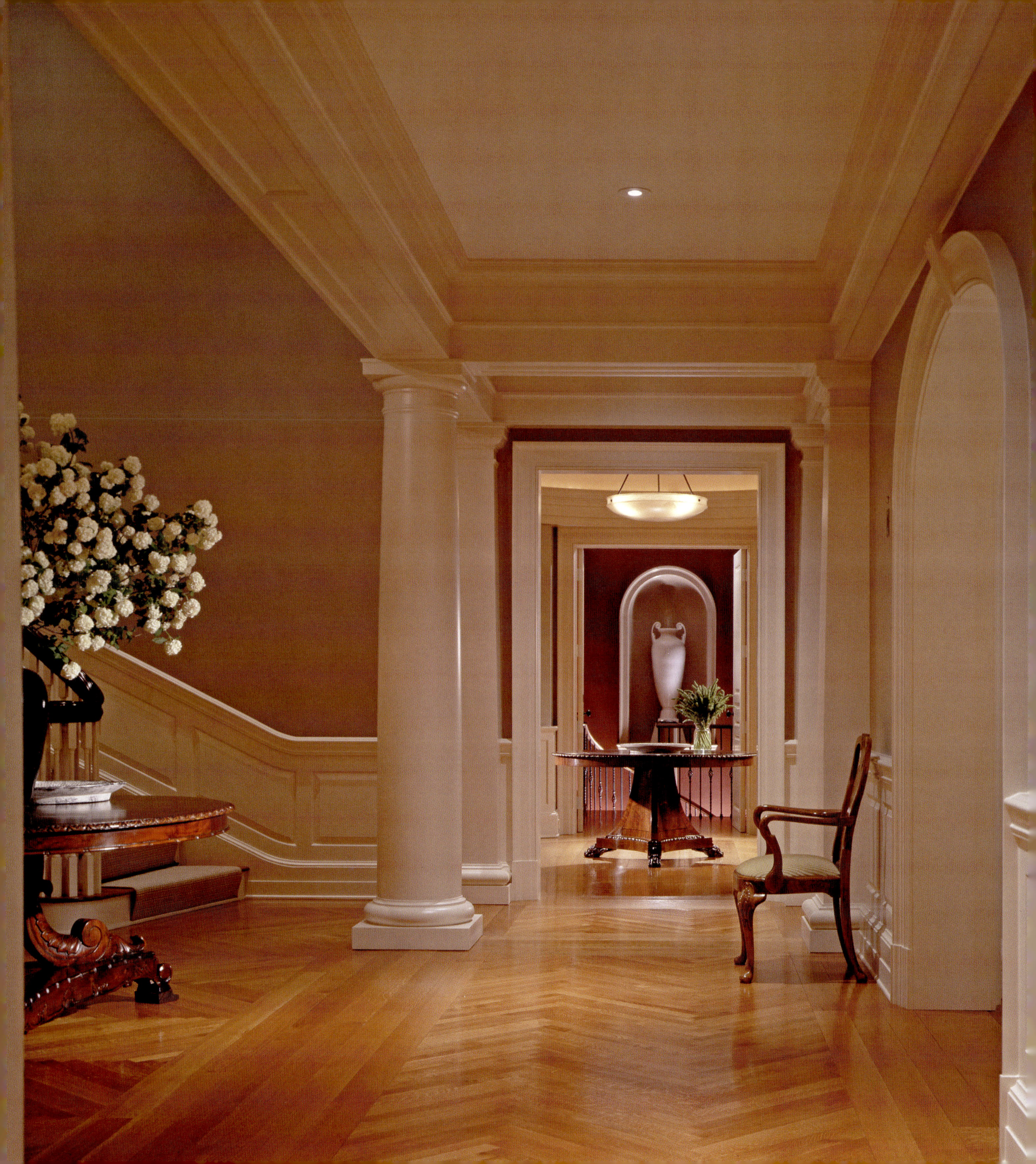

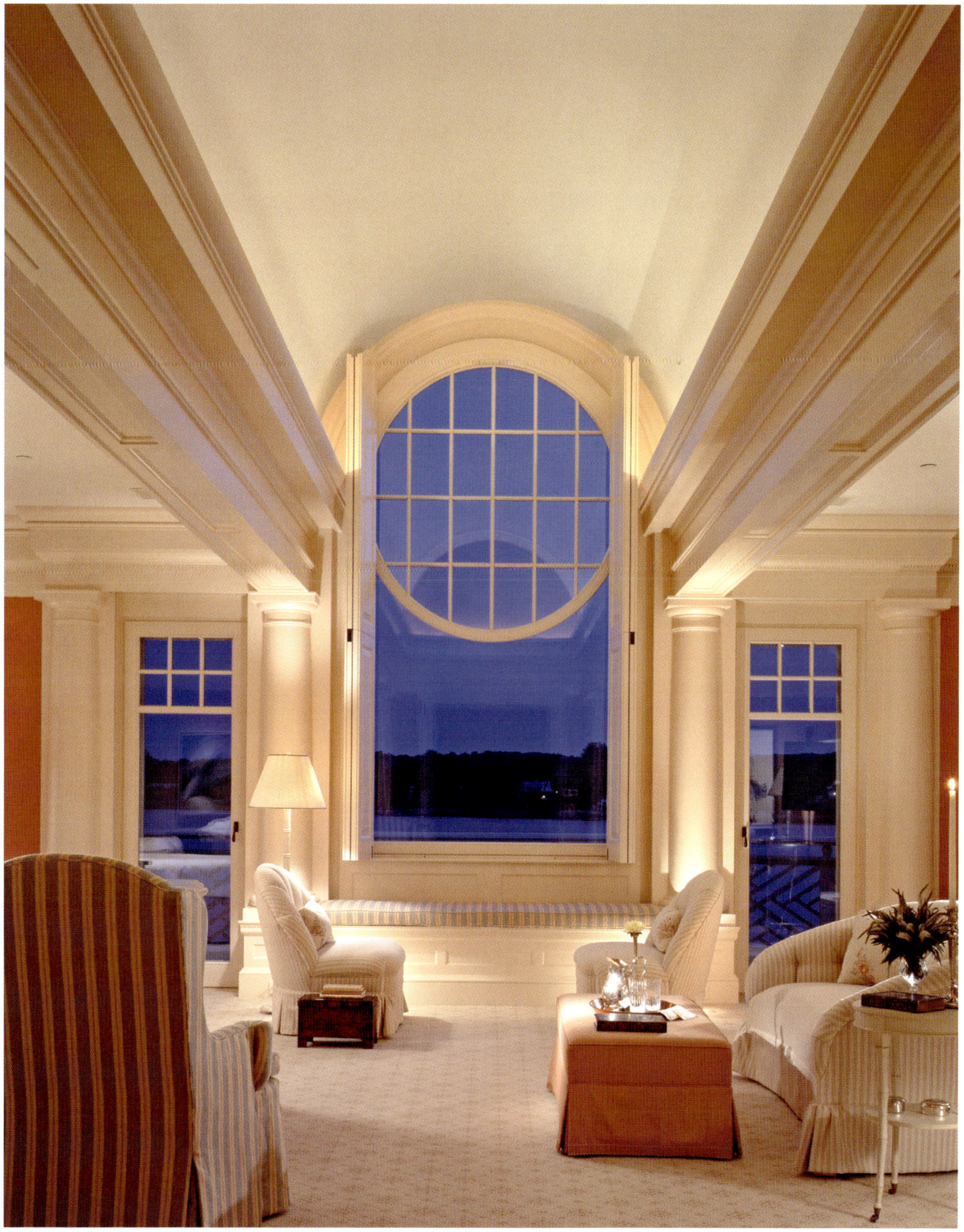

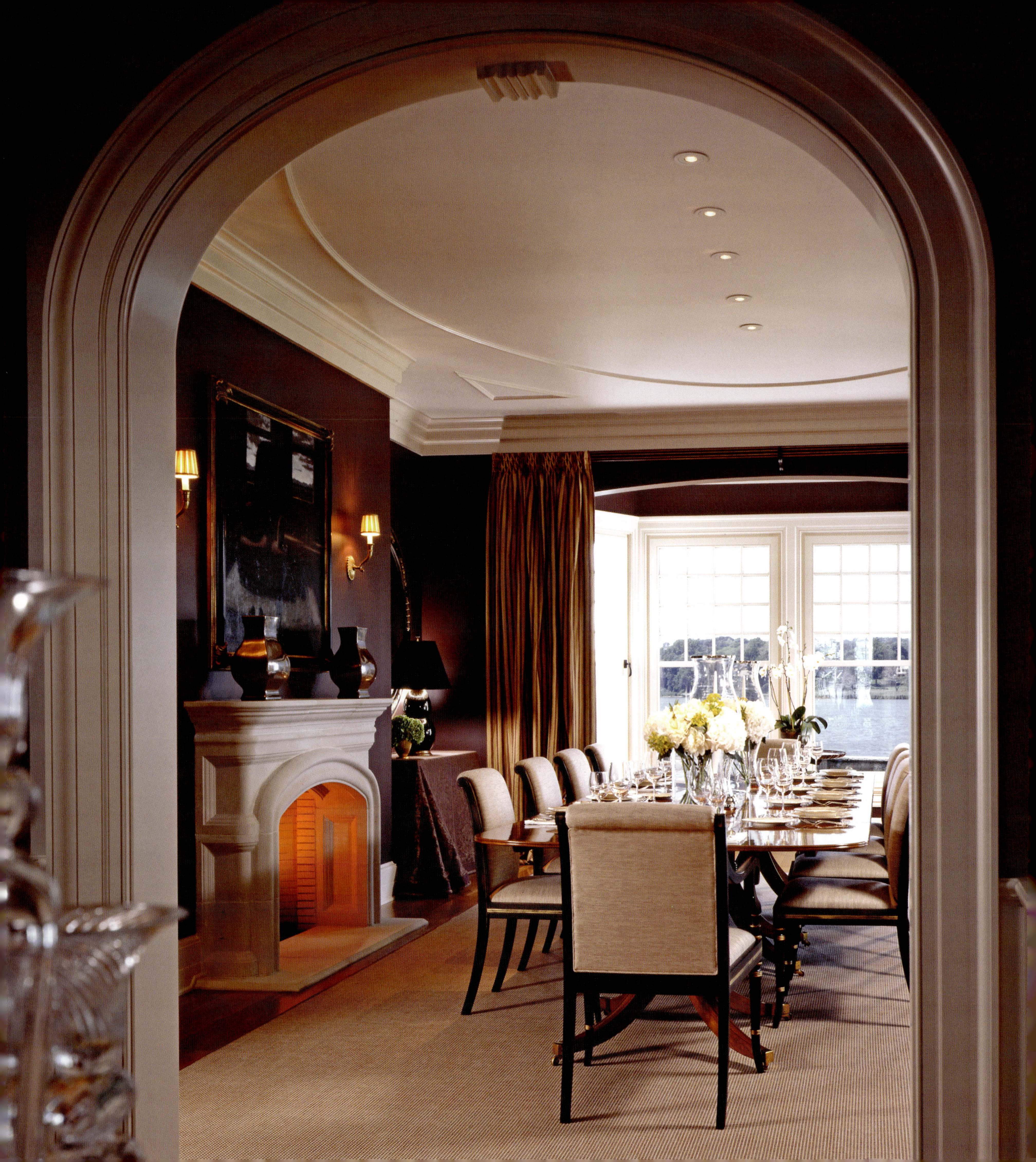

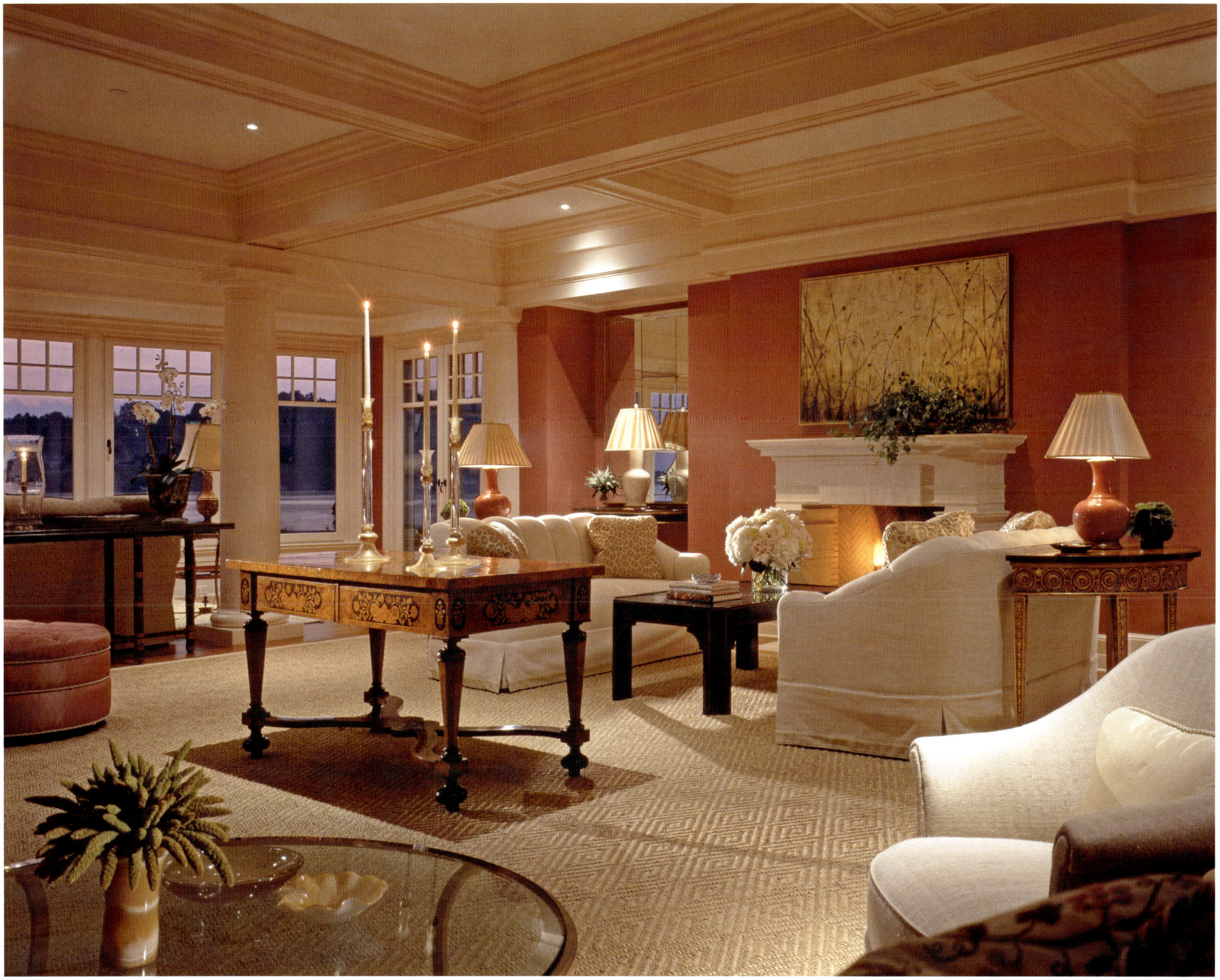

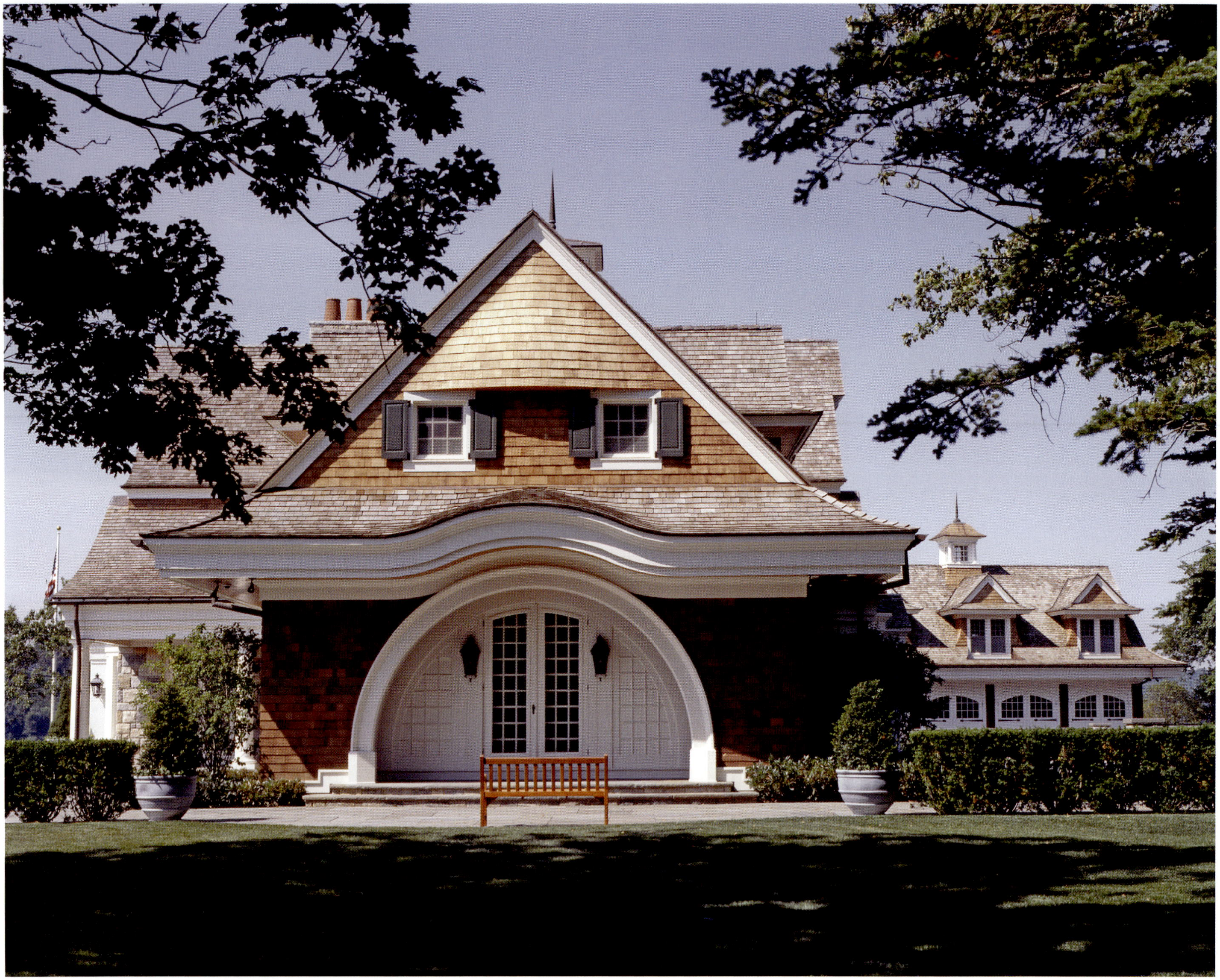

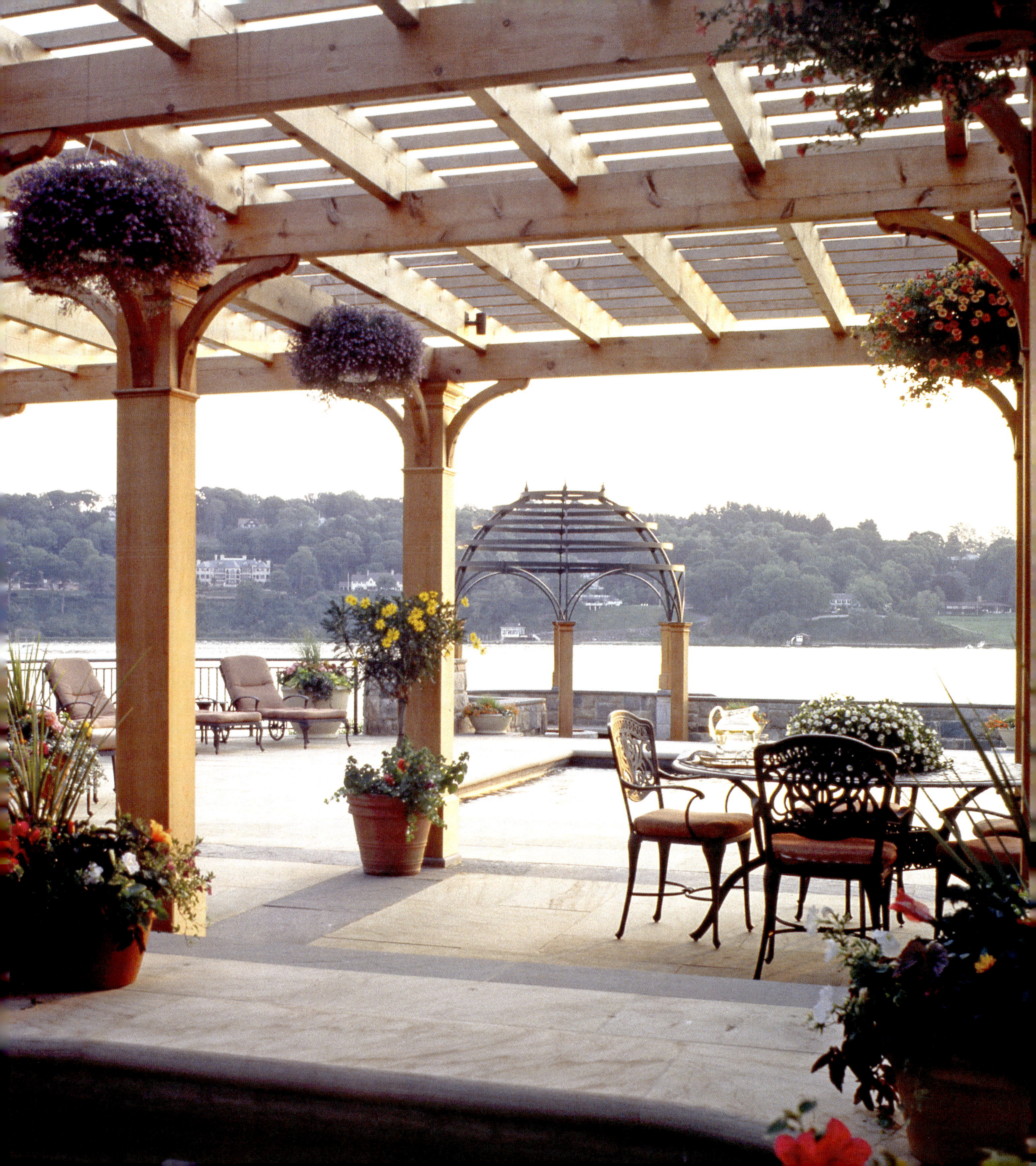

SITE PLAN

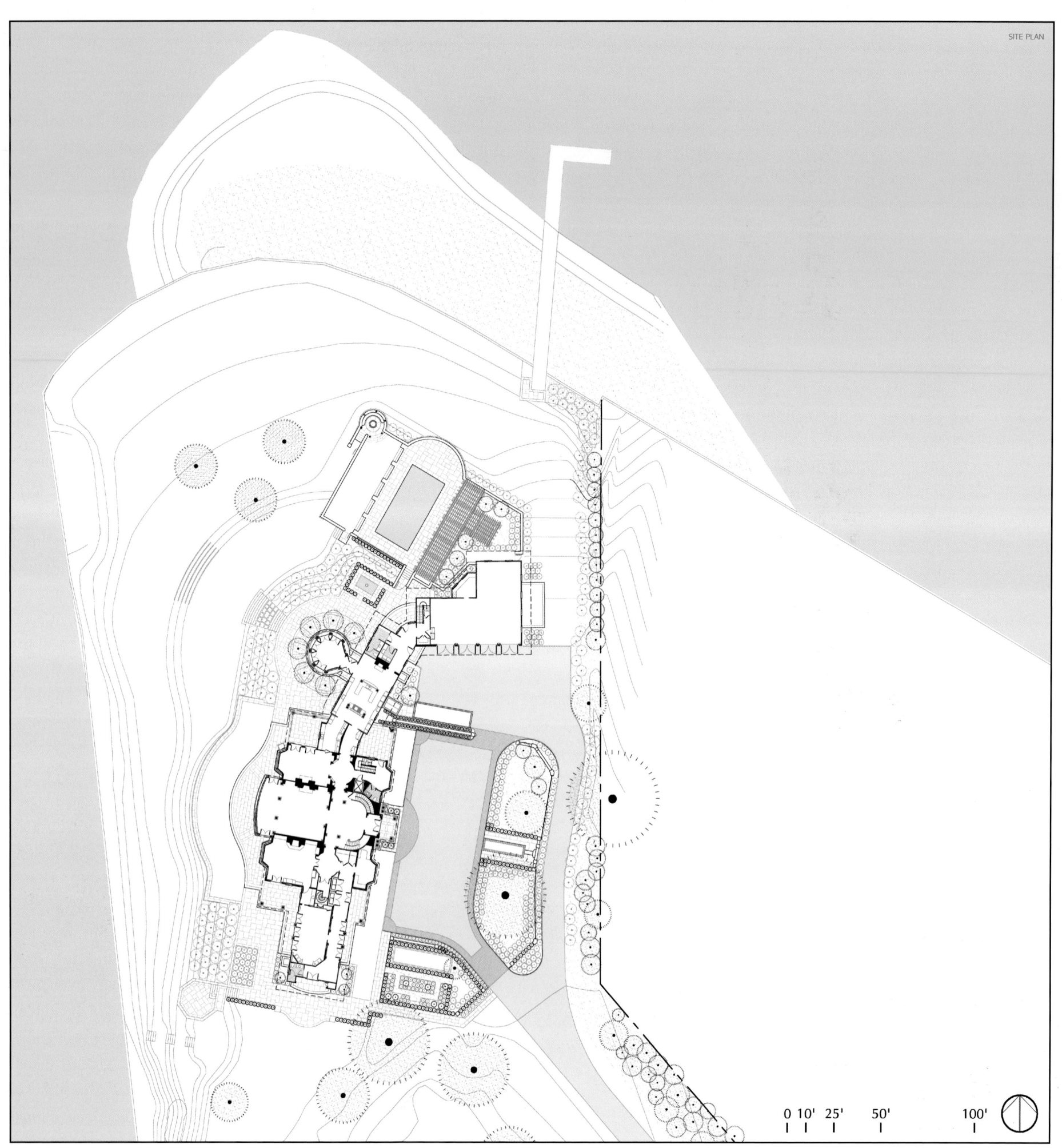

0 10' 25' 50'   100'

FIRST FLOOR

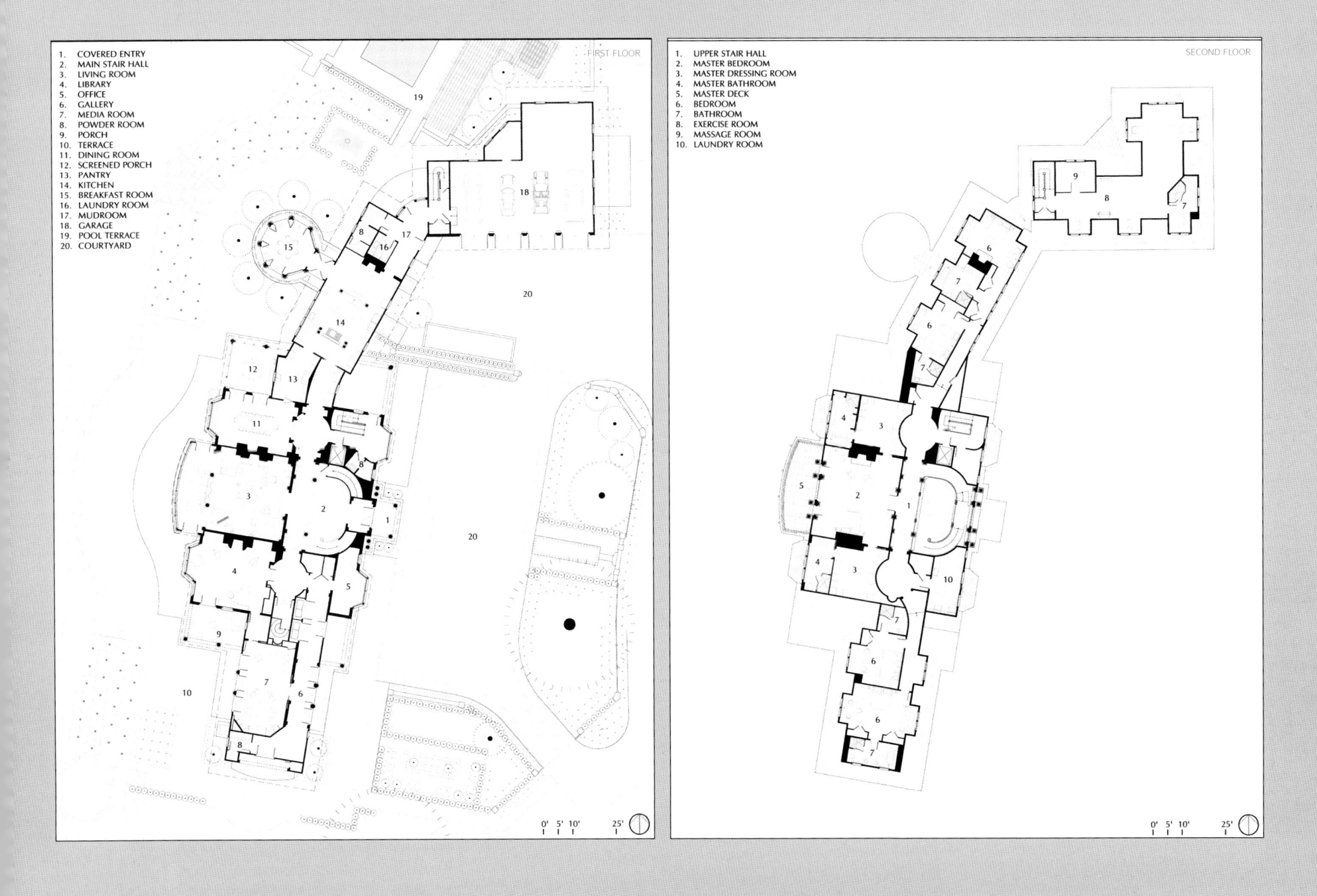

1. COVERED ENTRY
2. MAIN STAIR HALL
3. LIVING ROOM
4. LIBRARY
5. OFFICE
6. GALLERY
7. MEDIA ROOM
8. POWDER ROOM
9. PORCH
10. TERRACE
11. DINING ROOM
12. SCREENED PORCH
13. PANTRY
14. KITCHEN
15. BREAKFAST ROOM
16. LAUNDRY ROOM
17. MUDROOM
18. GARAGE
19. POOL TERRACE
20. COURTYARD

SECOND FLOOR

1. UPPER STAIR HALL
2. MASTER BEDROOM
3. MASTER DRESSING ROOM
4. MASTER BATHROOM
5. MASTER DECK
6. BEDROOM
7. BATHROOM
8. EXERCISE ROOM
9. MASSAGE ROOM
10. LAUNDRY ROOM

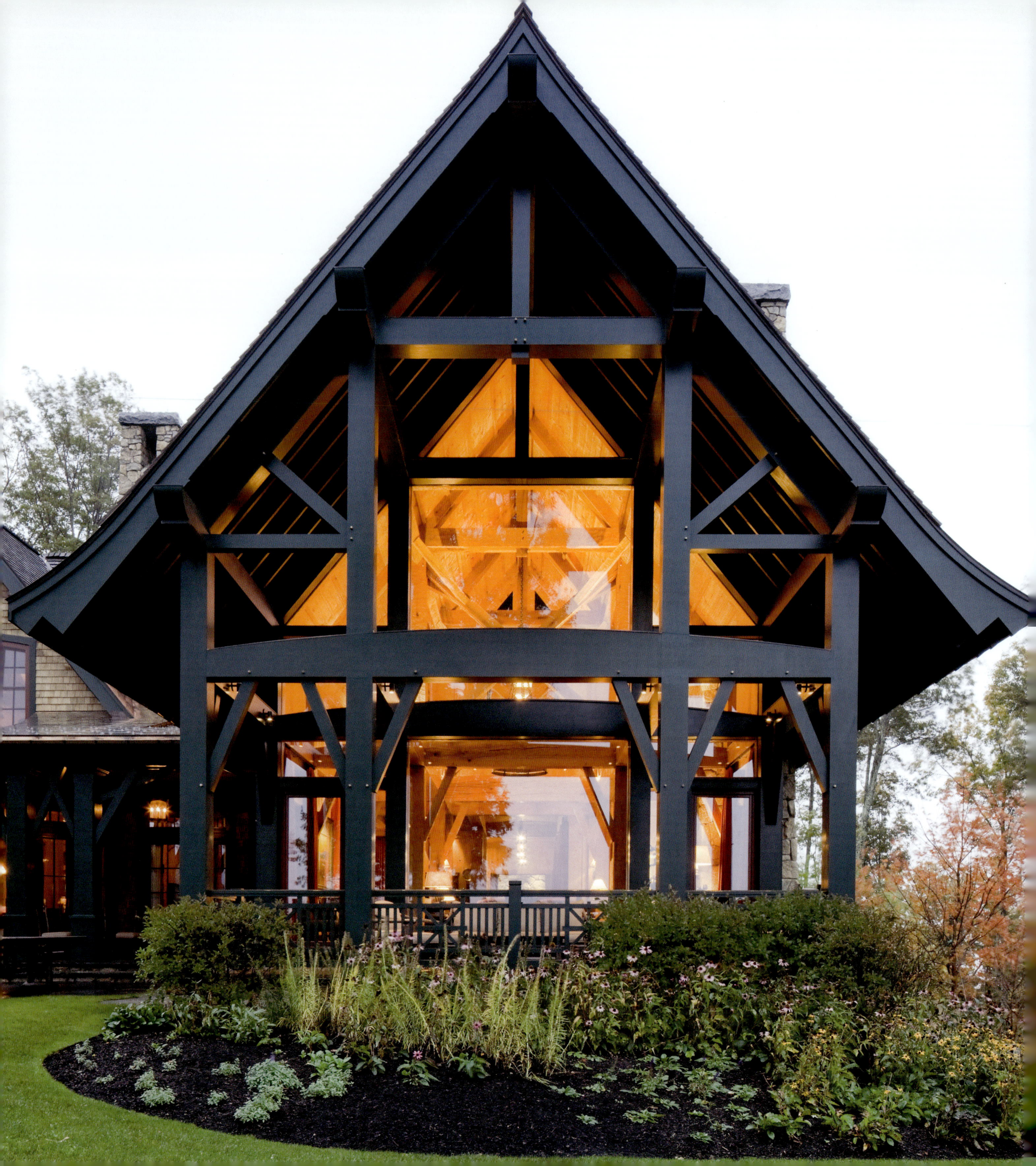

EXPANSES OF GLASS AND AN OPEN FLOOR-PLAN ALLOW FOR A HOME THAT TAKES IN MAJESTIC VIEWS

THE CLIENTS A young couple, with an affinity for exploring the outdoors, wanted a house that would place them close to hiking and cross-country skiing trails, as well as provide them with stunning views of the countryside.

THE DESIGN BRIEF The 140-acre site, on a hilltop overlooking the quaint skiing village of Stowe, Vermont, offered panoramic views of the east, which looked up the valley, and of the west, which faced Mount Mansfield, the state's highest mountain. The clients wanted the house to open up to both of these views, and they asked that it be done in a charming, rustic style that was both roomy and sophisticated.

THE SOLUTION The 10,600 square-foot house, clad in cedar shingles and vertically thrusting stone chimneys, has dark-painted trim that helps it to visually blend in with the trees on the property. The residence is composed of a number of wings that spread across the brow of a hill, creating unexpected angles. The low roofline of the clustered sections gives an illusion of the house embracing the earth. An entire wall of glass opens to the land outside, inviting it in. The front door is located at a point where several of the wings meet. The first floor is an open post-and-beam construction with crossing oak timbers that span the entire space. The living room, dining room, and kitchen areas below flow smoothly into one another. Each of these rooms are anchored by a massive stone fireplace. New York interior designer Victoria Hagan, with an aesthetic to "keep it simple, keep it comfortable, keep it interesting, but most importantly, keep it fun," decorated the rooms with sturdy furniture appropriate to a 1940s ski lodge. Leather wing-chairs and maple-framed rockers surround the living-room fireplace and the 12 tall Louis XIII-style chairs around the dining table are upholstered in leather with plaid fabric backs. The bedrooms are paneled in broad horizontal planks of knotty pine. From a second floor overlook, one sees through the timber frame above the living room, and then through a glass wall, to Mount Mansfield.

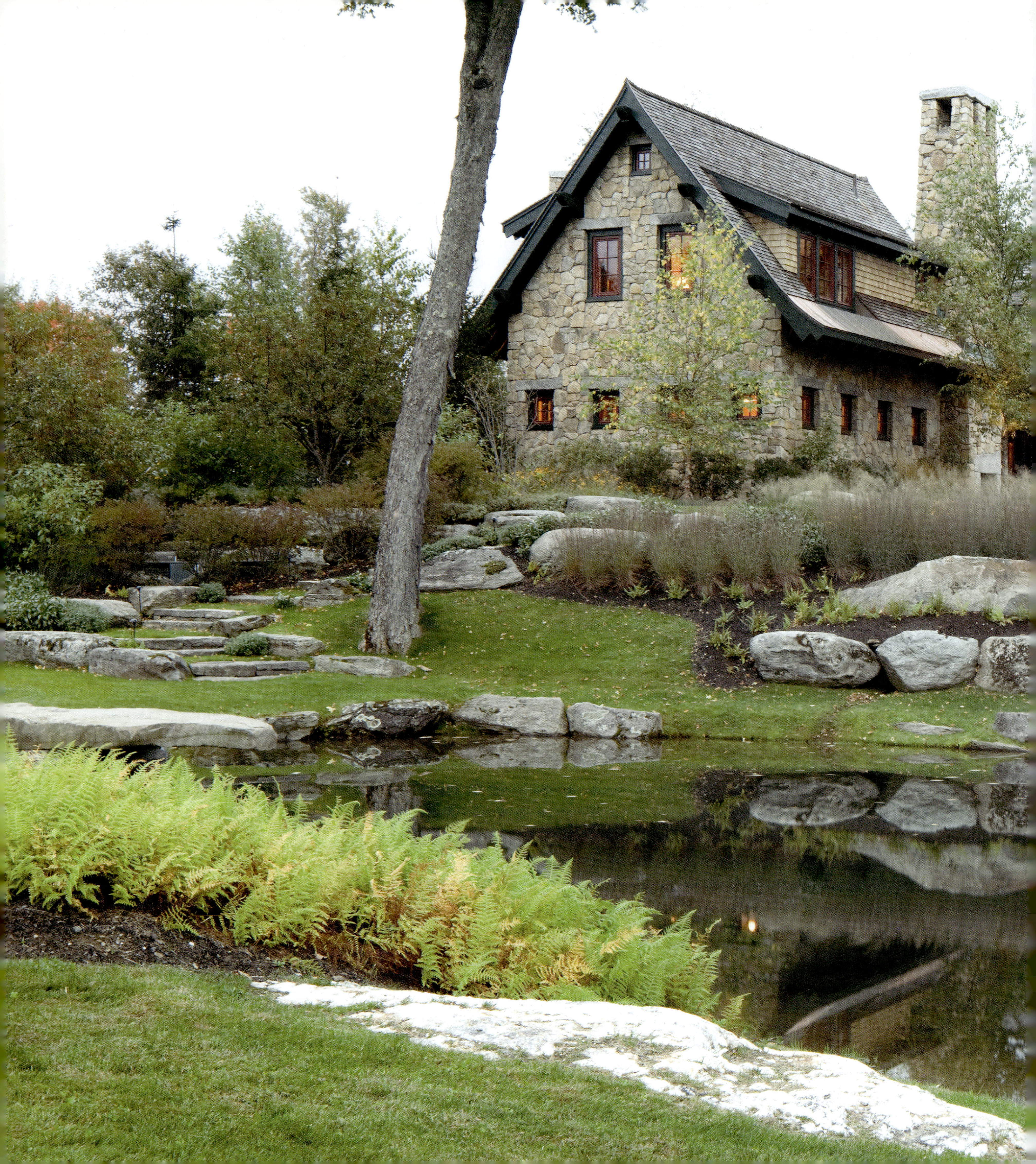

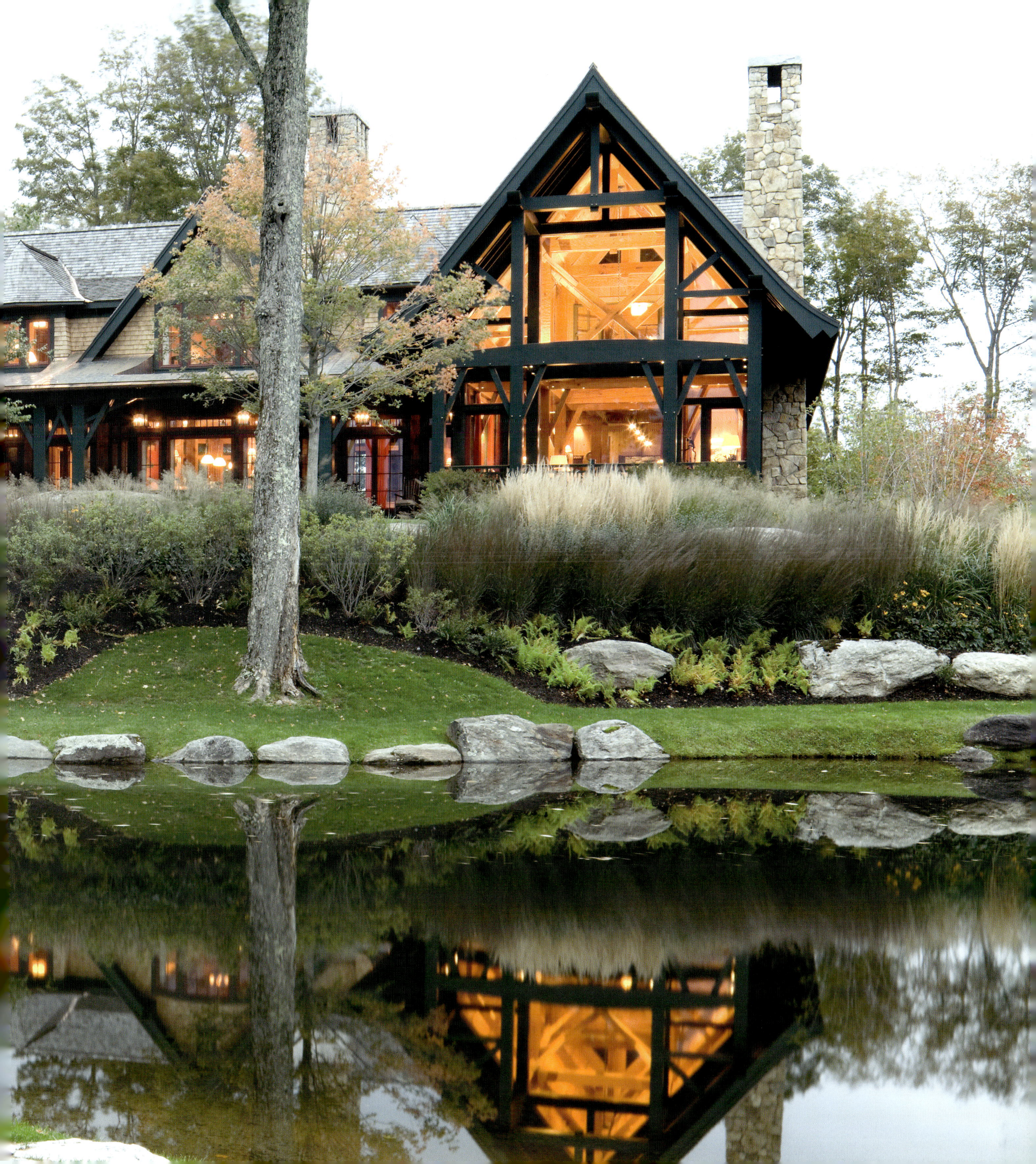

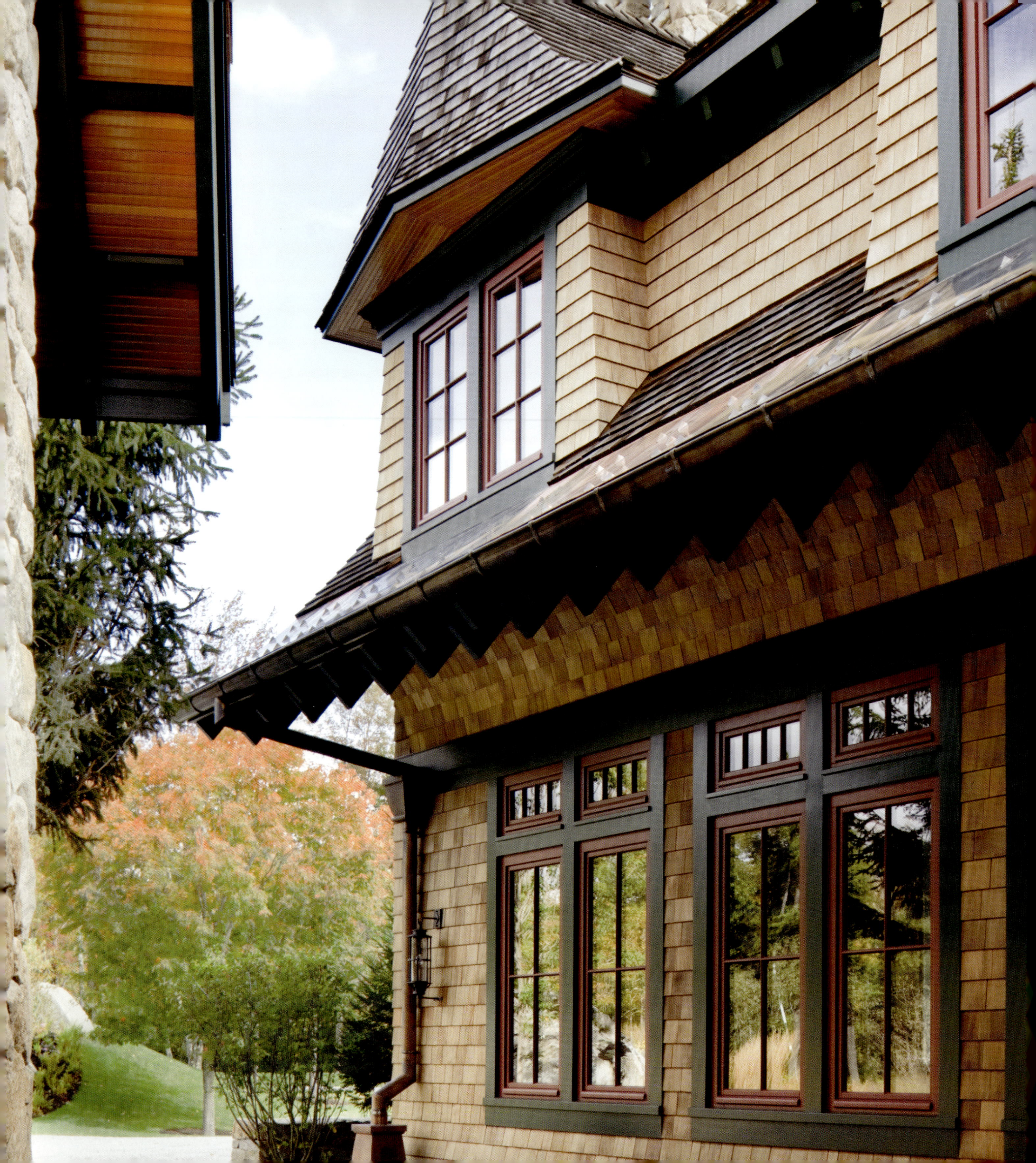

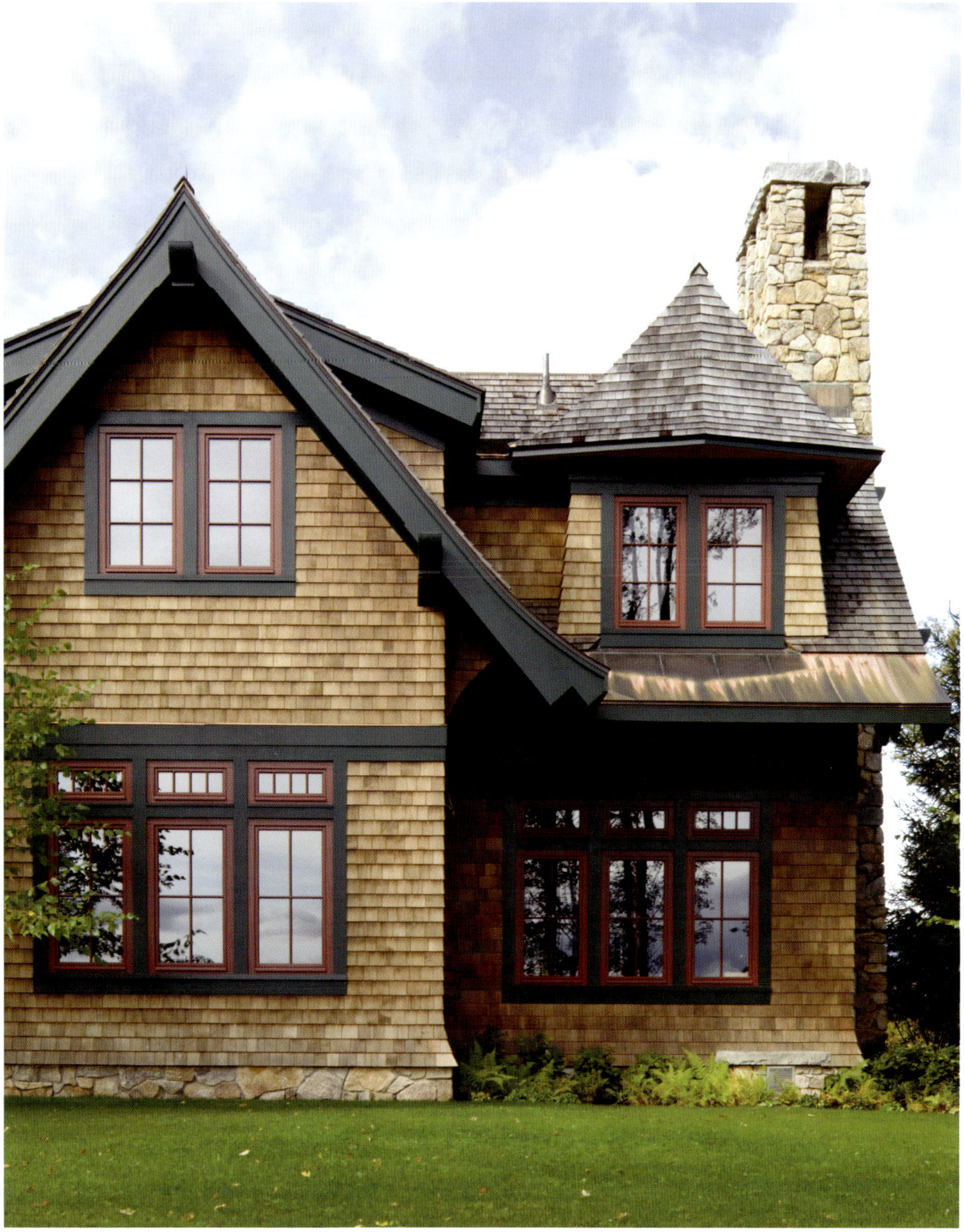

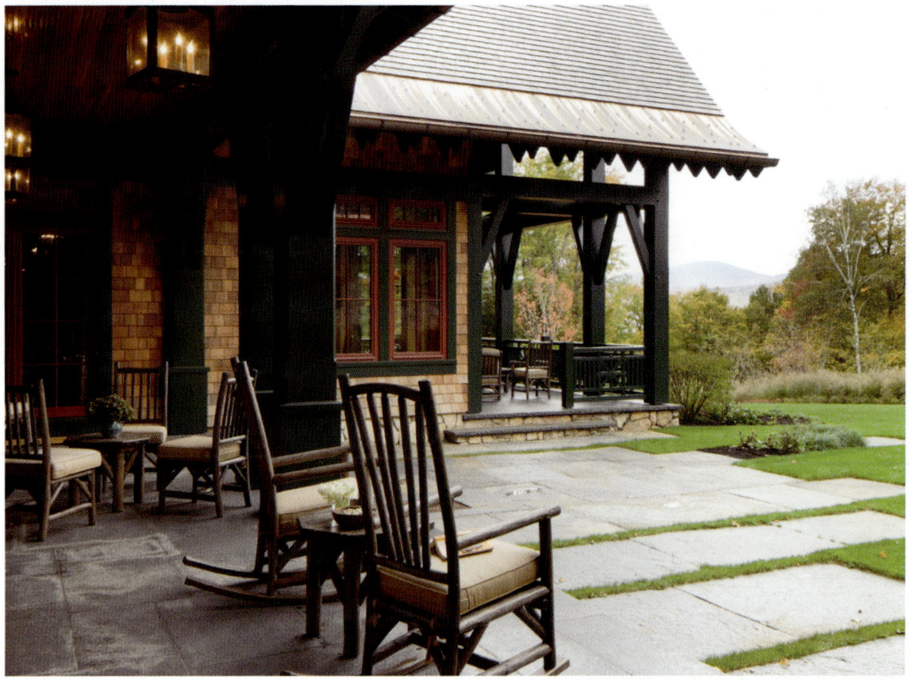

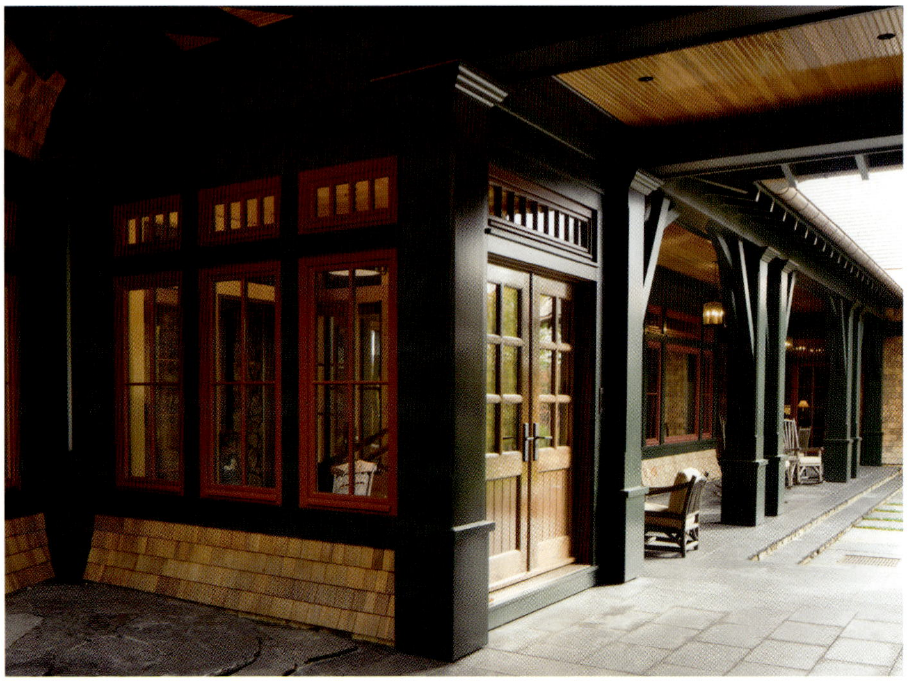

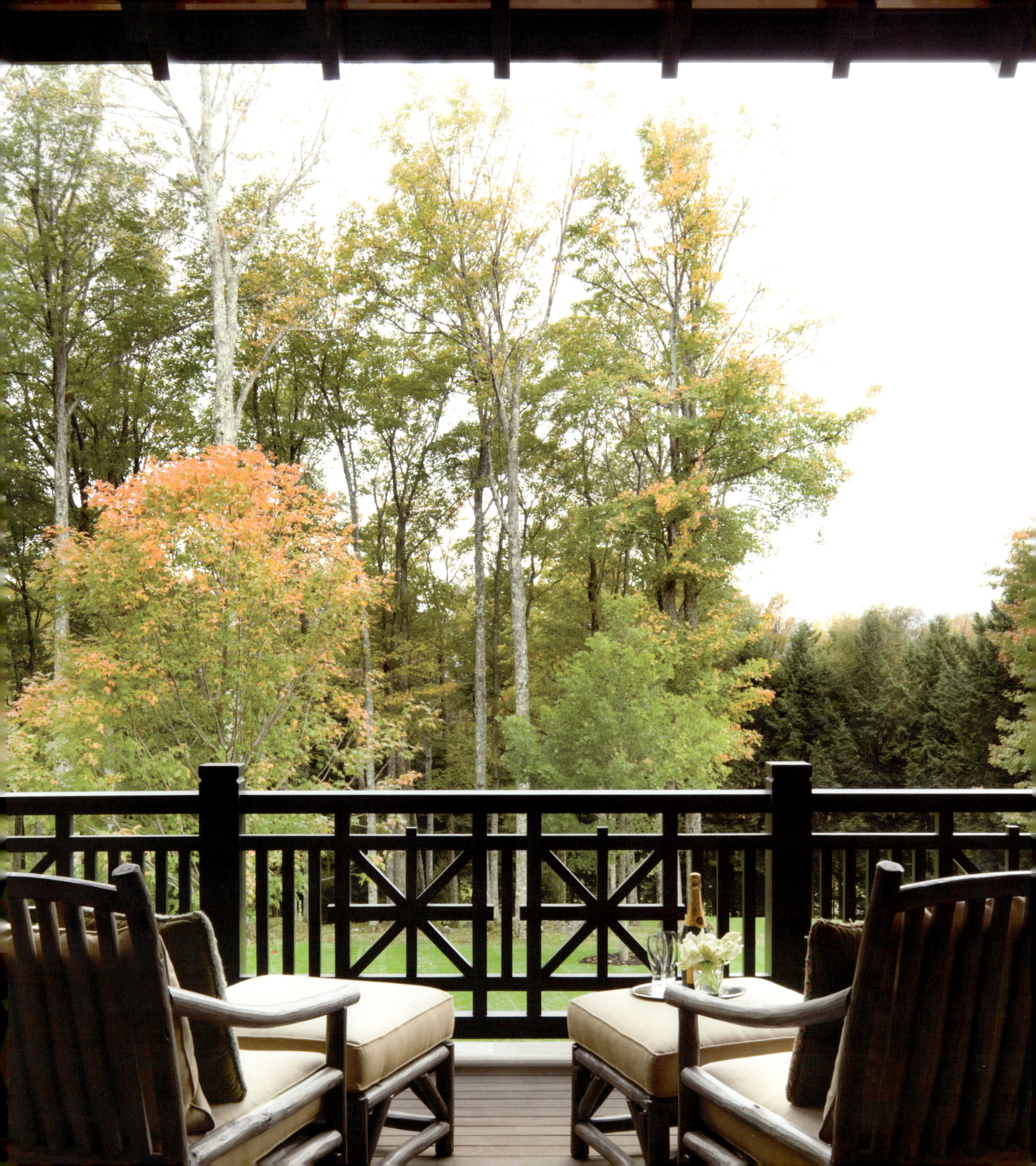

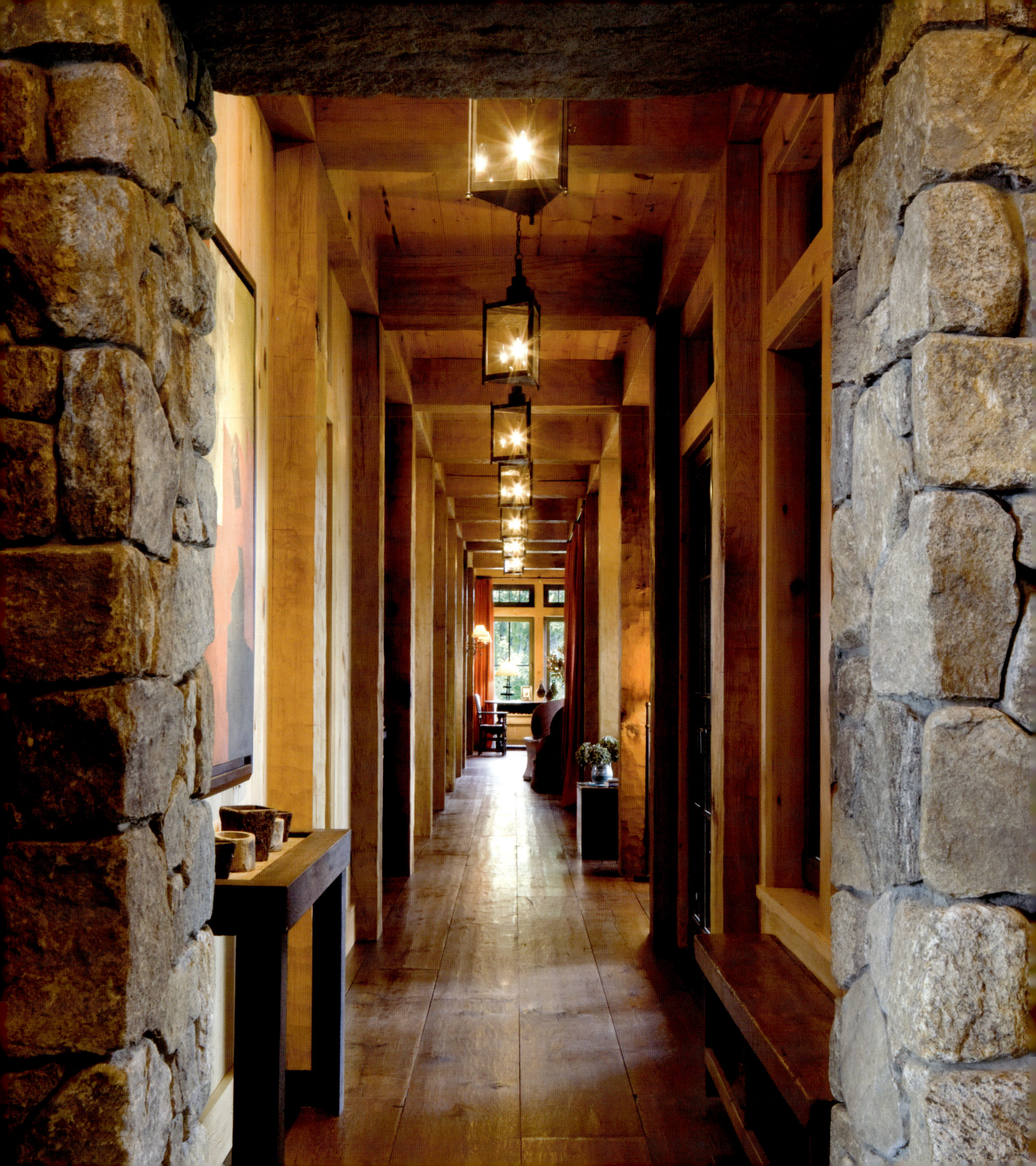

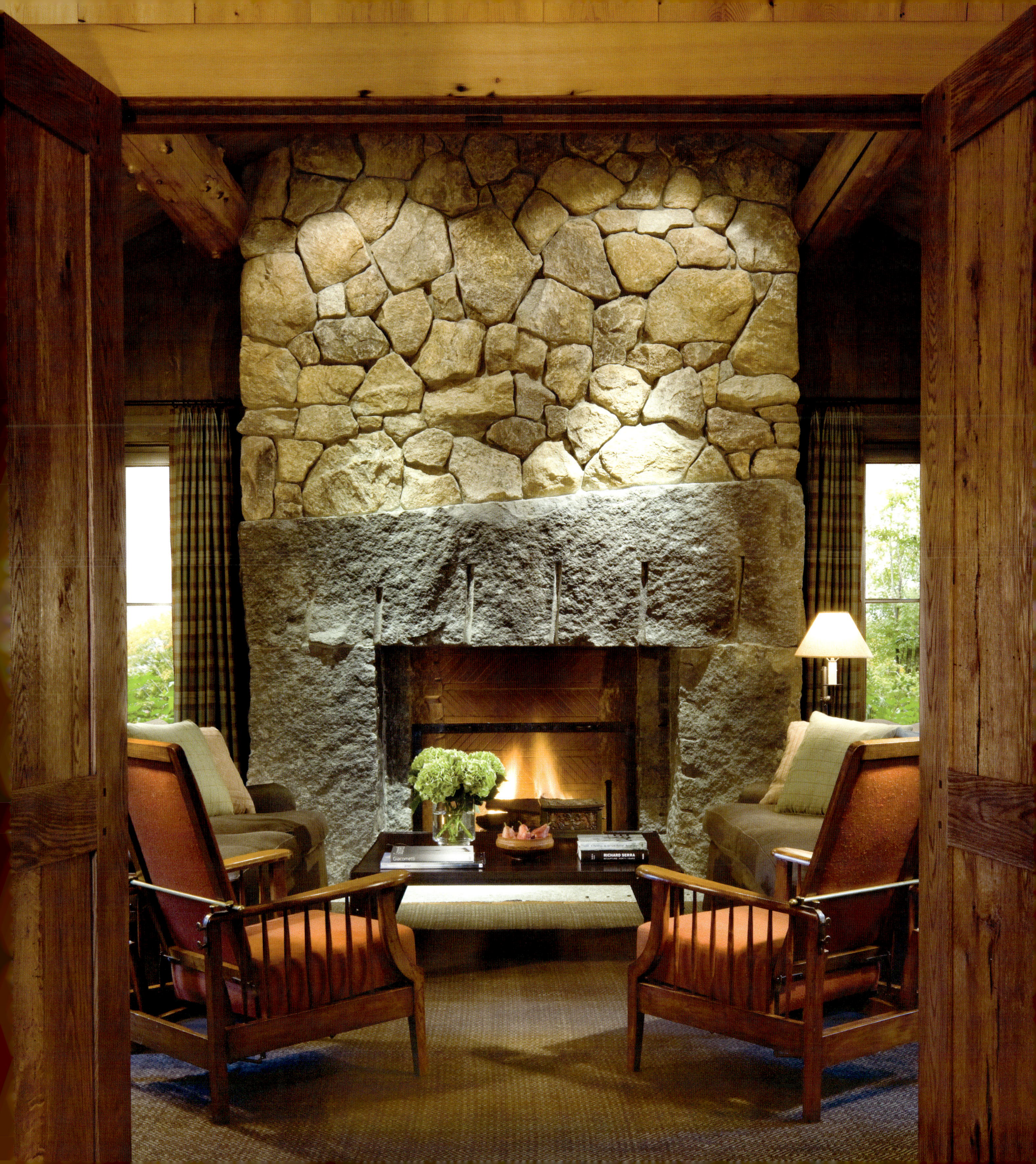
Giacometti
RICHARD SERRA

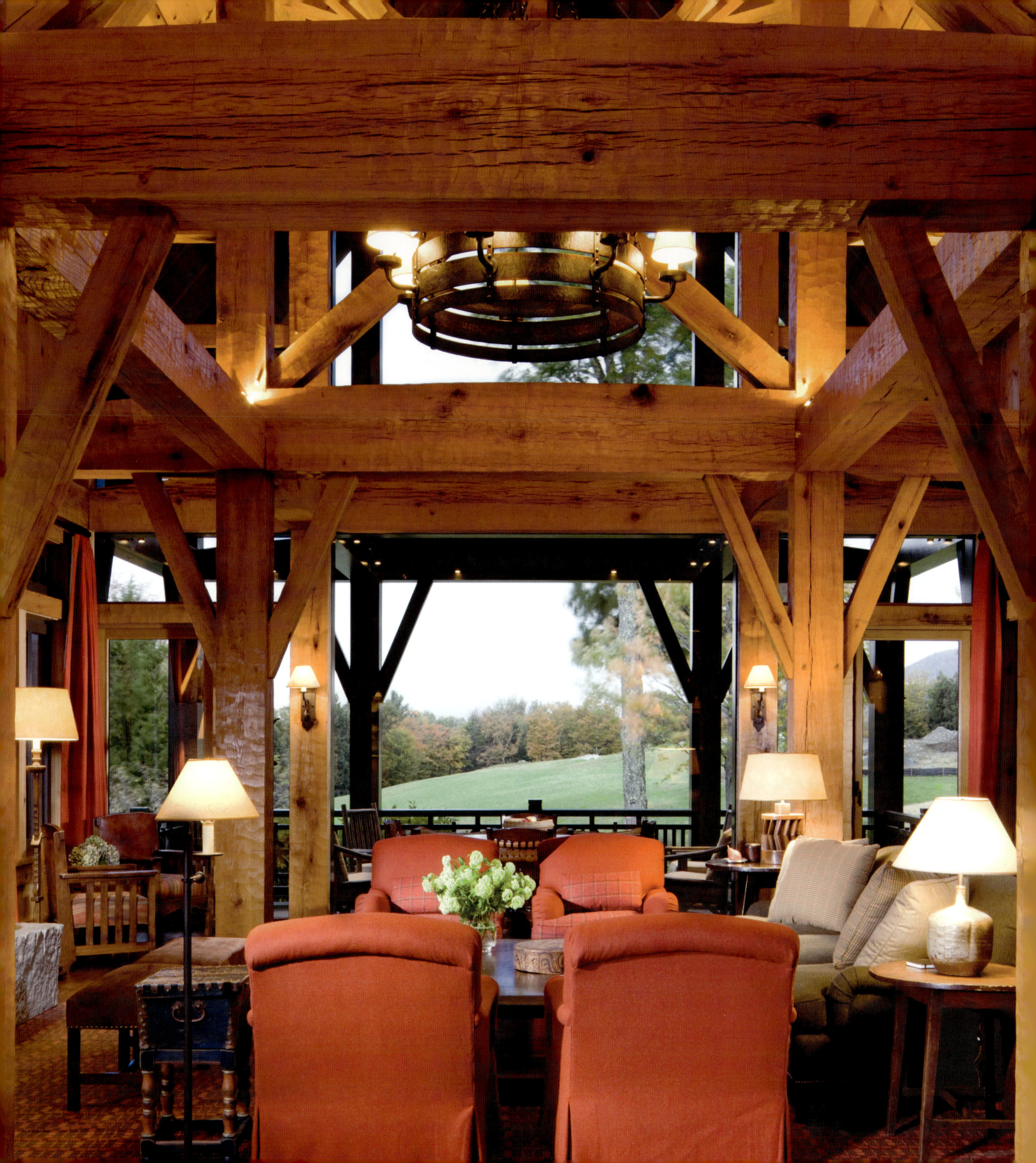

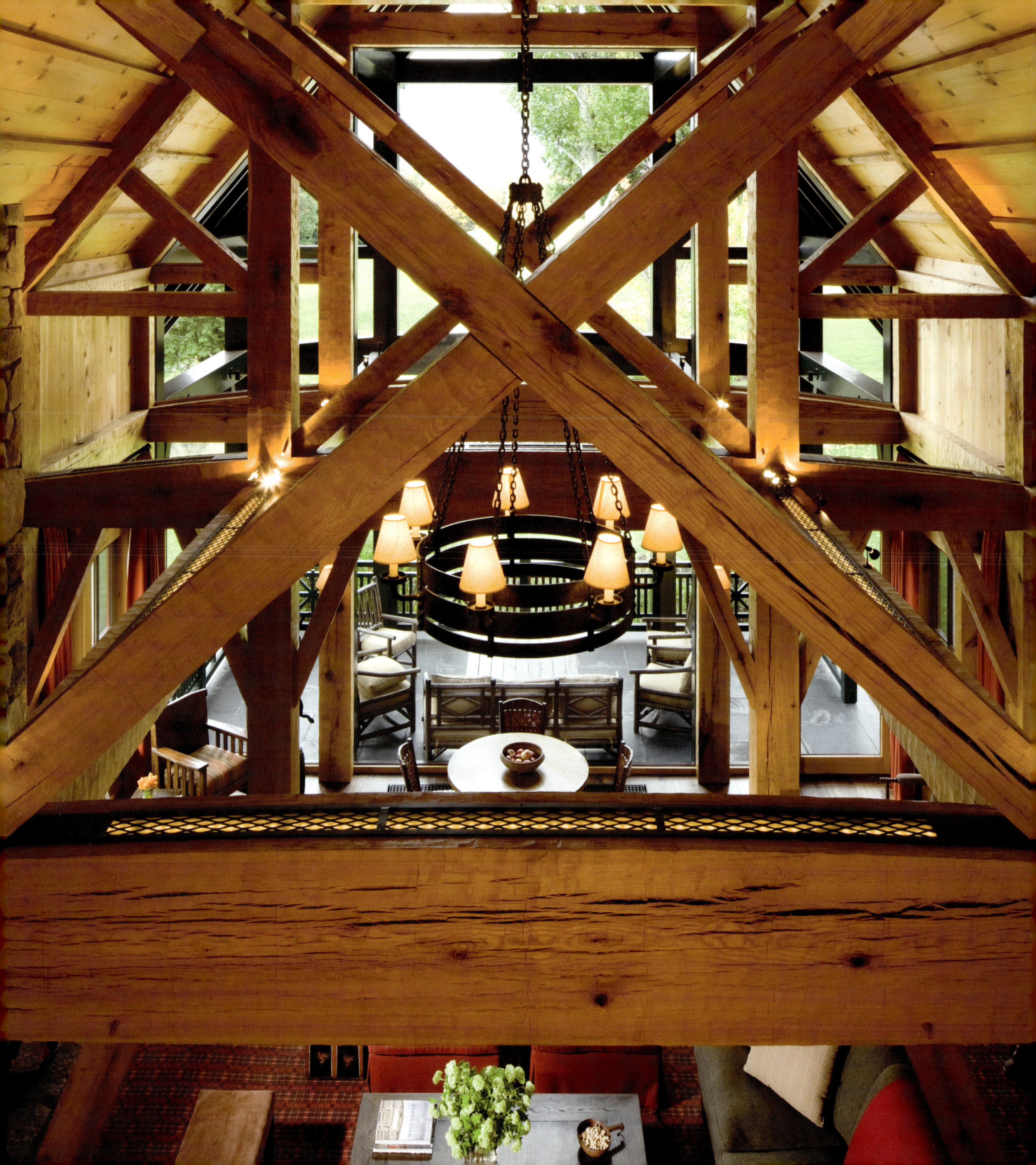

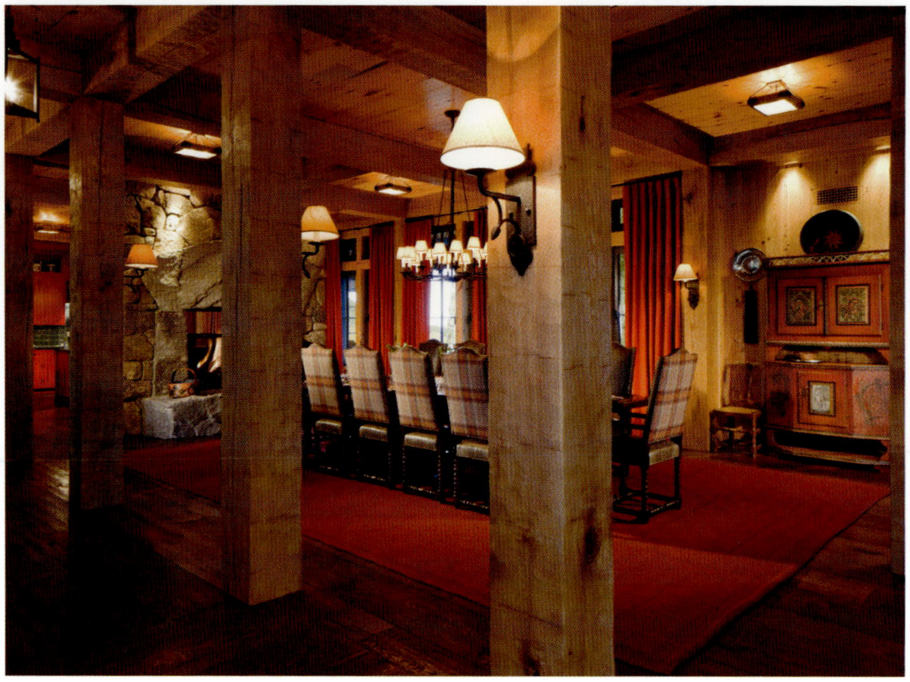

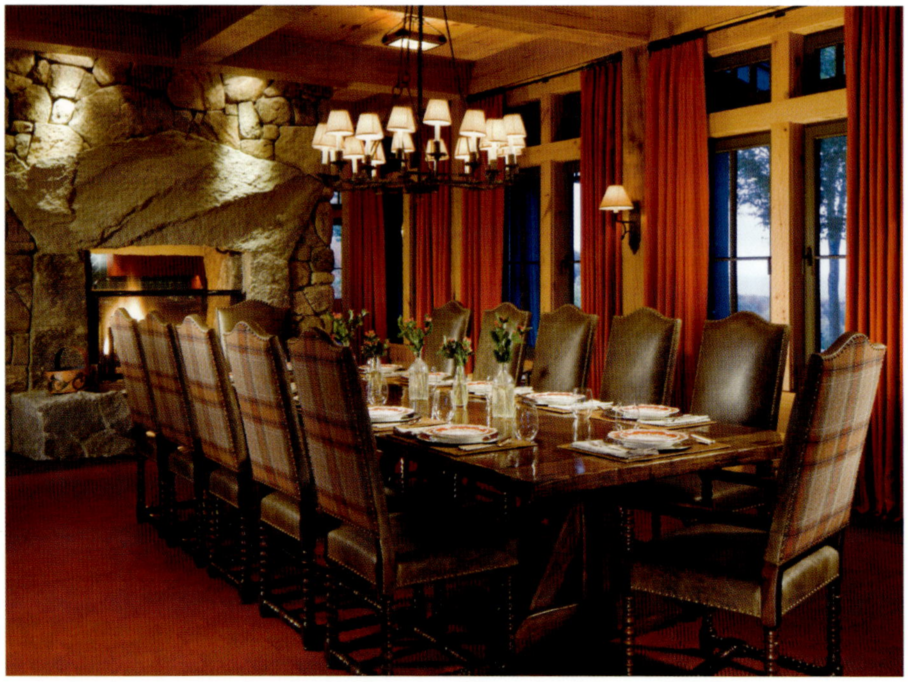

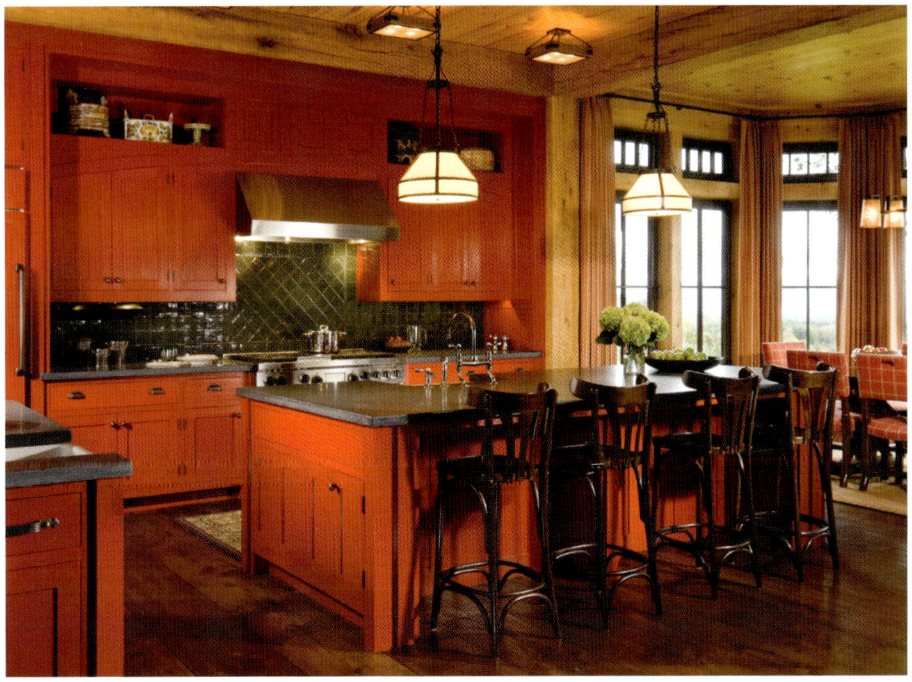

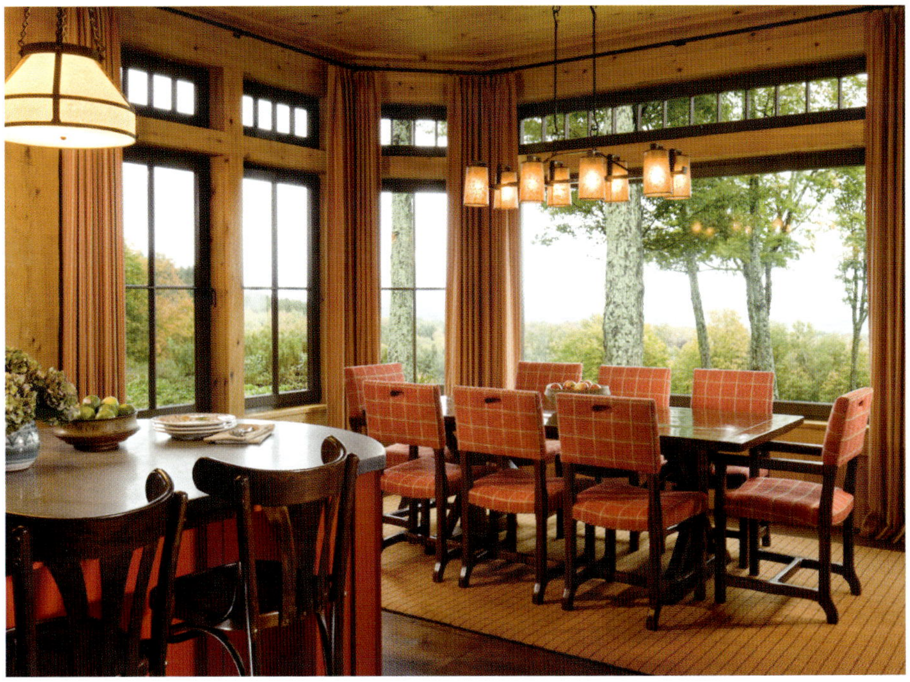

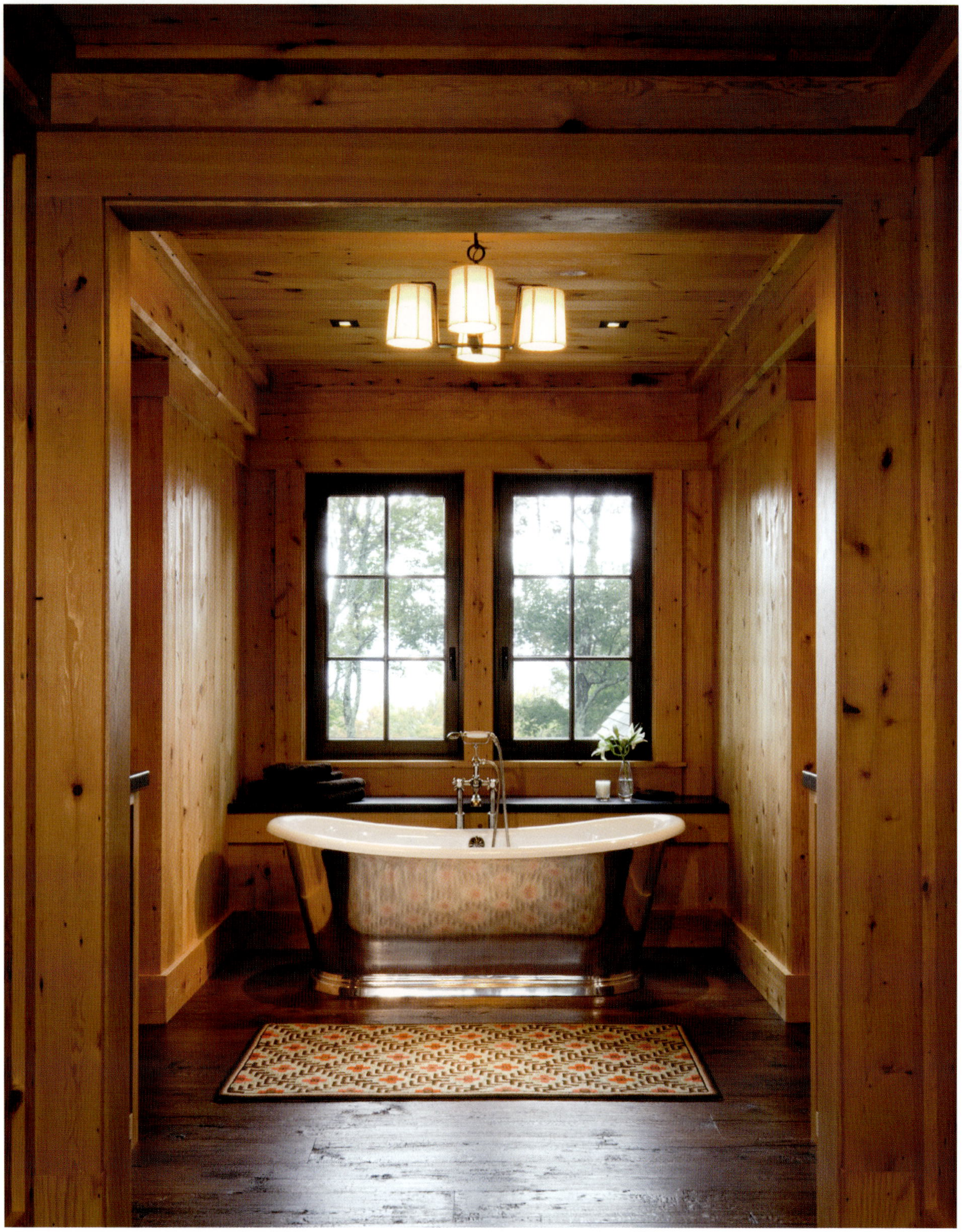

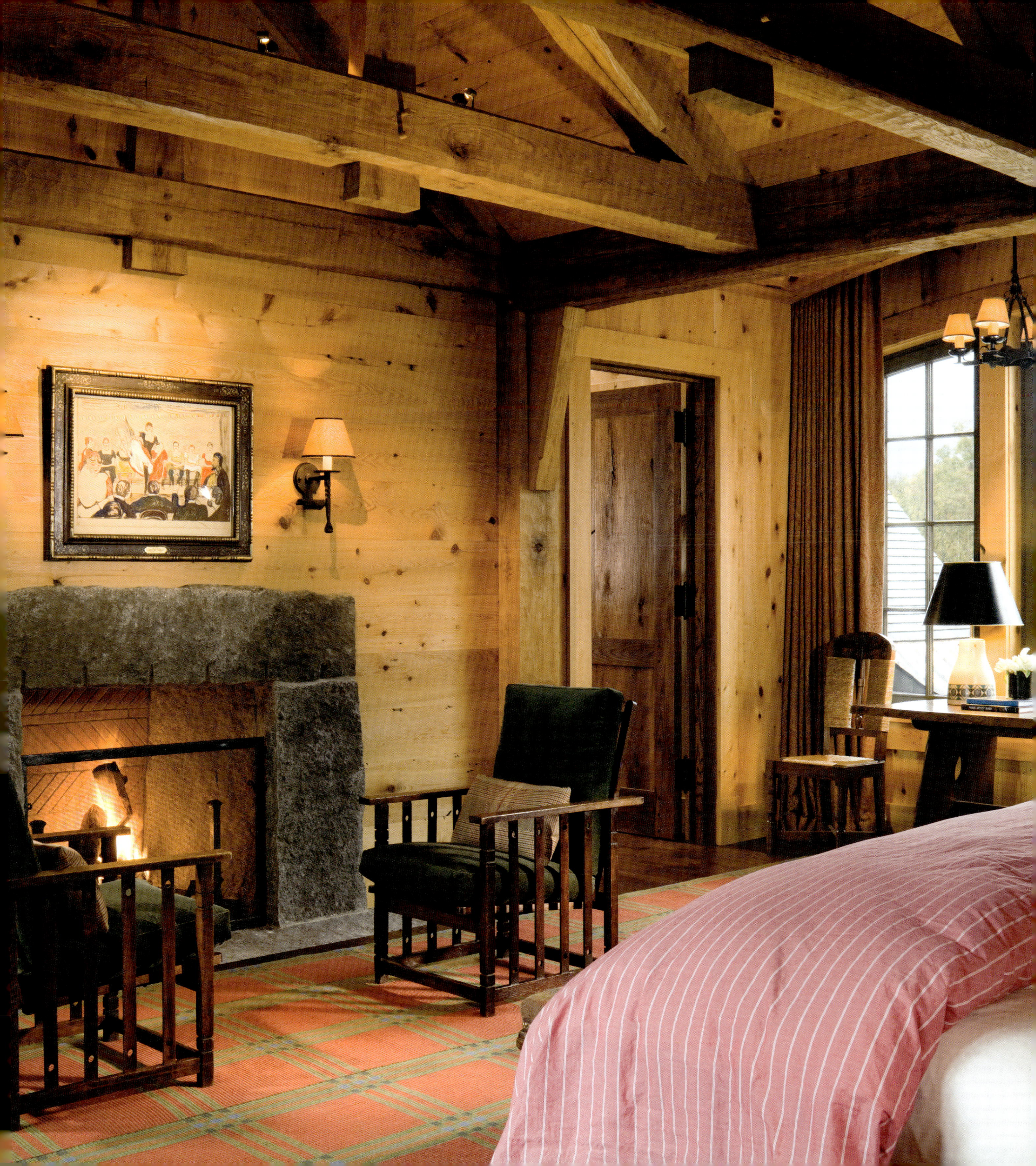

SITE PLAN

0 10' 25' 50' 100'

FIRST FLOOR

1. ENTRY
2. VESTIBULE
3. GALLERY
4. SKI ROOM
5. MUDROOM
6. POWDER ROOM
7. PORCH
8. OFFICE
9. KITCHEN
10. PANTRY
11. BREAKFAST NOOK
12. DINING ROOM
13. LIVING ROOM
14. SOUTH BALCONY
15. WET BAR
16. CAVE
17. GARAGE
18. COURTYARD
19. GRASS TERRACE

SECOND FLOOR

1. UPPER STAIR HALL
2. LOFT
3. BEDROOM
4. BATHROOM
5. MASTER BEDROOM
6. MASTER DRESSING ROOM
7. MASTER BATHROOM
8. OFFICE
9. OPEN TO BELOW

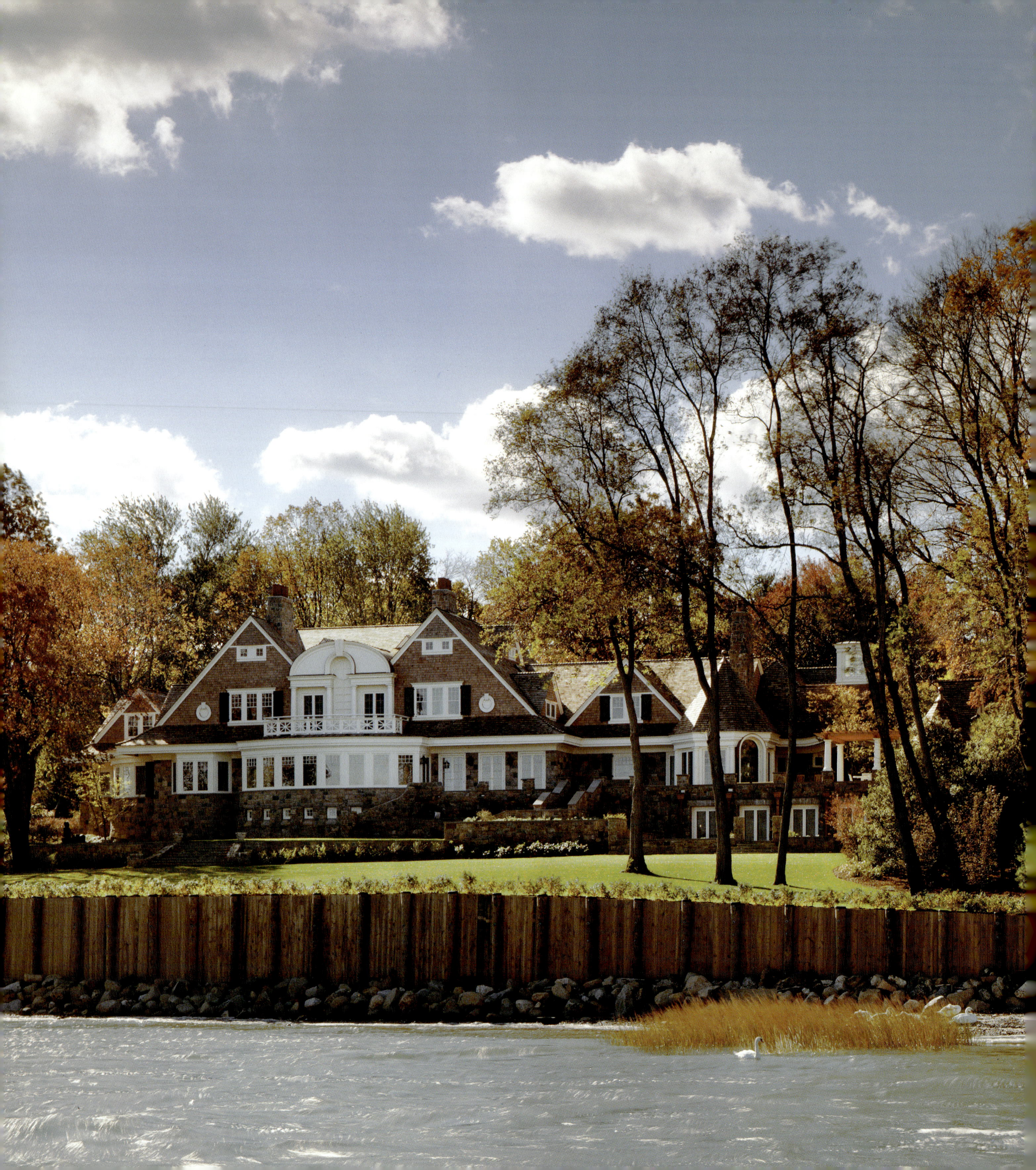

CEDAR-SHINGLED GABLES AND TALL CHIMNEYS DEFINE A HOUSE THAT CAN BE APPRECIATED FROM LAND OR SEA

THE CLIENTS These clients, a Manhattan lawyer and his wife, have long admired the period of the 1880s and 1890s when the Shingle Style in architecture flourished. When they were going to build a new house on a high bluff above Long Island Sound, on the North Shore of New York's Long Island, they knew they wanted it to be in this style.

THE DESIGN BRIEF The great Shingle Style houses in Newport, Rhode Island, that are often referred to as cottages, designed by the prestigious New York firm of McKim, Mead & White, were accented by cedar shingles and included details from classical architecture. This house is one of the heirs to the Shingle Style, with its classical embellishments. The relationship of this five-acre site to the Sound was a principal reason for building there, and the clients wanted the water to be visible from most of the rooms.

THE SOLUTION Cedar shingle gables and tall granite chimneys rise above a stone base. Because the lighter upper floors rest on the stone plinth that encloses the lower floors, the massing of the 10,300 square-foot house is visually cut almost in half. The courtyard is an indication of how the house will unfold. Between the house's wings, there are an unusual pair of libraries, one for him and one for her, and a large Palladian window above the entry portico. The window provides a powerful punctuation point on the façade. Wharton says of the entrance: "It is not just the front portico, but the whole composition, with the two library wings flanking the door." Passing through the front door, one sees the water through the windows in the living room. The interior of the house holds a tension between the finishes and the elaborate detailing of traditional pilasters and pediments, and the asymmetrical interior scheme and open plan, which are strictly modern—the better to accommodate the art. Among the pieces in the collection are paintings by René Magritte, Roberto Matta and Fernando Botero, and sculpture by Mimmo Paladino, Alberto Giacometti, Henry Moore, and Marino Marini. *The Artist and His Model 1964*, a painting by Pablo Picasso, hangs above the fireplace in the wife's library; a sculpture by Joan Miró is tucked beneath the curve of the grand staircase in the two-story entrance hall. The furniture, ranging from the late eighteenth-century to the late nineteenth-century, mixes very traditional American pieces with European gilt. A separate second-floor environment was created for visiting children and grandchildren. "The clients really needed a house that could contain their life in all its variety," Wharton says, "as well as their eclectic tastes. This house can be grand and comfortable at the same time, and it can also kick up its heels."

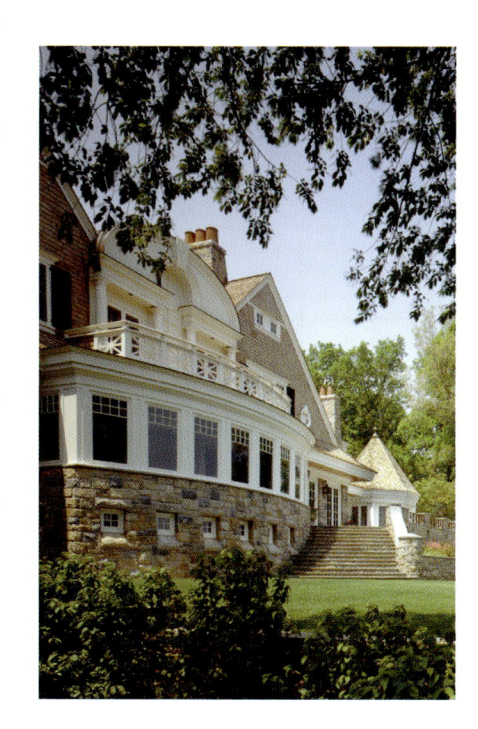

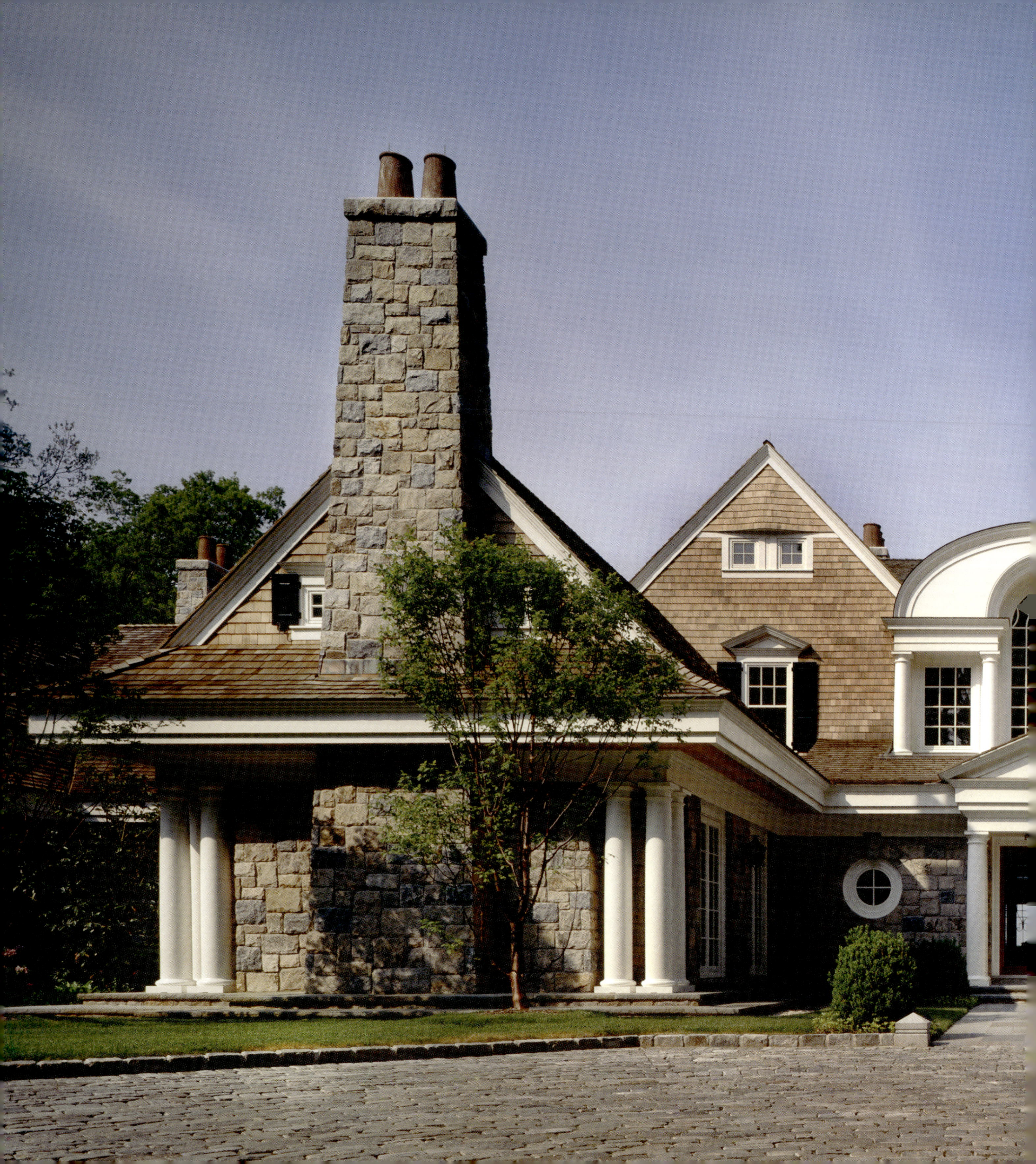

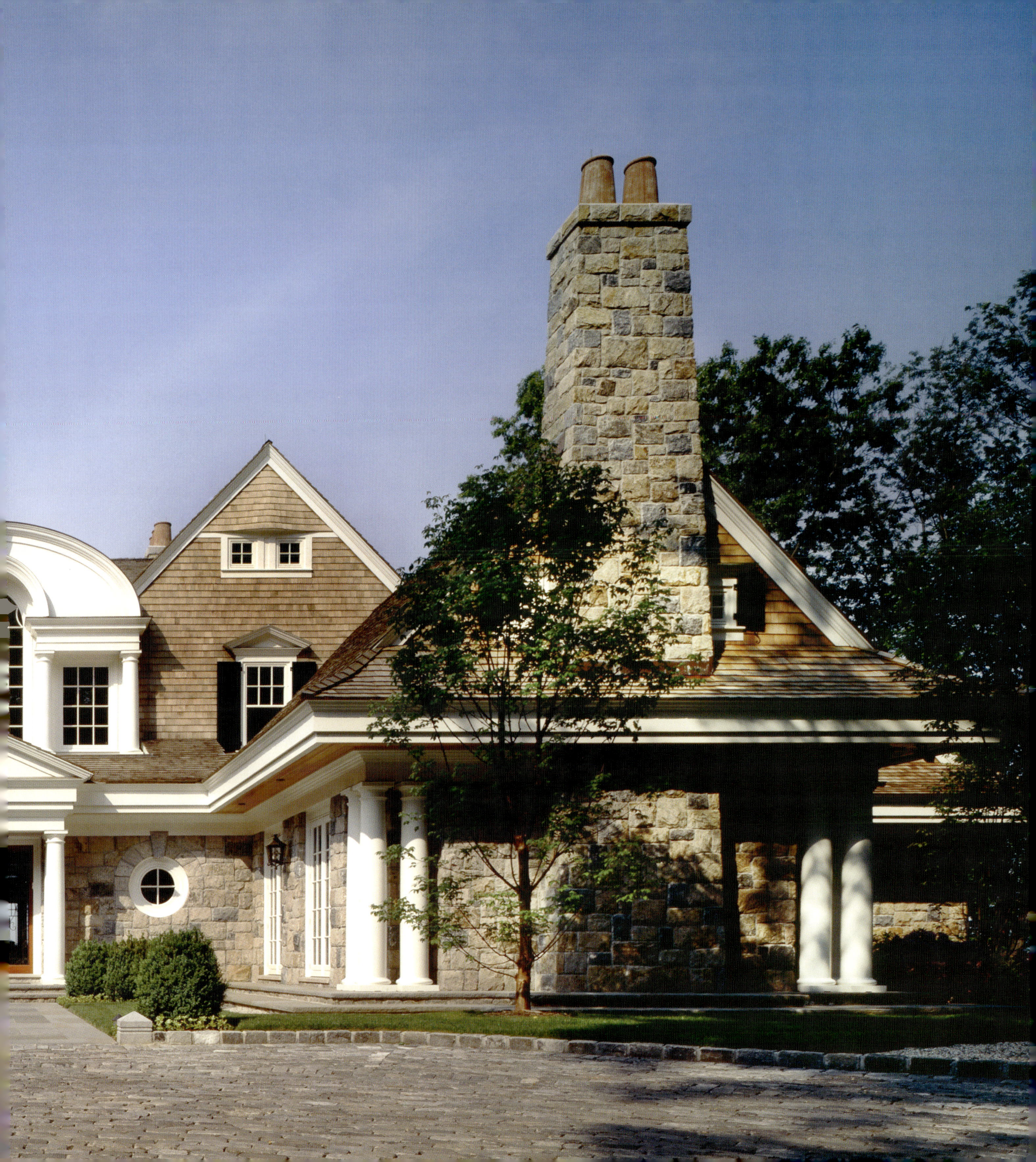

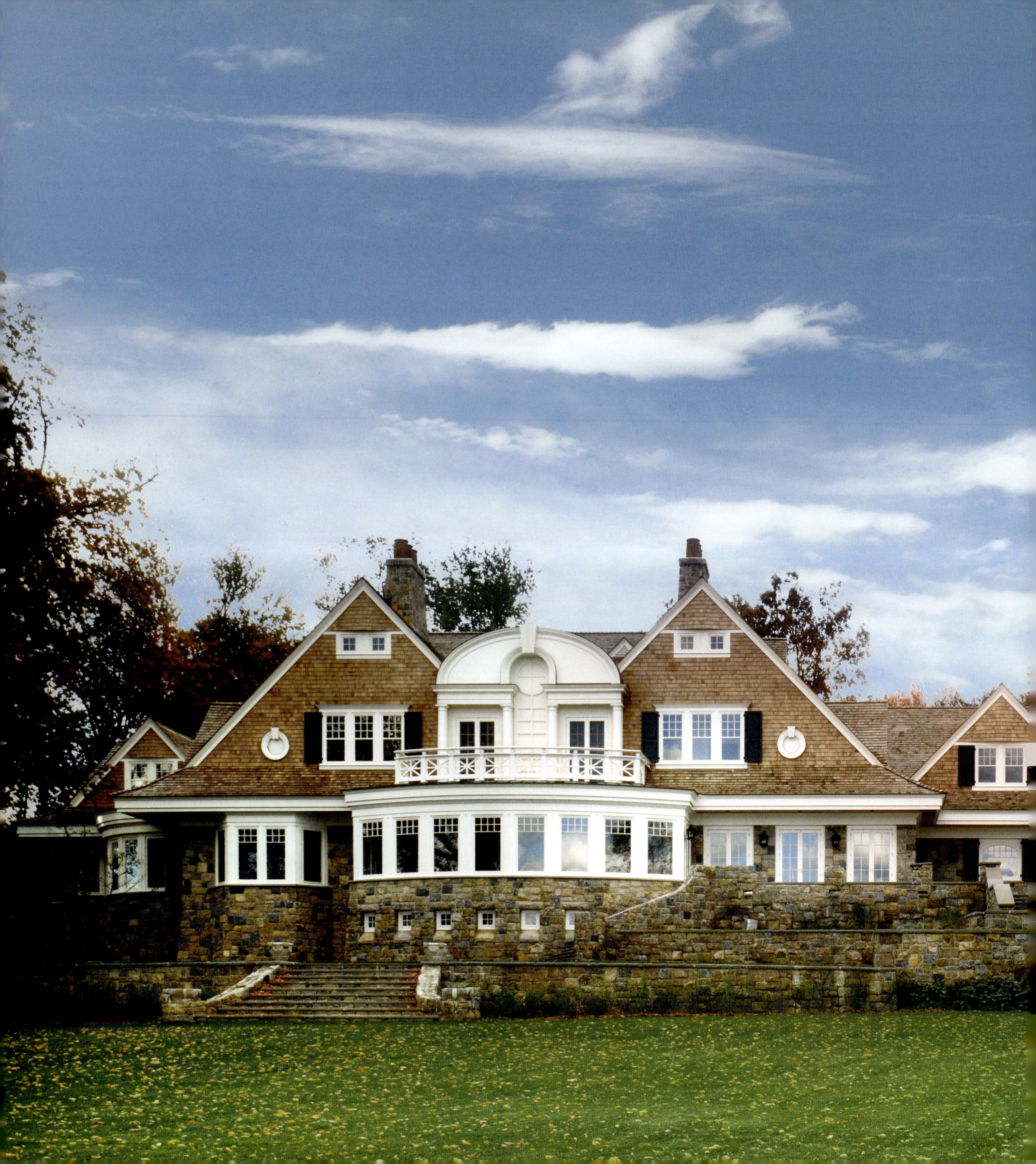

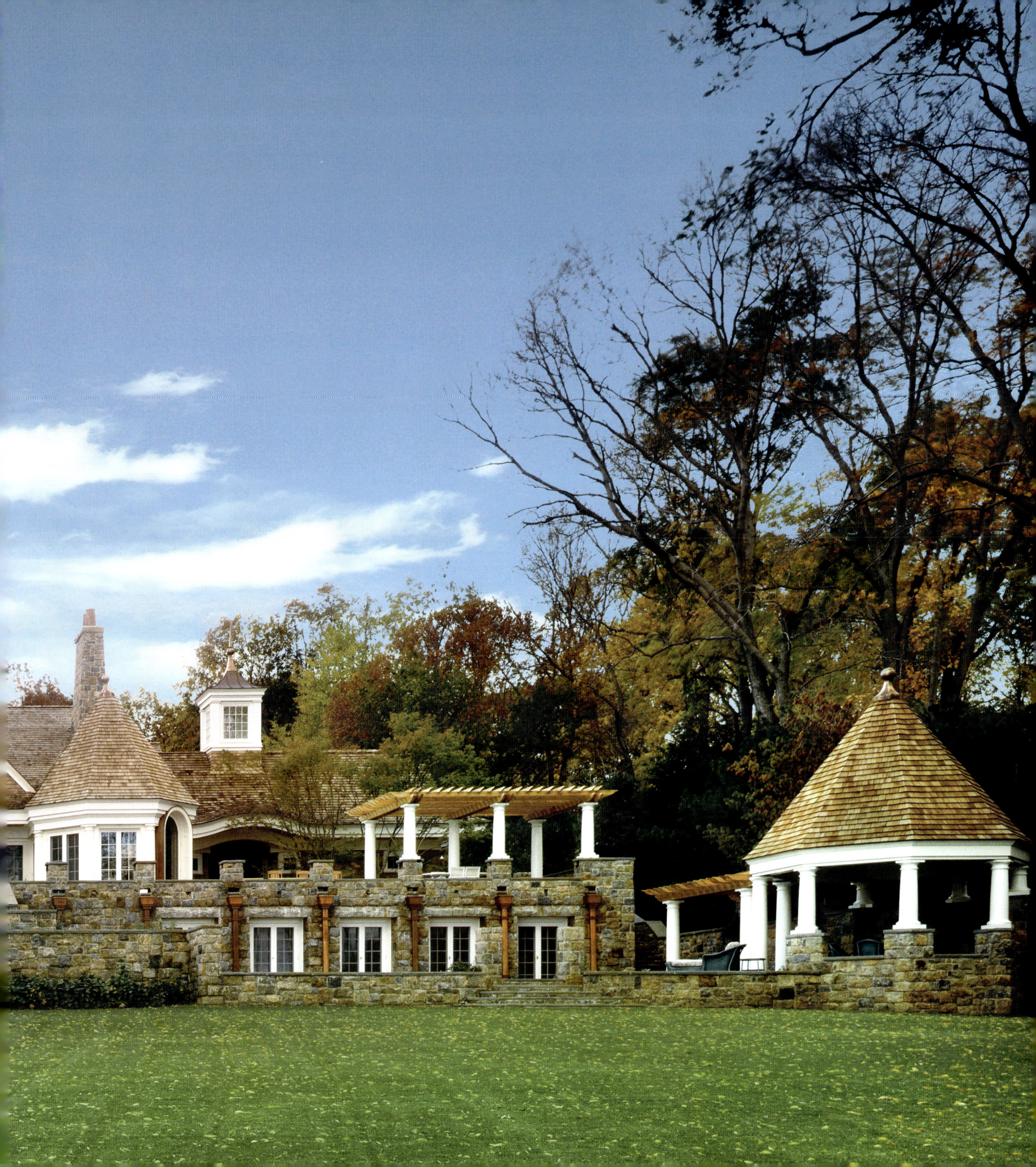

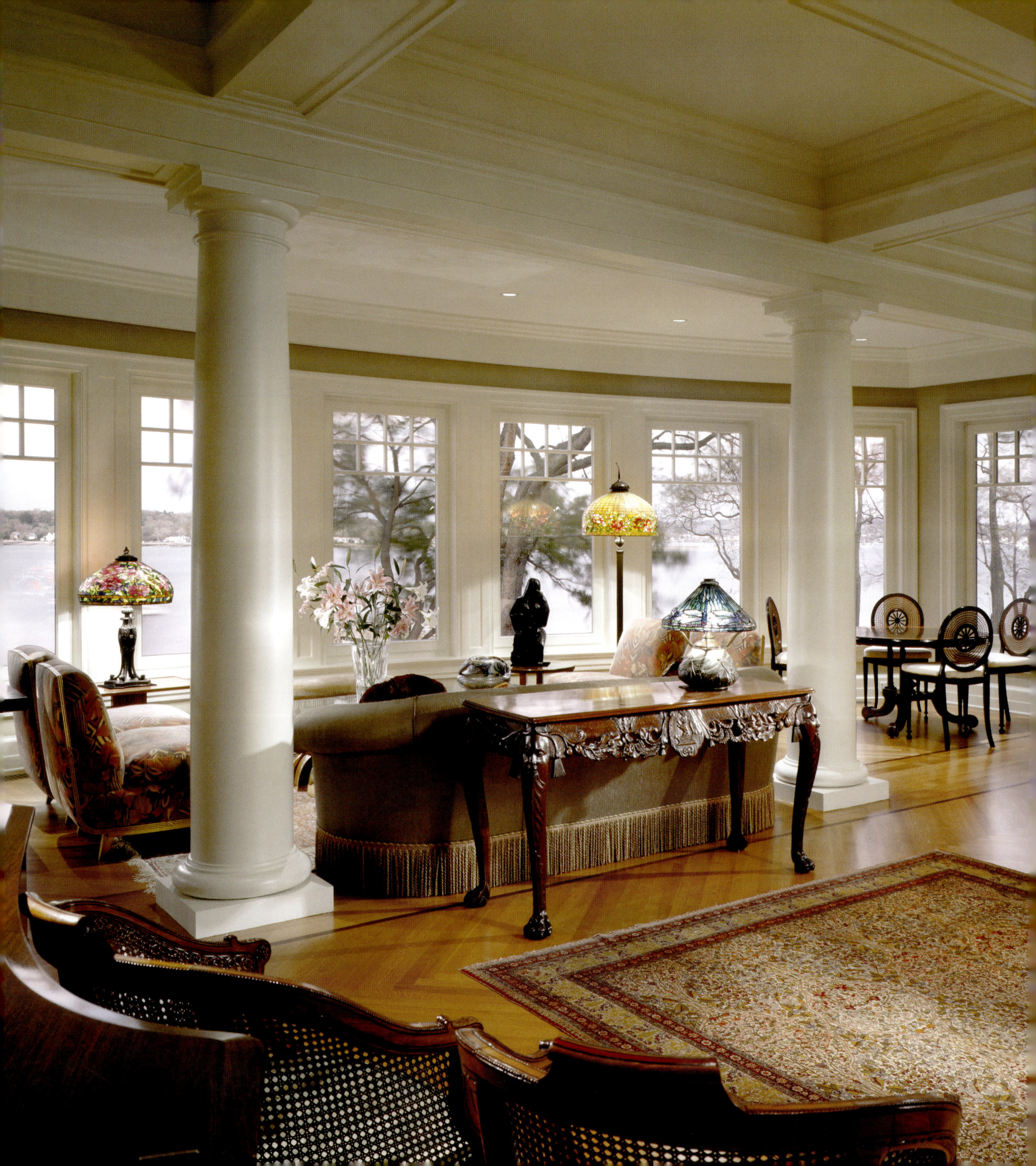

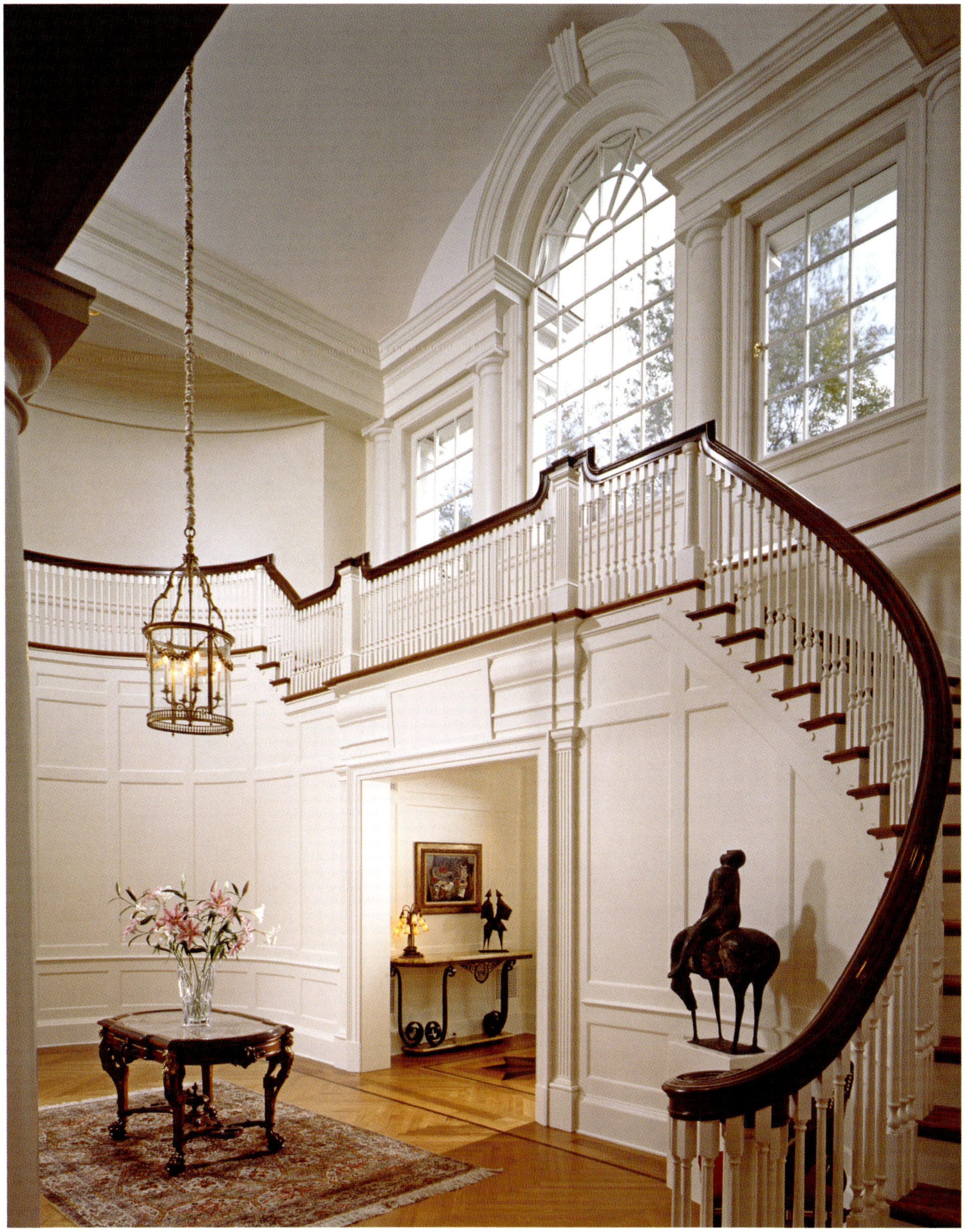

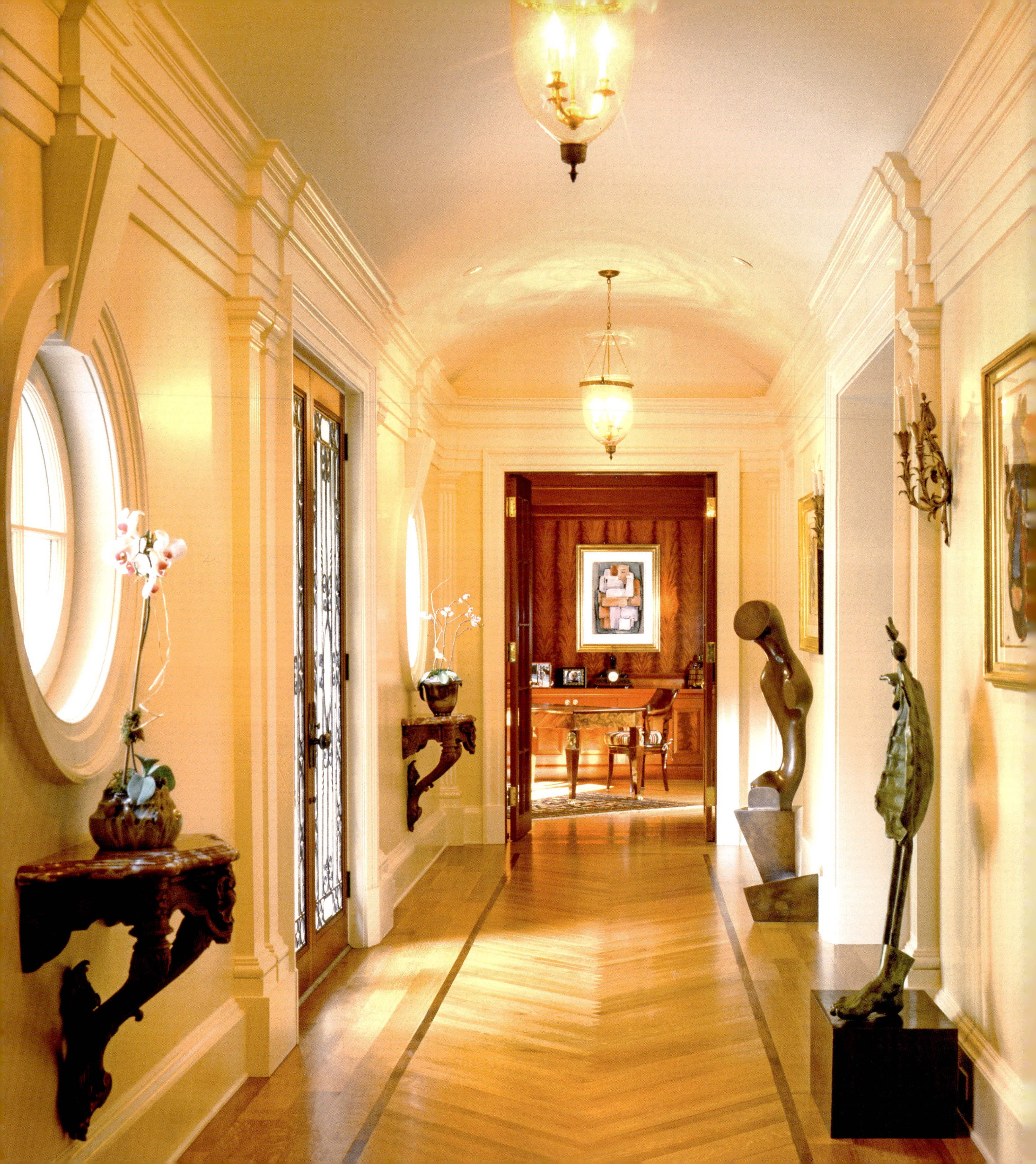

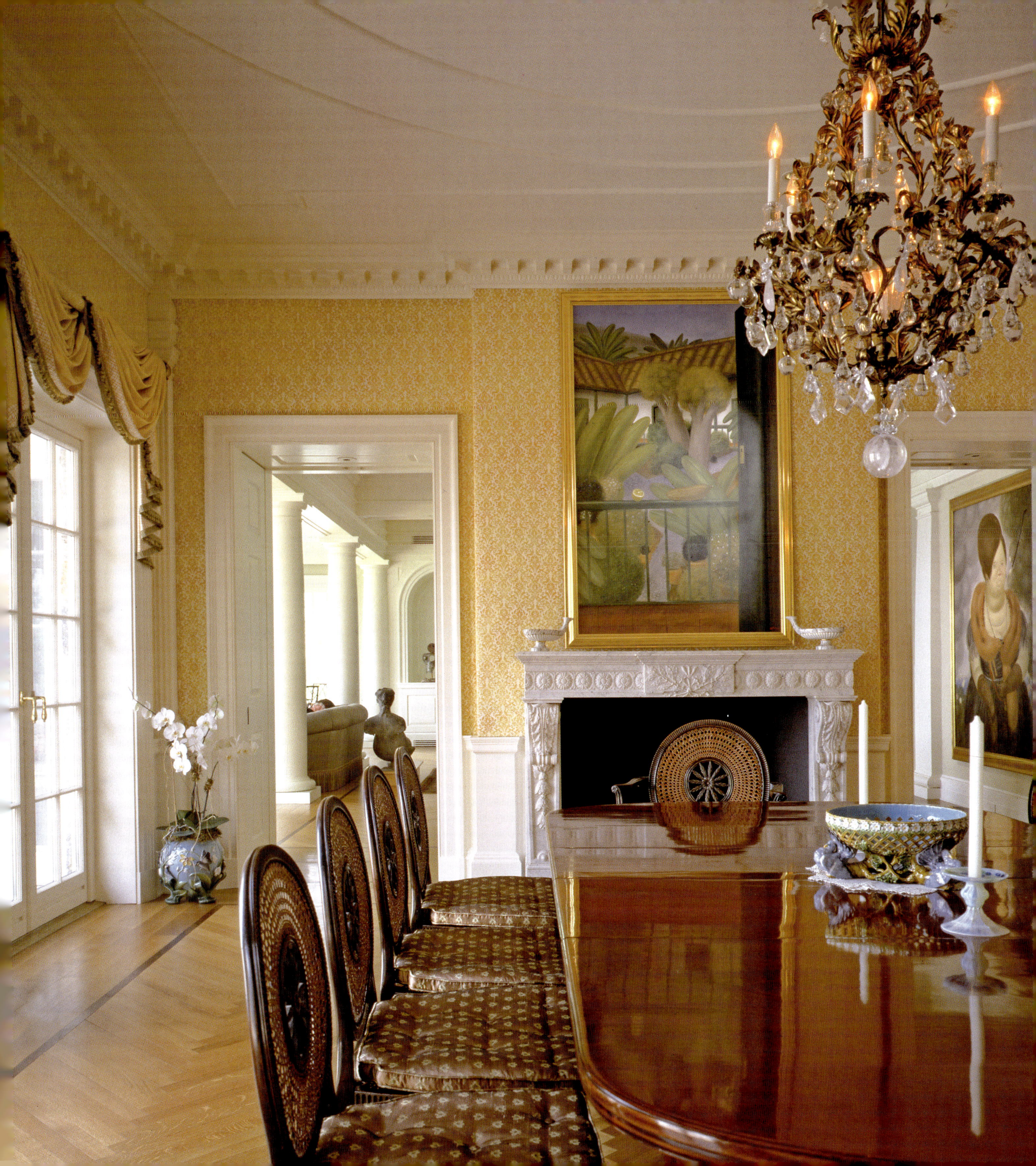

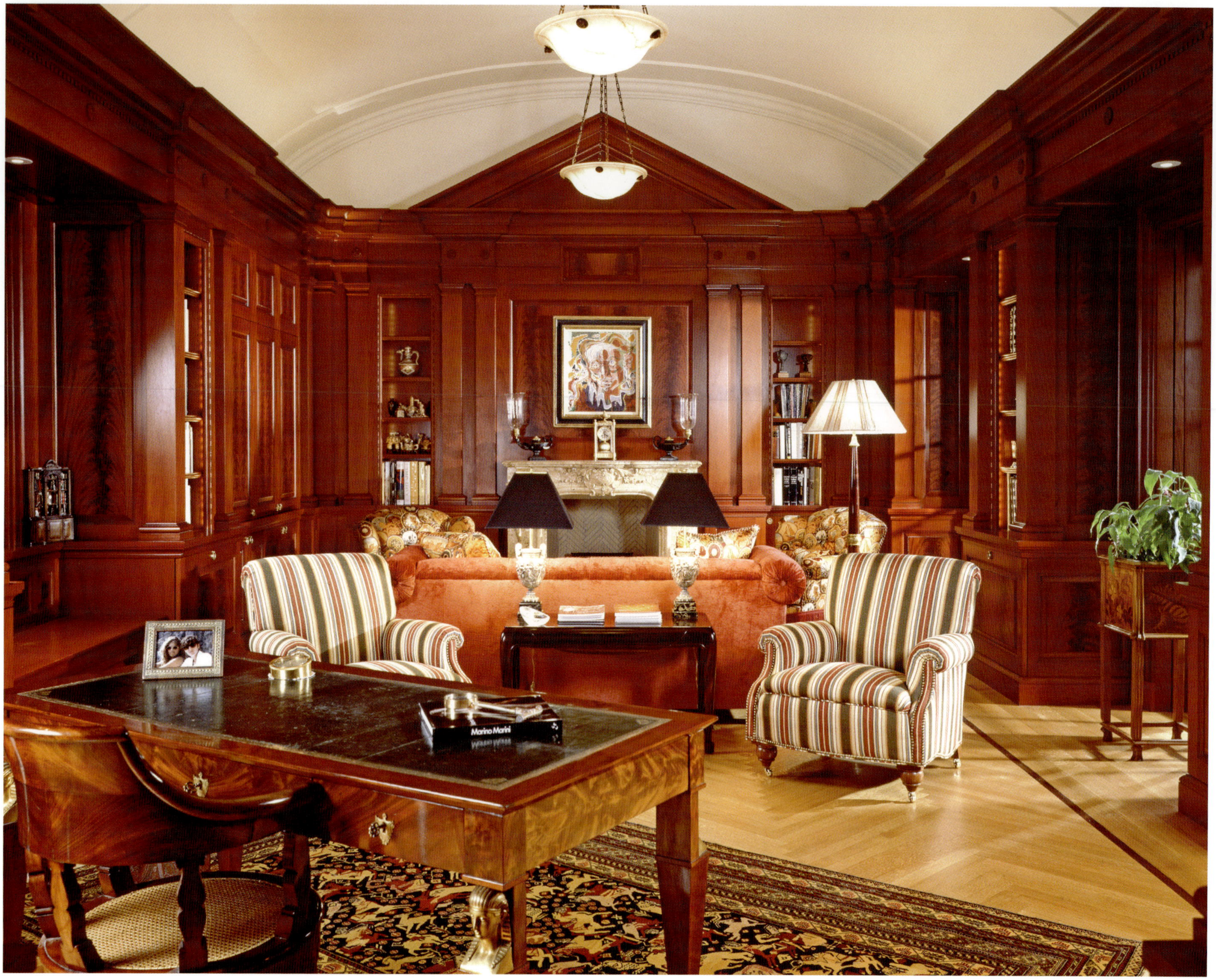
Marino Marini

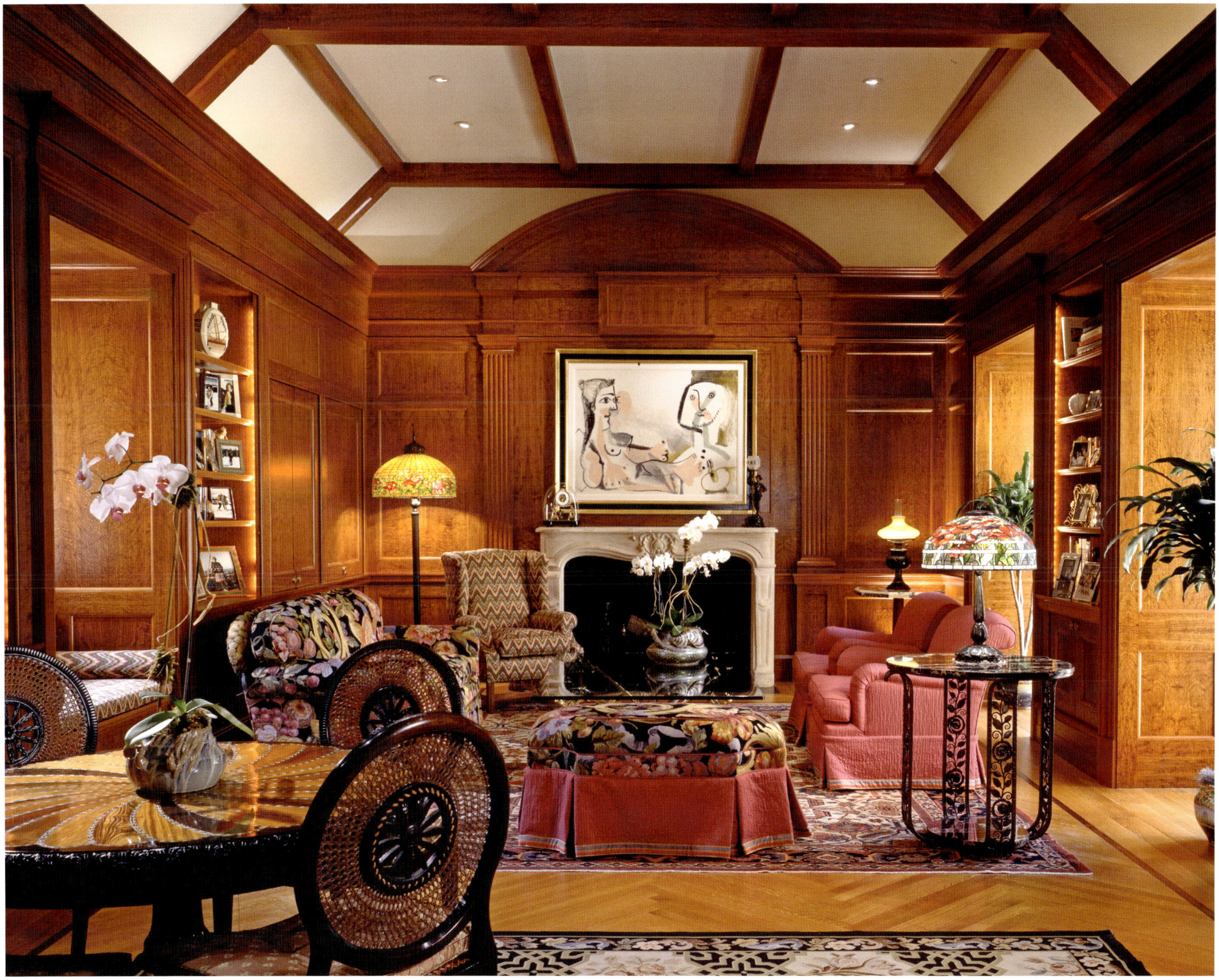

SITE PLAN

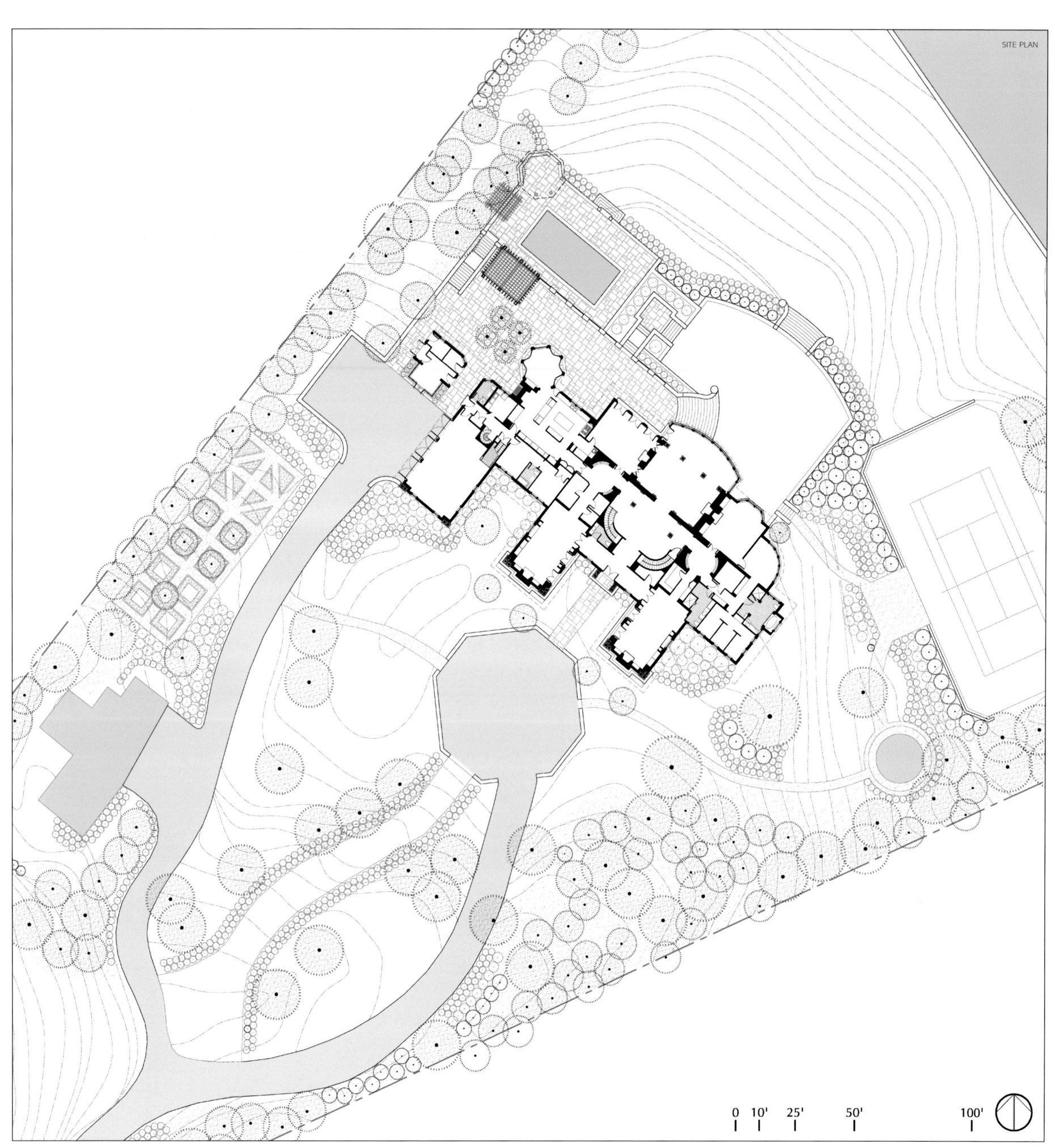

0 10' 25'   50'   100'

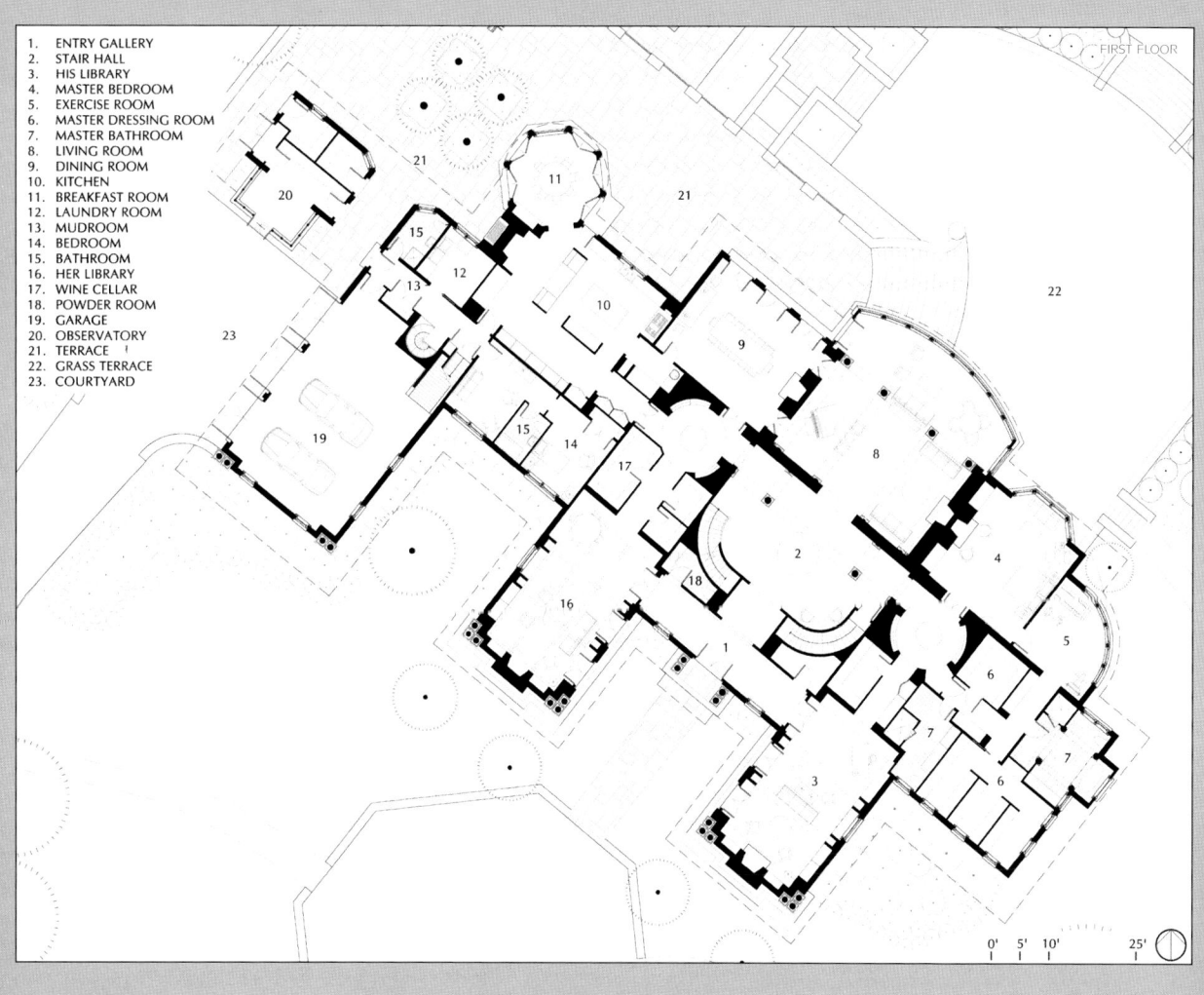

FIRST FLOOR

1. ENTRY GALLERY
2. STAIR HALL
3. HIS LIBRARY
4. MASTER BEDROOM
5. EXERCISE ROOM
6. MASTER DRESSING ROOM
7. MASTER BATHROOM
8. LIVING ROOM
9. DINING ROOM
10. KITCHEN
11. BREAKFAST ROOM
12. LAUNDRY ROOM
13. MUDROOM
14. BEDROOM
15. BATHROOM
16. HER LIBRARY
17. WINE CELLAR
18. POWDER ROOM
19. GARAGE
20. OBSERVATORY
21. TERRACE
22. GRASS TERRACE
23. COURTYARD

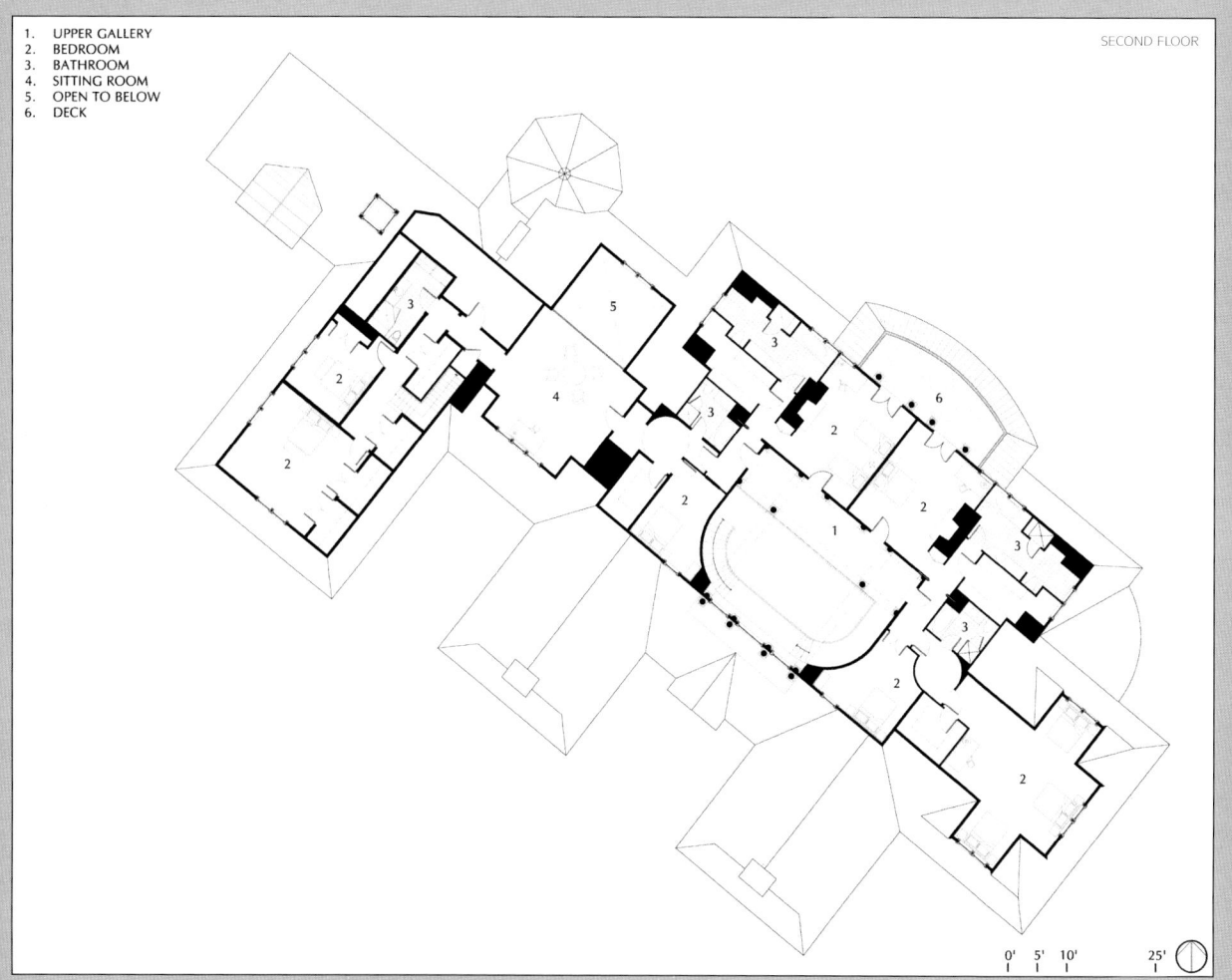

SECOND FLOOR

1. UPPER GALLERY
2. BEDROOM
3. BATHROOM
4. SITTING ROOM
5. OPEN TO BELOW
6. DECK

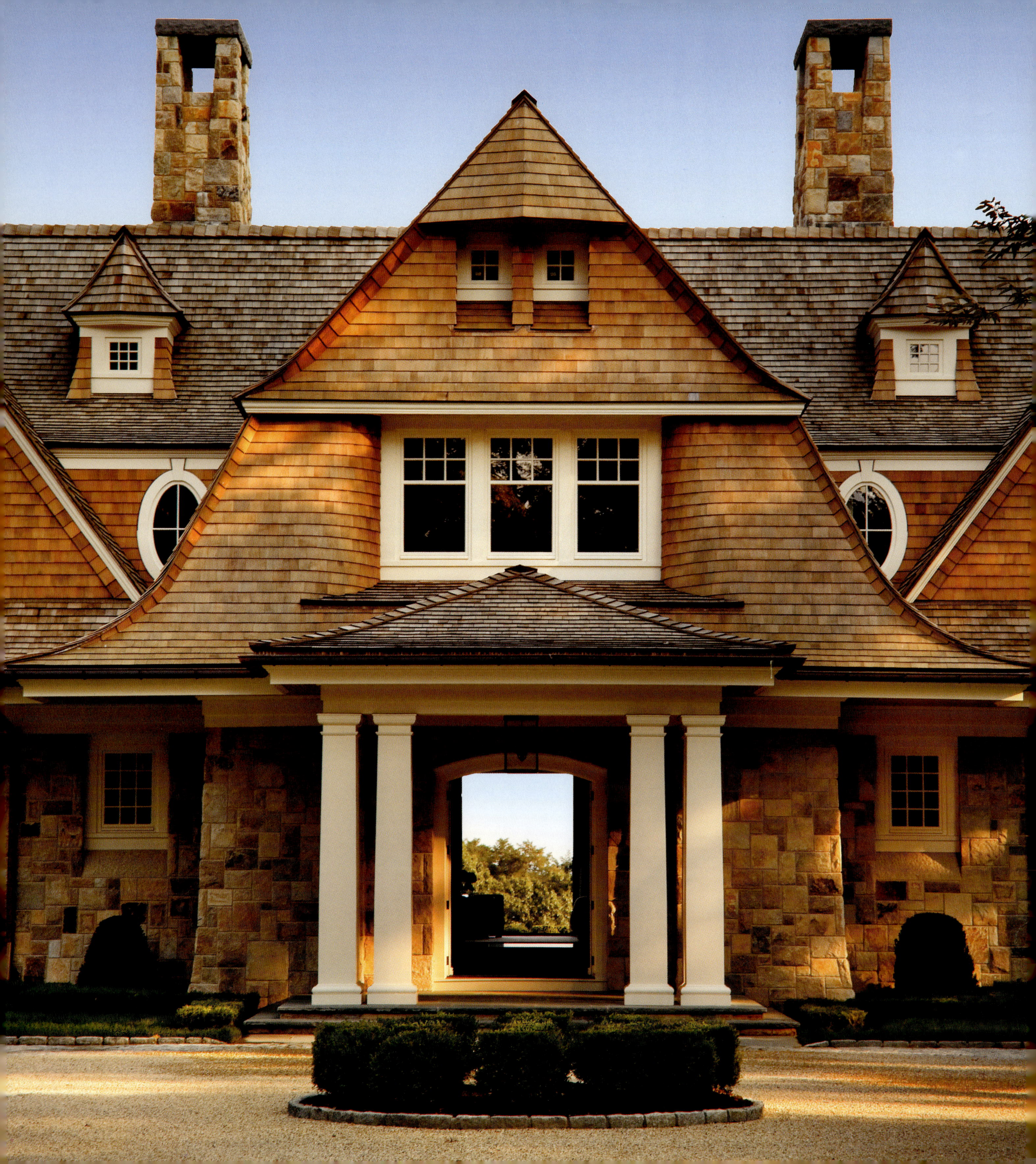

SITUATED ON A HIGH BLUFF, A HOUSE IN THE SHINGLE STYLE TAKES ON A CONTEMPORARY AIR

THE CLIENTS A young couple with three children wanted to build a house on the Connecticut shore. When they found a two-and-a-half acre site on the water, they envisioned a house that would be a comfortable home, where they could create their own family traditions.

THE DESIGN BRIEF Situated on a bluff, the house had to be one with its site. It had to be elegant yet low key. Scale and proportion, as related to the site, were paramount. The house had to show flexibility in plan, to accommodate the needs of a growing family. Stone and red cedar shingles, which are user-friendly and time-tested materials, were used in the construction of the house. The house had to evoke a feeling of permanence and timelessness. Although alluding to history in its imagery, the house had to be modern in plan.

THE SOLUTION Located above the harbor, the house has a strong presence in its relationship to the water. Visually, the house is long and meandering, with strong horizontal massing. Tall chimneys and the stair tower add vertical punctuation to the house's imagery. A generous motor court introduces you to the house, the backdrop of this court being the entry façade of the house. The entry portico is defined by pairs of columns, with the entry door framed by them. The house is long and thin, so as one enters the house, he or she is very aware of the living room and the water beyond. All the major rooms on the first and second floor have a view of the water. The house's configuration is guided by the client's desire to frame important views. While the symmetry and detailing of the entry façade is understated, the water view façade supports three Dutch gables, exaggerated almost to the dimensions of a house pictured in a fairytale illustration. The inside of the house is detailed with an assemblage of coffered ceilings, window seats, curving galleries, and paneling. The interior of the house has been beautifully decorated by Victoria Hagan, who kept the palette white, which nineteenth century proponents of the more traditional Shingle Style probably would not have done, but which seems eminently appropriate today. The house is striking in its attention to detail, but its strengths are derived from its low-key elegance.

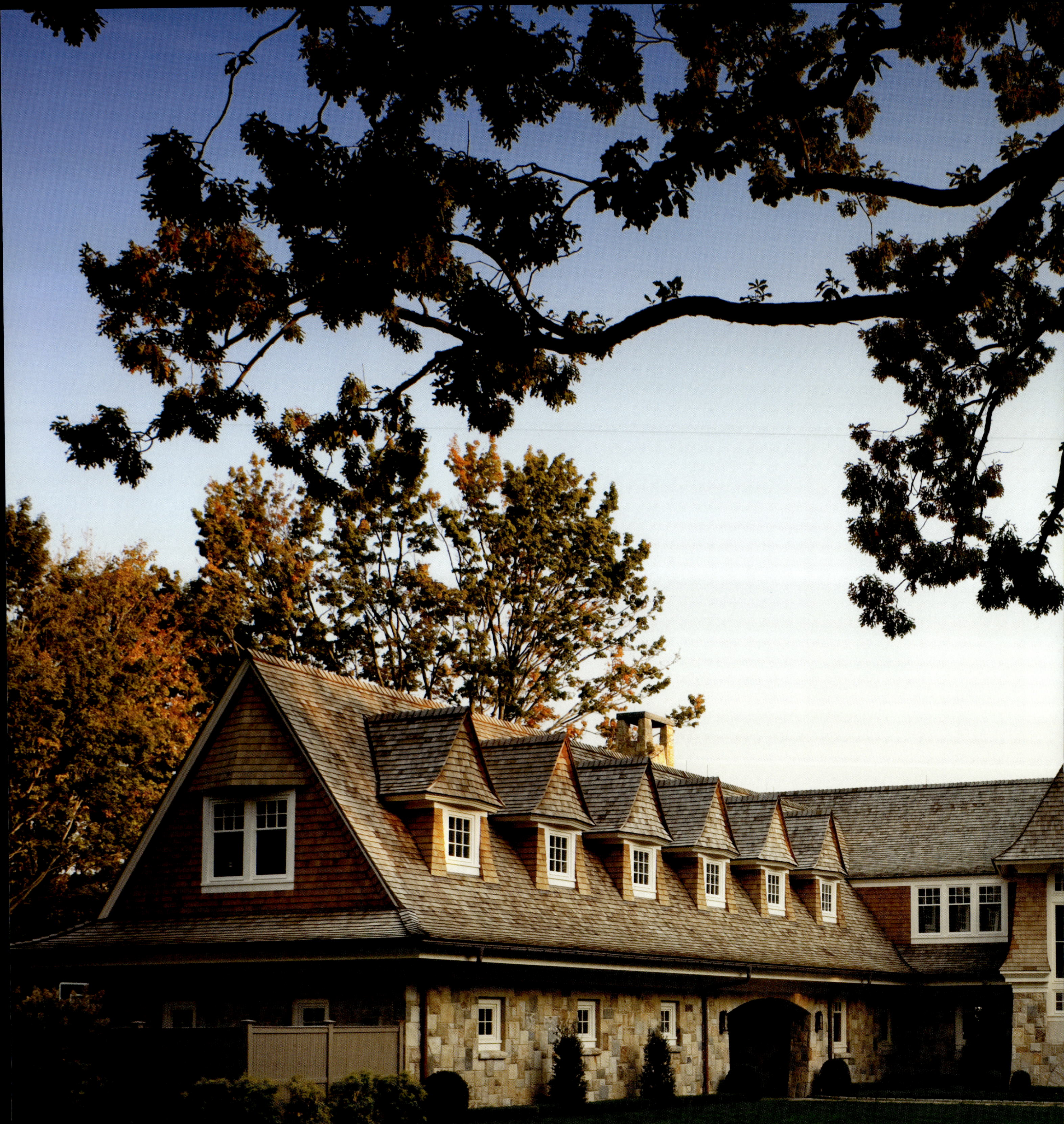

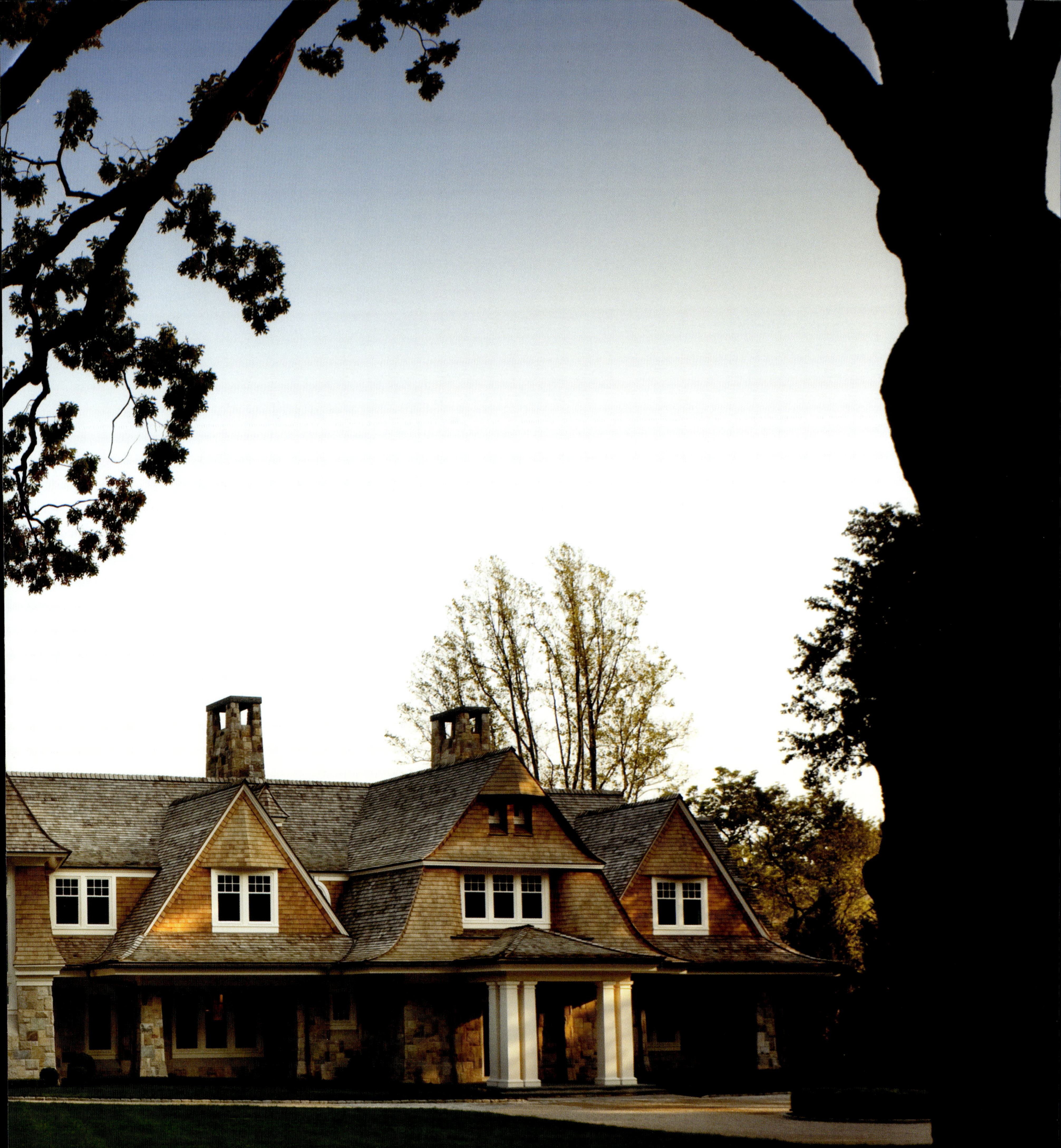

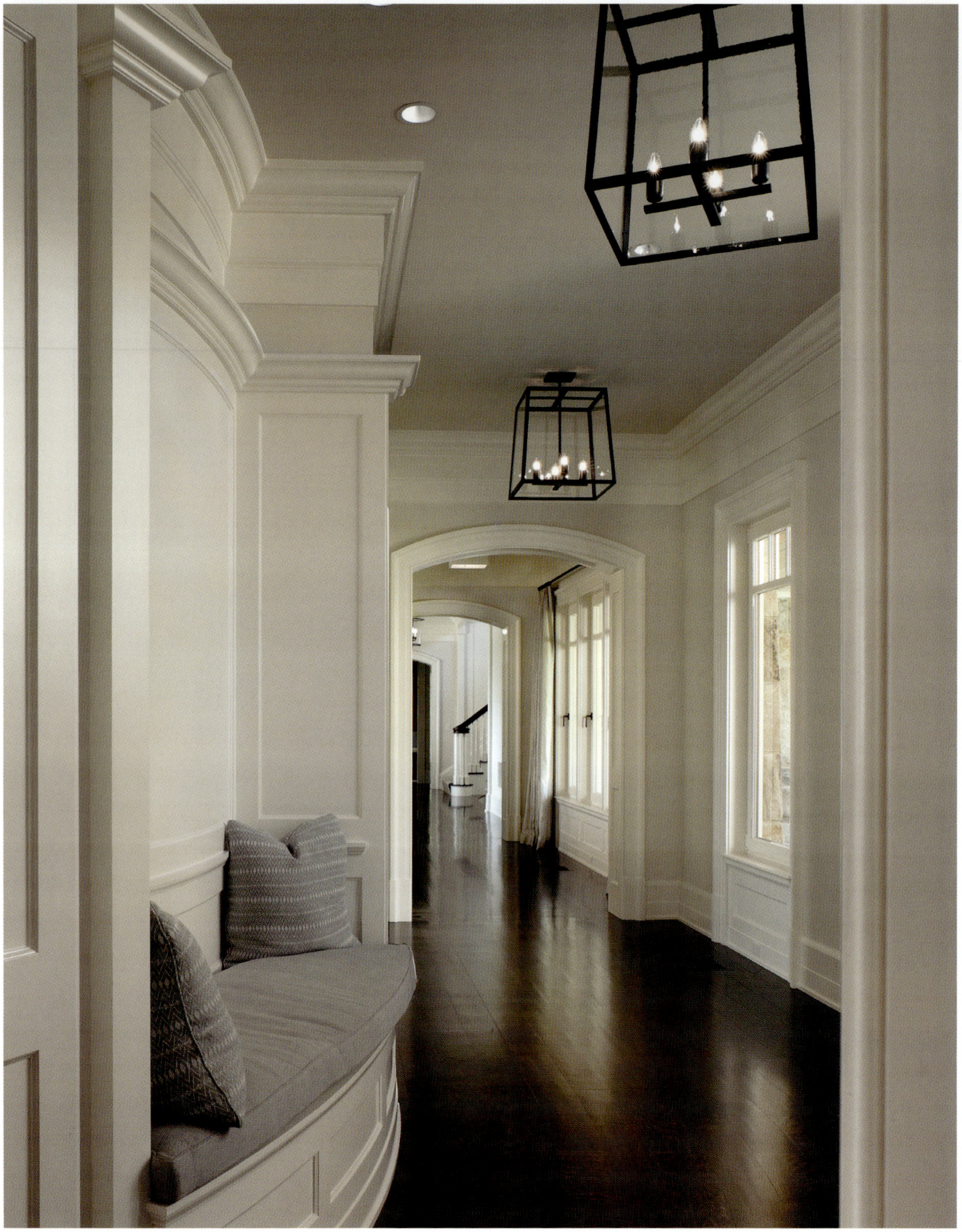

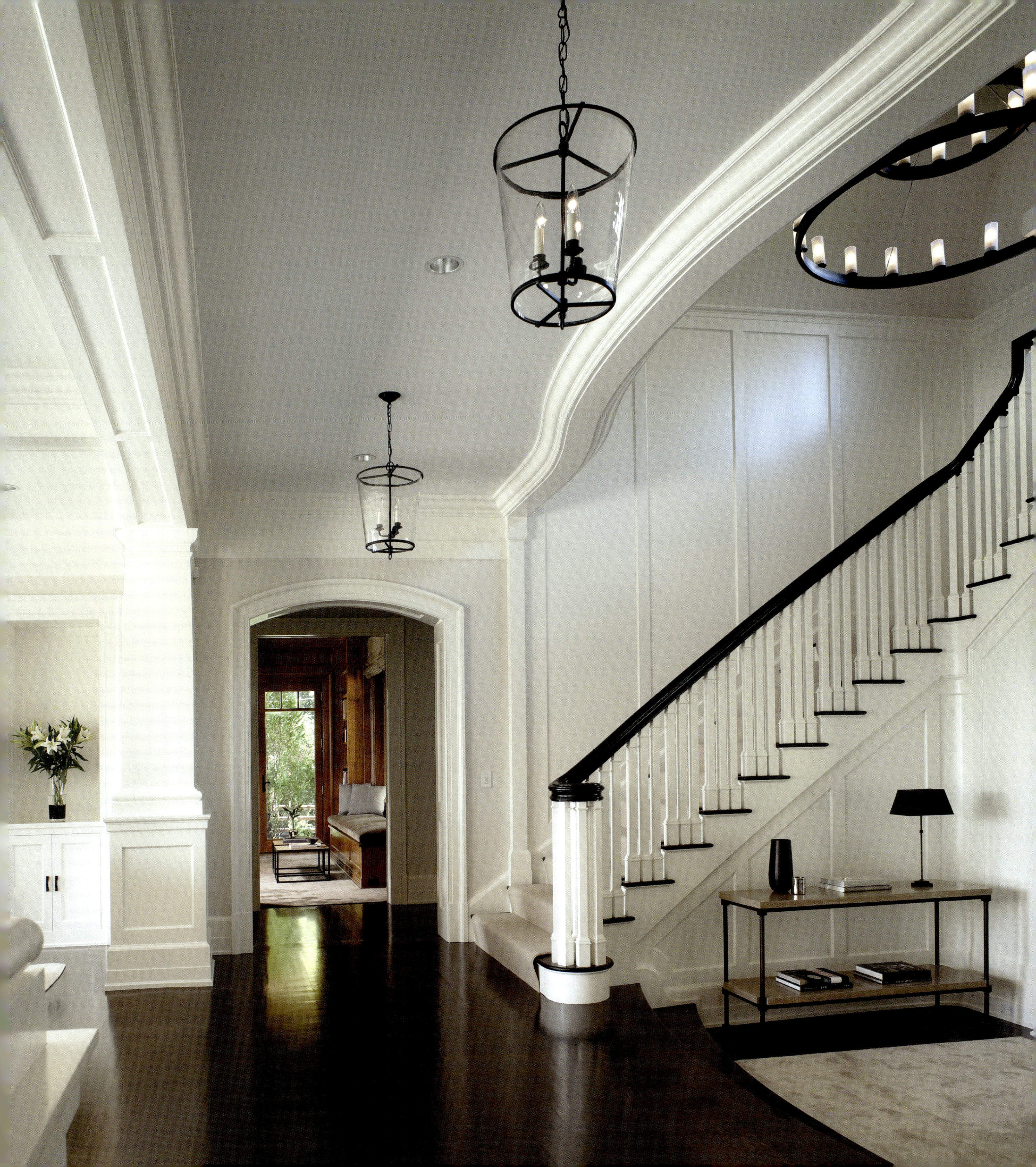

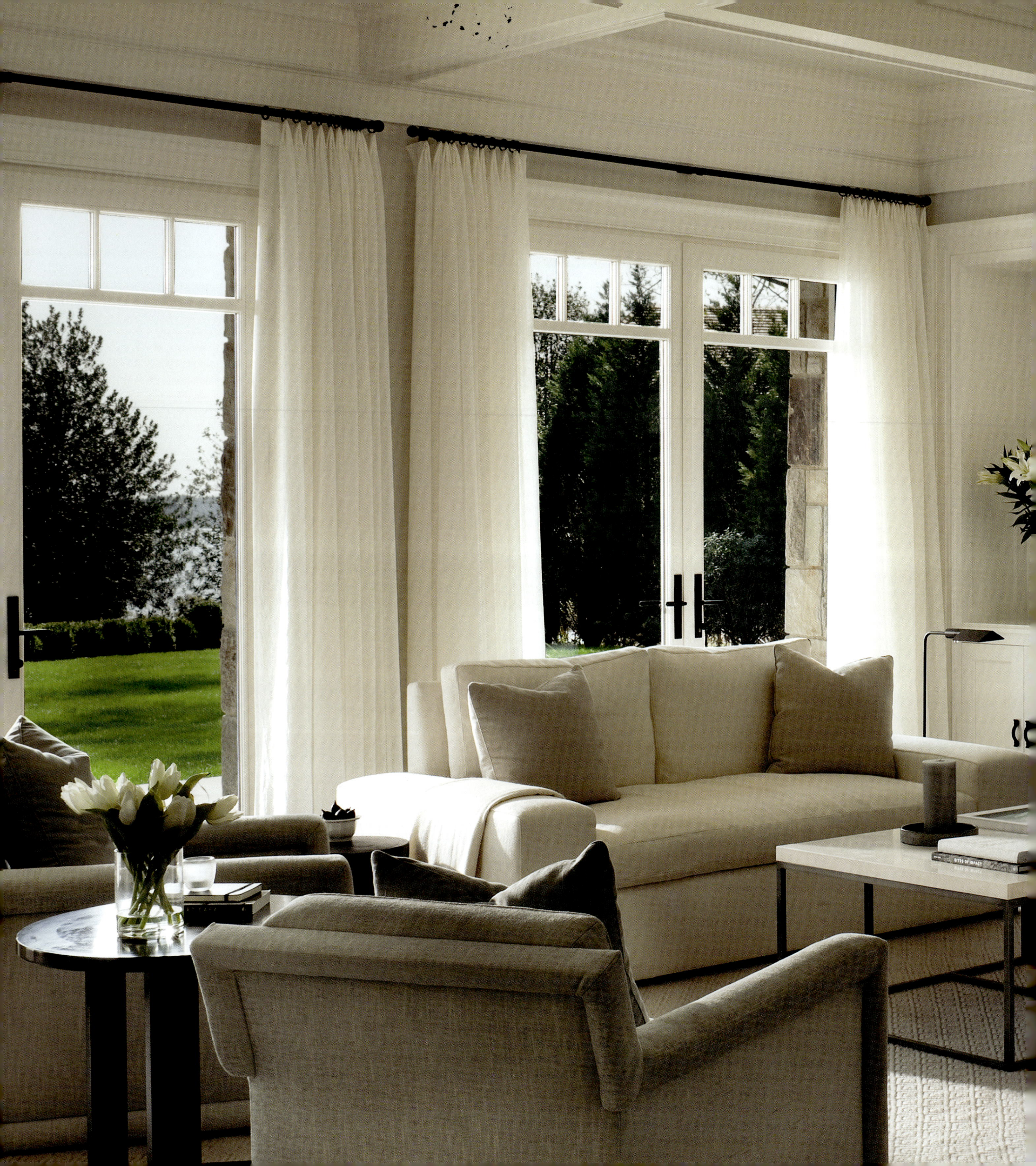

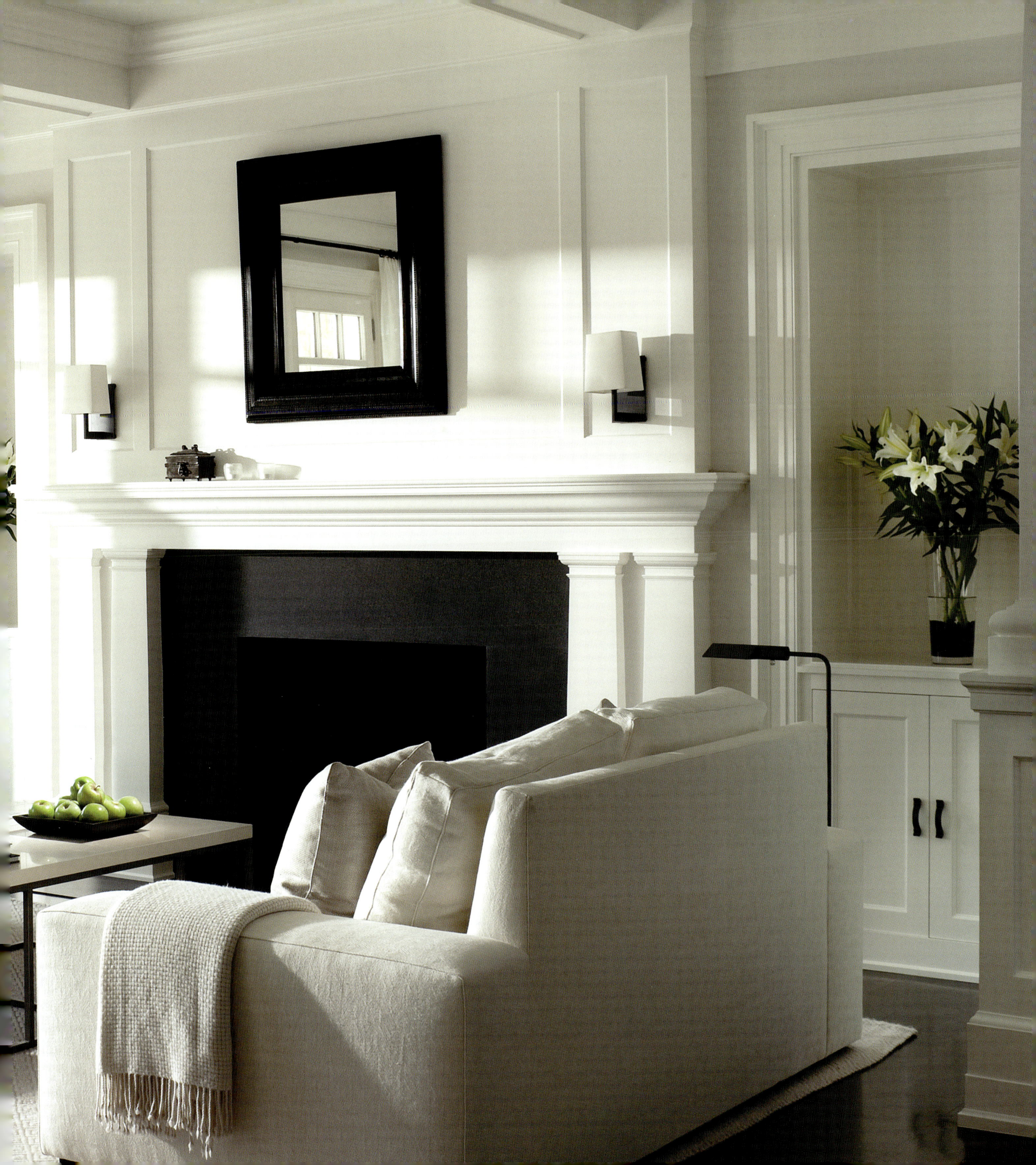

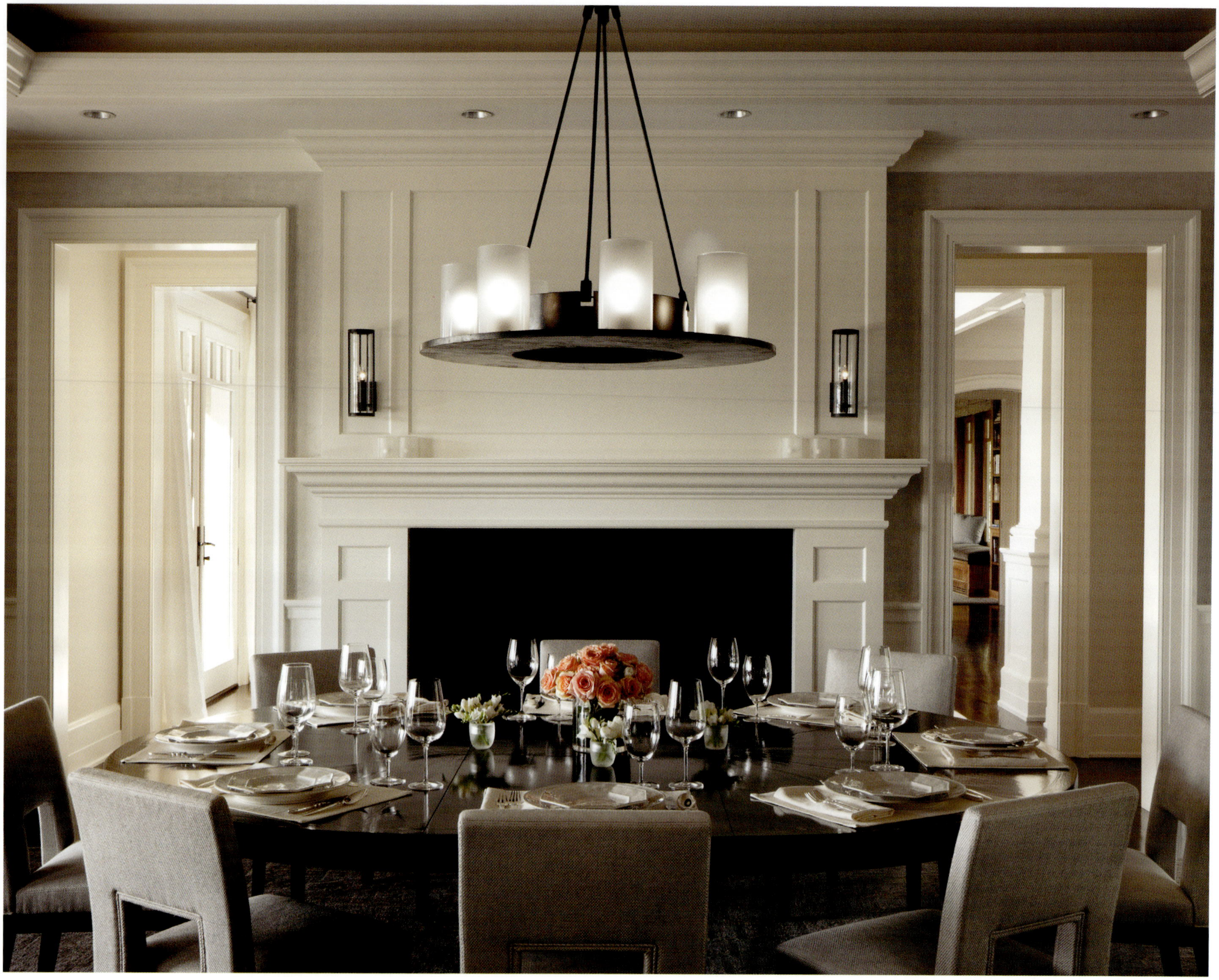

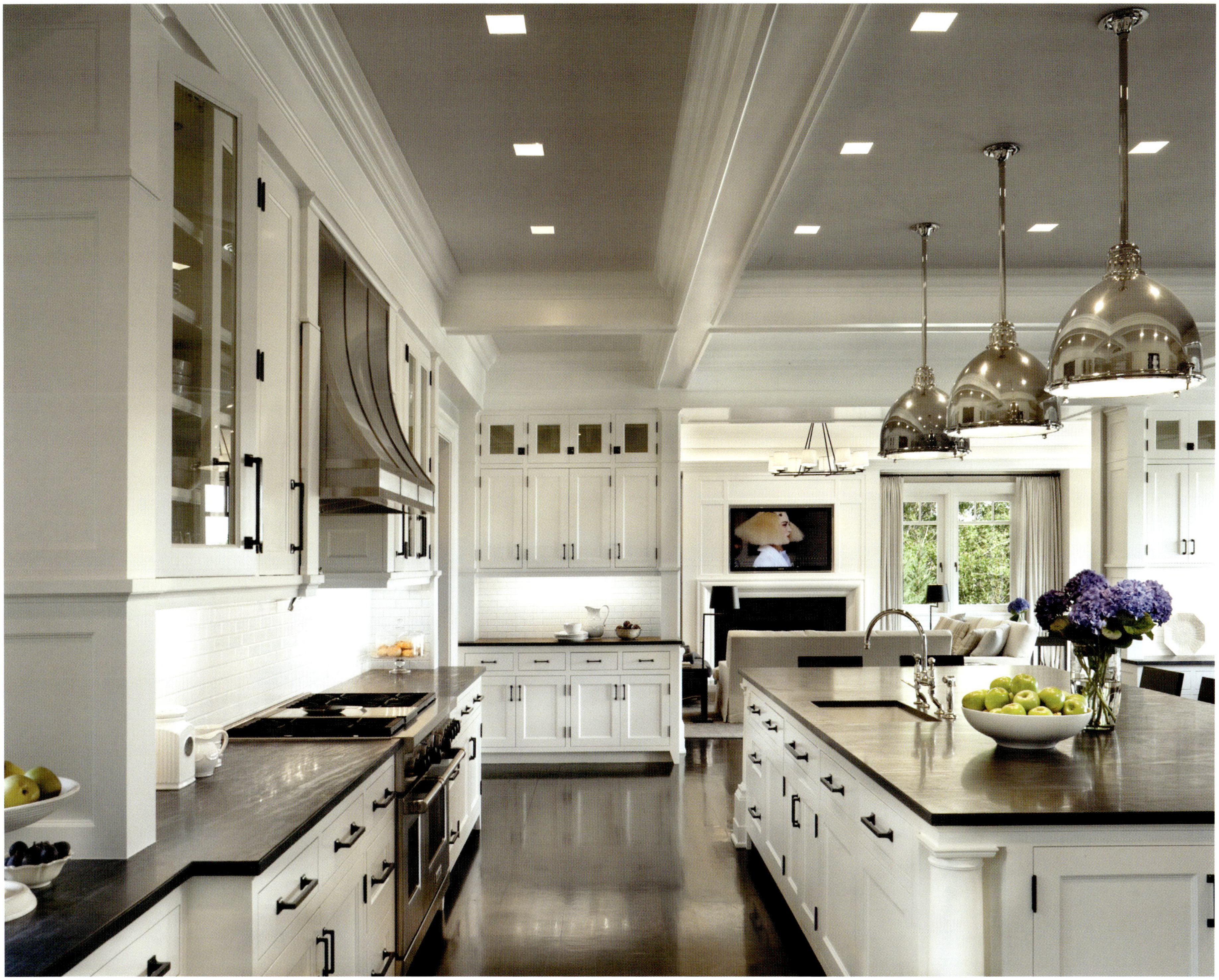

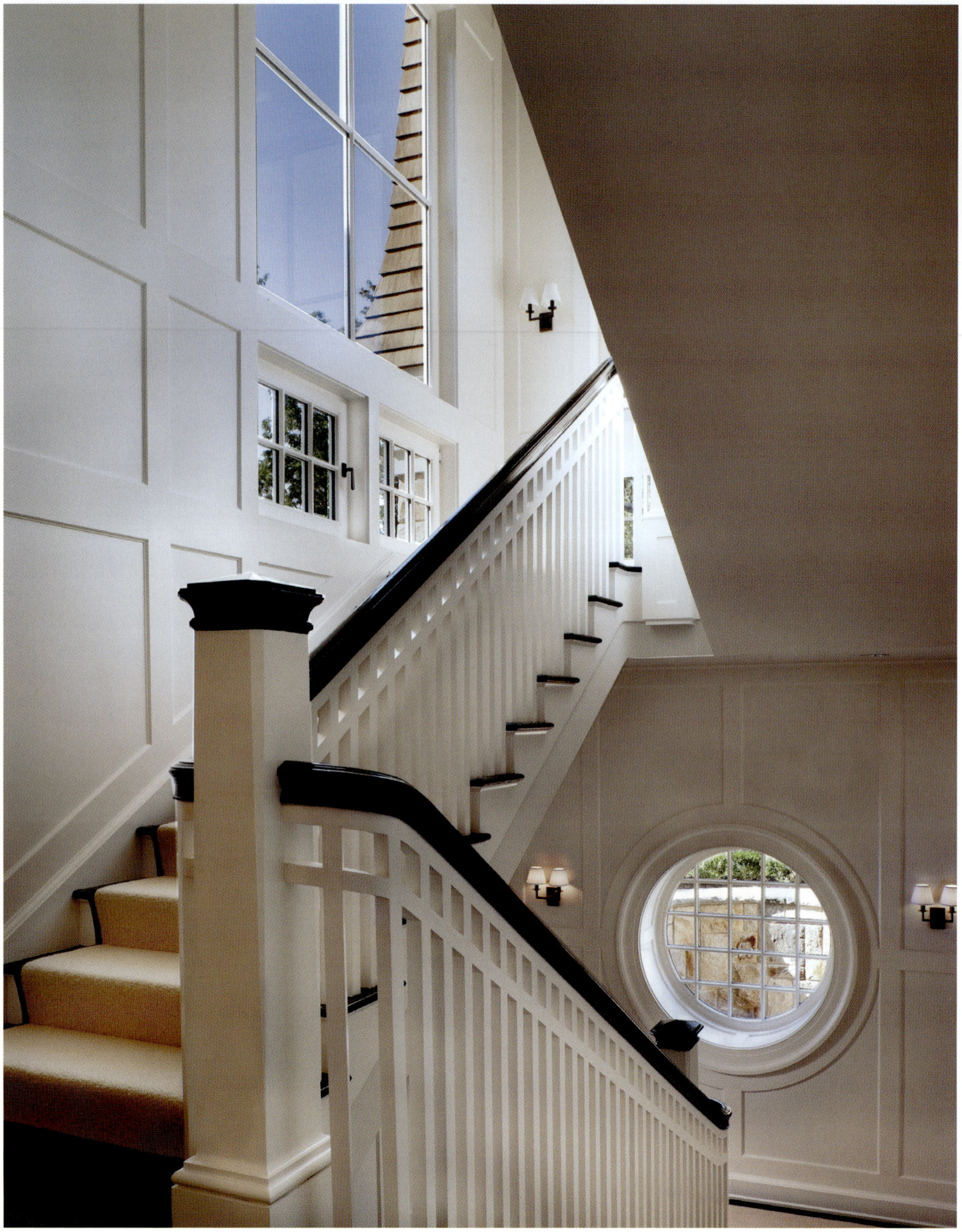

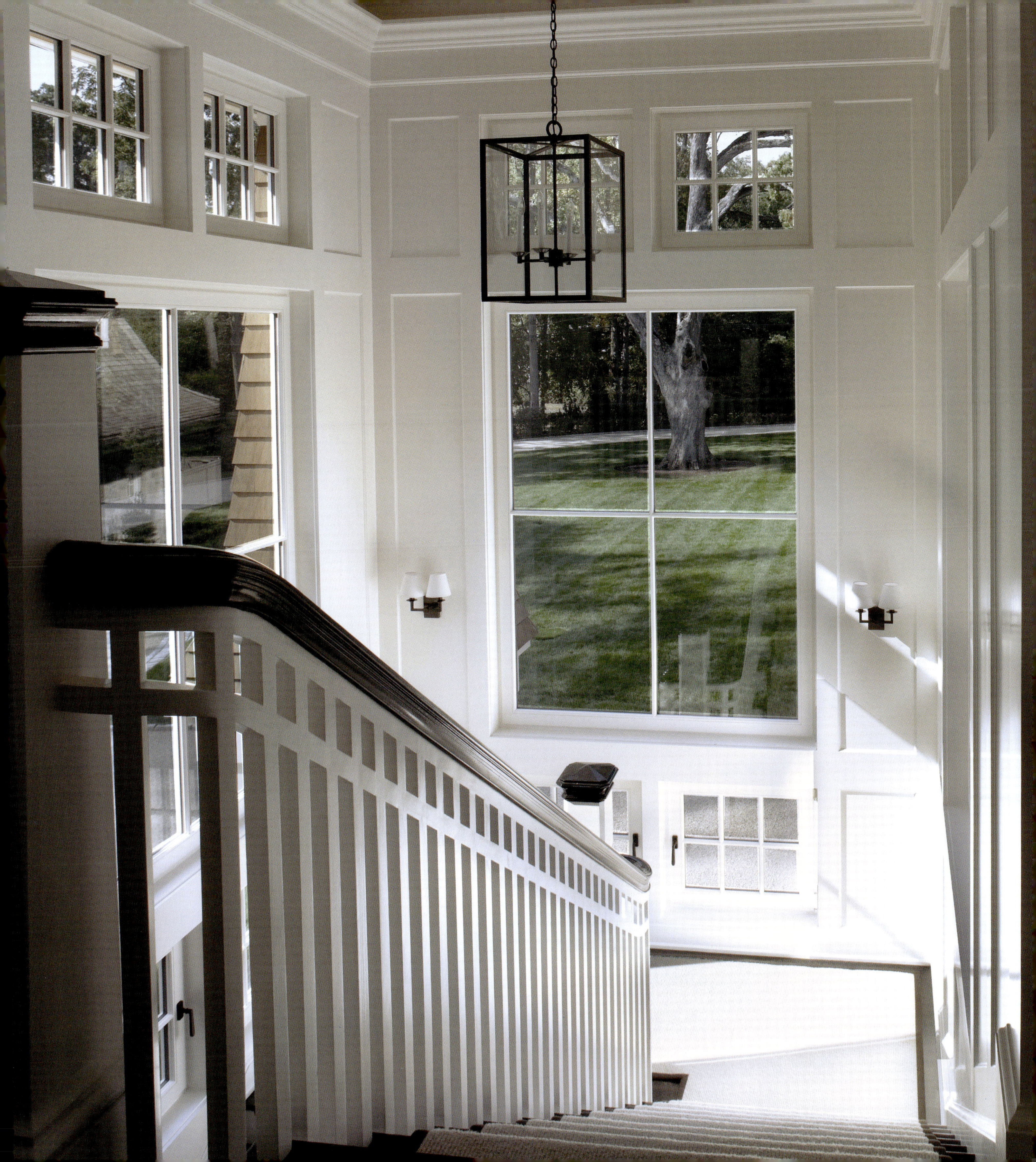

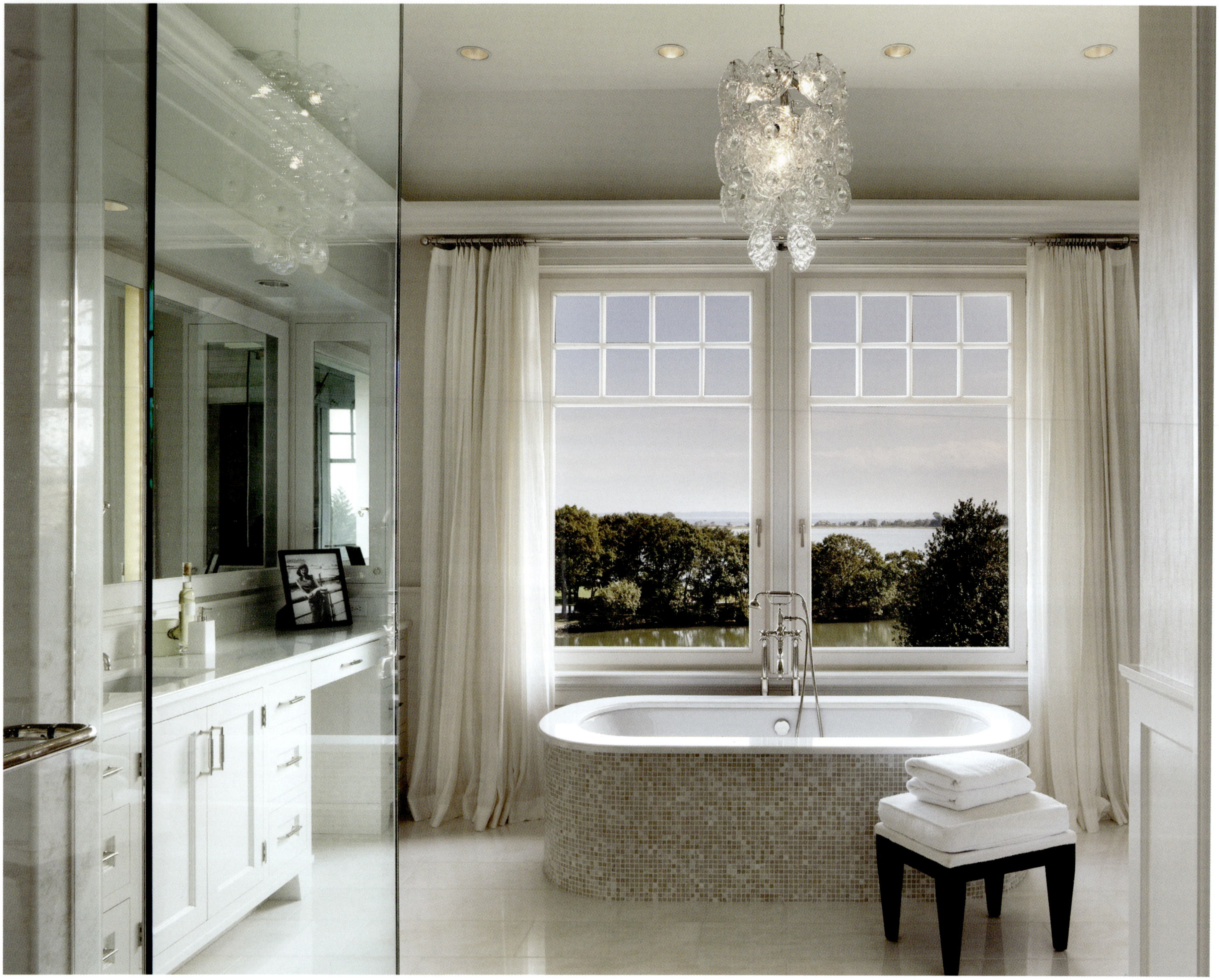

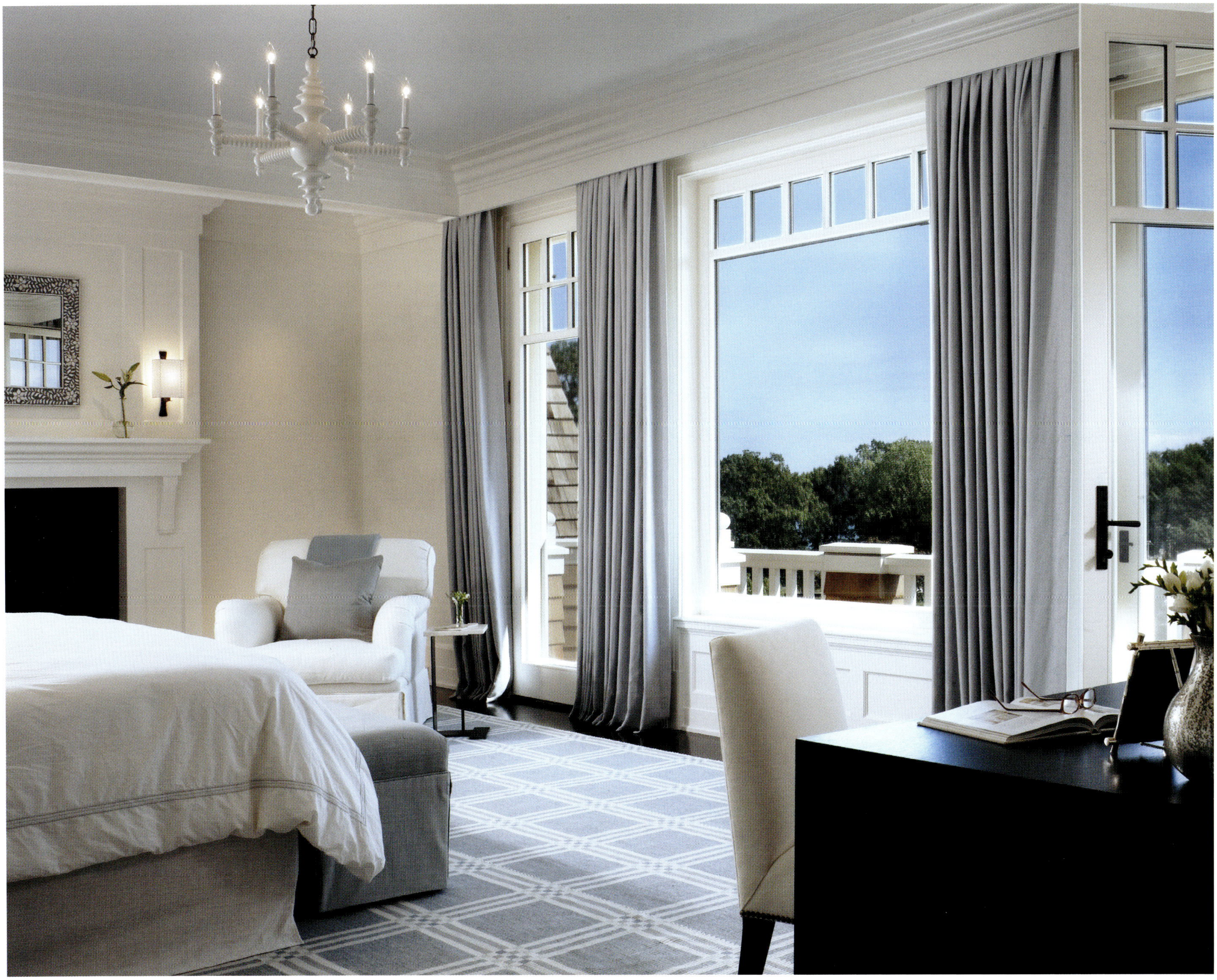

SITE PLAN

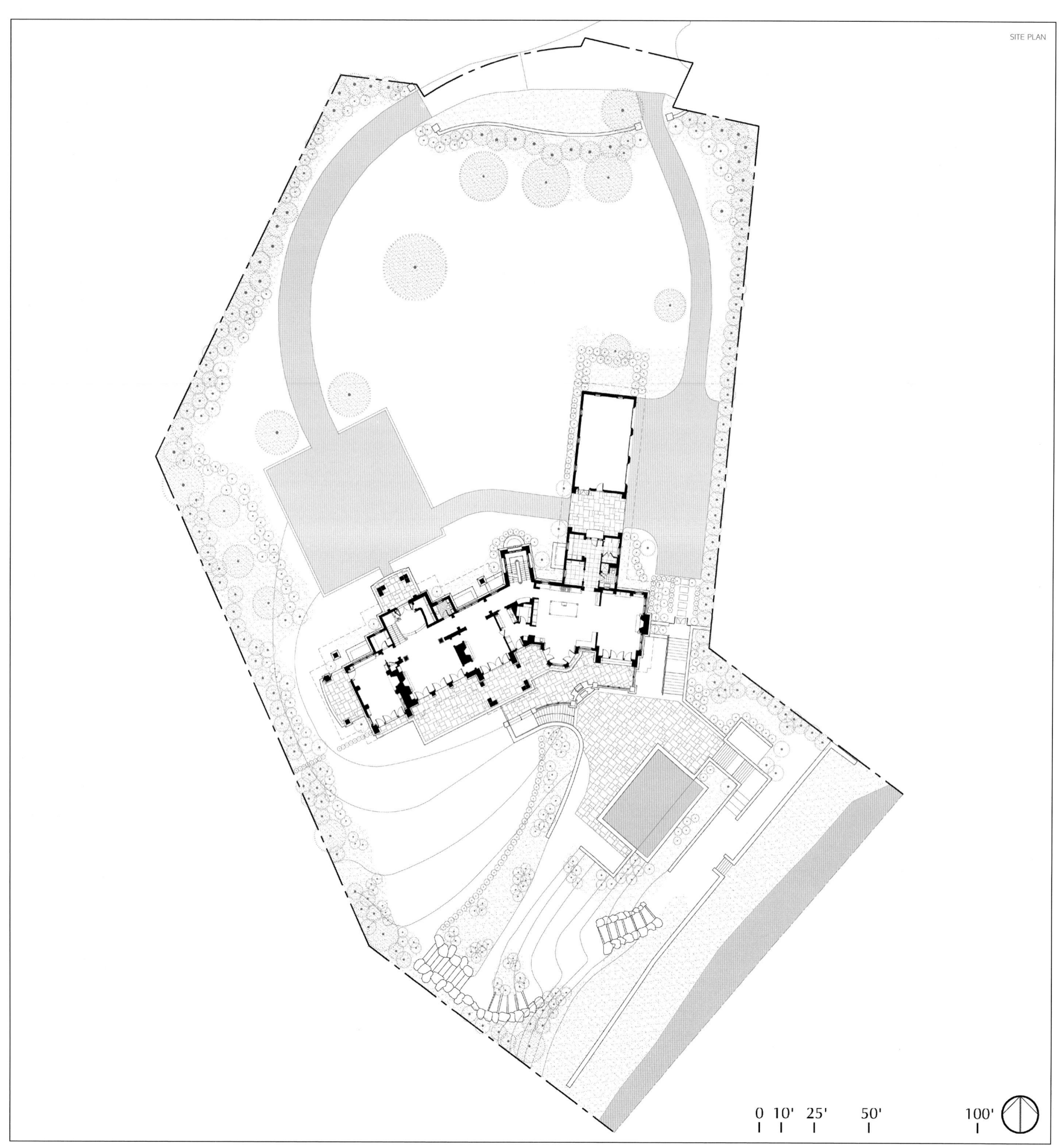

0 10' 25'   50'   100'

FIRST FLOOR

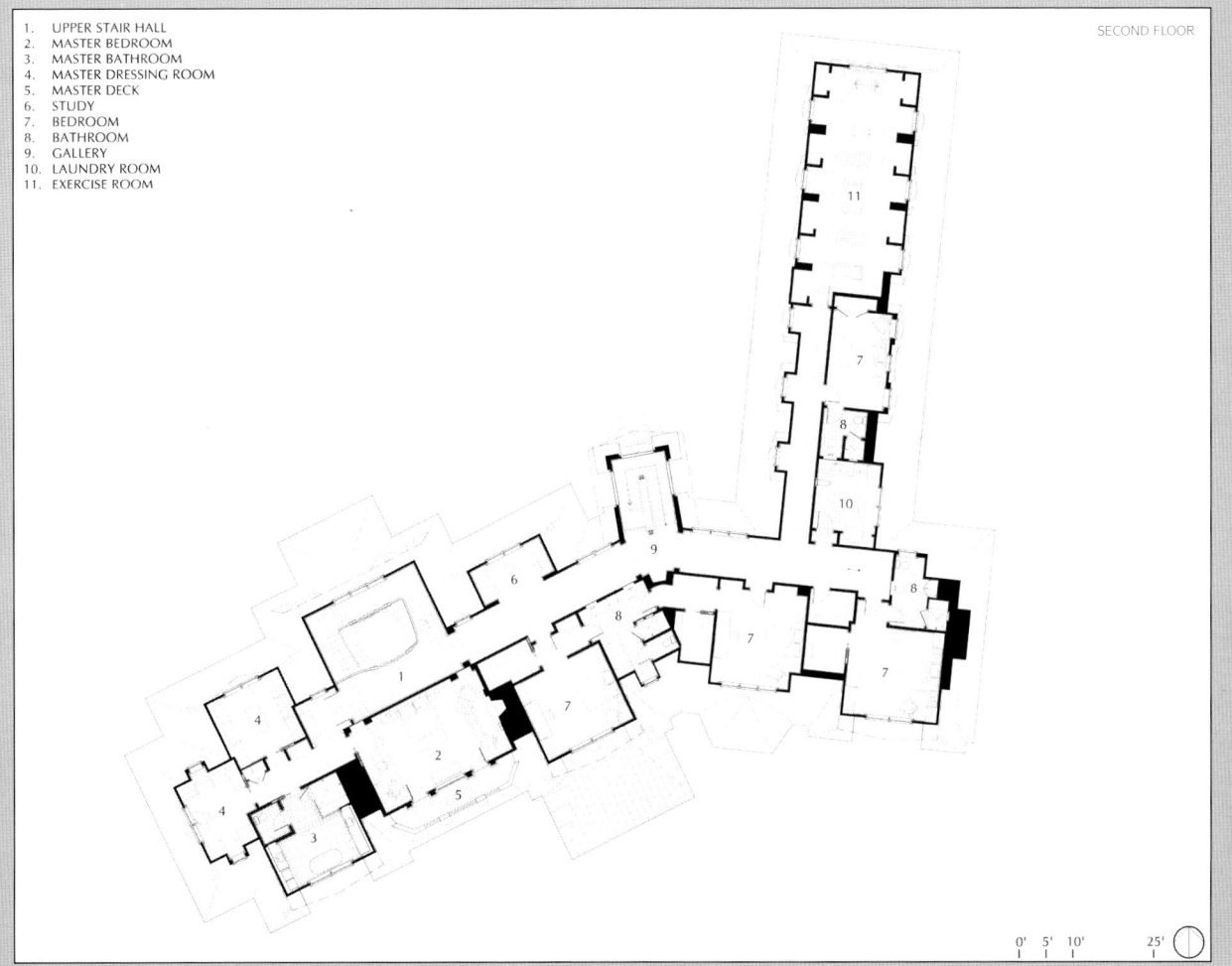

1. COVERED ENTRY
2. ENTRY STAIR HALL
3. LIVING ROOM
4. LIBRARY
5. PORCH
6. GALLERY
7. DINING ROOM
8. BUTLER'S PANTRY
9. KITCHEN
10. BREAKFAST NOOK
11. FAMILY ROOM
12. OFFICE
13. MUDROOM
14. POWDER ROOM
15. PORTE COCHERE
16. GARAGE
17. TERRACE
18. POOL TERRACE
19. ENTRY COURTYARD
20. GARAGE COURTYARD

SECOND FLOOR

1. UPPER STAIR HALL
2. MASTER BEDROOM
3. MASTER BATHROOM
4. MASTER DRESSING ROOM
5. MASTER DECK
6. STUDY
7. BEDROOM
8. BATHROOM
9. GALLERY
10. LAUNDRY ROOM
11. EXERCISE ROOM

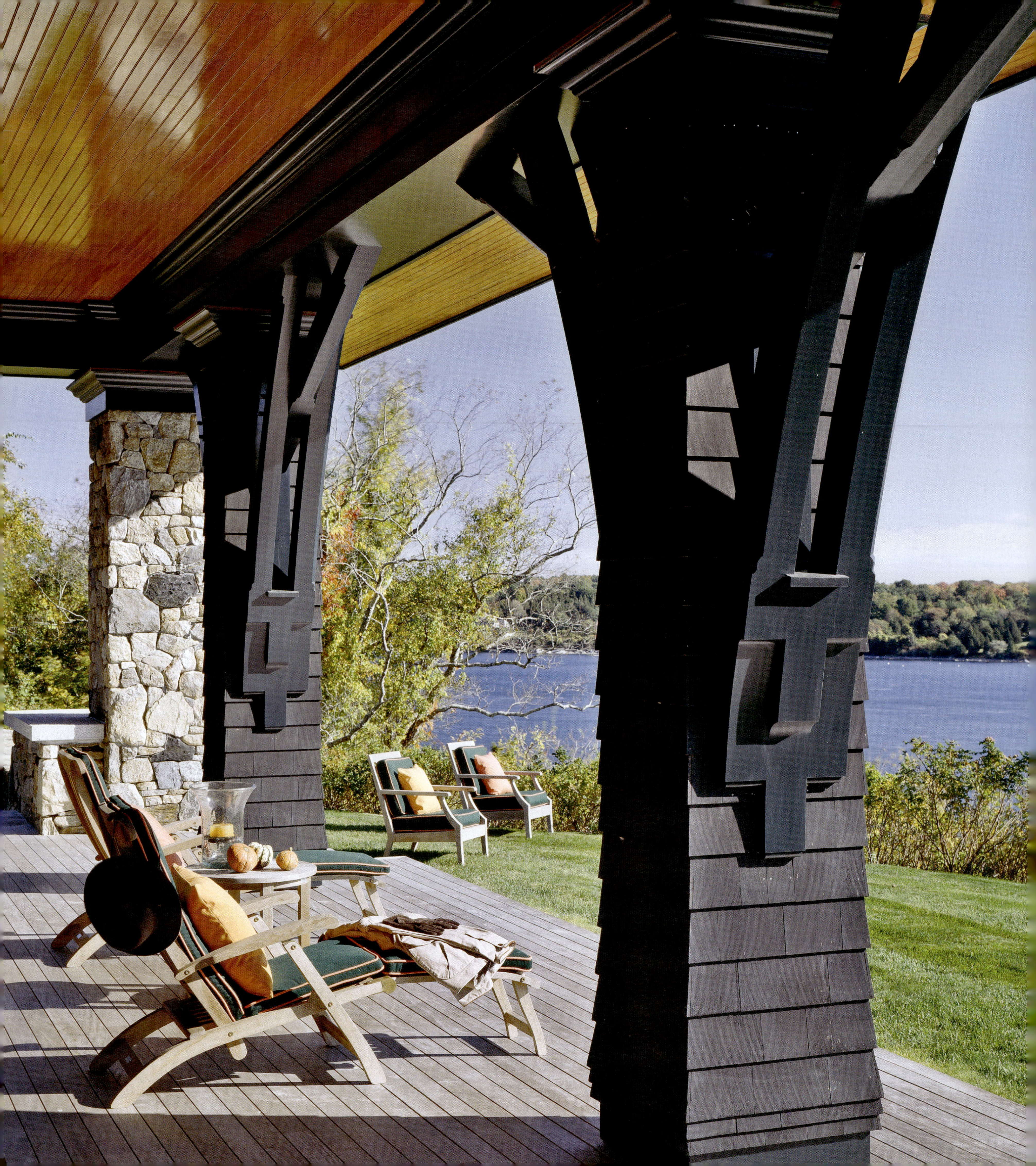

BLACK-PAINTED WOOD SHINGLES AND STEEPLY PITCHED ROOFS ARE AN ARCHITECT'S SIGNATURE

THE CLIENTS An architect with a long-established practice, and his wife, a photographer, decided to build a weekend house on an island in Narragansett Bay, where the architect's family has summered for almost 130 years.

THE DESIGN BRIEF Wharton has adapted and used the late-nineteenth-century Shingle Style and its Japanese influences for much of his 30-year career. Feeling humbled by the beauty and associations of the site, he wanted to use everything that he had learned to do justice to it.

THE SOLUTION Wharton drew nearly a dozen plans for a house for the eight-and-a-half-acre site before he came up with a seventeen-room, 3,900 square-foot residence that satisfied him. Contrary to any usage of color he had employed before, he painted the wooden shingles black, so that the house, when viewed from the water, would recede into the surrounding cedars. From the land, the color and the positioning of the house perpendicular to the coastline deflect the eye toward the water. Steeply pitched overscale roofs are one of the architect's trademarks. Here, they have what he calls "a gentle kick at the end, where the Japanese influence really comes through to give the house a sense of lightness." The large overhangs of the roofs provide space for a porch on the seaward end of the house. Brackets reminiscent of tree branches seem to grow out of shingle support posts, lightening the weight of the roof over the porch. In this environmentally sensitive structure, the overhangs provide shade and cooling in the summer and the dark exterior color absorbs the sun's heat in the winter. An underground irrigation system is another one of a number of ecological aspects to the property. Inside, an entrance gallery and the great room, which looks out to the sea through large-paned windows, form an enfilade. The great room, which is defined by a dining area at one end, and a massive granite fireplace at the other, is further delineated by the timber framework made from reclaimed timbers that have been shaped to the architect's design. The design contains curved "ships knees," which were originally made from tree roots to support the deck beams of wooden sailing ships. These come from the same bogs in Maine that were the source for the knees of the *U.S.S. Constitution*. The rooms are furnished with a comfortable mix of family antiques, contemporary pieces, and artworks. Adirondack chairs that belonged to the client's great-great grandmother allude to what is called the Adirondack heritage of the porch's branching support brackets. A set of photographs by Ansel Adams, known for his great images of the American West, and a pair of silkscreen print portraits of Mao Zedong by Andy Warhol, the iconic Pop Art artist, hang in the house. Through the large windows of the master bedroom, "you can see the sailing activity on the bay," says the architect. This house expresses his avocation of sailing, and celebrates his heritage.

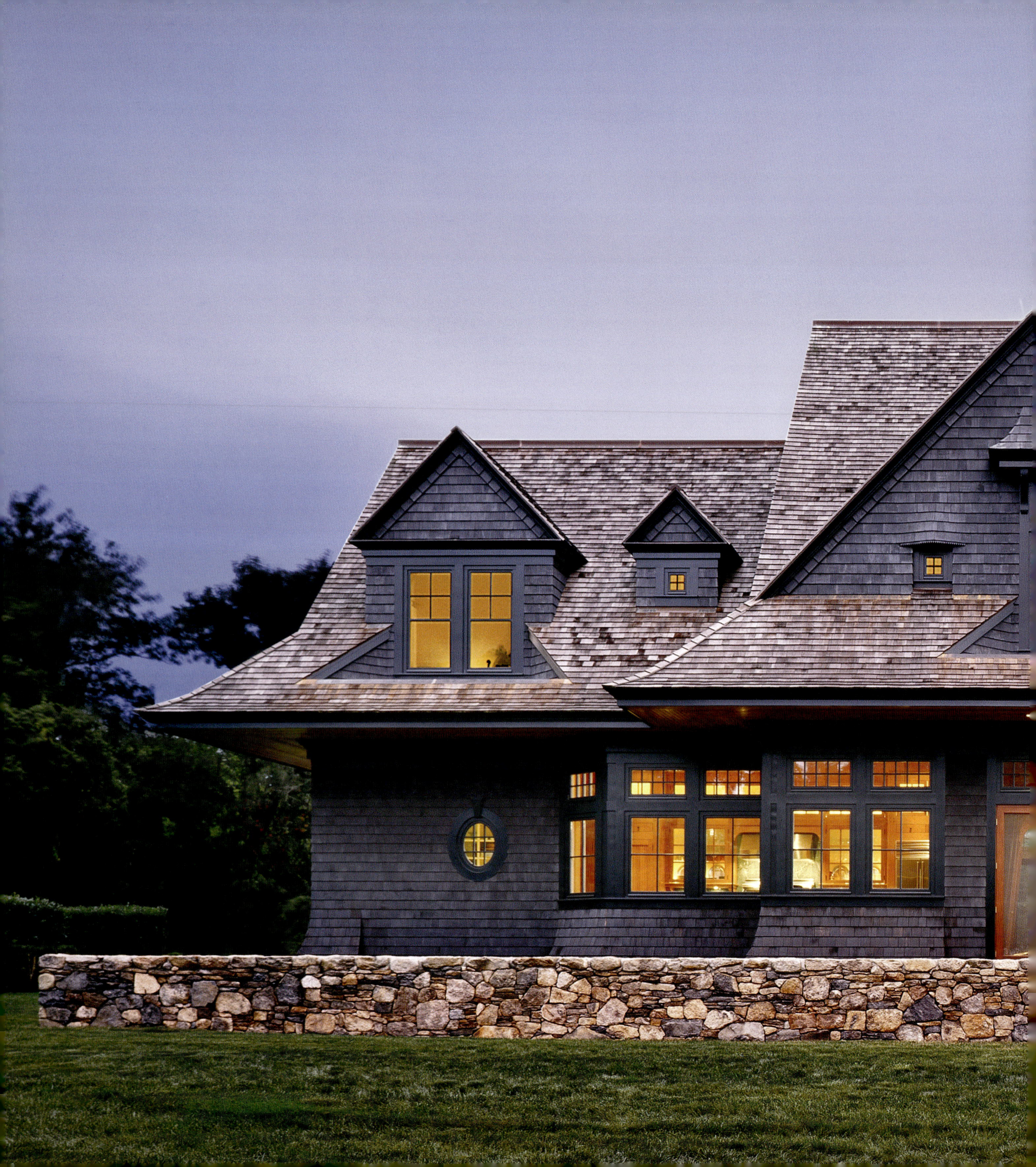

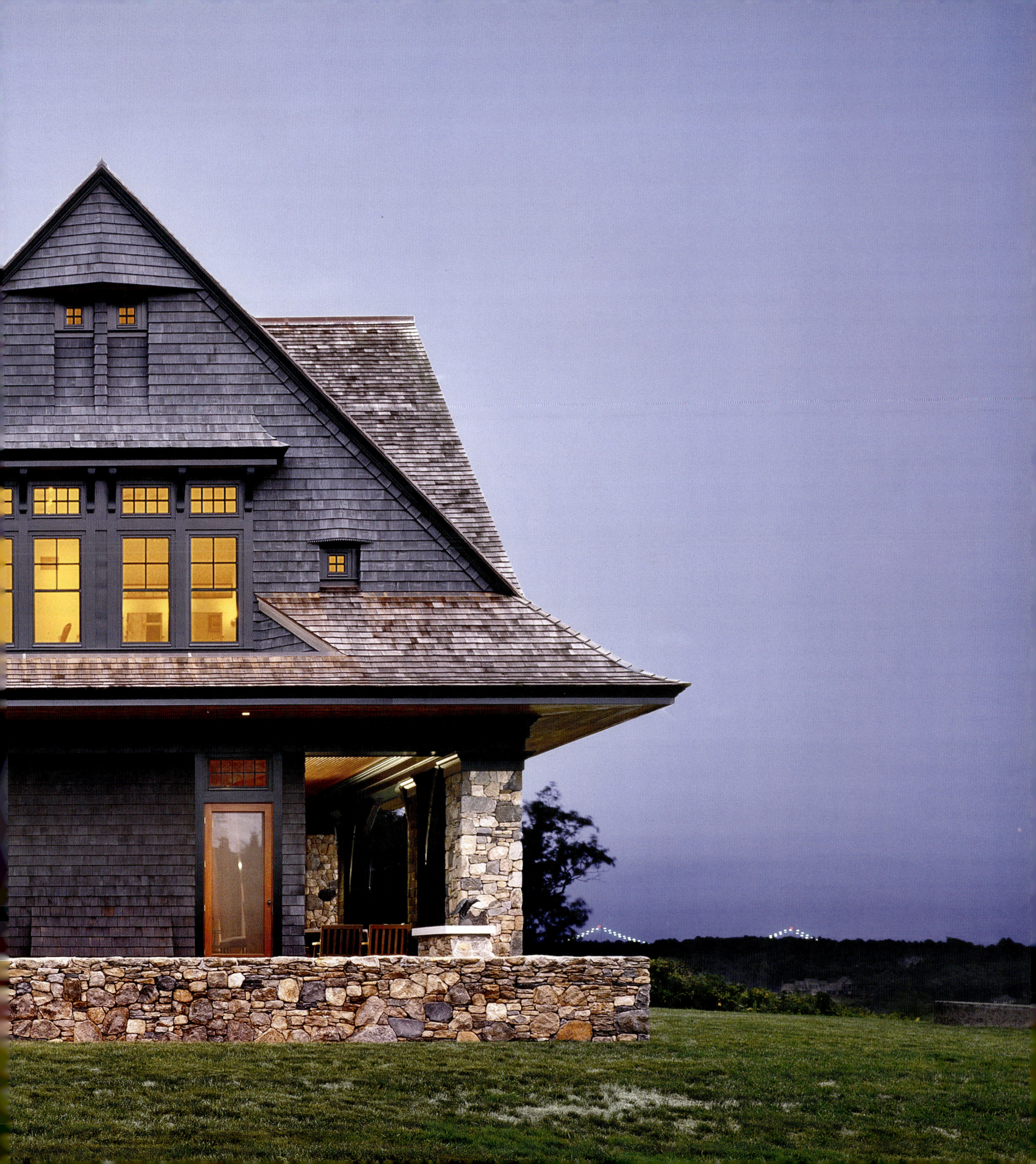

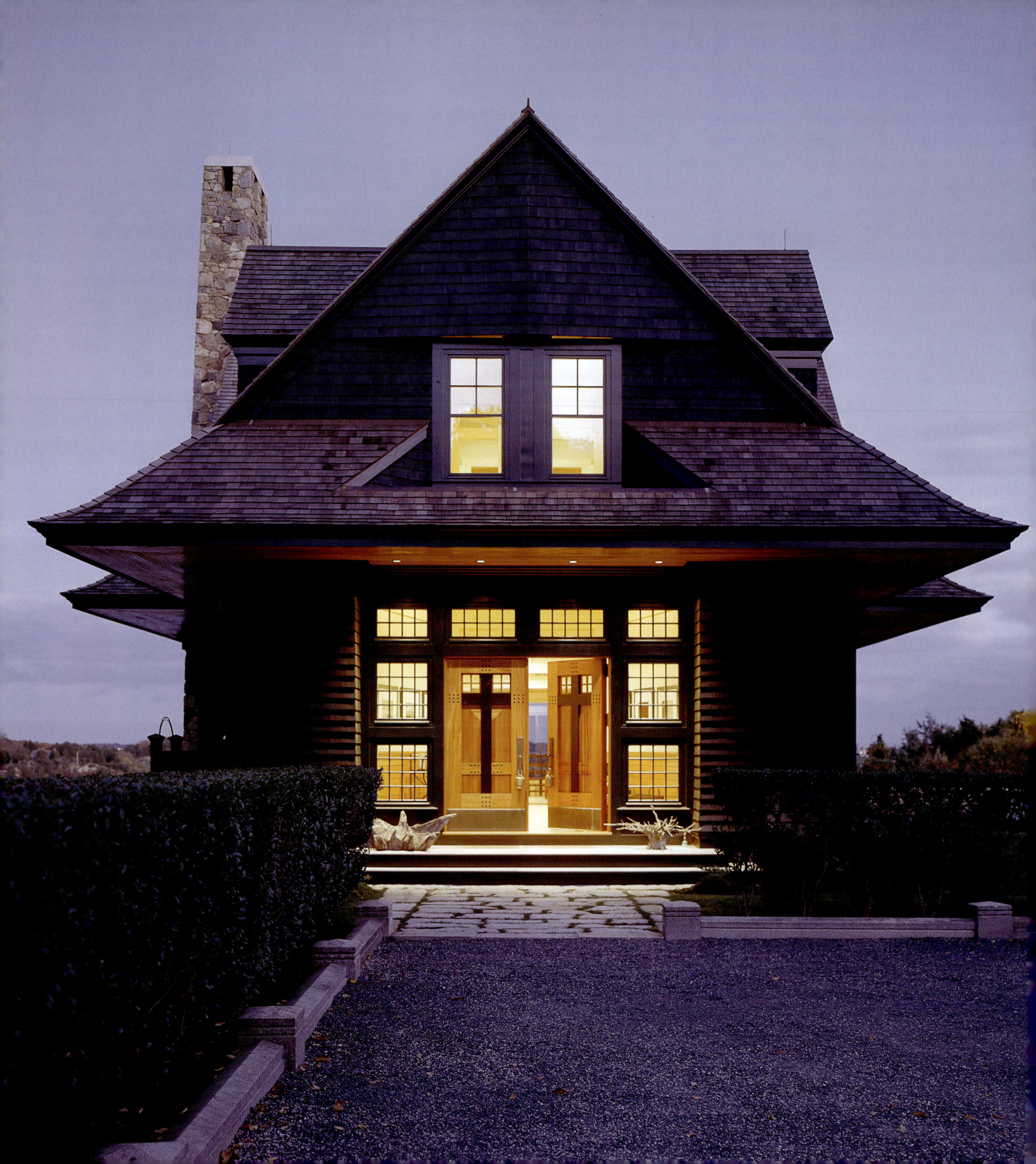

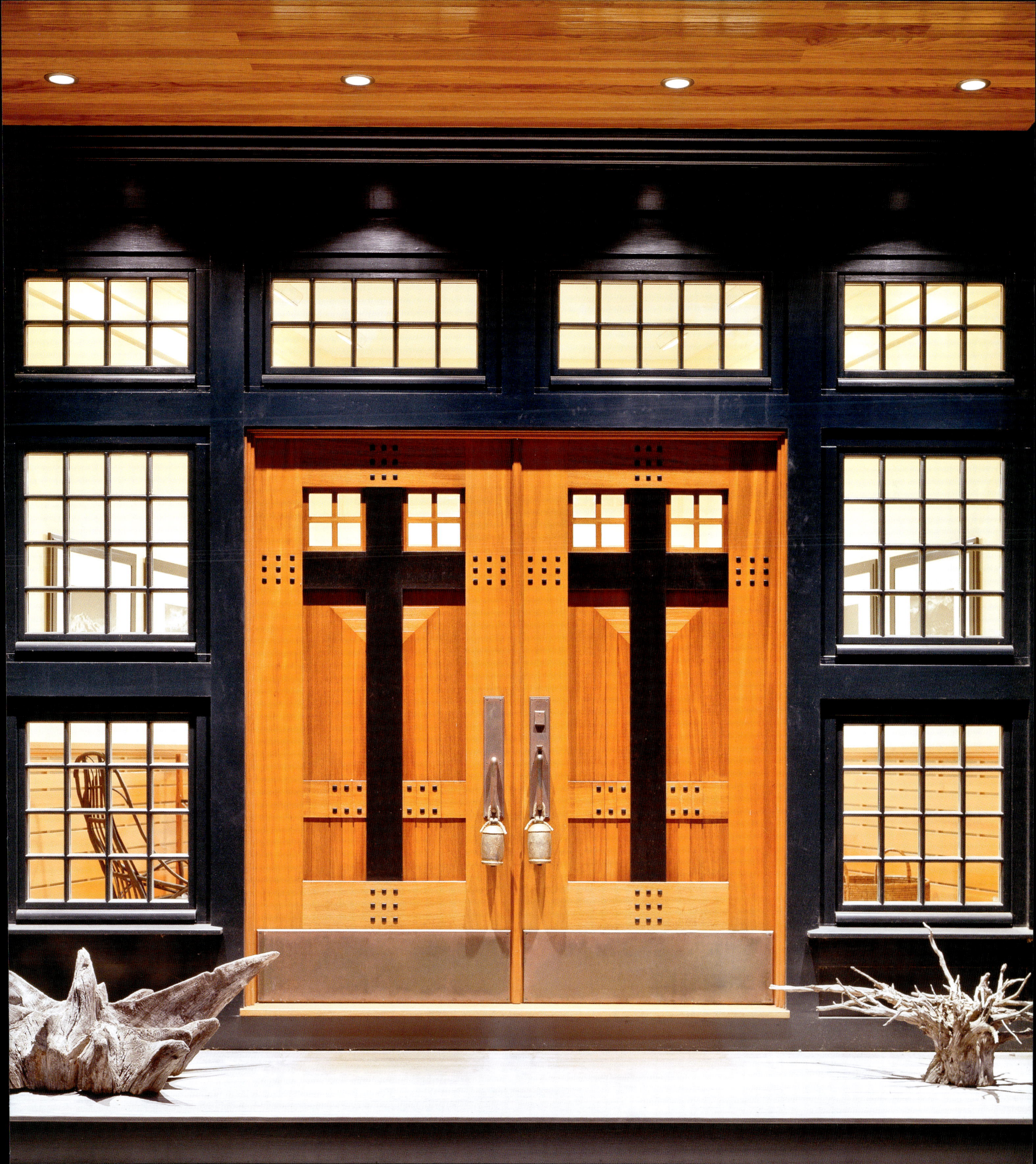

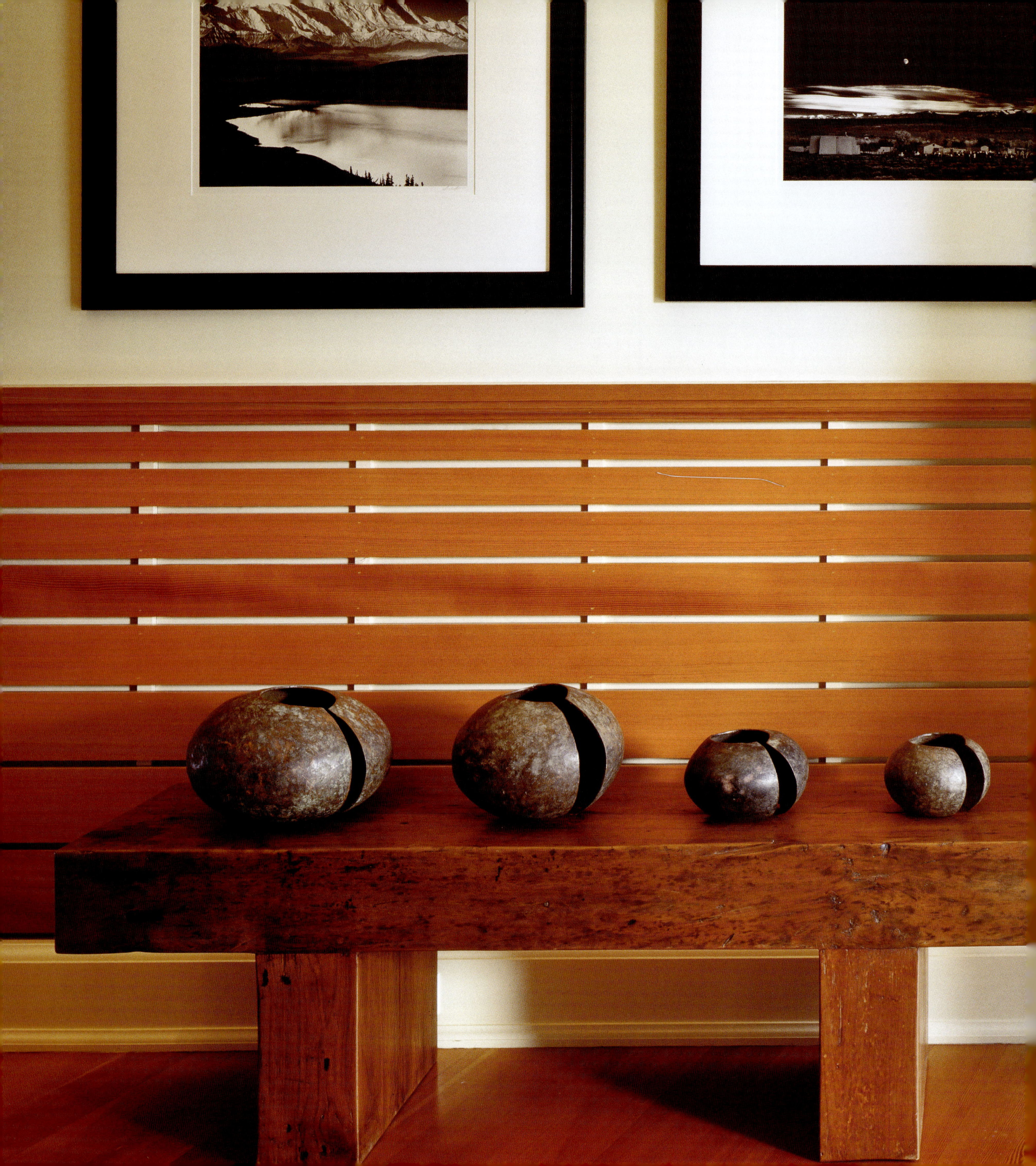

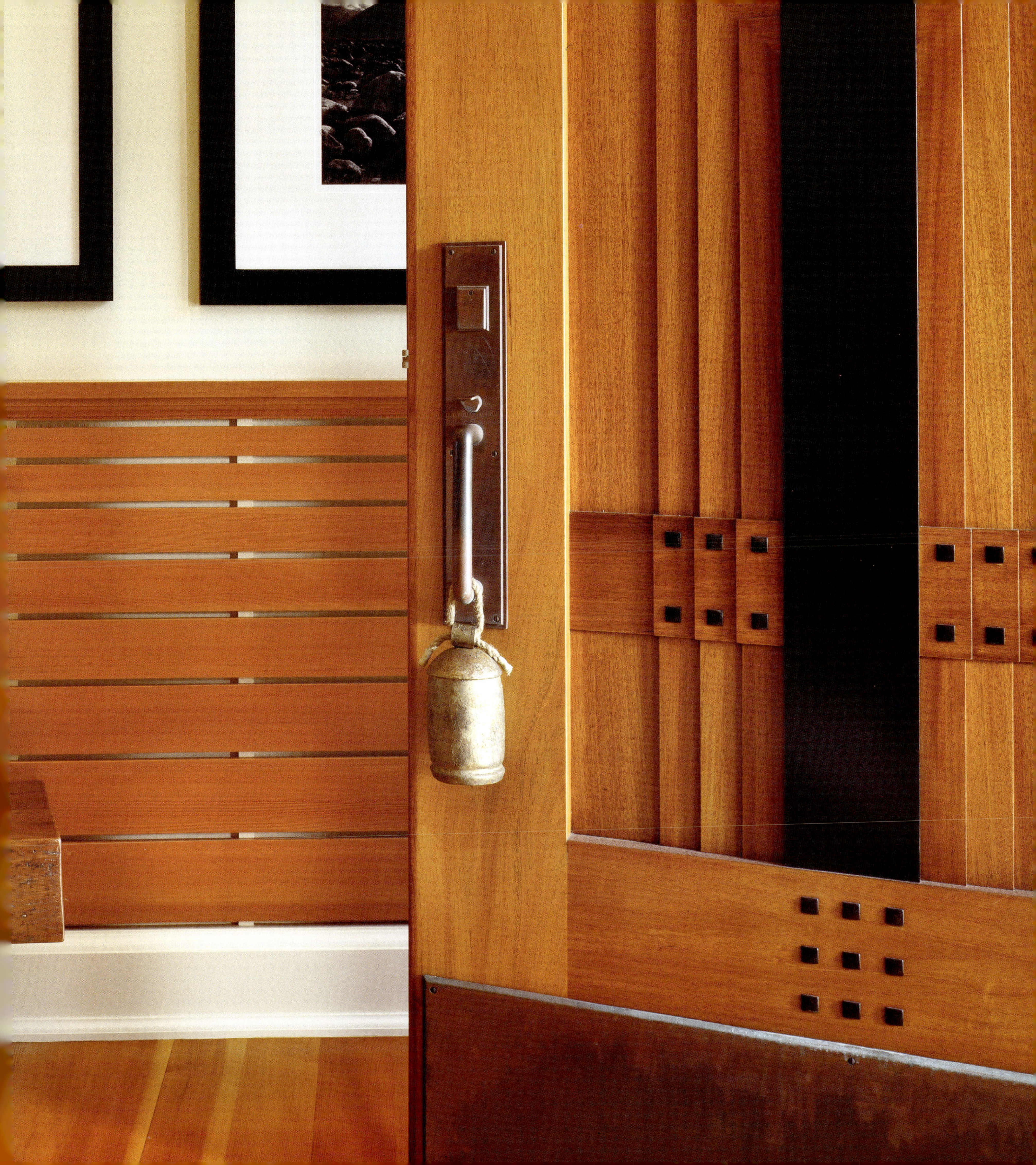

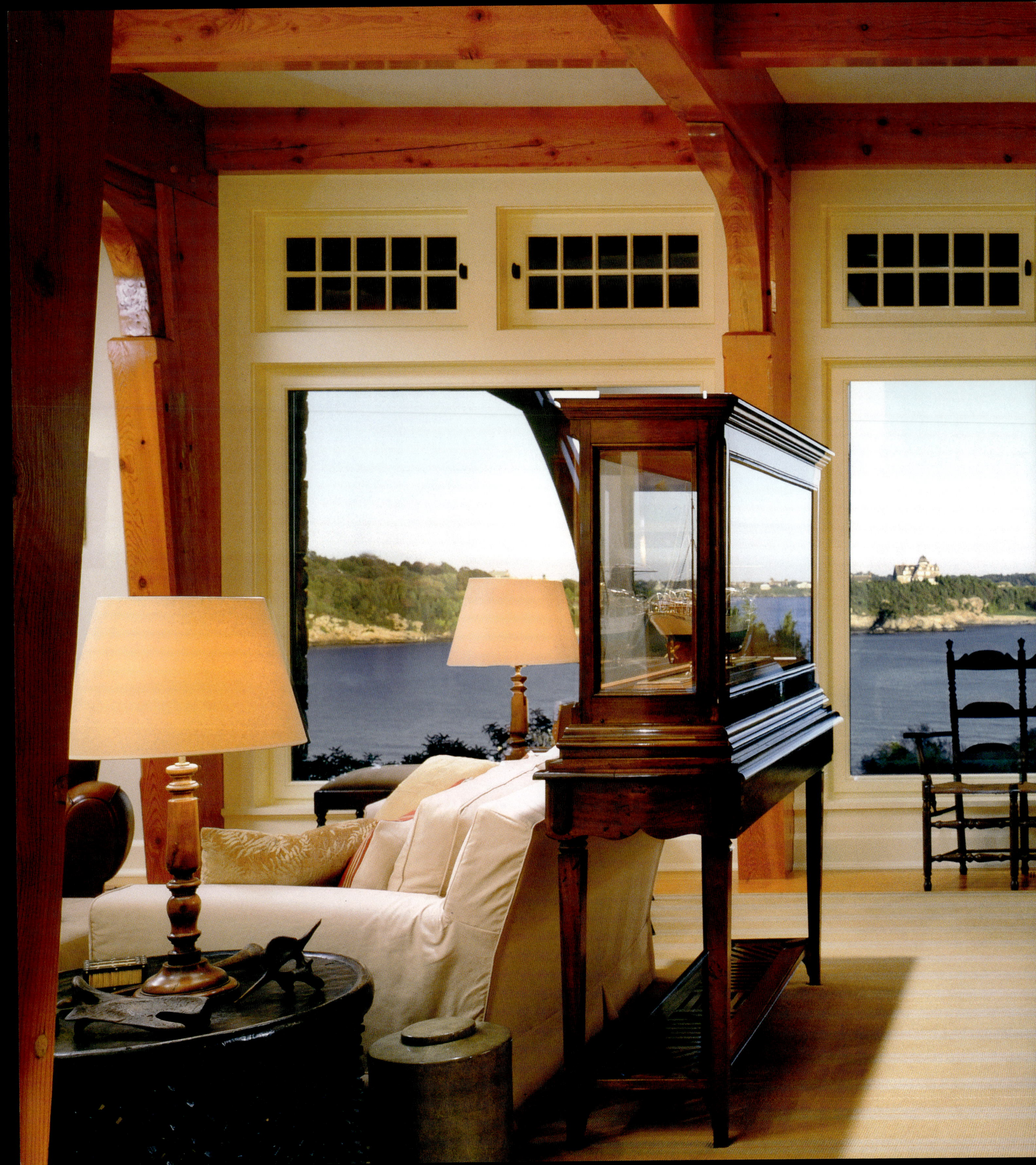

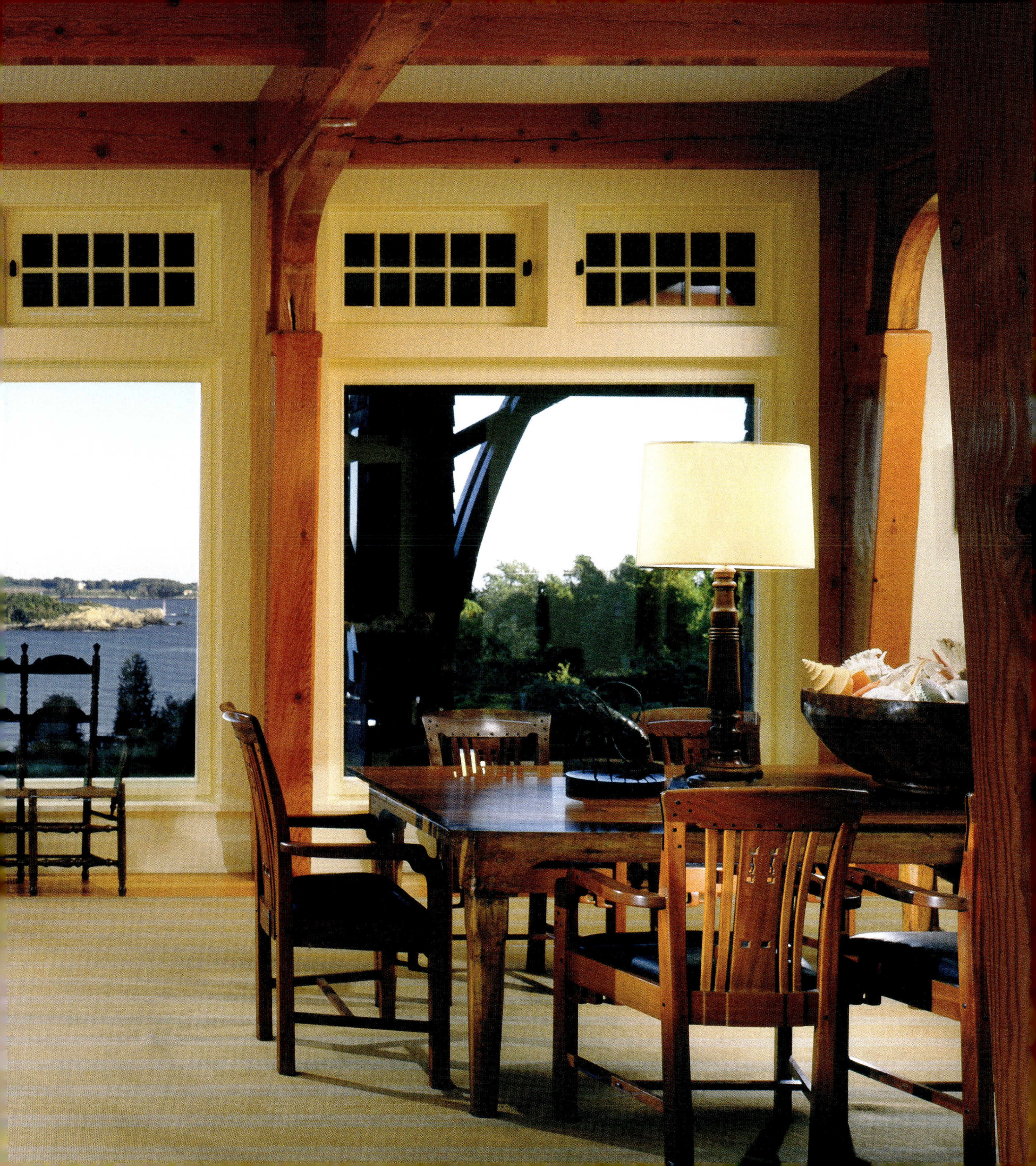

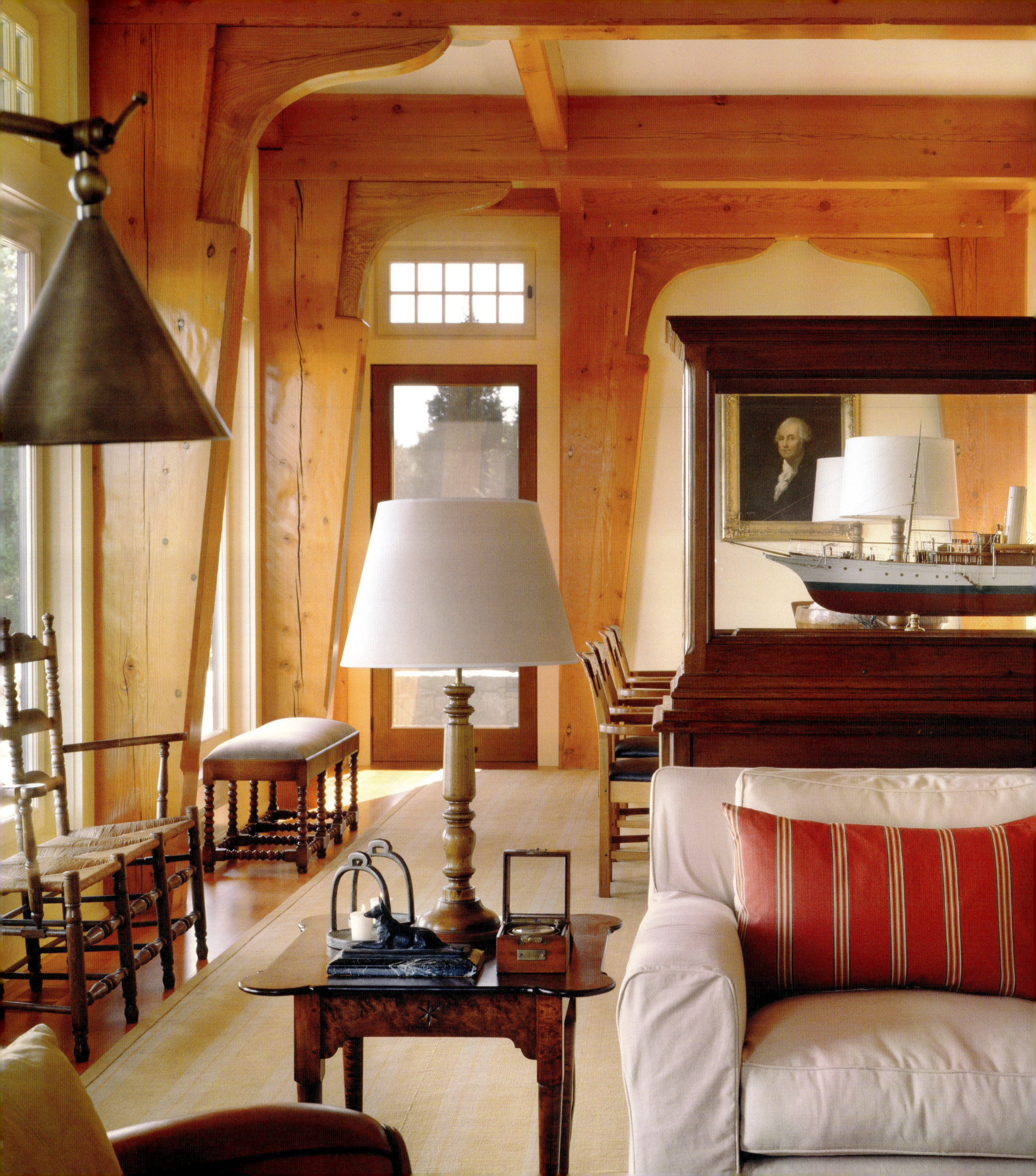

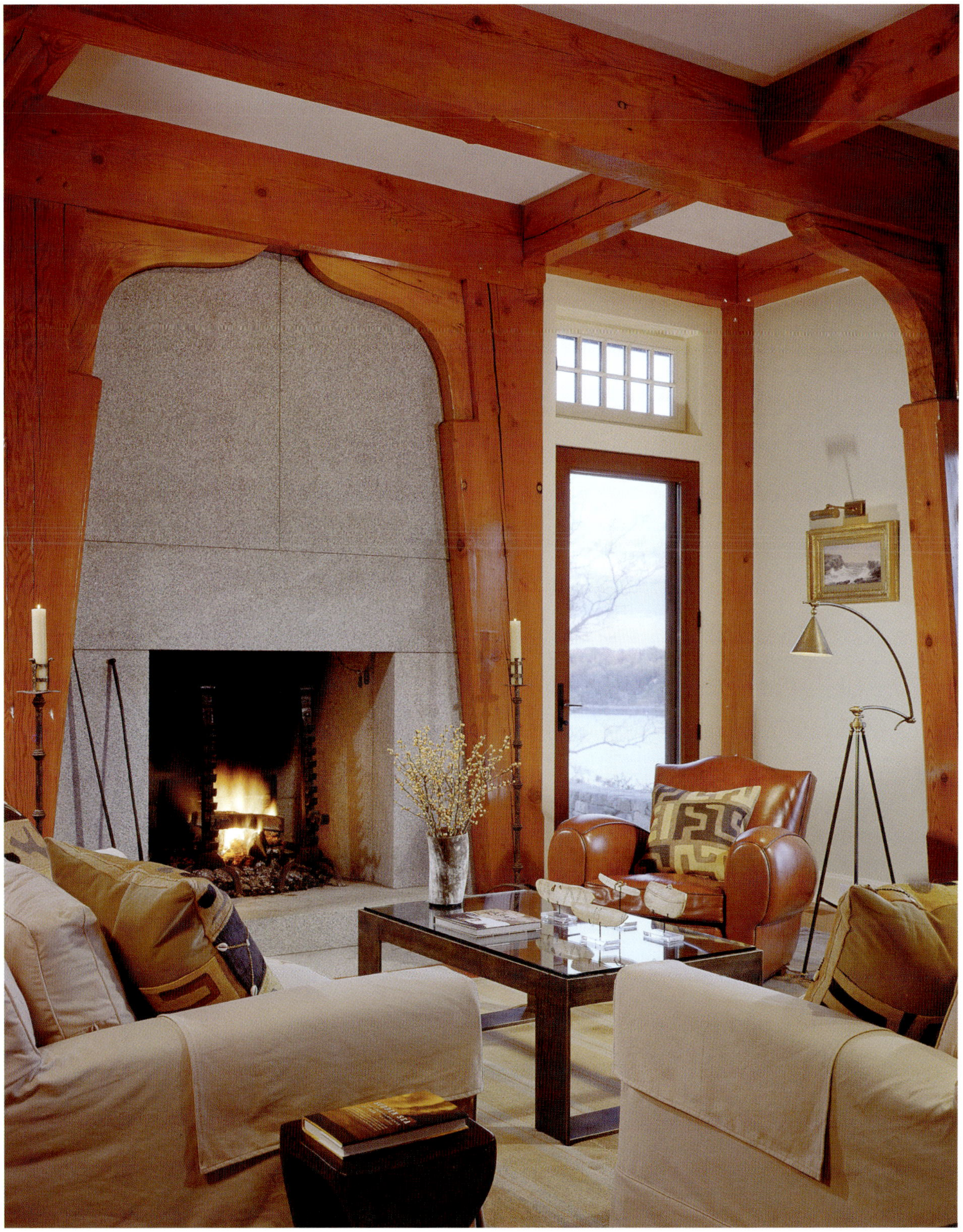

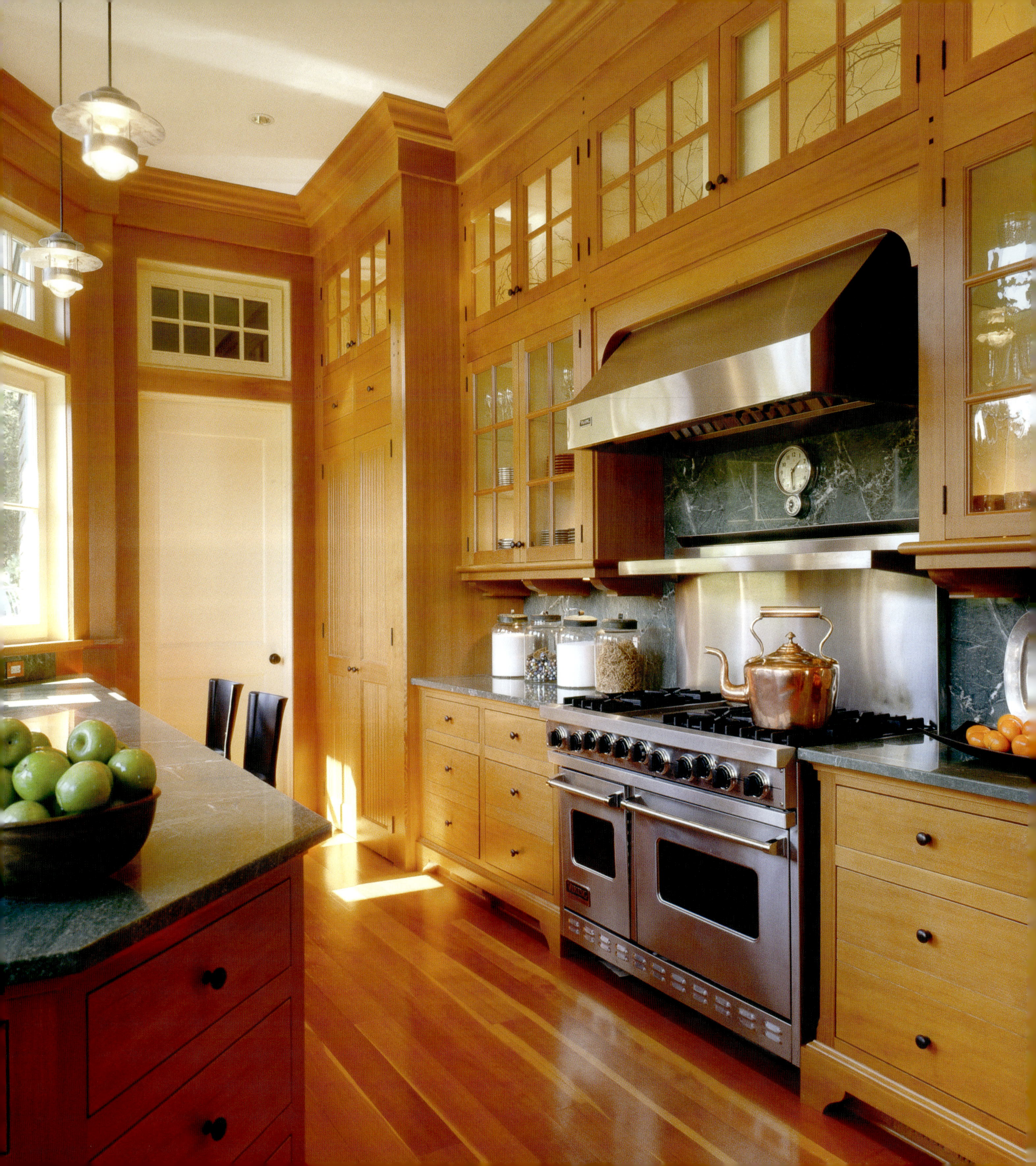

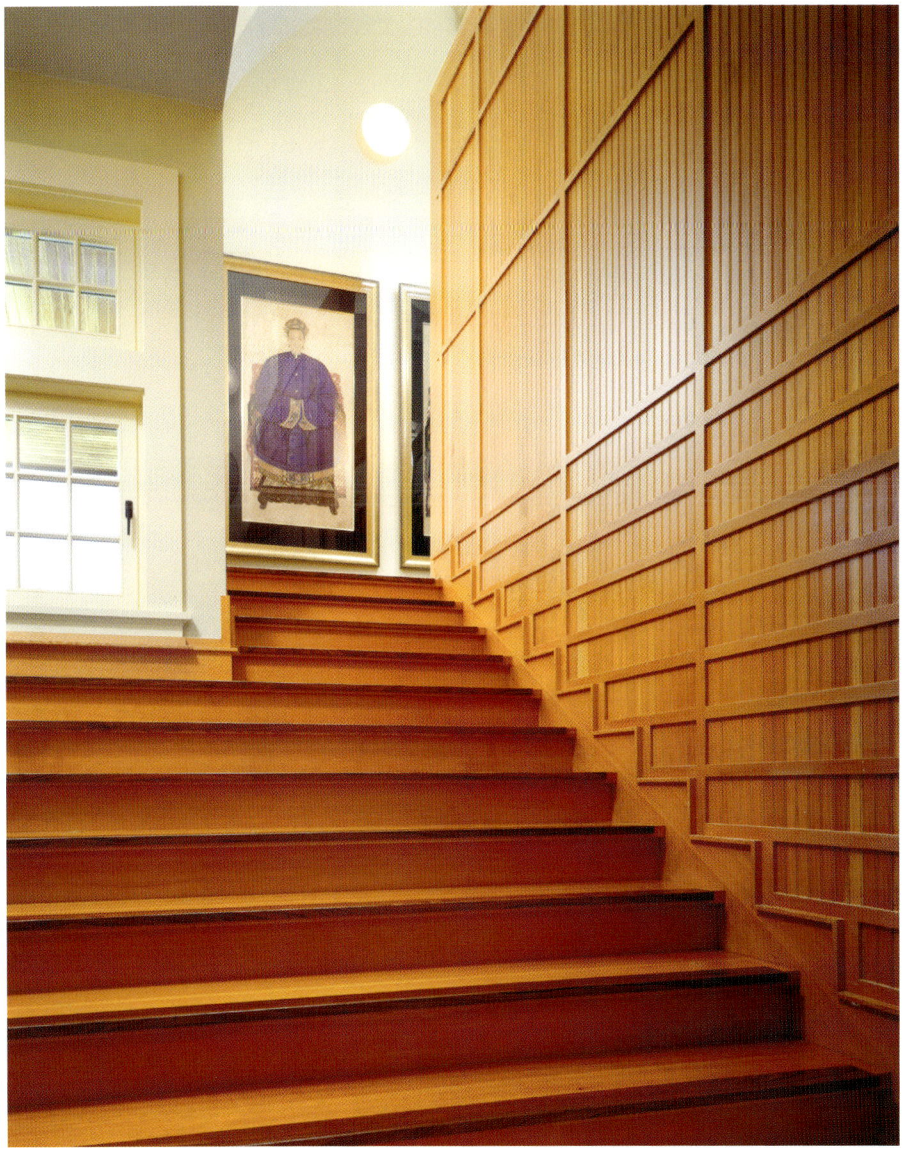
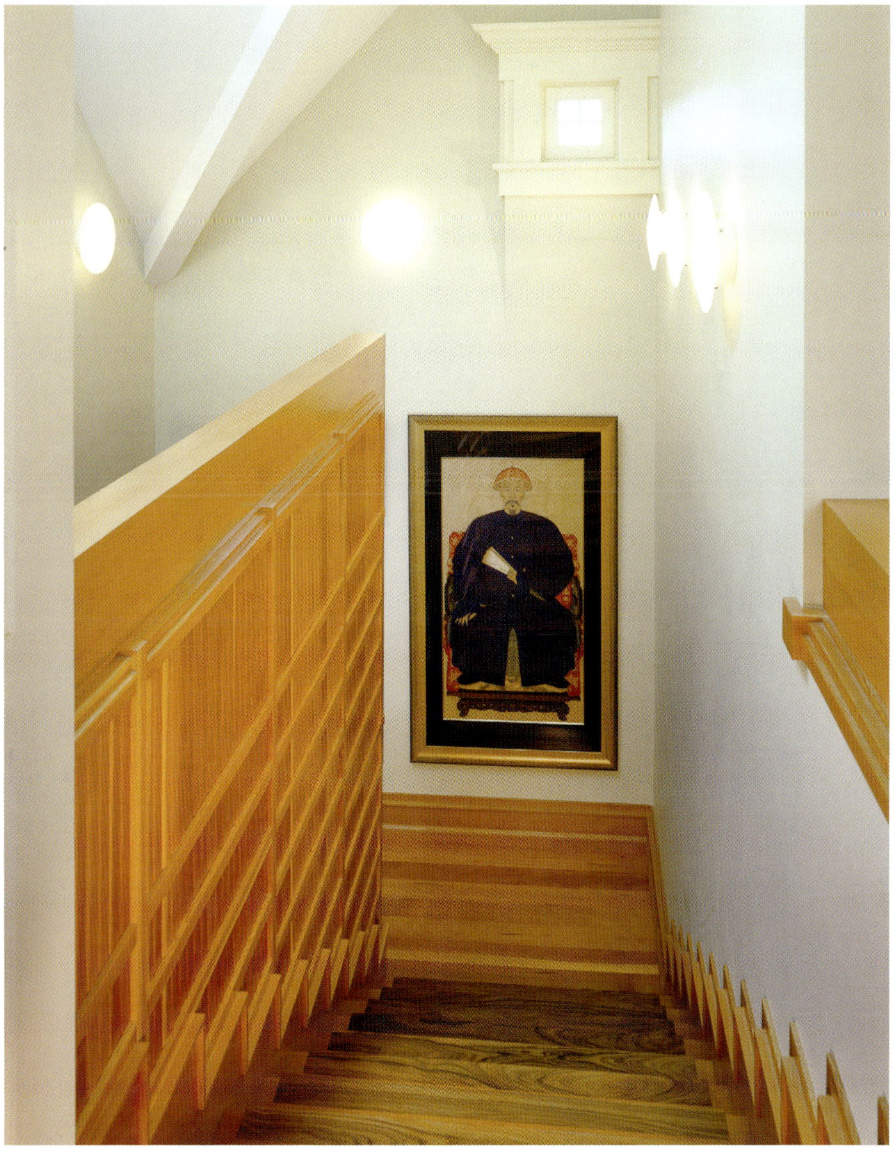

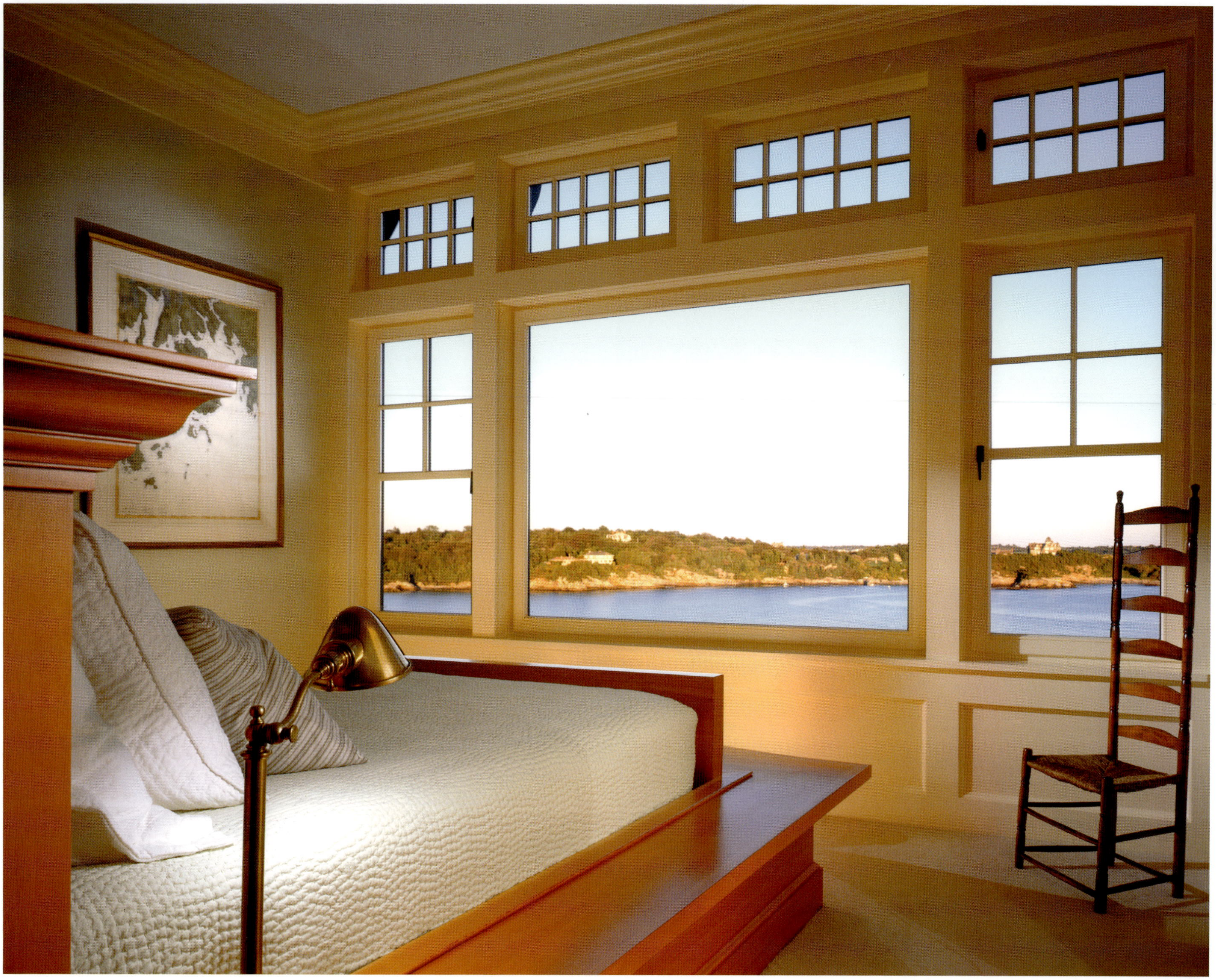

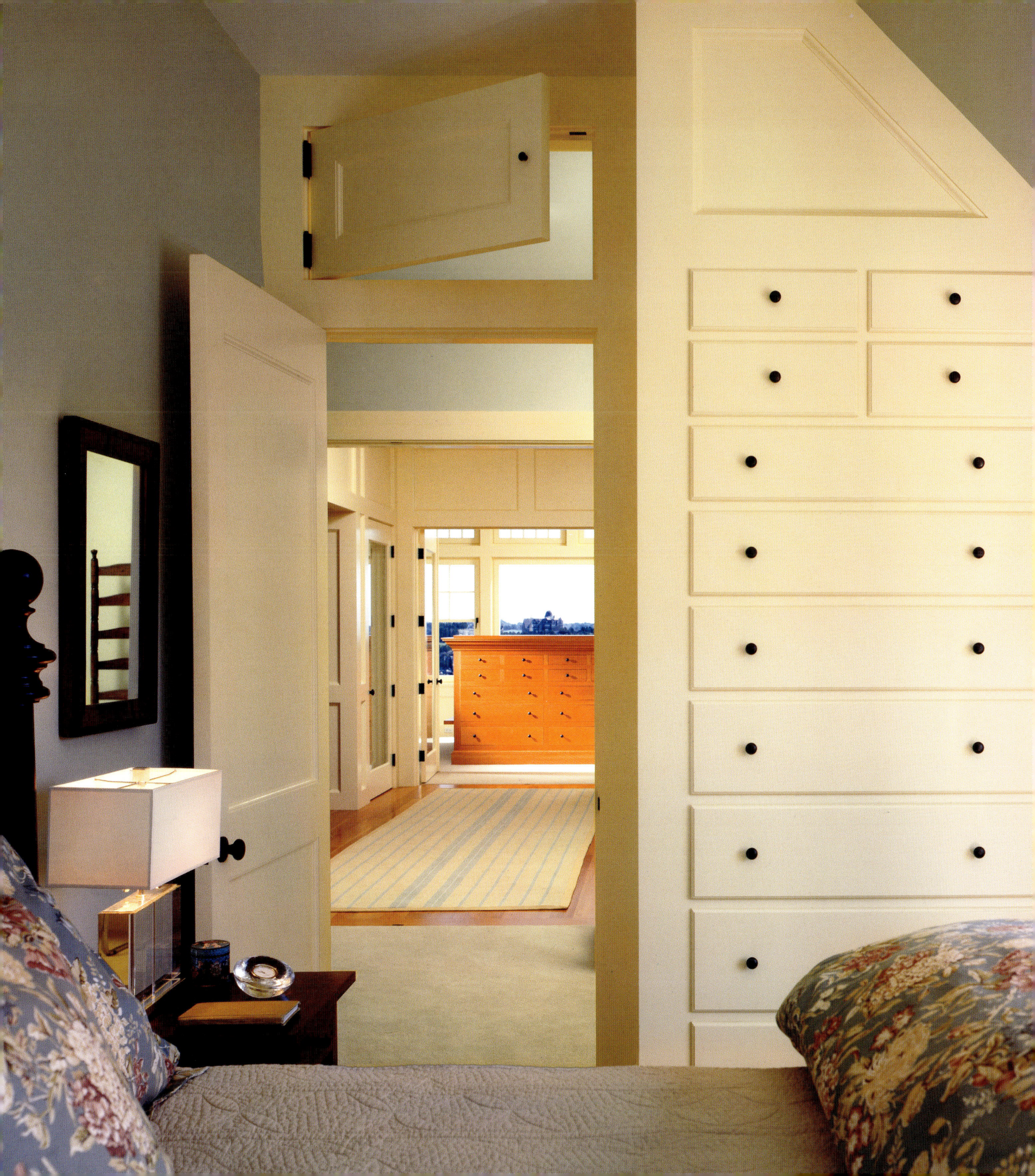

SITE PLAN

0 10' 25' 50' 100'

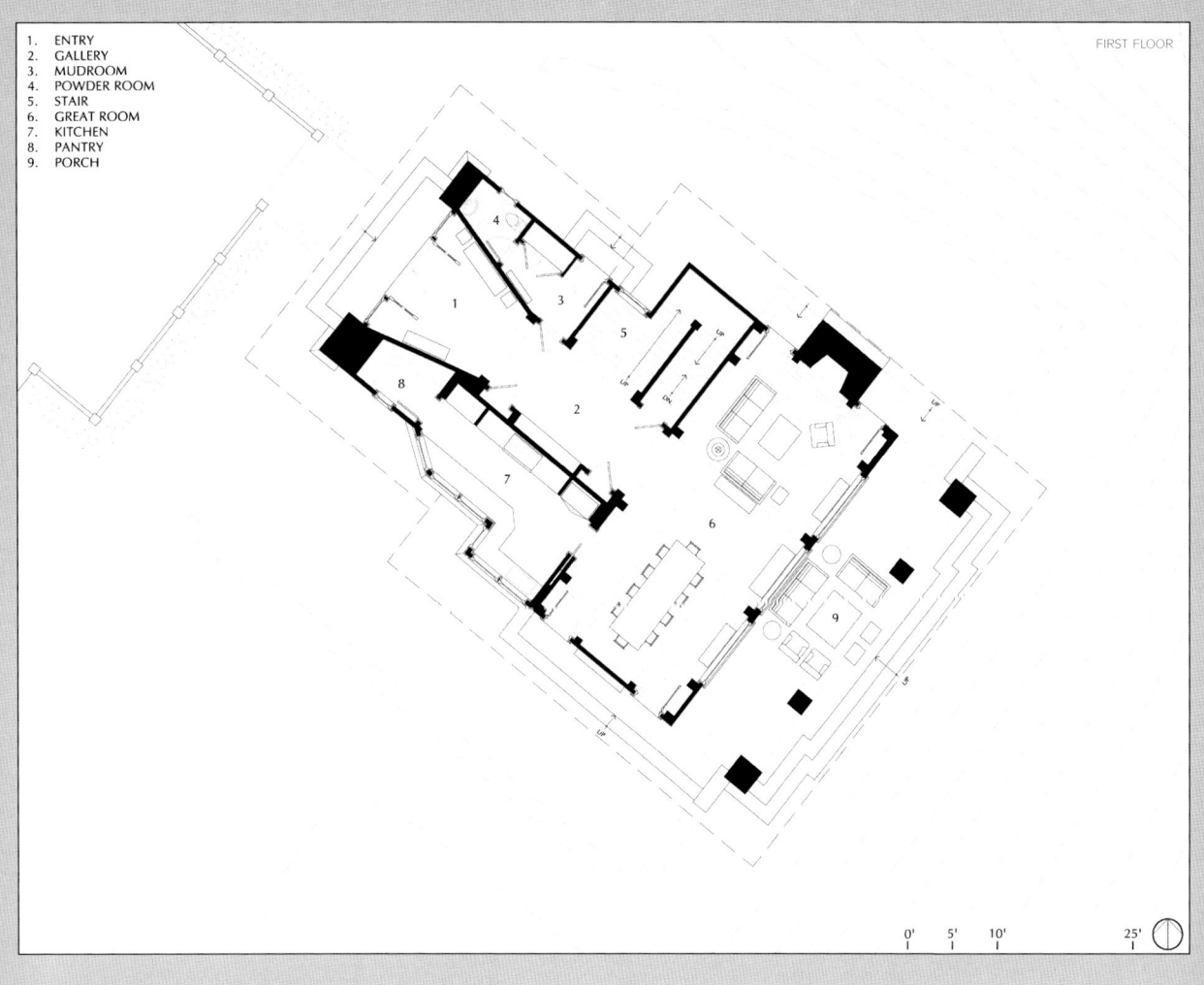

1. ENTRY
2. GALLERY
3. MUDROOM
4. POWDER ROOM
5. STAIR
6. GREAT ROOM
7. KITCHEN
8. PANTRY
9. PORCH

FIRST FLOOR

1. UPPER HALL
2. MASTER BEDROOM
3. MASTER DRESSING ROOM
4. MASTER BATHROOM
5. SITTING ROOM
6. SLEEPING NICHES
7. BEDROOM
8. BATHROOM

SECOND FLOOR

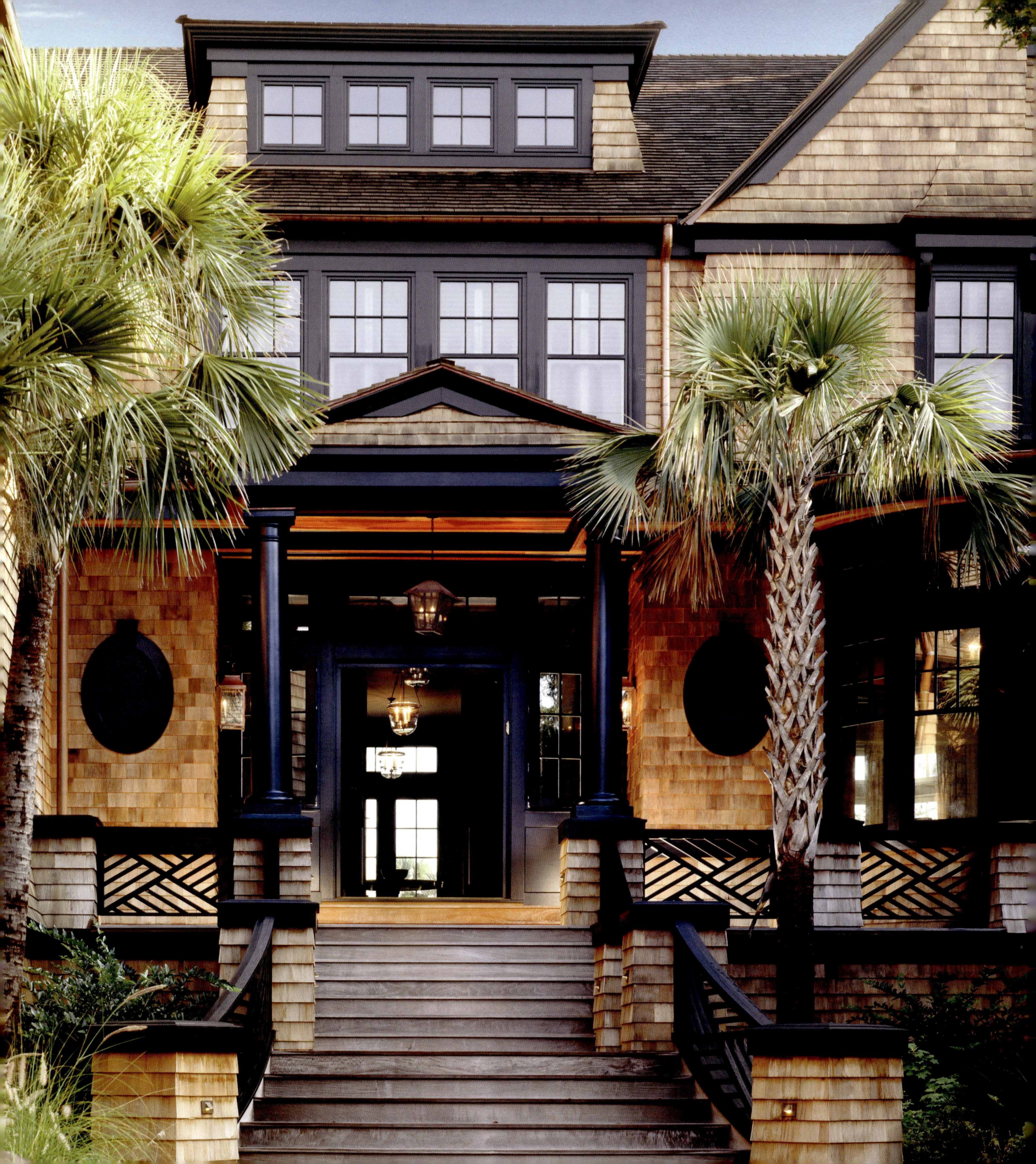

A VARIETY OF PORCHES AND TERRACES ALLOW A HOUSE TO RESPOND TO ITS LOWCOUNTRY LOCALE

THE CLIENTS An American businessman and his wife who spend most of the year in London, England, learned of the work of Shope Reno Wharton after visiting a residence and a private club the architecture firm had built on Kiawah Island in South Carolina. The clients wanted their own house on Kiawah to be a place to entertain guests as well as a retreat for their adult children. The architects also knew that the clients "wanted their house to take full advantage of the semi-tropical site, but not to tread on it in a hard way."

THE DESIGN BRIEF The site was full of challenges and opportunities. It is set upon a tidal marshland at the confluence of three rivers—a beautiful peninsula with fingers of land reaching out from the South Carolina Low Country. The land expands and contracts with the ebb and flow of the tide. Palms and live oaks rise from the land and punctuate the panoramic views. The clients wanted their home to resonate with the style of the Low Country, without it being a literal interpretation of the local plantation style with its broad porches and low roofs. The architects believed that the rambling shapes of Shingle Style architecture were very sympathetic to the Low Country. The flood zone regulations on the island dictated that the house be raised at least fourteen feet above the ground. This house needed to take into account, aside from the immediate physical beauty of the surrounding land, the ever-present dramatic views.

THE SOLUTION Because of its tidal marsh siting, the house had to be raised fourteen feet above the ground. From a distance, the 15,300 square-foot, 42-room house seems to be a clustered collection of buildings, almost like a village. The house has many wings—their position dictated by natural light, use requirements, and views. One unique feature is that the house has both a Sunrise Porch and a Sunset Porch, the former looking over the salt marshes, and the latter, which has a fireplace, looking over the river. The Washington, D.C.-based firm Oehme, van Sweden & Associates, Inc., worked with the natural flora of the 12-acre property so that the house would feel as if it were built around the existing landscape. Atlanta interior designer Jacquelynne Lanham combined eighteenth-century Georgian English furniture, bought on trips to London, with a pale palette of sea-glass and grassy olive green, gray, lavender, and various shades of blue, which are the natural colors of the island. Regarding the evocation of the Low Country in this house, Wharton says: "Good architecture is all about respect—placing the traditions and conditions and all the intangibles of the site above sheer creative impulse."

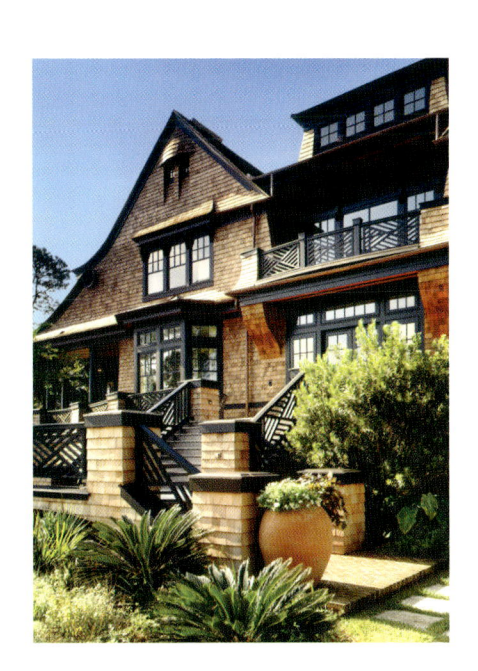

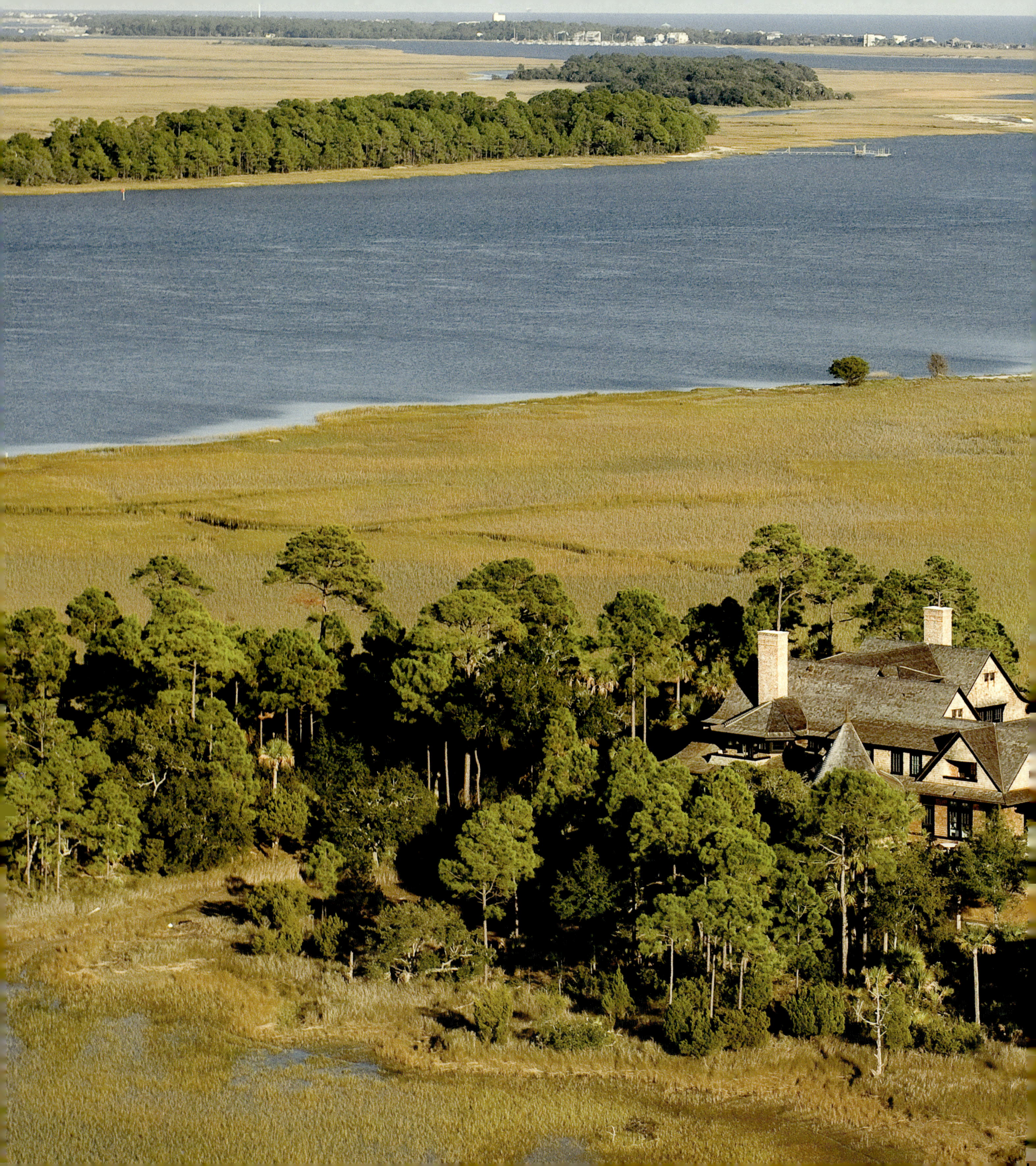

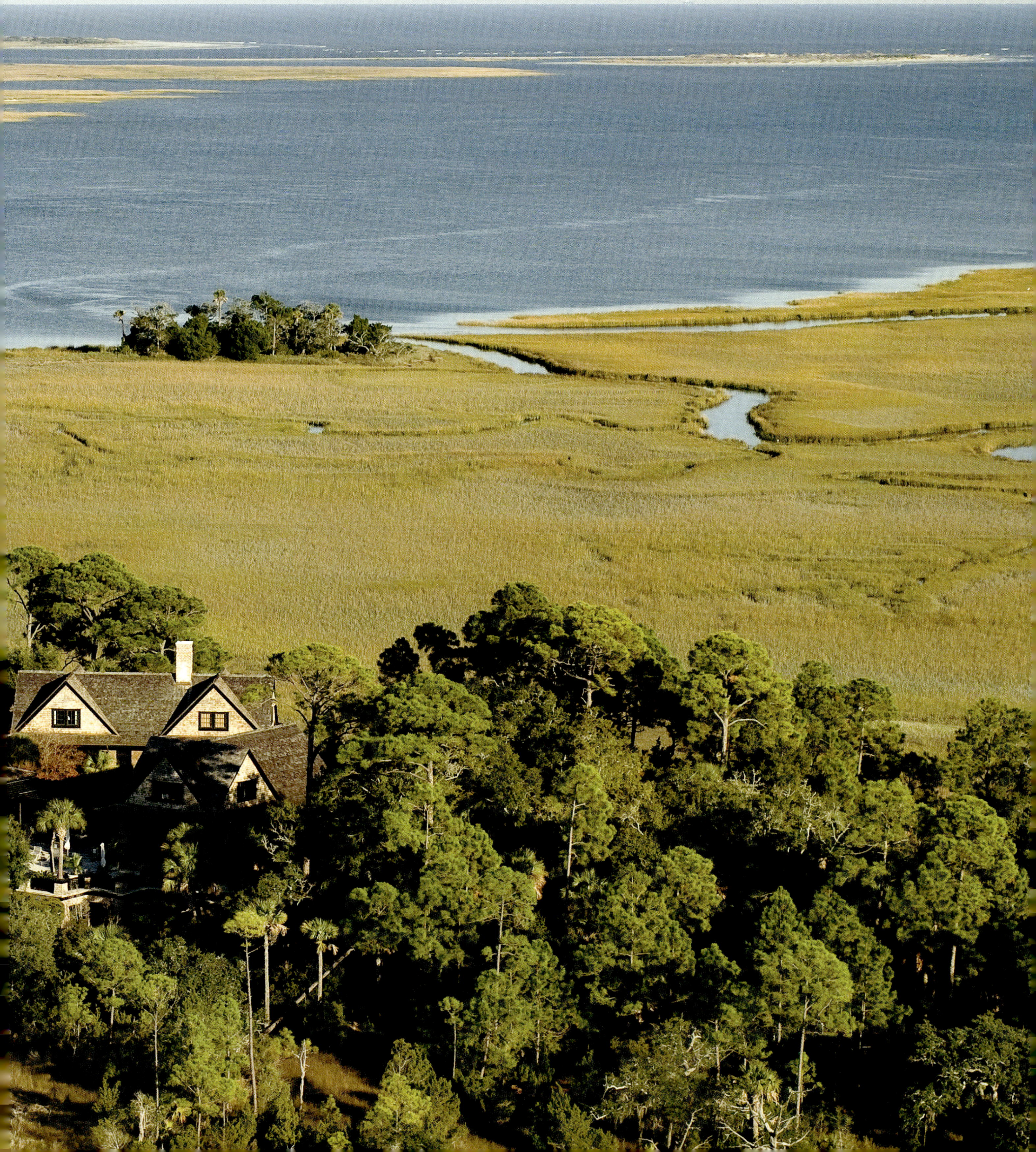

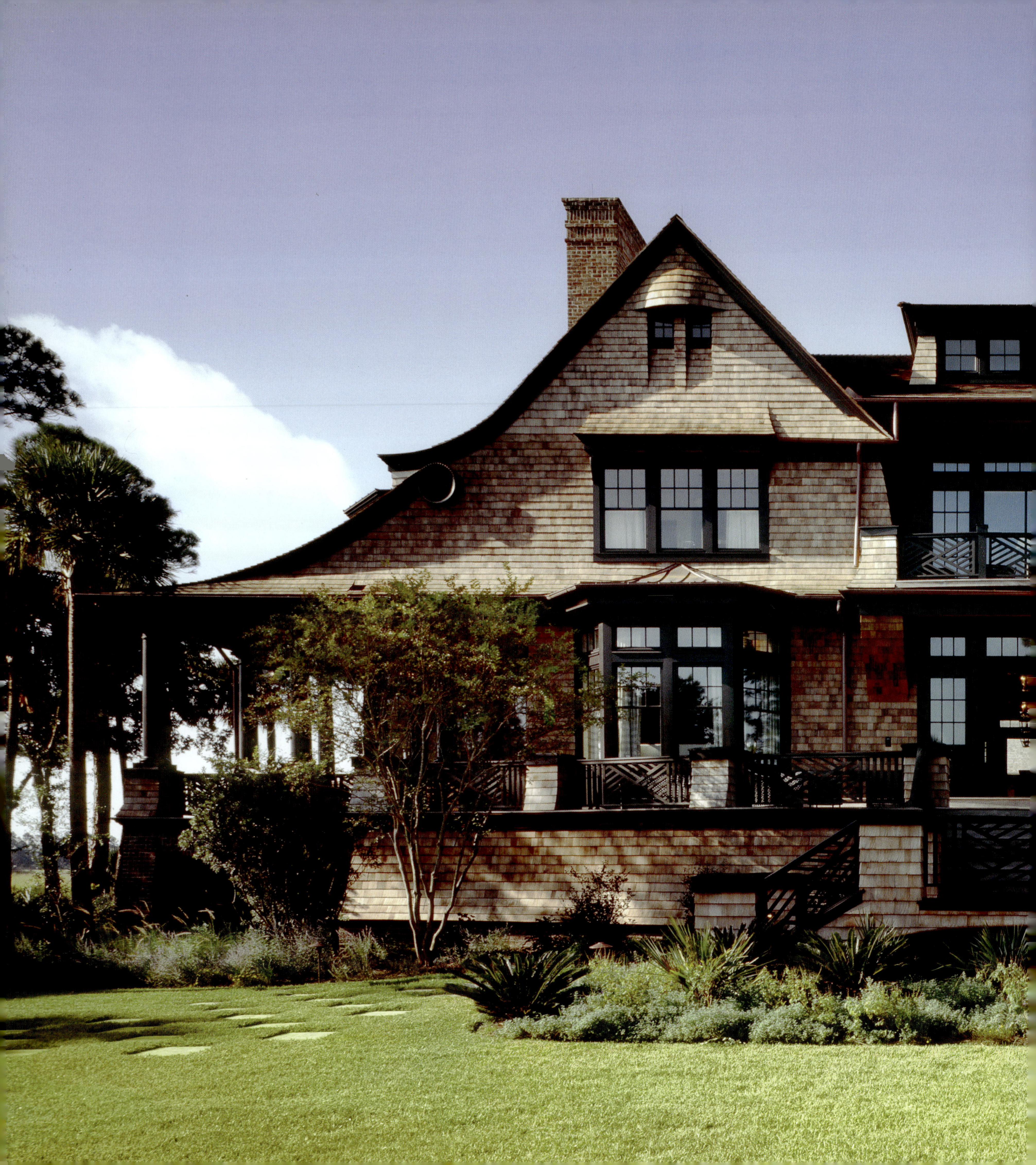

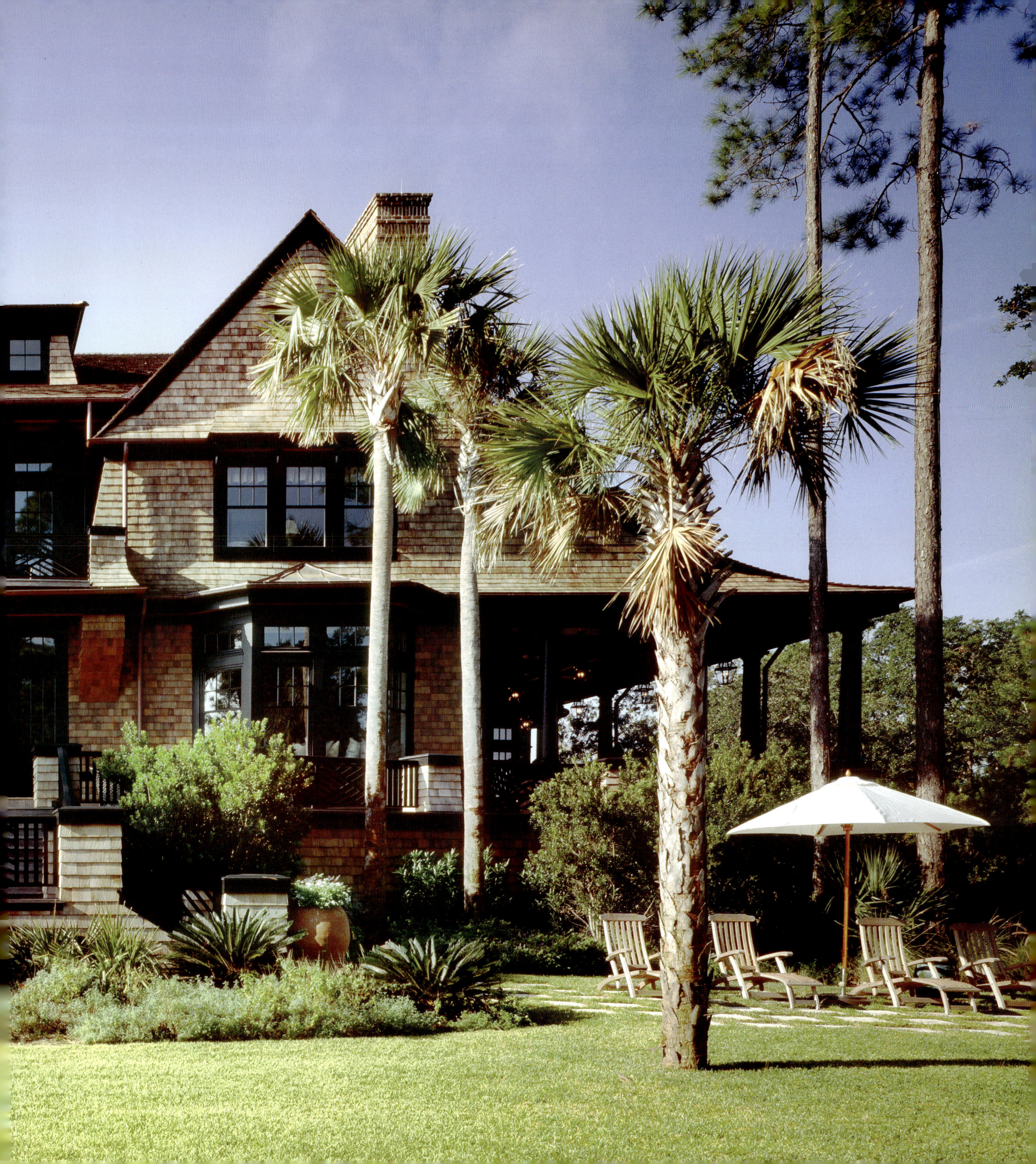

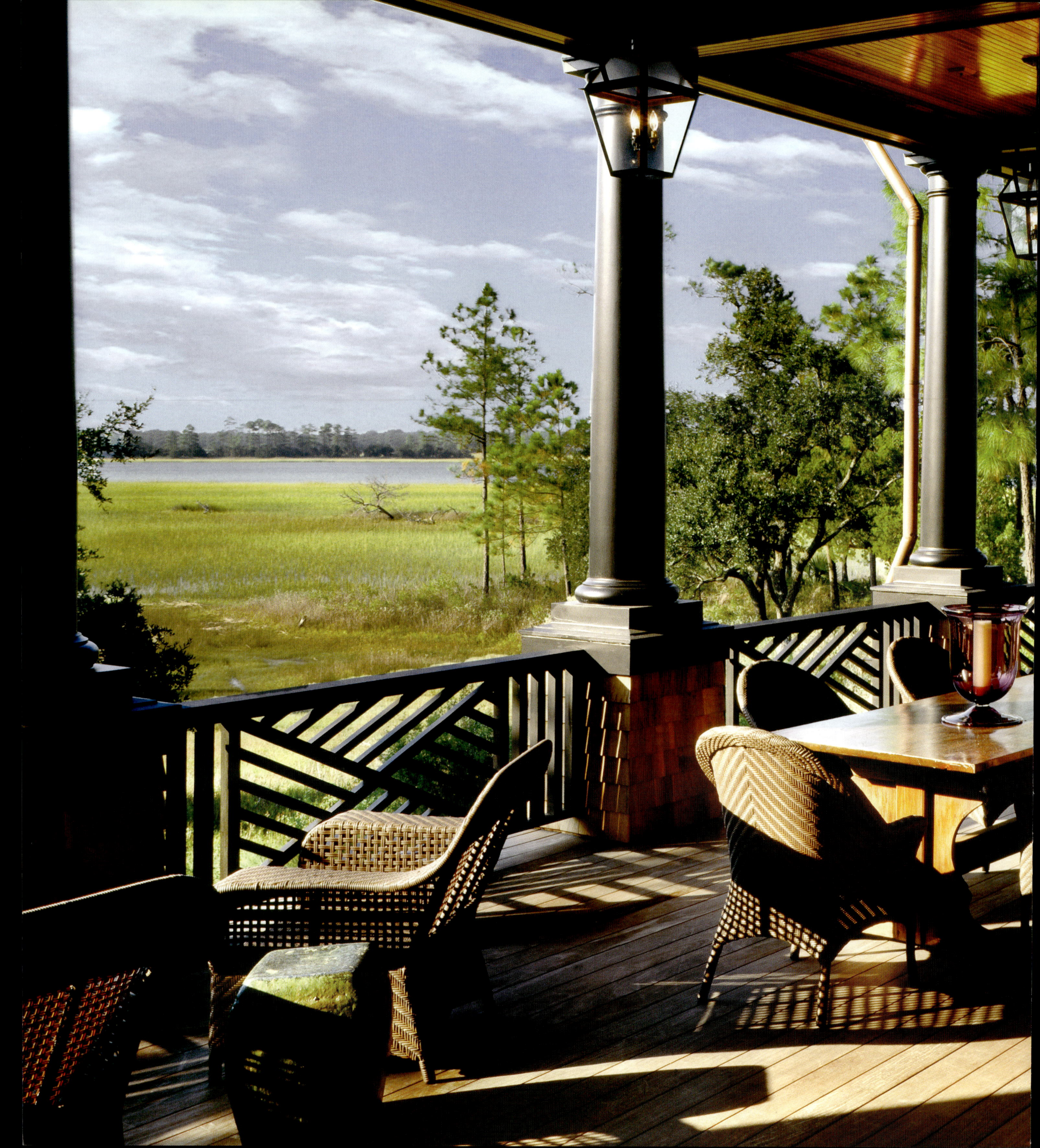

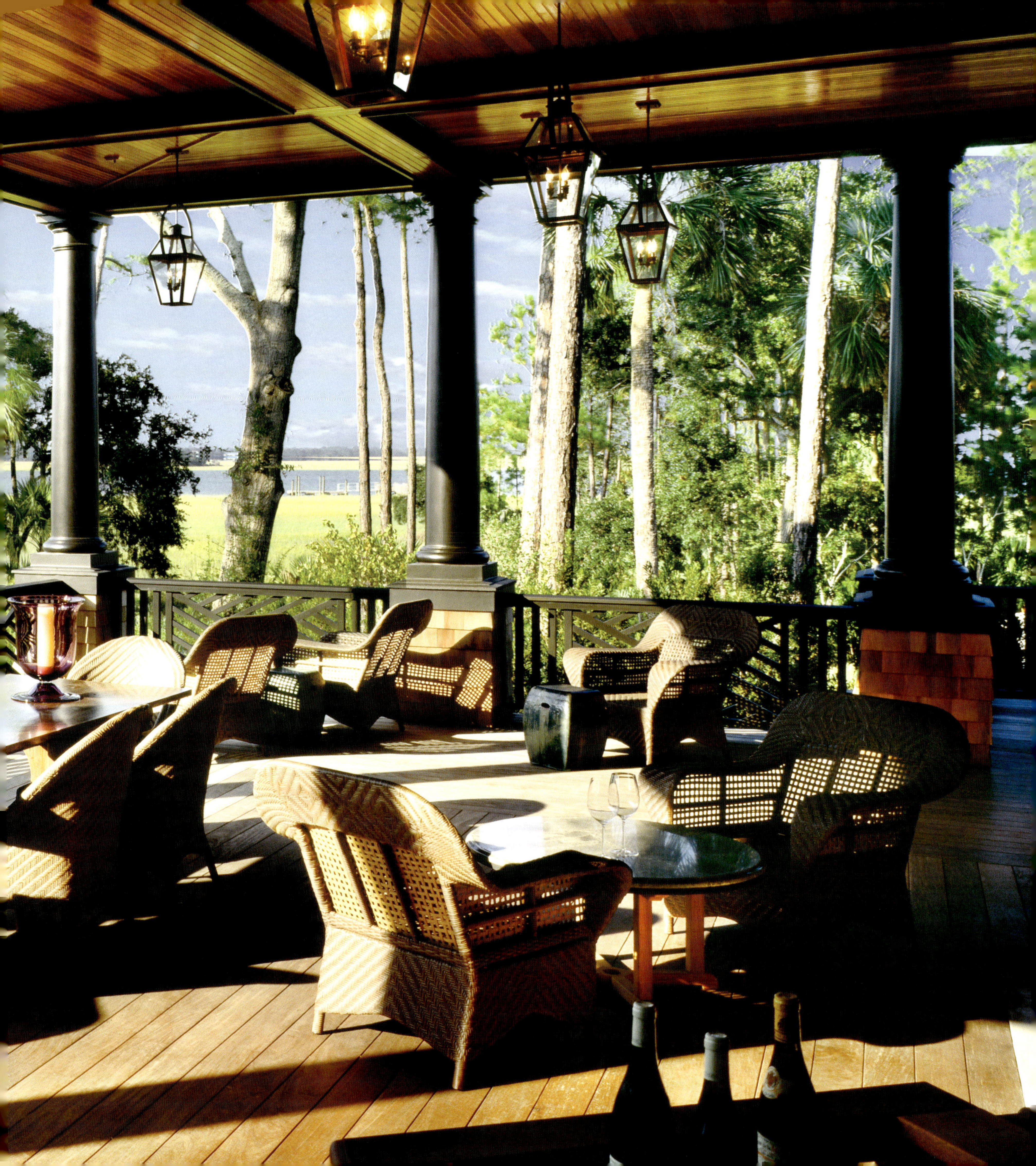

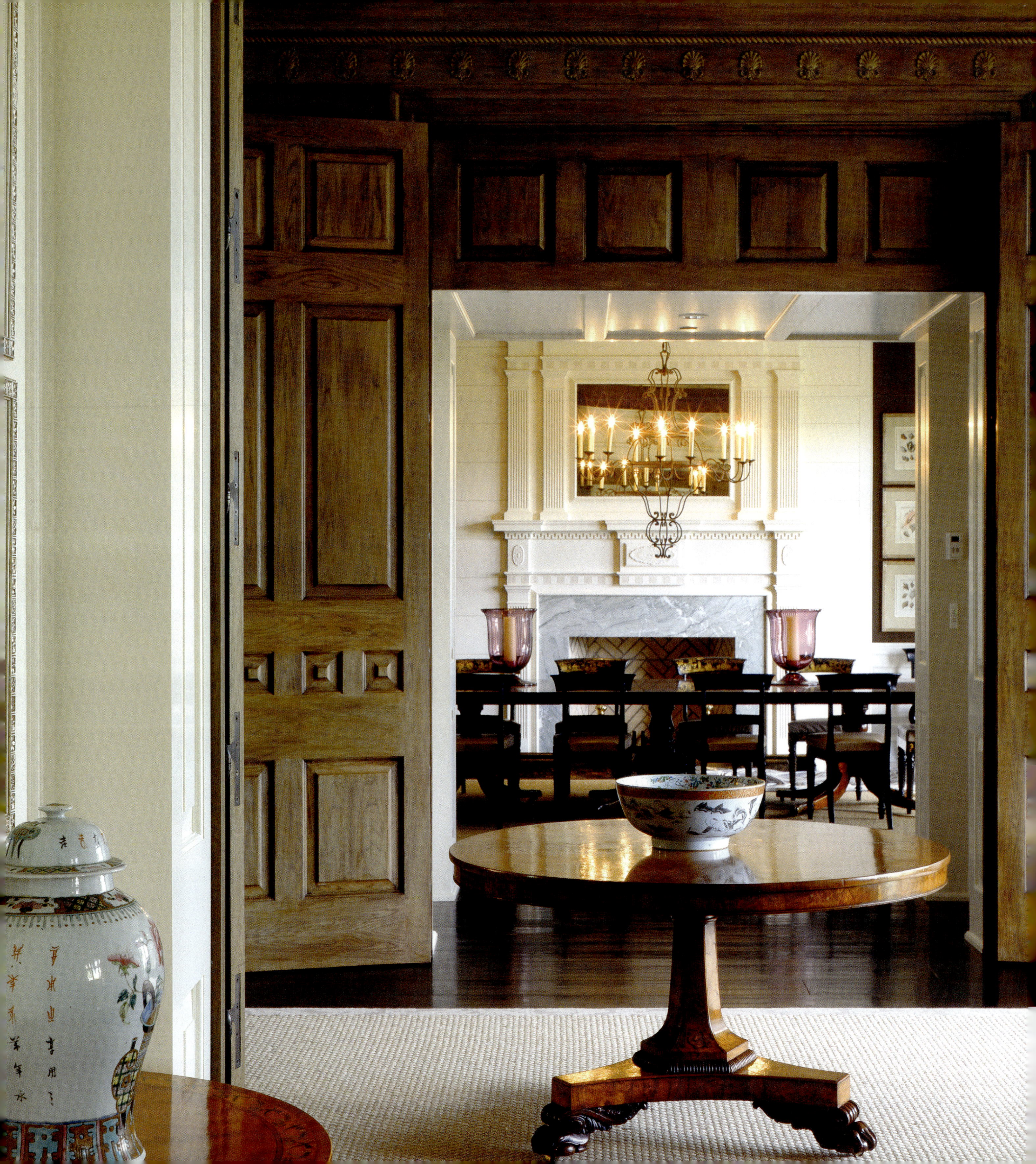

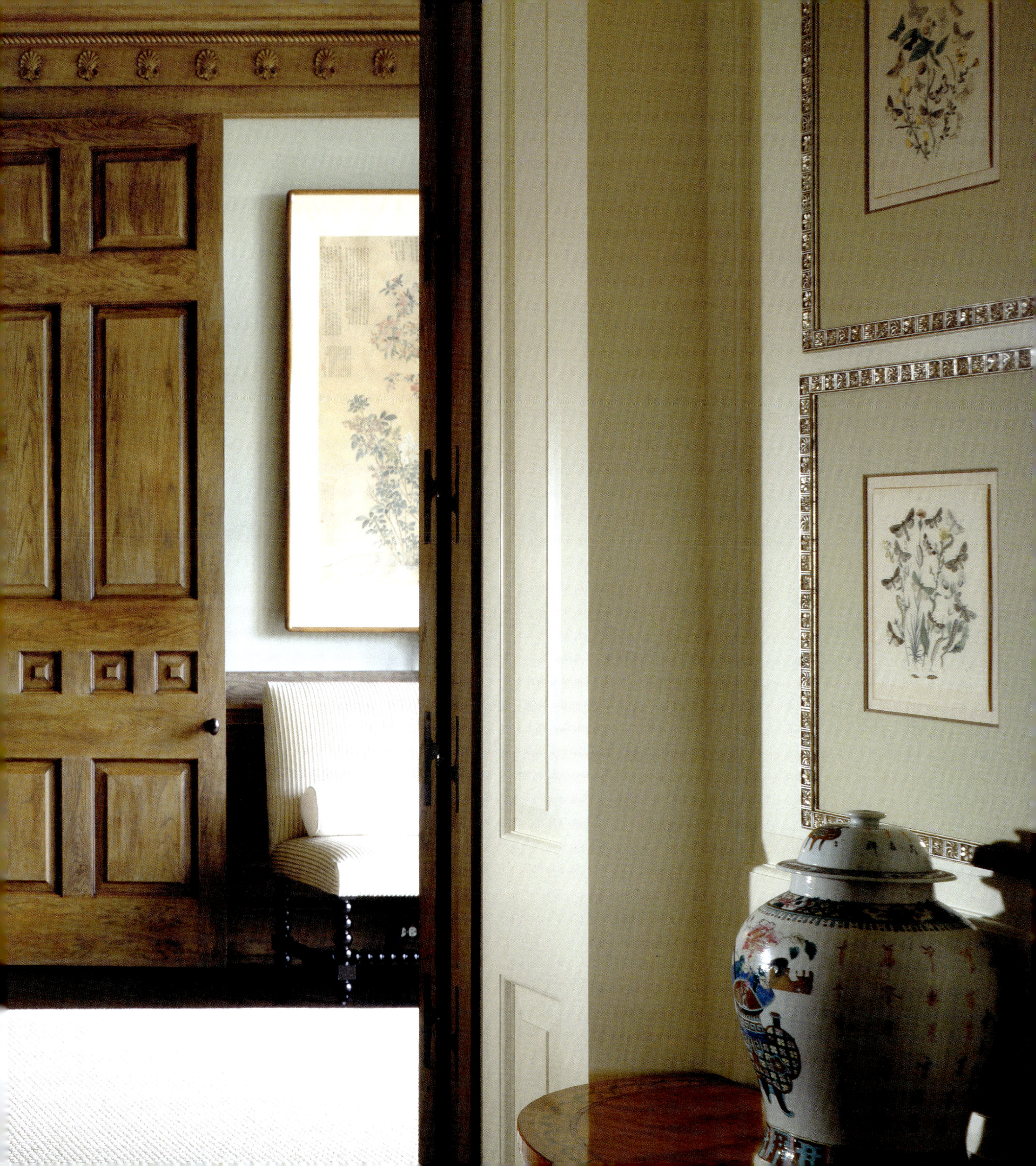

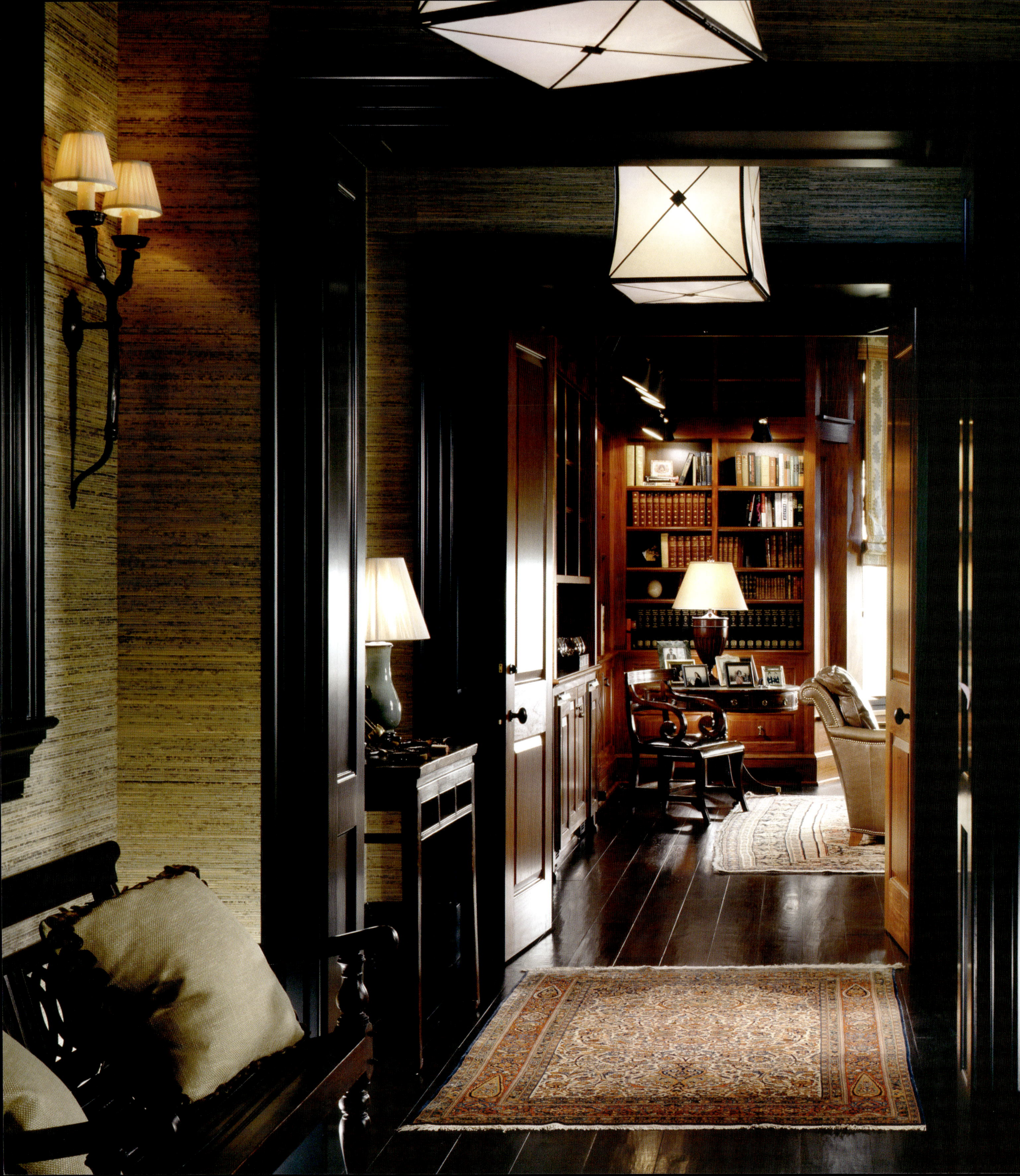

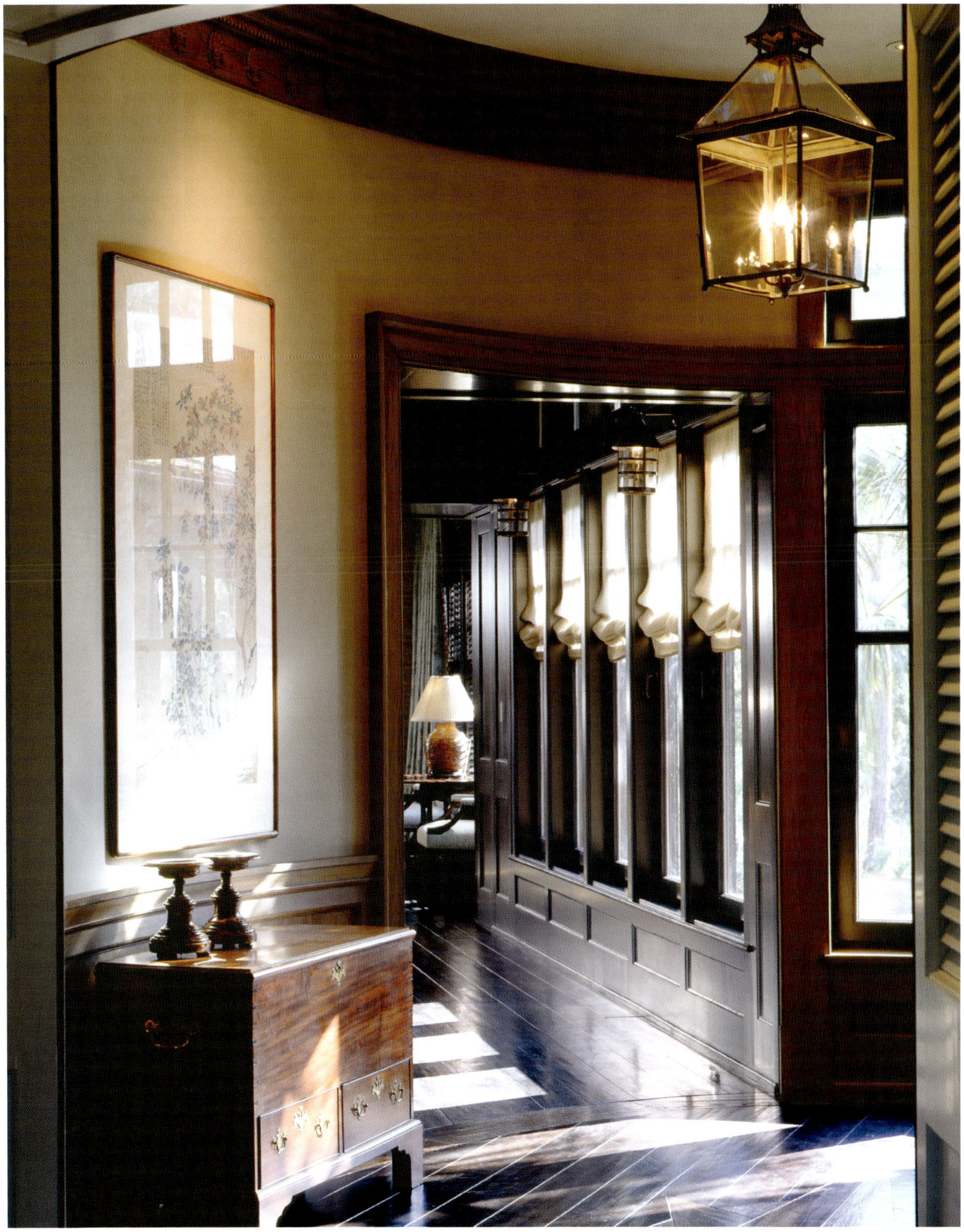

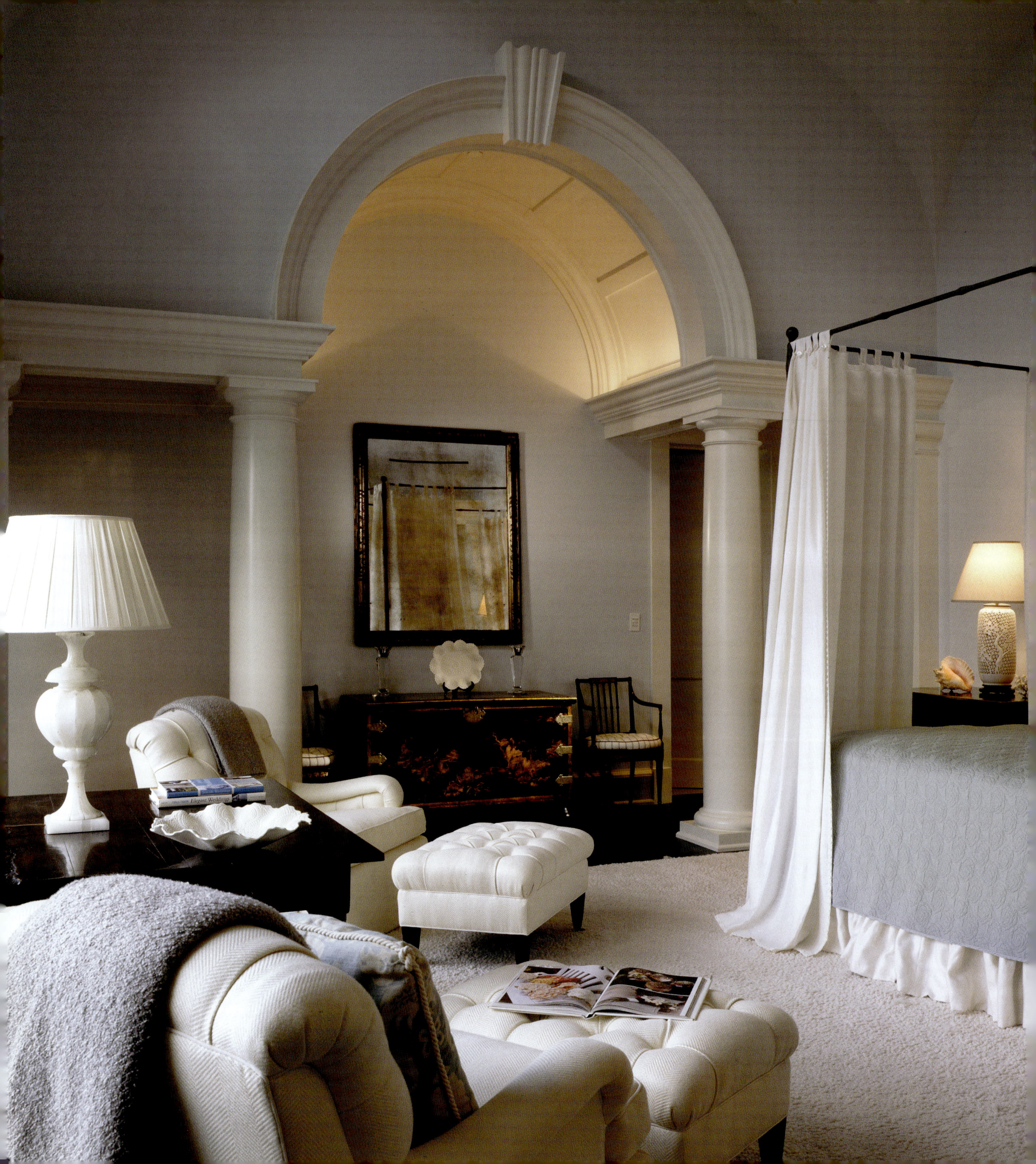

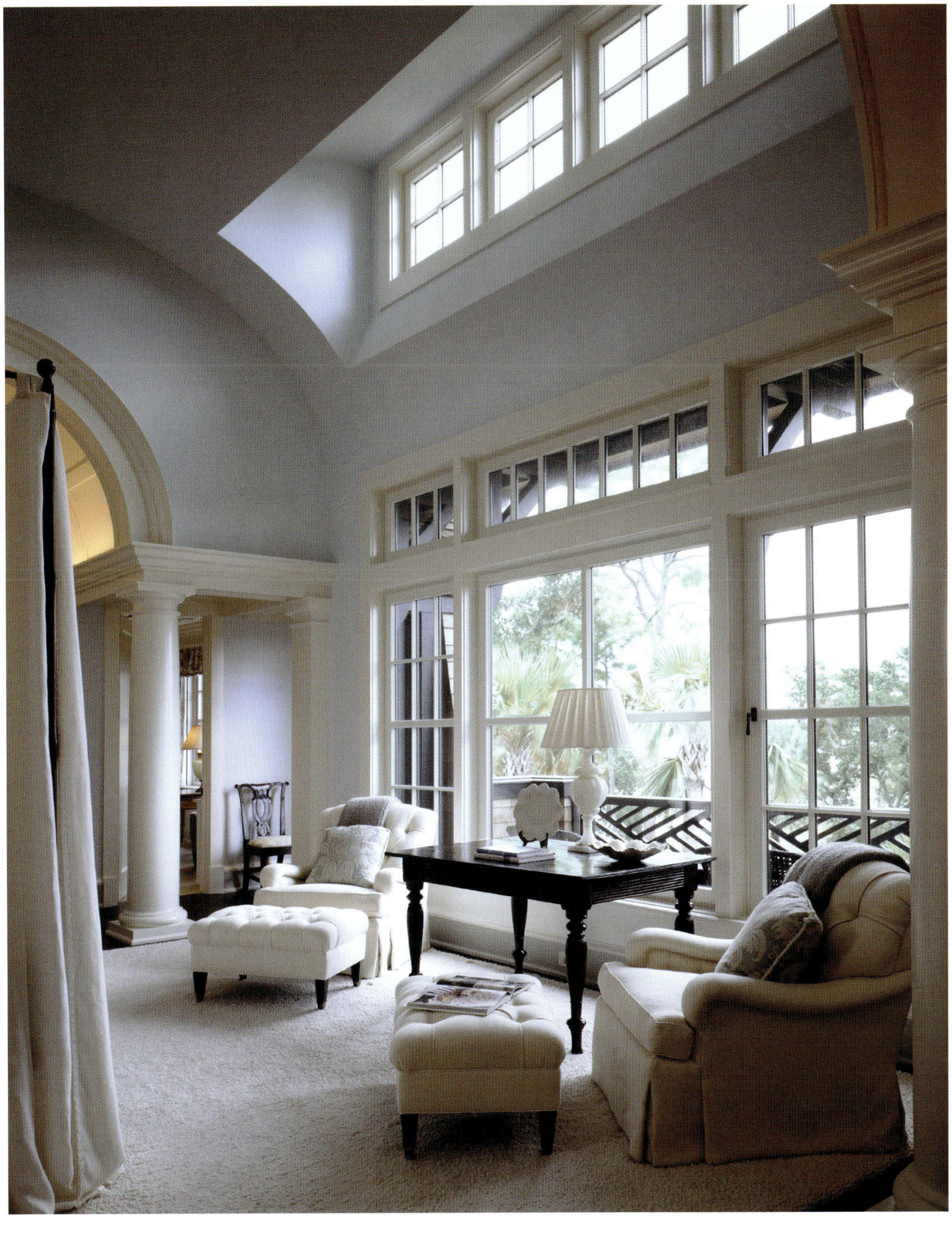

SITE PLAN

0 25' 50' 100'

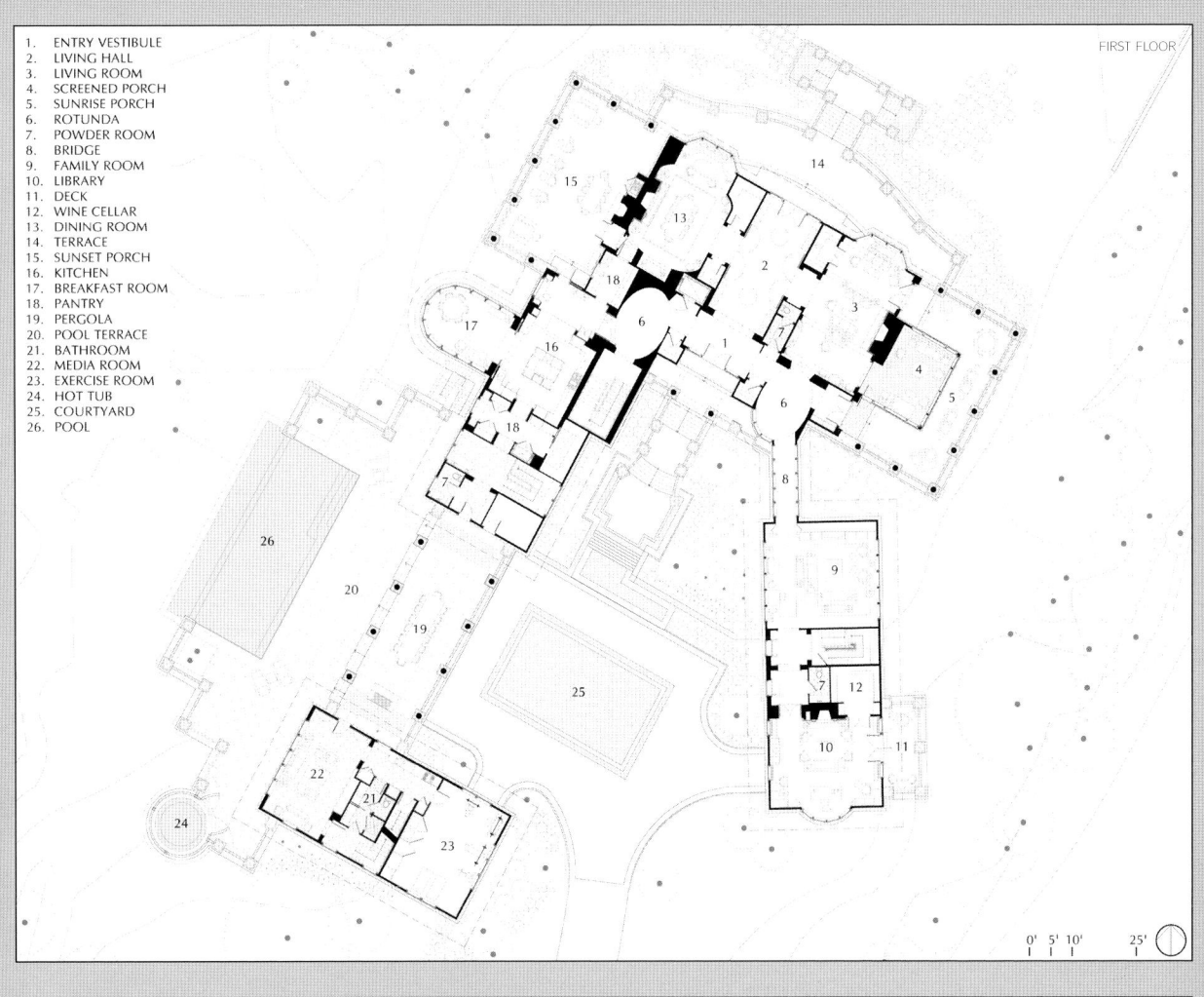

FIRST FLOOR

1. ENTRY VESTIBULE
2. LIVING HALL
3. LIVING ROOM
4. SCREENED PORCH
5. SUNRISE PORCH
6. ROTUNDA
7. POWDER ROOM
8. BRIDGE
9. FAMILY ROOM
10. LIBRARY
11. DECK
12. WINE CELLAR
13. DINING ROOM
14. TERRACE
15. SUNSET PORCH
16. KITCHEN
17. BREAKFAST ROOM
18. PANTRY
19. PERGOLA
20. POOL TERRACE
21. BATHROOM
22. MEDIA ROOM
23. EXERCISE ROOM
24. HOT TUB
25. COURTYARD
26. POOL

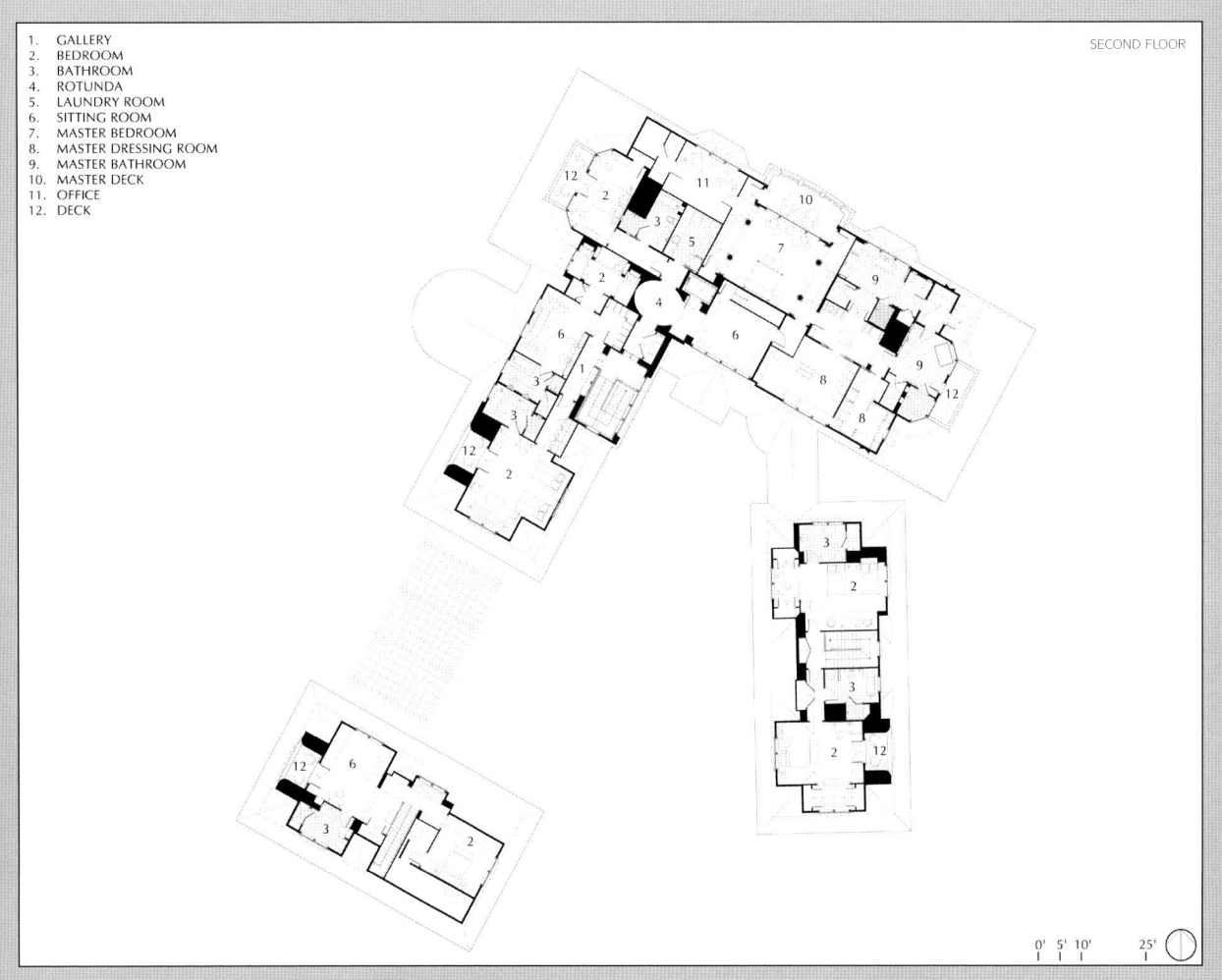

SECOND FLOOR

1. GALLERY
2. BEDROOM
3. BATHROOM
4. ROTUNDA
5. LAUNDRY ROOM
6. SITTING ROOM
7. MASTER BEDROOM
8. MASTER DRESSING ROOM
9. MASTER BATHROOM
10. MASTER DECK
11. OFFICE
12. DECK

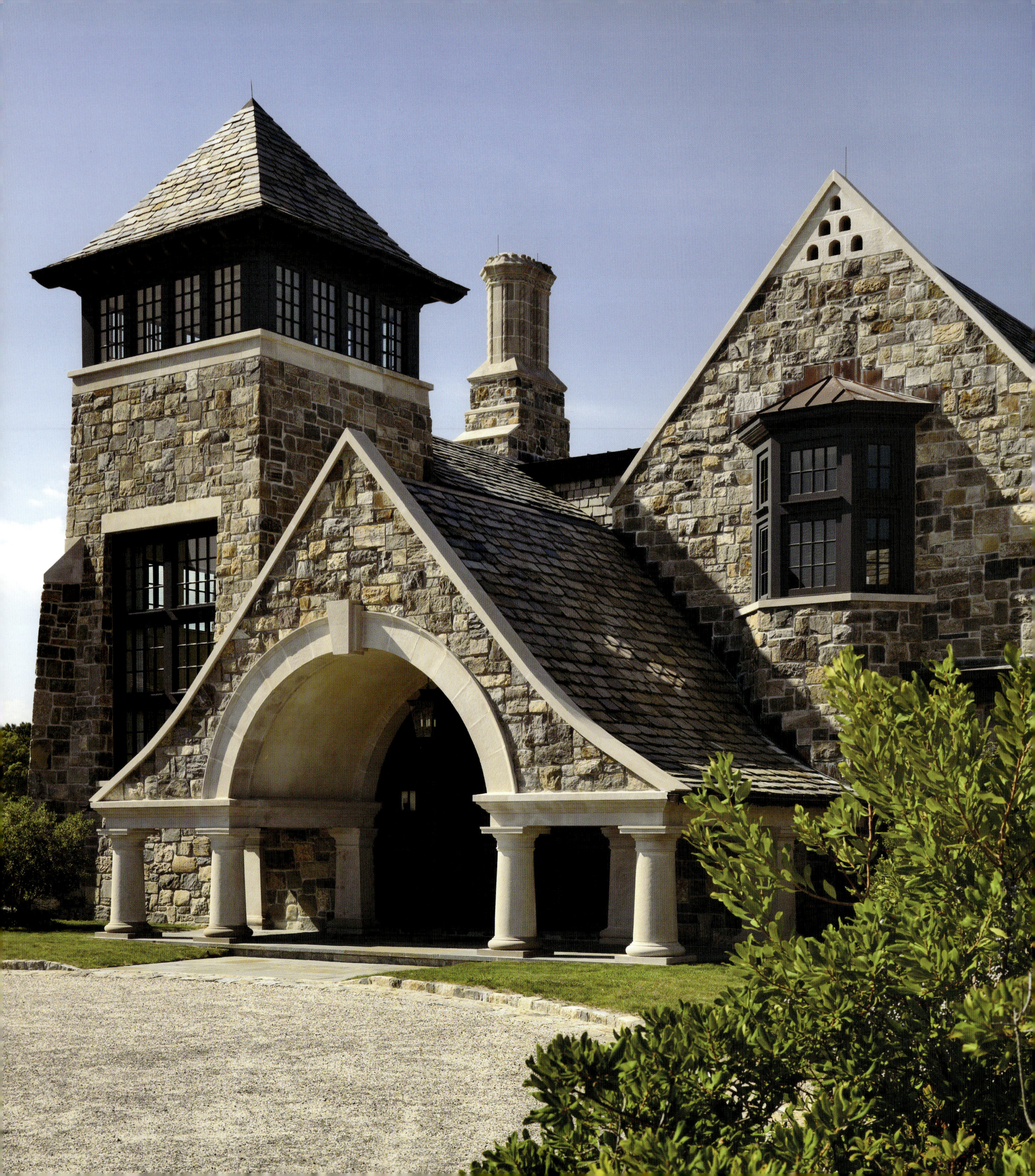

STEEPLY PITCHED ROOFS, DORMERS, AND EYEBROW WINDOWS DISTINGUISH THE DESIGN OF A NEW CLUBHOUSE

THE CLIENT Friar's Head is a recently opened golf course located in the hamlet of Baiting Hollow, where Long Island's North Shore turns into the North Fork. The name Friar's Head comes from a sand formation ringed with natural shrubbery, which nineteenth century sailors thought looked like a monk's tonsure, using it as a navigational reference point.

THE DESIGN BRIEF Because the course is windswept, near the water, and dotted with natural grasses and sand dunes, it has similarities to a links course—the oldest style of golf courses that were first developed in Scotland. The architects wanted the clubhouse to take advantage of this in the design of the clubhouse. The course is exposed to severe weather, so a stone clubhouse seemed appropriate.

THE SOLUTION The 17,400 square-foot club house was constructed of stone in a style reminiscent of a manor house from the turn of the twentieth century. Although it is built of stone, the building borrows elements from the Shingle Style with its steeply pitched overhanging roofs, dormers, eyebrow windows, a stair tower, and two massive chimneys that rise out of the spreading mass of the building. The New York-based firm Alex Papachristidis Interiors was responsible for the decoration of the 30 rooms that make up the complex. A building containing women's and men's locker rooms and lounges is covered in cedar shingles. It is placed in relation to the clubhouse as a carriage house would be to its manor. The two buildings embrace a circular court that faces the water on its open side. A masonry arch, supported on small columns, spreads across the entry to the clubhouse. The stair tower to one side is anchored by a massive stone buttress in acknowledgment of the building's medieval antecedents. An octagonal living hall, one of the clubhouse's 30 rooms, is built with intricately detailed Romanesque stone arches. A gallery with glass doors leads on to the golf course. Exterior terraces—one of which looks over the green and fairway at the 18th hole—are anchored by wood-framed pergolas mounted on granite columns. A large round porch where wooden columns rise from granite bases is placed on the north side of the building, from which one can look out over the golf course and to the water. A porch on the south side, where meals are served, is warmed by an outdoor fireplace. The Friar's Head golf course is recognized as one of the best golf courses in the country, and its clubhouse is a dignified tribute to its prestige among golfers.

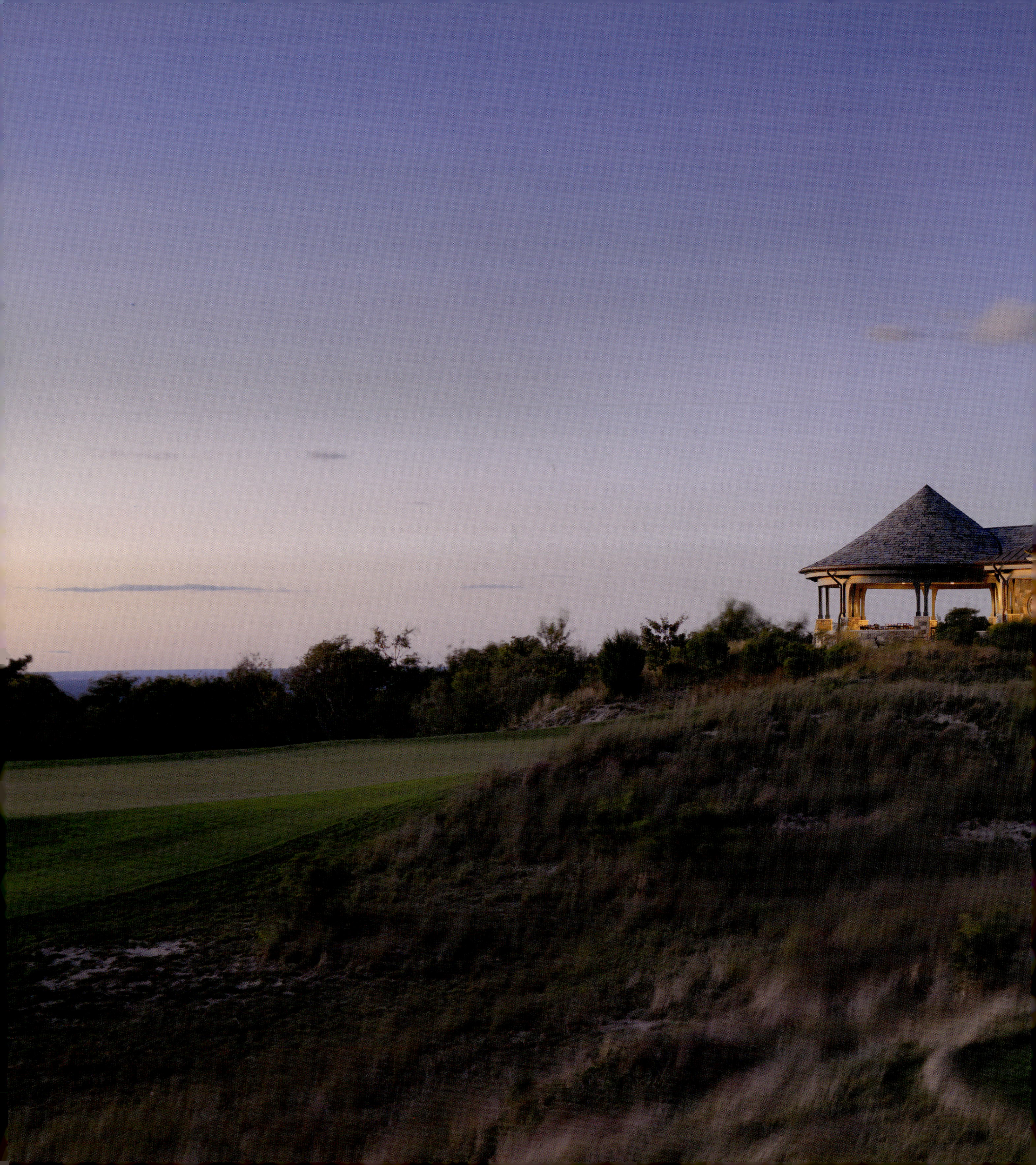

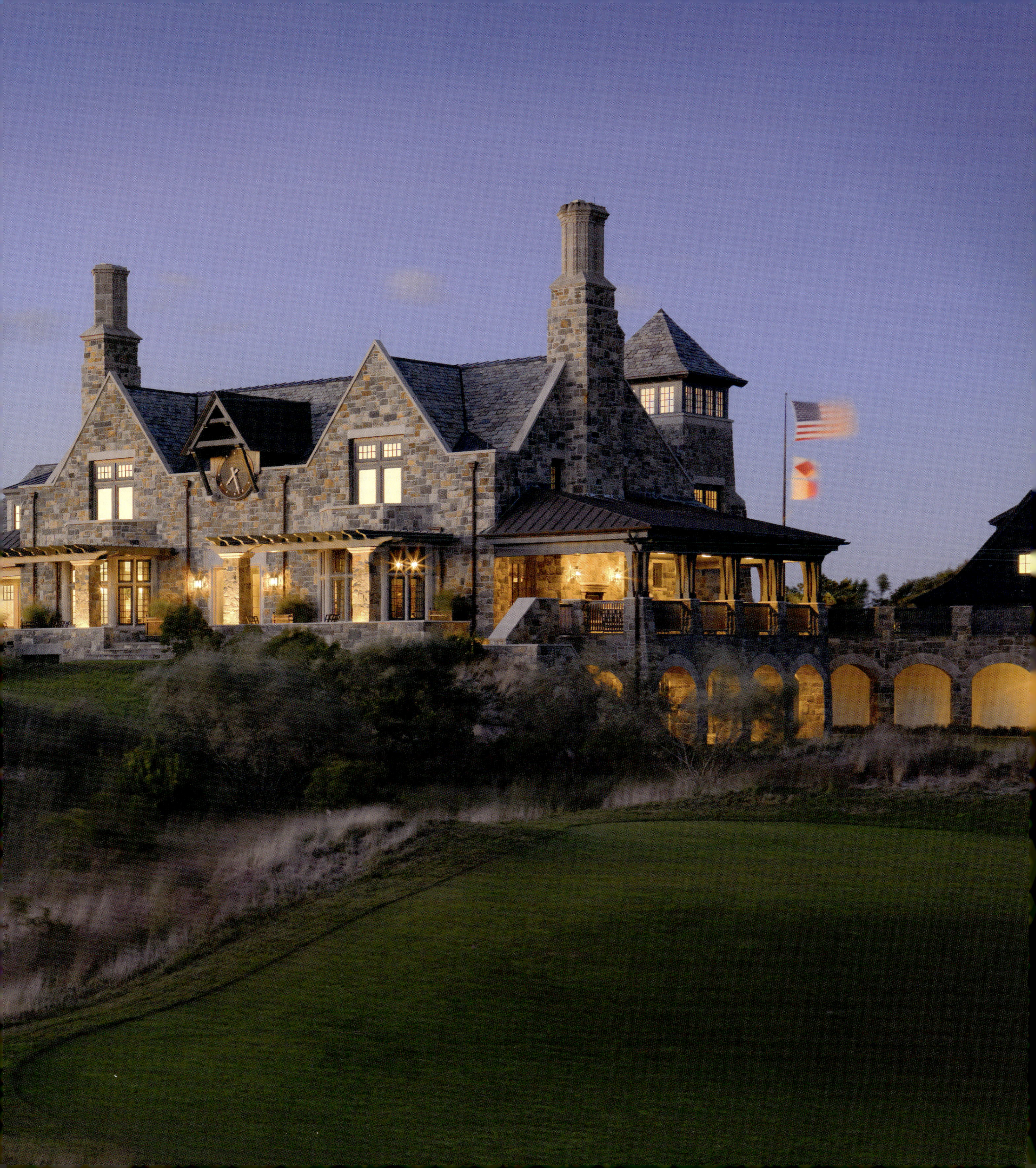

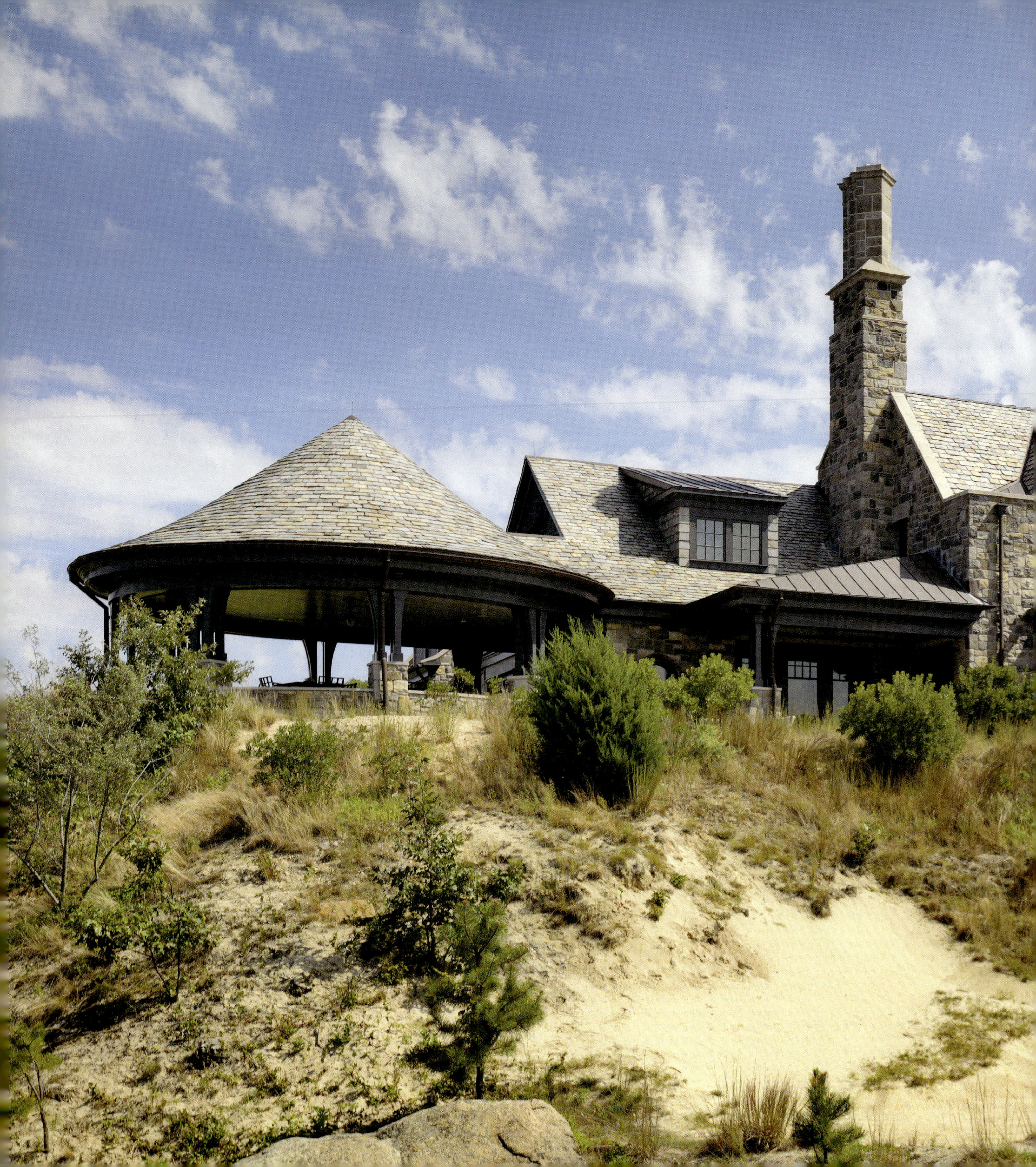

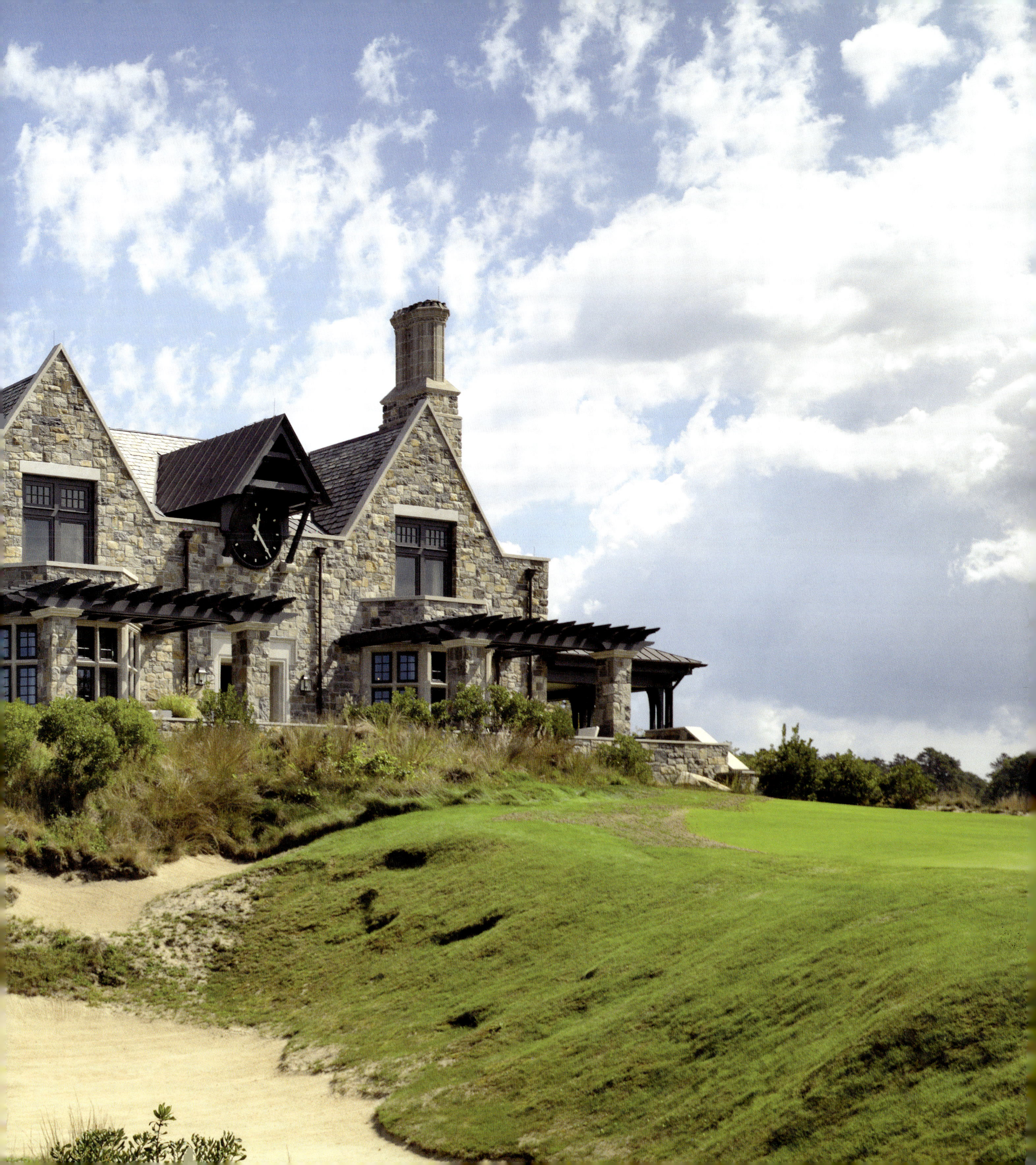

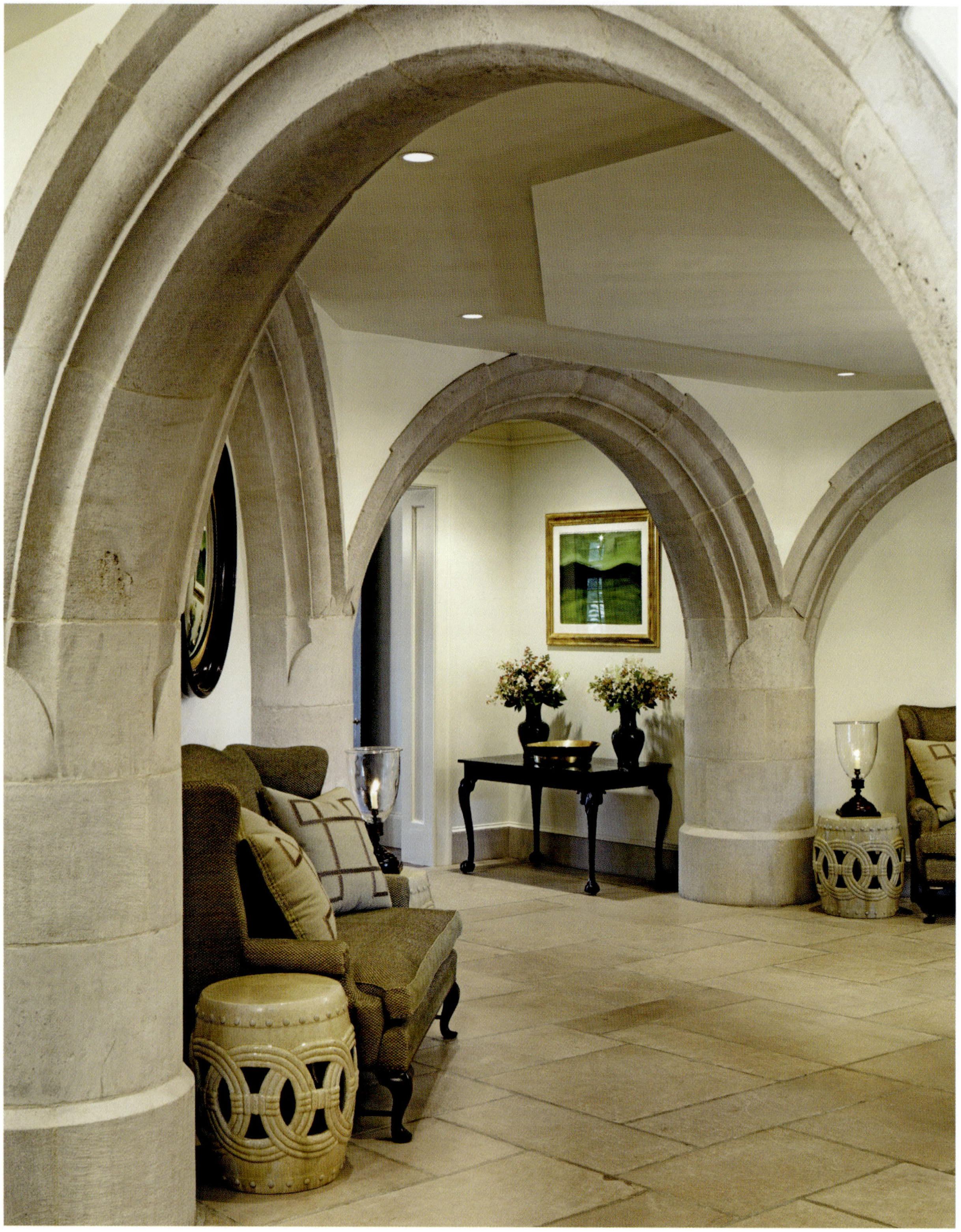

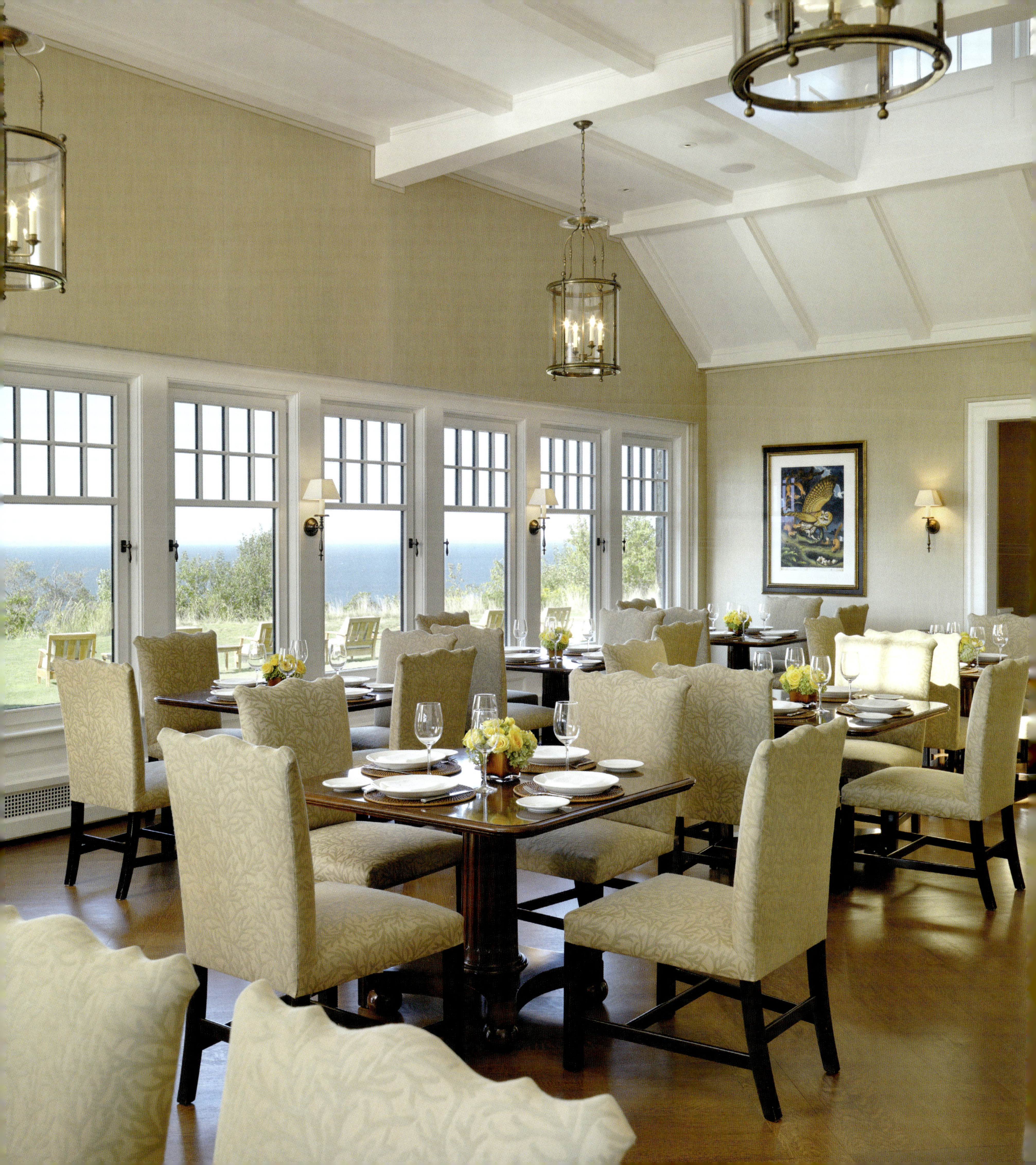

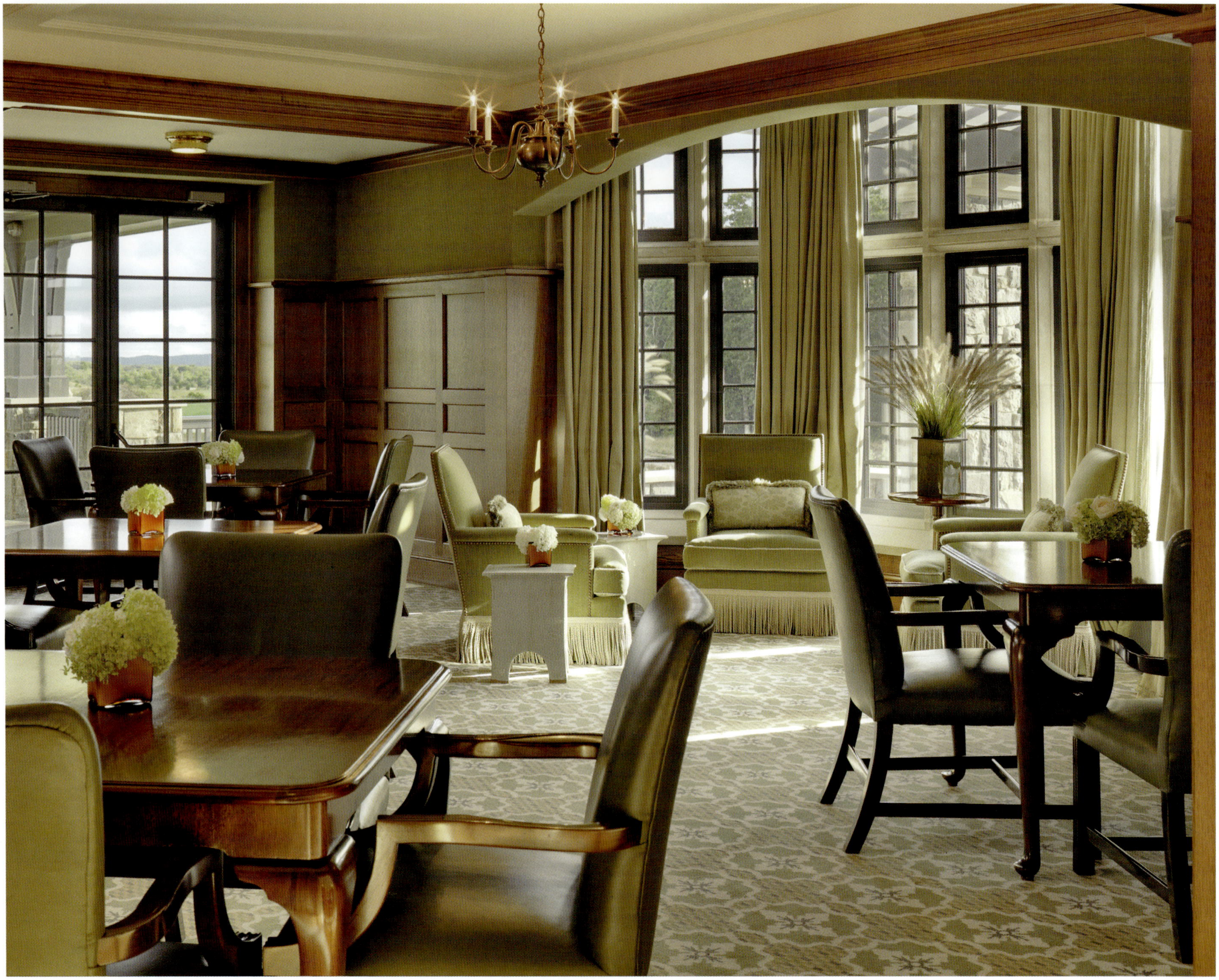

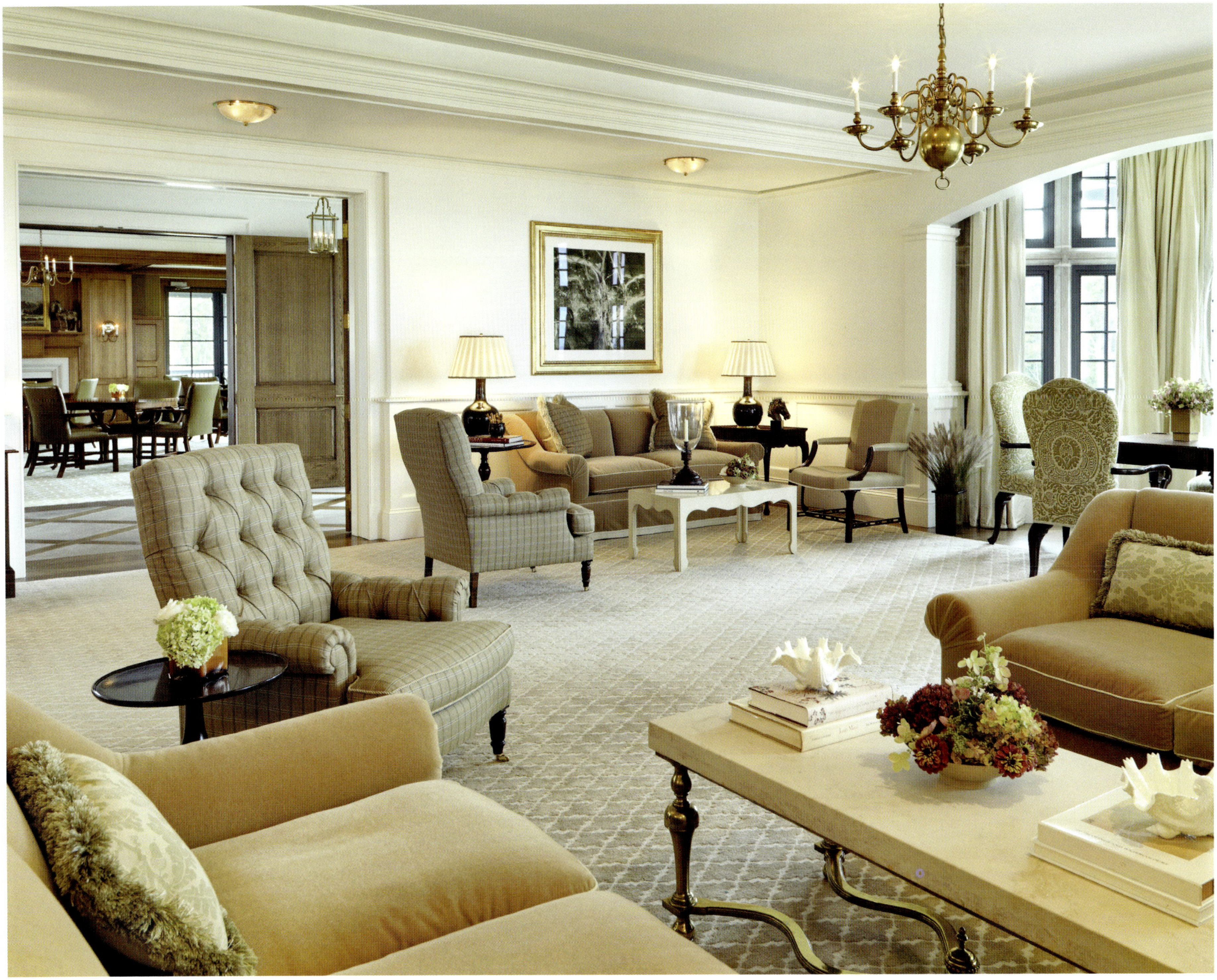

SITE PLAN

0 10' 25' 50' 100'

FIRST FLOOR

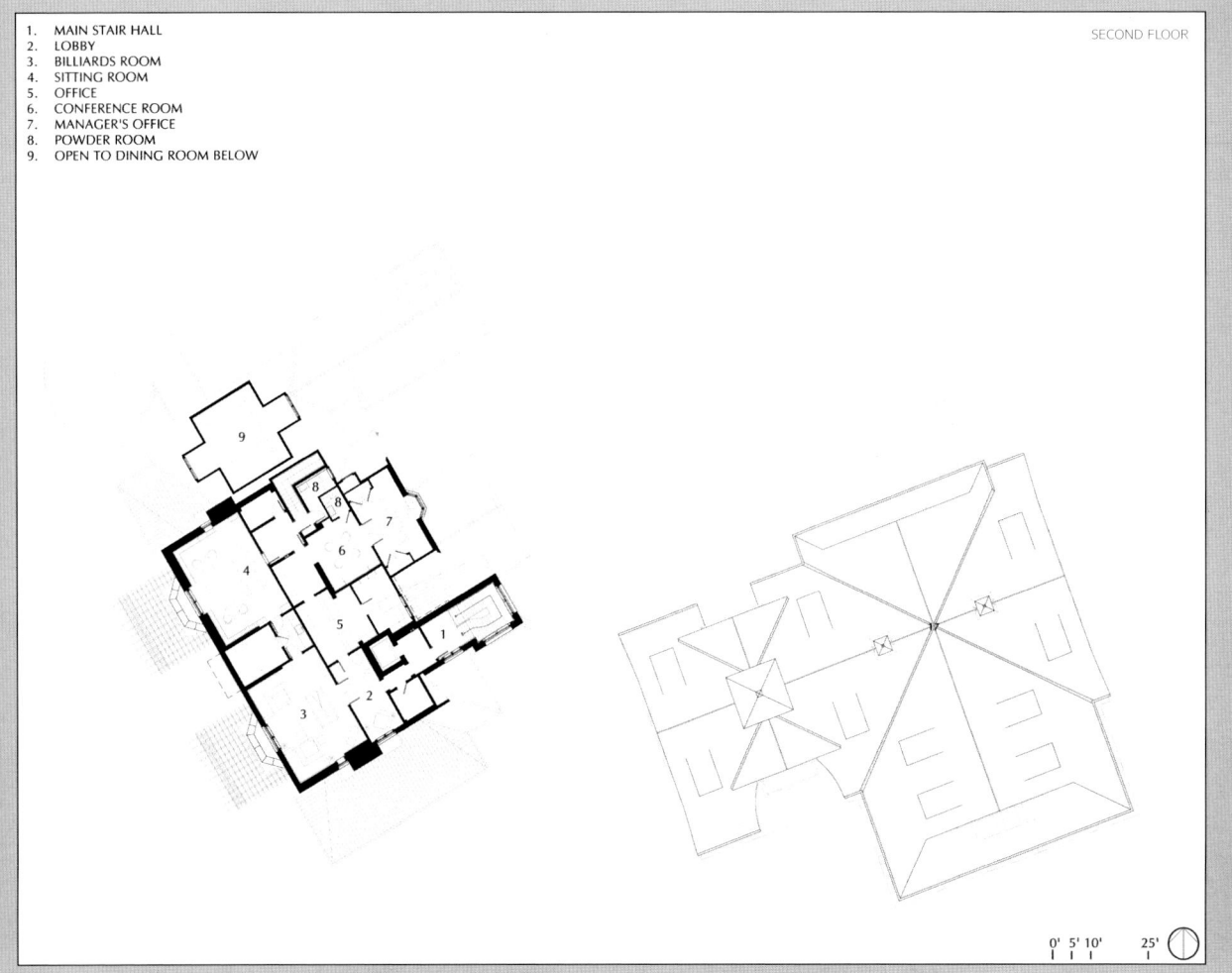

1. COVERED ENTRY
2. VESTIBULE
3. ROTUNDA
4. RESTROOM
5. GALLERY
6. LIVING ROOM
7. DINING ROOM
8. KITCHEN
9. PORCH
10. TERRACE
11. 19TH HOLE
12. MAIN STAIR
13. COURTYARD
14. OVERLOOK
15. ENTRY
16. GENTLEMEN'S LOUNGE
17. POWDER ROOM
18. BAR
19. LOCKER ROOM
20. LOCKER ROOM BATHROOM
21. PUTTING GREEN BELOW
22. 18TH HOLE WALK-UP

SECOND FLOOR

1. MAIN STAIR HALL
2. LOBBY
3. BILLIARDS ROOM
4. SITTING ROOM
5. OFFICE
6. CONFERENCE ROOM
7. MANAGER'S OFFICE
8. POWDER ROOM
9. OPEN TO DINING ROOM BELOW

223

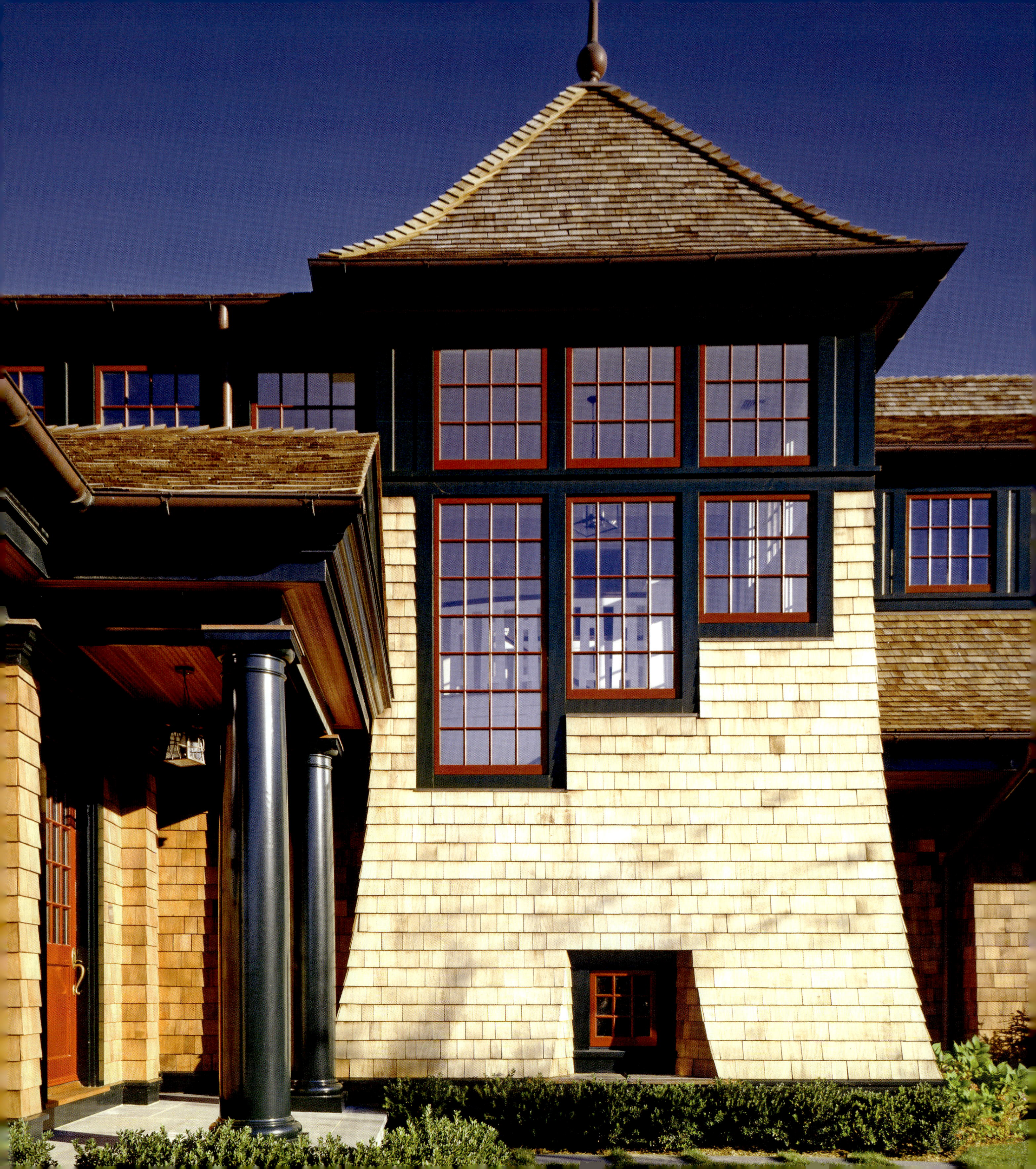

AN L-SHAPED PLAN OFFERS A VERSATILE SOLUTION TO A FAMILY HOUSE WITH WIDE-OPEN VIEWS

THE CLIENTS Family life was important to the clients, a young couple with two children. They liked living in interesting and spacious rooms which gained their strength through their simplicity. They also wanted their dog and cats to be comfortable in every part of their home. The husband was a Manhattan businessman who had always wanted a shingled house by the sea.

THE DESIGN BRIEF The three-and-a-half–acre property offered wonderful views across Long Island Sound. The clients were thinking in terms of an open informal interior within a traditional shell, oriented toward the water. The architects envisioned a Shingle Style-house that would stretch horizontally across the low-lying site. As opposed to the constraints of symmetrical Georgian architecture, the Shingle Style-architecture offered an opportunity to be whimsical.

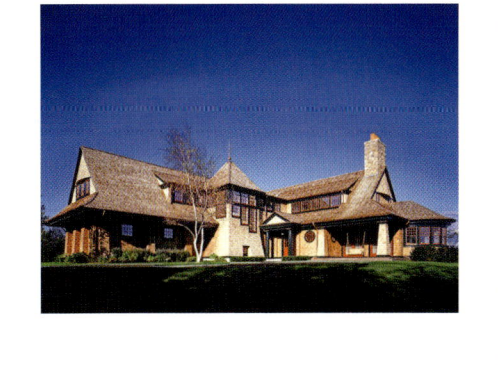

THE SOLUTION The architects designed a 7,300-square foot, 25-room house that sports a collection of dormers behind which the second floor is tucked in order to keep the profile of the house as low as possible. Limestone chimneys at each end of the house give a vertical thrust to offset the building's overall horizontality. According to Michael McClung, a member of the Shope Reno Wharton team, the deck railings, eyebrow windows set below steep peaks on the dormers, sloped-flaring porch posts that look as though they were grasping the earth, and a stair tower reminiscent of a pagoda, hint at the playfulness of the house. None of the play is gratuitous, however, because Wharton also points out that each aspect of the façade reflects a different interior function. For instance, on the façade of the staircase tower, which spreads its base at right angles to the entrance, there are three windows, which decrease in height as the stair rises. The tower is capped with a roof with upturning eaves that recalls the fascination with Japanesque things at the height of the Shingle Style's popularity in the 1880s. The plan of the house is L-shaped; the main wing contains in enfilade a family room, a kitchen and breakfast room, a combined living and dining room, and the office, all of which face the water, many of them through French doors. New York interior designer Mariette Himes Gomez says, "I always want to emphasize the architecture, so I kept the interior simple. The paneling and use of wood was very rich so I chose neutral colors and simple carpets to give that full play." Gomez describes the lighting that she chose for the house as "wisps that don't impose on your vision." A bold statement with lighting was made over the dining table where Gomez placed a square glass and iron lantern-within-a-lantern chandelier, which she designed. The architects describe the house as whimsical and playful, representing the light-hearted yet responsible creativity that came from the long years of discipline in their craft.

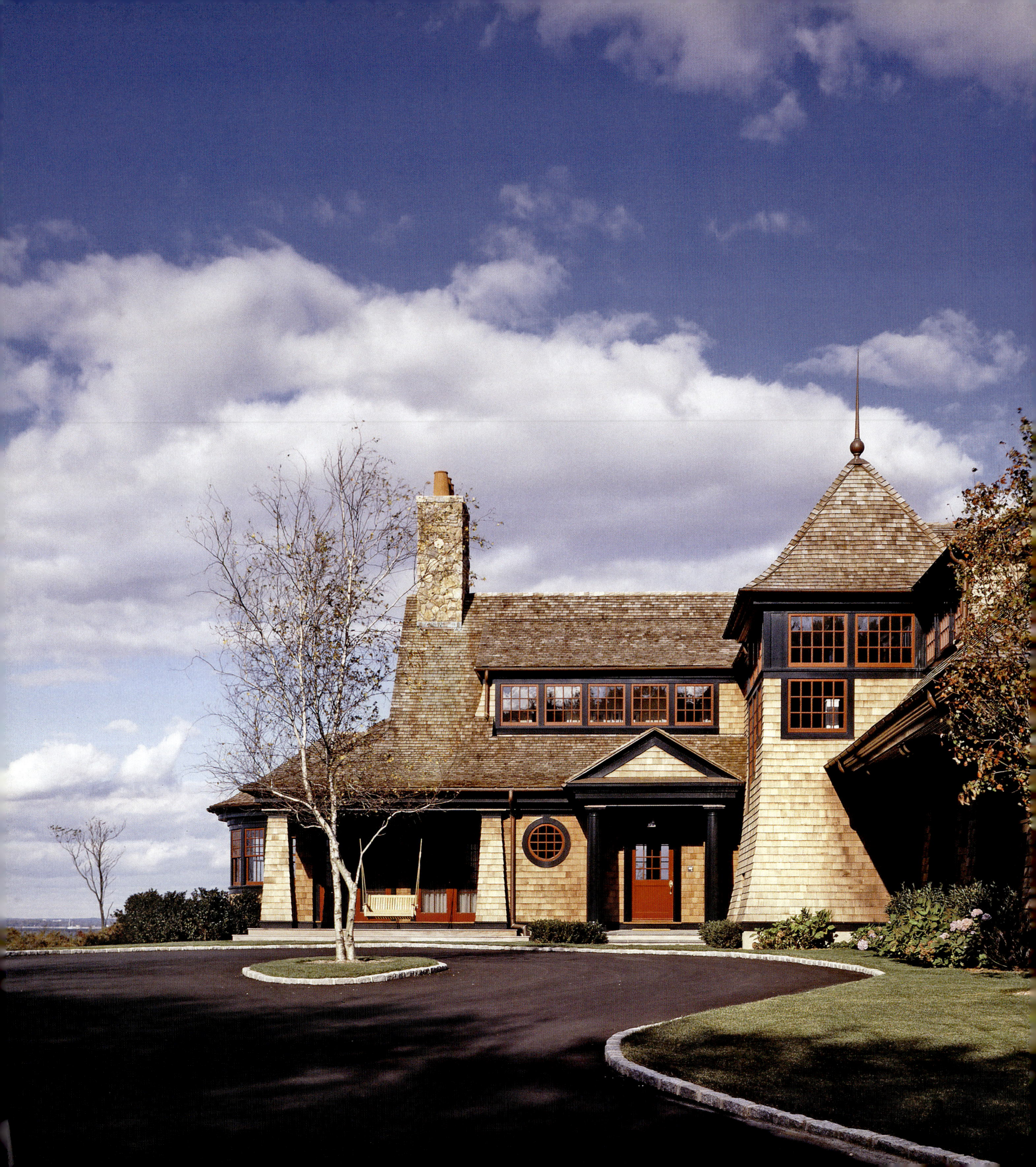

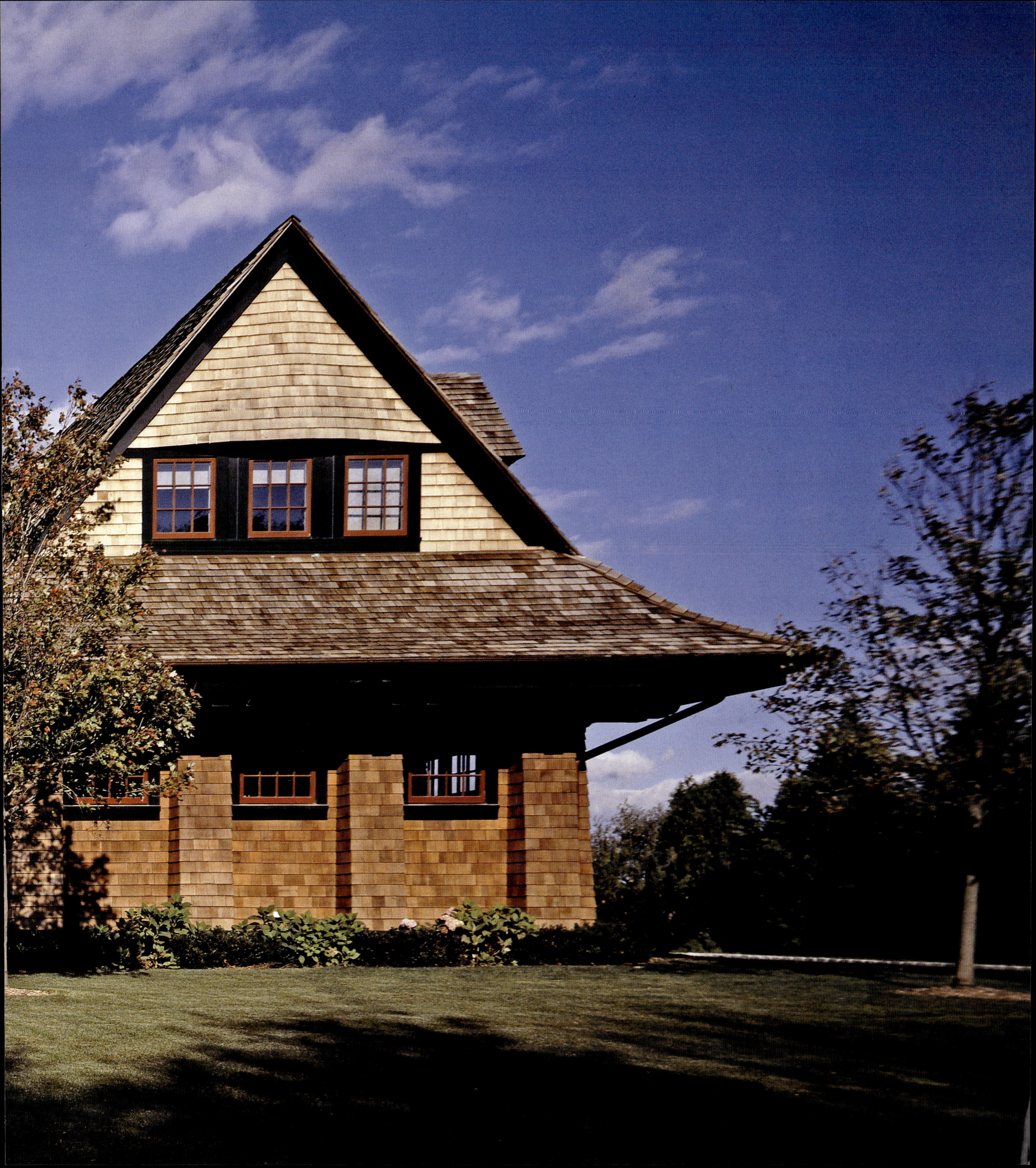

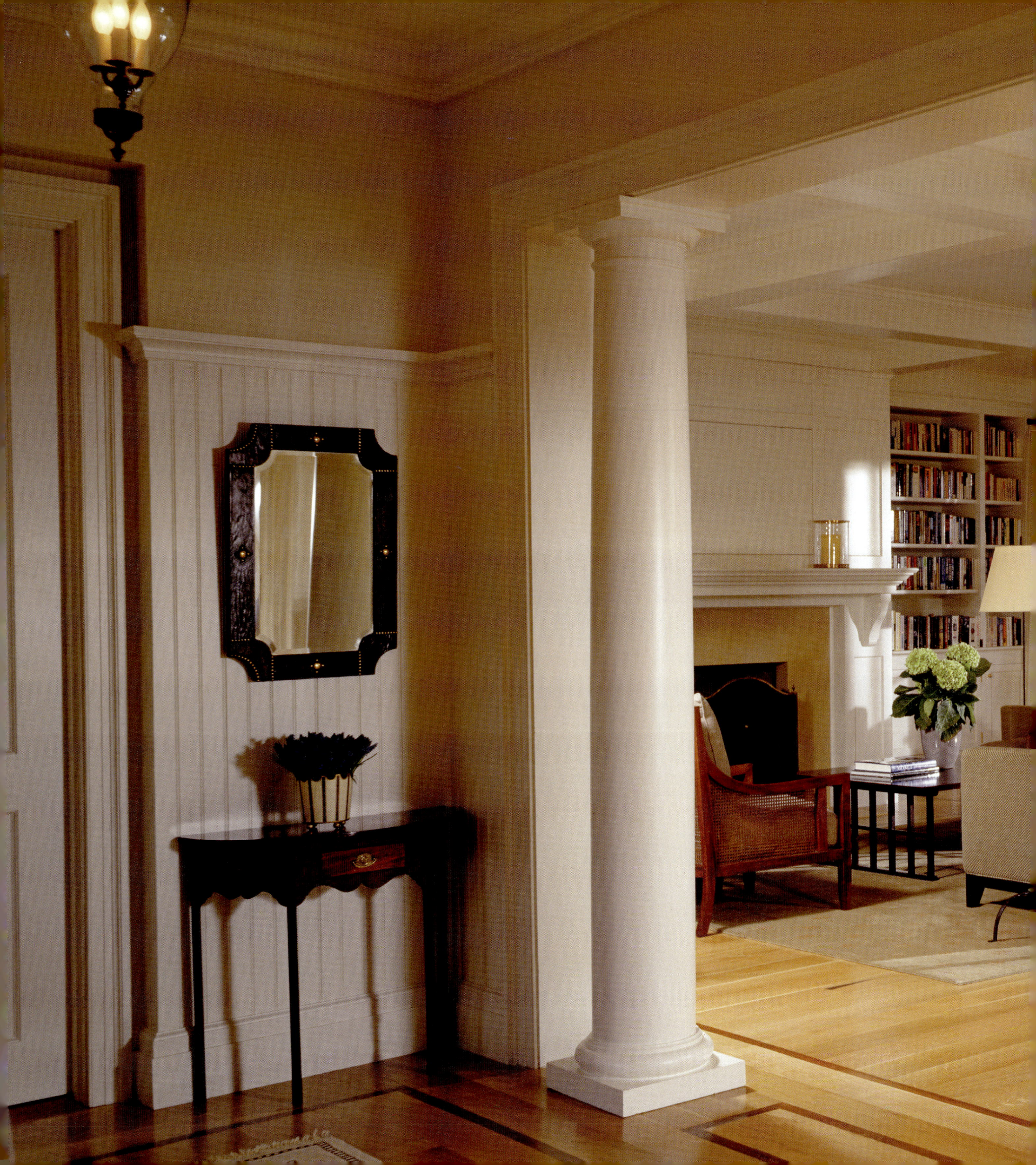

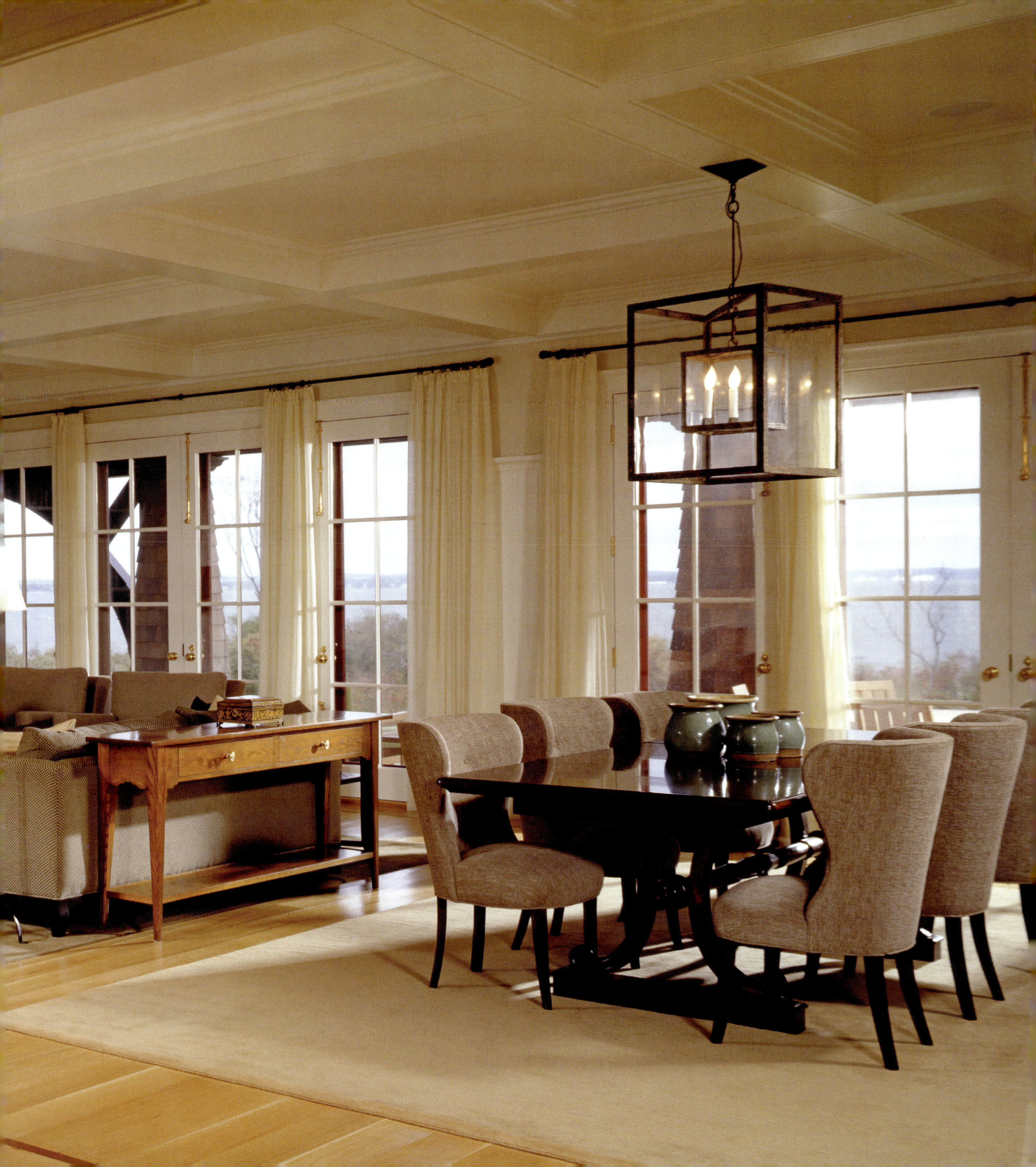

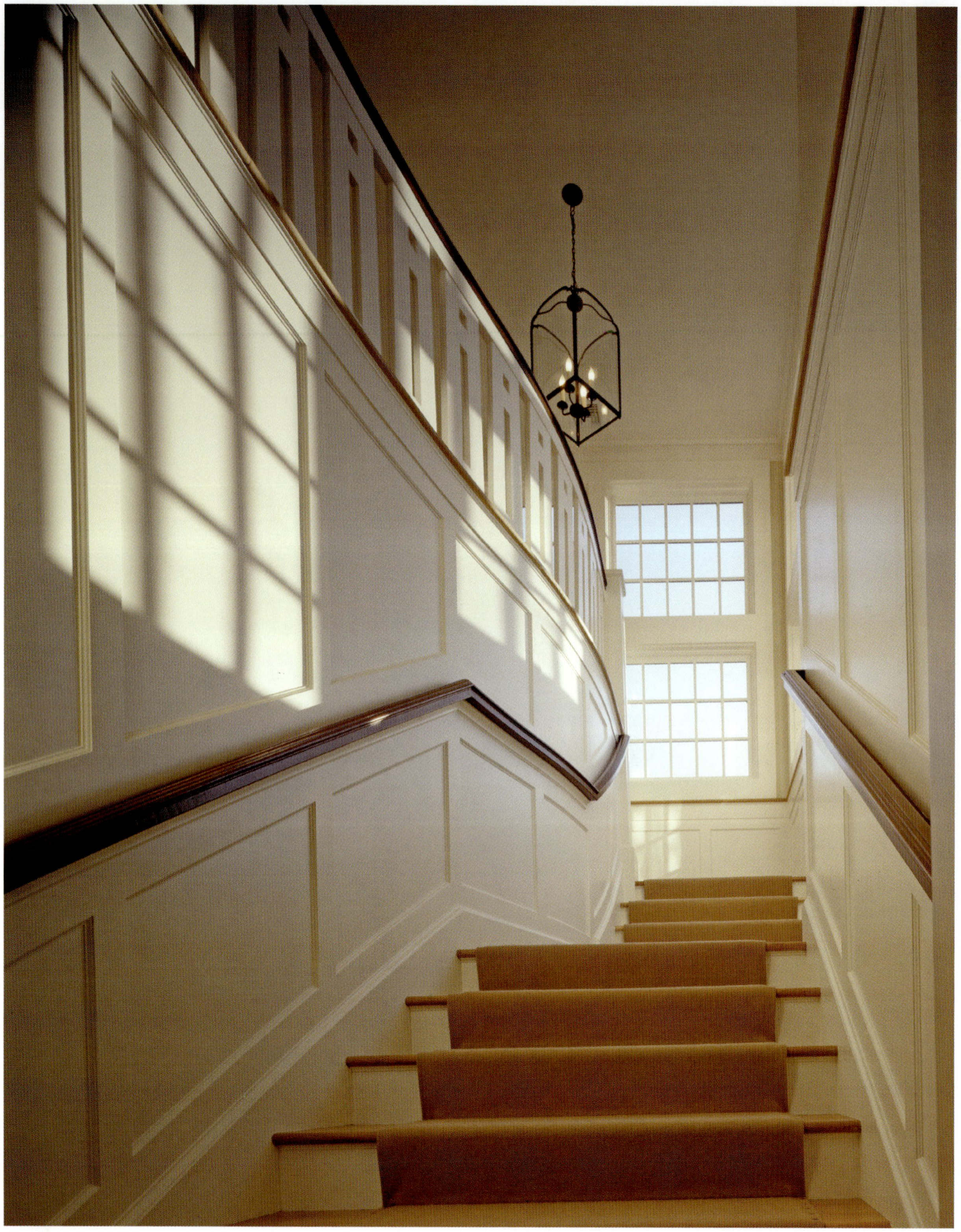

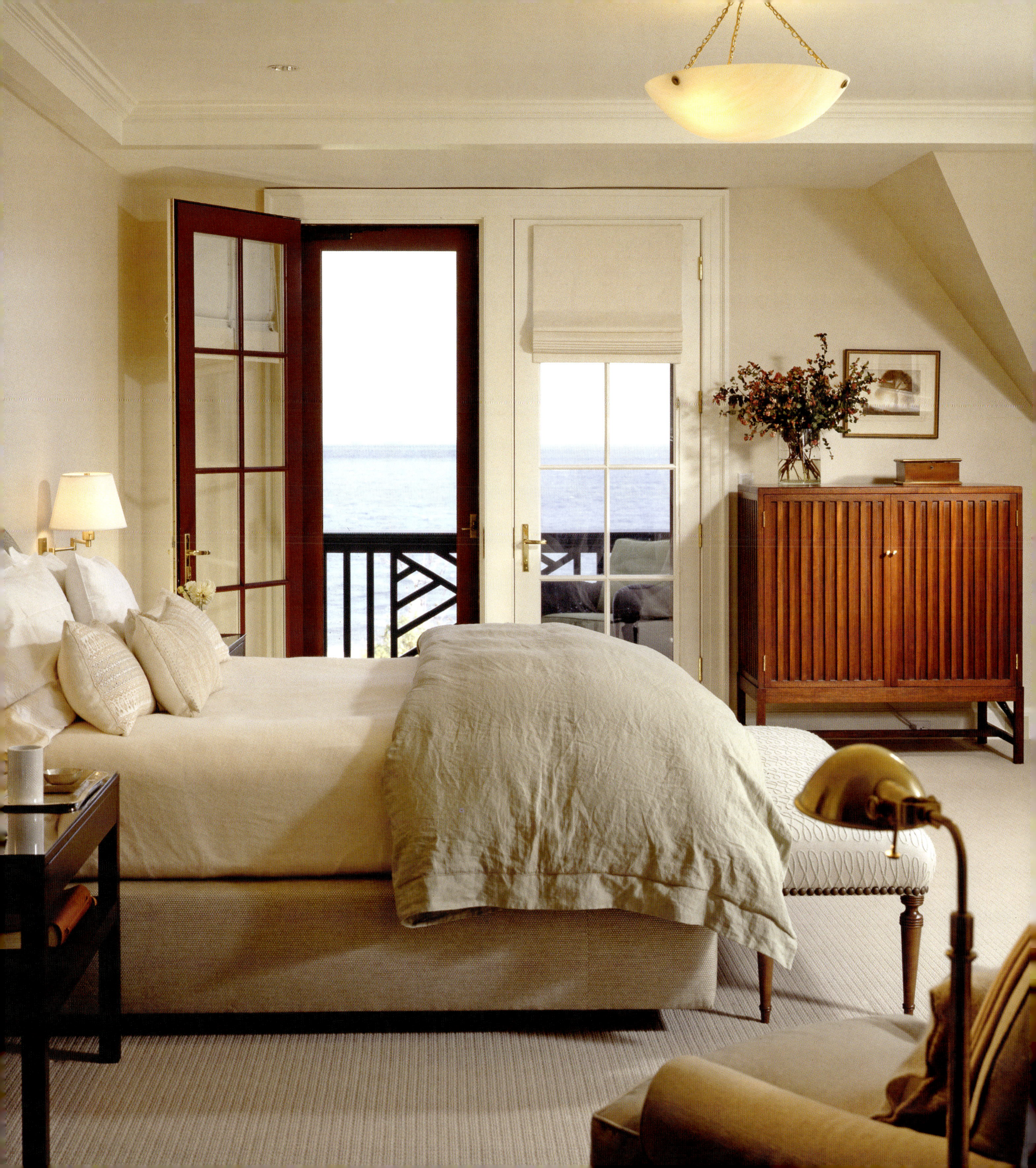

SITE PLAN

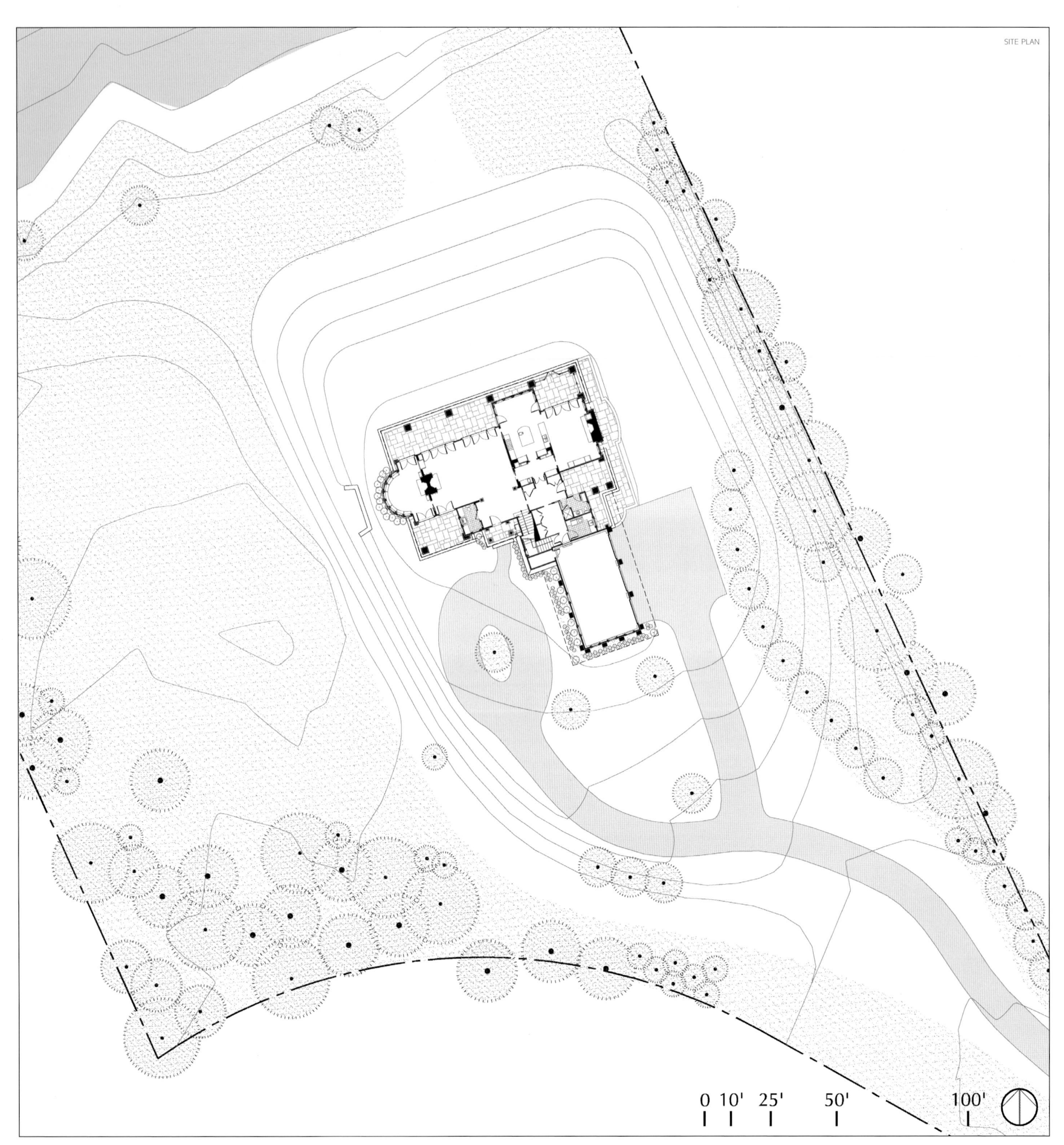

0 10' 25'   50'   100'

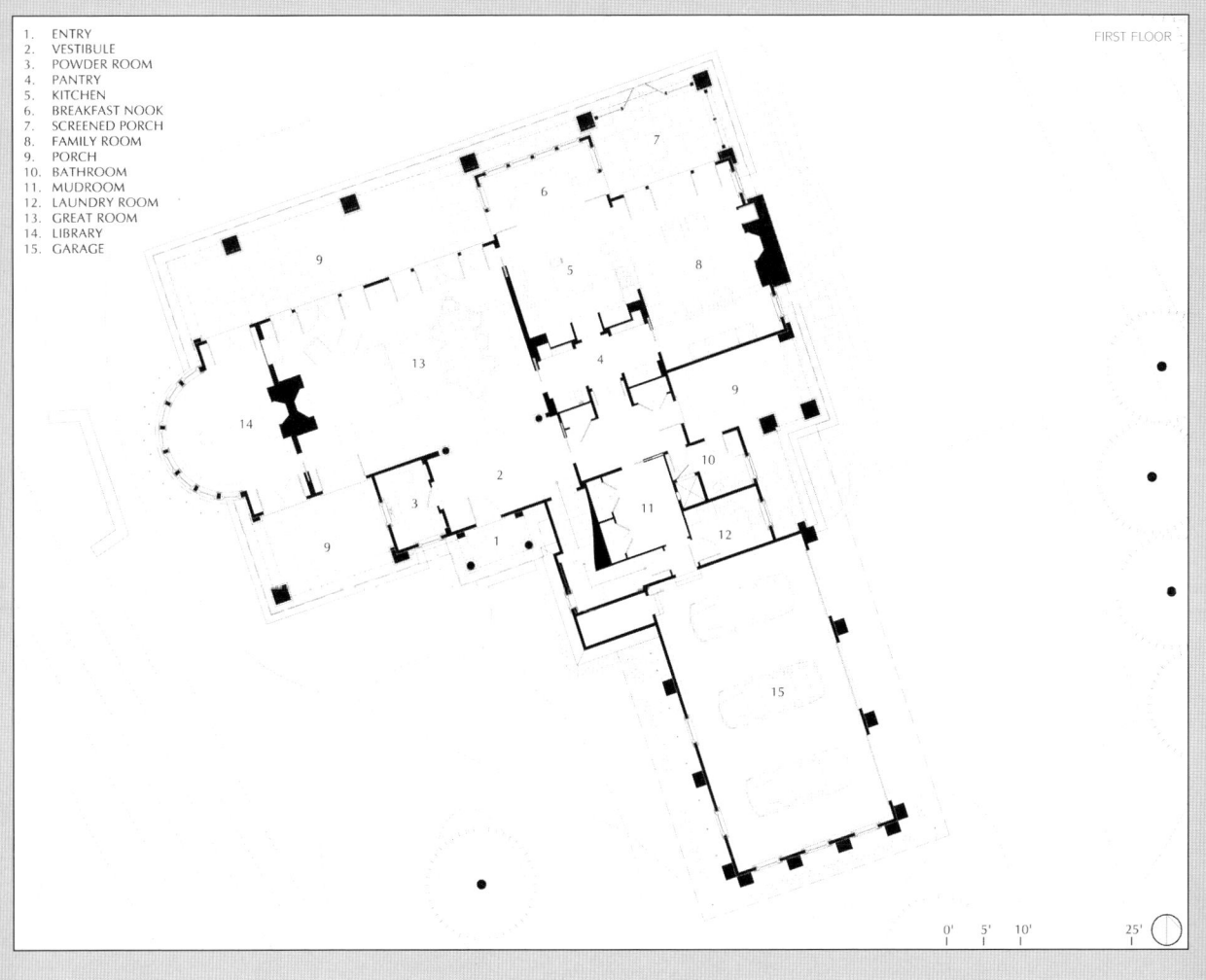

FIRST FLOOR

1. ENTRY
2. VESTIBULE
3. POWDER ROOM
4. PANTRY
5. KITCHEN
6. BREAKFAST NOOK
7. SCREENED PORCH
8. FAMILY ROOM
9. PORCH
10. BATHROOM
11. MUDROOM
12. LAUNDRY ROOM
13. GREAT ROOM
14. LIBRARY
15. GARAGE

SECOND FLOOR

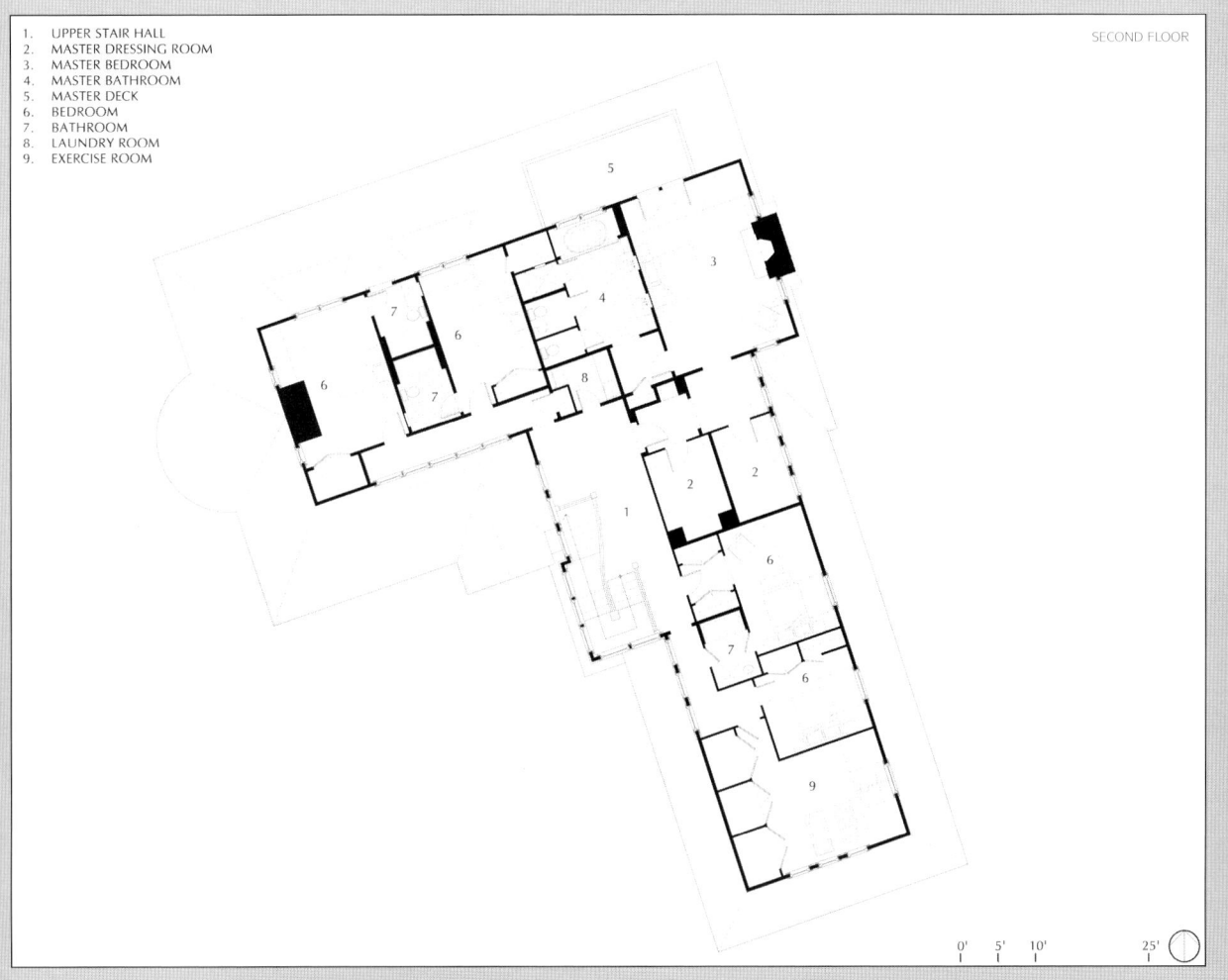

1. UPPER STAIR HALL
2. MASTER DRESSING ROOM
3. MASTER BEDROOM
4. MASTER BATHROOM
5. MASTER DECK
6. BEDROOM
7. BATHROOM
8. LAUNDRY ROOM
9. EXERCISE ROOM

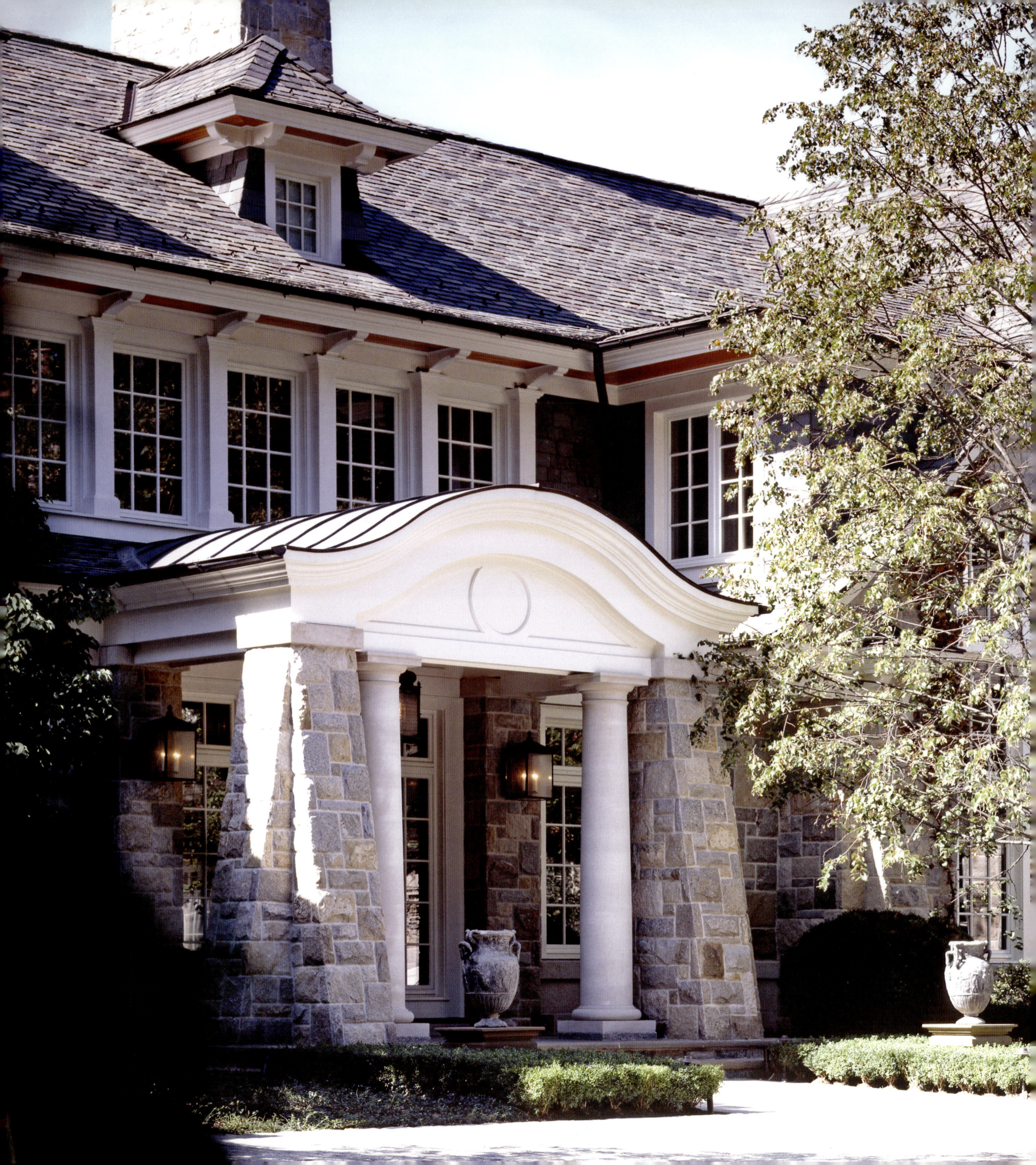

FAMILY GATHERINGS AND ROOMS FOR ENTERTAINING DEFINE THE LOOK OF A STONE COUNTRY HOUSE

THE CLIENTS The couple, both of whom are Manhattan philanthropists in the areas of art and medicine, had spent weekends on New York's North Shore of Long Island for many years. With four married children and many grandchildren coming to visit them, they found their previous house to be too small—and needed a home that would be more accommodating.

THE DESIGN BRIEF In addition to wanting a home that could be a haven for family gatherings, and where they could entertain large numbers of friends, the clients also desired an elegant country house where they could display their contemporary paintings. The clients also wished a house that looked as though it had been there for a long time—something that was reminiscent of an English manor house, with a stone exterior and sloping slate roofs. The 22-acre site is wooded and secluded, with a rolling topography to the land that makes it ideal for taking long walks. The sound and presence of water also play an important role. The house is large—240 feet long—so the challenge for the architects was to make sure it was well integrated with the property, rather than reading like a massive giant block.

THE SOLUTION Careful attention has been given to the proportion, scale, and rhythm of the house, which is made up of a series of wings that stretch out into the landscape—designed by Armstrong Berger of Dallas, Texas. The house had to be broken down into elements that relate to one another but that can work individually. Each wing captures a different view and has different functions. The several roofs interact with each other like a series of waterfalls. One is conical, capping a short tower next to a tall chimney; together they suggest rocks sticking up out of a waterfall. The masonry on the house is granite, in soft mixed colors of gray, tan, and brown. Inside, the spaces are generously scaled, but not intimidating, evoking the rooms of a rambling English manor. Windows and doors frame picturesque views. The New York interior design firm Sills Huniford helped their clients to arrange their important collection of contemporary paintings and sculpture in such a way that it created a dialogue between the art and the antique furniture throughout the house. For instance, in the two-story front hall, a painting by the American abstract painter Brice Marden hangs above a 1730 boulle marquetry table, while a sculpture by Catalán Surrealist artist Joan Miró anchors the space below an elegant Regency-style stair railing. On each side of the living room fireplace are paintings by the contemporary German artist Gerhard Richter, and the American painter, Robert Ryman. There are other works by such masters as Pablo Picasso, Henri Matisse, and Mark Rothko throughout the house. A photograph by Cindy Sherman hangs over the dining room fireplace on damask-covered walls treated to resemble embossed antique leather. Scale and rich visual variety are very important in the creation of a comfortable mood for a family that spans four generations.

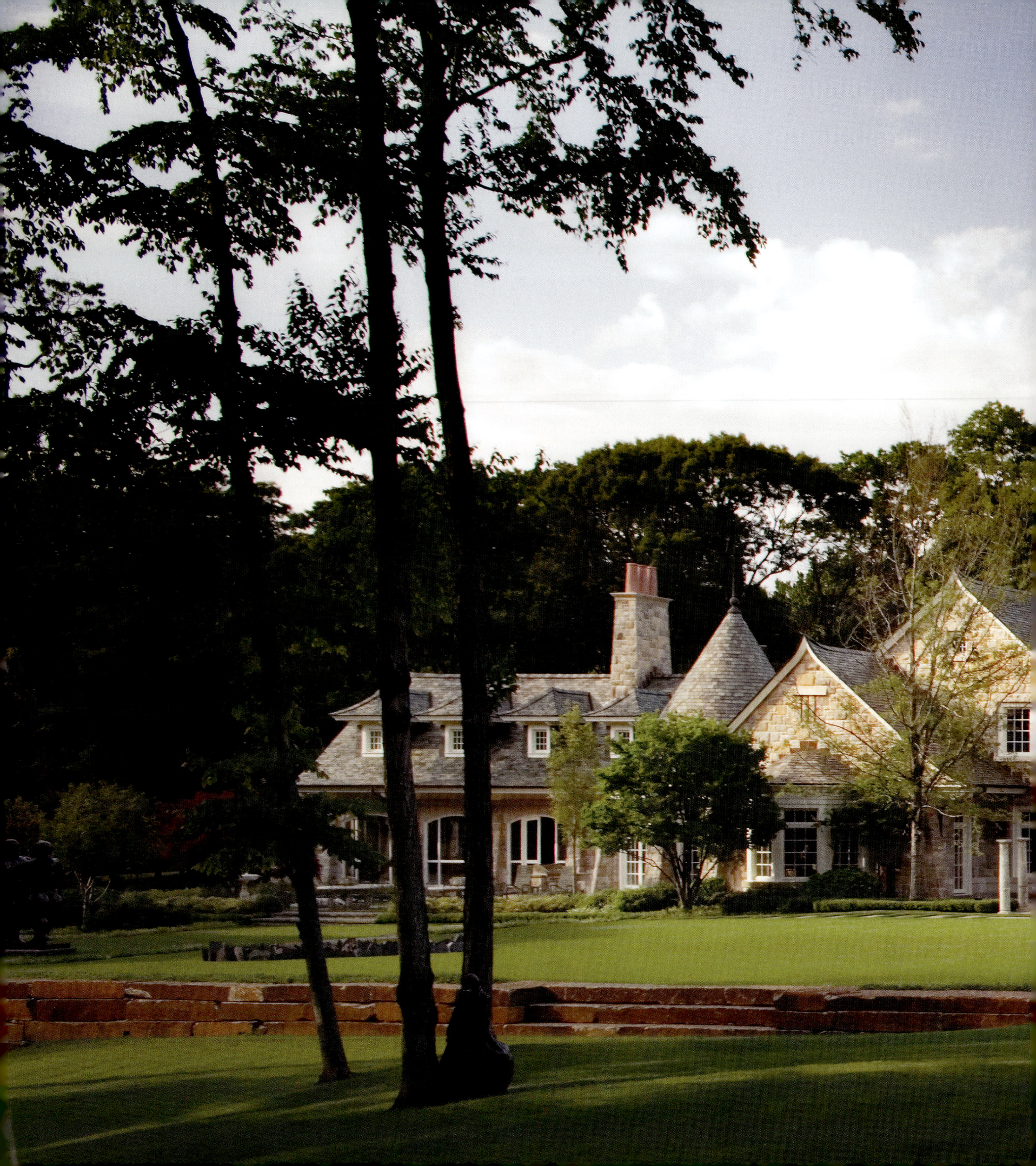

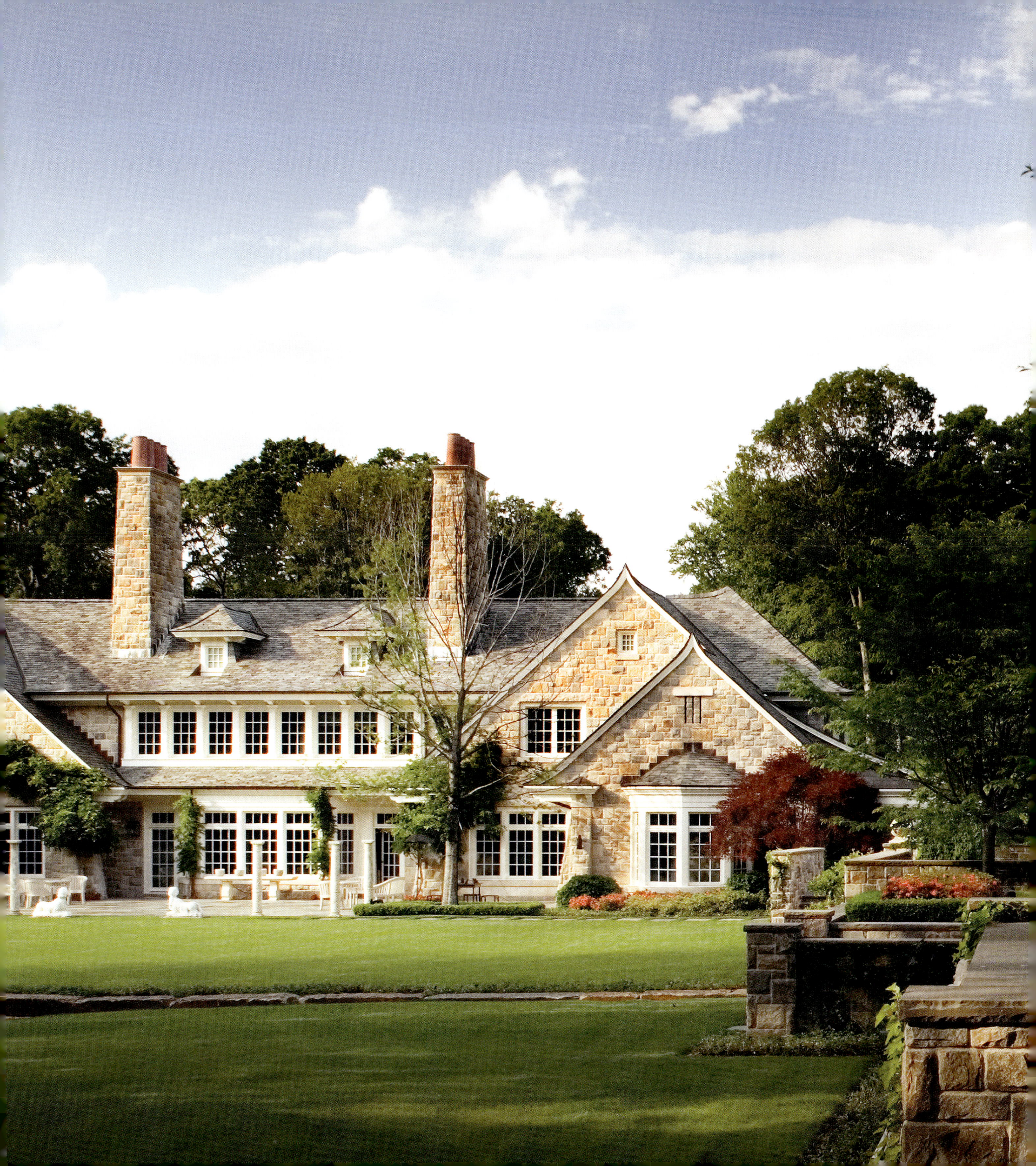

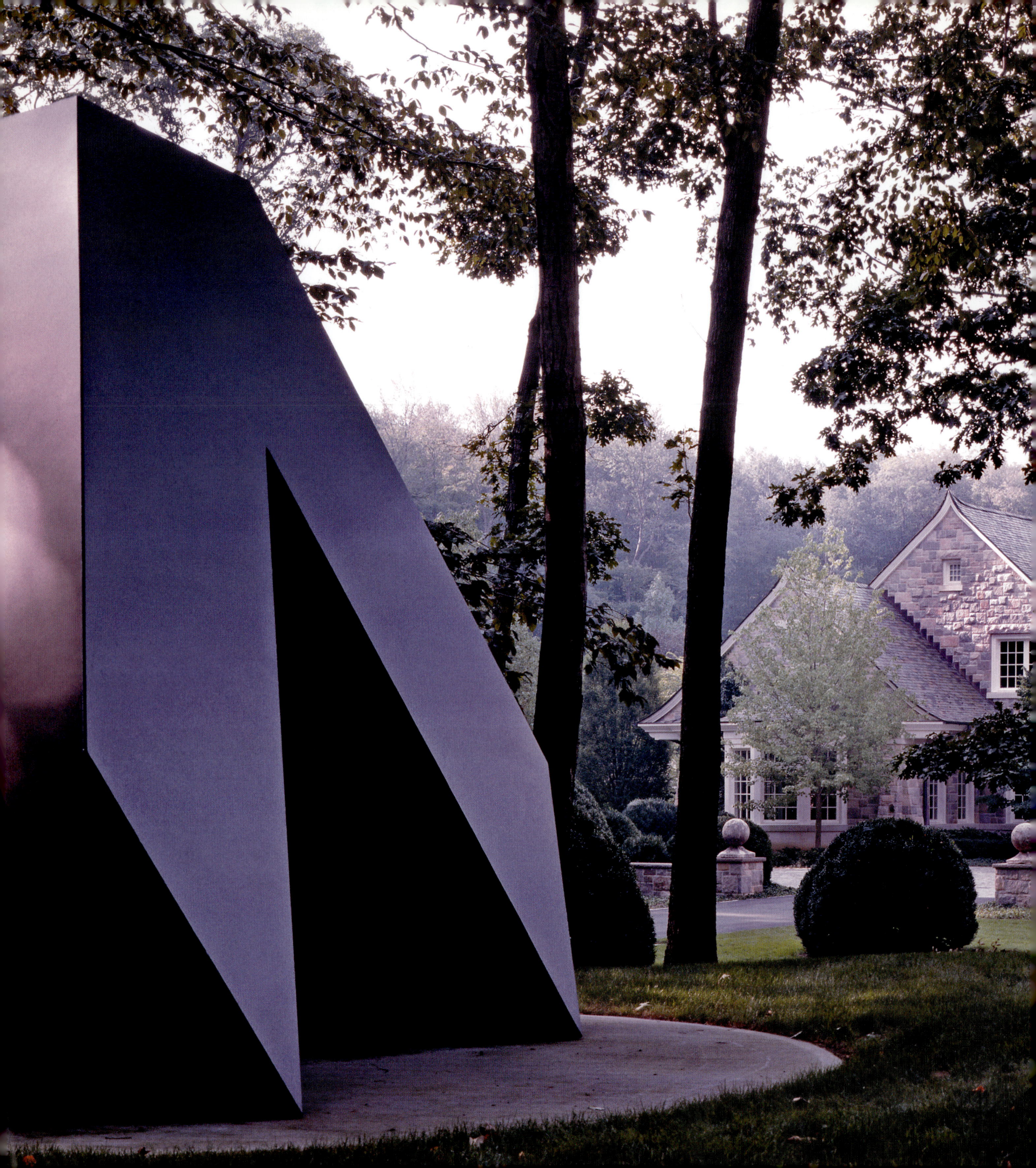

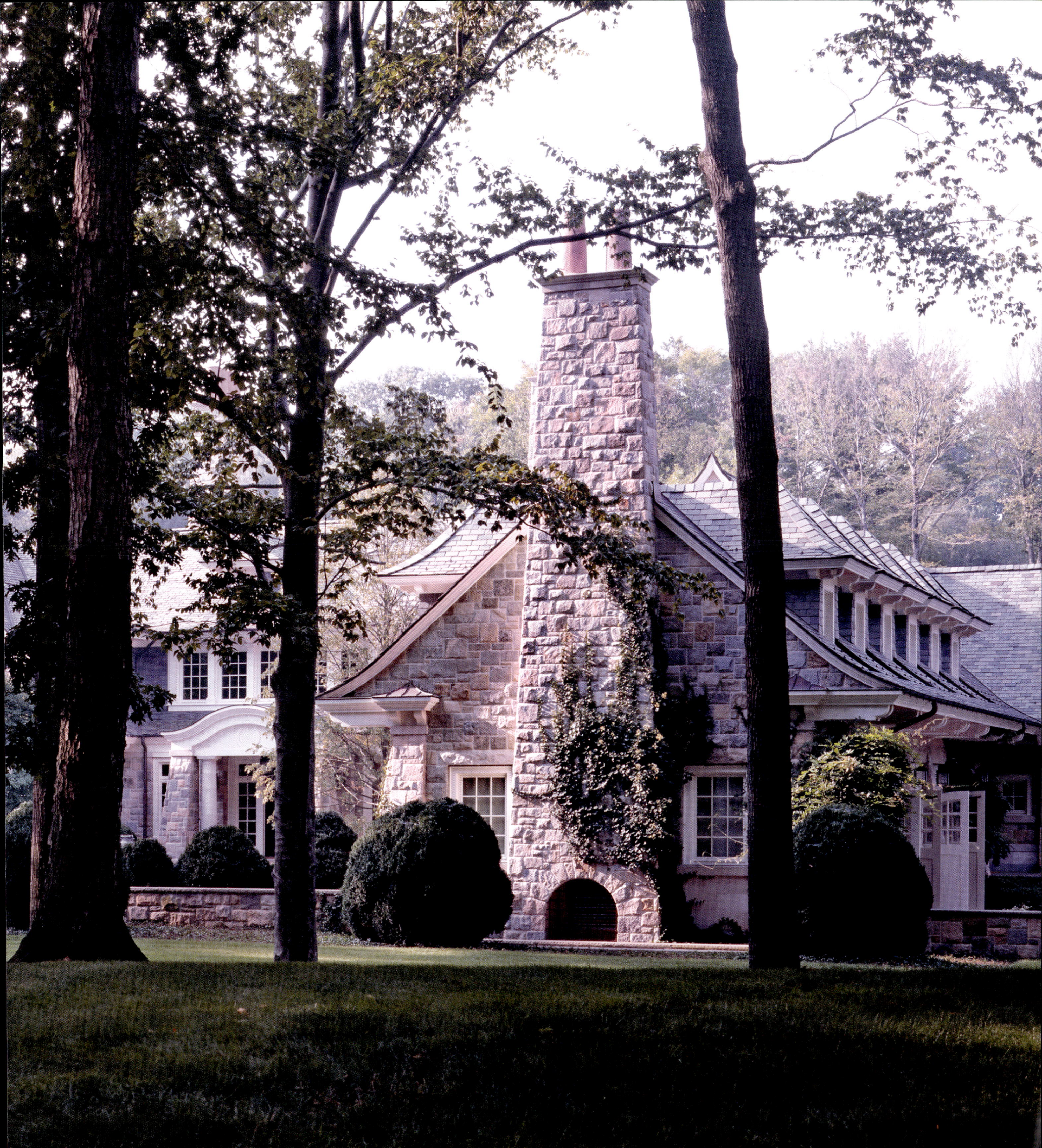

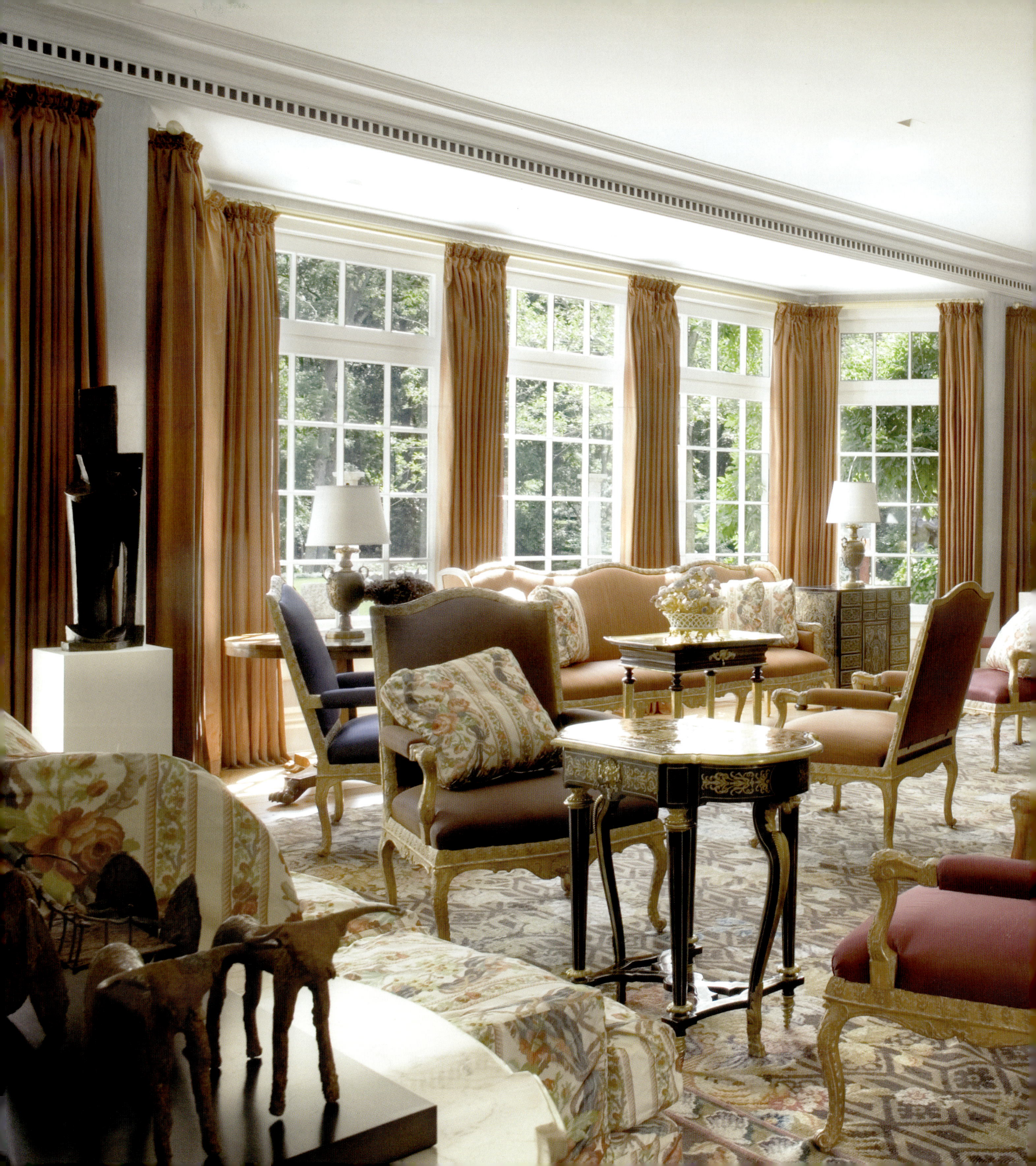

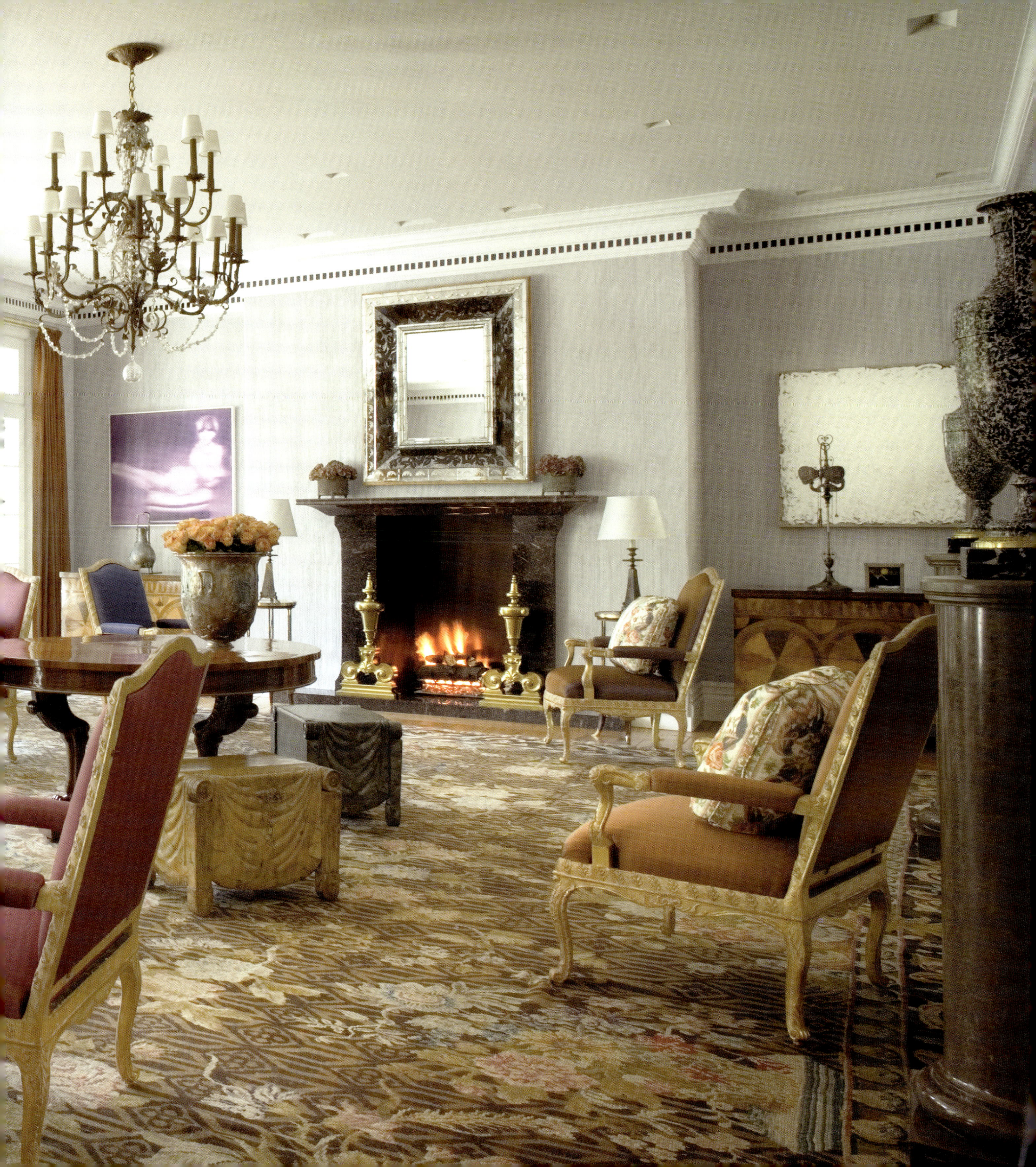

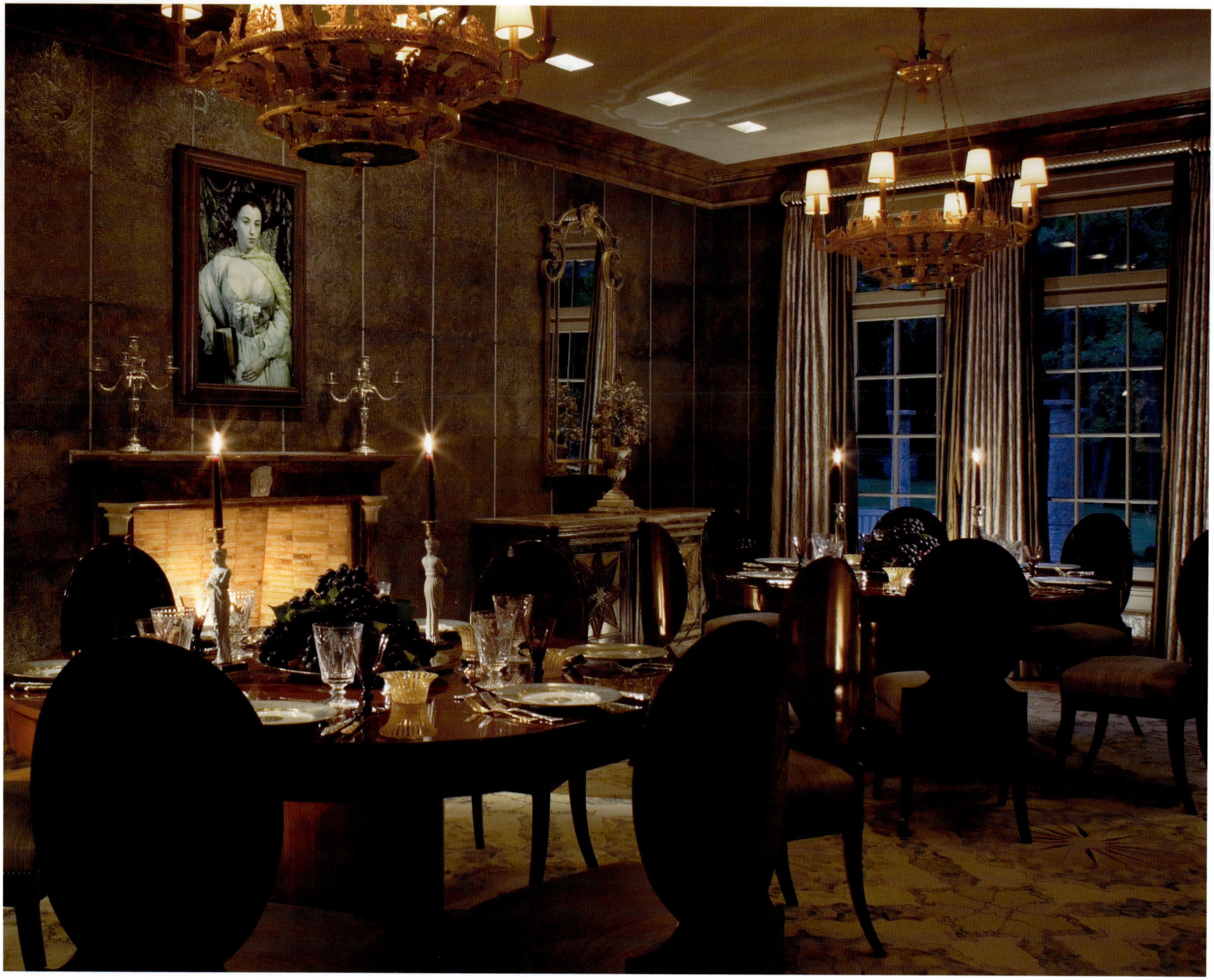

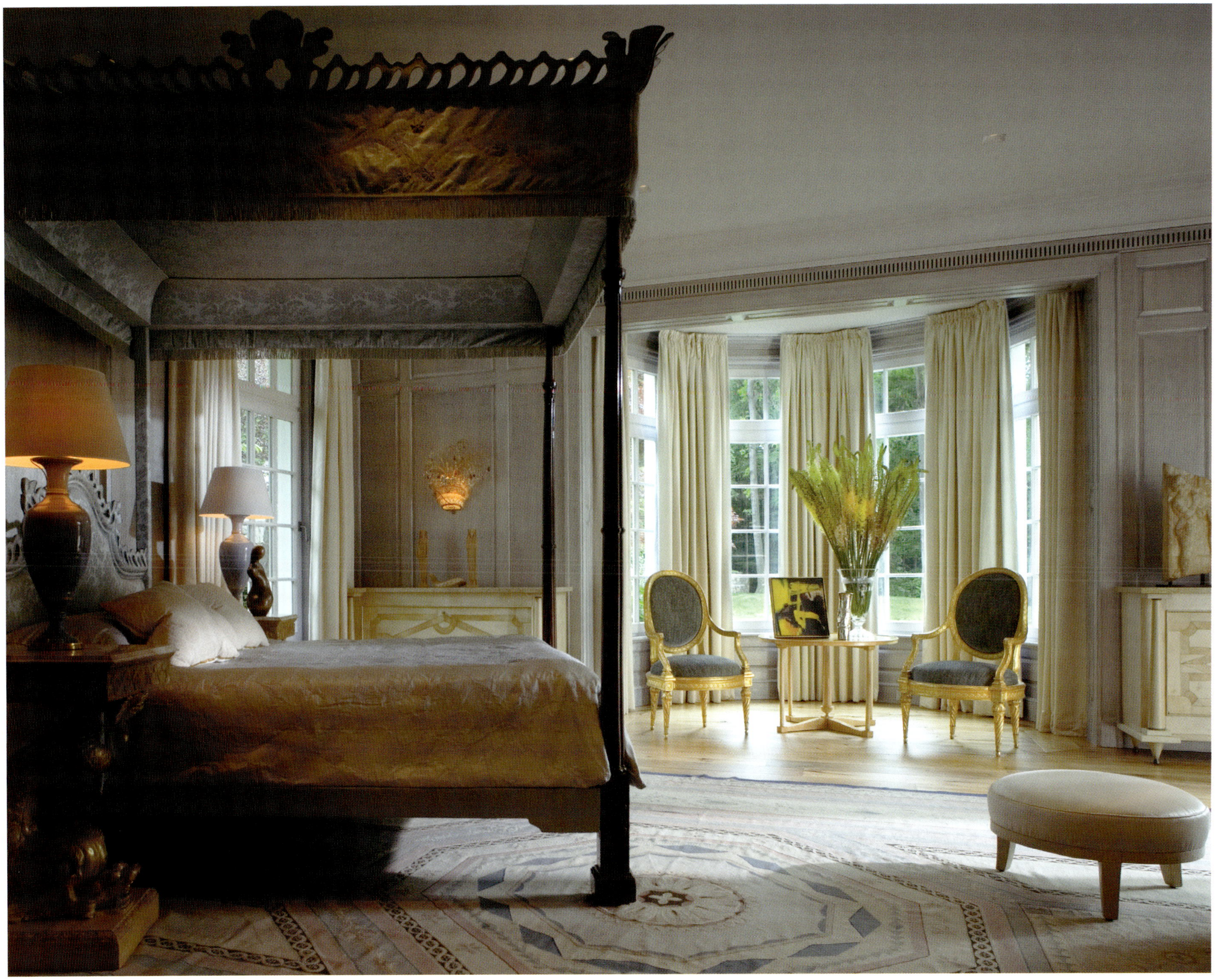

SITE PLAN

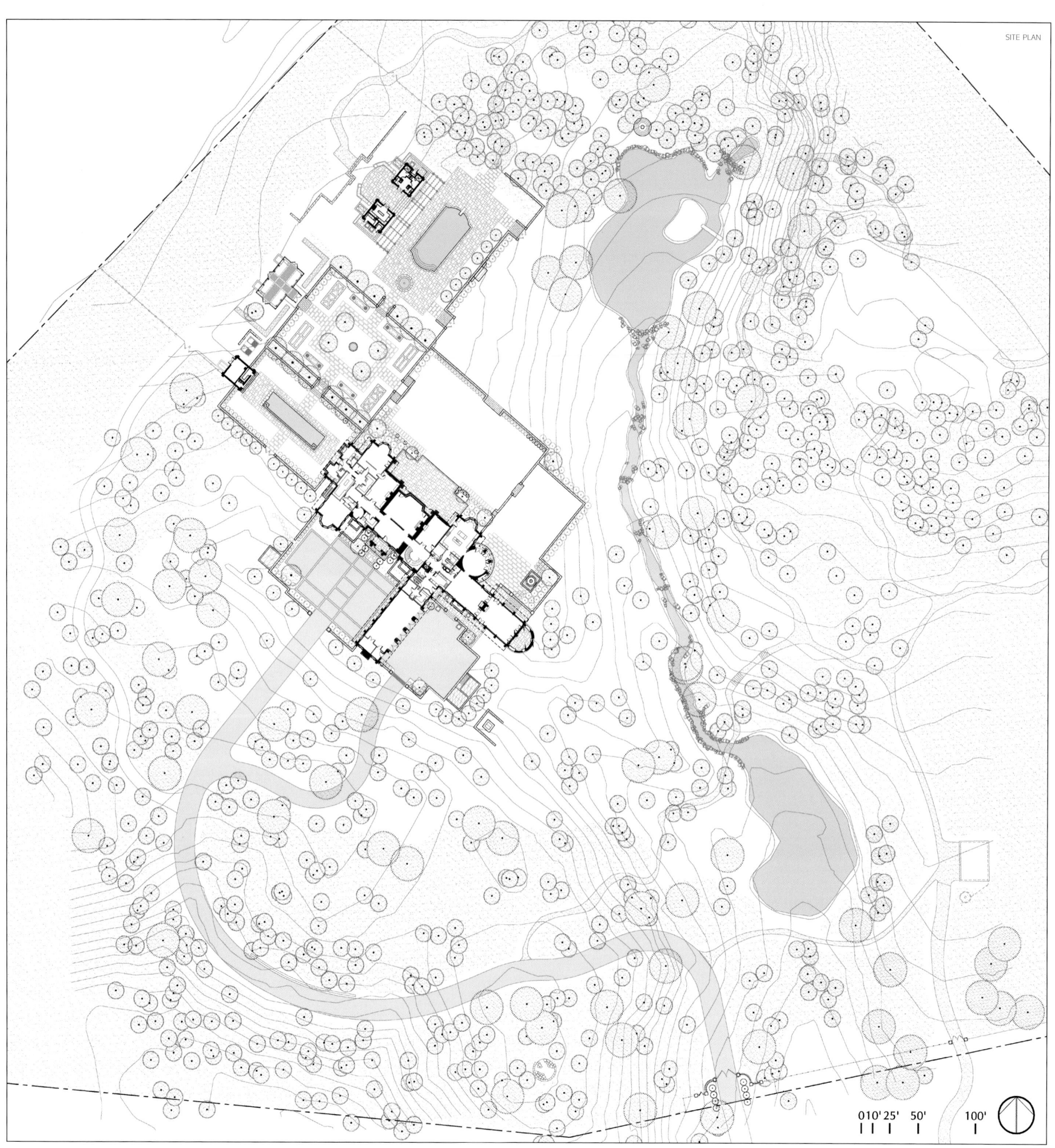

244

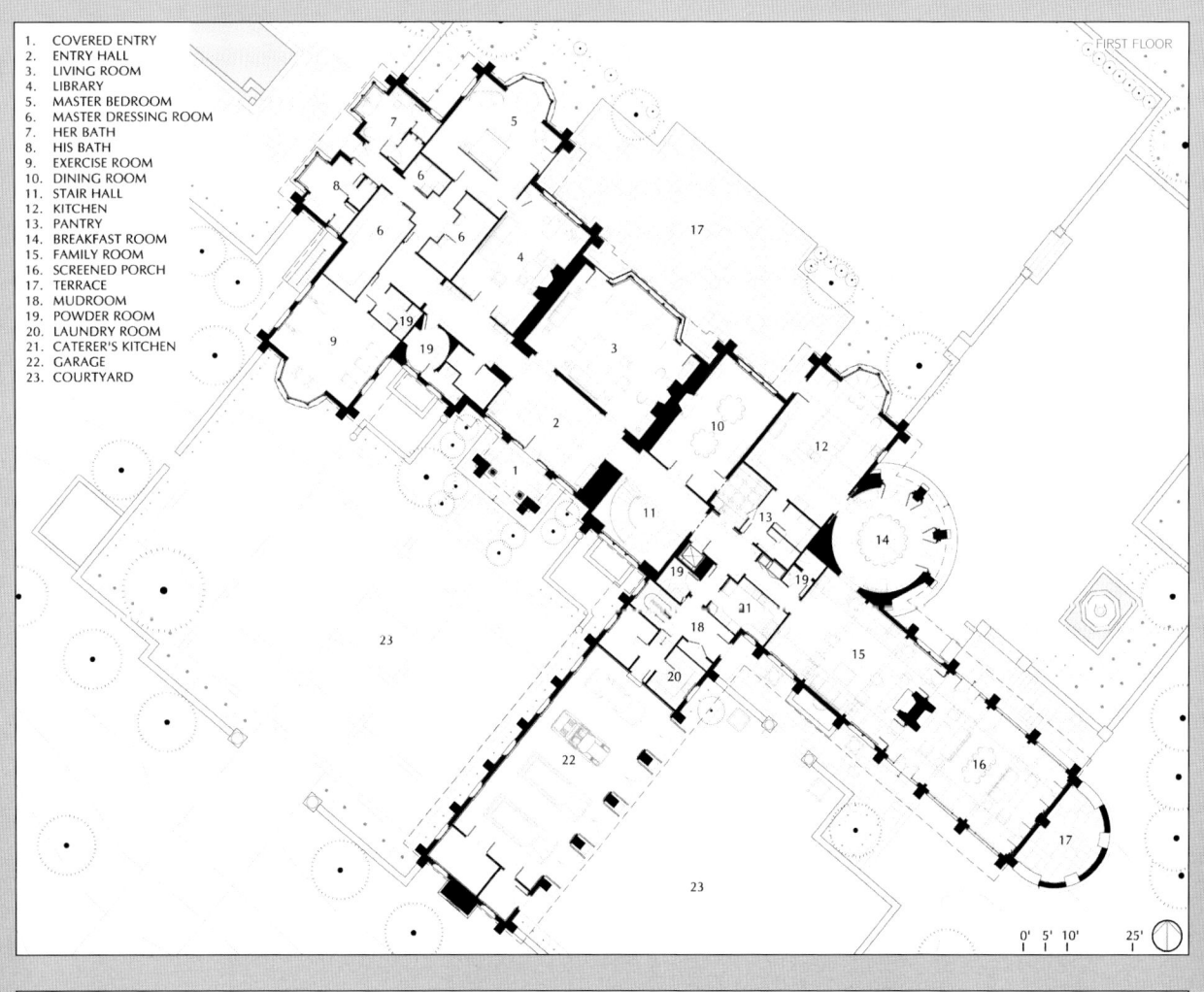

FIRST FLOOR

1. COVERED ENTRY
2. ENTRY HALL
3. LIVING ROOM
4. LIBRARY
5. MASTER BEDROOM
6. MASTER DRESSING ROOM
7. HER BATH
8. HIS BATH
9. EXERCISE ROOM
10. DINING ROOM
11. STAIR HALL
12. KITCHEN
13. PANTRY
14. BREAKFAST ROOM
15. FAMILY ROOM
16. SCREENED PORCH
17. TERRACE
18. MUDROOM
19. POWDER ROOM
20. LAUNDRY ROOM
21. CATERER'S KITCHEN
22. GARAGE
23. COURTYARD

SECOND FLOOR

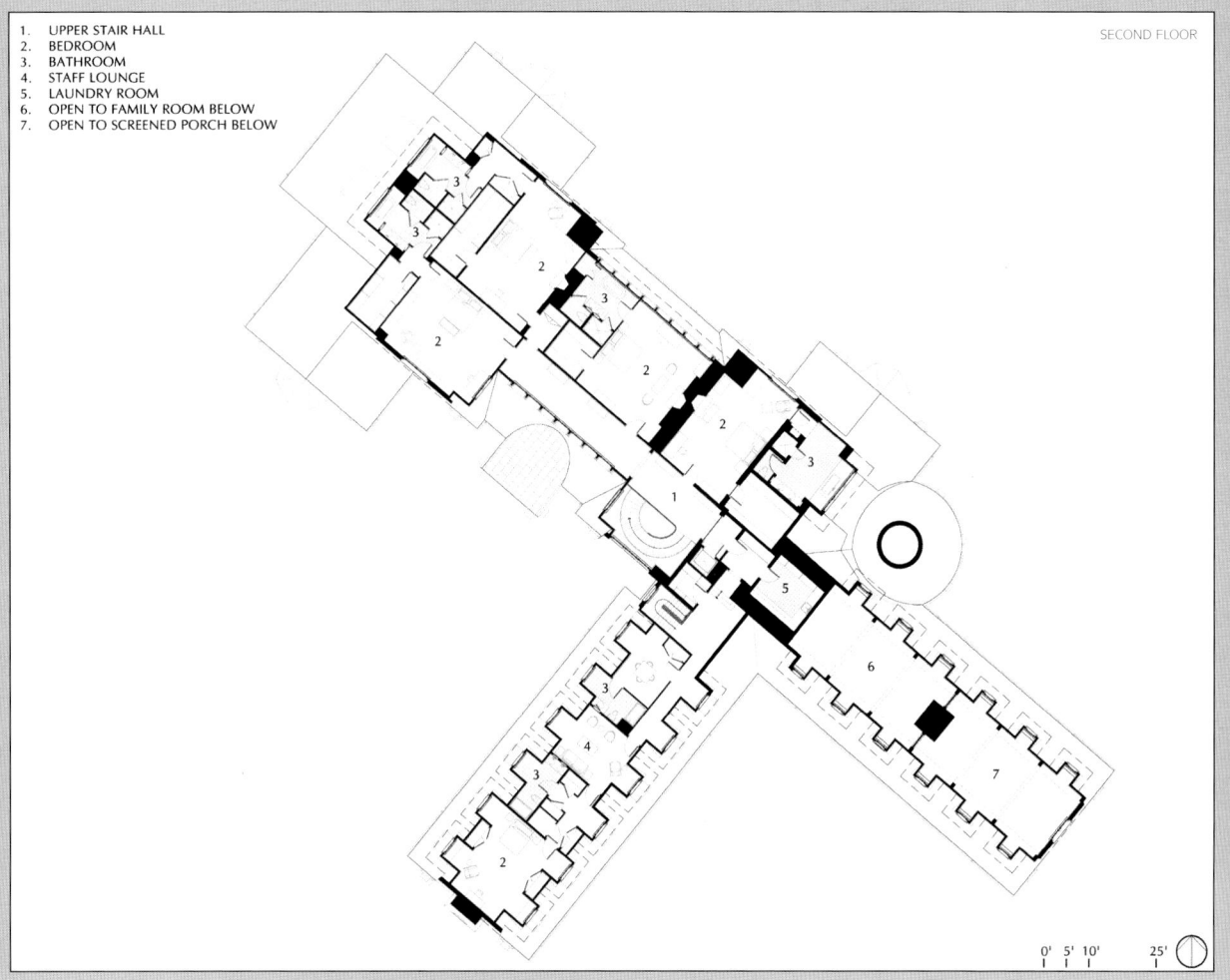

1. UPPER STAIR HALL
2. BEDROOM
3. BATHROOM
4. STAFF LOUNGE
5. LAUNDRY ROOM
6. OPEN TO FAMILY ROOM BELOW
7. OPEN TO SCREENED PORCH BELOW

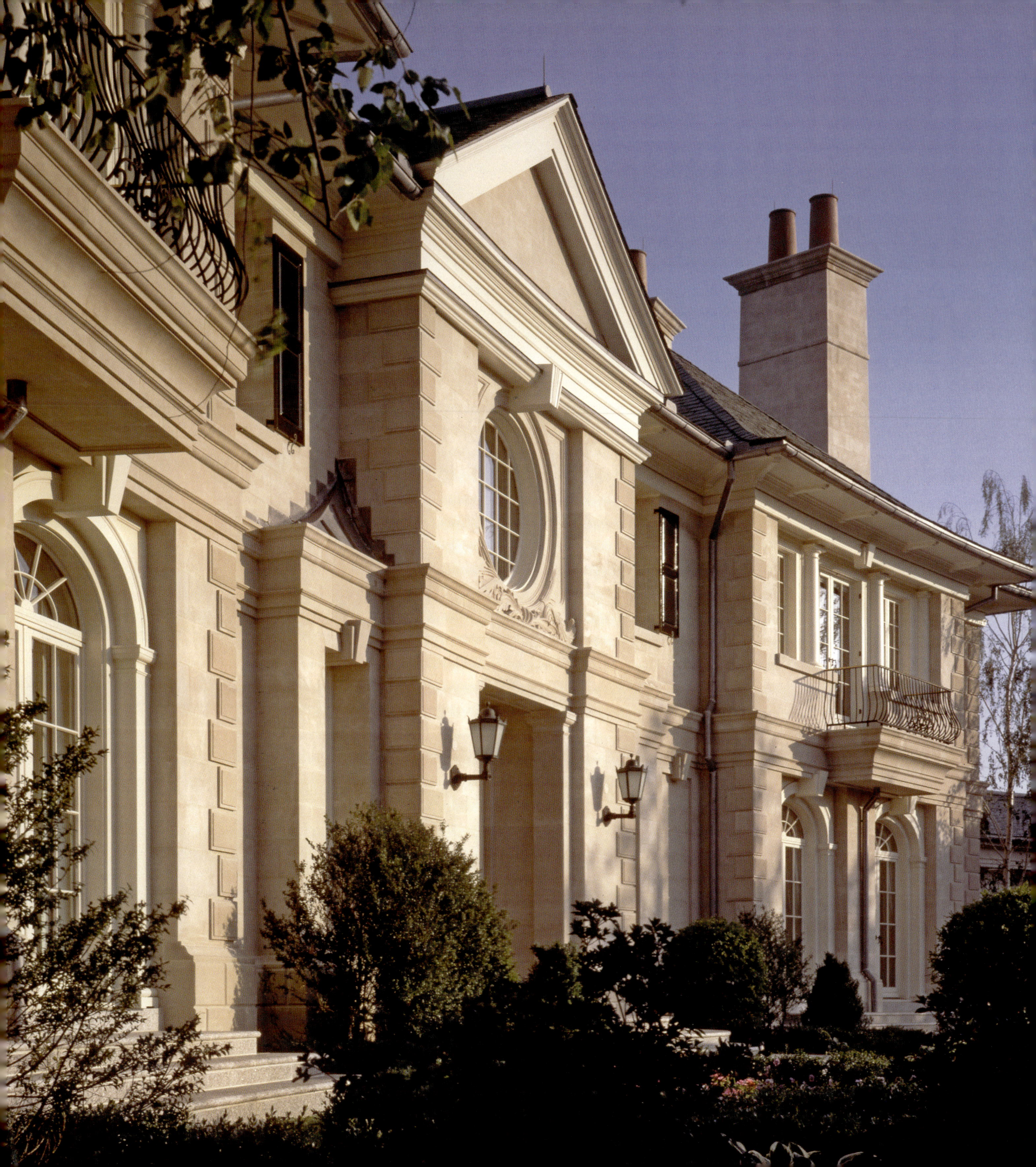

GALLERY-LIKE SPACES FOR A COLLECTION OF MODERN ART IN A LIMESTONE COUNTRY HOUSE.

THE CLIENTS The client is an entrepreneur and philanthropist who lives in a suburb of Boston. He and his wife have grown children. They had been looking for a dignified home with generous space for their important collection of late nineteenth and early twentieth century art.

THE DESIGN BRIEF The clients liked English Georgian architecture because of its formality, symmetry, and even the predictability of its building style. They favored cut stone, rather than brick or wood. While a certain symmetrical effect was desired, the clients also wanted some individual distinction that would set the house apart from other Georgian Revival mansions. And inside there had to be gallery-like rooms for their art collection.

THE SOLUTION The 12-acre site, adjacent to a golf course, has an abundance of trees. Colorful flowerbeds line the winding drive, which hugs a large pond. At the end of the drive, a central fountain plays in the entrance courtyard, which is elliptical to fit the curve of the façade. All of these elements—the concave bow of the façade, the fountain, even the flowers on the approach—conspire to relieve what would otherwise be the rather forbidding mass of a formal Georgian building with its rows of windows, ranked quoins marching up the corners, and a sharply defined pediment that looms over the entrance door. The severity of the cut limestone, used as the building material throughout, is lightened by its pinkish-tan hue. On the side of the 22,000-square-foot house that faces the back garden, the center section is recessed between two wings. This façade is opened up by the placement of large French windows topped by fanlights across the entire expanse. Fronting a wing to the left, a porch with wooden columns and a wooden railing introduces an informal note. Indoors, a curving staircase with an ornamental iron banister, which rises to ring a circular gallery on the second level, distinguishes the three-story-high vestibule. A cupola of small-paned windows caps a high dome. A conservatory opens up to the terraces and the garden beyond, while a sculpture by Fernando Botero, the Colombian artist, is one of the first pieces to greet a visitor. To one side of the vestibule lies the living room, to the other, the dining room. A convex wall in each room reflects the curved walls of the exterior façade; the rooms have deeply coffered ceilings, which draw the eye upward. Boston-based interior designer Judith Ross helped the clients place their works of art. This is a house in which, as in the best eighteenth-century buildings, formality provides a setting for the artful life.

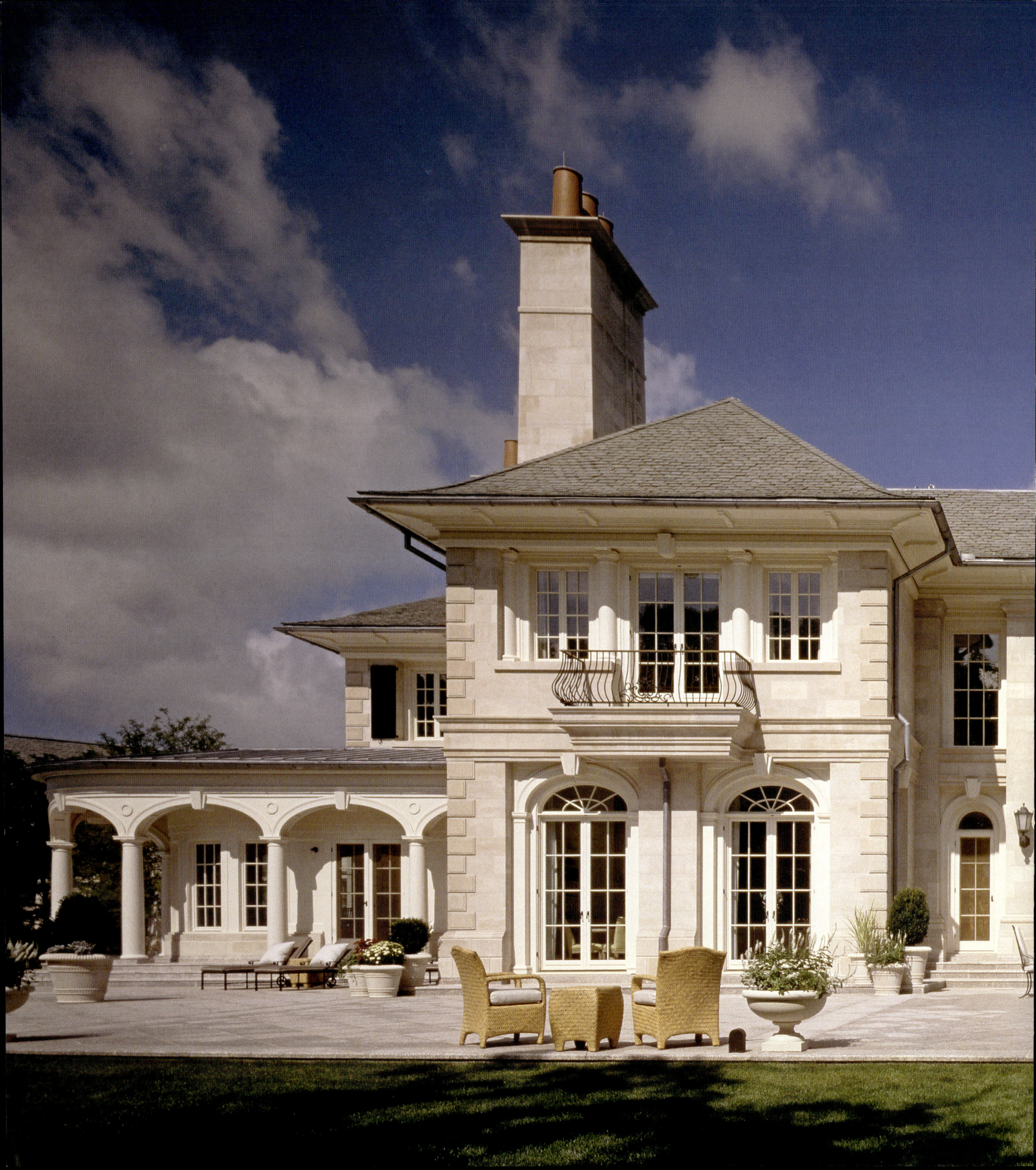

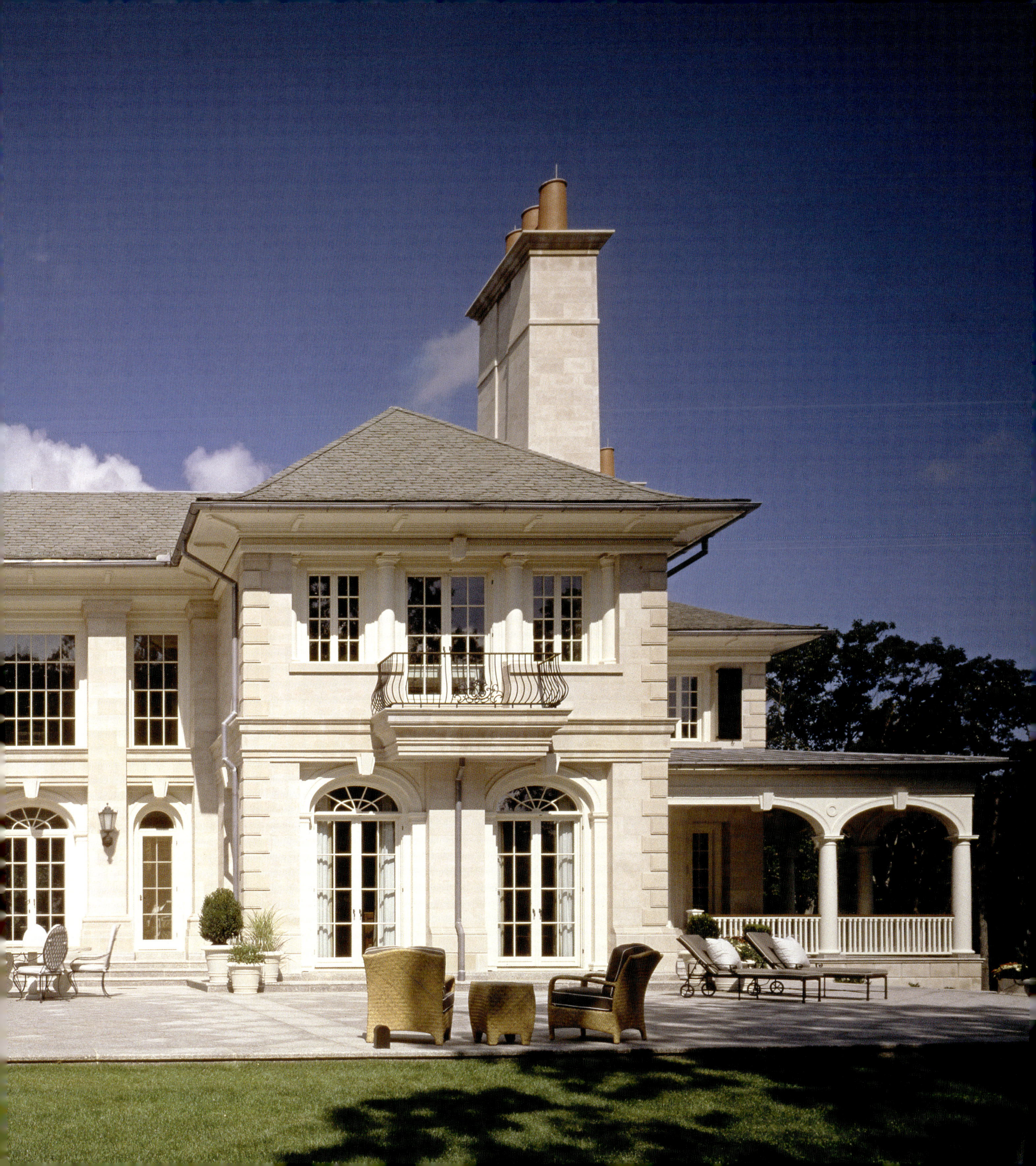

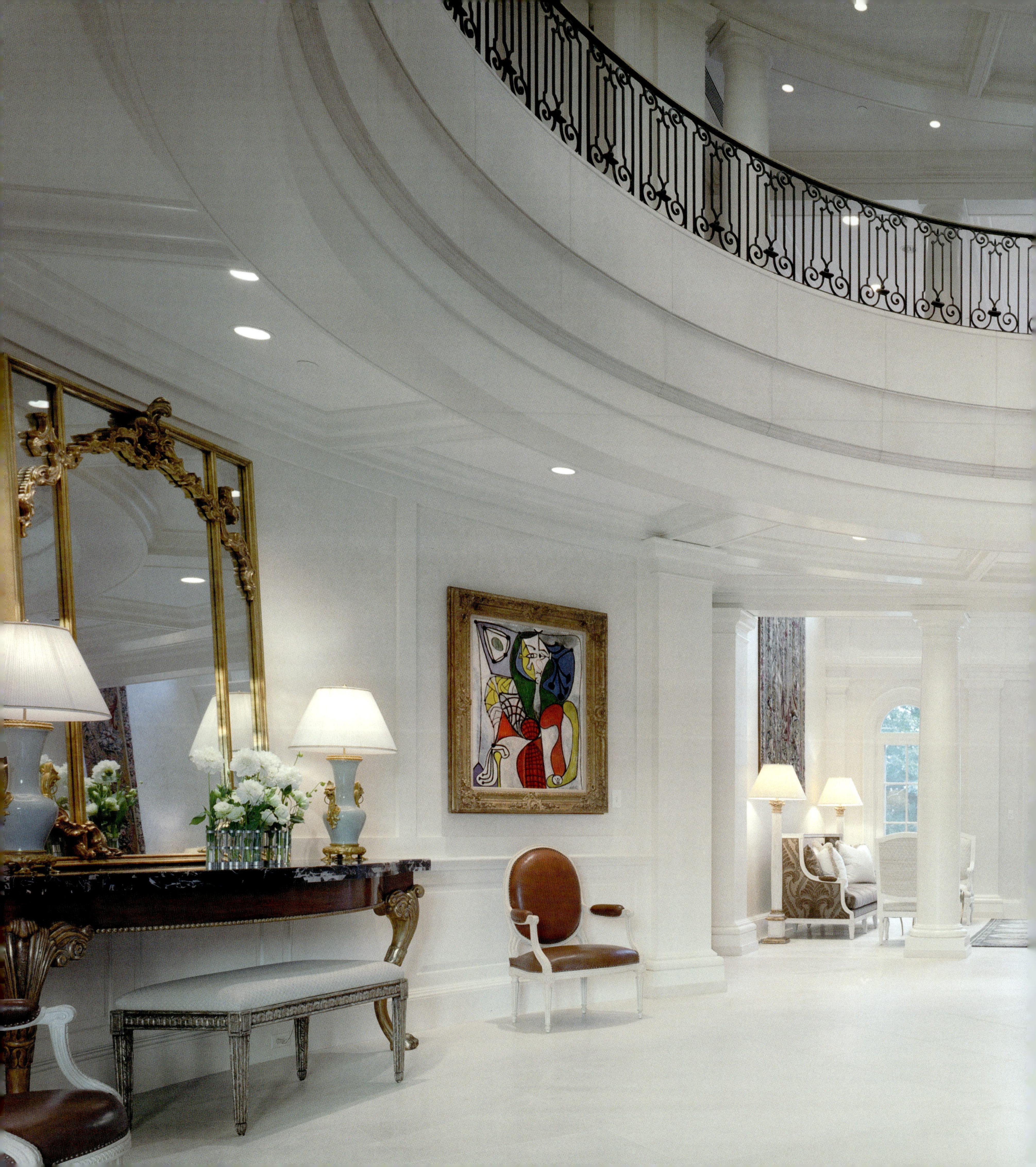

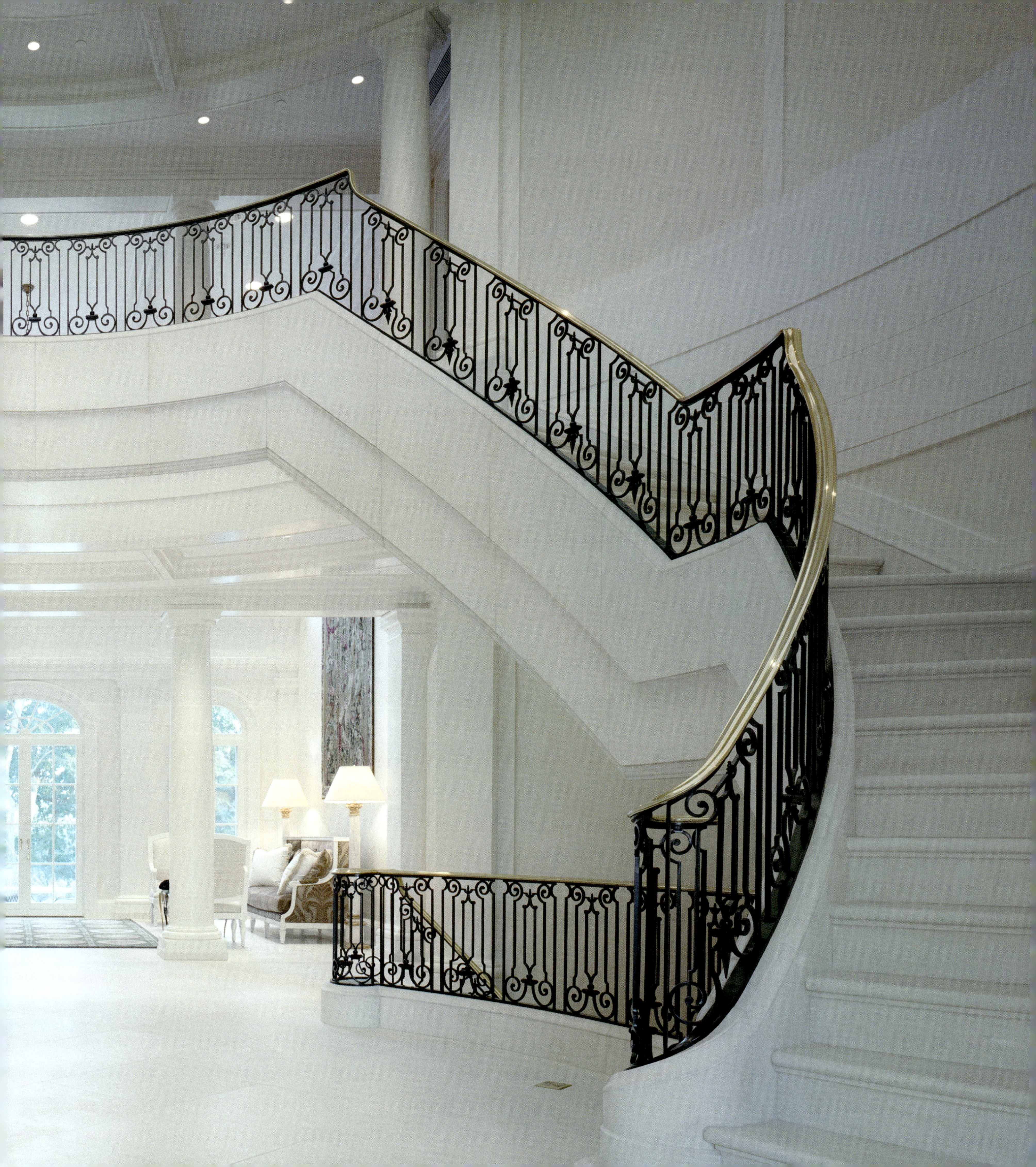

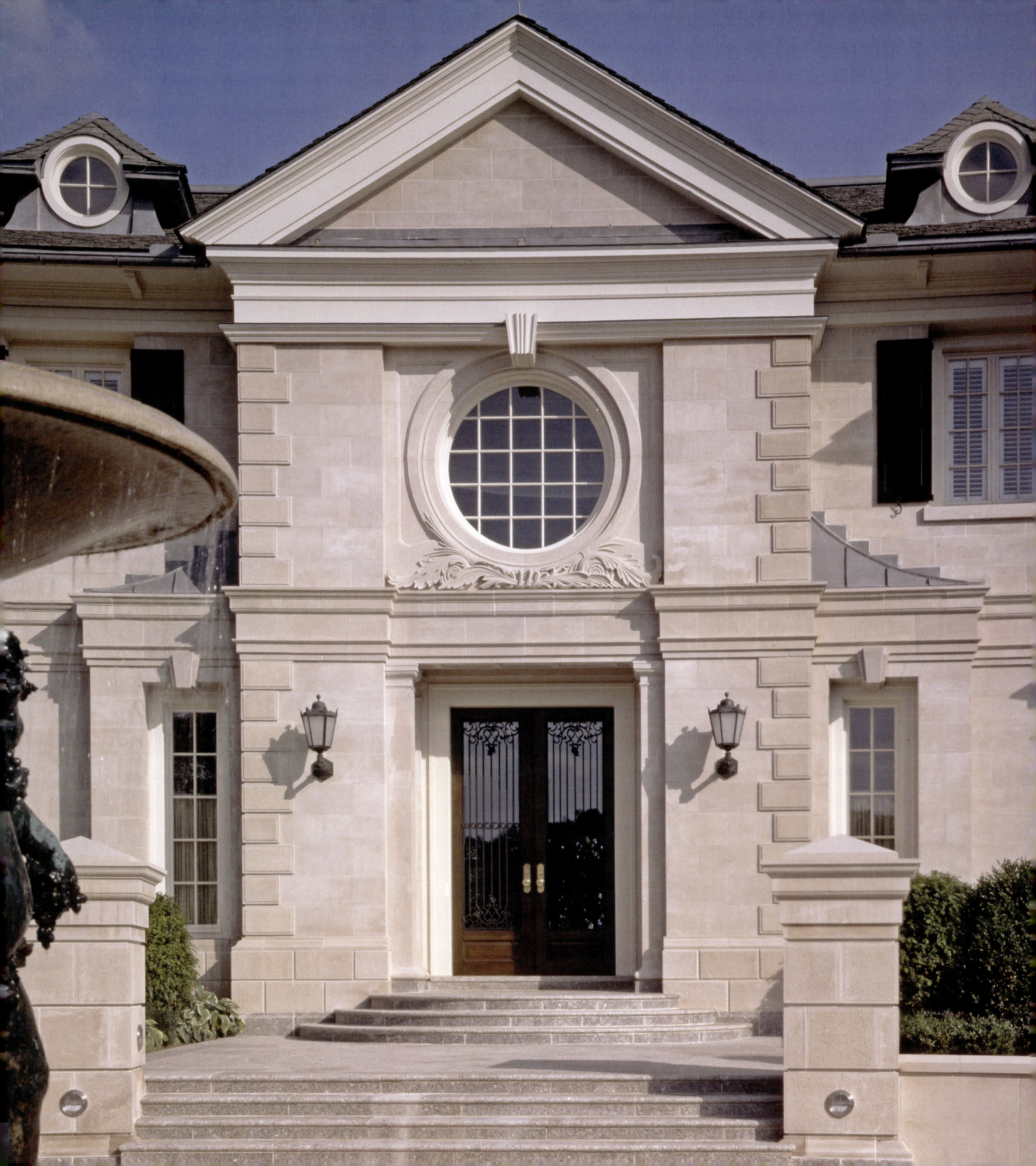

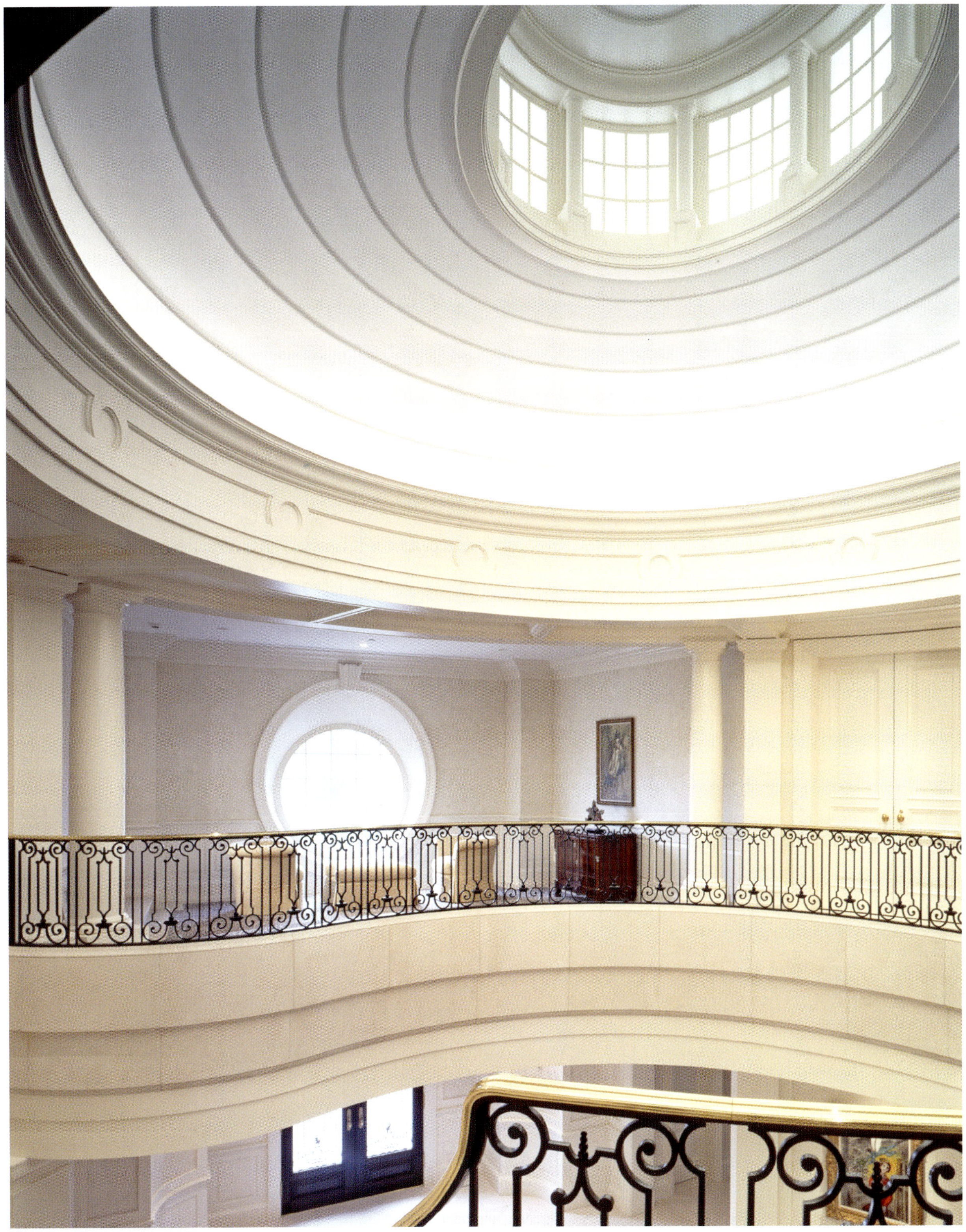

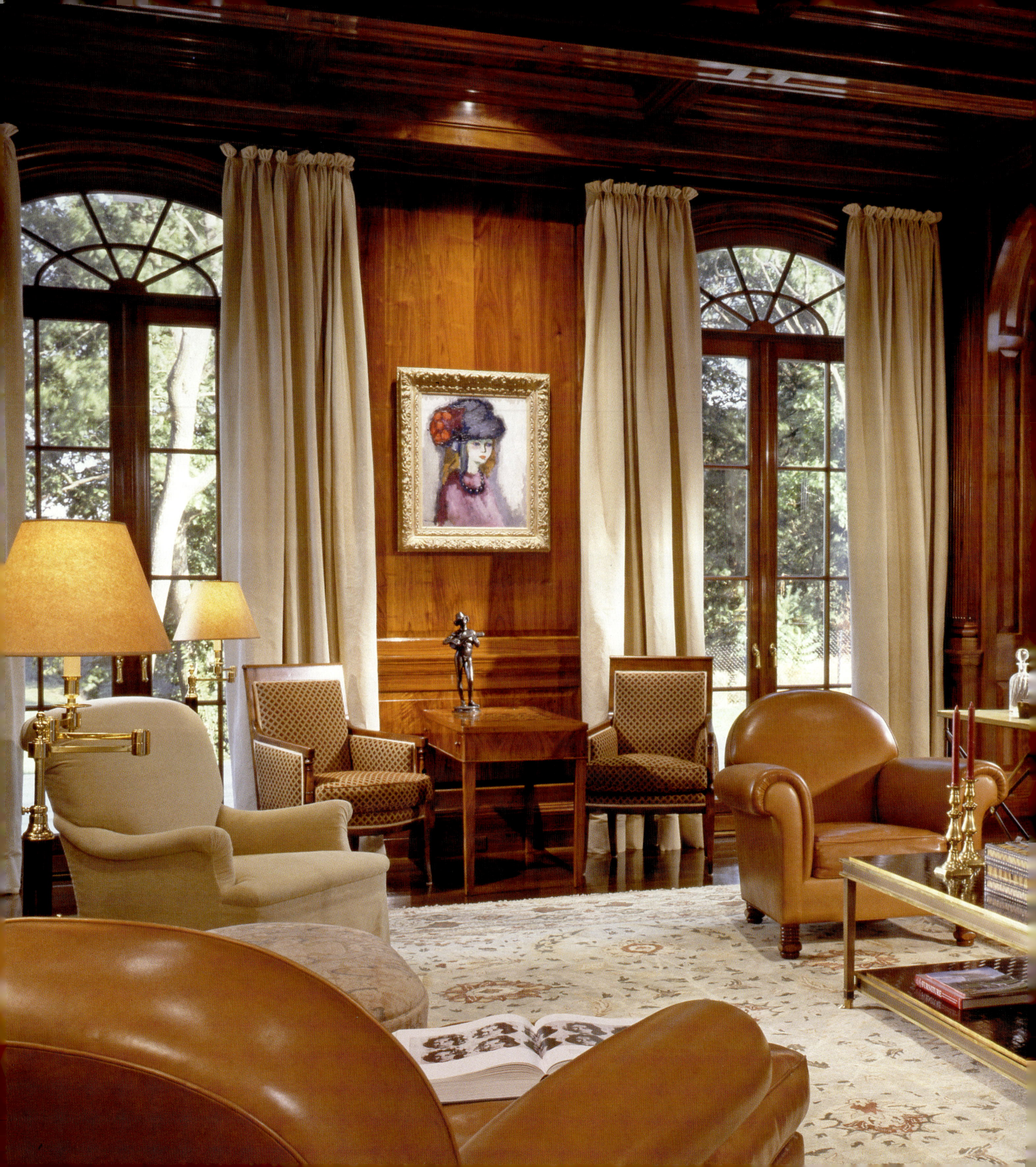

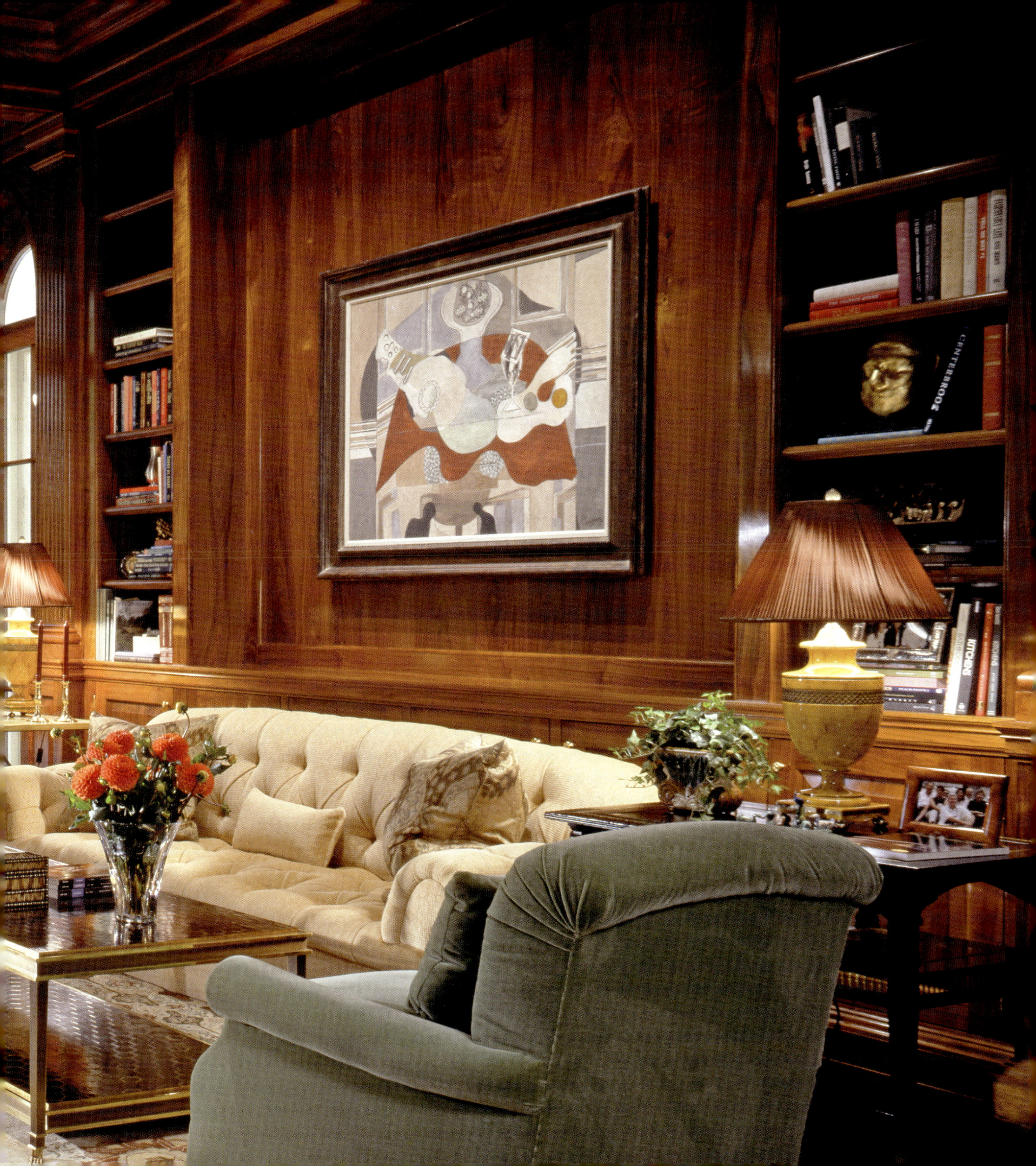
CENTERBROOK
KITCHENS

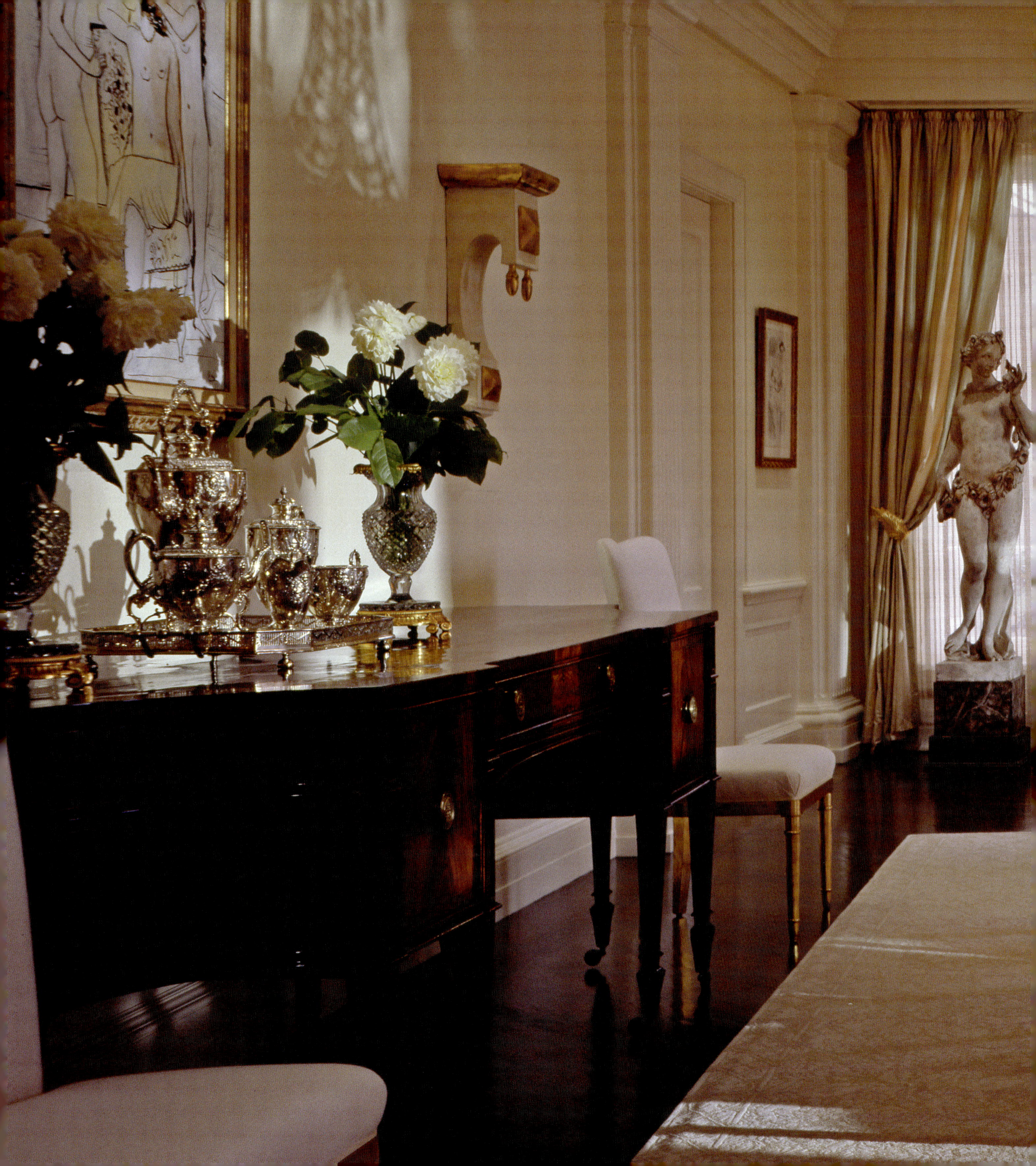

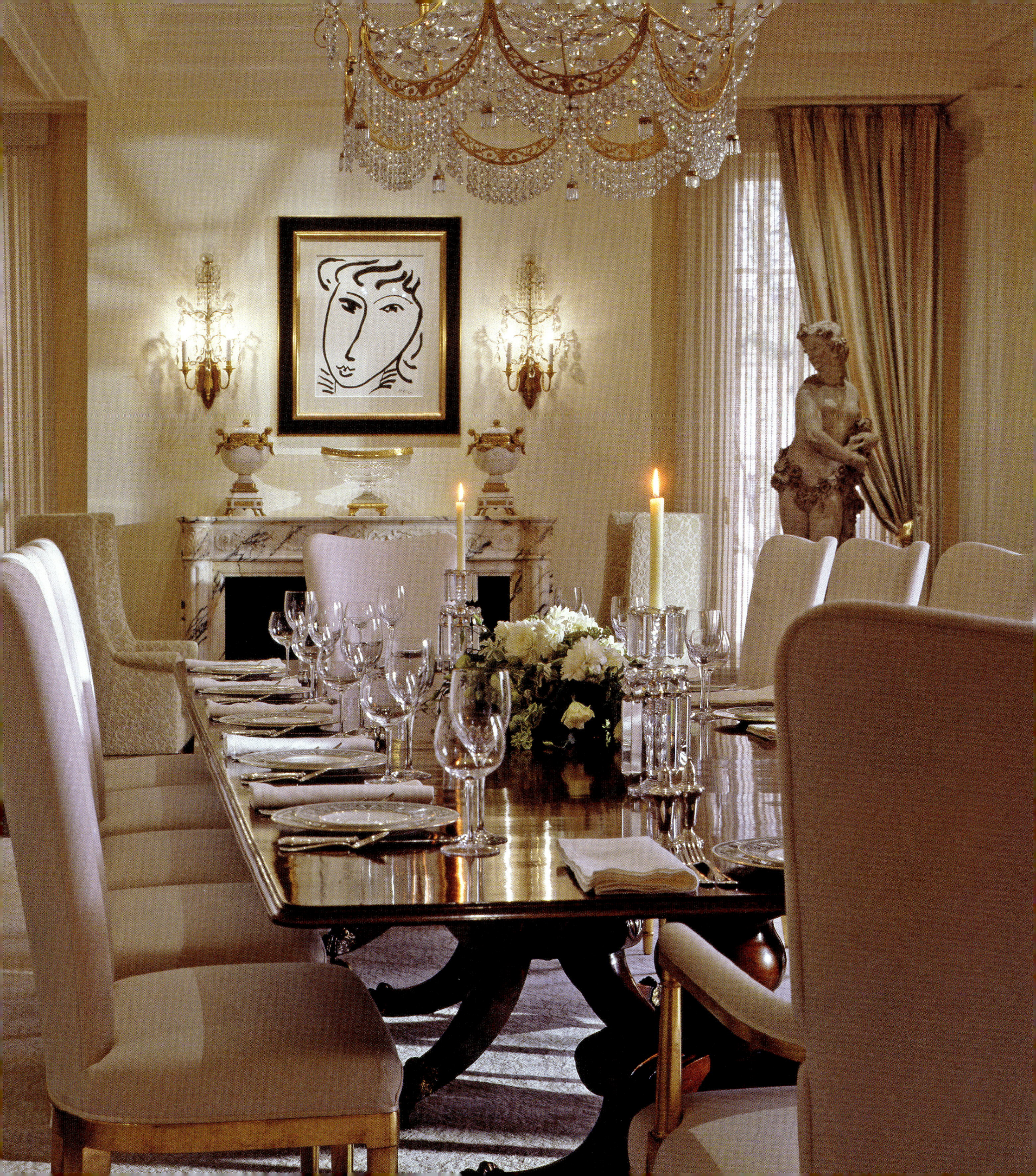

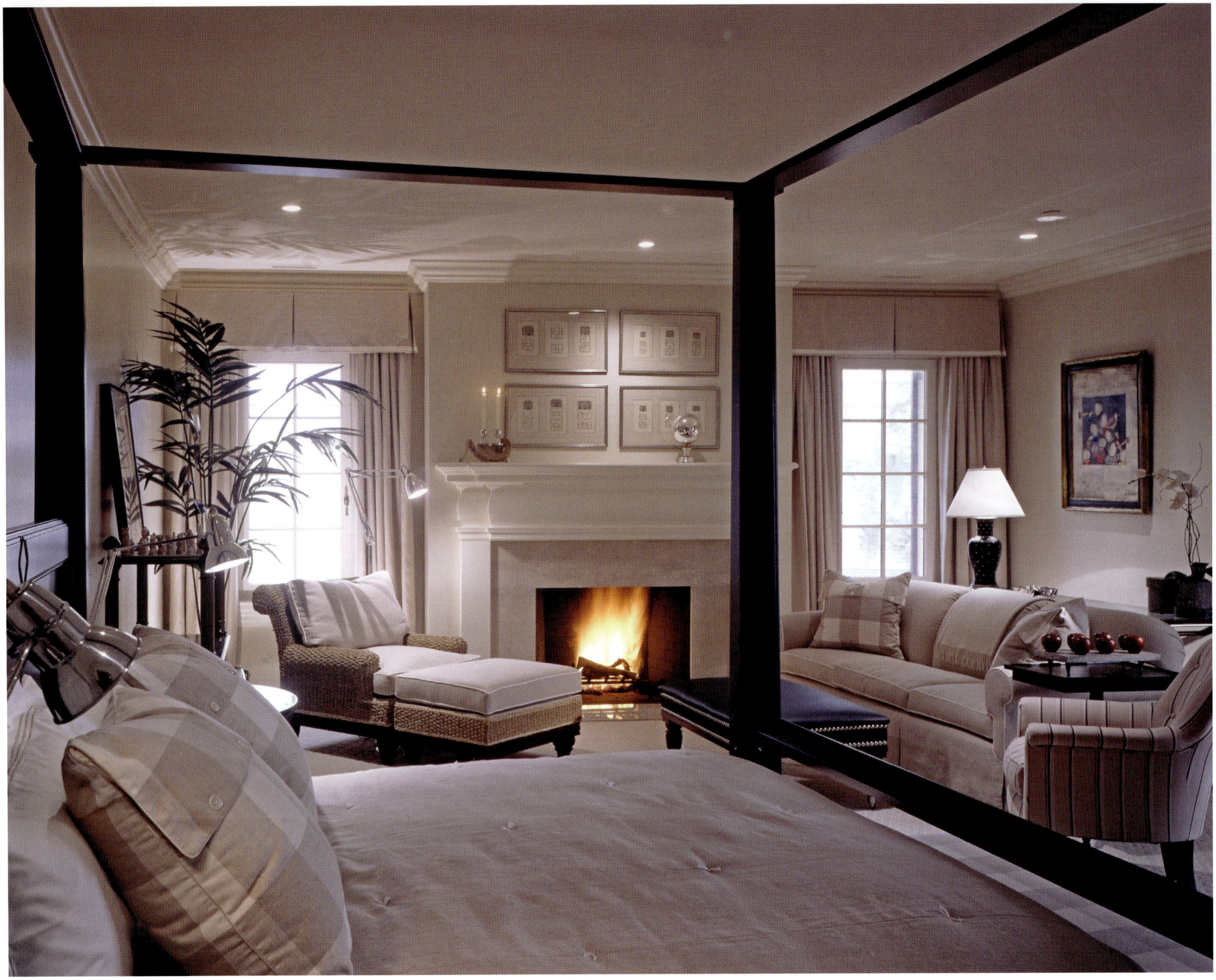

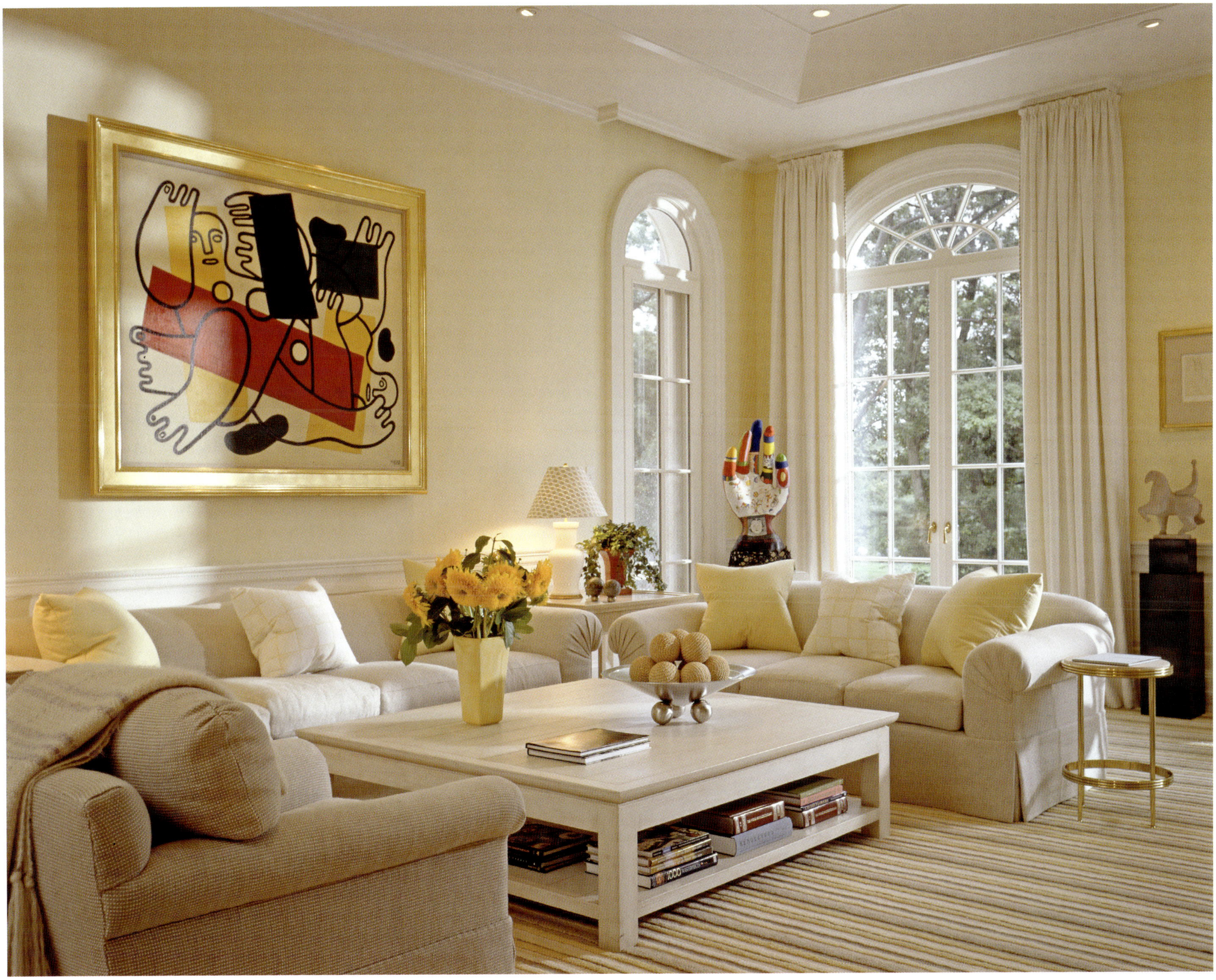

SITE PLAN

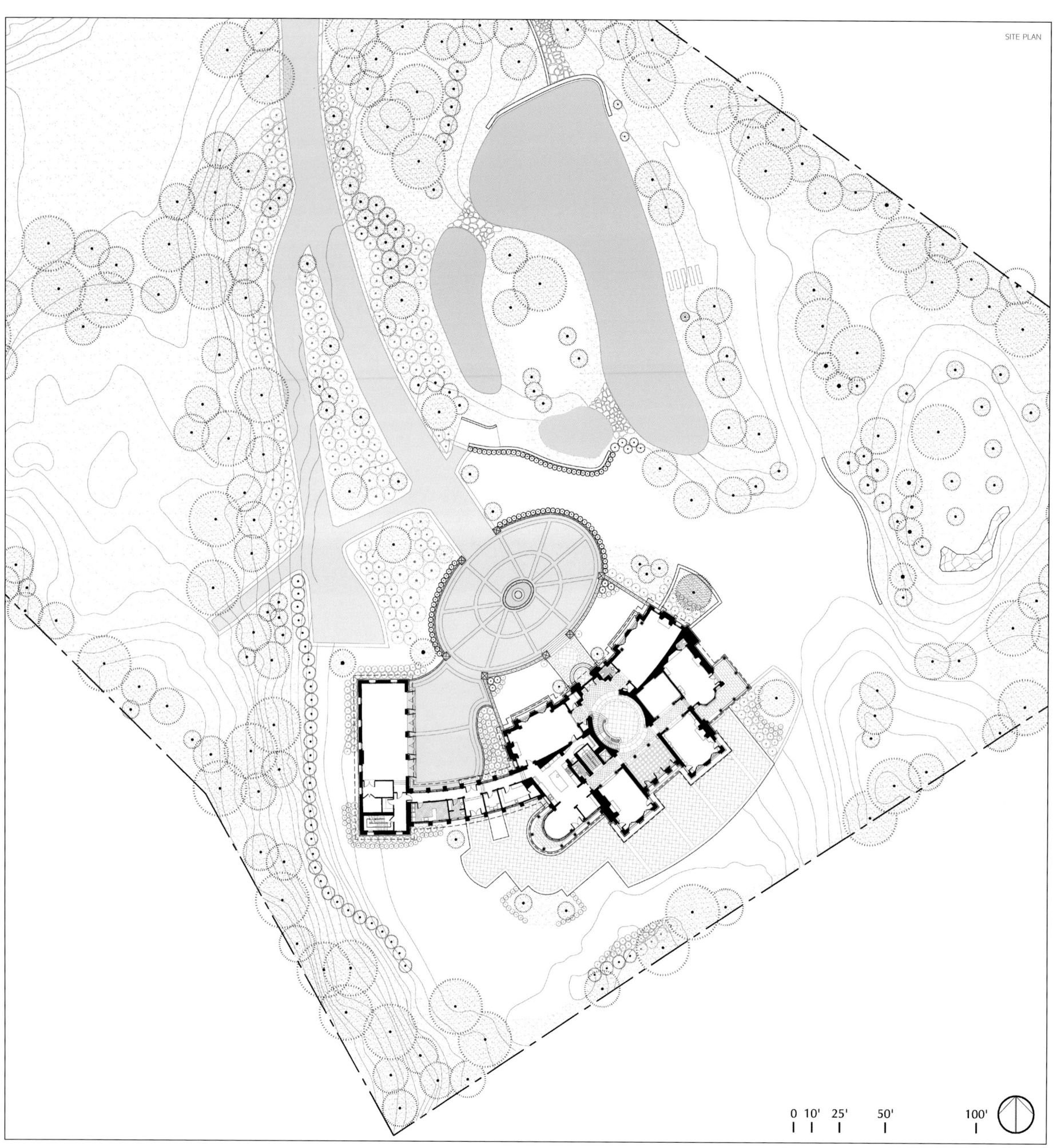

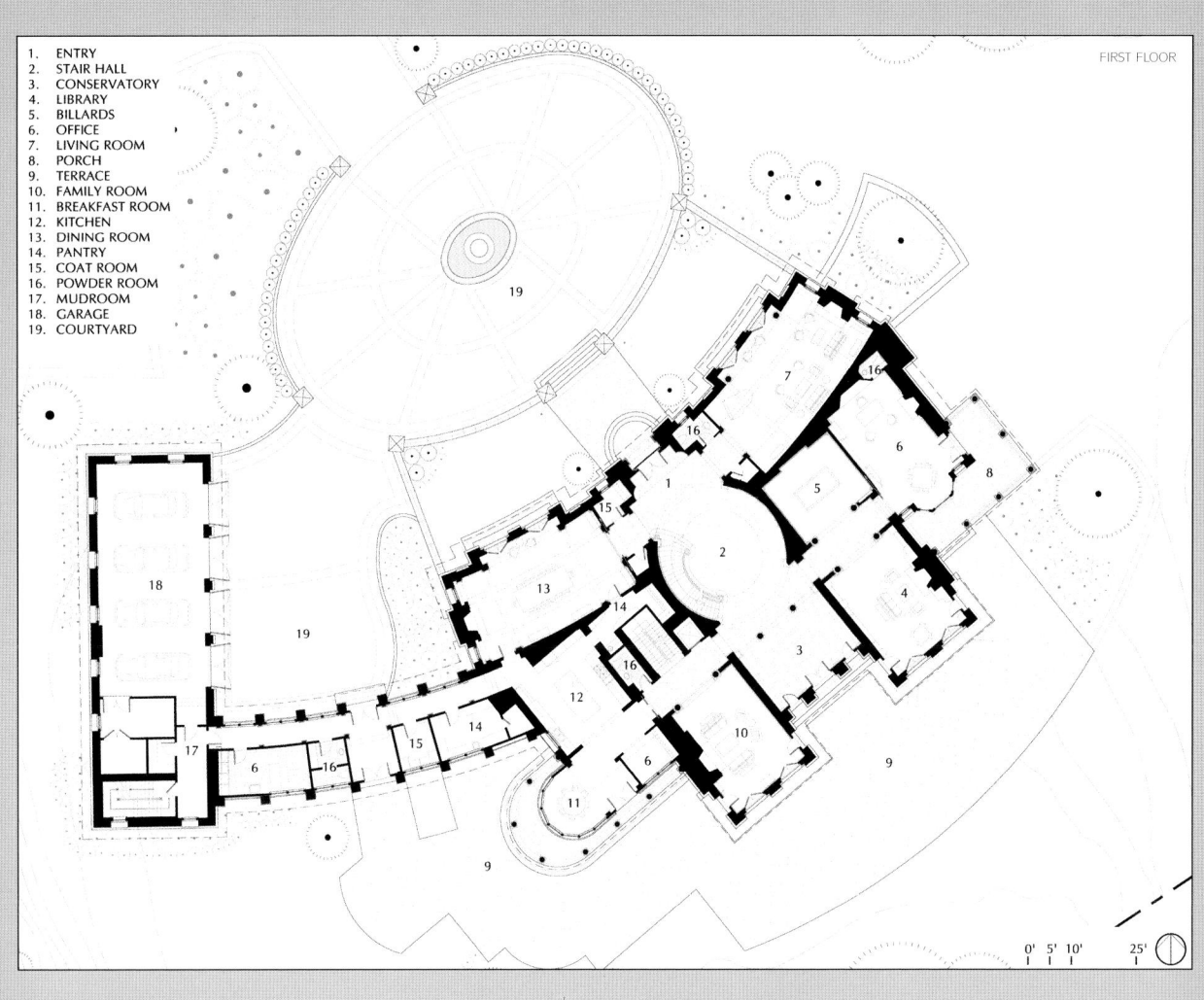

FIRST FLOOR

1. ENTRY
2. STAIR HALL
3. CONSERVATORY
4. LIBRARY
5. BILLARDS
6. OFFICE
7. LIVING ROOM
8. PORCH
9. TERRACE
10. FAMILY ROOM
11. BREAKFAST ROOM
12. KITCHEN
13. DINING ROOM
14. PANTRY
15. COAT ROOM
16. POWDER ROOM
17. MUDROOM
18. GARAGE
19. COURTYARD

SECOND FLOOR

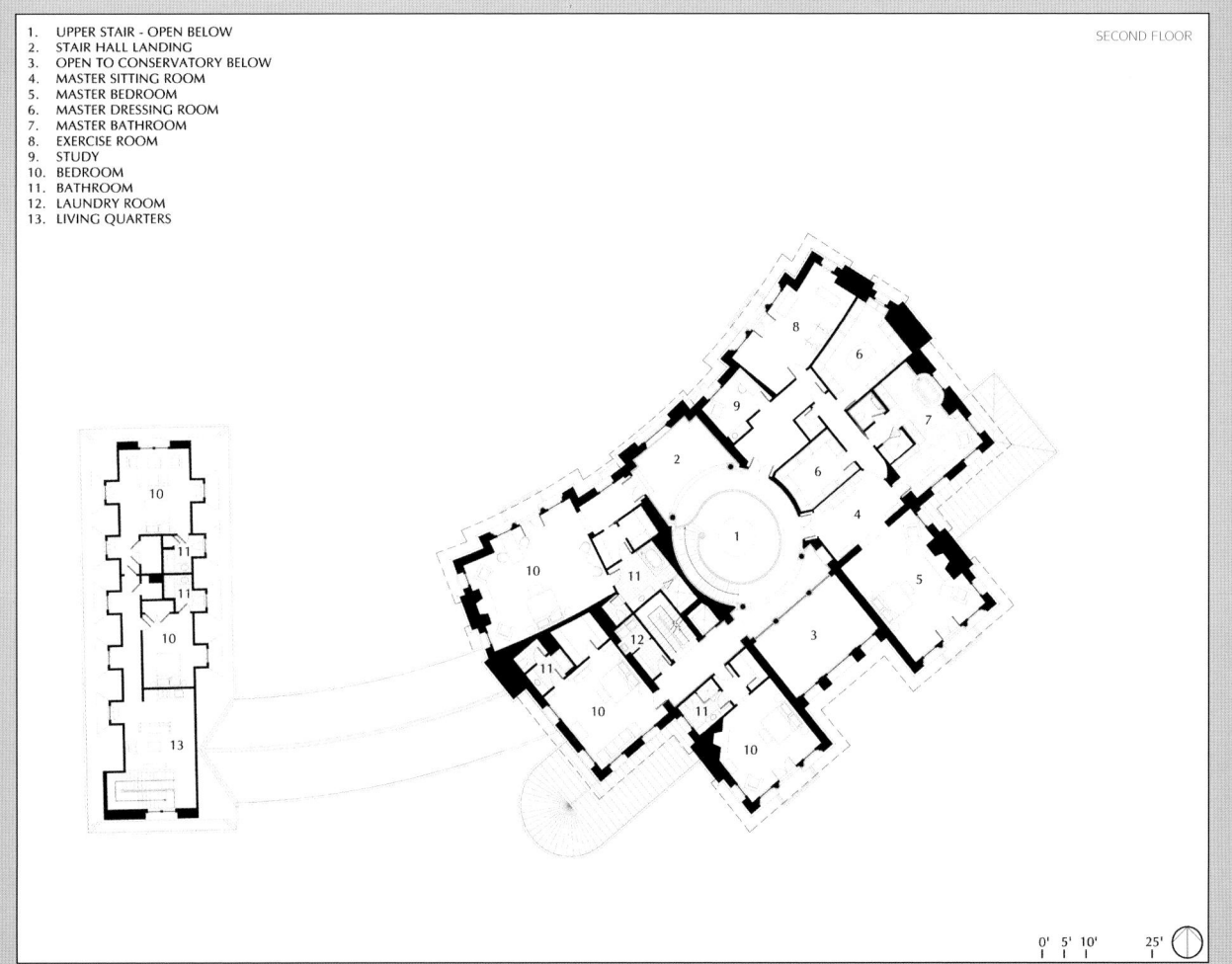

1. UPPER STAIR - OPEN BELOW
2. STAIR HALL LANDING
3. OPEN TO CONSERVATORY BELOW
4. MASTER SITTING ROOM
5. MASTER BEDROOM
6. MASTER DRESSING ROOM
7. MASTER BATHROOM
8. EXERCISE ROOM
9. STUDY
10. BEDROOM
11. BATHROOM
12. LAUNDRY ROOM
13. LIVING QUARTERS

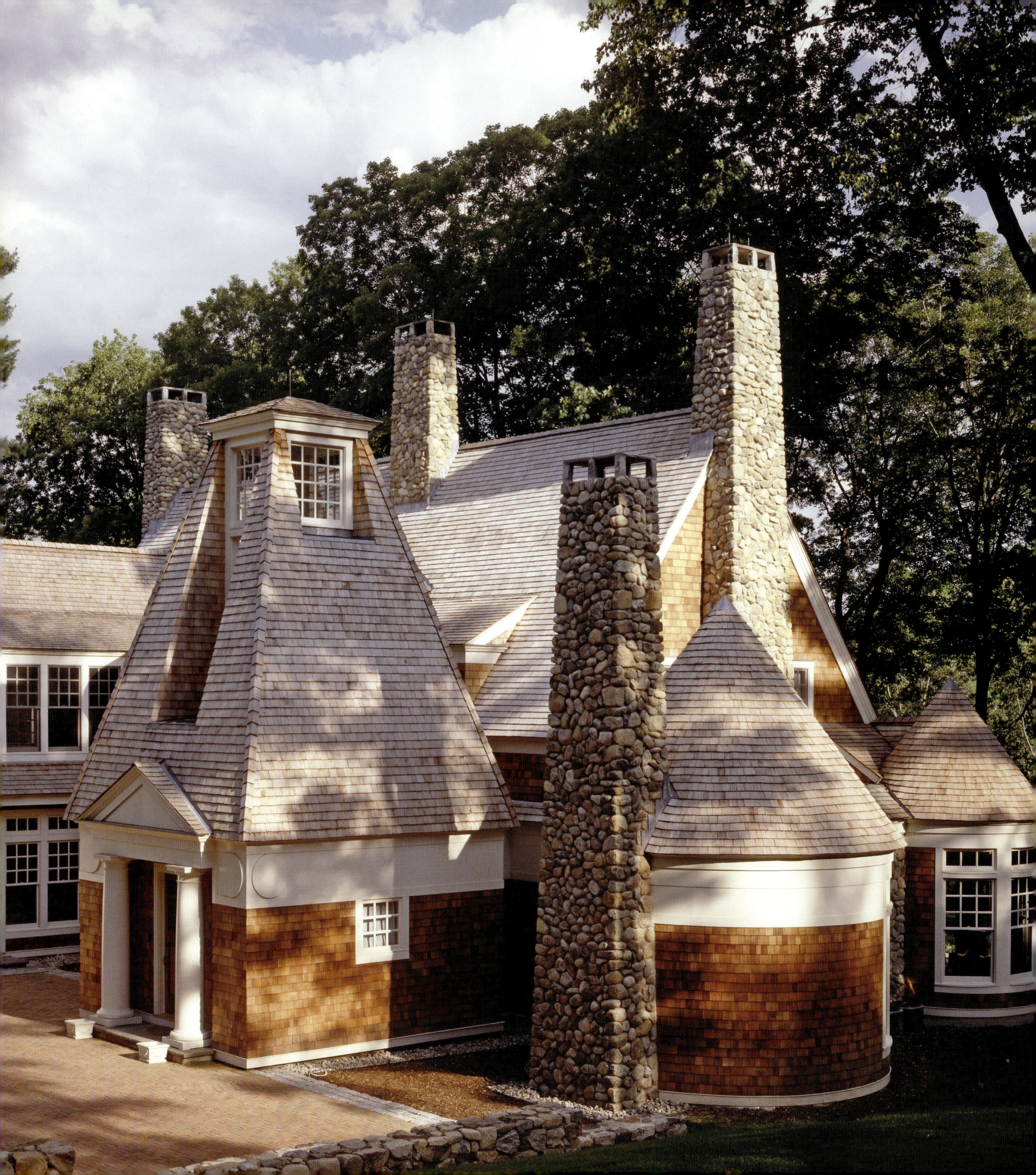

A STRIKING OBELISK AND STEEPLY PITCHED ROOFS CONTRIBUTE TO A WHIMSICAL AND HAPPY FEELING

THE CLIENTS A businessman and his wife, a graphic artist, who shared a strong interest in architecture, knew the work of Shope Reno Wharton. The clients felt that the architects' Shingle Style houses "blended into the landscape because of their weathered surfaces." The couple had one-year-old twin boys and plans for the wife's parents to live in a renovated eighteenth-century house that already existed on the property.

THE DESIGN BRIEF The site encompasses ten acres above the Ramapo River and its flood plain in Mahwah, New Jersey. It is a dramatic location, and there were many opportunities for the creation of a special house. Wharton referred to the work of the late nineteenth- and early-twentieth-century English architect Sir Edwin Lutyens, who often adapted traditional Arts and Crafts styles. The wife encouraged the Lutyens-esque degree to which the architects took the Shingle Style in this case, which they described as having a playfulness among all the elements.

THE SOLUTION The 8,000-square foot house, which is shingle-clad, consists of steeply pitched roofs, tall chimneys, and an obelisk that contains the entry vestibule. The architectural elements are separate but related in the overall massing of the house. Following Lutyens' style, the roofs are placed like hats on various sections of the house. The stair tower, which is next to the obelisk, is studded with a series of small-paned windows that follow the line of the stair's ascent; the library occupies a conical shaped room, anchored by a chimney. Most of the roofs are pulled low, which lends a feeling of intimacy. The individual architectural elements are both classically grand and whimsically combined. The house works with the eighteenth-century farmhouse and the old and new barns on the property to evoke the feeling of a village, while the tall chimneys and the vertical aspects of the main house echo the trees surrounding the buildings. The barn has three cupolas and an arched rear entrance. The first floor houses horse stalls, while the second gives way to a beautiful, naturally lit studio two stories high, with a magnificent view of the main house and the river beyond. The house has well-resolved rooms that were designed by John Saladino, who is based in New York and California. Classical details help define the modern, open spaces that are punctuated with pockets of intimacy, such as an inglenook in the living room. At the rear, a row of French doors graciously open onto a bluestone terrace, at the end of which lies a colonnaded porch with a swing. All of the major rooms have a river view. "We used roof shapes that define the spaces below and give them a more human scale, character, and a certain unpredictability," Wharton says of the second floor. The master bedroom has a huge half-moon window set in a dormer, giving the room the feeling of a tree house.

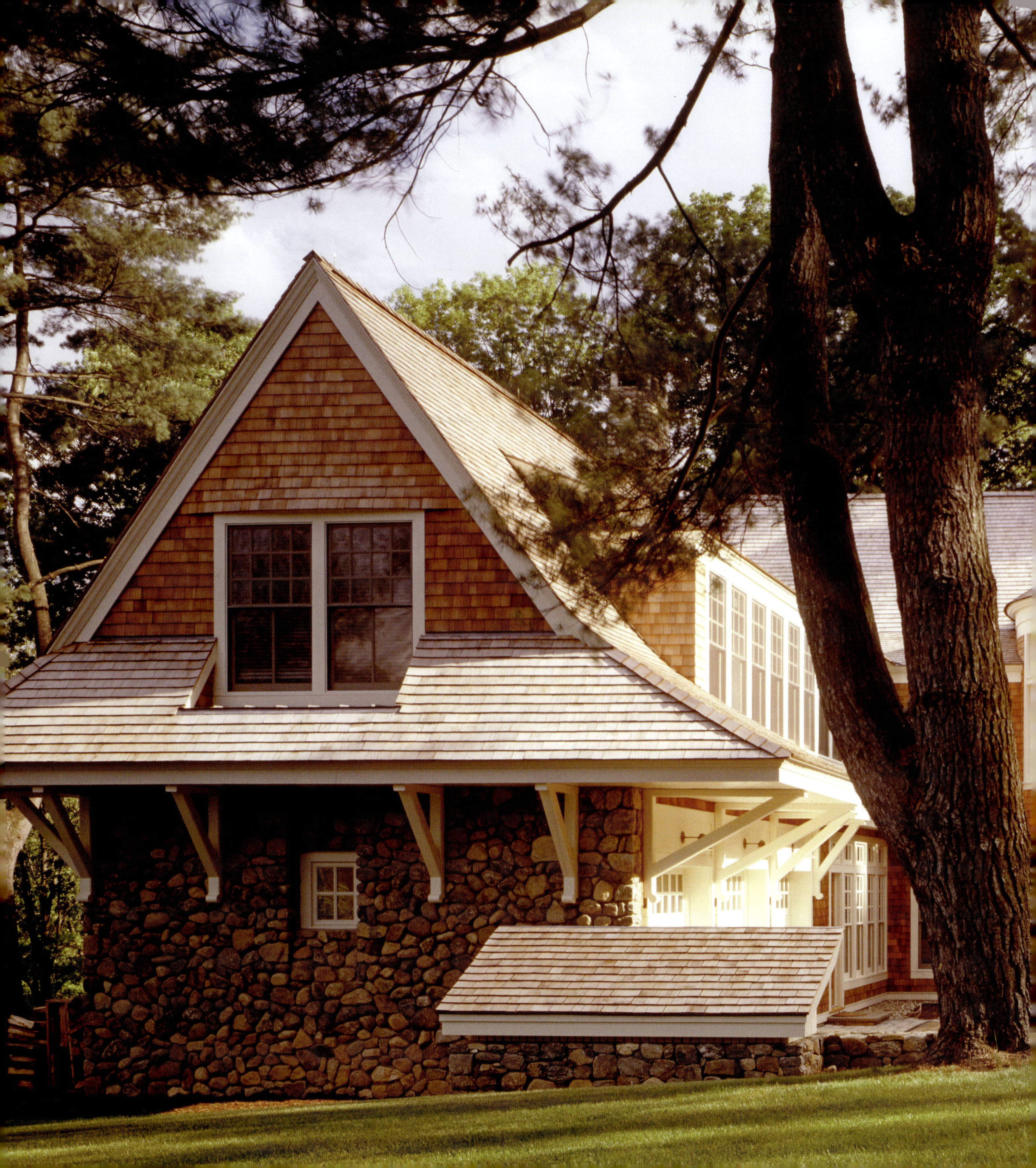

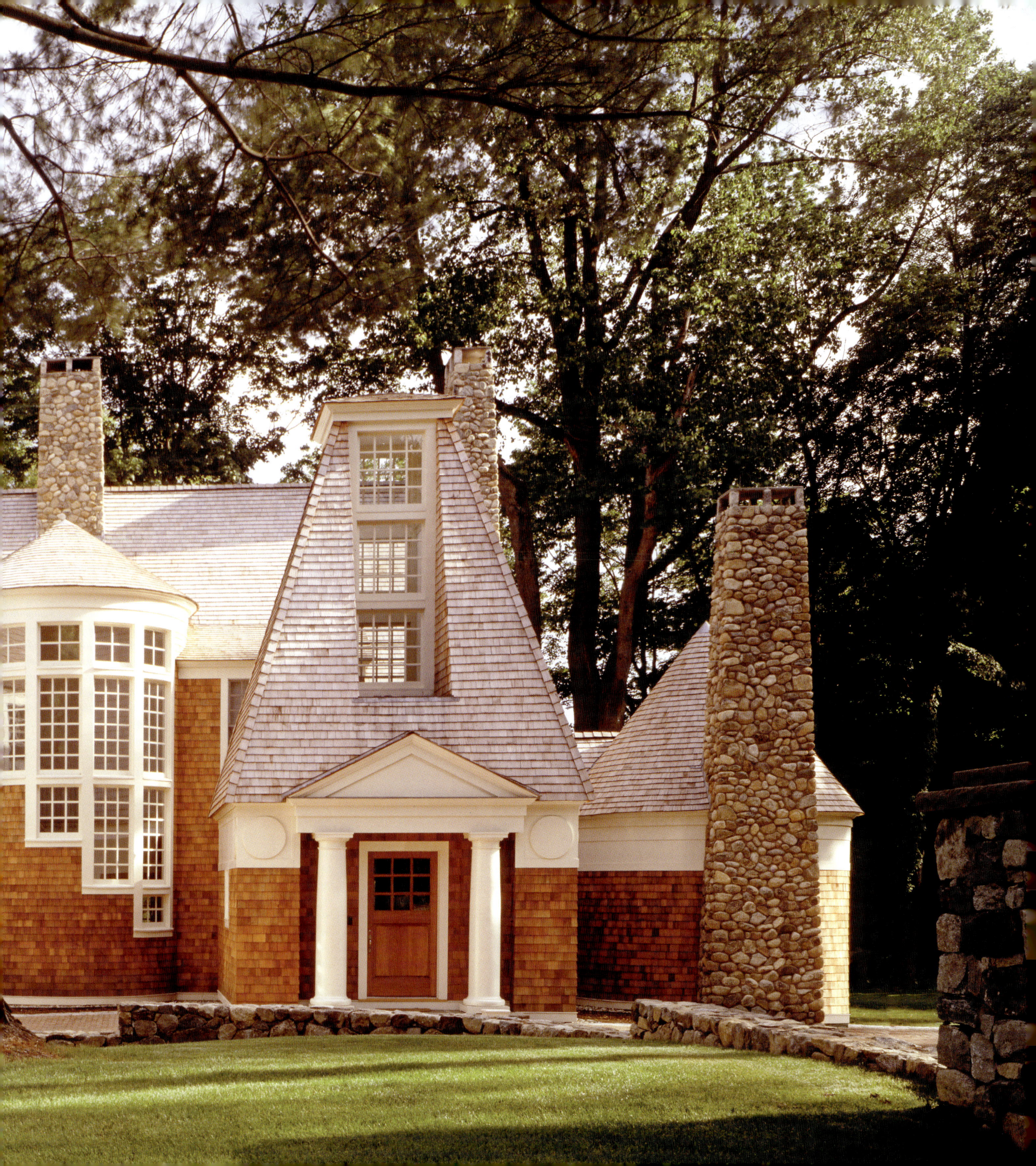

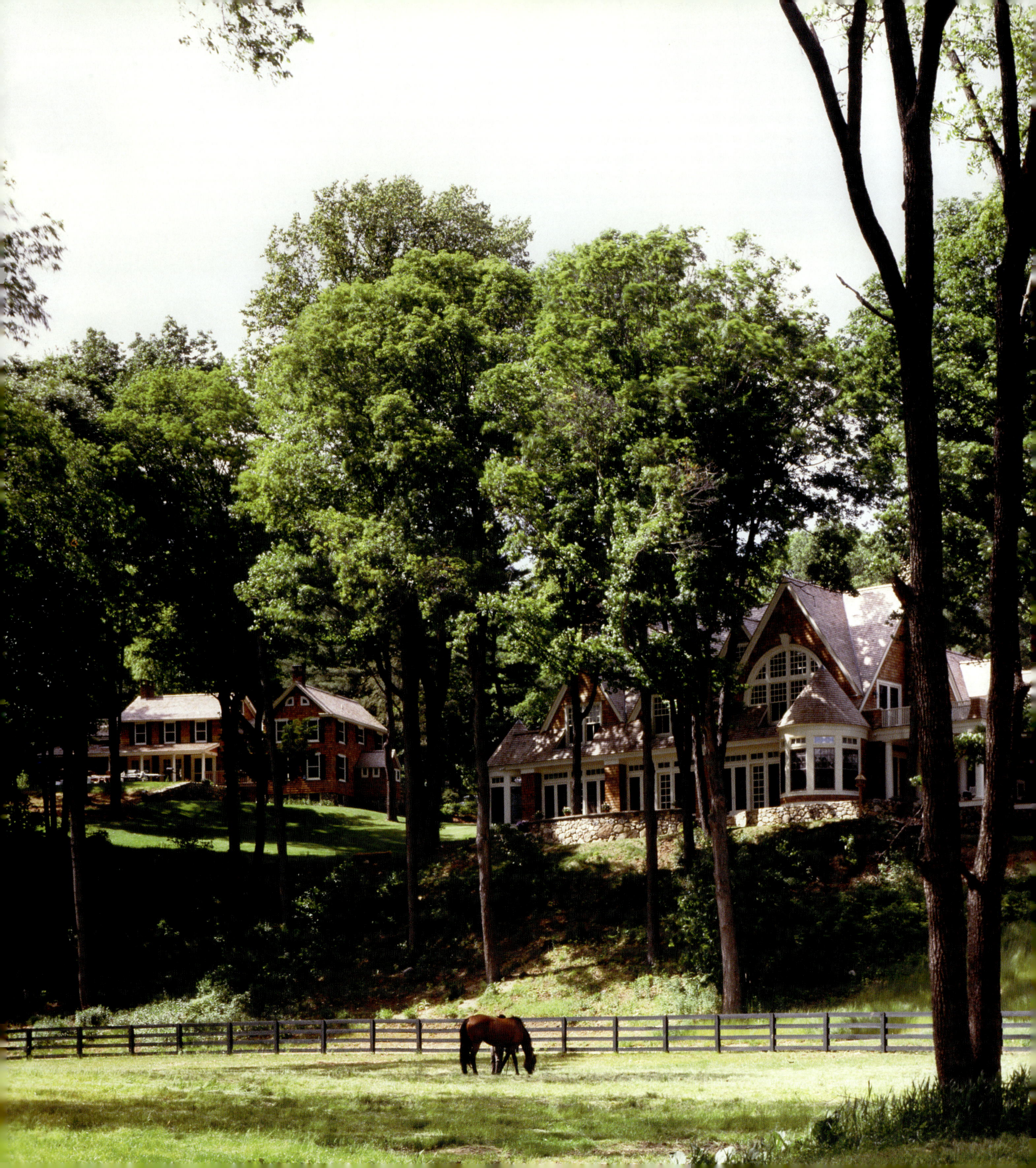

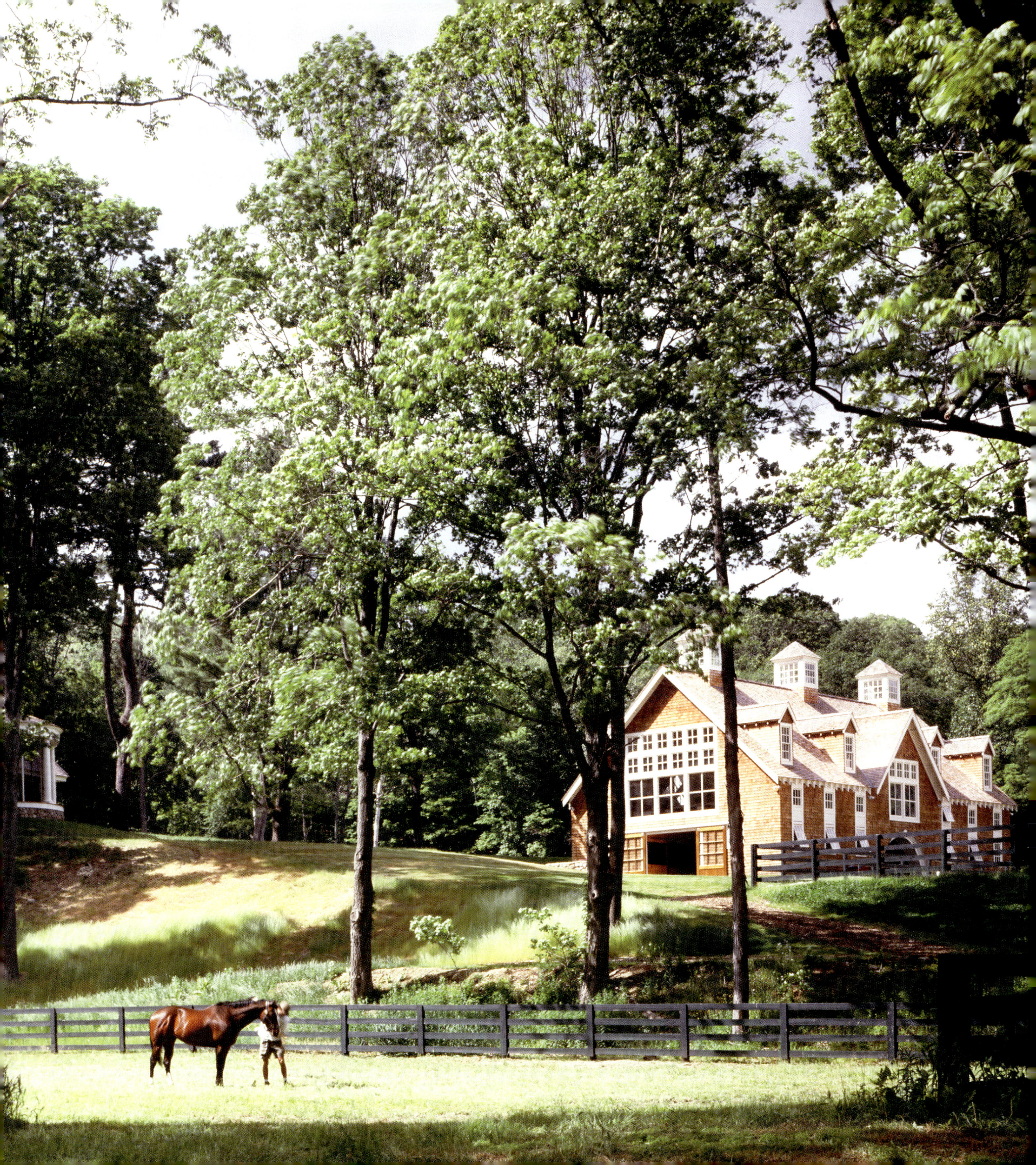

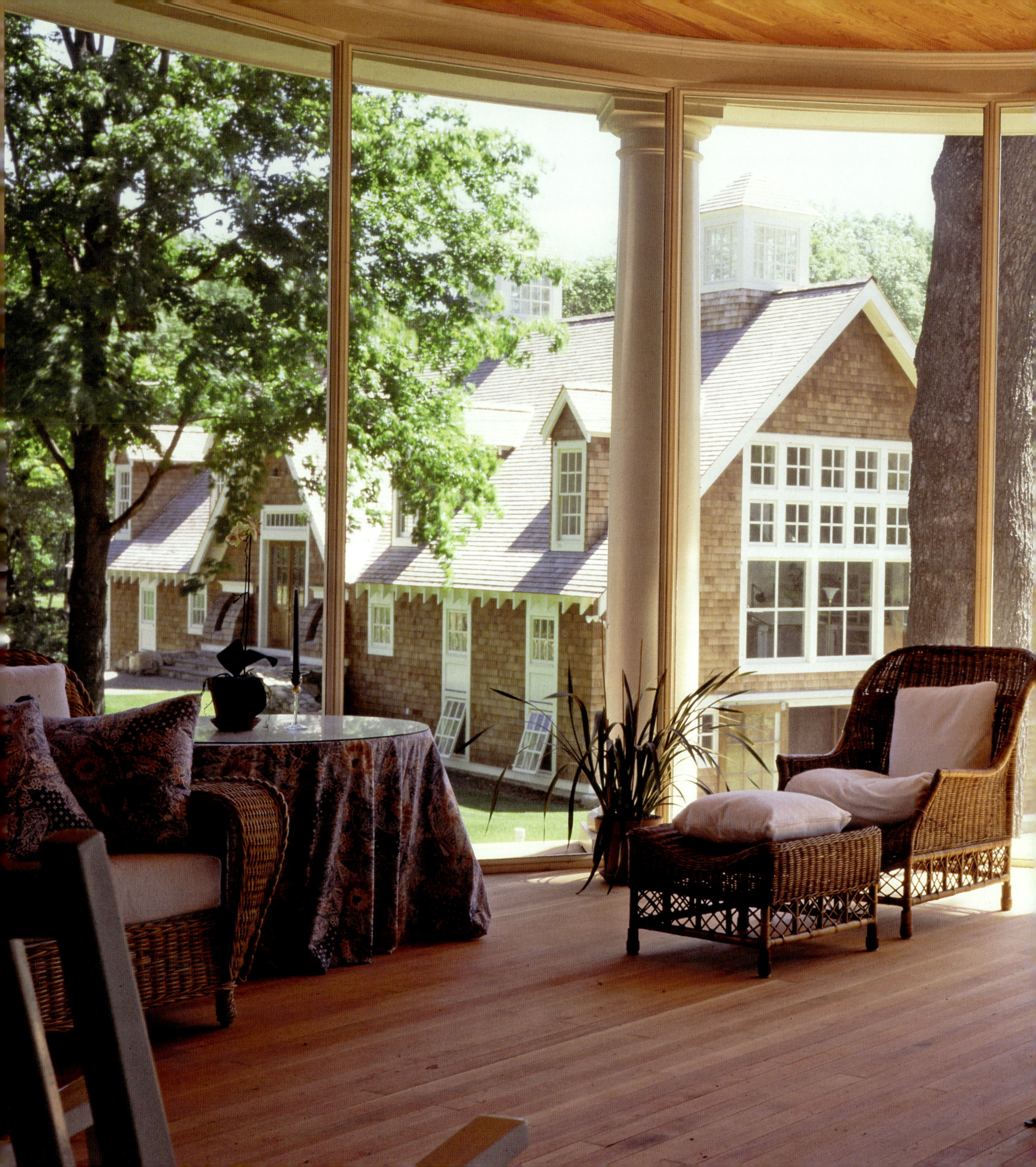

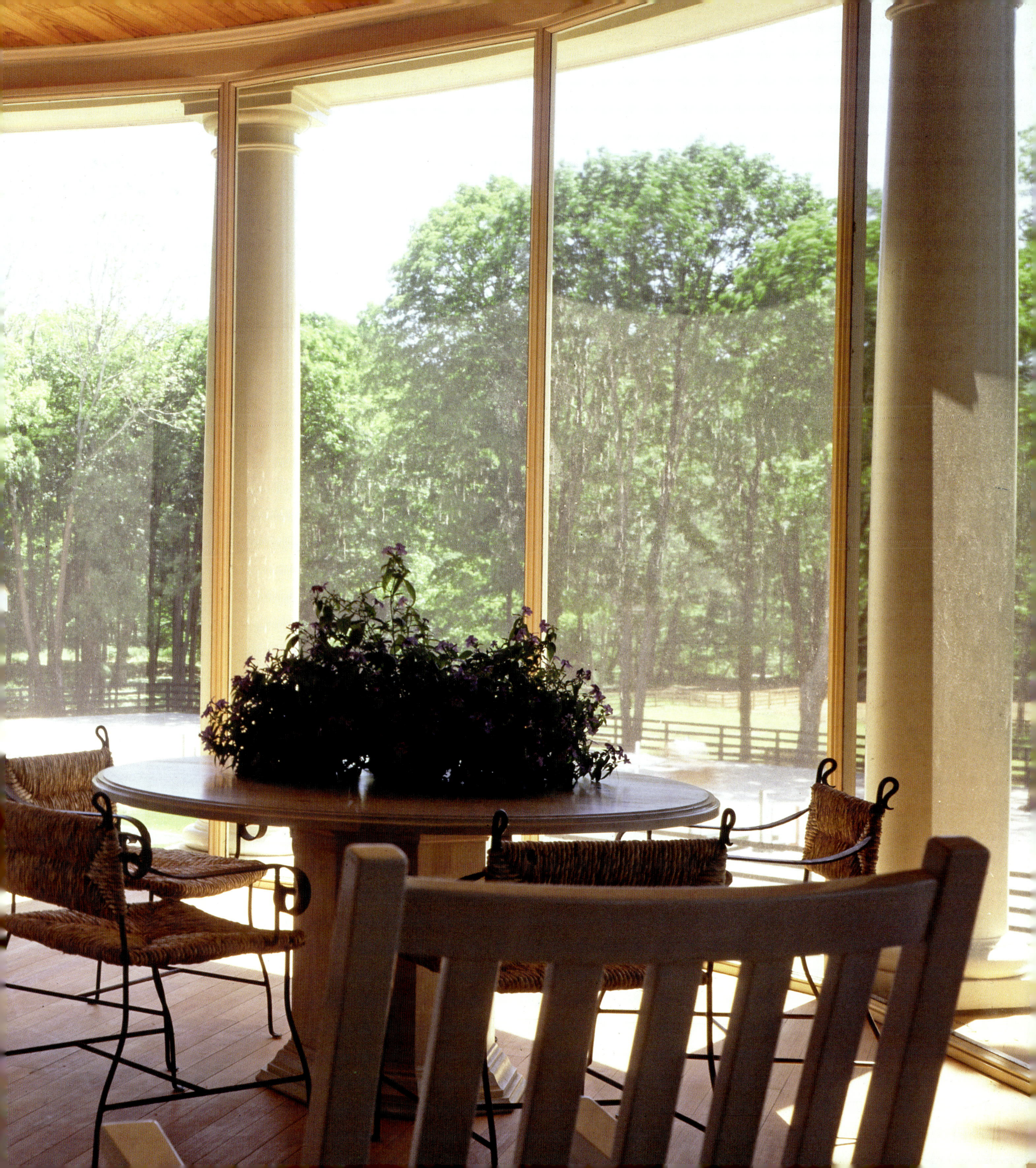

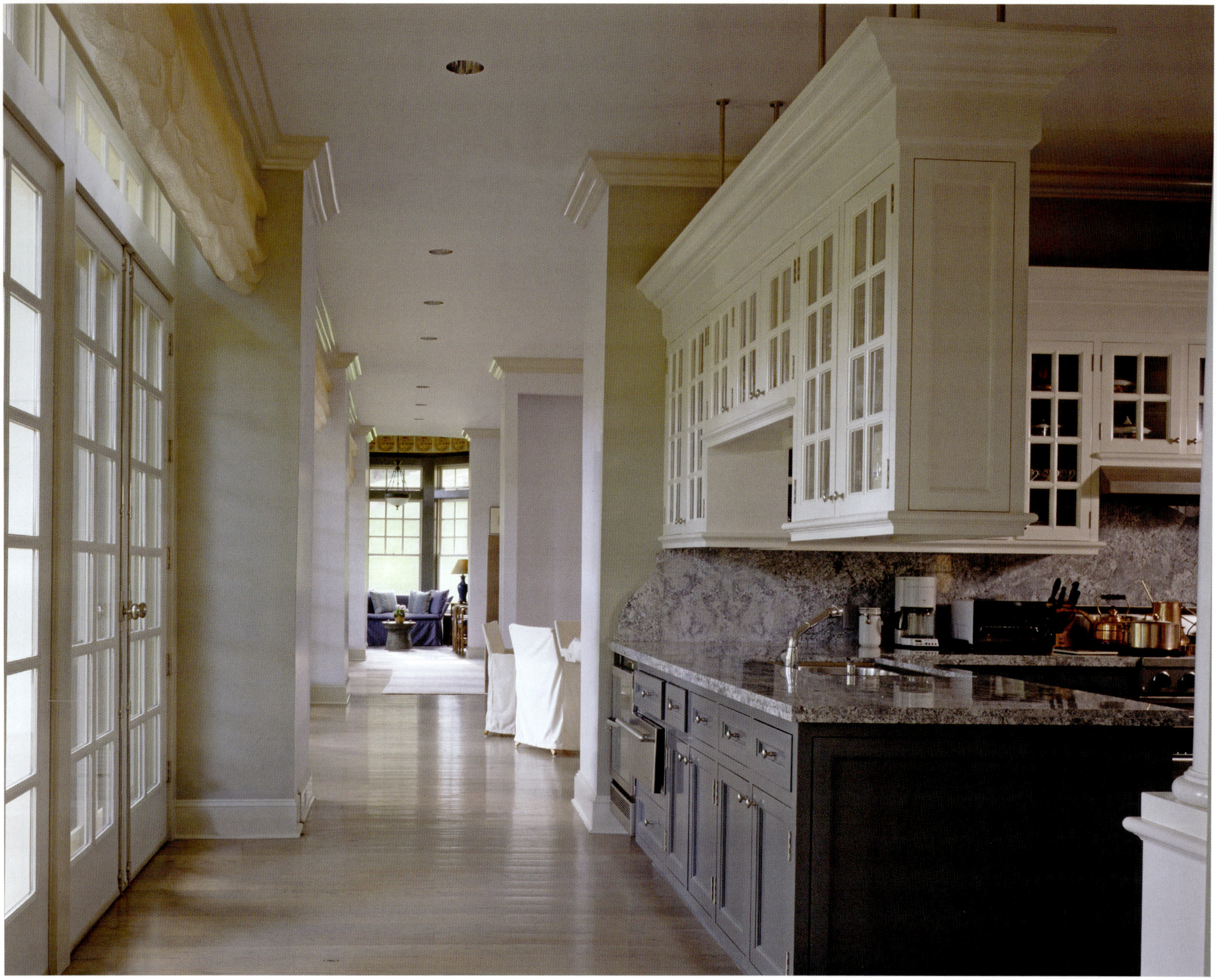

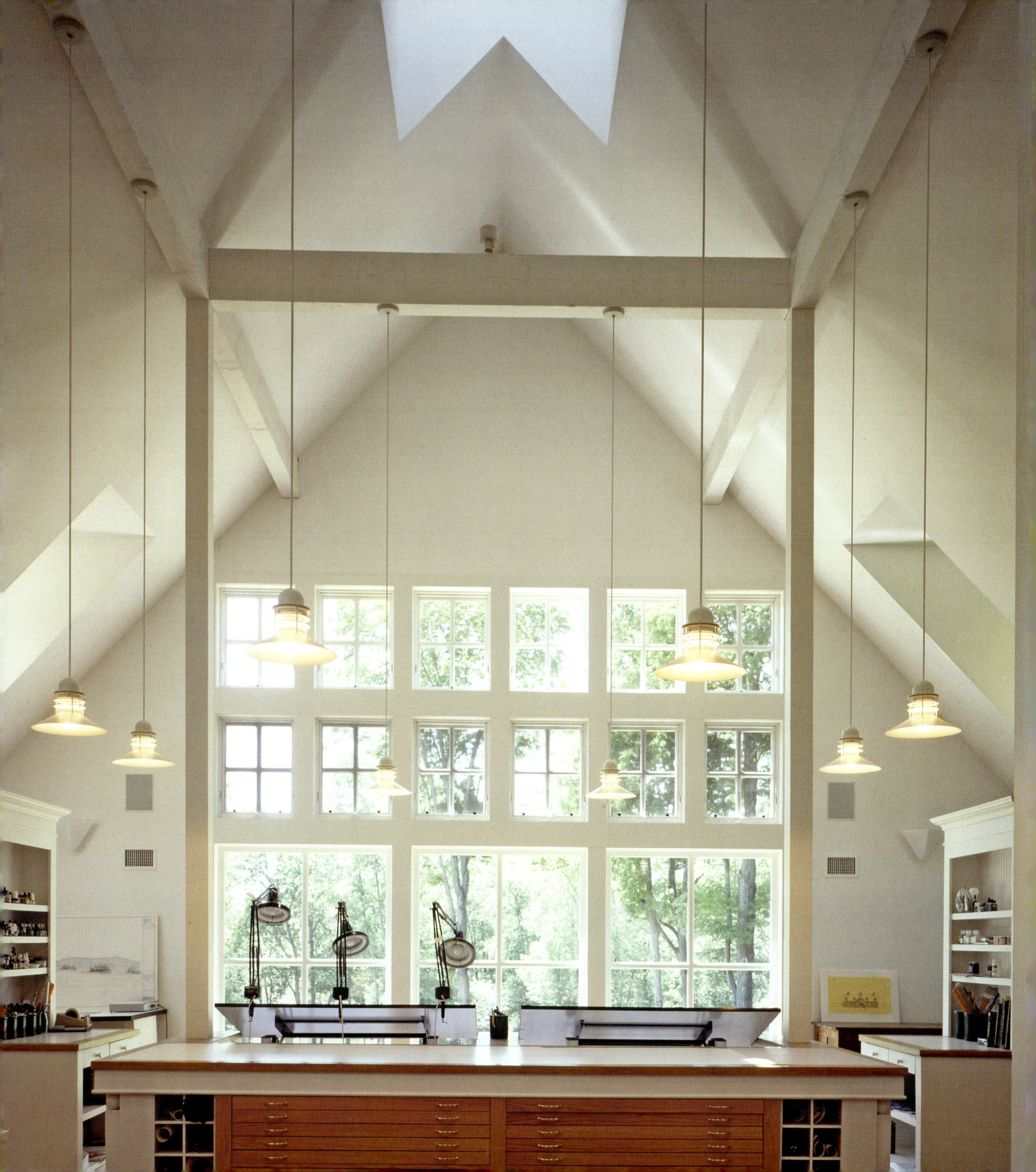

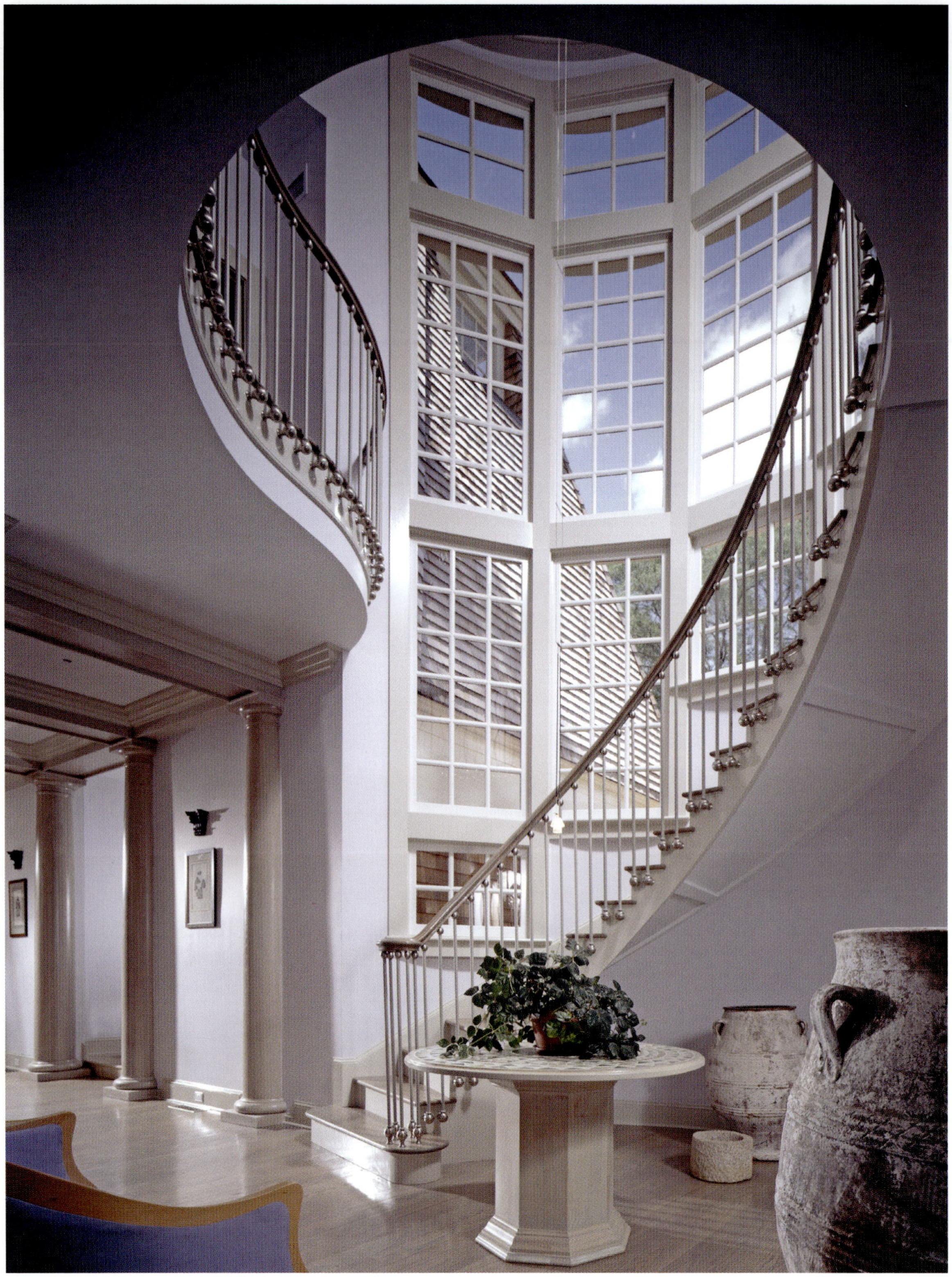

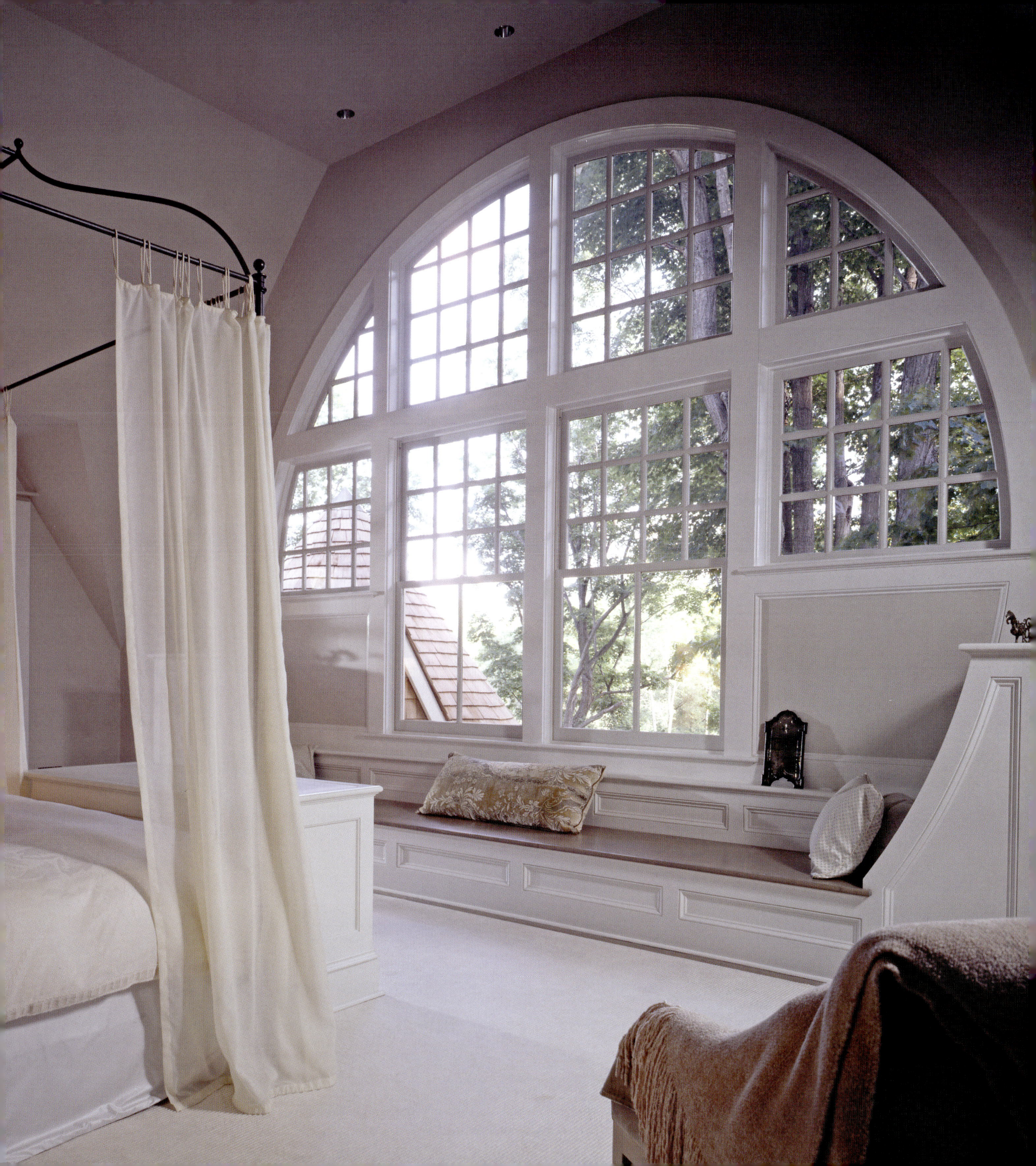

SITE PLAN

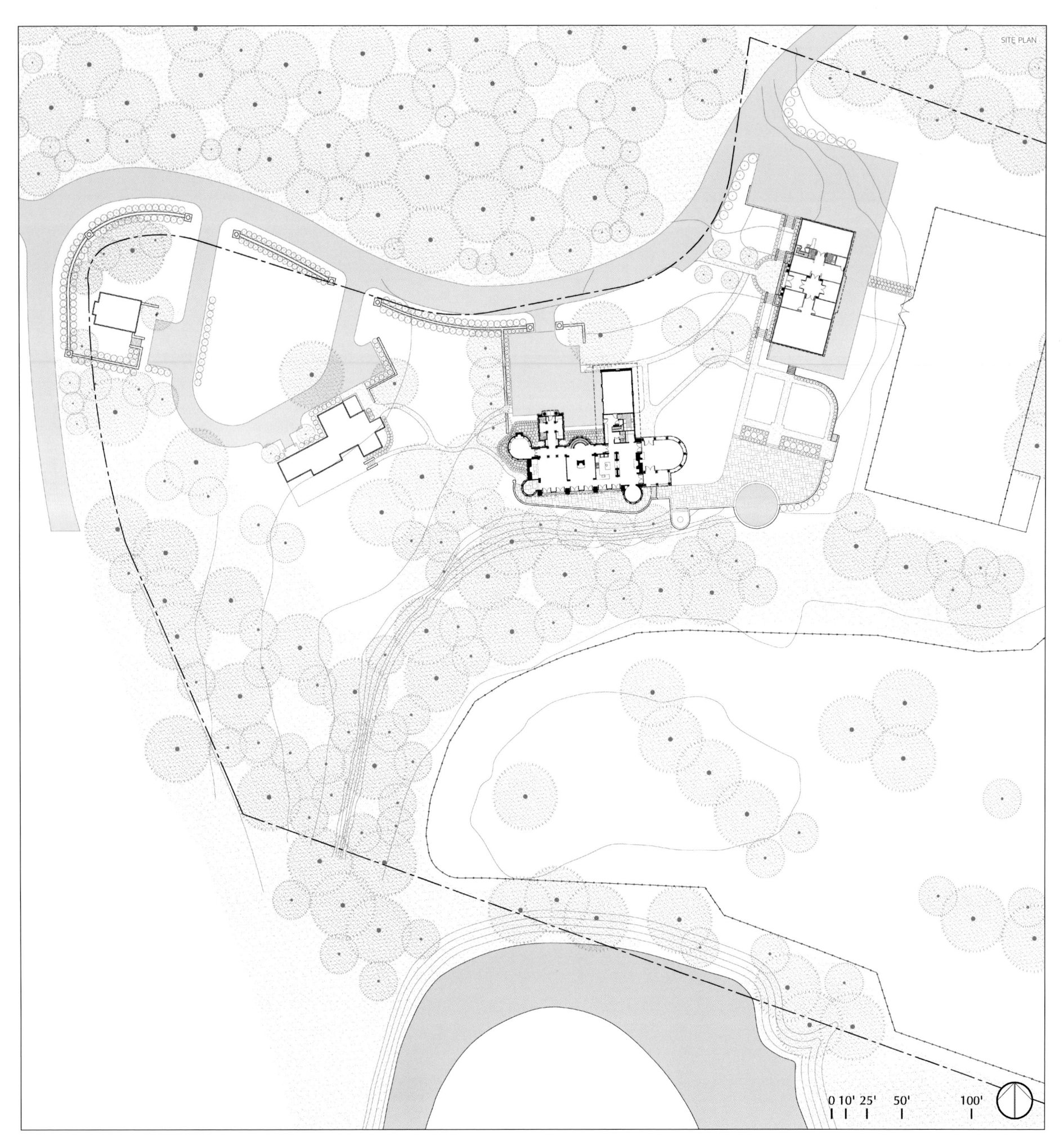

0 10' 25' 50'   100'

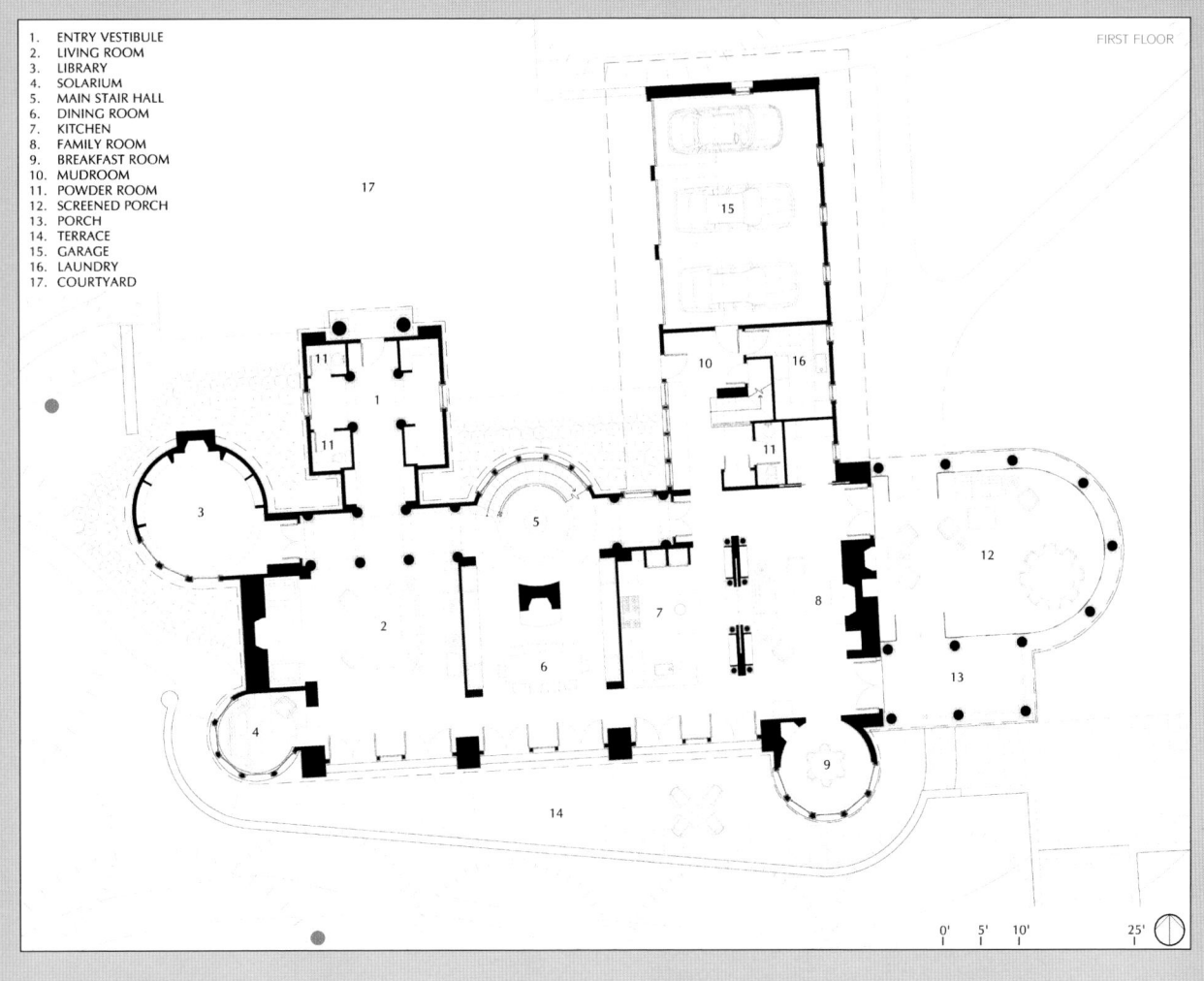

FIRST FLOOR

1. ENTRY VESTIBULE
2. LIVING ROOM
3. LIBRARY
4. SOLARIUM
5. MAIN STAIR HALL
6. DINING ROOM
7. KITCHEN
8. FAMILY ROOM
9. BREAKFAST ROOM
10. MUDROOM
11. POWDER ROOM
12. SCREENED PORCH
13. PORCH
14. TERRACE
15. GARAGE
16. LAUNDRY
17. COURTYARD

SECOND FLOOR

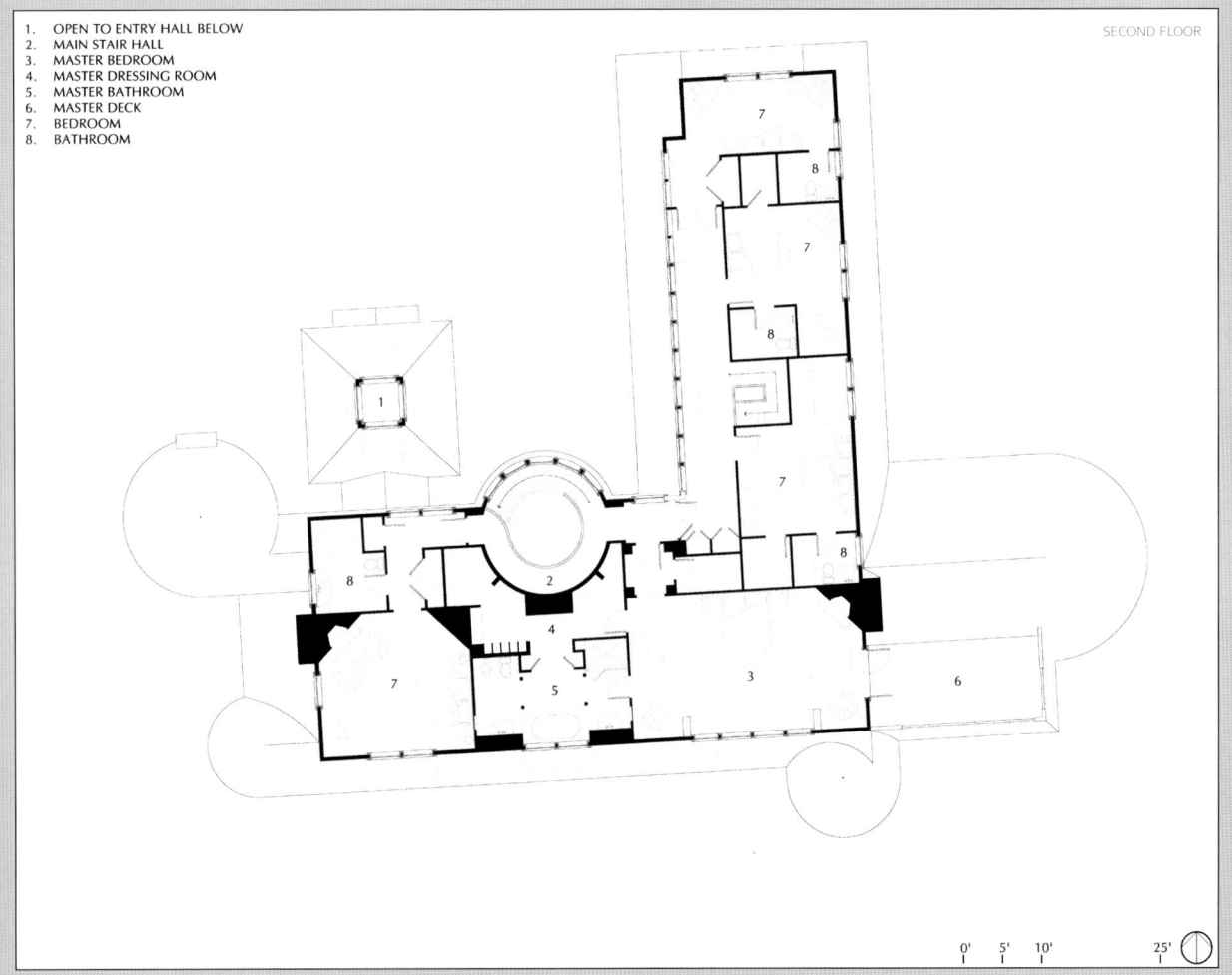

1. OPEN TO ENTRY HALL BELOW
2. MAIN STAIR HALL
3. MASTER BEDROOM
4. MASTER DRESSING ROOM
5. MASTER BATHROOM
6. MASTER DECK
7. BEDROOM
8. BATHROOM

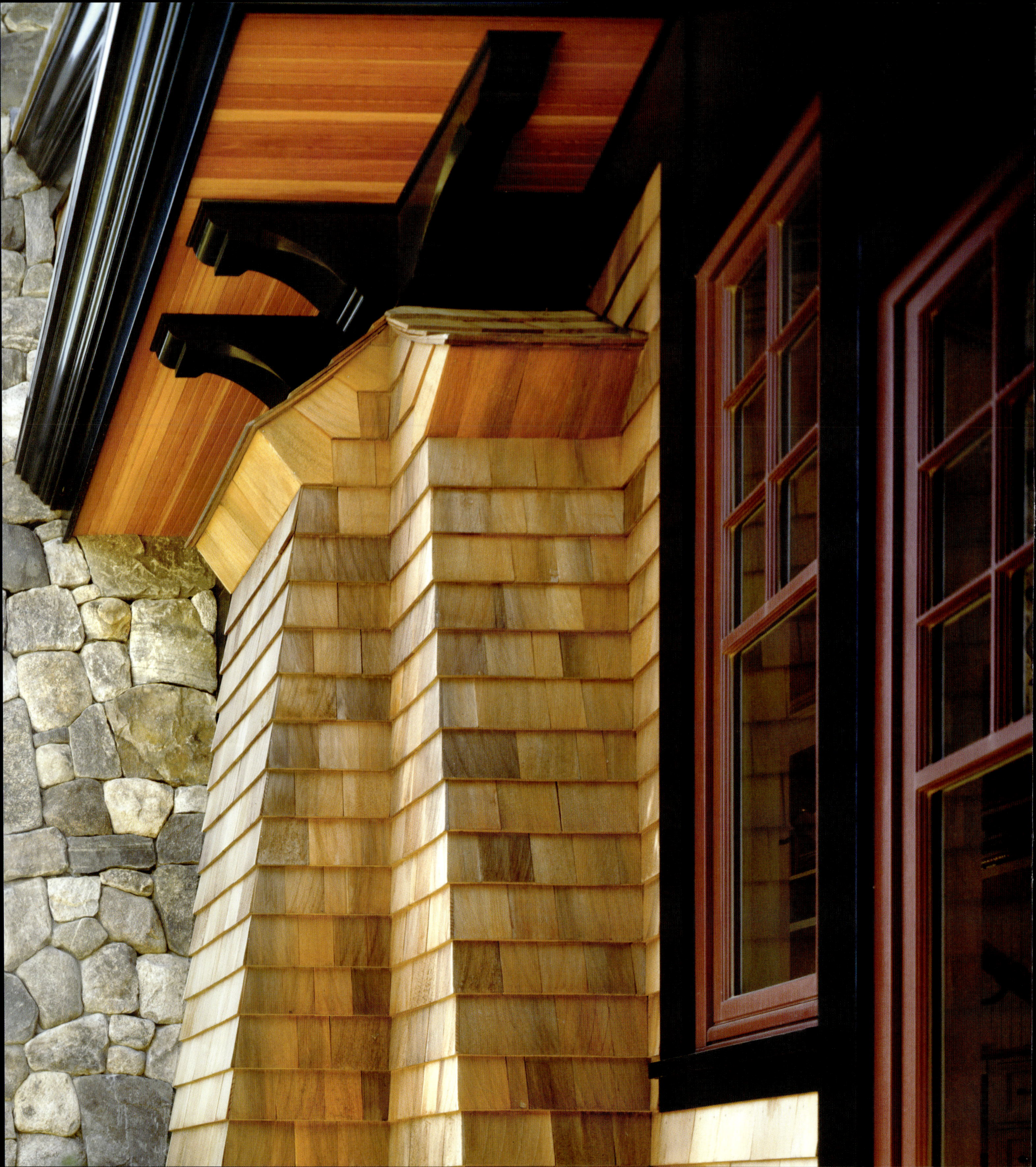

A HILLTOP HOME MADE UP OF A TRIO OF RED-CEDAR SHINGLE-CLAD BUILDINGS RESPECTS ITS LOCATION

THE CLIENTS A Boston financier, his physician wife, and their grown-up son wanted to build a house on a six-acre piece of land on a hilltop in Chilmark, Massachusetts, a town on the southwestern tip of the island of Martha's Vineyard. The site had sweeping views of both the Atlantic Ocean and a local body of water, known as Squibnocket Pond. The clients wanted to be respectful of the property's strict conservation regulations.

THE DESIGN BRIEF The land-use restrictions required the maximum height of any building on the six-acre property to be no more than eighteen feet high, and the entire floor plan to be contained within one-and-a-half acres, as defined by the boundary of the property and neighboring wetlands. Wharton rose to the challenge. "What first appeared as a set of terrible constraints became a wonderful opportunity to design a house very different from what we usually do," he says. There had once been barns on the property, so Wharton began to conceive of a design that would resemble a series of rural barns. The house would be low-lying and earth-hugging across the brow of the hill, and would be broken up into different sections. Although seemingly modest from a distance, the buildings would become more complex as their details emerged.

THE SOLUTION The architects decided to step three interconnected barn-like buildings gradually downward from the high point on the hill. They created three separate roof-ridge heights, one ridge with four cupolas, and three separate floor levels to avoid a linear look. The wife loved views of the Atlantic and the husband enjoyed views of the pond. Accordingly, each wing was oriented slightly differently so that they could both enjoy their favorite vista. Each wing is composed of trussed bays reinforced by wood-framed, shingle-covered buttresses. The buttresses create a rhythm on the facades, alternating with the pattern of windows and French doors. Chimneys did not have to remain within the roof height stricture, so the architects designed three massive ones—one to anchor each wing. The interior plan of this 5,600-square-foot house is clean and open. Coming in through a small entrance hall, one steps into a Great Room twenty-two feet wide by seventy feet long. New York-based Mariette Himes Gomez, known for her richly textured style, designed the interiors. Because of the narrowness of the Great Room, it had to have an axial arrangement of living, dining, and kitchen spaces. Gomez says, "We created boundaries with the floor surfaces, rugs, and furniture placement, but the entire room is unified by the continuity of the ceiling and the subtlety of the palette of paint, wood finishes, and fabrics." The interior designer also worked with New York color consultant Donald Kaufman to get the right stains and finishes for the walls. They chose clear finishes that strengthened the color and grain of the wood, so in the Douglas fir trusses, the wainscoting, and the cabinetry in the main wing, the redness of the wood comes through. Where the walls are plaster, they are painted in neutral tones that echo the color of the exterior shingles. The interior detailing has a serene, Shaker feeling, and it furnishes a perfect background for the couple's collection of American folk art sculpture and paintings.

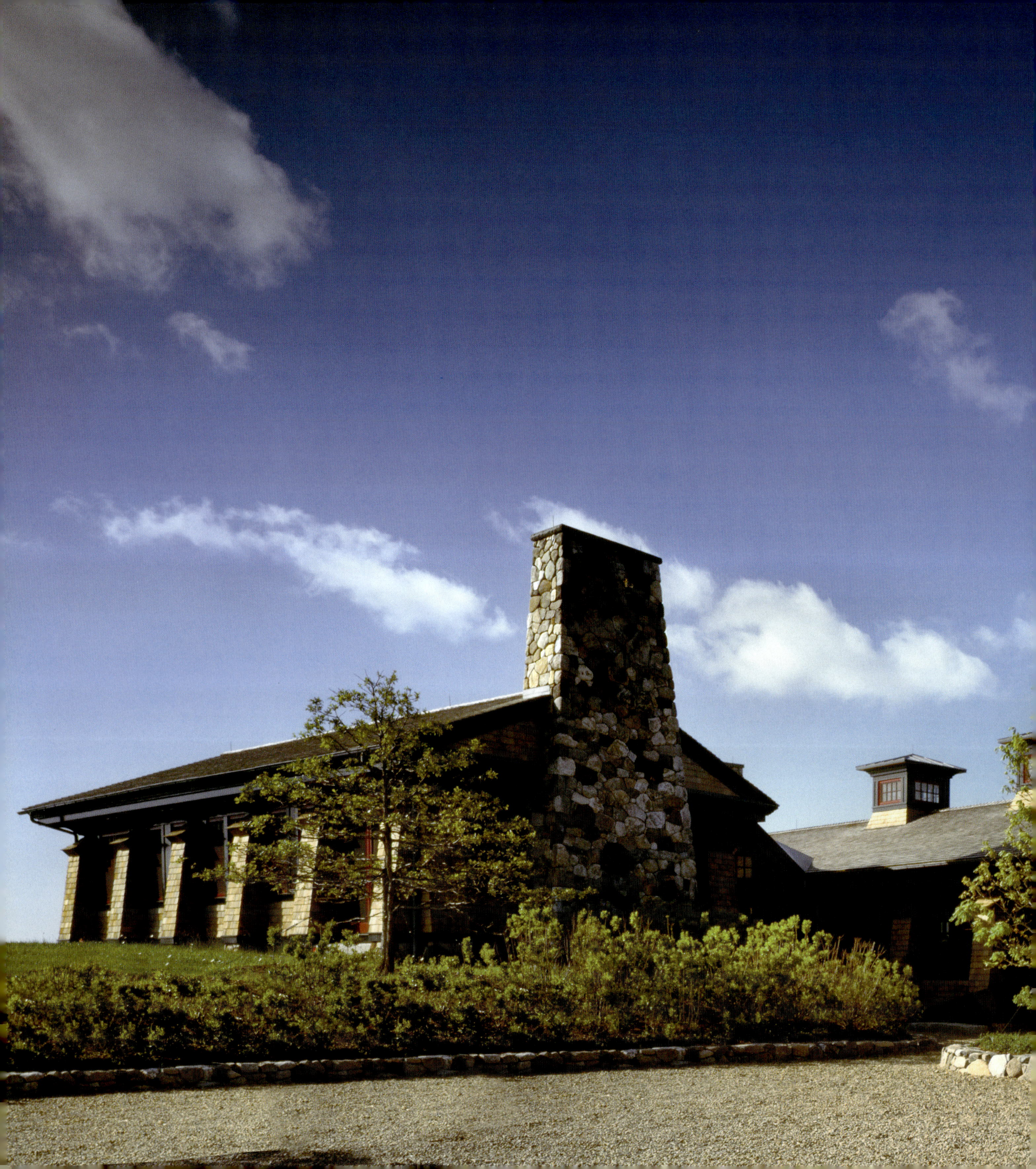

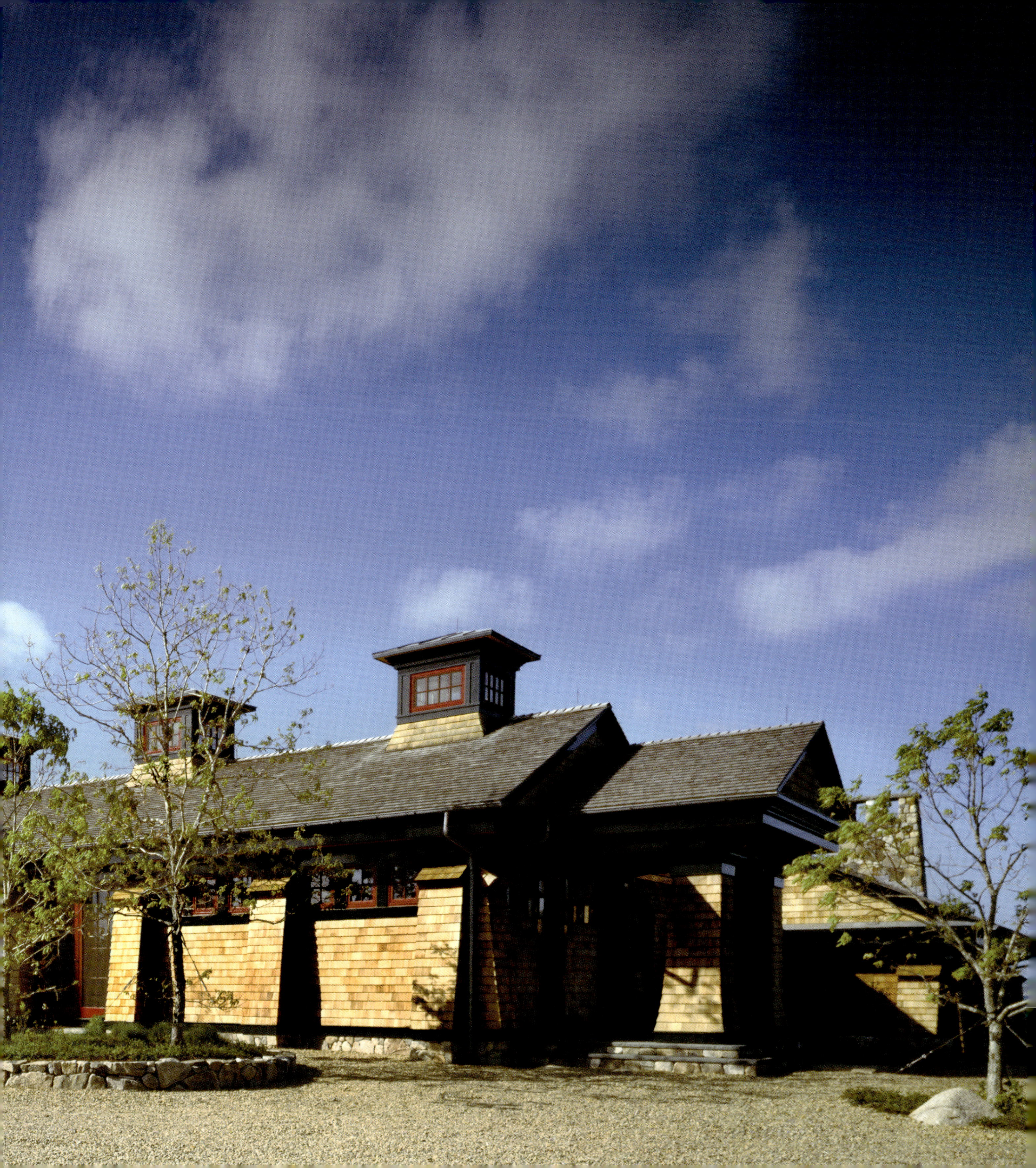

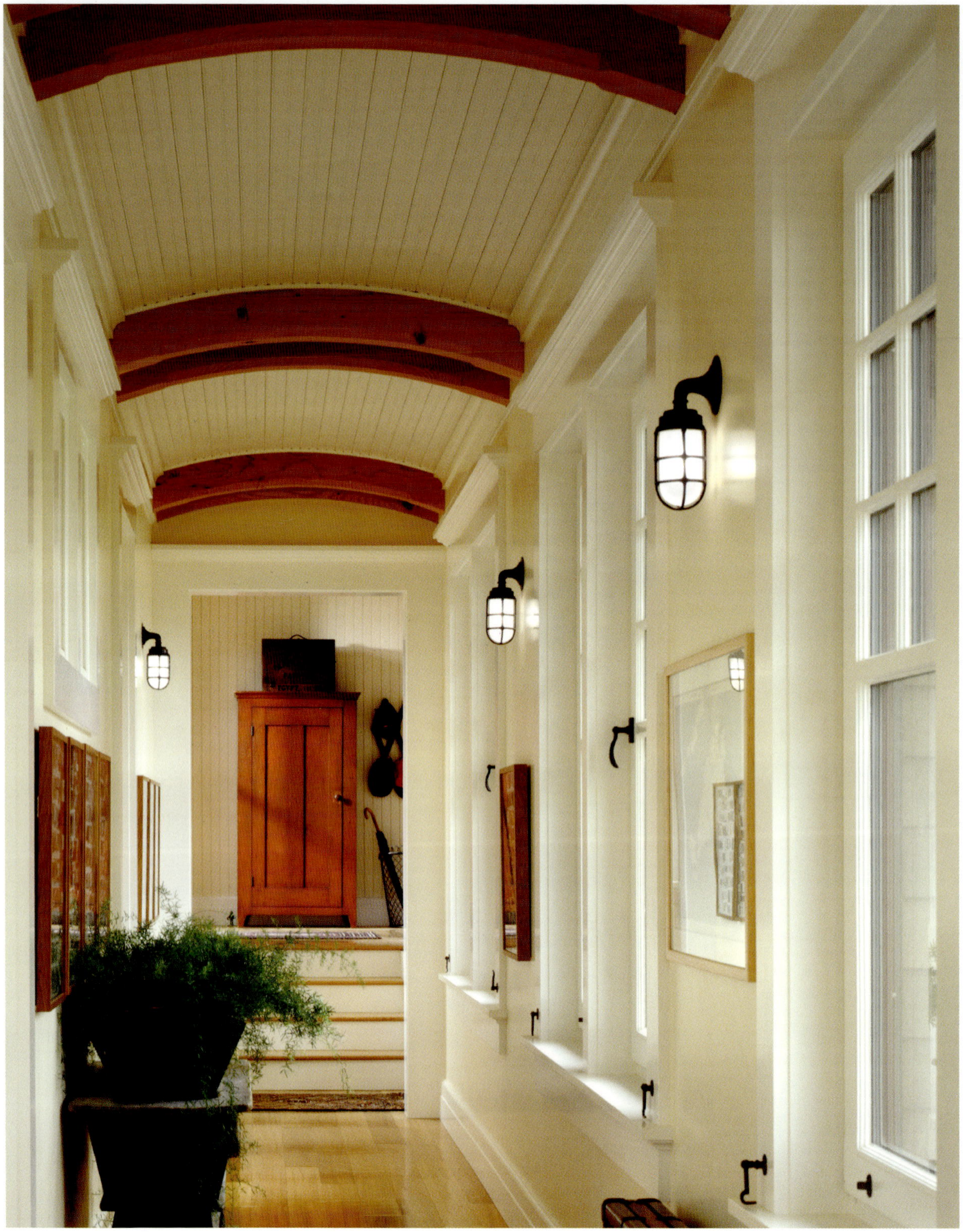

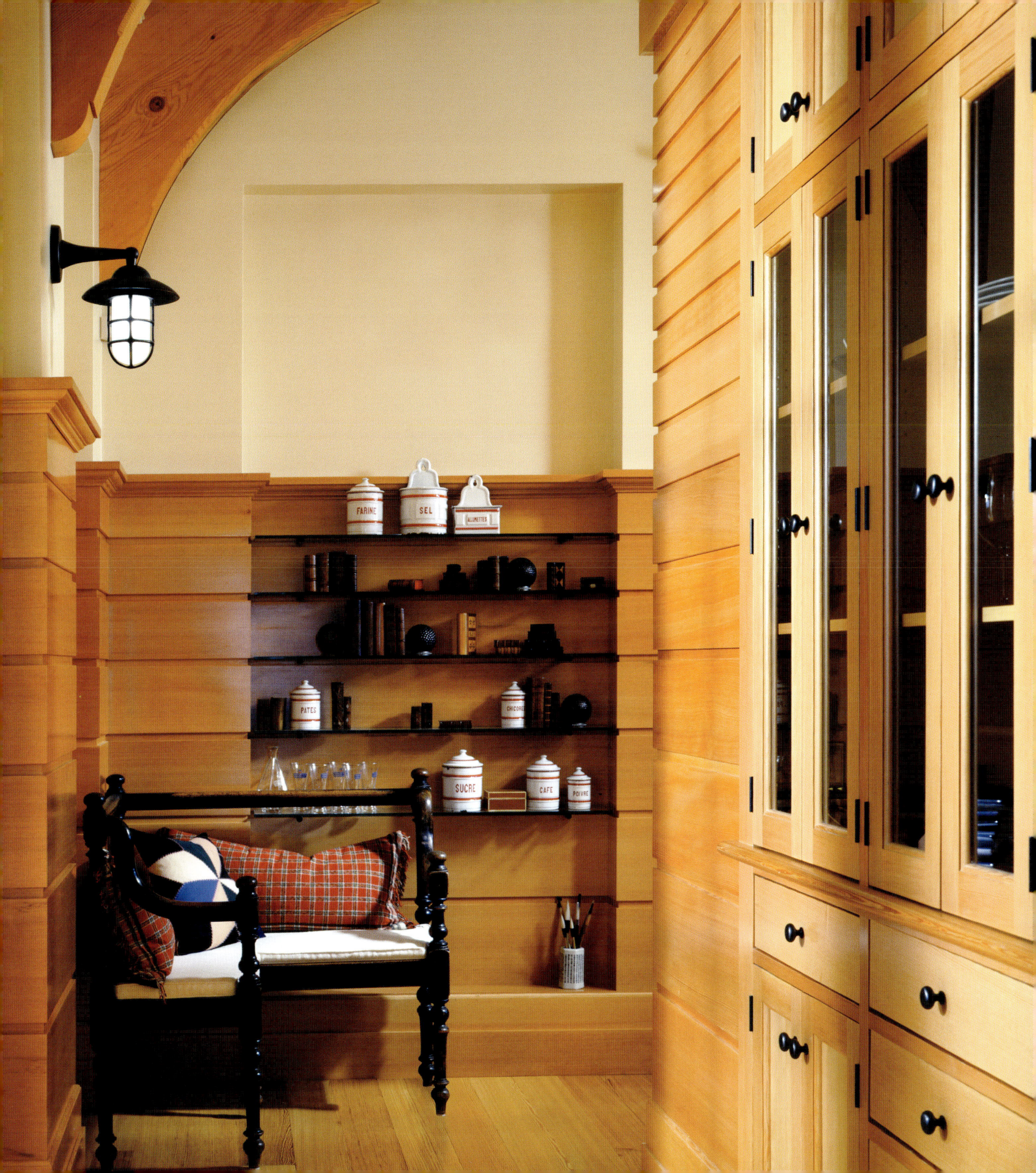
FARINE
SEL
PATES
SUCRE
CAFE
POIVRE

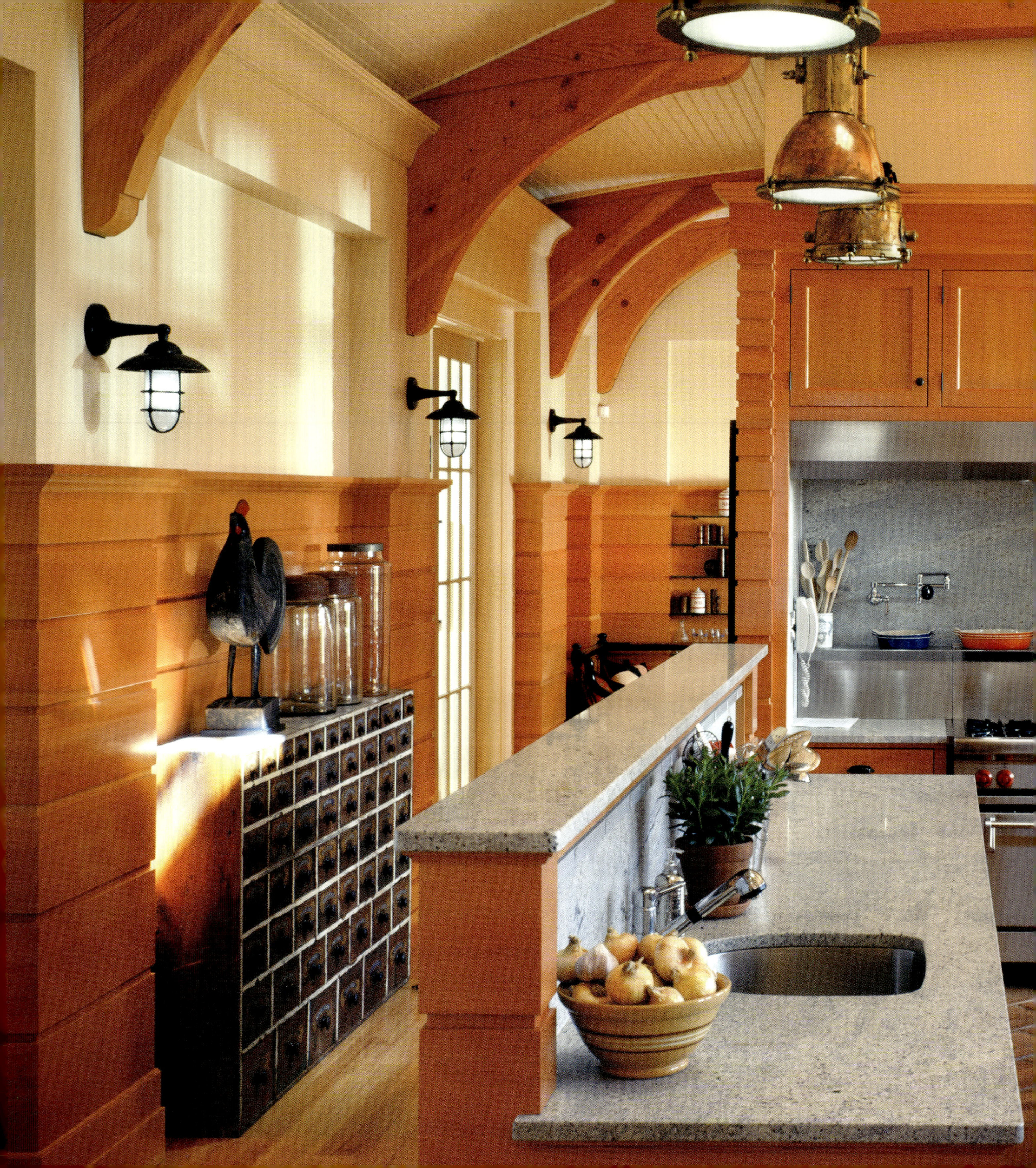

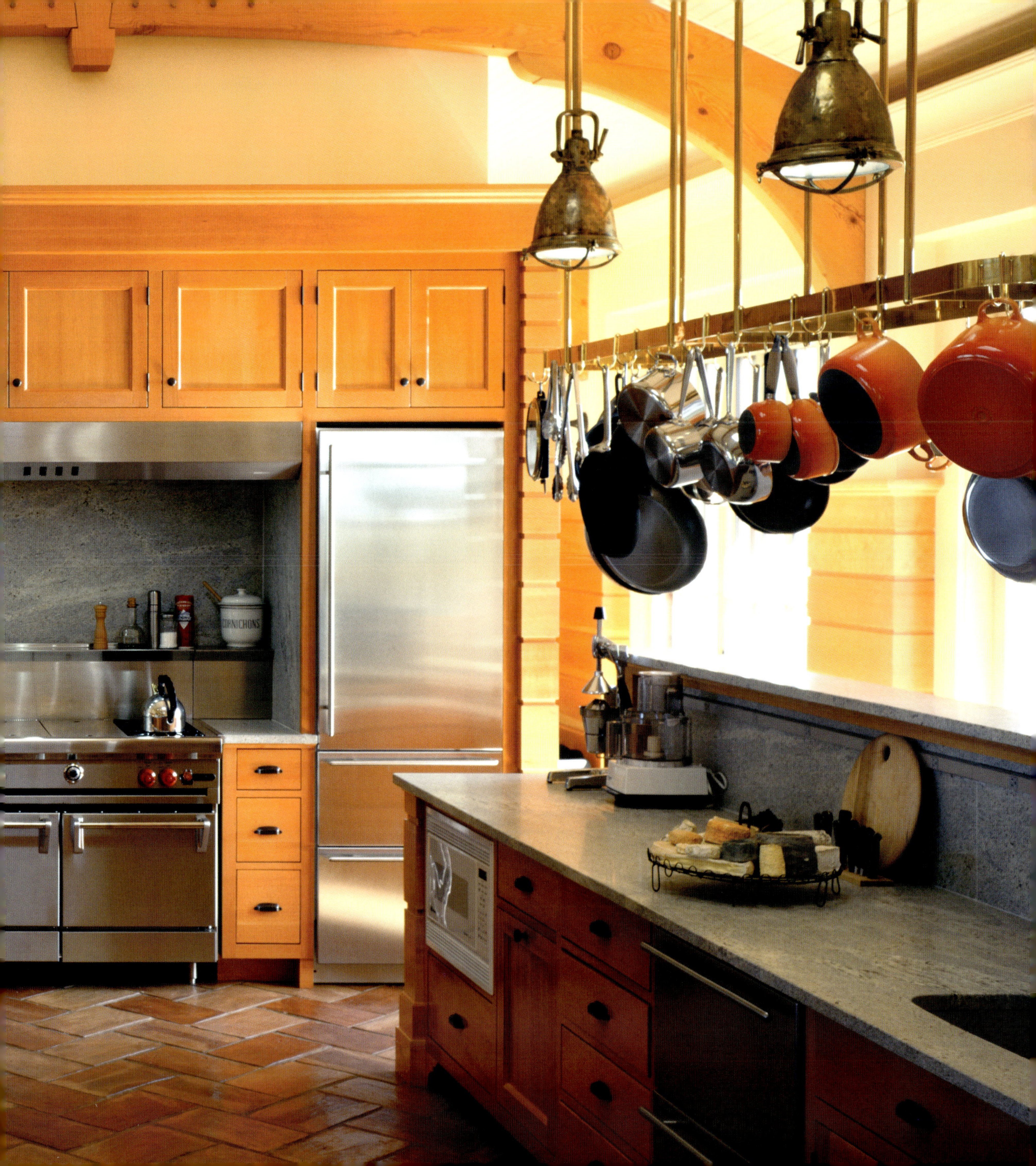
CORNICHONS

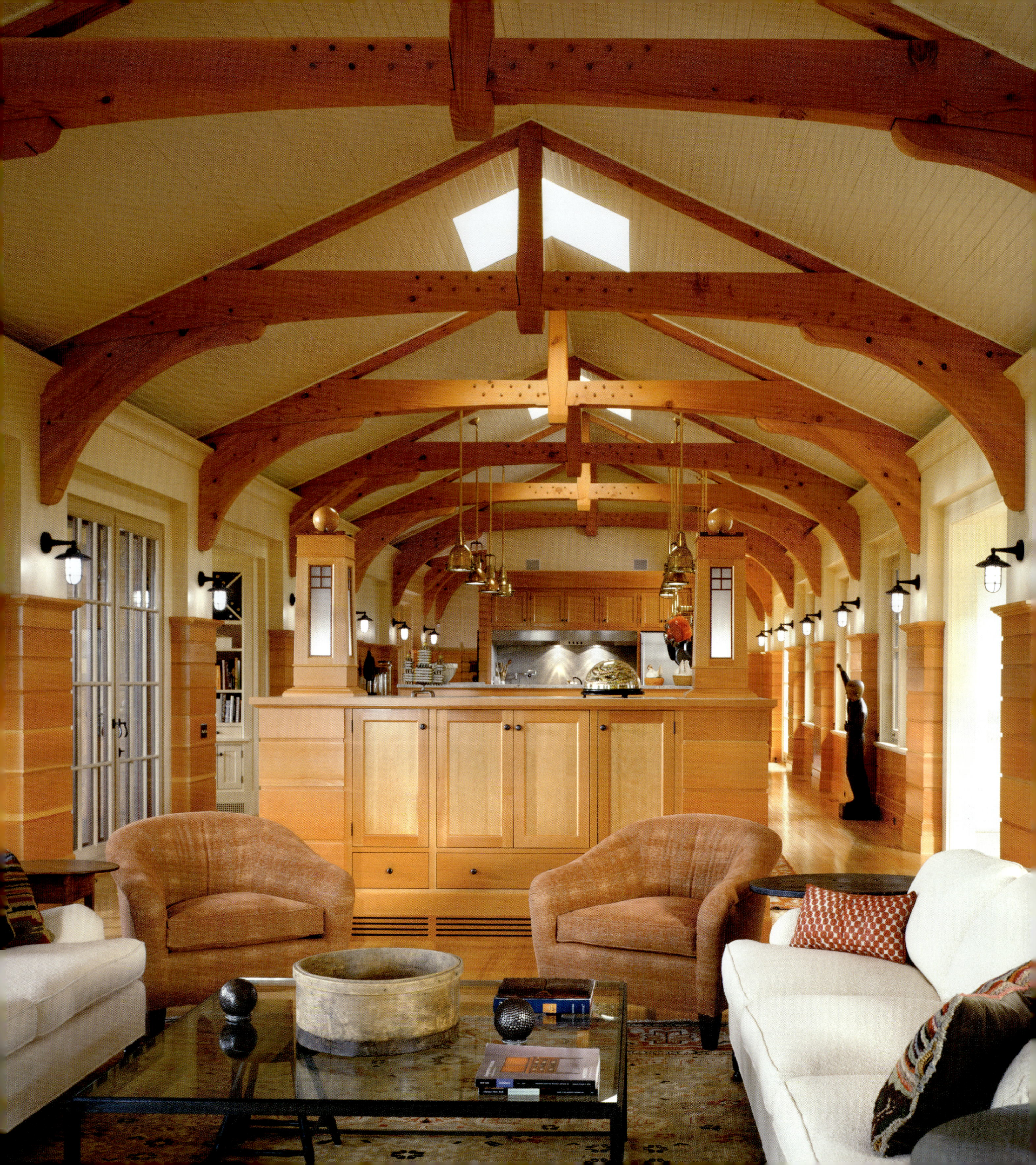

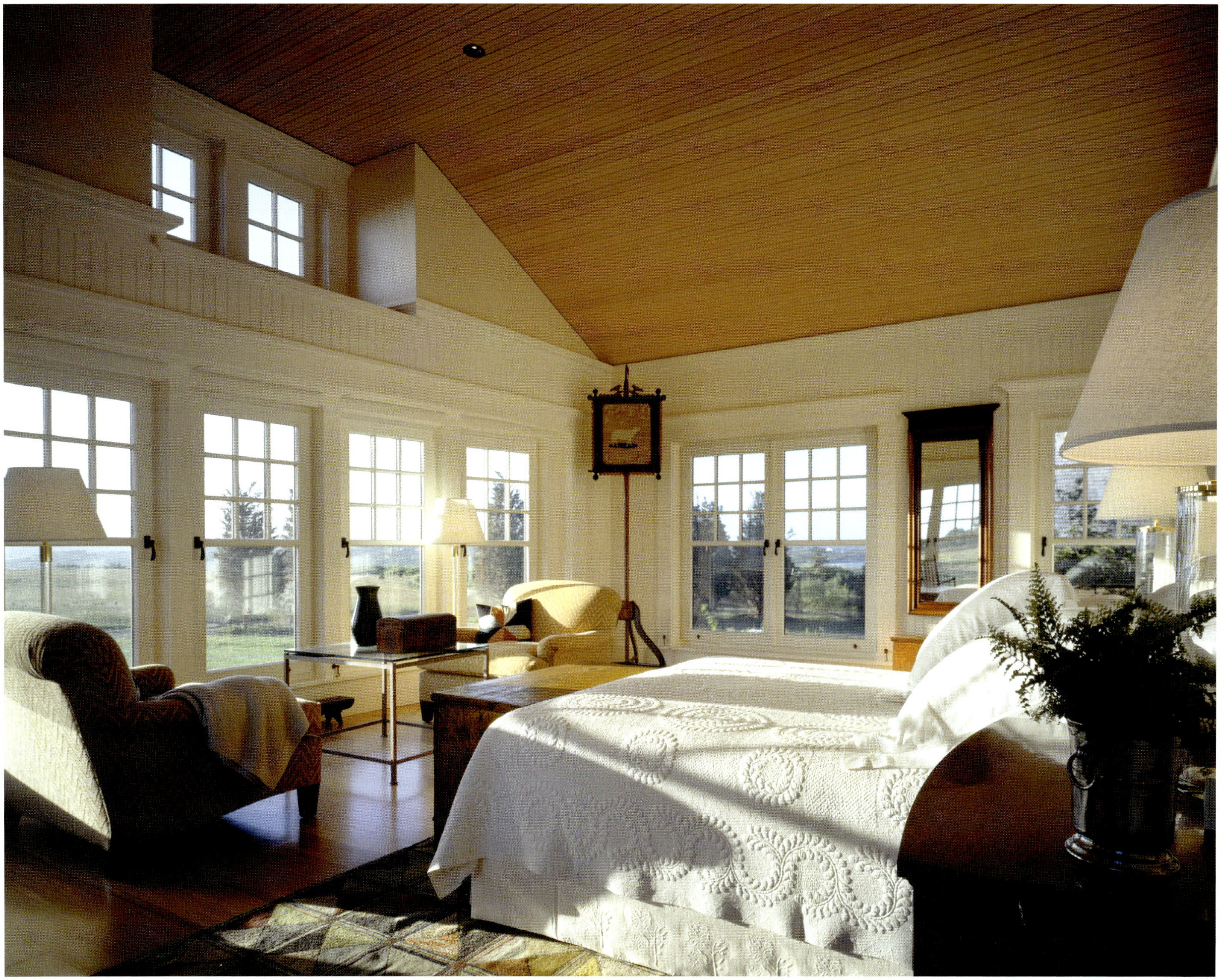

SITE PLAN

0 10' 25' 50'   100'

FIRST FLOOR

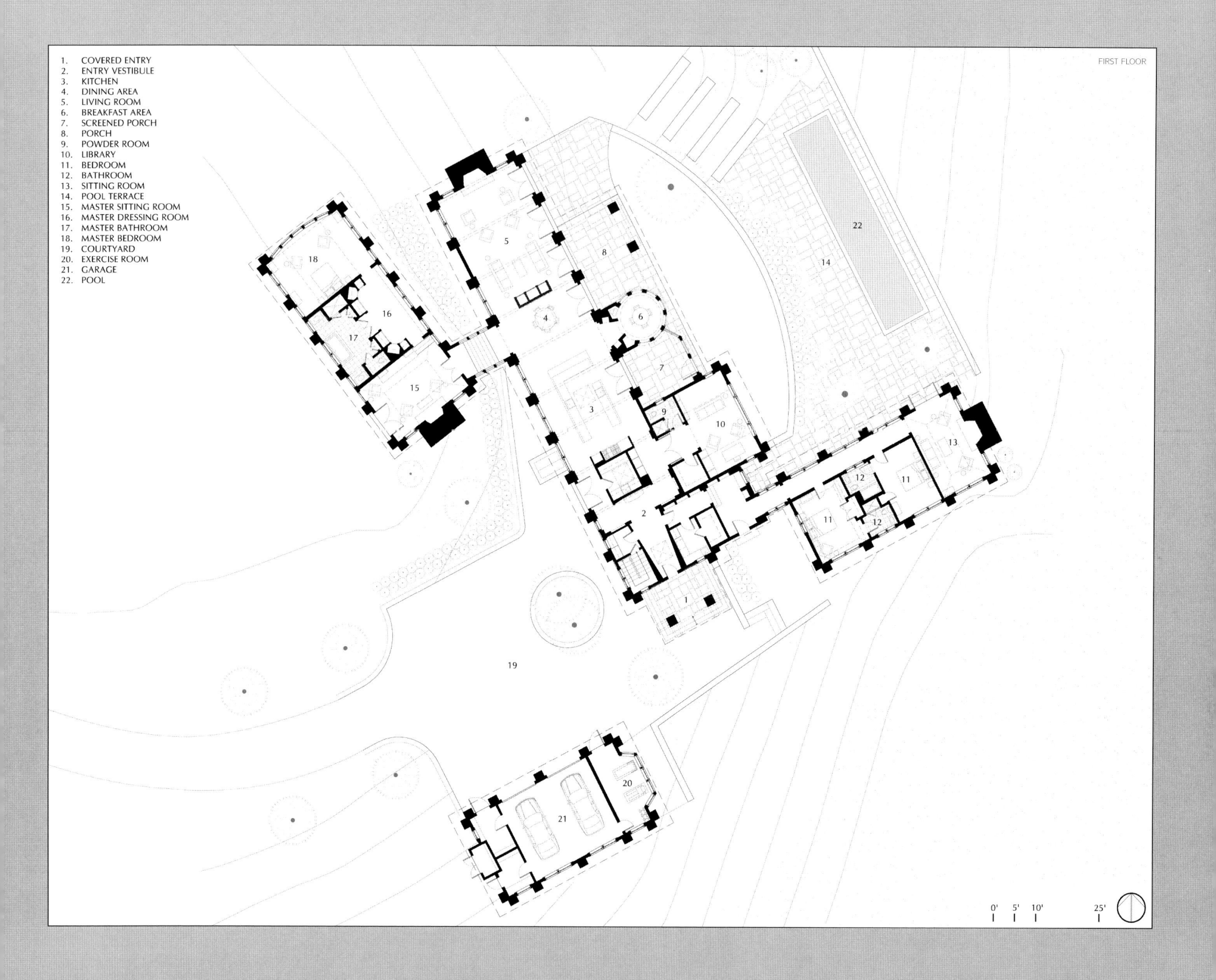

1. COVERED ENTRY
2. ENTRY VESTIBULE
3. KITCHEN
4. DINING AREA
5. LIVING ROOM
6. BREAKFAST AREA
7. SCREENED PORCH
8. PORCH
9. POWDER ROOM
10. LIBRARY
11. BEDROOM
12. BATHROOM
13. SITTING ROOM
14. POOL TERRACE
15. MASTER SITTING ROOM
16. MASTER DRESSING ROOM
17. MASTER BATHROOM
18. MASTER BEDROOM
19. COURTYARD
20. EXERCISE ROOM
21. GARAGE
22. POOL

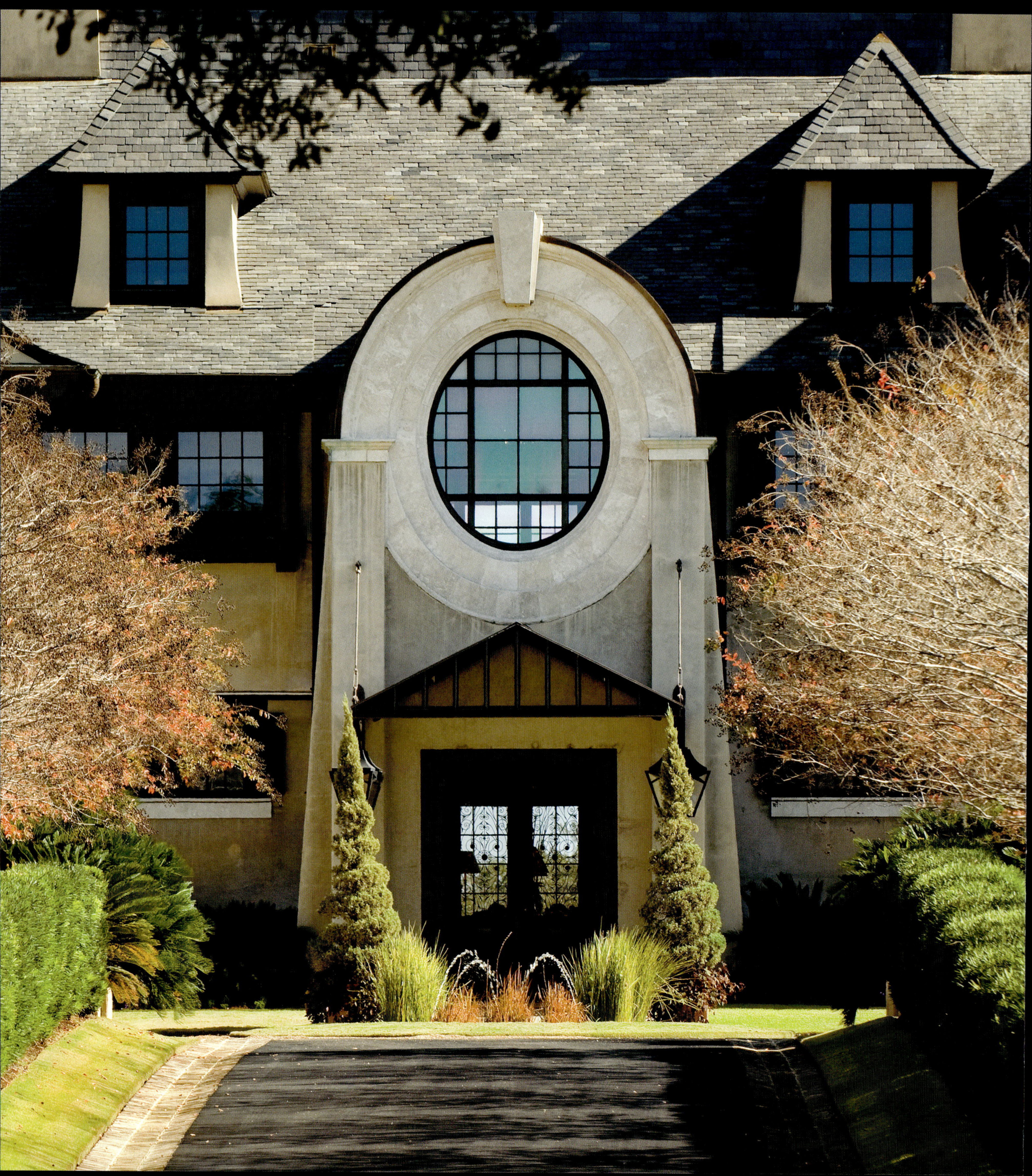

AN ARTS AND CRAFTS AESTHETIC WAS CHOSEN FOR A GOLF CLUB BUILT IN THE LOWCOUNTRY

THE CLIENTS The Cassique Golf Club was established by the Kiawah Island Development Corporation on a tidal island near Charleston, South Carolina. The eighteen-hole course is a links course, of which there are only about a dozen in the United States. Links developed in Scotland where golf originated, and it remains the oldest kind of golf course in the world. The first links courses were near the shore, and they are often still located near water, where they tend to be characterized by sand dunes, natural topography, and sparse vegetation.

THE DESIGN BRIEF The clients wanted a clubhouse that would be traditional and harmonious with the heritage of the links course. The rough terrain and grasses called for an English manor house in the Arts and Crafts style that might have been found on the treeless, windswept moors.

THE SOLUTION Wharton has always been enthusiastic about the turn of the twentieth century designs of English architects Sir Edwin Lutyens and Charles Voysey. In this case, Voysey seemed to offer the right precedent. His buildings were largely derived from the English vernacular architecture of the sixteenth- and early-seventeenth centuries, with white roughcast walls, rows of small windows, and generously pitched roofs. Stucco was chosen for the walls of the 20,000-square-foot, 24-room clubhouse, as it would age and acquire an antique weathered look over time. Visitors drive across acres of former tomato fields and ascend up a drive flanked by an allee of trees, to the glassed-front entry canopy. The appearance of the courtyard, which has an overscale round window, small-paned windows, and heavy roofs sloping down to end in sharply pointed eaves, is domestic rather than institutional. Nonetheless, the impression conveyed is powerful, with two massive chimneys contributing to the brooding atmosphere. Atlanta-based interior designer Jacquelynne Lanham used antique blue-gray English Yorkstone paving in the entry and a lot of darkened oak floors inside the clubhouse: "I wanted them to be the color of pluff mud, which is the gray, chocolaty brown soil that is left on the Carolina coast when the tide goes out," adds the designer. To maintain a seventeenth-century feeling, Lanham imitated English manor houses, which often displayed a collection of armor, by arranging antique golf clubs in patterns of circles and half-circles on the ceiling of the entry. To lighten the sense of antique moodiness, the fabrics and upholstery of the clubhouse interiors feature island colors—blues and greens—rather than the more traditional English colors such as reds and yellows. Among the 24 rooms of the clubhouse, there is a large living room on the main floor with views of the course beyond, as well as a pro shop and a meeting room. The dining facilities, which include a private dining room, are on the second floor, at the top of a dramatic stairway.

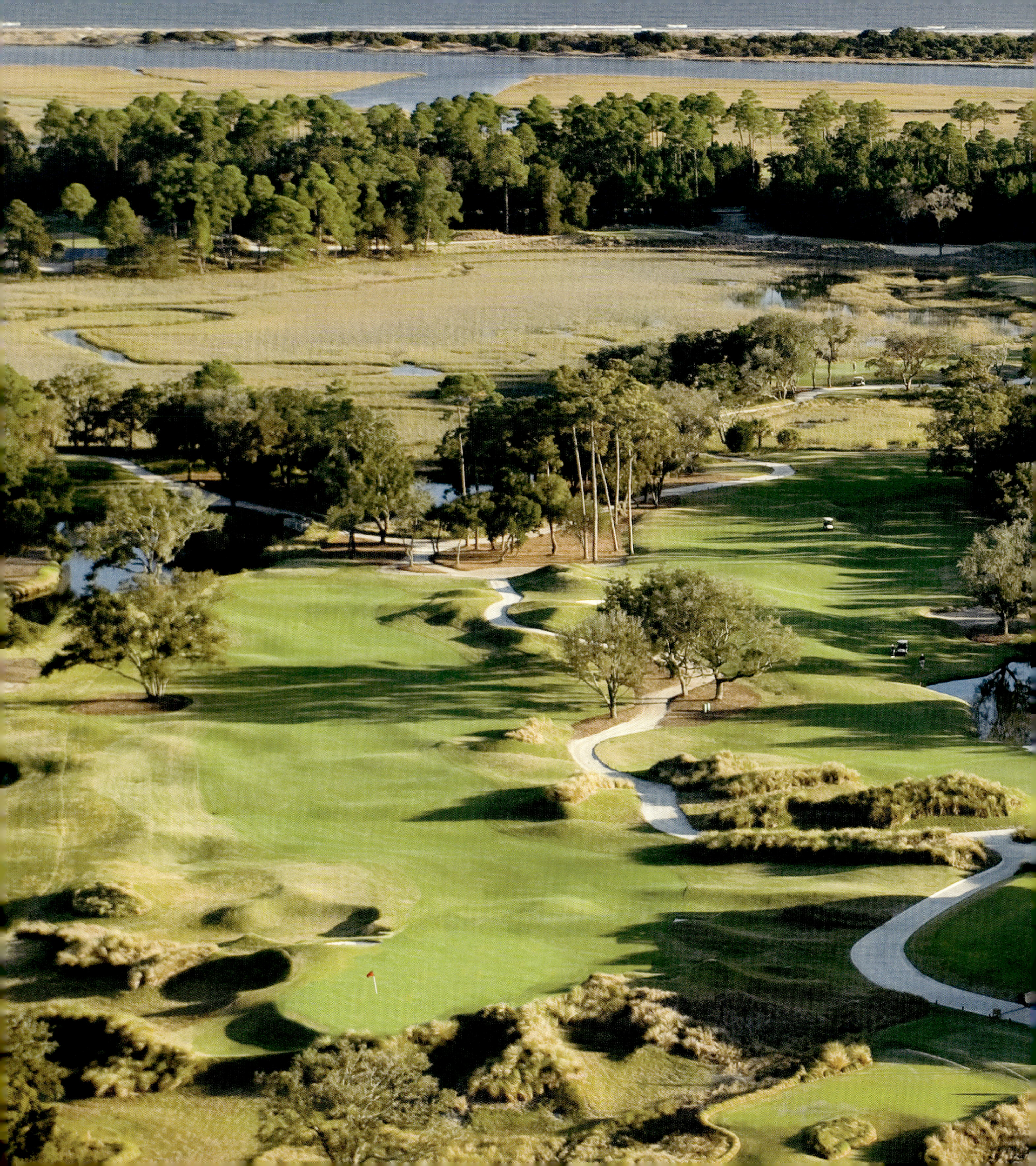

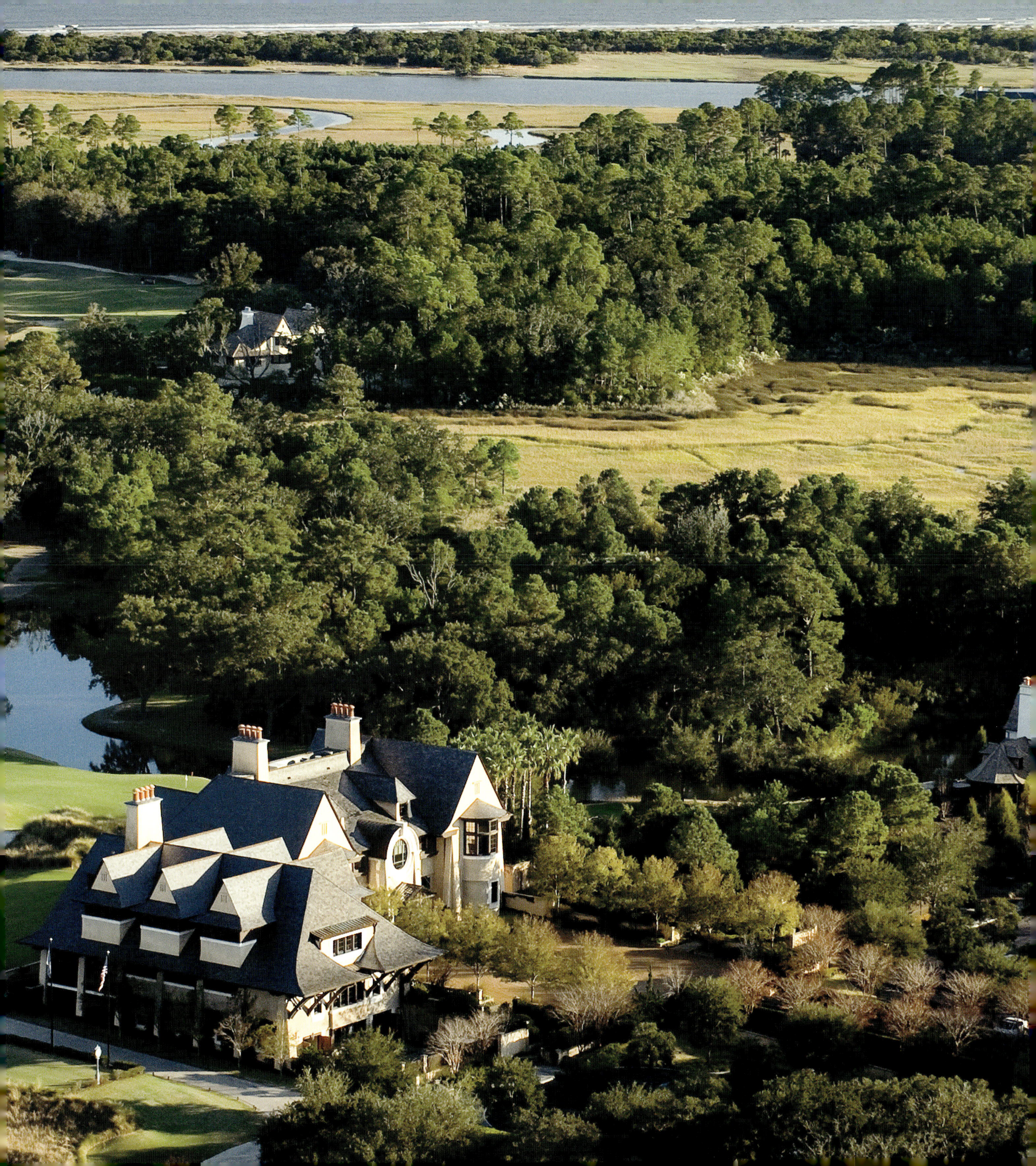

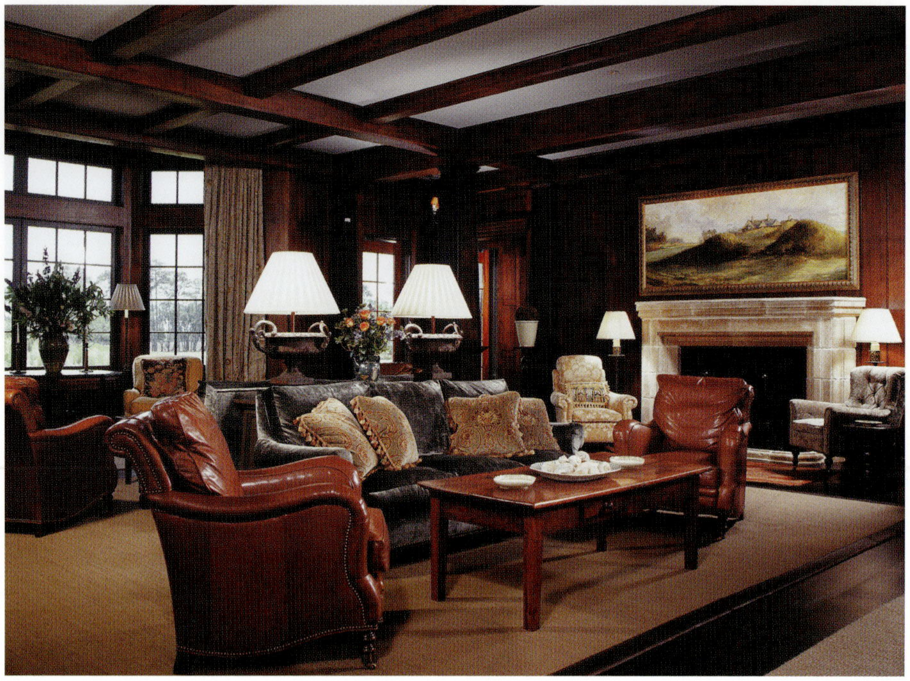

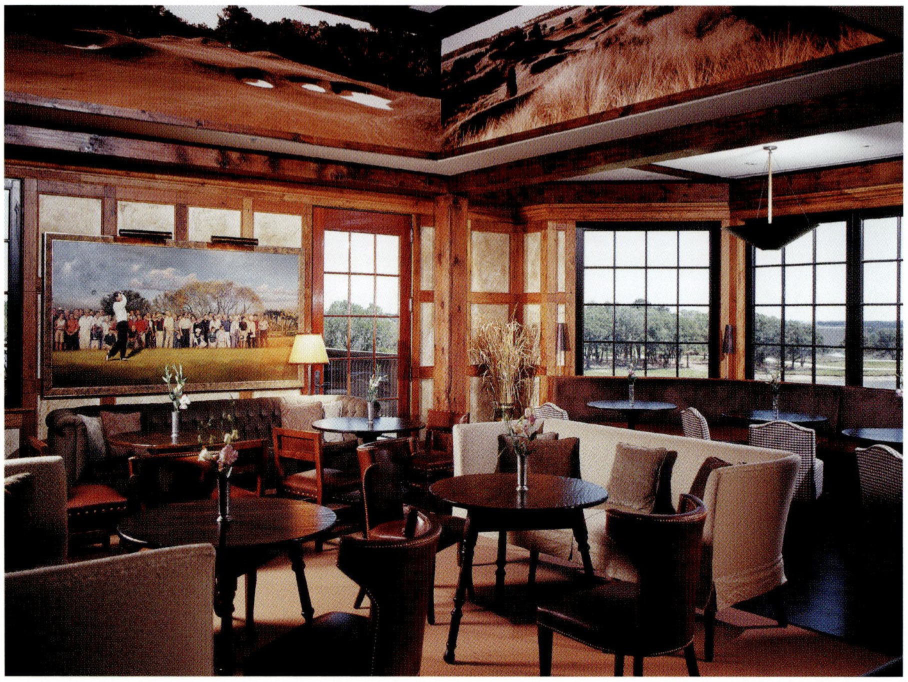

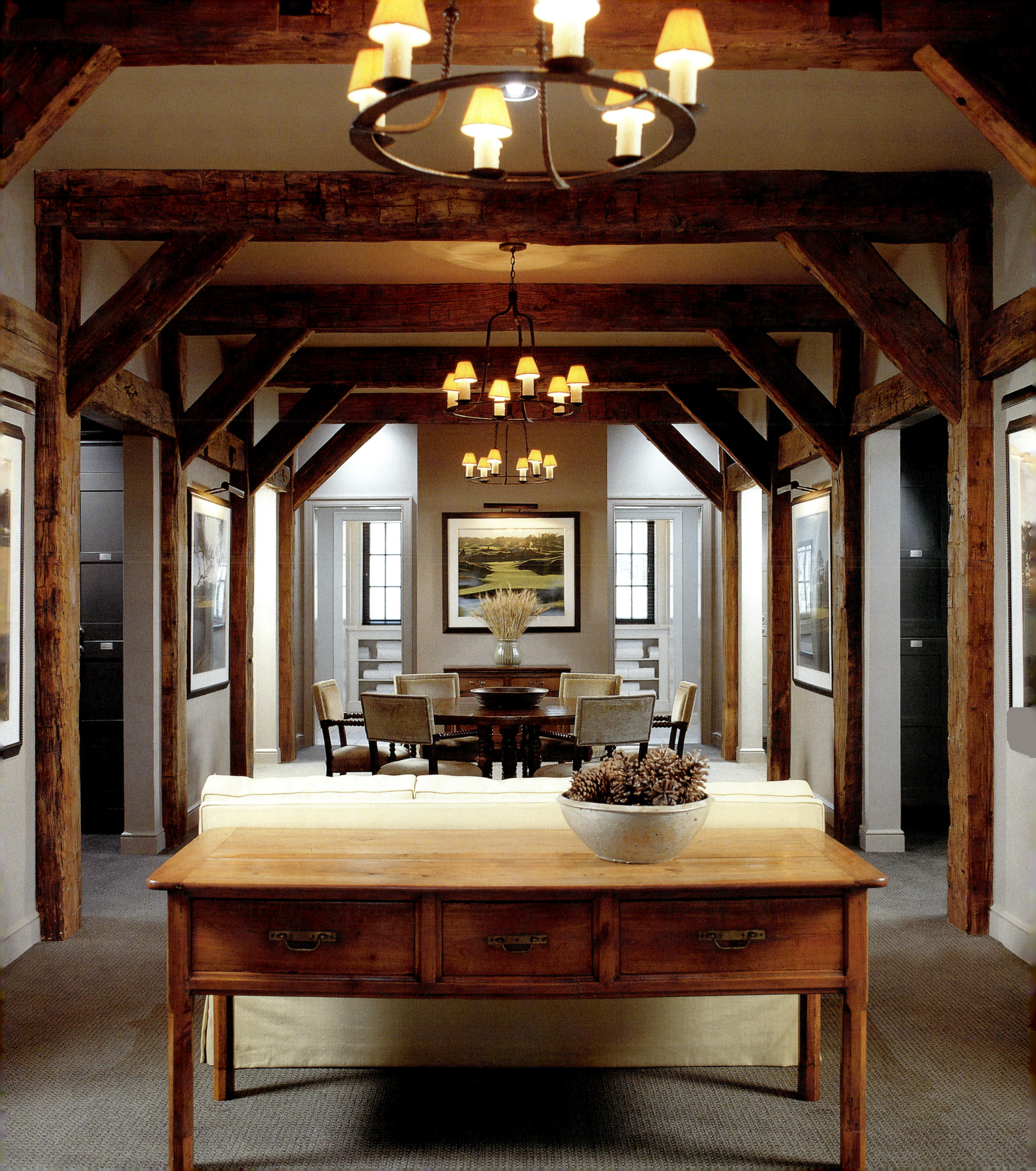

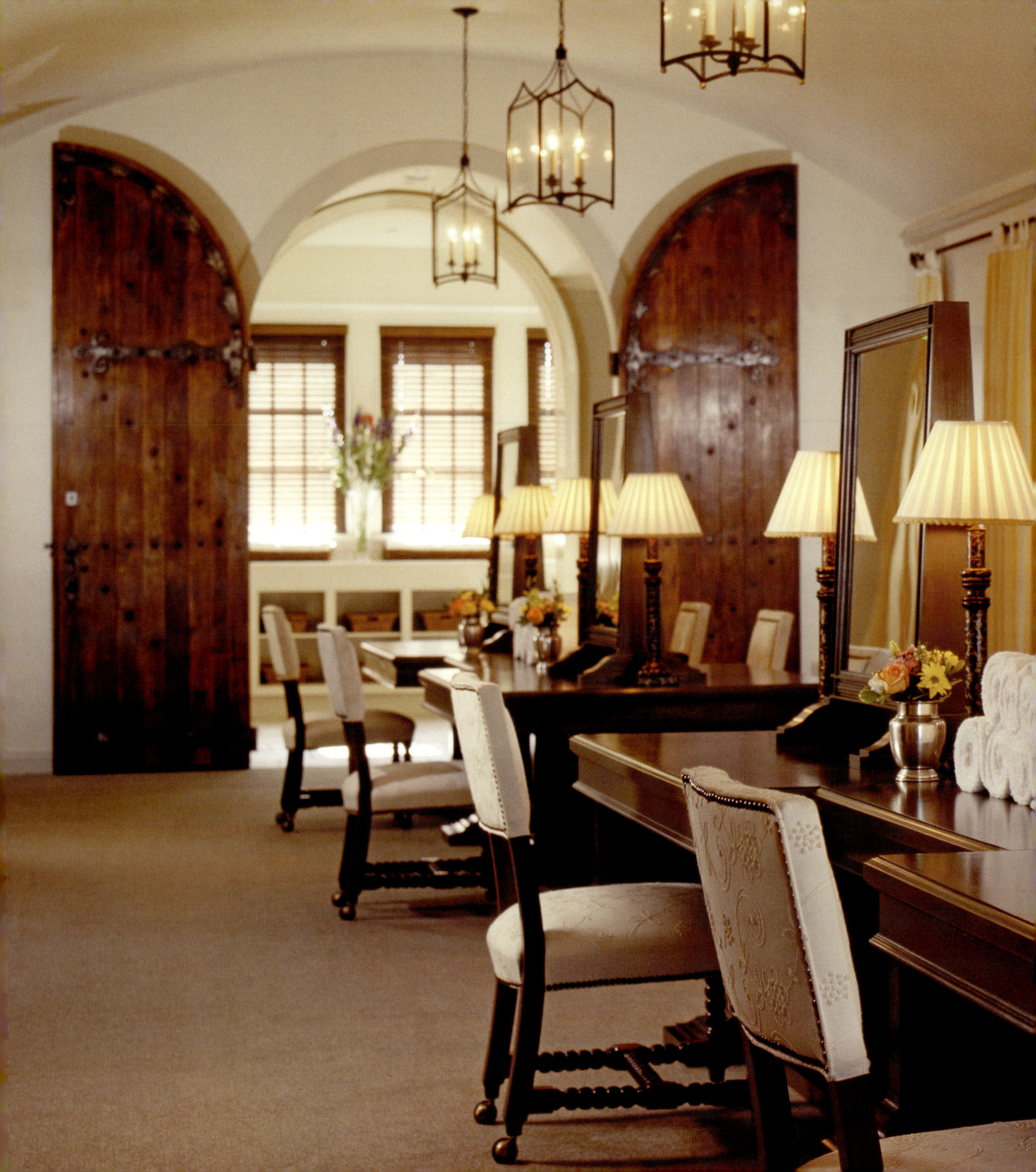

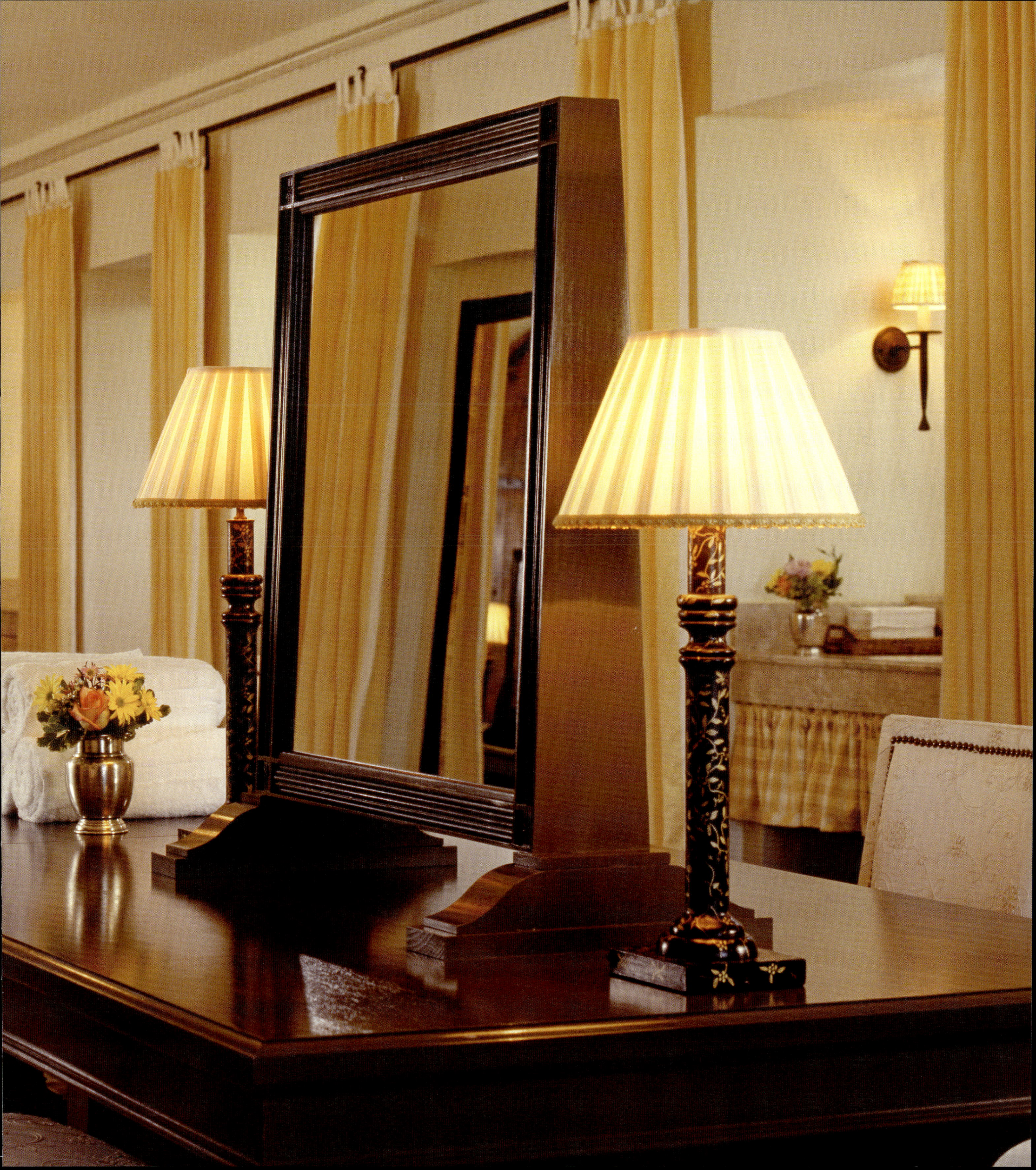

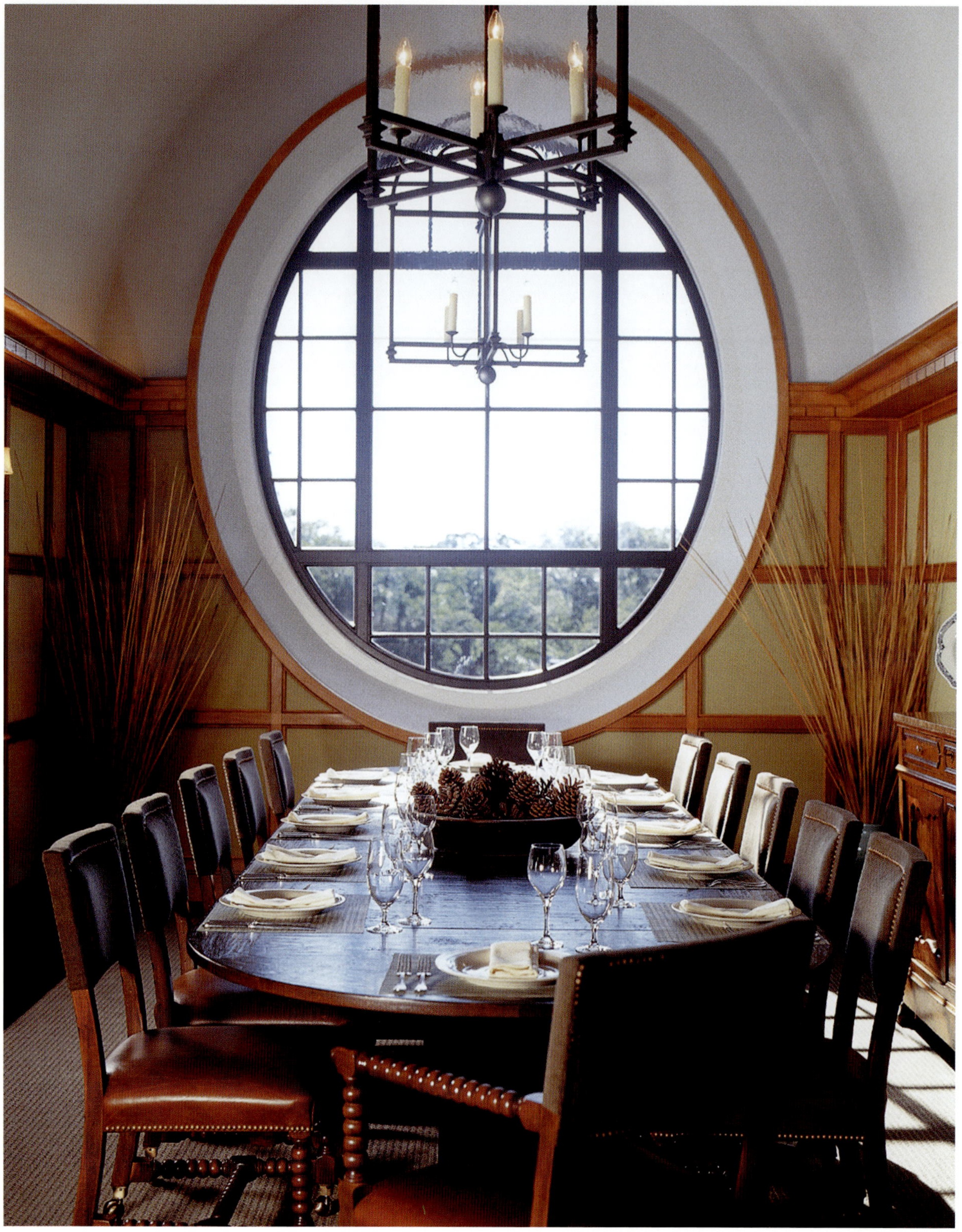

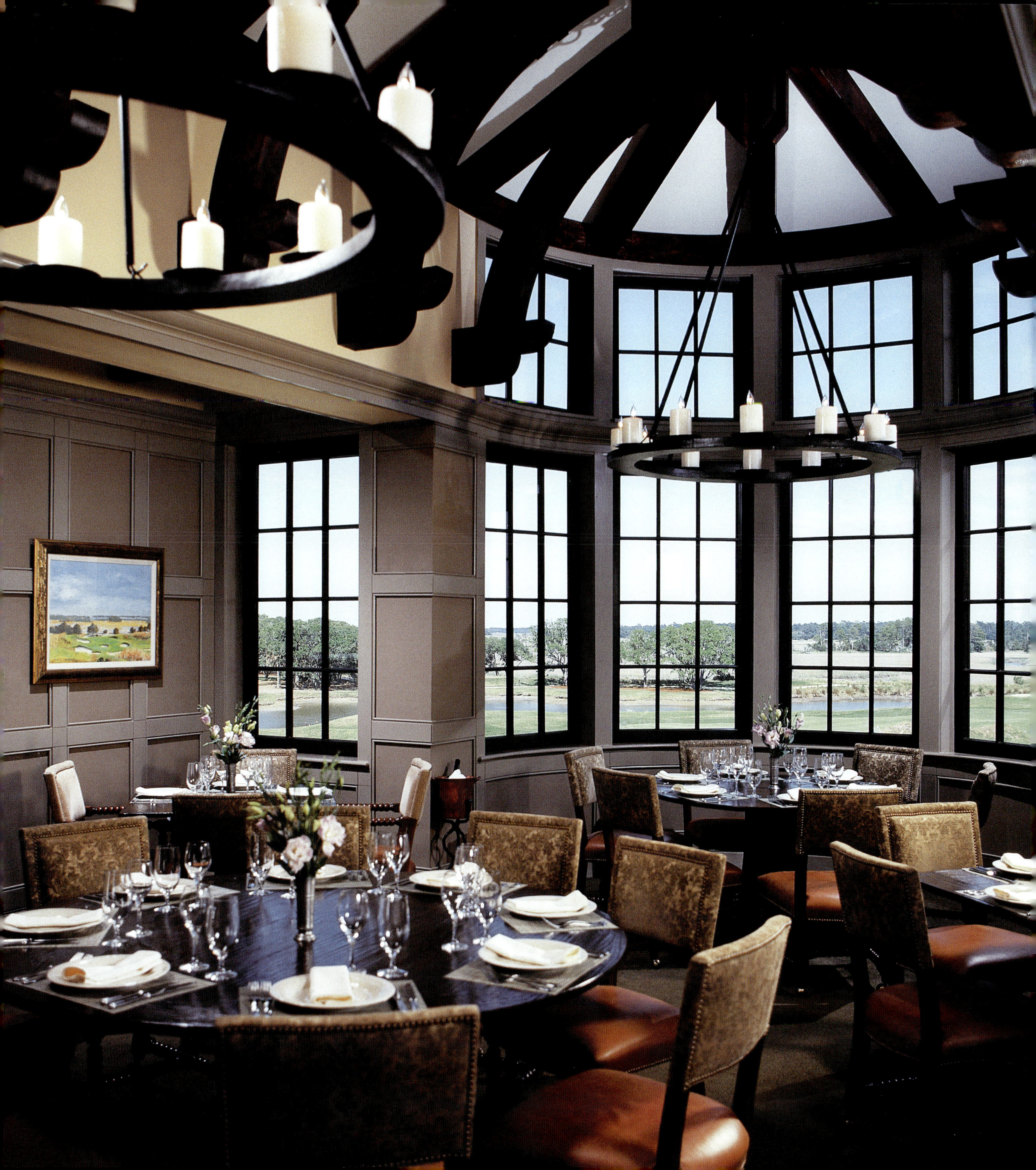

SITE PLAN

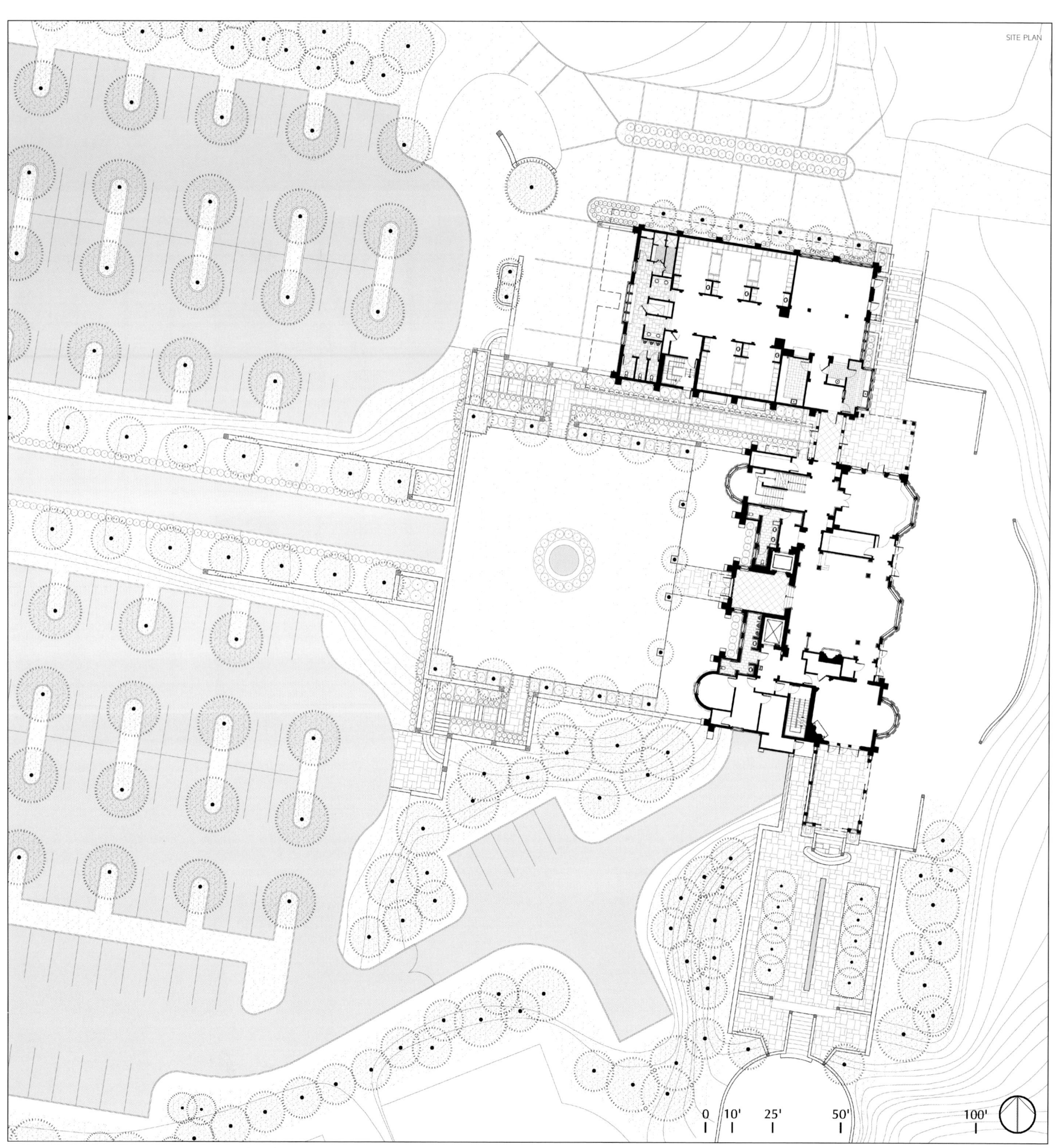

0 10' 25' 50' 100'

FIRST FLOOR

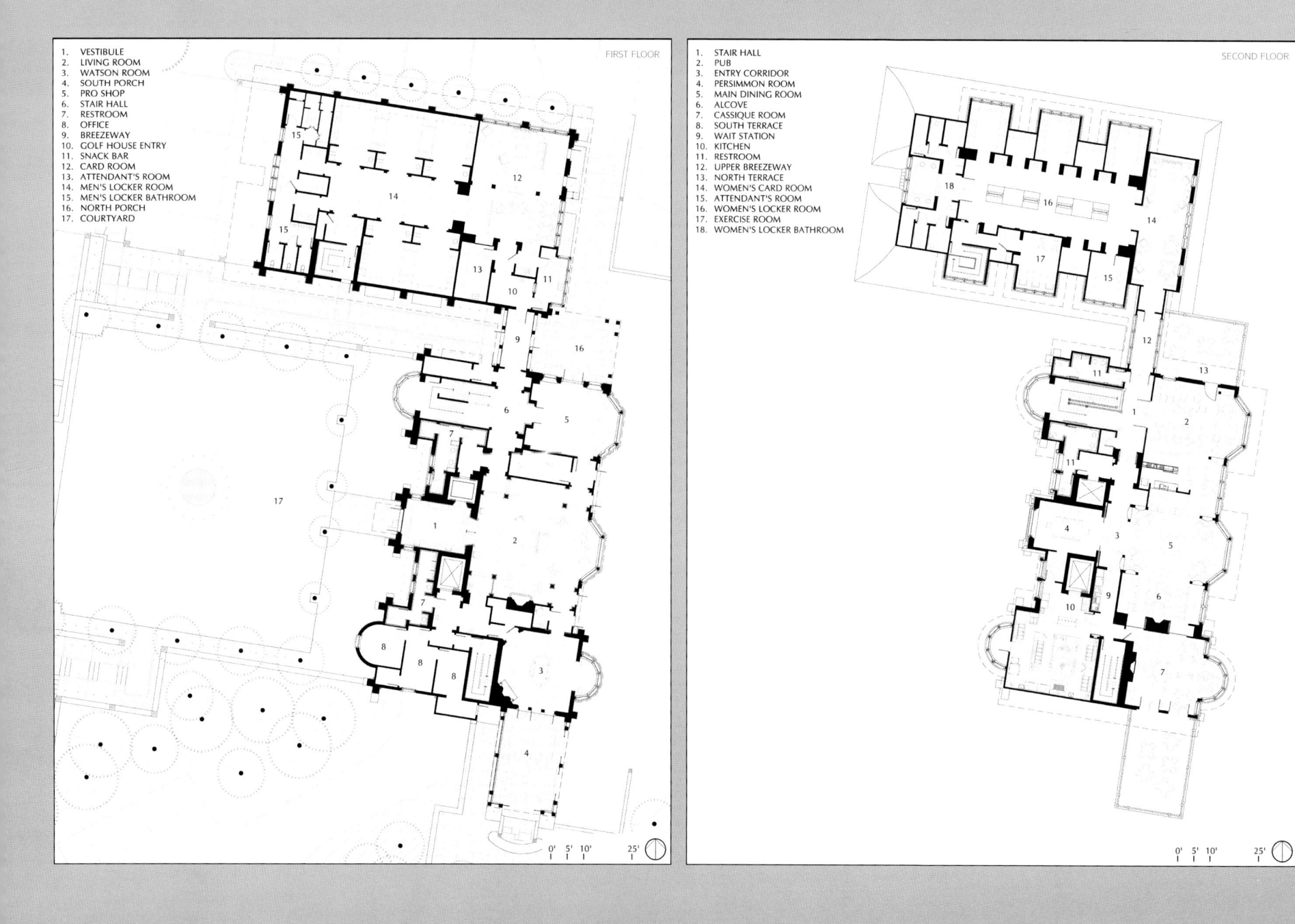

1. VESTIBULE
2. LIVING ROOM
3. WATSON ROOM
4. SOUTH PORCH
5. PRO SHOP
6. STAIR HALL
7. RESTROOM
8. OFFICE
9. BREEZEWAY
10. GOLF HOUSE ENTRY
11. SNACK BAR
12. CARD ROOM
13. ATTENDANT'S ROOM
14. MEN'S LOCKER ROOM
15. MEN'S LOCKER BATHROOM
16. NORTH PORCH
17. COURTYARD

SECOND FLOOR

1. STAIR HALL
2. PUB
3. ENTRY CORRIDOR
4. PERSIMMON ROOM
5. MAIN DINING ROOM
6. ALCOVE
7. CASSIQUE ROOM
8. SOUTH TERRACE
9. WAIT STATION
10. KITCHEN
11. RESTROOM
12. UPPER BREEZEWAY
13. NORTH TERRACE
14. WOMEN'S CARD ROOM
15. ATTENDANT'S ROOM
16. WOMEN'S LOCKER ROOM
17. EXERCISE ROOM
18. WOMEN'S LOCKER BATHROOM

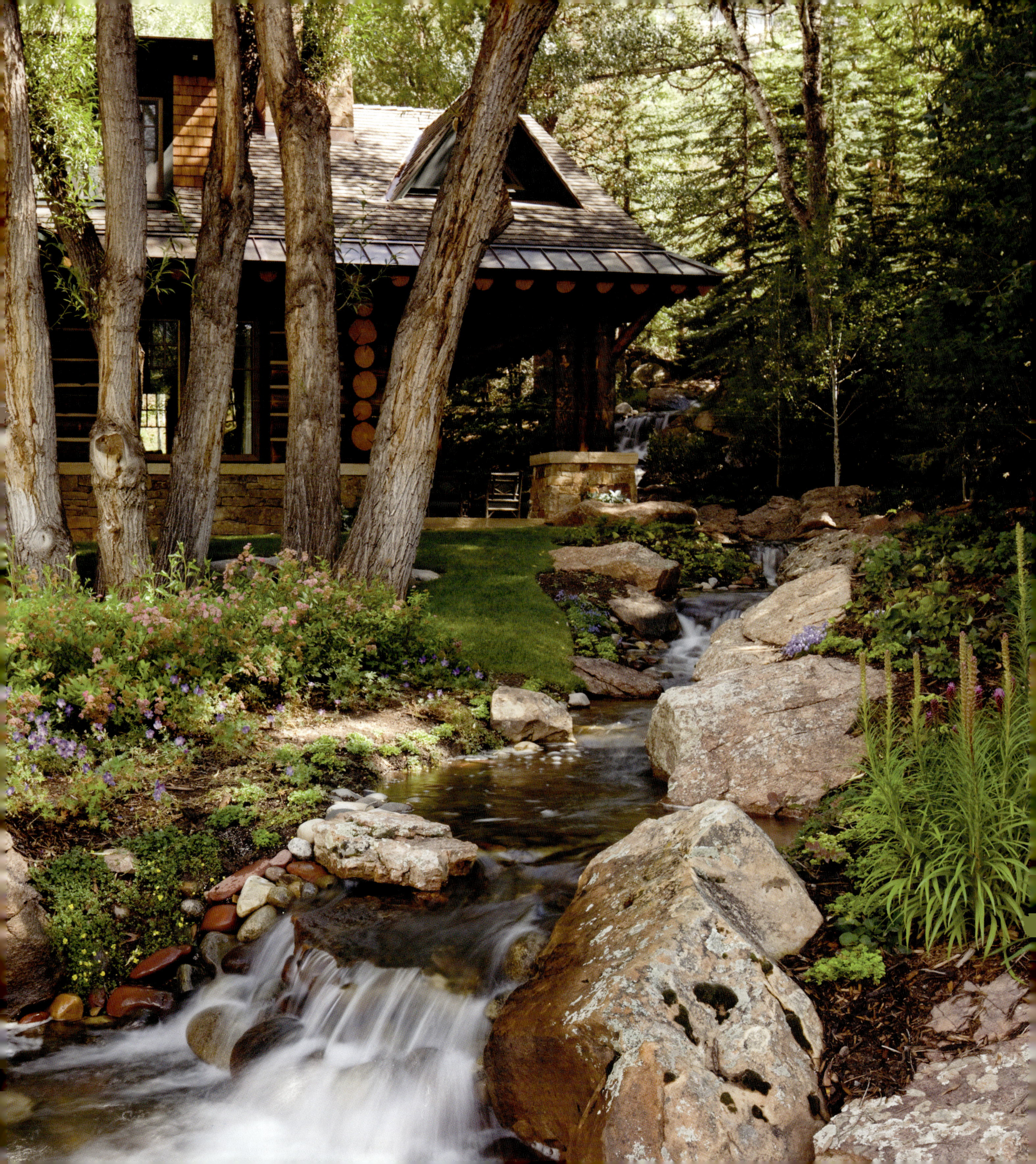

SITED ON A POND, A SOPHISTICATED RUSTIC RETREAT SUITS A FAMILY'S LOVE FOR THE GREAT OUTDOORS

THE CLIENTS An East Coast financier and his wife bought a wonderful three-acre site at the foot of a fir-clad hillside by a pond in Aspen, Colorado. They enjoy skiing, hiking, and swimming and, with both children still living at home and children in college, they wanted a house that the entire family could use all year round.

THE DESIGN BRIEF The clients wanted their home to reflect the architectural heritage of the area, without looking like a Western pastiche. The property's pond and mountain views had to be featured prominently in the house's orientation, and they also had to remain visible from the interior of the house.

THE SOLUTION The architects decided that a log residence in the style of an old Western lodge would honor the site and the history of the region. The house spreads dramatically across the pond's shore at the foot of the mountain. Upon entering the property, one notes the driveway leading to an intimate courtyard where a stone stair tower is pierced by a long window with small panes. The canopy over the entrance is the first instance of the log motif, which is continued throughout the architecture of the house. The large, welcoming double-entrance door has nine small-paned windows in each panel. Inside, the double-height living room anchors the center of the house. It has two entrances that flank the stone fireplace wall. There is an intricate post-and-beam arrangement of logs that crosses the space below the peaked roof. The walls of most of the 26 rooms in this 7,800-square-foot house are paneled in sawn horizontal wood planks. Large expanses of glass that make way for breathtaking views of the mountains lighten the paneling and bring in the sense of the outdoors. The living room leads to the dining room and the library, each of which is anchored by its own fireplace. The kitchen is one of the lighter rooms in the house, where the pine paneling is painted white, and rather delicate Windsor chairs surround a pine table in the bay-windowed breakfast nook. New York-based interior designer Victoria Hagan furnished most of the house in a style that reflects its Western heritage. The Morris chairs in the living room are upholstered in red leather, and gray upholstered sofas on each side of the fireplace sport pillows in a gray and red plaid. Images by Ansel Adams, the photographer known for his black-and-white Western landscapes, hang on the living room walls, and a nineteenth-century weathervane is placed by the window. On the second floor, a gallery overlooking the living room leads to the bedrooms. Most of the bedrooms maintain a minimalist decor; however, they still have Western touches, such as classic Hudson Bay blankets on the beds. Nestled securely in the mountains and reflected in the pond, this is a house that is sympathetic with the beautiful environments of the West.

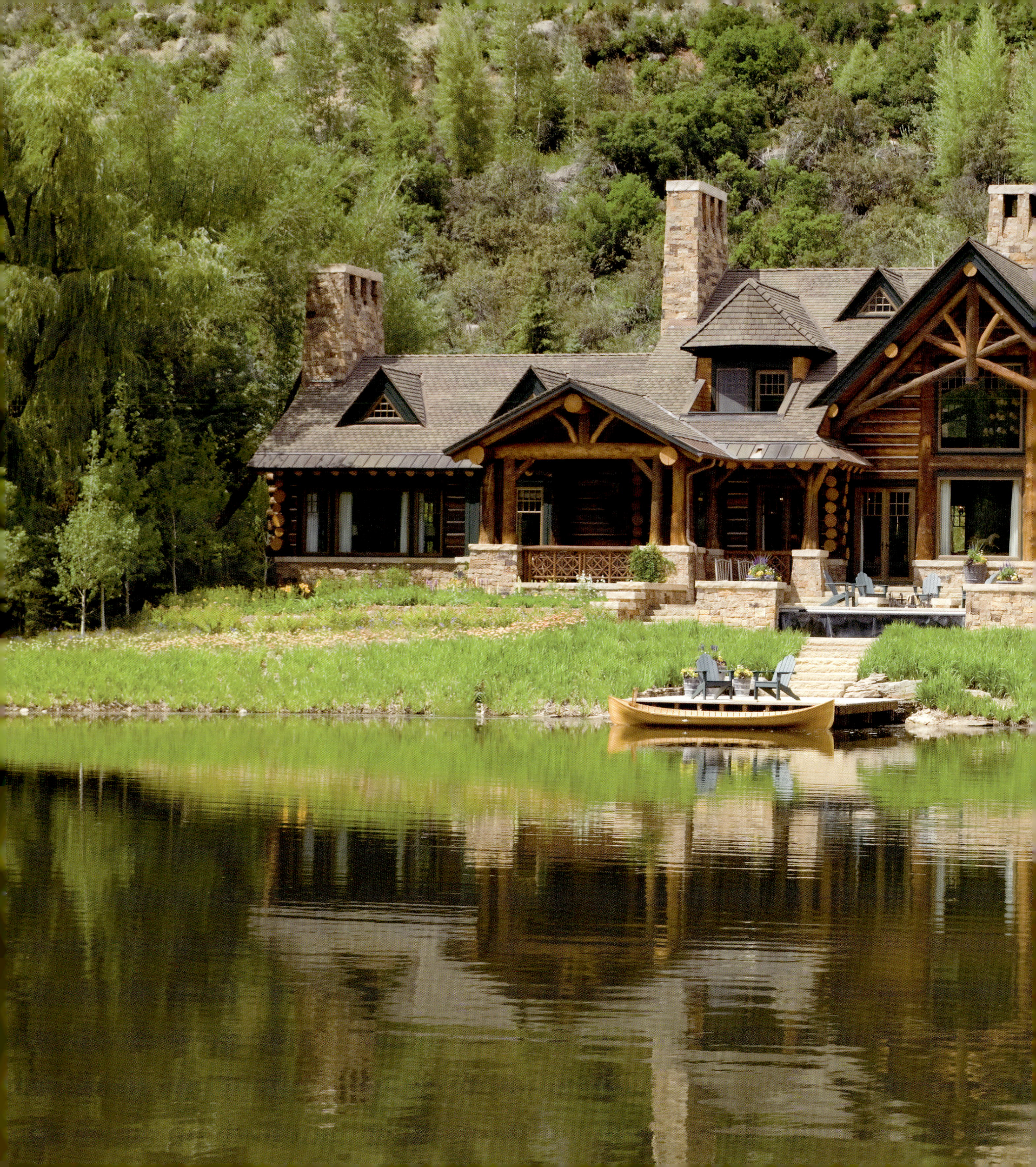

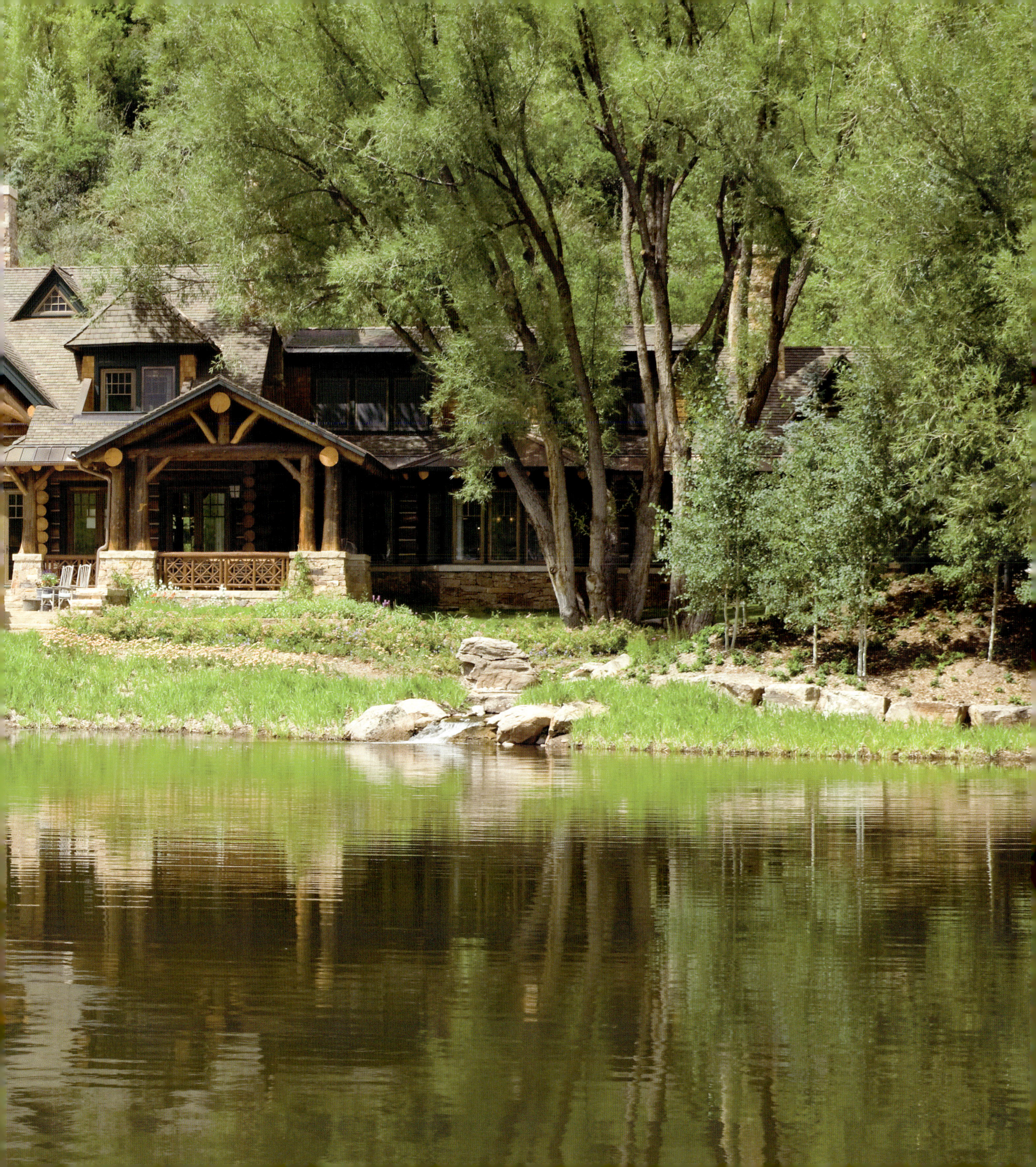

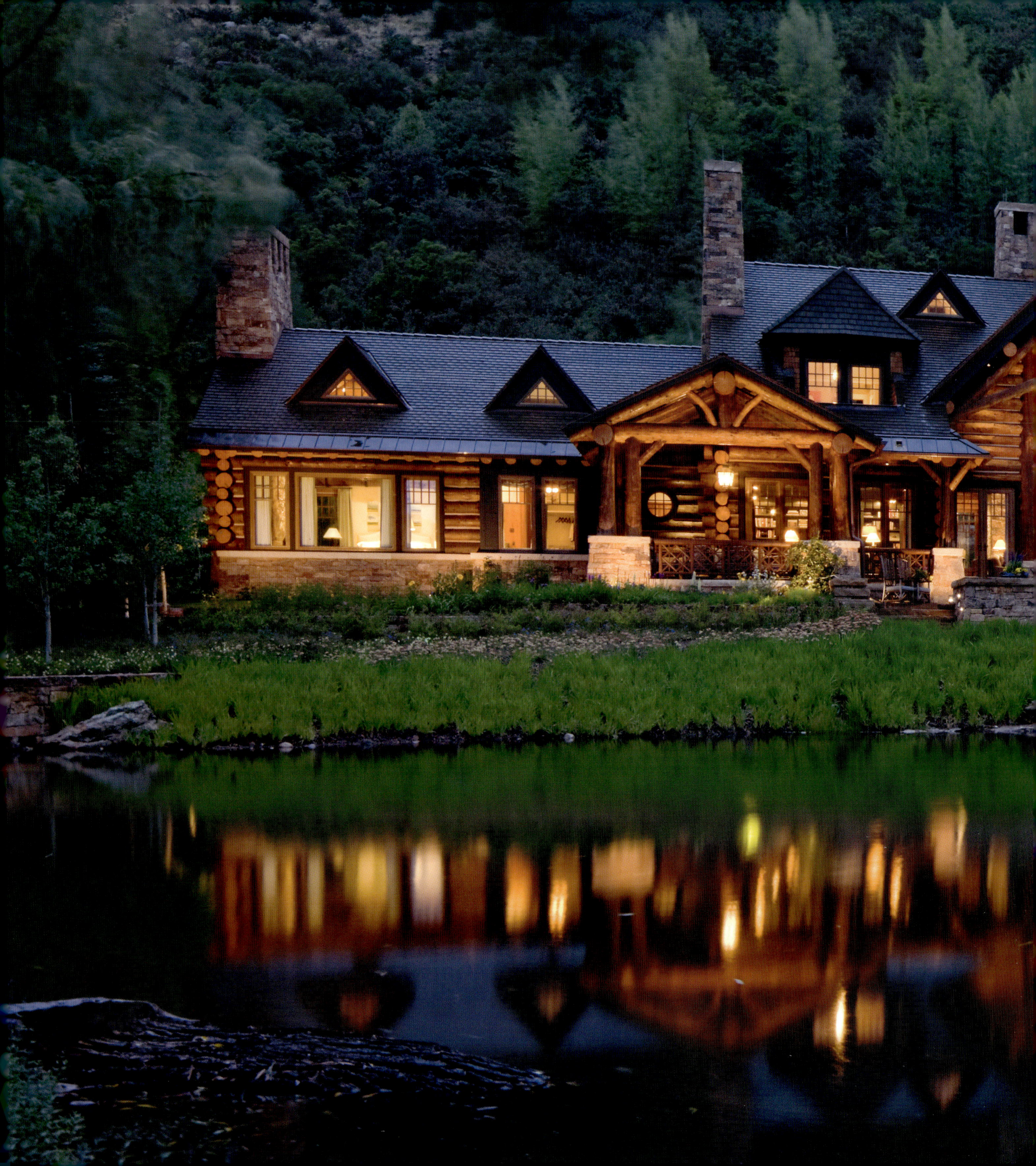

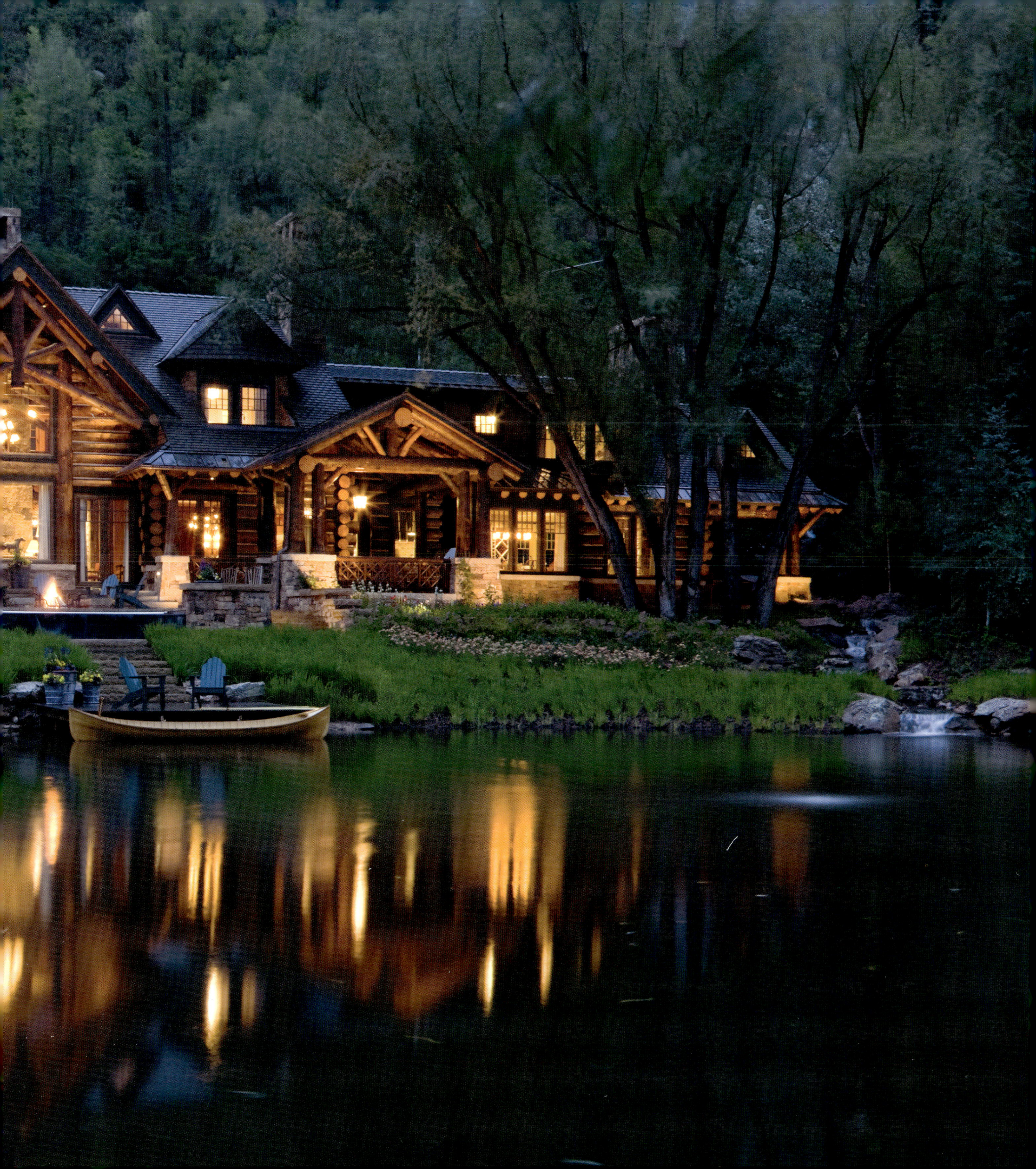

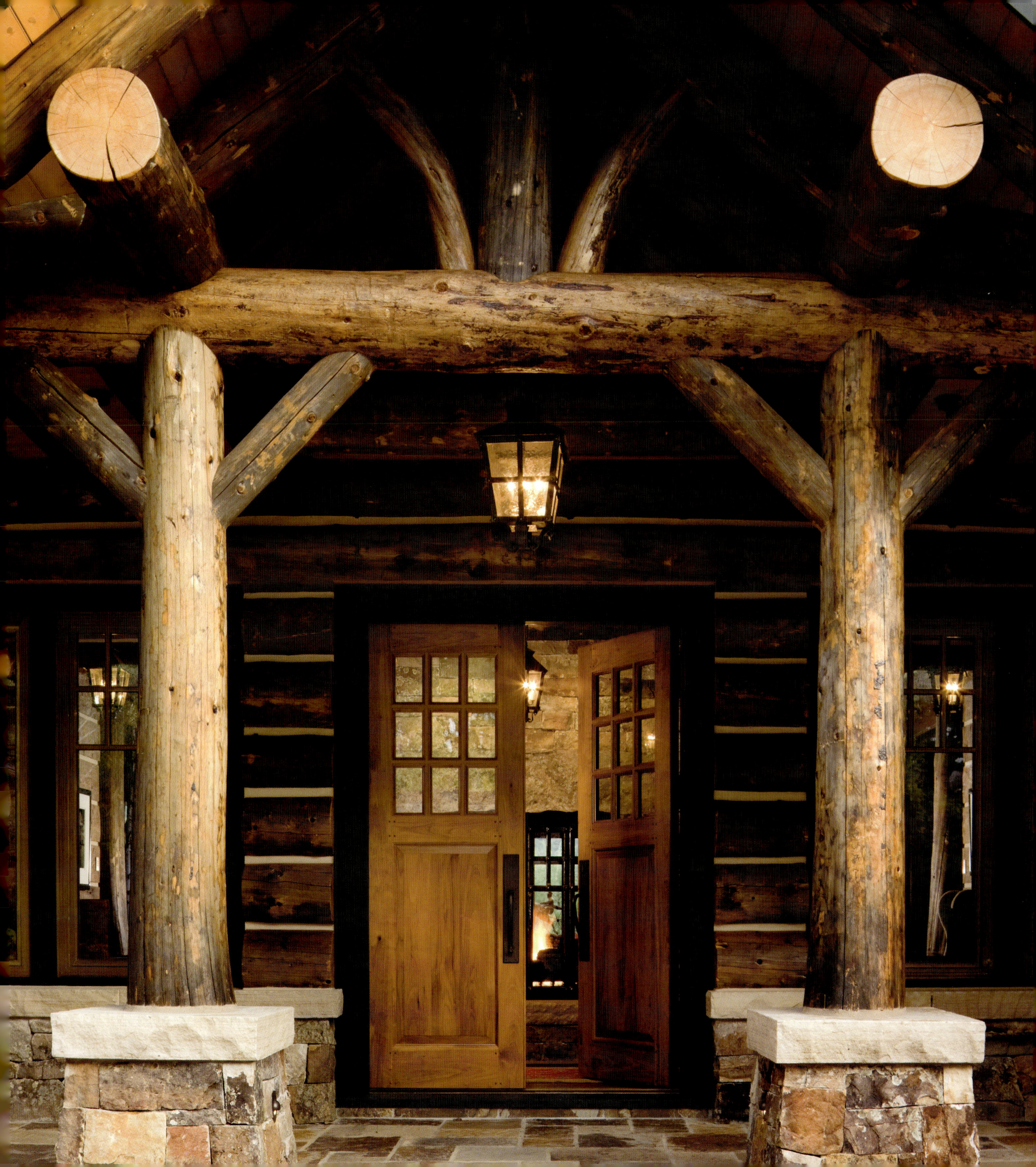

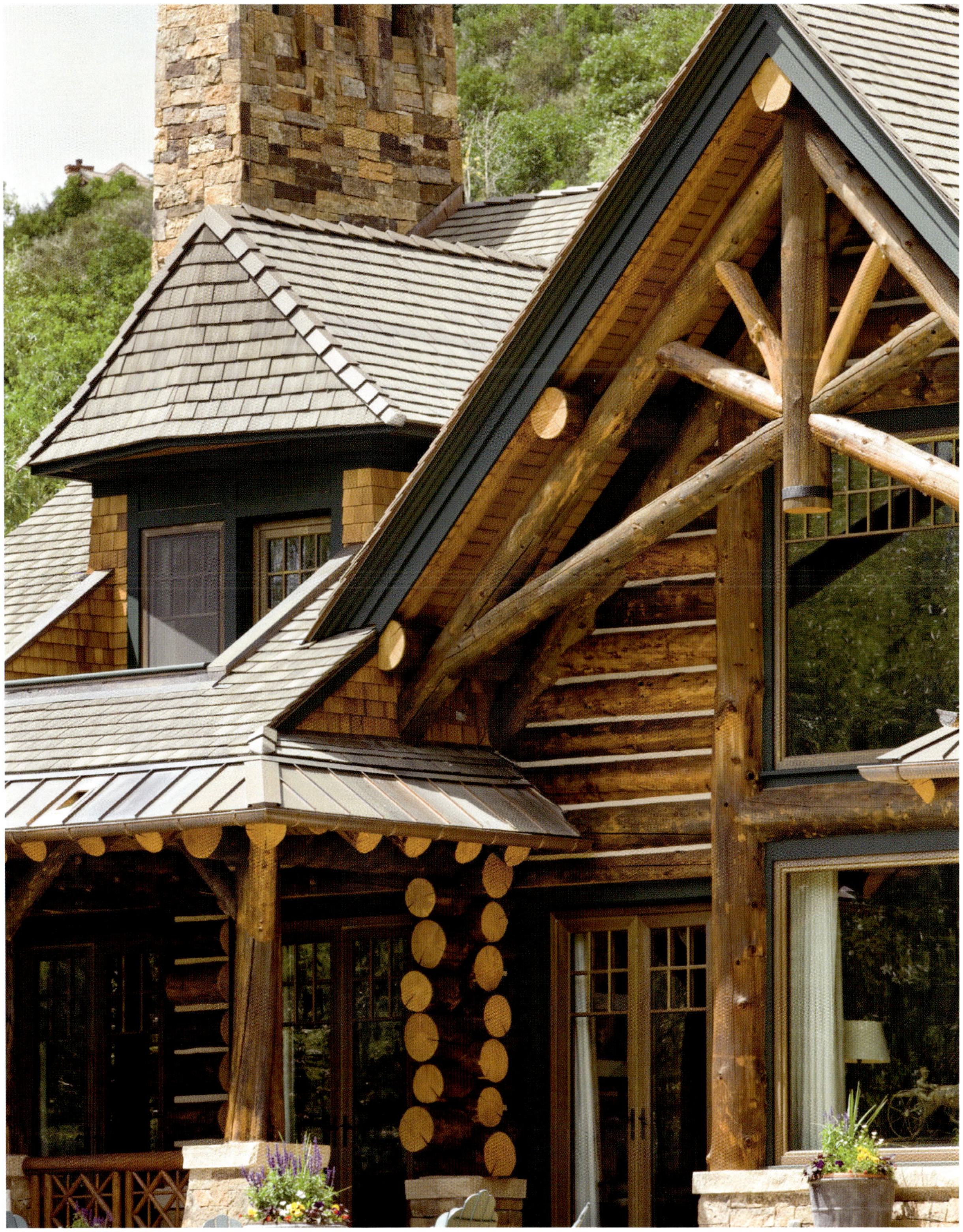

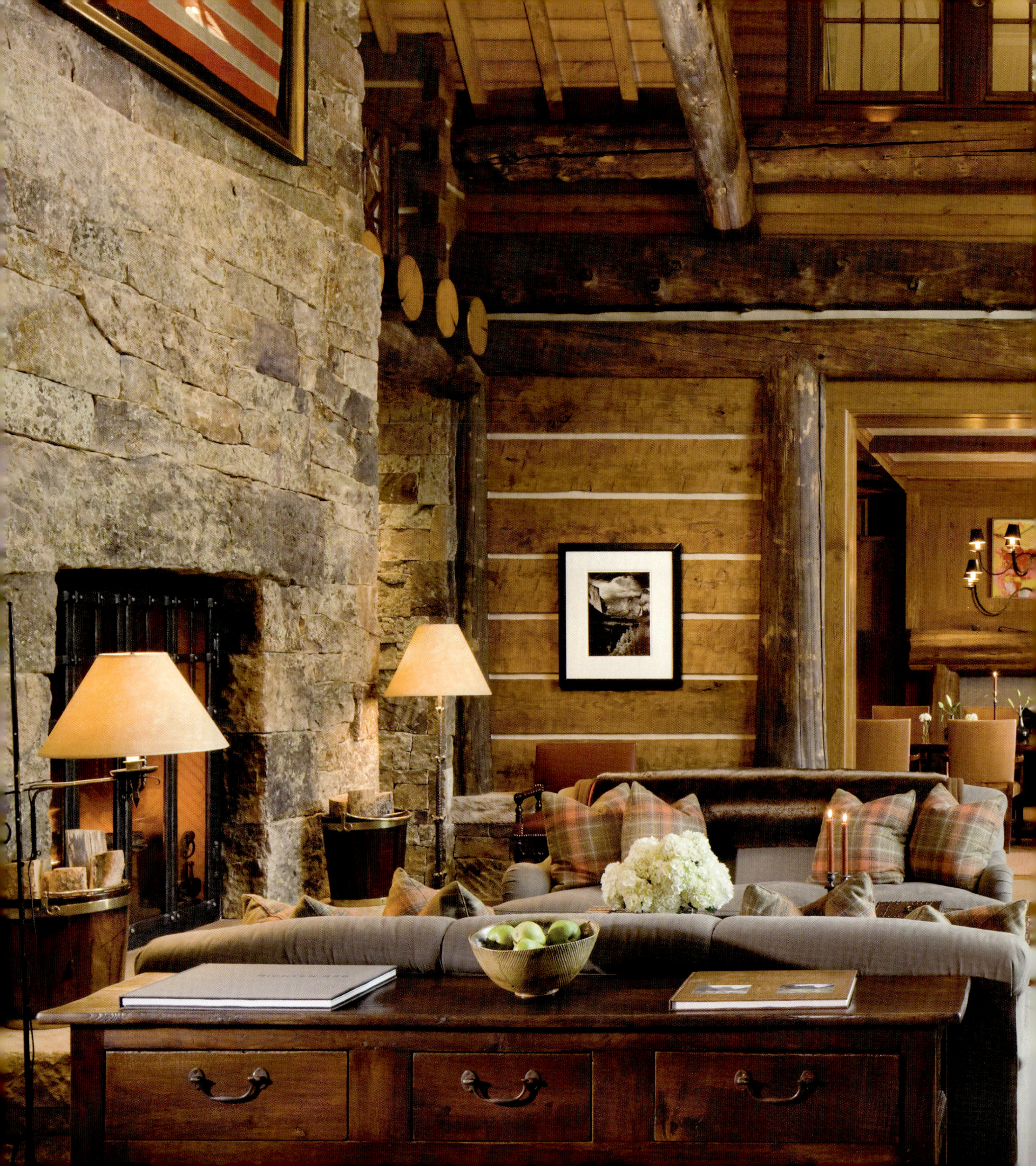

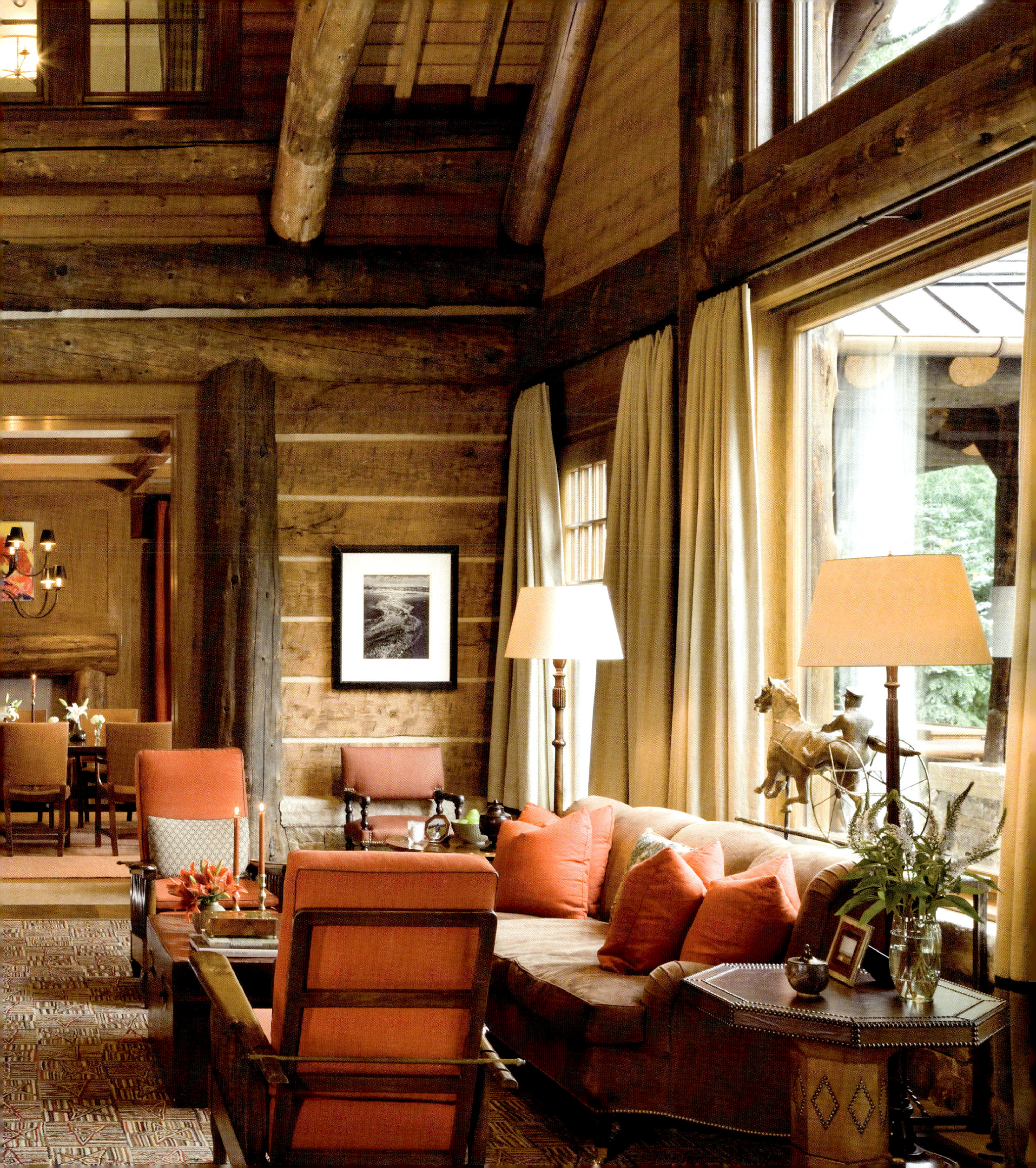

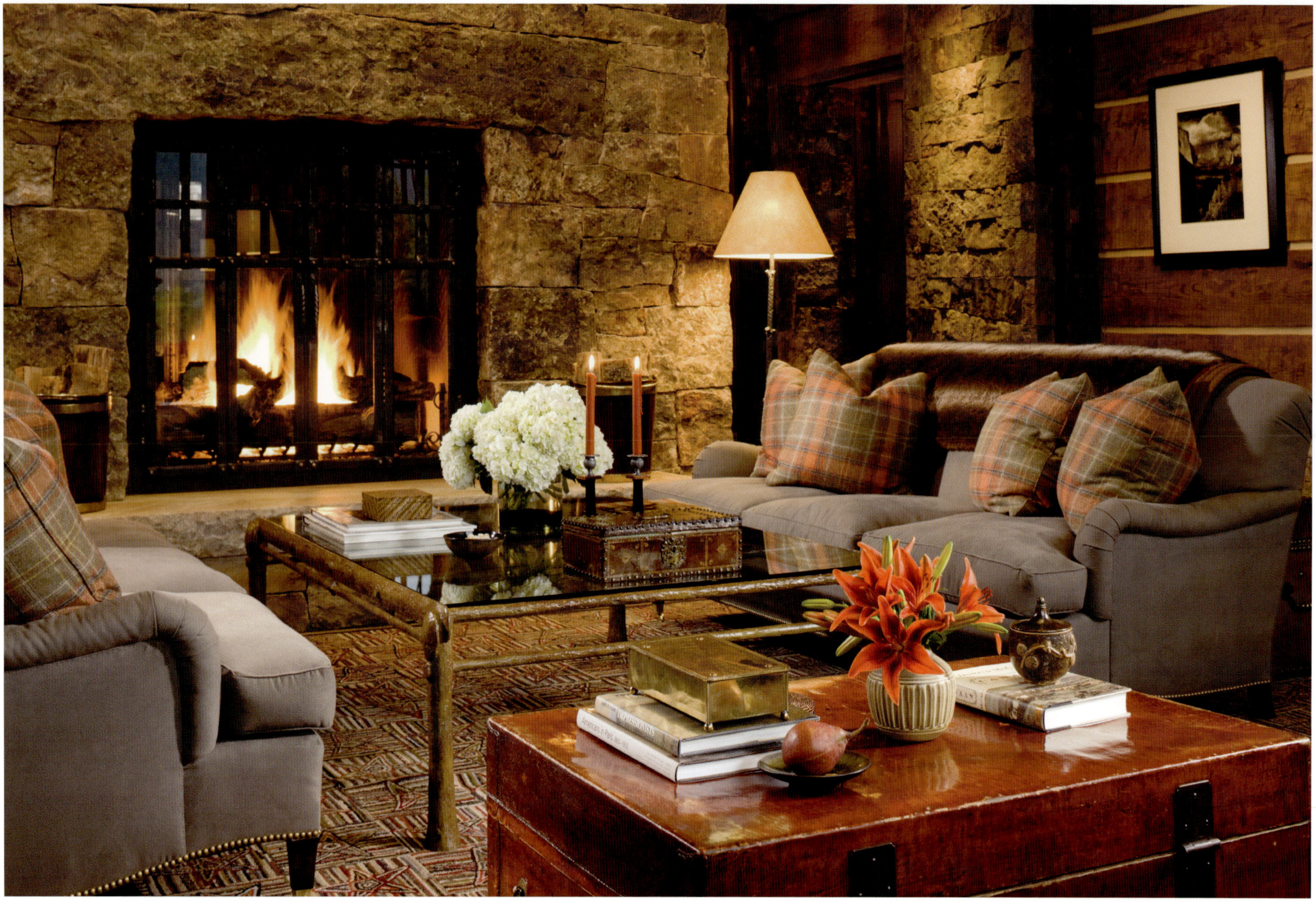

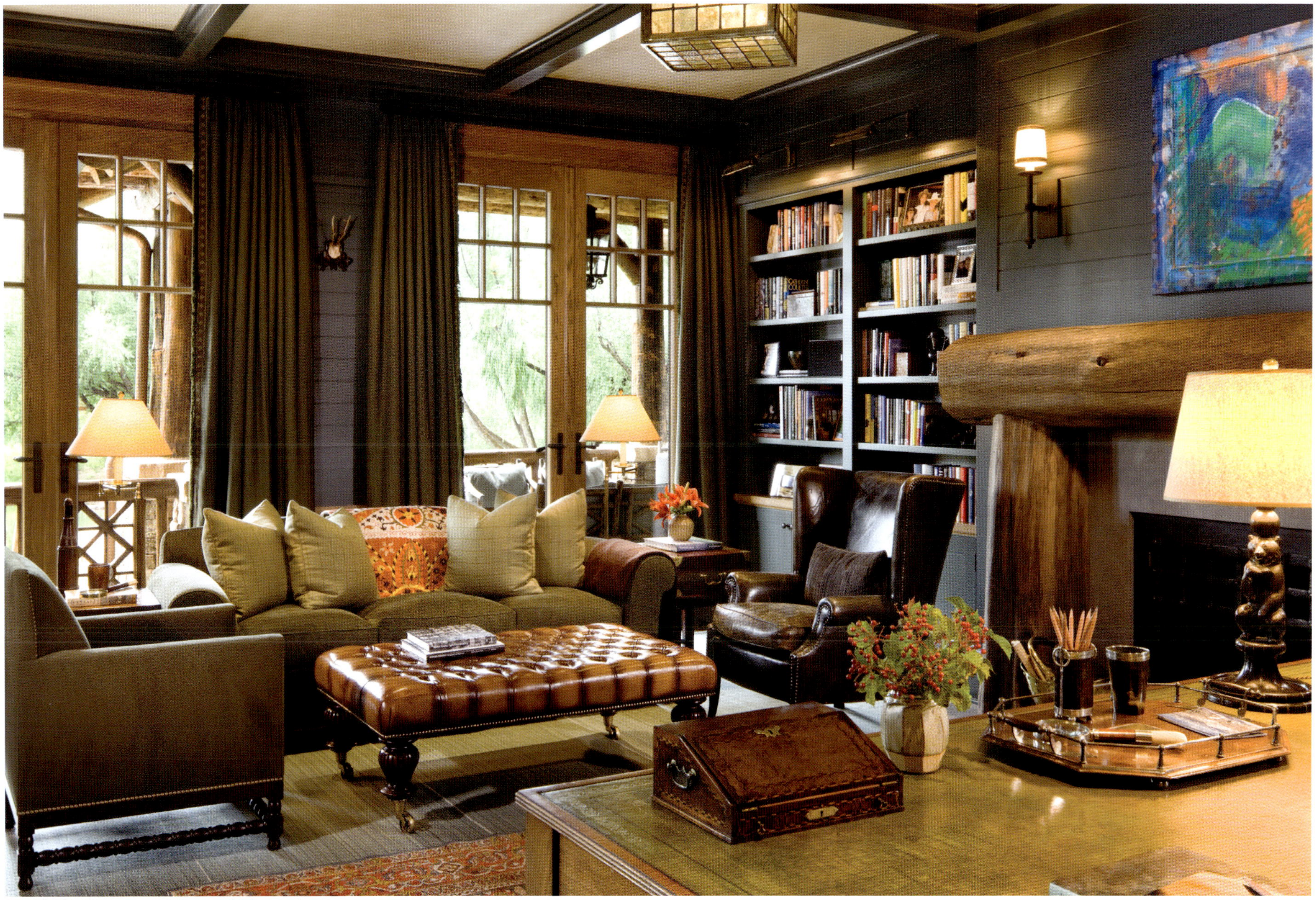

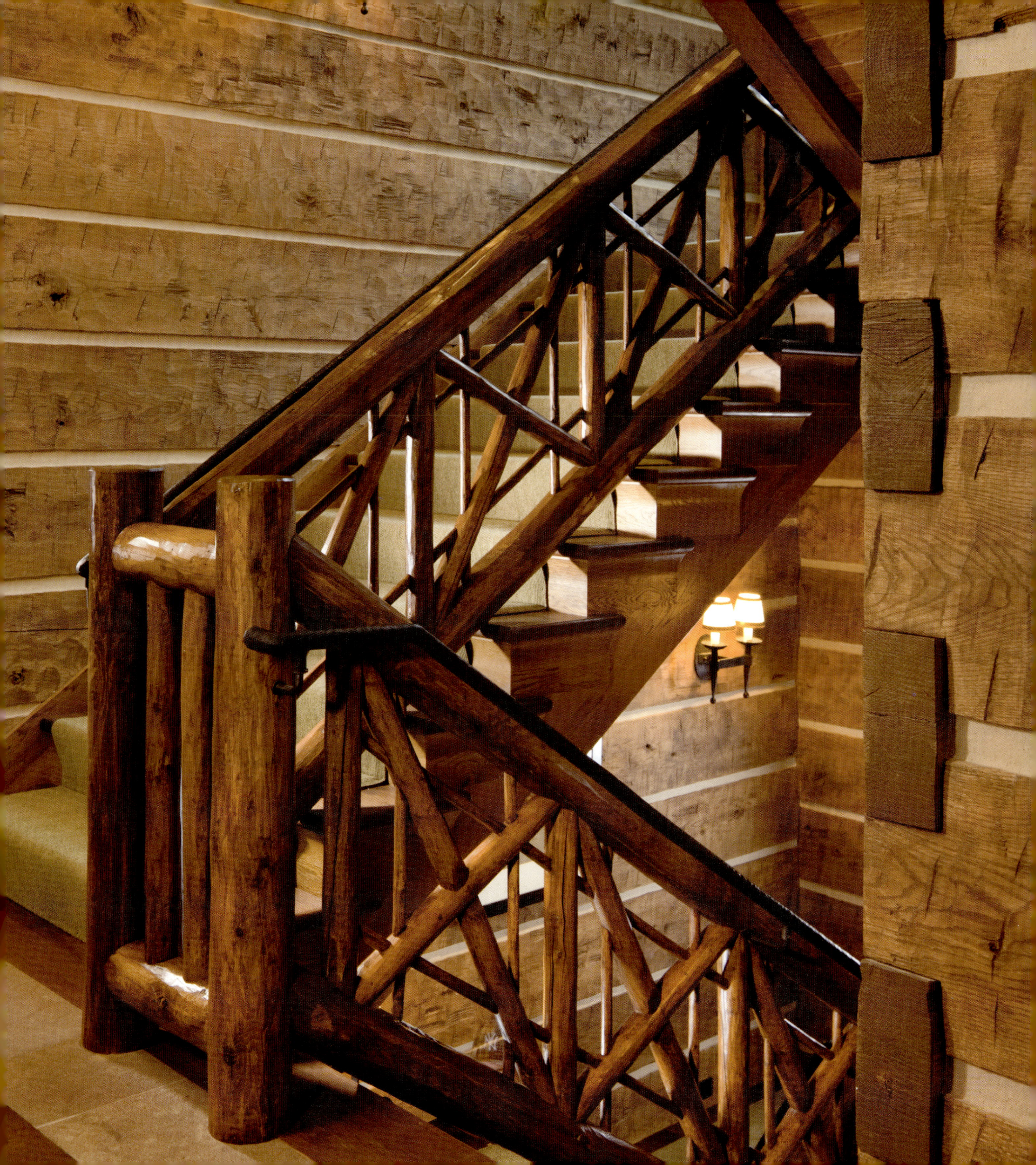

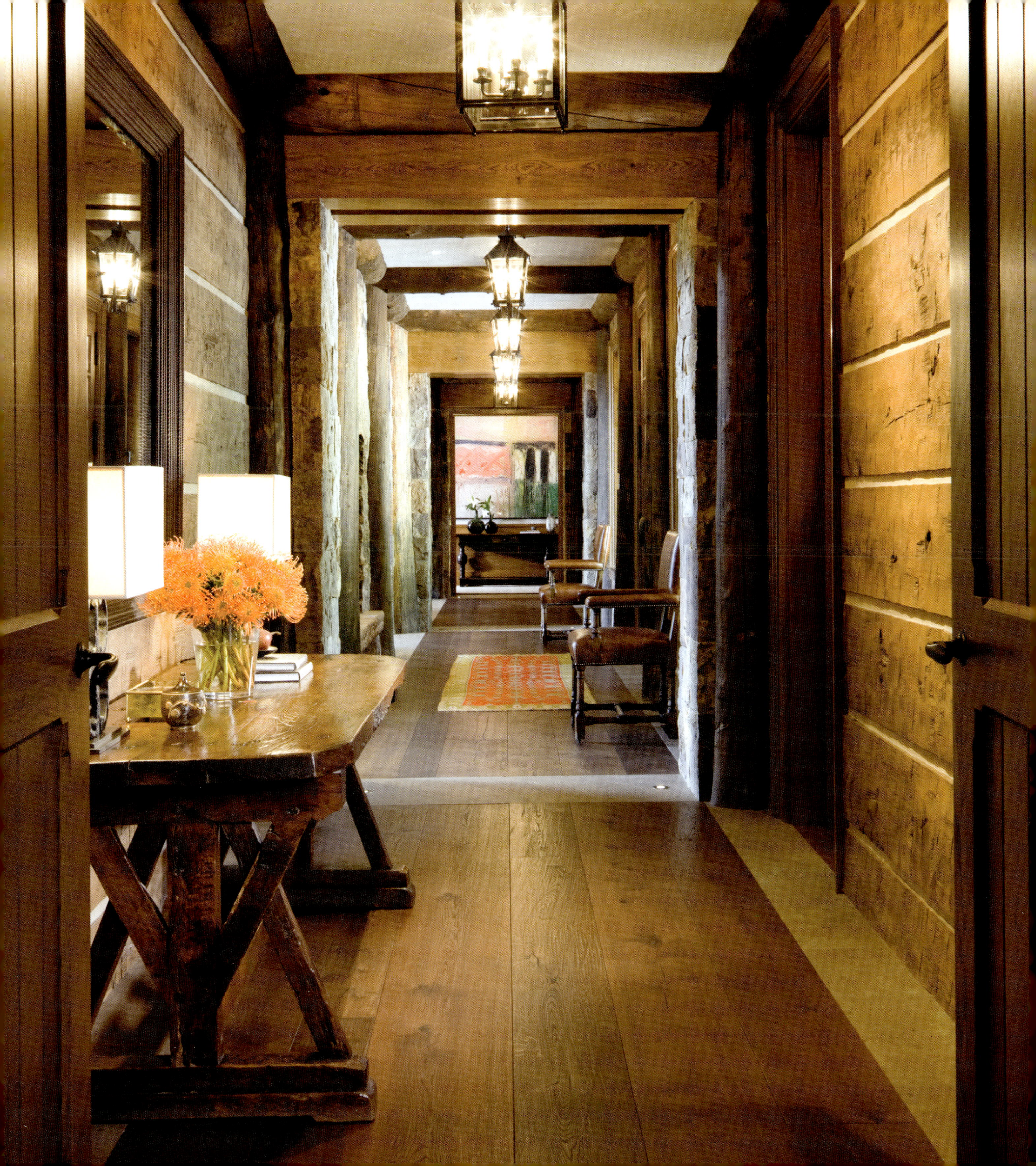

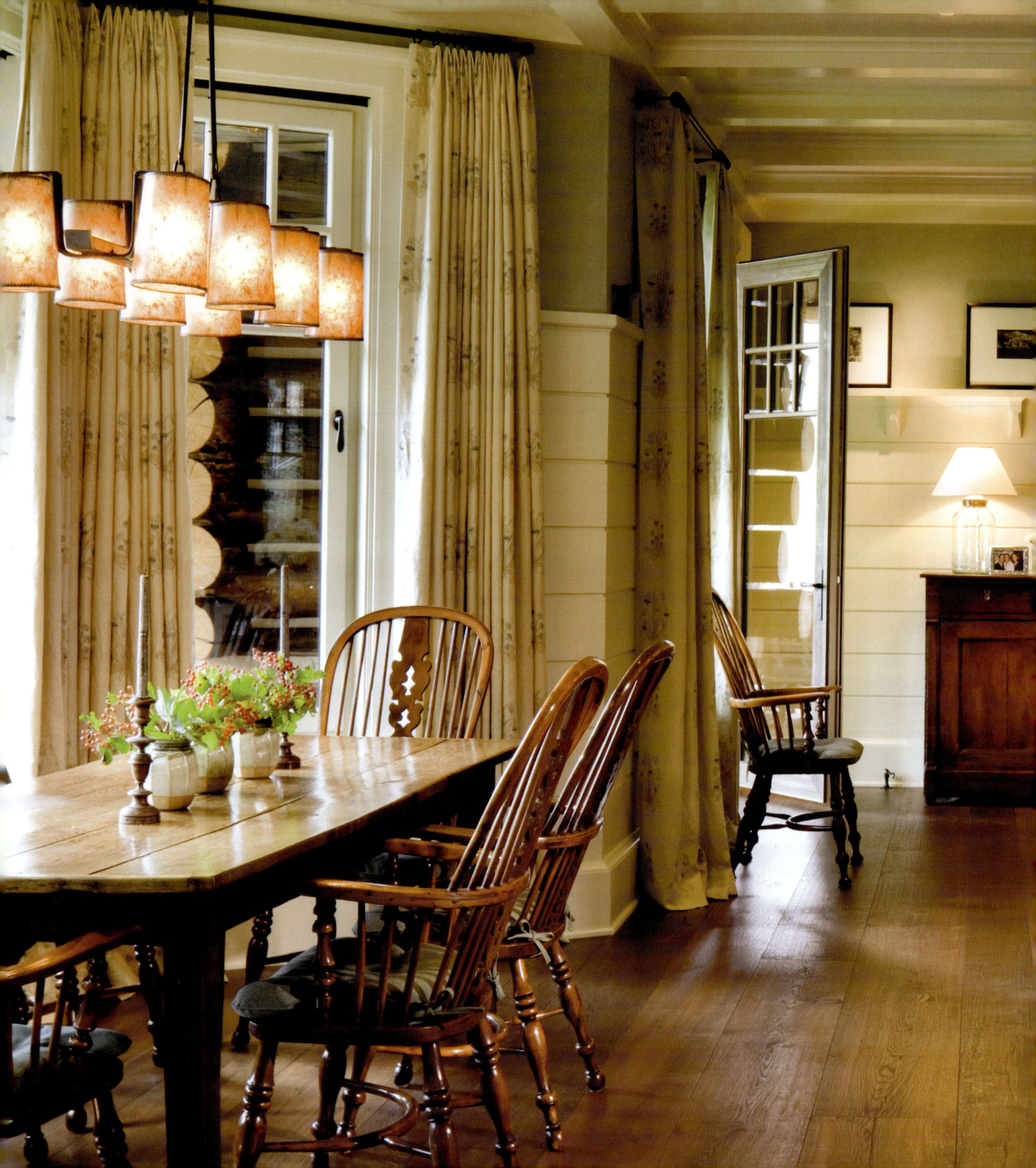

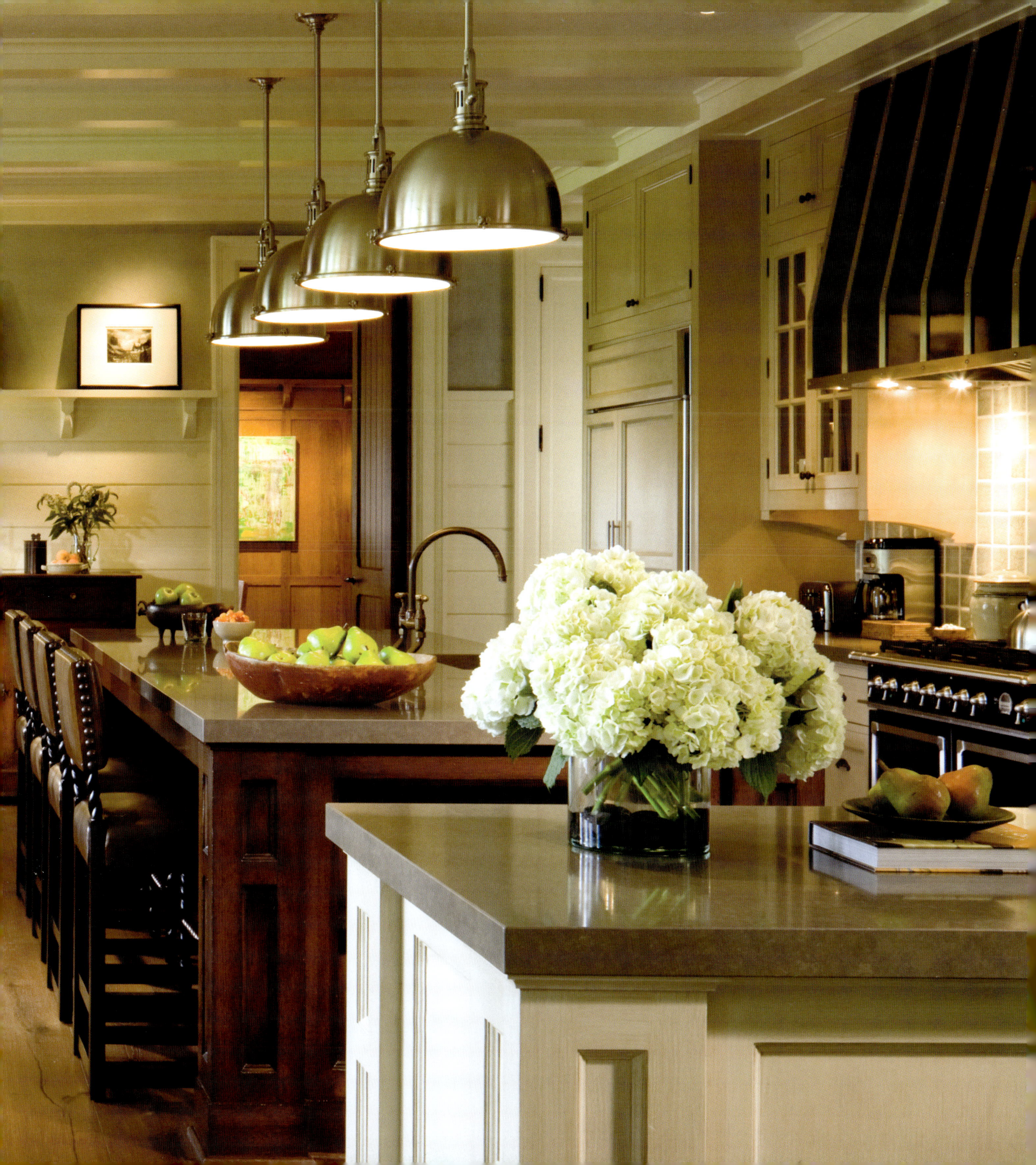

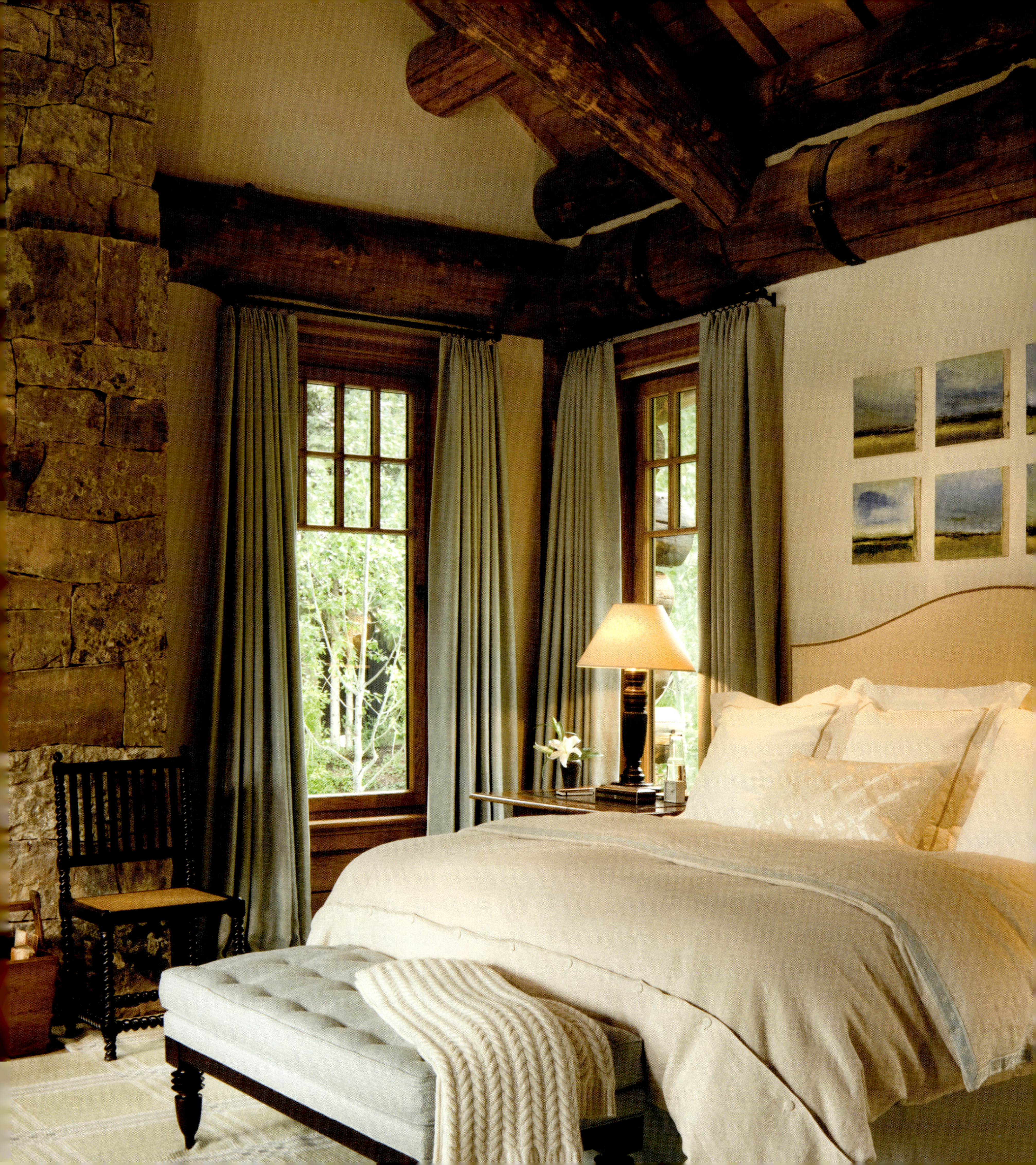

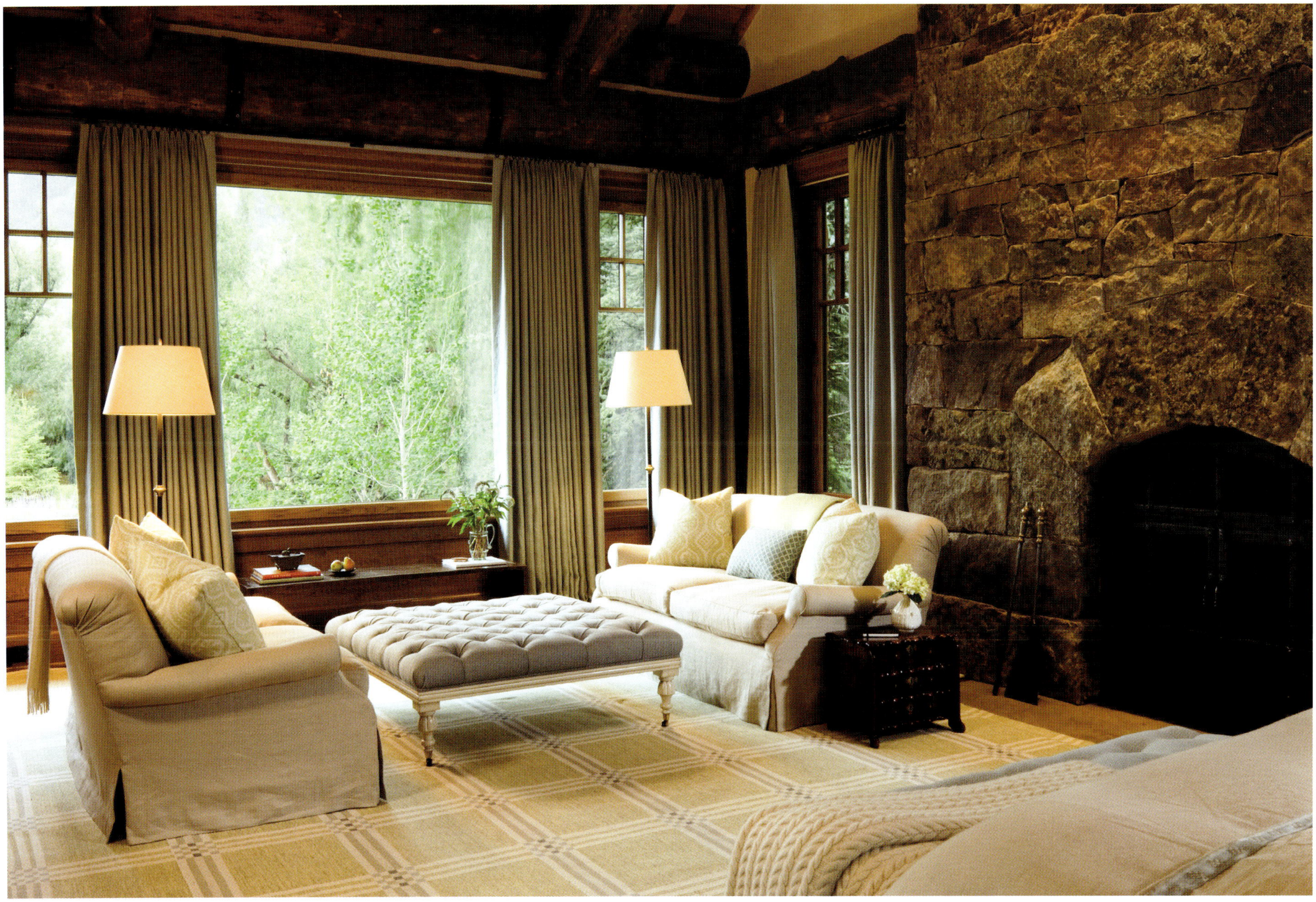

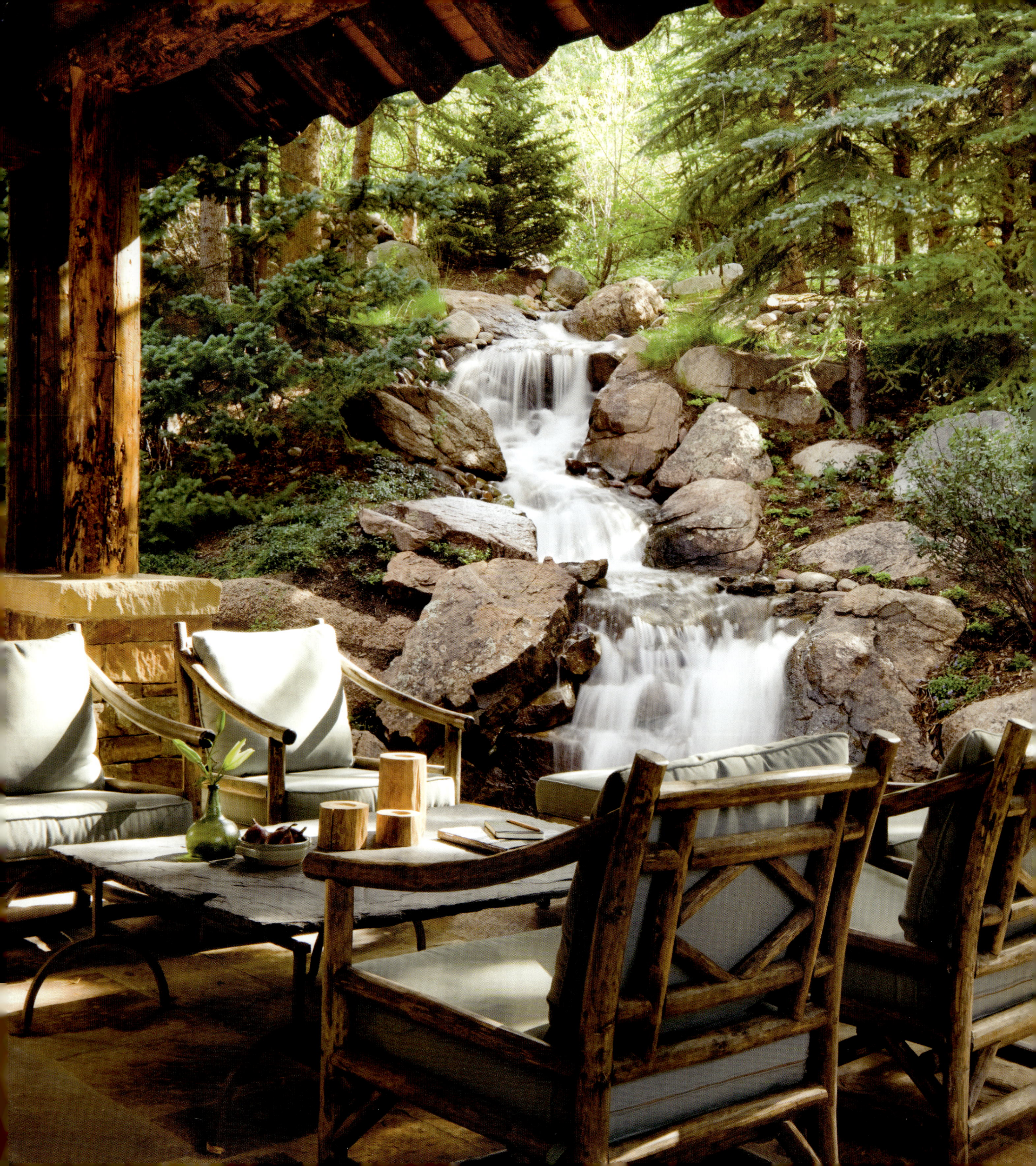

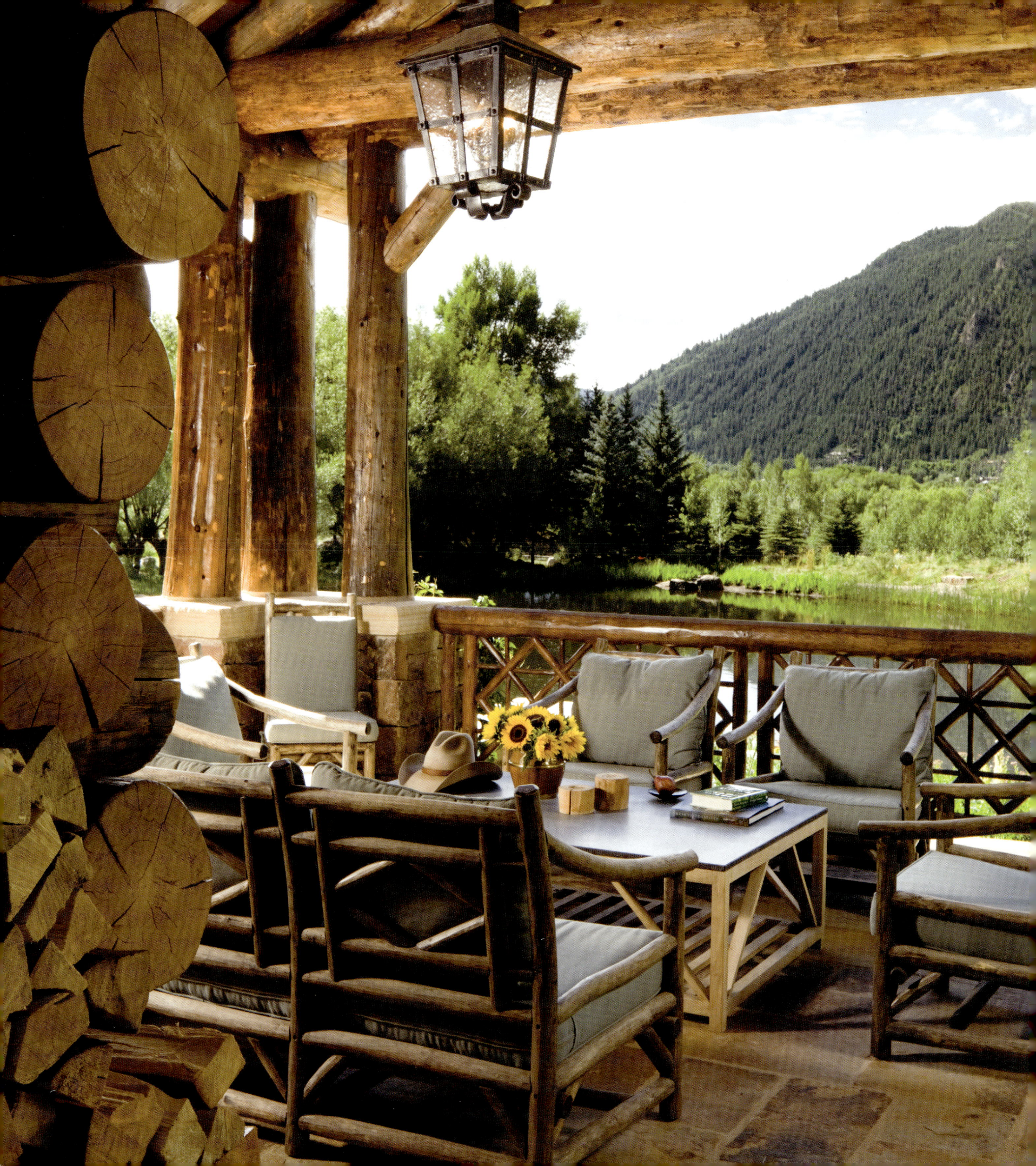

SITE PLAN

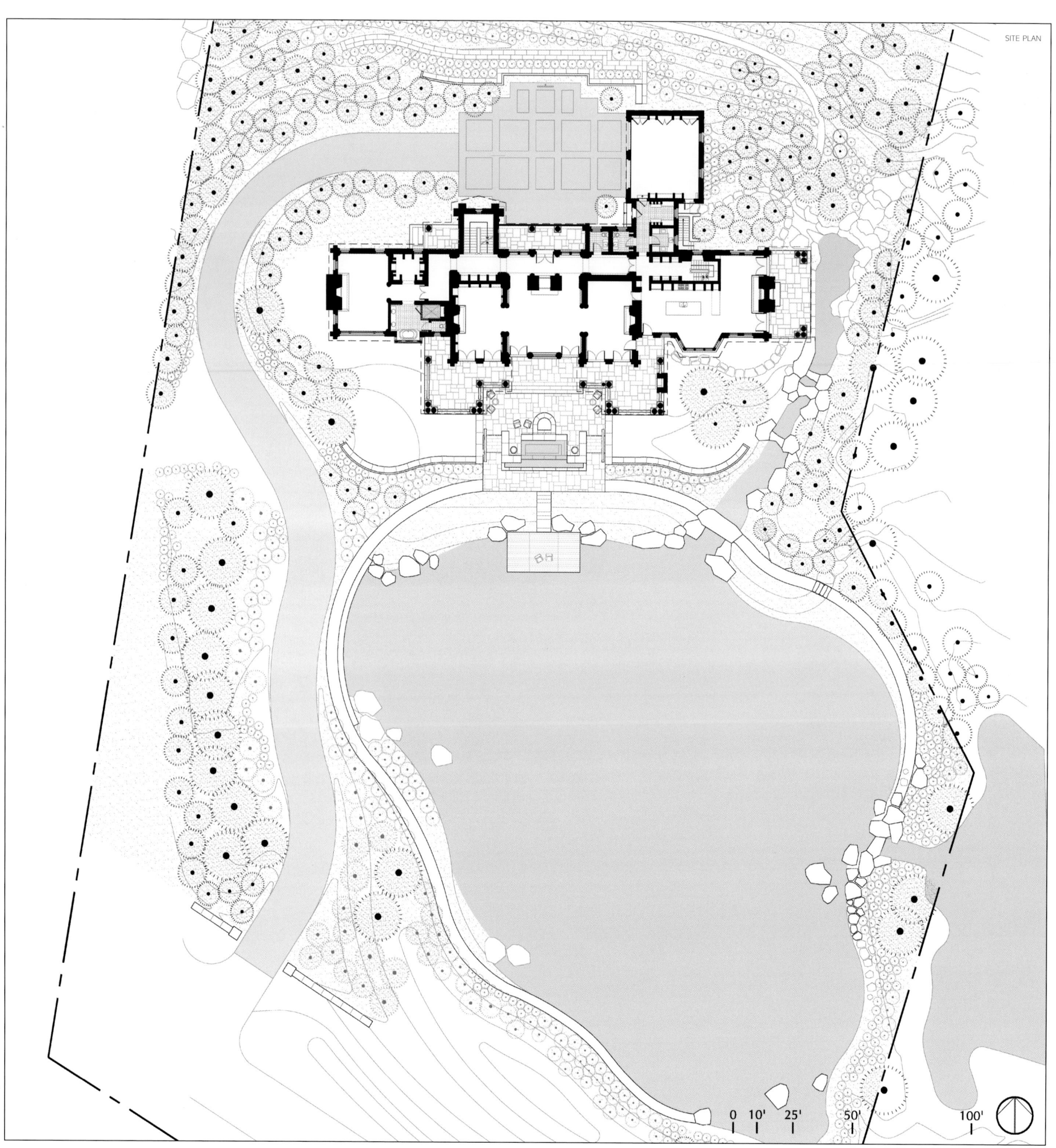

0 10' 25'   50'   100'

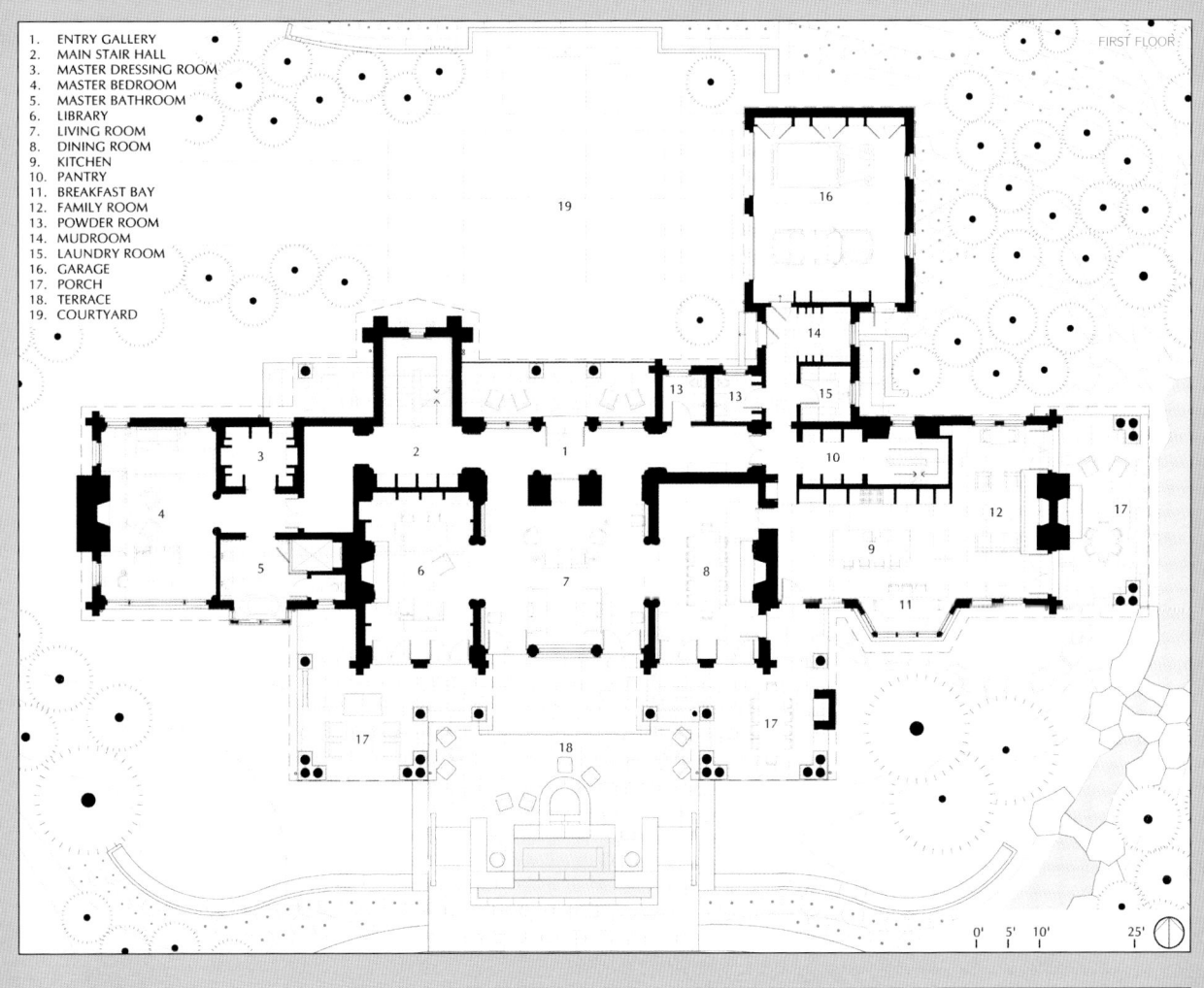

FIRST FLOOR

1. ENTRY GALLERY
2. MAIN STAIR HALL
3. MASTER DRESSING ROOM
4. MASTER BEDROOM
5. MASTER BATHROOM
6. LIBRARY
7. LIVING ROOM
8. DINING ROOM
9. KITCHEN
10. PANTRY
11. BREAKFAST BAY
12. FAMILY ROOM
13. POWDER ROOM
14. MUDROOM
15. LAUNDRY ROOM
16. GARAGE
17. PORCH
18. TERRACE
19. COURTYARD

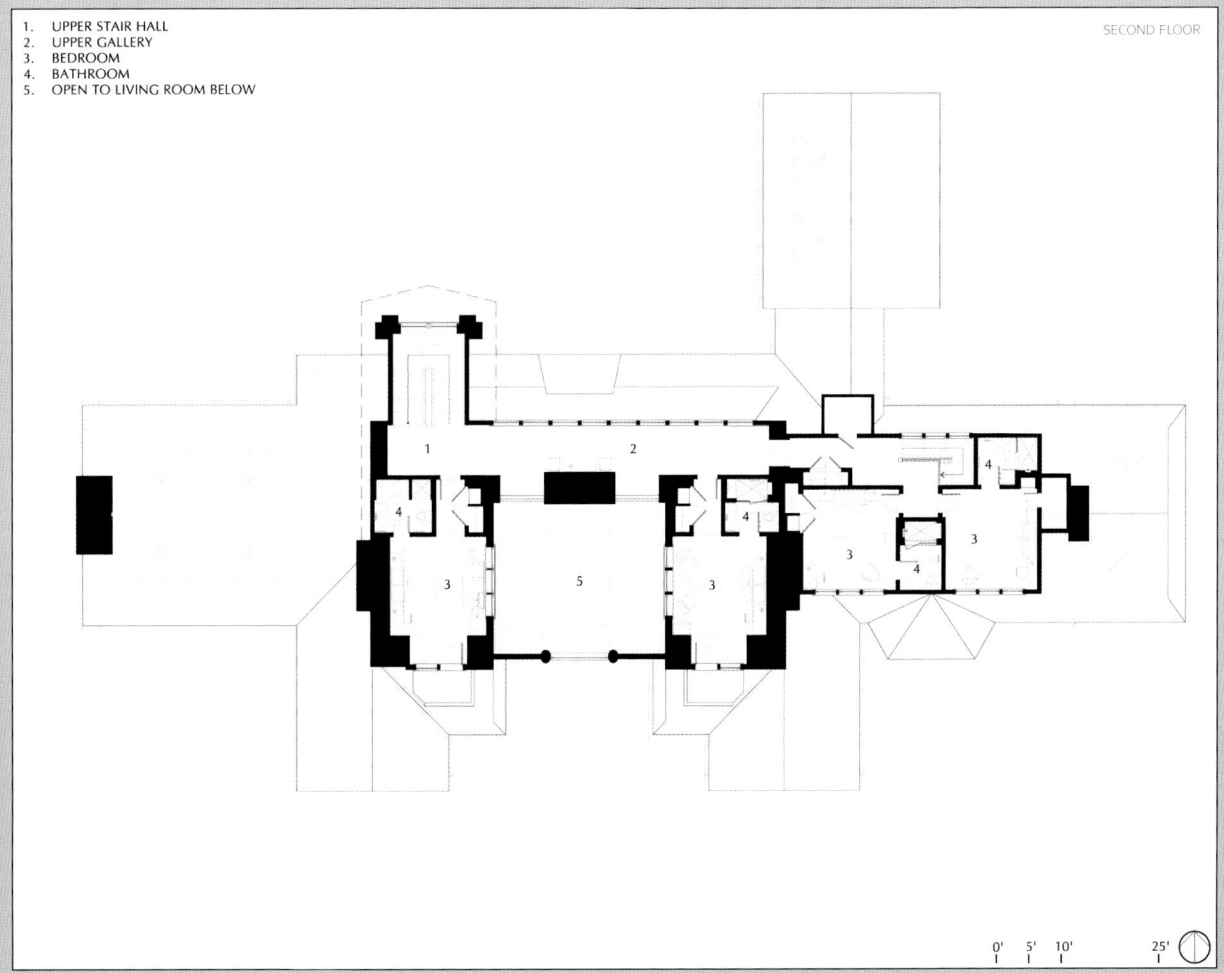

SECOND FLOOR

1. UPPER STAIR HALL
2. UPPER GALLERY
3. BEDROOM
4. BATHROOM
5. OPEN TO LIVING ROOM BELOW

INDEX AND PHOTOGRAPHY CREDITS

Adams, Ansel, 179, 301
Adirondacks, 15, 47, 49, 65, 179
Aitken, Don, 22, 47
antiques, 81, 99, 117, 179
arches, 81; masonry, 213; Romanesque stone, 213
architecture: American, 22; as art, 49; classical, 149; English Georgian, 247; English vernacular, 289; French Renaissance, 16; future outlook and, 21–22; Georgian, 16, 17, 225; heritage of the American West, 301; history and, 16, 21–22; holistic view of, 22; Japanese, 22, 81; medieval style, 81; Mediterranean, 16; pluralism and, 17; reinvention, 15; Renaissance, 17; traditions of, 15, 17; Tudor, 16–17; whimsical, 225
Armstrong Berger, 235
art, 179; American folk, 277; contemporary, 81, 235; paintings, 235; sculpture, 235
Arts and Crafts style, 263, 289
artwork, display of, 235, 247
Aspen, Colorado, 301

Baiting Hollow, New York, 213
barns, 263, 277
bays, trussed, 277
Big Rock. see Adirondacks
boathouse, 65
Boston, Massachusetts, 81, 247. see also Brookline, Massachusetts
Boston suburb, 247
Botero, Fernando, 149, 247
"brag book", 48
breakfast nook, 301
breakfast room, 117
brick, 81, 247
Brookline, Massachusetts, 81
buildings: interconnected, 277; land and, 22; weathering, 49
buttresses, 81, 213, 277

Cape Cod cottages, 15
Carolina coast, 289
carpets, 225
Cassique Golf Club, 289
ceiling beams, 99
ceilings, coffered, 163
chairs: Adirondack, 179; Louis XIII-style, 131; maple-framed rockers, 131; Windsor, 301
chandelier, 225
Charleston, South Carolina, 289
Chilmark, Massachusetts, 277
chimneys, 213, 263, 277, 289; stone, 131; tall, 149, 163
color palette, 81, 197, 225
composition, architectural, 15–17
conical shaped room, 263
Connecticut waterfront, 15, 16, 99
conservation regulations, 277
conservatism, 17
contemporary art, 179, 235
courtyard, 99, 289, 301
craftspersons, 49

Cummin Associates, Inc., 99, 117
cupola, 247, 263, 277

designs, turn of the 20th century, 289
details, classical, 263
dining room, 131, 301, 179, 289
door, double-entrance, 301
dormers, 213, 225
driveway, 99, 117, 301

Eastlake style, 22
eaves, upturning, 225
ecology, 179
enfilade, 179
English country house, 15
English Georgian architecture, 247
English manor house, 235, 289
entrance hall, 99, 225, 277

façades, 81, 225, 247, 277
family room, 225
fanlights, 247
farmhouse, 263
fire towers, 65
fireplace, 131, 179, 301
flood zone regulations, 197
floors, oak, 289
French doors, 99, 225, 263, 277
French windows, 247
Friar's Head golf course, 16, 213
furniture: 1940s ski lodge, 131; antique, 235; Georgian English, 197; plans and, 48

gables, 149, 163
galleries, 163, 213, 301
Gassett, John, 22, 47
Georgian architecture, 16, 17, 225
Georgian English furniture, 197
Georgian Revival mansions, 247
Giacometti, Alberto, 149
glass, 17, 131, 289, 301
Goldberger, Paul, 16
golf courses, 289
Gomez, Mariette Himes, 225, 277
granite, 81, 99, 235
Great Rooms, 65, 179, 277
Greenwich, Connecticut, 17

Hagan, Victoria, 131, 163, 301
Hanlon, Arthur, 22, 47, 65
Hudson Bay, 301
Huniford, Sills, 235
Hupy, Jerry, 22, 47

inglenook, 263
interior detailing, 277
interior hardscape, 49
irrigation system, underground, 179

Japanese influences, 22, 81, 179, 225

Kahn, Wolf, 81
Kaufman, Donald, 117, 277
Kiawah Island Development Corporation, 289
Kiawah Island, South Carolina, 197

kitchen, 65, 99, 117, 131, 277, 301; breakfast room and, 225; open plan, 117; knotty pine, 131

L-shaped plan, 225
land-use restrictions, 277
Lanham, Jacquelynne, 197, 289
leather wing-chairs, 131
Lewis, Nannette, 81
library, 81, 99, 149, 263, 301
limestone, 225, 247
living room, 131, 225, 263, 289, 301
locker rooms, club house at Friar's Head golf course, 213
logs, 301
Long Island, 16; North Shore of, 149, 213, 235
Long Island Sound, 99, 149, 225
lowcountry, 197, 289
Lutyens, Sir Edwin, 15, 263, 289

Magritte, René, 149
Mahwah, New Jersey, 263
Maine, 179
manor house, English, 235, 289
Marden, Brice, 235
Marini, Marino, 149
Martha's Vineyard, 277
masonry, 235
master bedroom, 65, 263; suite, 117
Matisse, Henri, 235
Matta, Roberto, 149
McClung, Michael, 22, 47, 225
McKim, Mead, & White, 149
McMansions, 15
meeting room, 289
millwork, 48
minimalist decor, 301
Miró, Joan, 149, 235
modernist, 15
Montecito, California, 17
Moore, Henry, 149
Morris chairs, 301
Mount Mansfield, 131

Narragansett Bay, 179
natural flora, 197
Navesink River, 117
Newport, Rhode Island, 149
Northeast, 17
Norwalk, Connecticut, 47
Nunnerly, Sandra, 117

obelisk, 263
O'Brien, Thomas, 99
Oehme, van Sweeden & Associates, Inc, 197
ornamental iron banister, 247
overhanging roofs, 179, 213
overhangs, 49, 179

palms, 197
paneling, 163, 225, 301
Papachristidis, Alex, 213
pavilion, 117
paving, antique English Yorkshire, 289
pediment, 247
pergolas, wood-framed, 213

Picasso, Pablo, 149, 235
piers, granite, 99
pine planks paneling, 301
pitched roof, 179, 289
plaid fabric, 131
plinth, stone, 149
pointed eaves, 289
Pop Art, 179
porches, 197, 263; colonnaded, 263; kitchen, 65; outdoor screen-in, 65; round, 213; sunrise, 197; sunset, 197; on waterfront house, 99
porte-cochère, 65
post-and-beam construction, 131
pro shop, 289

railings, 225; Chinese Chippendale, 117; Regency style, 235
Ramapo River, 263
Richardson, Henry Hobson, 22, 81, 99
Richarsonian Romanesque, 22, 81
Richter, Gerhard, 235
river views, 263
roof overhangs, 179
roofs, 225, 235, 263, 277
Ross, Judith, 247
Rothko, Mark, 235
rotundas, 117
Rumson, New Jersey, 117
rustic style, 131
Ryman, Robert, 235

sailing ships, 179
Saladino, John, 263
Santa Fe, New Mexico, 17
scale, 81, 117, 235
scale model, 48
sconces, vintage, 81
Scotland, 213, 289
Shackleton, Ernest, 21
Shakers, 277
Sherman, Cindy, 235
Shingle Style, 15, 81, 117, 149, 163, 179, 197, 213, 225, 263
shingles, 65, 117, 131, 179, 213, 277
Shope Reno Wharton firm (SRW), 15, 46–49, 117, 197, 225, 263; skylights, 99
South Carolina Low Country, 197
Spanish colonial houses, 17
Squibnocket Pond, 277
stair tower, 65, 81, 163, 263; pagoda styling, 225
stairway, 247, 289
Starn, Doug, 81
Starn, Mike, 81
stone, 163; cut, 247; slate, 81
Stowe, Vermont, 131
structure, environmentally sensitive, 179
studio, 263
swimming pool, 99

table, 1730 boulle marquetry, 235
terraces, 213
tidal marshland, 197
topography, 289

trusses, Douglas fir, 277
Tudor, 16, 17

Usonian houses, 22
U.S.S. Constitution, 179

vestibule, 3-story, 247
views, 17, 47, 163
Voysey, Charles, 289

walls: convex, 247; curved, 247; damask-covered, 235; glass, 131; plaster, 277; stucco, 289; white roughcast, 289
Warhol, Andy, 179
Washington, D.C., 197
waterfront setting, 22, 99, 225
Western lodge, 301
Wharton, Bernard M., 149, 197, 263, 277, 289; clients and, 22; compositional skill of, 16–17; initial sketches, 48; Northeast and, 17; partners of, 22; plans for house in Narragansett Bay, 179; sailing and, 22
whimsy, 16, 81, 225, 263
window seats, 163
windows: bay, 301; eyebrow, 213, 225; half-moon, 263; overscale round, 289; Palladian, 117, 149; pattern of, 277; rows of, 247; Serlian, 16; small-paned, 289, 301
wings, 117, 131, 235
wood, 247
Wright, Frank Lloyd, 22

PHOTOGRAPHY CREDITS

Every effort has been made to locate the copyright holders, any omissions will be corrected in future printings.
Durston Saylor, 14, 18-19, 24-25, 28-35, 38-45, 63, 64-79, 116-127, 148-159, 162-175, 186-188, 190, 191 (left), 192-193, 196-197, 200-203, 206-209, 224-231, 234-235, 238-239, 246-259, 262-273, 276-285
Brian Vanden Brink, 12, 36-37, 178-185, 189, 191 (right)
Scott Frances, 4-5, 80-95, 98-113, 236-237, 240-243
Tim Lee, 46
Richard Mandelkorn, 212-221
David O. Marlow, Dust Jacket front and back, 8-9, 26-27, 130-145, 300-319
Patrick O'Brien, 6-7, 198-199, 288-291
Shope Reno Wharton, 62
Jason Stemple, 23
Steve Uzzell, 10-11
Peter Vitale, 204-205, 292-297
Jennifer Walsh, 20

322

BIBLIOGRAPHY

Residential Architect 50: The Short List of Architects We Love; Hanley Wood, LLC; November/December 2010
Connecticut Cottages & Gardens; Cottages & Gardens Publications, LLC; February 2010
Architectural Digest, The New AD 100; The World's 20 Greatest Designers of All Time; The Condé Nast Publications Inc.; January 2010
Connecticut Cottages & Gardens; Cottages & Gardens Publications, LLC; November 2009
New England Home; Network Communications, Inc.; September/October 2009
Better Homes and Gardens Special Interest Publications; Beautiful Kitchens; Meredith Publishing Group; Summer 2009
Architectural Digest; The Condé Nast Publications Inc.; June 2009
Architectural Digest; The Condé Nast Publications Inc.; April 2009
Connecticut Cottages & Gardens; Cottages & Gardens Publications, LLC; January 2009
Hamptons Cottages & Gardens; Cottages & Gardens Publications, LLC; July 1-15, 2008
At Home by the Sea; Dow East Books; 2008
Connecticut Home & Garden; Connecticut Magazine and Journal Register Company; Spring 2008
Architectural Digest; The Condé Nast Publications Inc.; February 2008
Architectural Digest; The Condé Nast Publications Inc.; December 2007
Architectural Digest; The Condé Nast Publications Inc.; September 2007
Architectural Digest, Designer's Own Homes; The Condé Nast Publications Inc.; September 2007
Connecticut Magazine; Michael Mims; July 2007
Connecticut Cottages & Gardens; Cottages & Gardens Publications, LLC; March 2007
Architectural Digest, The AD 100, International Directory of Interior Designers and Architects; The Condé Nast Publications Inc.; January 2007
Architectural Digest; The Condé Nast Publications Inc; November 2006
Departures; American Express Publishing Corporation; October 2006
Architectural Digest; The Condé Nast Publications Inc.; June 2006
Club Management; Finan Publishing Co., Inc.; April 2006
Architectural Digest, Architecture Issue; The Condé Nast Publications Inc.; May 2005
Real Estate & Construction Review – New York Tri-state Edition; Construction Communications; Volume 4, 2005 Edition
Architectural Digest, The AD 100, The World's Top Designers and Architects; The Condé Nast Publications Inc.; January 2004
The Franklin Report; An Allgood Press Publication; 2003
Architectural Digest, The New AD 100, Today's Designers & Legendary Design; The Condé Nast Publications Inc.; January 2002
Architectural Digest; The Condé Nast Publications Inc.; September 2001
Architectural Digest; The Condé Nast Publications Inc.; July 2001
Architectural Digest; The Condé Nast Publications Inc.; November 2000
Architectural Digest; The Condé Nast Publications Inc.; May 2000
Architectural Digest; Interior Design Legends; Special Section: The AD 100 Designers and Architects; The Condé Nast Publications Inc.; January 2000
The New American Cottage, Innovations in Small-Scale Residential Architecture; Whitney Library of Design; 1999
Architectural Digest; The Condé Nast Publications Inc.; October 1999
Architectural Digest; The Condé Nast Publications Inc.; June 1999
Architectural Digest, 100 Years of Design; The Condé Nast Publications Inc.; April 1999
Connecticut Magazine; Communications International, March 1999
Architectural Digest; The Condé Nast Publications Inc.; February 1999
Architectural Digest; Advance Magazine Publishers Inc.; October 1998
Links Magazine; Purcell Enterprises, Inc.; March 1998
Legends Magazine; Kiawah Island Publishing, Inc.; 1997 Vol. 8, #1
Architectural Digest; Advance Magazine Publishers Inc.; June 1997
Architectural Digest; Advance Magazine Publishers Inc.; May 1997
Audio Video Interiors; Arcom Publishing, Ltd.; May 1996
Architectural Digest; Advance Magazine Publishers Inc.; February 1996
Architectural Digest; Advance Magazine Publishers Inc.; October 1995
Architectural Digest; Special Section: The AD 100 Designers & Architects; Advance Magazine Publishers Inc.; September 1995
Style, Baltimore's Magazine For Smart Living; The Baltimore Jewish Times; May/June 1995
Mary Emmerling's Country; The New York Times Company Women's Magazine; August/September 1994
Architectural Digest; Advance Magazine Publishers Inc.; June 1994
House Beautiful; The Hearst Corporation; February 1994
American HomeStyle; New York Times Women's Magazines; January/February 1994
Architectural Digest; Advance Magazine Publishers Inc.; October 1993
Greenwich Magazine; Moffly Publications, Inc.; September 1993
The New York Times Magazine; The New York Times Company; February 28, 1993
Architectural Digest; Architectural Digest Publishing Corporation; February 1993
Architectural Record; McGraw-Hill Inc.; January 1993
Greenwich Magazine; Moffly Publications, Inc.; April 1992
Decorating Remodeling; The New York Times Company; February/March 1992
Architectural Digest; Architectural Digest Publishing Corporation; October 1991
Architectural Digest. The AD 100 Architects; Architectural Digest Publishing Corporation; August 1991
Decorating Remodeling Custom Kitchen Planner; The New York Times Company; Spring 1991
Greenwich Magazine; Moffly Publications, Inc.; April 1991
Home Magazine's Best Ideas Kitchen & Bath; Knapp Communications; Spring 1991
Architectural Digest; Architectural Digest Publishing Corporation; December 1990
Greenwich Magazine; Moffly Publications, Inc.; November 1990
Home Magazine's Best Kitchen & Bath Ideas; Knapp Communications; September 1990
Architectural Digest; Architectural Digest Publishing Corporation; September 1990
Architectural Detailing in Residential Interiors; Wendy W. Staebler, Whitney Library of Design; 1990
Home Magazine's Remodel!; Knapp Communications; May 1990
Architecture; Affiliated Publications, Inc.; April 1990
Metropolitan Home; Magazine Group of Meredith Corporation; April 1990
Fine Homebuilding; The Taunton Press, Inc.; Spring 1990
Decorating Remodeling; The New York Times Company; March 1990
Decorating Remodeling; The New York Times Company; December 1989
House Beautiful; The Hearst Corporation; November 1989
Home Magazine's Best Remodeling Ideas; Knapp Communications Corporation; Fall 1989
Home Magazine; Knapp Communications Corporation; April 1989
Home Magazine's Best Kitchen Ideas; Knapp Communications Corporation; Spring 1989
Architectural Digest; Architectural Digest Publishing Corporation; April 1989
New England Monthly; New England Monthly, Inc.; December 1988
Connecticut Magazine; Communications International; March 1988
House Beautiful's Home Remodeling; The Hearst Corporation; Spring 1988
Profiles Magazine; Jan Press; October 1987
The New York Times Magazine, Home Design; The New York Times Company; October 18, 1987
Home Magazine; Knapp Communications Corporation; August 1987
Profiles Magazine; Jan Press; April 1987
Northeast Magazine; The Hartford Courant; April 12, 1987
House Beautiful's Building Manual; The Hearst Corporation; Spring 1987
House Beautiful's Home Remodeling; The Hearst Corporation; Fall 1986
Home Magazine; Knapp Communications Corporation; June 1986
Remodeling; A Hanley-Wood, Inc. Publication; May 1986
House Beautiful; The Hearst Corporation; March 1986
Profiles Magazine; Jan Press; March 1986
New Jersey Monthly; Aylesworth Communications Corporation; February 1986
Progressive Architecture; Reinhold Publishing, News Report; January 1986
Atlantic City Press; January 1986
Chicago Tribune; December 8, 1985
Austin, Texas, American Statesman; December 7, 1985
Newark Star-Ledger; 1985
Houston Chronicle; November 28, 1985
News-Free Press; Chattanooga, Tennessee; November 26, 1985
Fort Lauderdale Sun-Sentinel; November 22, 1985
The Denver Post; November 22, 1985
Profiles Magazine; Jan Press; November 1985
House Beautiful, Home Remodeling; The Hearst Corporation; Fall 1985
Beyond The Kitchen; Thomas Cowan, Running Press Book Publishers; 1985
The Home; Susan S. Szenasy, Macmillan Publishing Company; 1985
New England Monthly; New England Monthly, Inc.; June 1985
Architectural Digest; Knapp Communications Corporation; April 1985
House Beautiful; The Hearst Corporation; 1985
Adding On; McGraw-Hill Publications; 1984
House Beautiful; The Hearst Corporation; 1984
News Day Magazine; News Day Publications; 1984
Making Space; Clarkson Potter Publications Inc.; 1983
Design Presentation; McGraw-Hill Publications; 1983
The New York Times, The Home Section; The New York Times Company; 1982
Progressive Architecture; Reinhold Publishing; 1982
Nutmegger Magazine; Nutmegger Publishing Corporation; 1982
Human Ecology Forum; Cornell University Press; 1982
Progressive Architecture; Reinhold Publishing; 1981

DEDICATION

This book is dedicated to those who believed in our ability to create timeless and meaningful architecture.

ACKNOWLEDGMENTS

Writing an architecture book is difficult without the help, energy, and dedication of those who believe in your mission. This book is a true testament to the creative spirit of everyone involved in the process, and Shope Reno Wharton would like to thank you not only for your contribution to the book, but to the ultimate success of the firm.

Many thanks to our publisher Suzanne Slesin, who has transformed our passion into this stunning and meaningful book, as well as her team: Regan Toews, Deanna Kawitzky, and Nyasha Gutsa at Pointed Leaf Press. Many thanks also to Stafford Cliff, whose unfailing insight and style gave a voice to our work, and to Dominick Santise, for all his hard work.

We are grateful for the support that we received from *Architectural Digest*'s Paige Rense. We would not be the firm that we are today without her. We would also like to thank James Huntington and Therese Bissell—two very special people at the magazine.

We have been blessed with creative and talented partners who have contributed immensely to the firm's success. Without Arthur Hanlon, Jerry Hupy, Michael McClung, John Gassett, Don Aitken, and their diligent staff, the work in this book would not be possible.

Thank you Jeffrey Simpson, for your patience, understanding, and wonderful writing, as architects, by nature, are not great writers.

We are honored to have Paul Goldberger's written words as part of our book. Paul has long been a vital link between all architects, and a legend in his own right.

Thank you to our agent, Karen Lehrman Bloch, whose insight guided us to the right publisher.

To the amazing and talented photographers Durston Saylor, David O. Marlow, Scott Frances, Richard Mandelkorn, Brian Vanden Brink, and Peter Vitale, each of whom has his own unique and distinctive style.

To the talented interior designers, we appreciate your voice and your commitment to enhancing our clients' daily experience.

Many thanks to the builders and artisans who made this architectural firm shine with their finesse and craftsmanship.

We are thankful to Dorothy Susko, Patrick Lau, and Jose Goncalves, who worked tirelessly, with conviction and enthusiasm.

To our office staff throughout the years: Without you this book would not be possible.

To our partner emeritus, Allan Shope, whose energy and enthusiasm were vital to the success of the firm.

Thank you to our families, who have always hung in there throughout the good, the bad, and the ugly.

Finally, this book would not be possible without our clients: You are our inspiration.

Bernard M. Wharton—Founding partner
Arthur Hanlon—Partner
Jerry Hupy—Partner
Michael McClung—Partner
John Gassett—Partner
Don Aitken—Partner
Dorothy Susko
W. Bayard Cutting
Terence O'Halloran
Paul Wise
Alice Weatherford
Patrick Lau
Sara Murray
Jose Goncalves

SHOPE RENO WHARTON ARCHITECTURE
18 MARSHALL STREET
SOUTH NORWALK, CT 06854
T: (203) 852-7250
WWW.SHOPERENOWHARTON.COM

DUST JACKET
From the project on pages 130–147; photographs by David O. Marlow.

COVER
Preliminary sketch of the façade of Big Rock, by Shope Reno Wharton.

INTERIOR AND LANDSCAPE DESIGNERS

Alex Papachristidis Interiors
300 East 57th Street, Suite 1C
New York, NY 10022
T: (212) 588-1777

Aero Studios
419 Broome Street
New York, NY 10013
T: (212) 966-4700

Armstrong Berger
2611 State Street
Dallas, Texas 75204
T: (214) 871-0893

Cummin Associates, Inc.
114 Water Street
Stonington, Connecticut 06378
T: (860) 535-4224

Donald Kaufman Color
336 W. 37th Street, Suite 801
New York, NY 10018
T: (212) 594-2608

Gomez Associates Inc.
504 East 74th Street
New York, NY 10021
T: (212) 288-6856

Huniford
210 11th Avenue, Suite 601
New York, NY 10001
T: (212) 717-9177

Jacquelynne P. Lanham Designs
472 E Paces Ferry Rd. NE
Atlanta, GA 30305
T: (404) 364-0472

John Saladino Group Design Services
200 Lexington Avenue, Suite 1600
New York, NY 10016
T: (212) 684-6805

Judith Ross & Company, Inc.
2 Newbury Street
Boston, MA 02116
T: (617) 267-5045

Nannette Lewis Interiors
45 Laurel Rd.
Chestnut Hill, MA 02467
T: (617) 739-3004

Oehme, van Sweden & Associates
800 G Street SE
Washington, D.C. 20003
T: (202) 546-7575

Sandra Nunnerley, Inc.
41 East 57th Street
New York, NY 10022
T: (212) 826-0539

Stephen Sills Associates
30 East 67th Street
New York, NY 10065
T: (212) 988-6100

Victoria Hagan Interiors
1790 Broadway, 19th Floor
New York, NY 10019
T: (212) 888-1178

Foreword ©2011 Paul Goldberger
©2011 Bernard M. Wharton
All rights reserved under international copyright conventions. No part of this book may be reproduced, utilized, or transmitted in any form or by any means, electronic or mechanical, including photocopying, recording, or by any information storage and retrieval system, or otherwise, without permission in writing from the publisher. Inquiries should be addressed to:
POINTED LEAF PRESS, LLC.
136 BAXTER STREET
NEW YORK, NY 10013
WWW.POINTEDLEAFPRESS.COM

Pointed Leaf Press is pleased to offer special discounts for our publications and can provide signed copies upon request. Please contact info@pointedleafpress.com for details.
Printed and bound in China
First edition
10 9 8 7 6 5 4 3 2 1
Library of Congress Control Number: 2011925226
ISBN 13: 978-0-9833889-0-6

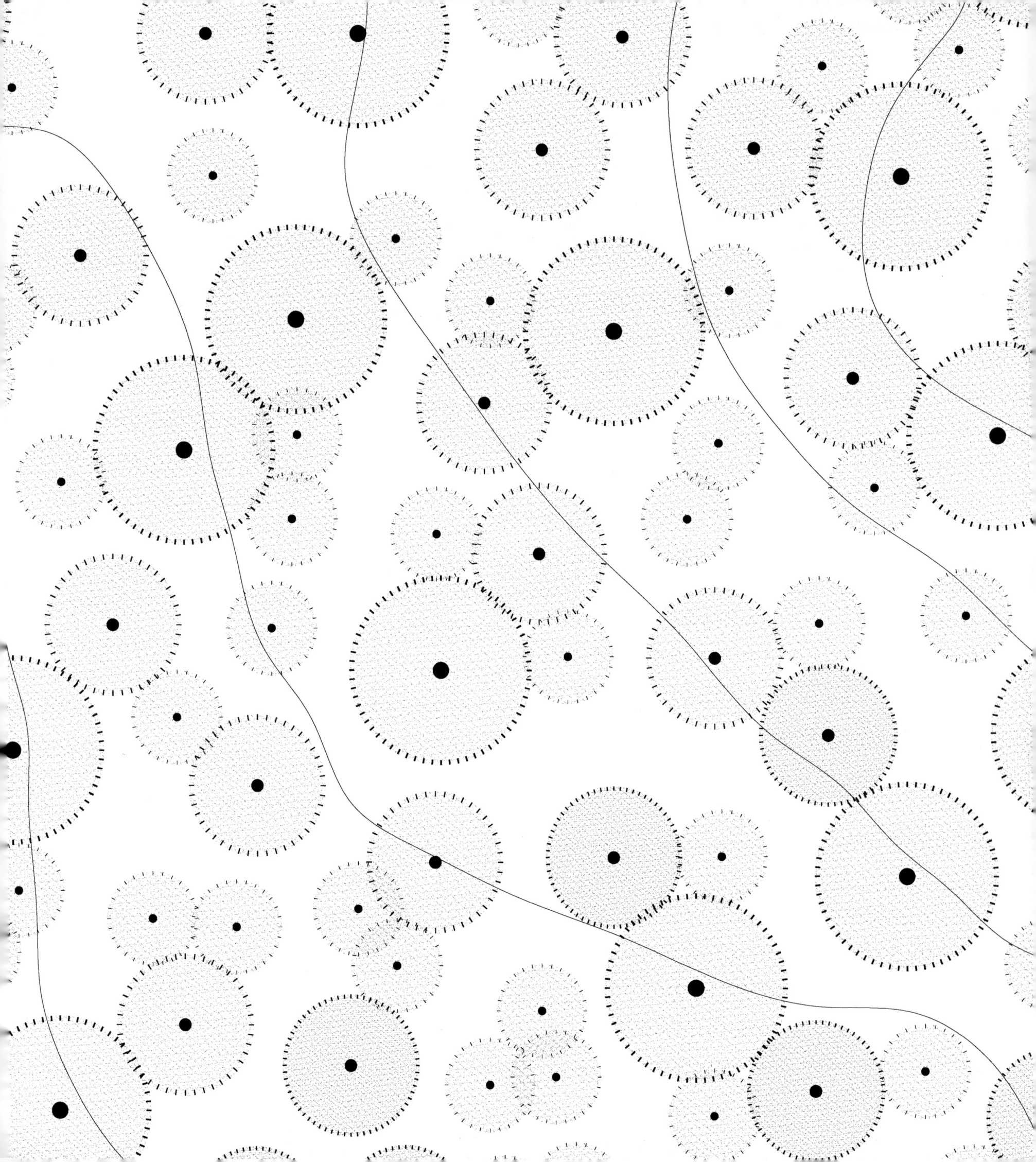